T

"Aimed at educated, experienced travellers, the [Berlitz Travellers] Guides capture the flavor of foreign lands."
—*Entrepreneur*

"Filling a needed niche in guidebooks . . . designed to eliminate the cumbersome lists of virtually every hotel and restaurant . . . . Special out-of-the-way places are detailed. . . . The books capture the personality and excitement of each destination."
—*Los Angeles Times*

"There's a different tone to these books, and certainly a different approach . . . information is aimed at independent and clearly sophisticated travellers. . . . Strong opinions give these books a different personality from most guides, and make them fun to read."
—*Travel & Leisure*

"Aimed at experienced, independent travellers who want information beyond the nuts-and-bolts material available in many familiar sources. Although each volume gives necessary basics, the series sends travellers not just to 'sights,' but to places and events that convey the personality of each locale."
—*The Denver Post*

"Just the right amount of information about where to stay and play."
—*Detroit Free Press*

CONTRIBUTORS

BARRY ANDERSON, a third-generation Californian, has written about the state for more than 30 years, first as a *Sunset Magazine* editor, then as a free-lance writer of magazine and newspaper articles and guidebooks. He has contributed to many publications, including the *Los Angeles Times* and the World of Travel series, and is a past president of the Society of American Travel Writers.

SHIRLEY MAAS FOCKLER is a member of the Society of American Travel Writers and the Travel Journalists Guild, and a contributor to *The Berlitz Travellers Guide to Australia.* She has written for many magazines and newspapers in North America and Oceania. A resident of the San Francisco Bay Area for 32 years, she now lives in Oregon.

MARK GORDON, author of *Once Upon A City,* a humorous history of San Francisco, has written for nearly all the major San Francisco newspapers and magazines. He also leads specialized tours of the city with Frisco Productions.

GEORGIA I. HESSE, Travel Editor of the *San Francisco Examiner and Chronicle* for 20 years, has contributed travel articles to almost every major North American newspaper and magazine. She is a contributor to *The Berlitz Travellers Guide to France.*

JACQUELINE KILLEEN writes about dining and travel for *San Francisco Focus* and other magazines. She is also the author of several books about the inns and restaurants of California and is a native San Franciscan.

CAROLE TERWILLIGER MEYERS, author of *Weekend Adventures for City-Weary People: Overnight Trips in Northern California* and *San Francisco Family Fun,* has lived in Berkeley for 24 years. She has been a columnist for the *San Francisco Examiner* and the *San Jose Mercury News.*

JEAN PIERCE is Editor of *Chevron Odyssey,* the magazine of the Chevron Travel Club. While Senior Editor at Rand McNally, her *National Parks Recreation Directory for Northern California* won a Lowell Thomas Award for Excellence in Journalism. A member of the Society of American Travel

Writers and a third-generation Californian, she resides in the Napa Valley.

BEA PIXA is a 30-year resident of San Francisco. She wrote a column for the *San Francisco Examiner* for many years and has contributed articles on a variety of subjects to many national publications.

SUSAN SHOOK has edited several guidebooks in the Berlitz series, as well as *The Backroads of Holland* and other travel books. A native Californian, she lives in San Francisco.

SHARON SILVA has written several books, including *Best Restaurants of the San Francisco Bay Area* and *Exploring the Best Ethnic Restaurants of the Bay Area*. Silva is a contributing editor at *San Francisco Focus* magazine, for which she writes a regular dining column, and a four-time recipient of the White Award for criticism.

ELOISE SNYDER was a reporter for the *San Francisco Examiner* before becoming a free-lance travel writer. She is based in Jackson, in California's Gold Country, where she has lived for 18 years.

DAVID W. TOLL, author of *The Compleat Nevada Traveler,* is a publisher and journalist. He divides his time between Healdsburg, California, and Gold Hill, Nevada.

THE BERLITZ
TRAVELLERS GUIDES

THE AMERICAN SOUTHWEST

AUSTRALIA

BERLIN

CANADA

THE CARIBBEAN

COSTA RICA

ENGLAND & WALES

FRANCE

GERMANY

GREECE

HAWAII

IRELAND

LONDON

MEXICO

NEW ENGLAND

NEW YORK CITY

NORTHERN ITALY AND ROME

PORTUGAL

SAN FRANCISCO &
NORTHERN CALIFORNIA

SOUTHERN ITALY AND ROME

SPAIN

TURKEY

THE BERLITZ TRAVELLERS GUIDE TO SAN FRANCISCO
& NORTHERN CALIFORNIA

Fourth Edition

ALAN TUCKER
General Editor

BERLITZ PUBLISHING COMPANY, INC.
New York, New York

BERLITZ PUBLISHING COMPANY LTD.
Oxford, England

THE BERLITZ TRAVELLERS GUIDE TO SAN FRANCISCO
& NORTHERN CALIFORNIA
Fourth Edition

Berlitz Trademark Reg U.S. Patent and Trademark Office
and other countries—Marca Registrada

Copyright © Root Publishing Company,
1991, 1992, 1993, 1994

Published by Berlitz Publishing Company, Inc.
257 Park Avenue South, New York, New York 10010, U.S.A.

Distributed in the United States by
the Macmillan Publishing Group

Distributed elsewhere by Berlitz Publishing Company Ltd.
Berlitz House, Peterley Road, Horspath, Oxford OX4 2TX, England

ISBN 2-8315-1705-2
ISSN 1057-4727

Designed by Beth Tondreau Design
Cover design by Dan Miller Design
Cover photograph by The Slide Library
Maps by Volti Graphics
Illustrations by Bill Russell
Edited by Susan Shook

Printed in the United States of America
1 3 5 7 9 10 8 6 4 2

THIS GUIDEBOOK

The Berlitz Travellers Guides are designed for experienced travellers in search of exceptional information that will enhance the enjoyment of the trips they take.

Where, for example, are the interesting, out-of-the-way, fun, charming, or romantic places to stay? The hotels described by our expert writers are some of the special places, in all price ranges except for the very lowest—not just the run-of-the-mill, heavily marketed places in advertised airline and travel-wholesaler packages.

We are *highly* selective in our choices of accommodations, concentrating on what our insider contributors think are the most interesting or rewarding places, and why. Readers who want to review exhaustive lists of hotel and resort choices as well, and who feel they need detailed descriptions of each property, can supplement the *Berlitz Travellers Guide* with tourism industry publications or one of the many directory-type guidebooks on the market.

We indicate the approximate price level of each accommodation in our description of it (no indication means it is moderate in local, relative terms), and at the end of every chapter we supply more detailed hotel rates as well as contact information so that you can get precise, up-to-minute rates and make reservations.

The Berlitz Travellers Guide to San Francisco & Northern California highlights the more rewarding parts of the city and region so that you can quickly and efficiently home in on a good itinerary.

Of course, this guidebook does far more than just help you choose a hotel and plan your trip. *The Berlitz Travellers Guide to San Francisco & Northern California* is designed for use *in* Northern California. Our writers, each of whom is an experienced travel journalist who either lives in or regularly tours the city or region of Northern California he or she covers, tell you what you really need to know, what you can't find out so easily on your own. They identify and describe the truly out-of-the-ordinary restaurants, shops, activities, and sights, and tell you the best way to "do" your destination.

Our writers are highly selective. They bring out the significance of the places they *do* cover, capturing the personality and the underlying cultural and historical resonances of a city or region—making clear its special appeal.

The Berlitz Travellers Guide to San Francisco & Northern California is full of reliable information. We would like to know if you think we've left out some very special place. Although we make every effort to provide the most current information available about every destination described in this book, it is possible too that changes have occurred before you arrive. If you do have an experience that is contrary to what you were led to expect by our description, we would like to hear from you about it.

A guidebook is no substitute for common sense when you are travelling. Always pack the clothing, footwear, and other items appropriate for the destination, and make the necessary accommodation for such variables as altitude, weather, and local rules and customs. Of course, once on the scene you should avoid situations that are in your own judgment potentially hazardous, even if they have to do with something mentioned in a guidebook. Half the fun of travelling is exploring, but explore with care.

ALAN TUCKER
General Editor
Berlitz Travellers Guides

Root Publishing Company
350 West Hubbard Street
Suite 440
Chicago, Illinois 60610

CONTENTS

MAPS

THE BERLITZ TRAVELLERS GUIDE TO SAN FRANCISCO

&

NORTHERN CALIFORNIA

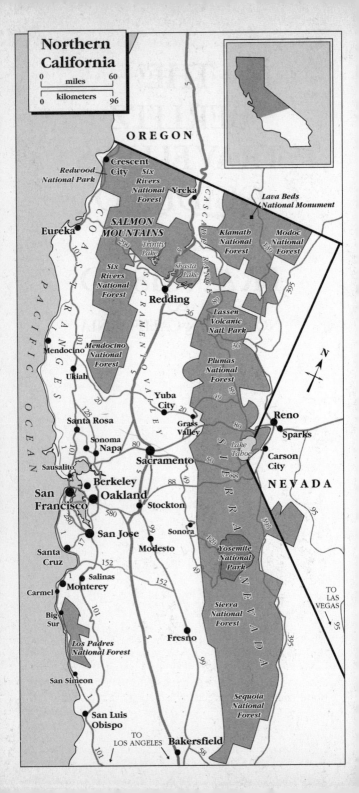

Northern California

0 miles 60

0 kilometers 96

OREGON

Crescent City

Redwood National Park

Six Rivers National Forest

Yreka

Lava Beds National Monument

Eureka

SALMON MOUNTAINS

Trinity Lake

Klamath National Forest

Modoc National Forest

CASCADE RANGE

Shasta Lake

Six Rivers National Forest

Redding

Lassen Volcanic Natl. Park

SACRAMENTO VALLEY

Mendocino National Forest

Plumas National Forest

Mendocino

Ukiah

COAST RANGES

Yuba City

Grass Valley

PACIFIC OCEAN

Santa Rosa

Sonoma

Napa

Sacramento

SIERRA

Lake Tahoe

Reno

Sparks

Carson City

NEVADA

Sausalito

Berkeley

Oakland

San Francisco

Stockton

Sonora

San Jose

Modesto

Santa Cruz

Salinas

Monterey

Carmel

Big Sur

Los Padres National Forest

San Simeon

San Luis Obispo

TO LOS ANGELES

Bakersfield

Yosemite National Park

Sierra National Forest

Sequoia National Forest

SIERRA NEVADA

TO LAS VEGAS

Fresno

OVERVIEW

By Georgia I. Hesse

Georgia I. Hesse, Travel Editor of the San Francisco Examiner
and Chronicle *for 20 years, has contributed travel articles to
almost every major North American newspaper and magazine. She is a contributor to* The Berlitz Travellers Guide to
France.

> "San Francisco's changing, changing,
> But no matter whatever comes,
> There'll still be Grace Cathedral
> And crumpets and tea at Blum's."

That memorable ditty from a forgettable musical ex-
pressed the character of the city (and much of Northern
California) in the late 1950s: stylish, optimistic, as self-
assured as the gloved and behatted ladies who sat in their
proper pews on Sundays, carried pink boxes of goodies
home from Blum's, and smiled "Good taste costs no more"
to each other, with a tip of the flowery hat to Gump's.

But Blum's is gone. Gump's is no longer a family affair.
Gays are married in Grace Cathedral. "Nostalgia," as Herb
Caen, the city's celebrator, reminds us, "is a thing of the
past." What's going on here?

The Age of Aquarius has waxed and waned; the flower
children have faded. This is the age of the activist, the
coming of the Greens. Battle lines have been drawn between the Earth First! protesters and the lumber companies
in the redwood and Douglas fir forests of Humboldt and Del
Norte counties. The streets of San Francisco are loud with
the cries and protests of the homeless, the underemployed,
and those suffering from AIDS.

The truth is, the woes of the world have come to Northern California, and residents don't like it one bit. After all, this is El Dorado, the earthly Utopia of which even the sophisticated Robert Louis Stevenson, riding the rails over the Sierra Nevada, could write, "All the passengers . . . thronged with shining eyes upon the platform. . . . At every turn we could look further into the land of our happy future. . . . For this indeed was our destination—this was 'the good country' we had been going to so long."

The trouble is, they just keep coming, bringing to the land of the sons of the pioneers diseases of development: overcrowding, erosion of personal safety, pollution, water worries, and the need to pay attention to the Big E's: environment, energy, and ecology.

The typical Northern Californian (a "native" who's been around five years or more) would close the Golden Gates, issue a Redwood Passport (but only to travellers with money and a round-trip ticket home), and buy a doormat reading *Go Away*.

In the mid-1970s Ernest Callenbach, an editor at University of California Press, gave the language a new word, even a new concept, when he wrote a visionary little novel entitled *Ecotopia*. In this book, set in 1999, Northern California, Oregon, and Washington seceded from the United States in the 1980s in order to create a more perfect union. In the resulting high-tech, low-energy society, bicycles have replaced BMWs, potholes have become flowerbeds, trees are Significant Others, and the president is female. (This last may happen some day, if California's Senators—Dianne Feinstein and Barbara Boxer—have their way.)

The idea was embraced by Joel Garreau in his 1981 study of new American realities, *The Nine Nations of North America*. He considers San Francisco the capital of Ecotopia, which stretches along the Pacific coast from Point Conception near Santa Barbara north to Anchorage, Alaska. In this compelling civilization, the clean silicon chip is king and sunshine heats the homes of the few poor as well as those with hot tubs.

The name California has an interesting origin, as described by historian George R. Stewart. Its first occurrence seems to have been in a long 16th-century poem, *Las Sergas de Esplandián,* by Garcí Ordóñez de Montalvo. The poem pictures California as an island in the ocean, inhabited by Amazon-like women, and rich in gold and precious stones. A Spanish exploration party in about 1524 spread rumors of the existence of such an island floating in the Pacific, and when Hernando Cortés came upon what is today the tip of peninsular Mexico, he named it California. Under Spanish-Mexican rule, what is today the American state was called Alta, or upper, California, while the skinny peninsula was, and is, Baja (lower) California in Mexico.

Place-names in Northern California are, in large part, Spanish, from Monterey to Del Norte, with San Francisco, Alameda, Sacramento, San Joaquin, and Santa Cruz in between, reflecting a Spanish-Mexican heritage that has a history of more than four centuries.

The first historic date verified in Alta California is September 28, 1542, when two ships under the command of Juan Rodriguez Cabrillo entered "a very good closed port" and christened it San Miguel; 60 years later, explorer Sebastián Vizcaíno would rename it San Diego. At the time, what is now California was home to some 300,000 indigenous people whose ancestors had arrived about 12,000 years before. They were at first of little interest to the Spaniards, who were concerned chiefly with protecting the coastal routes along which the treasures of the Orient arrived at the port of Acapulco.

Then, in the 1760s, challenged by the growing powers of Britain, France, and Russia in the New World, Spain awoke and began to deliberately colonize Alta California. The colonization took three forms: Franciscan missions, *presidios* (military settlements), and *pueblos* (towns). Evidence of all three remains. Of the 21 missions along the California coast, a few are little more than shells but most have been intelligently restored and some are still in use (see Mission Dolores in the San Francisco chapter). The four presidios completed before the end of the 18th century exist today as major cities: San Diego, Santa Barbara, Monterey, and San Francisco. Two pueblos also survive as major cities: Los Angeles and San Jose, while a third, Branciforte, disappeared; its site is now Santa Cruz.

Alta California was considered a mere extension of New Spain, as Mexico was known, until New Spain threw off its Spanish yoke in 1822 and declared itself the Republic of Mexico. Under Spanish rule, about two dozen private individuals had been given rights to occupy specific tracts of land (*ranchos*), and under Mexican rule these land grants were expanded to some 500, many of them important contributions to the life of early Northern California: the vast Rancho San Antonio (today's Alameda, Albany, Berkeley, Emeryville, Oakland, Piedmont, and part of San Leandro near San Francisco), Rancho Carne Humana (upper Napa

Valley), and Rancho San Francisquito (Stanford University) among them.

Between 1835, when Mexico turned down a United States offer to purchase San Francisco Bay, and 1846, relations between Mexico and the expanding U.S. deteriorated badly. The American annexation of Texas in 1845 led to war between the two countries, and on June 14, 1846, a little band of Yankees captured the commander of the presidio of Sonoma and raised the Bear Flag of California over its plaza (see Sonoma Plaza in the Wine Country chapter). On July 17, John D. Sloat raised the American flag at the customs house of Monterey and claimed California for the United States. Some skirmishes followed, but after more than 300 years, the official Spanish-Mexican history of the state was over.

Northern California can be said to live in a room of its own, with walls near Carmel-Monterey in the south and the Oregon border in the north, windows looking out onto the Pacific, and the back doors of Lake Tahoe and Reno, Nevada, on the east. Even outsiders admit there's something different about it. Witness a William Hamilton cartoon in the *New Yorker:* At a cocktail party, presumably someplace Back East, the hostess makes introductions: "Nan and Gordon are from California, but Northern California."

Nan and Gordon may be from a separate state properly named Northern California some day soon if assemblyman Stan Statham from rural Shasta County has his way. His proposal, introduced in the State Legislature in January 1992, would create a new state about the size of Iowa running just north of San Francisco and Sacramento to the Oregon border. The point is, the residents of the intensely rural, dramatically beautiful, thinly populated north view with some alarm the state as becoming overrun with urban angst, drug gangs, noise polluters, water thieves, and addicts of radicchio, blackened redfish, Perrier, and porcini. Although attempts to split the state have been suggested before (25 times since statehood itself in 1850), the latest try is a reaction to Proposition 13, an anti-tax measure passed in 1978 that limited property taxes, thus passing costly services such as welfare and criminal courts on to the counties and threatening the sparsely populated top-third of the state with bankruptcy.

The compulsive chauvinism of Northern Californians irritates everybody else, especially their neighbors. In Oregon, cars wear bumper stickers reading, "Don't Californicate Oregon." John Steinbeck's *Travels with Charley* deals with the subject: "We who were born here [in his case, in Salinas], and our parents also felt a strange superiority over newcomers, barbarians, *forestieri,* and they, the foreigners, resented us and even made a rude poem about us: The miner came in forty-nine, The whores in fifty-one/And when they got together, They made a native son."

No question about it: The people here are different from those elsewhere. "Have a nice day now, honey," croons the waitress in a far north Eureka café; you think to step on her toes, but you don't because she smiles, and she means it. (Elsewhere, her tone might imply, "I hope your legs drop off.") "What do *you* think of leveraged buyouts?" asks the parking-garage attendant, handing you a receipt. Or, "Well," the doorman grins as he helps a mink-wrapped dowager into her flashy Alfa-Romeo Spyder, "so much for stereotypes." Then there is the urban Oz of Marin County, where a child sniffles, "Sorry. I always cry at Tchaikovsky."

If Northern Californians are different, it may be because of the land: big, bold, of immense variety, and sparsely inhabited (even though the latest census results show that more than one in ten Americans lives in California).

In the recent past, travellers believed that San Francisco was all there was in the north. They placed Carmel, Monterey, even Yosemite, and perhaps a drop of Wine Country, within their mental borders of the city, eyes glazing over at talk of Eureka, even of Mendocino, certainly of Sacramento. Foreign visitors unused to the grandeur of American geography still imagine San Francisco to be a rather European suburb of Los Angeles.

Without a doubt, the traveller's Northern California does begin in **San Francisco** (unless you drive south from Washington or Oregon states); it probably always will. The city is the transportation hub, after all, and still the major lure. San Franciscans consider theirs the quintessential city: cosmopolitan (and growing more so all the time), civilized, and eccentric, not to mention self-centered. It is large enough to provide infinite cultural, culinary, and competitive diversions, yet small enough to comprehend; its hills, valleys, homes, and parks are suited to a human scale.

Yet the city is only one intriguing element in the composition called the **Bay Area**, with the counterpoints of Marin County to the north; to the east, the cities of Berkeley and Oakland; to the south, Palo Alto and Stanford University, and the rugged coast and hills, beaches, and parks of San Mateo County.

Visitors who want to stay in San Francisco can easily

acquaint themselves with these stellar surroundings on day trips, which is what we have done in this text. Then there are the delights beyond the immediate Bay Area:

Wine Country is a world of its own. Increasingly, all of California is wine country; one would not be shocked should a sprig of Sirah spring up in Death Valley. In Northern California, however, Wine Country means, in the main, Napa and Sonoma counties, with significant swatches in Mendocino and Lake counties. Wine Country feels, smells, tastes, and even looks like southern France or central Italy, and its mood is definitely Mediterranean. Days stretch out and slow down near the vineyards, breezes blow more fragrantly, the sun shines more salubriously, city strife slips into *la dolce vita*. It's possible to see a corner of Wine Country in one day, but more fun if you spend at least three.

If Wine Country evokes the Old Country, the **Redwood Country** speaks of ancient Earth. Long, long thoughts follow you as you stroll in the shadows of giants that were young when Christianity was born, descendants of ancestors that lived before the glacial ages. Sun, shade, blistered hills and pelting rains, wave-battered shores and craggy cliffs: This is elemental earth. The welcoming inns, warming fireplaces, and well-set tables come as civilizing dividends.

The call of the lonesome wild still echos in the big northeast, in the little-known, often untracked counties of Siskiyou, Modoc, Shasta, and Lassen, called here **Northeastern California**. This area remains almost as unfamiliar to most Californians as it is to people from beyond the state's borders. Here ghost towns fade and crumble; great peaks remain snow-capped right into summer; limestone caverns reveal an underworld of fluted columns, stone draperies, and stalactites and stalagmites studded with crystals; wrinkled lava beds hint at the growing of the globe. For the adventurous wanderer, this is hunting, fishing, hiking, and being-alone country at its most compelling.

"Boys, I believe I have found a gold mine," said James W. Marshall in measured tones, standing near a sluice gate on the south fork of the American River. The date was January 24, 1848, and the West—and the whole world—was listening. The Gold Rush really began that day. **Gold Country** still lives in the little mining towns that sleep along Highway 49; towns with names like Angels Camp, Sutter Creek, Fiddletown, Volcano, and Rough 'N Ready. Gone with the wind are Freeze-Out, Bed Bug, and Mme. Pantaloons. (The latter's spirit lingers in the bar of the Louisiana House and National

Hotel in Jackson, where a piano and gutbucket still beat out the stomping songs of the bawdy old days.)

The Central Valley stretches from old-gold Butte County in the north through the Sacramento and San Joaquin valleys. Stockton, born in 1847, watched as thousands of Argonauts poured through in the early 1850s, bound for the gold fields. The state's capital, **Sacramento**, boasts the Old Sacramento Historical Park, the elaborate State Capitol, and one of the world's finest train-oriented collections in the California State Railroad Museum.

To roam Gold Country best, follow Highway 49 south along its length from Downieville, in the north, to its end south of spectacular **Yosemite National Park**, which is also covered in the Gold Country chapter.

To Northern Californians, their backyard begins at **Lake Tahoe**, which bathes the California–Nevada state line, and reaches east into Nevada at least as far as **Carson City** and **Reno**. Here, the range of the Sierra Nevada holds its spine against the sky, and of the sapphire cup of Lake Tahoe Mark Twain wrote, "The air . . . is very pure and fine, bracing and delicious, and why shouldn't it be? It is the same air angels breathe."

This is family vacation country par excellence, with summer water sports, dinner cruises on paddle-wheel boats, more than 20 winter ski resorts (Heavenly Valley is the largest in the country), many historical spots, and the gaming-dining-entertainment complexes.

"Everyone was delighted with the appearance of things," wrote Richard Henry Dana, Jr., in *Two Years Before the Mast*. It was the 1830s, and he had just arrived off the coast of Monterey. "[This], as far as my observation goes, is decidedly the pleasantest and most civilized-looking place in California." France celebrates its Grande Corniche, Italy boasts its Amalfi Drive, but Northern California claims to best any oceanside stretch with the Pacific Coast Highway, Highway 1, which winds south of San Francisco along the **Central Coast** to Monterey and beyond.

Monterey and **Carmel** are endlessly seductive; sea lions sport and bark off Point Lobos, and anyone with an eye for smashing seascapes should stop to picnic along **Big Sur** of Henry Miller fame. Eventually, you arrive at **Hearst Castle** near Cambria, the house that William Randolph built.

Inland, don't miss a call at **San Juan Bautista**, one of the finest examples of California missions; collectors of such wonders will wander as far as Mission San Antonio at Jolon.

In Northern California, you can have almost any weather you want. The snow stays up in the mountains where it belongs (usually), and in winter the San Franciscan can ski and sail on the same long weekend. If the coastline is too chilly, drive up and over the Coast Range and into a near-permanent summer. When Sacramento scorches, you can answer the foghorns calling from San Francisco.

The search for the essence of Northern California is perhaps a futile one, stretching as it does from the nearly untracked wilderness of the Redwood Country's Lost Coast to the downtown Club DV-8 in San Francisco's SoMa. Is that essence a European one, born of Spanish political and religious expansion? (Even today, many visitors from overseas describe San Francisco as "the most European city in America.")

Is the essence American, involving the special challenge of the unconquered frontier, the Manifest Destiny to civilize a heathen land, the ineffable attraction of the "west of the West" (in Theodore Roosevelt's felicitous phrase)?

Is Northern California *Ultima Thule,* the final jumping-off place? (The hundreds of people who have leapt from the Golden Gate Bridge may have believed that; interestingly, they tend to jump facing toward the beautiful city by the bay rather than looking west toward nothingness.)

Are Northern Californians the restless heirs of what was called the Great California Lottery, the rush for gold? "Vice seems more alluring here," one William Swain wrote home from the fields in 1850. "Sabbath days here are spent by miners mostly hunting, prospecting for gold, and gambling. Very little attention is paid to morals . . . Say to all my friends: stay at home. Tell my enemies to come" (from *The World Rushed In,* J. S. Holliday).

The Northern California experience is all these things and many more. Travellers come to it expecting sun and find fog; wanting momentary craziness and discovering a very permanent culture; anticipating, perhaps, a rush of the risqué, the kooky, and the hipped-out, only to recognize an old-fashioned, determined, all-American work ethic. All the signs of our times are here, from "Welcome" in 40 languages to "Trespassers will be violated."

The quest remains; one thing Northern California is not is static. With Walt Whitman, it looks west toward the Far East and asks: "But where is what I started for so long ago? And why is it yet unfound?"

USEFUL FACTS

When to Go

Northern California is a complexity of microclimates; in some seasons there can be a difference of 30 degrees Fahrenheit between the coast and 30 miles inland or between San Francisco and the areas north and south of it. Usually, and in most regions, rain falls between December and February, thus making mid-September to mid-November and mid-March through June the most pleasant months to visit San Francisco proper, although fog can creep in at any time. August in the city is cold, clammy, and overcast almost every year.

In the Sierra Nevada temperatures fall below zero in winter and soar to over 100 degrees in midsummer; Gold Country is much the same. In the summertime, Redwood Country temperatures average from 50 to 60 degrees F along the coast and 75 to 90 degrees inland, and in winter, around 40 to 50 degrees. Snow is very rare except on the highest inland elevations. In Yosemite National Park winter temperatures range from 25 to 50 degrees F and in summer from 50 to 90 degrees F. Similar conditions pertain throughout the northeast part of the state such as in Lassen National Park. Because of varying altitudes it's always wise to pack a windbreaker or heavy sweater.

Entry Documents

The United States no longer requires visas from citizens of Great Britain, Canada, Japan, most western European countries, Australia, or New Zealand under a 90-day visa waiver plan for pleasure trips only. Citizens of Hong Kong are required to obtain visas from the local American consulate.

Arrival at Major Gateways by Air

San Francisco, Oakland, and San Jose international airports are the major air gateways in the northern part of the state.

Just 16 miles (25 km) south of the city **San Francisco International Airport** (SFO) is the seventh-busiest airport in the world, served by more than 46 major carriers, including Air Canada, American, British Airways, Canadian, Delta, Japan, Lufthansa and its charter arm Condor, Northwest, Qantas, TWA, United, and UTA (of the Air France group). The complex comprises three buildings: the South, International, and North terminals, each with an upper level for departures and a lower level for arrivals. A complimentary shuttle bus circles the upper roadway every five minutes and stops in front of each terminal. A $2.4 billion expansion project begun in 1993 is scheduled for completion in 1997.

SFO's widely known medical clinic in the International Terminal offers the services of a doctor or registered nurse and special assistance to the handicapped. From the airport call 70444 from a white courtesy phone; from outside, Tel: (415) 877-0444.

No charge is made for baggage carts in the international arrival area; in the domestic arrival area, the charge is $1, with a 25-cent refund if the cart is returned to a rack. Foreign exchange is available in all three terminals.

SFO was the country's first airport to establish a Bureau of Exhibitions and Cultural Education and is unusual in having a curator and museum professionals on the premises. Five gallery areas host 40 exhibitions annually.

SFO is connected to the eastern, downtown part of San Francisco by Highway 101; visitors to the western half of the city (largely residential) can take 101 north to the Interstate 380 interchange, then west to the interchange with Interstate Highway 280 (marked Daly City). Follow 280 to State Highway 1 and into town via 19th Avenue and Golden Gate Park. This is also the most direct route for visitors headed for Marin County or other points north. Watch for Golden Gate Bridge direction signs.

Complimentary shuttle service between the airport and several nearby hotels and motels is available; use the courtesy phone at the hotel/motel board in the baggage claim areas.

Taxi service from the airport to downtown San Francisco costs about $29 and takes 20 to 30 minutes. Ride-sharing for two or more people to a maximum of three destinations is permitted.

SFO Airporter (buses) charges $8 one way, $14 round trip between the airport and Union Square in the heart of town, stopping at several central hotels. The first departure from SFO is at 5:00 A.M. and the last at 11:00 P.M., with departures every 20 minutes in between; no reservations are required. Pickups are on the lower level at the luggage claim area; Tel: (415) 495-8404. (The second half of the round-trip ticket is valid for one year.)

Door-to-door Airport Express leaves SFO every 30 minutes from 5:30 A.M. to 10:30 P.M. to any San Francisco hotel. The fare is $9; Tel: (415) 775-5121.

Door-to-door transportation is offered 24 hours a day by Super Shuttle vans. Pickup is on the upper level at American and USAir. For rates (credit cards accepted) and reservations to or from SFO, call (415) 558-8500.

Airport Connection serves SFO, San Francisco, the East Bay, and the Peninsula; reservations, which should be made at least six hours prior to pickup, are recommended; Tel: (415) 885-2666 or (800) AIRPORT. From SFO use the white courtesy telephones and dial 70901. The current fare is $11 to San Francisco, more to other locations (credit cards accepted); pickup is on the upper level in the red-and-white zones.

Yellow Airport Shuttle offers 24-hour door-to-door service from residences and hotels in San Francisco to either SFO or Oakland International. Reservations are required and the fare between SFO and downtown is $9; Tel: (415) 282-7433.

Marin Airporter maintains scheduled bus service every half hour from SFO to the Marin County cities of Novato, Ignacio, Terra Linda, San Rafael, Larkspur, Mill Valley, and Sausalito from 5:30 A.M. to midnight and from 4:30 A.M. to 11:00 P.M. in the opposite direction; Tel: (415) 461-4222. All suburban boarding is at the center island, lower level. Fares run from $10 to $13 each way.

The BayPorter Express connects SFO, Oakland International, and San Jose International hourly and provides service to any location in the suburbs east and south of San Francisco (Tel: 415-467-1800 or, from the airport, 800-287-6783). Call to inquire for departures and fares. Reservations are required.

There is bus transportation from SFO to cities in the East Bay and north. For Sacramento, Vacaville, and Davis, call Gray Line (Tel: 916-371-3090); for Napa and Vallejo, Evans Airport Service (Tel: 707-255-1559); for Berkeley, Bay Area Shuttle (Tel: 415-873-7771). Transportation to the farthest point, Sacramento, is $25; to Berkeley, $10.

From SFO there is also transportation to the East Bay and south. For Fremont, Union City, and Newark, Fun Connexion (Tel: 510-791-7160); for Alamo, Dublin, Livermore, Pleasanton, San Ramon, etc., San Ramon Valley Airporter Express (Tel: 510-484-4044).

Rental-car companies with desks at SFO include Alamo, Alpine, American International, Apple, AVCar, Avis, Budget, Dollar, General, Hertz, National, Payless RPM, Showcase, Snappy, Thrifty, and Wheels for Rent. Rental-car booths are located in the baggage-claim areas.

Oakland International Airport (OAK) is 11 miles (17 km) southeast of Oakland, on Highway 880 (take the Hegenberger exit), and 19 miles (30 km) southeast across the Bay

Bridge from San Francisco. Taxis charge about $20 between downtown Oakland and OAK, $35 and up (plus $1 bridge toll) to locations in San Francisco.

Oakland International is served by nine airlines, including Alaska, American, Delta, Morris Air, Northwest, Southwest, and United Express.

The Air-BART shuttle (BART is the Bay Area's subway) departs from the shelter on the center island outside the main airport entrance every five minutes from 6:00 A.M. to midnight Mondays through Saturdays, and from 8:00 A.M. on Sundays. The ride to the Coliseum station of BART is $2. To Oakland City Center from there take the Richmond train; the fare is 80 cents. To downtown San Francisco (Embarcadero, Montgomery, Powell, or Civic Center stations) take the Daly City train for $1.90.

AC Transit Bus number 58 goes from the airport to downtown Oakland every 30 to 60 minutes depending upon the time of day; Tel: (510) 839-2882.

For bus service to points east such as Pleasanton and Castro Valley, call Airporter Express at (510) 484-4044; to Napa, Vallejo, and nearby towns, call Grapevine Airport Service at (707) 253-9093.

Rental-car companies at OAK are Alamo, Avis, Budget, Dollar, General, Hertz, and National.

San Jose International Airport (SJC) is 3 miles (5 km) northwest of San Jose via Highways 101 and 17/880. In 1990 Terminal A was opened, the airport's first new facility in 25 years, and is now used by American and American Eagle airlines (all others use Terminal C). Thirteen commercial airlines now serve SJC, including Alaska, American, Continental, Delta, Mexicana, Northwest, TWA, and United.

A taxi ride to downtown San Jose takes only 10 to 15 minutes, at a cost of about $10. Santa Clara County Transit bus number 65 departs from the shelters outside baggage claim in both terminals for downtown stops and connections to BART and CalTrain every hour between 6:03 A.M. and 9:33 P.M. Adult fares are $1 one way, $2 for a day pass, with lower rates for children and seniors. On weekdays between 9:30 A.M. and 2:30 P.M., the fare is only 50 cents; Tel: (408) 321-2300.

In addition, SJC is served by Metro/Light Rail/Airport Van (Tel: 408-248-4810), Peerless Stages (Tel: 408-297-8890), Santa Cruz Airporter (Tel: 800-223-4142), South Bay Airport Shuttle (Tel: 408-559-9477), Airport Connection (Tel: 408-730-5555), and BayPorter Express (Tel: 415-467-1800).

In 1991, SJC opened the only KidPort on the West Coast in Terminal C's main lobby. Designed for children aged 3 to 14, it offers such distractions as airport maps, video telephones to the control tower, and TV monitors for watching the airfield activity.

Rental-car companies at the airport include Alamo, Avis, Budget, Dollar, and Hertz, with desks on the lower level off the lobby.

Arrival by Train

Amtrak trains connect San Francisco with Portland and Seattle to the north and Los Angeles to the south daily via the Coast Starlight. The superliner California Zephyr runs to and from Chicago via Omaha, Denver, and Salt Lake City, and provides daily service to Stockton, Merced-Yosemite, Fresno, Bakersfield, and San Joaquin Valley points. The San Joaquin links the Bay Area with Merced (gateway to Yosemite National Park) and Bakersfield.

Shuttle buses meet arrivals at the Oakland depot at 16th and Wood streets and transfer passengers to the Transbay Terminal in San Francisco at First and Mission streets, where you can take a bus or taxi to your destination. For information and rates call (800) 872-7245 in the U.S. and (800) 4-AMTRAK in Canada.

Arrival by Bus

San Francisco and the Bay Area are served by Greyhound-Trailways Bus System (Transbay Terminal, First and Mission streets, San Francisco; Tel: 415-558-6789) and various charter companies from across the country.

Arrival by Cruise Ship

The official passenger terminal is Pier 35, within walking distance of Pier 39, a complex of shops and restaurants east of colorful and lively Fisherman's Wharf.

At this writing cruise companies calling regularly in San Francisco include Cunard, Holland America Line, Princess Line, Regency Cruises, Royal Cruise Line, Royal Viking Line, and Special Expeditions. Ships of other major lines make periodic calls as well.

Passenger facilities are primitive by international standards and a constant source of dispute.

Renting a Car

Visitors from other countries who wish to rent a car in the U.S. must be 25 years or older, present a valid passport and driver's license from the country of residence, and show a return ticket for air or sea travel. In some cases prepayment may be required. Almost all major international credit cards are accepted.

A word to the wise: Don't get a standard shift unless you know how to shift into gear from a stop on a very steep hill, with cars stopped behind you—especially if you're going to drive in San Francisco.

Local Time

All of Northern California is in the Pacific Standard time zone, three hours behind New York and Montreal (Eastern Standard), two hours behind Chicago and Winnipeg (Central Standard), one hour behind Denver and Calgary (Mountain Standard), eight hours behind London, 18 hours behind Sydney, and 20 hours behind Auckland. (If you fly west across the Pacific from San Francisco, you lose a day; travelling in the other direction, you gain a day.) During daylight savings time there will be an hour's variance, because countries and cities go on and off daylight savings on different dates.

Currency

In San Francisco major foreign-exchange brokers are American Foreign Exchange, 315 Sutter Street, Tel: (415) 391-9913; Associated Foreign Exchange, Inc., 201 Sansome Street, Tel: (415) 781-7683; Foreign Exchange, Ltd., 415 Stockton Street, near Union Square, Tel: (415) 397-4700; and Pacific Foreign Exchange, 527 Sutter Street, Tel: (415) 391-2548. Four Bank of America branches, including one at SFO, provide exchange services, as does the Wells Fargo bank at 1 Montgomery Street. Thomas Cook Foreign Exchange provides exchange and associated services at 75 Geary Street, Tel: (415) 362-3452, at Pier 39, Tel: (415) 362-6271, at Stanford Shopping Center in Palo Alto, Tel: (415) 321-3308, at the Village Shopping Center in Corte Madera (Marin County), Tel: (415) 924-6001, and at San Jose International Airport.

The $1 coin, rarely seen in most of the United States, is common in Nevada, where slot gambling machines are legal.

Telephoning

The international country code for the United States is 1. Northern California uses six area codes: 415 for San Francisco and cities in the Northern Peninsula; 510 for the East Bay, including Berkeley and Oakland; 408 for Southern

Peninsula cities such as San Jose, Santa Cruz, and Monterey-Carmel; 707 for Napa, Eureka, and general Redwood Country locations north to the Oregon border; 916 for inland and northern towns such as Sacramento, locations in Modoc, Lassen, and Shasta national forests up to the Oregon line, and Lake Tahoe; and 209 for Gold Country spots. All of Nevada employs area code 702.

Electrical Current
Current in the U.S. is 110/120 volts. Foreign-made appliances may require adapters and North American flat-blade plugs.

Business Hours and Holidays
Normally, business hours are 9:00 A.M. to 5:00 P.M. Mondays through Fridays; some of the largest banks have extended their hours to conform to these times and are open even on Saturdays for certain hours. Shopping malls, major department stores, supermarkets, and all but the smallest businesses operate seven days a week. In San Francisco several large food markets and some drugstores are open 24 hours a day, 365 days a year.

Government agencies, banks, and post offices close for several national holidays: January 1 (New Year's Day); January 18 (Martin Luther King Jr.'s birthday); President's Day, honoring George Washington and Abraham Lincoln (observed in mid-February on a Monday between their birthdays); the last Monday in May (Memorial Day); July 4 (Independence Day); the first Monday in September (Labor Day); the second Monday in October (Columbus Day); November 11 (Veterans Day); the fourth Thursday in November (Thanksgiving Day); and December 25 (Christmas).

Credit Cards
Major credit cards from overseas affiliated with Visa or MasterCard are widely accepted, as are foreign-held cards such as American Express, Diner's Club, and the like.

Accommodations
Hotels and motels of most major national chains have members in San Francisco and Northern California. (See details under Accommodations Reference at the end of each chapter.) In addition, several smaller groups operate throughout the region. Prestigious France-based Relais & Châteaux has five members in Northern California: Sherman House in San Francisco, Timberhill Ranch near Cazadero on the Sonoma County coast, Meadowood Resort

Hotel in St. Helena and Auberge du Soleil in Rutherford, both in the Napa Valley, and Stonepine in Carmel Valley. Small Luxury Hotels of the World counts among its six Northern California members Carmel's Highlands Inn, Big Sur's Post Ranch Inn, San Francisco's Huntington, and the above-mentioned Auberge du Soleil, Meadowood, and Sherman House.

Bed-and-breakfast inns are booming in popularity; several regional referral services can supply information about them: California Association of Bed & Breakfast Inns, Tel: (800) 284-4667; Bed & Breakfast Innkeepers of Santa Cruz County, Tel: (408) 425-8212; The Inns of Point Reyes, Tel: (415) 663-1420; Bed & Breakfast Inns of Sonoma Valley, Tel: (800) 284-6675; Mendocino Coast Innkeepers Association, Tel: (800) 7-COAST-0; Bed & Breakfast Inns of the Gold Country, Box 462, Sonora, CA 95370 or Fax: (916) 626-6136; Historic Inns of Grass Valley and Nevada City, Tel: (916) 477-6634; Sacramento Innkeepers' Association, Fax: (916) 441-3214; Yosemite Mariposa Bed & Breakfast Association, Tel: (209) 742-7666. A brochure package of lodging choices on the north coast is available from The Porters, P.O. Box 999, Gualala, CA 95445; Tel: (800) 726-9997.

Reservation/Referral Services

Several firms in San Francisco and the Bay Area can assist travellers in finding accommodations throughout Northern California. The most reliable are listed here in alphabetical order. All are within the 415 area code unless otherwise indicated.

Accommodations Referral of Napa Valley: Located in St. Helena, this free reservation line has information on 150 Napa Valley bed and breakfasts, hotels, and resorts, as well as regional excursions such as balloon rides; Tel: (707) 963-VINO or, in California, (800) 499-8466; Fax: (707) 963-1762.

American Property Exchange: This real estate broker features deluxe condominiums and apartments in San Francisco. All units are fully equipped for short-term stays; Tel: 863-8484 or (800) 747-7784; Fax: 255-8865.

Bed & Breakfast International: Bed-and-breakfast rooms in San Francisco, the Wine Country, and the Monterey Peninsula in reasonably priced homes, luxurious Victorians, country inns, and houseboats; Tel: 696-1690 or (800) 872-4500; Fax: 696-1699.

Bed and Breakfast San Francisco: Reservations may be made in bed and breakfasts in San Francisco, Marin County, the Wine Country, Monterey/Carmel, the Pacific coast north and south of San Francisco, and Yosemite, and in inns, homes, and yachts; Tel: 479-1913 or (800) 452-8249; Fax: 921-BBSF.

Boat & Breakfast USA: Sixteen yachts with kitchens and complimentary breakfasts may be reserved for from one person to families at locations at San Francisco's Pier 39, Sausalito, and Oakland; Tel: 291-8411 or (800) BOAT-BED; Fax: 291-8477.

California Suites: Fully furnished one- or two-bedroom condominium suites can be booked throughout the Bay Area; Tel: (510) 429-9700 or (800) 782-9577; Fax: (510) 429-6780.

Coastal Lodging of Point Reyes National Seashore: Ten cottages, inns, and guest homes in Point Reyes, Inverness, and Bolinas in ocean, bay, and rural settings are represented, accommodating from 4 to 12 people; Tel: 663-1351.

Gerson, Bakar & Associates: Studios, one- to three-bedroom apartments, condominiums, and townhouses may be booked, from San Francisco south to Santa Clara, some with health facilities and pools. There's a one-month minimum stay; Tel: 391-1313; Fax: 391-1895.

Golden Gate Reservations: Discounts are offered on more than 200 properties in San Francisco, the Wine Country, and Monterey/Carmel; Tel: 771-6915, (800) 576-0003 (from the western U.S.), or (800) 423-7846 (from the eastern U.S.); Fax: 771-1458.

Inns by Design: This service offers homestays, bed and breakfasts, boutique hotels, corporate condominiums, flats, and short-term rental homes in San Francisco, the East Bay, the Wine Country, Mendocino, the Gold Country, Monterey, and Carmel; Tel: 382-1462; Fax: 382-1491.

San Francisco Reservations: This is a free, central hotel reservation service for more than 225 hotels in all price ranges; Tel: 227-1500 or (800) 677-1550; Fax: 227-1520.

Trinity Properties: Fine, furnished apartments are available in San Francisco's most interesting areas, ranging from $500 to $5,000 per month; Tel: 433-3333; Fax: 989-9390.

Wine Country Inns of Sonoma County: This service offers farmhouses, Victorians, and ranches, all serving country breakfasts; Tel: (707) 433-INNS or (800) 354-4743.

For Further Information

The San Francisco Visitor Information Center, in Benjamin Swig Pavilion on the lower level of Hallidie Plaza at Market and Powell streets, answers questions and distributes maps and information brochures weekdays from 9:00 A.M. to 5:00

P.M., Saturdays until 3:00 P.M., and Sundays from 10:00 A.M. to
2:00 P.M.; Tel: (415) 391-2000, 24 hours a day.

For travel details and a handbook with maps, listings of
accommodations, restaurants, museums, and more, contact
the Redwood Empire Association, Humboldt Bank Building,
785 Market Street, 15th Floor, San Francisco, CA 94103-2022;
Tel: (415) 543-8334. (If ordered by mail, the Redwood Empire publication costs $3 prepaid.)

A general source of information is the California Office of
Tourism, Department of Commerce, 1121 L Street, Suite 103,
Sacramento, CA 95814; Tel: (916) 322-1396.

For weather information call (916) 646-2000 or (415) 364-
7974; for road conditions call Caltrans, Tel: (415) 557-3755.

For information on camping, weather, and road conditions in the national parks, call (415) 556-0560 or 556-6030;
for state park information call (415) 456-1286.

In San Francisco a free (if called from within area code
415) Cityline now gives news and information 24 hours a
day in more than 150 categories, from national news to
weather, sports, finance, and even historical trivia; Tel: (415)
512-5000.

—*Georgia I. Hesse and Jean Pierce*

BIBLIOGRAPHY

JOAN ABBOTT, *Jack London and His Daughters* (1990). London's eldest daughter recalls her Oakland childhood, her
love for her novelist father, and his abandonment of her.

THOMAS R. AIDALA, *Hearst Castle, San Simeon* (1985). Illustrated. William Randolph Hearst was an insatiable collector
of European arts and artifacts and much of what he collected
ended up at Hearst Castle, San Simeon, a baronial estate that
is now a state park.

RICHARD BATMAN, *The Outer Coast* (1985). The human-interest
side of history—from Father Serra's feuds with the military
commander at Monterey to Richard Henry Dana's nostalgic
return to California and San Francisco in 1859—enlivens this
study of the first decades of California settlement.

MORTON BEEBE, *San Francisco* (1985). Beebe photographed
his hometown from every angle for this popular volume. His
photographs are accompanied by words from such local
writers as Herb Caen, Tom Cole, Herbert Gold, and Kevin
Starr.

GEOFFREY BELL, *The Golden Gate and the Silver Screen*
(1984). The San Francisco Bay Area was a movie-producing

center early in the century, with such companies as Essanay churning out Westerns at Niles in Alameda County. This volume provides an illustrated history of the action.

PAUL BERTOLLI AND ALICE WATERS, *Chez Panisse Cooking: New Tastes and Techniques* (1988). An exploration of the philosophy behind the cooking at Waters's trend-setting Berkeley restaurant, as well as recipes, special menus, and sources for fresh and pure ingredients.

JOHN BOESSENECKER, *Badge and Buckshot: Lawlessness in Old California* (1988). A San Francisco attorney peers into the past at famous outlaws and the men who tracked them down, from Rattlesnake Dick to John C. Boggs, sheriff of Calaveras County and nemesis of badmen.

SARA HOLMES BOUTELLE, *Julia Morgan, Architect* (1988). A leading figure in Northern California architecture, Morgan designed some 700 buildings, including Hearst Castle.

JOSEPH E. BROWN, *Monarchs of the Mist* (1982). A fascinating (and illustrated) collection of information about Redwood National Park and the ever-magnificent Coast Redwoods.

HERB CAEN, *Baghdad-by-the-Bay* (1949). Newspaper columnist Caen has chronicled the San Francisco that is, was, and never was for more than four decades. This 40-year-old volume is pure nostalgia for those who knew the city "when."

THOMAS W. CHINN, *Bridging the Pacific: San Francisco Chinatown and Its People* (1989). An examination of San Francisco's Chinatown and its people, past and present.

PAT CODY, *Cody's Books: The Life and Times of a Berkeley Bookstore, 1956–1977* (1992). Publisher Chronicle Books describes this volume as "a look at the building of one of the country's great bookstores." The text is a collection of letters and articles about the bookstore founded by the late Fred Cody and his wife, Pat.

DAVID COHEN AND RICH SMOLAN, *A Day in the Life of California* (1988). On April 1, 1988, a team of 100 photographers captured the people and places of California. Images from the day's record clearly define the differences between north and south.

JAMES CONAWAY, *Napa* (1990). This history of the Napa Valley wine industry focuses on the people who settled the valley, planted the vineyards, and produced the world-famous wines. Conflicts, from personal feuds to the modern fight to stop development in the valley, add drama to the story.

STEVE COUCH, *Steinbeck Country* (1973). A photographic essay on the places and people of Steinbeck's Salinas Valley, Monterey Peninsula, and Big Sur. Excerpts from Steinbeck's books introduce each section.

ROBERT X. CRINGELY, *Accidental Empire: How the Boys of Silicon Valley Make Their Millions, Battle Foreign Competitors, and Still Can't Get a Date* (1992). San Jose and neighboring towns in the Santa Clara Valley south of San Francisco have become known collectively as Silicon Valley, high-tech home for the computer and electronics industry. This gossipy volume explains how and why the personal computer industry there works.

RICHARD HENRY DANA, JR., *Two Years Before the Mast* (1840). The writer, a seaman on a brig engaged in the California tallow-hide trade, recorded his observations of life in Mexican California in the late 1830s.

DAVID DARLINGTON, *Angels' Visits: An Inquiry into the Mystery of Zinfandel* (1991). Writer Darlington considers Zinfandel "sheer joy." He unravels the "mystery" of the wine's character and origin with an exploration of the vineyards of Sonoma and Napa counties.

NARSAI M. DAVID AND DORIS MUSCATINE, *Monday Night at Narsai's* (1987). From 1972 to 1984, Narsai's was a Marin County restaurant on the cutting edge of California cuisine. This volume reproduces the menus for chef David's famous fixed-menu Monday night dinners.

ROY ANDRES DE GROOT, *The Wines of California, the Pacific Northwest and New York* (1982). The author begins with an introduction to American wines and then turns to the "best wines of the best vineyards and wineries." His choices of the top 200 American vineyards and wineries include fewer than two dozen from outside California, and most of his California choices are in the north. He concludes with profiles of the vineyards, wineries, and leading wine makers.

IDA RAE EGLI, ED., *No Rooms of Their Own: Women Writers of Early California* (1992). The voices of 15 mid-19th-century California women are presented in journal entries, stories, and poems.

CURT GENTRY, *The Last Days of the Late, Great State of California* (1968). Gentry tackles the ultimate disaster scenario: An earthquake lurches out of the sea at Point Arena, California trembles, the earth cracks along fault lines, and everything west of the chasm disappears into the sea. Breathless reading.

ALLEN GINSBERG, *Collected Poems 1947–1980* (1984). Ginsberg was the poet laureate of San Francisco's 1950s Beat Generation; his angry, pungent verse of that era brought him into court on obscenity charges.

HERBERT GOLD, *Dreaming* (1989). Gold, a fixture of San Francisco's contemporary literary scene, writes about a none-too-successful wheeler-dealer who moves across a familiar cityscape, ranging from Enrico's in North Beach to the Marina and the Avenues. In *Travels in San Francisco* (1990), Gold provides a guide to "hanging out" in a city he considers to be the last great American metropolitan village.

Great Chefs of San Francisco (1983). Thirteen cooking classes presented on public television by San Francisco Bay Area kitchen greats were compiled in this masters' cookbook with recipes and details on the chefs and their workplaces. Includes such chefs as Jeremiah Tower (Stars, formerly with Santa Fe Bar & Grill), Mark Miller (Fourth Street Grill), and Masataka Kobayashi (Masa's).

Guide to California Wine Country (1979, frequent revisions). Most of this practical guide from Sunset Books focuses on wine in Northern California. Winery descriptions are accompanied by regional maps.

GARY HAMILTON AND NICOLE WOOLSEY BIGGART, *Governor Reagan, Governor Brown* (1984). An examination of the gubernatorial styles and philosophies of two very different men—one an ex-actor, the other, his successor, a young ex-theologian who was nicknamed Governor Moonbeam.

DASHIELL HAMMETT, *The Maltese Falcon* (1929). Detective Sam Spade works the foggy streets of San Francisco in this classic mystery.

HANK HARRISON, *The Dead* (1990). A two-volume history in words, photographs, and art of 25 years of San Francisco underground music.

JAMES D. HART, *A Companion to California* (1987). Director of the Bancroft Library at the University of California, Berkeley, the late Hart compiled an encyclopedic guide to people, places, and events in the state.

BRET HARTE, *Luck of Roaring Camp* (1868), *The Outcasts of Poker Flat* (1869). These classics, written when Harte edited the *Overland Monthly,* present a picturesque, sentimental view of Gold Rush days. (Found today in anthologies.)

MIKE HIPPLER, *So Little Time* (1990). A collection of 50 essays on gay themes; most are reprinted from this San Francisco writer's *Bay Area Reporter* column.

J. S. HOLLIDAY, *The World Rushed In* (1981). A masterful account of the 1849 stampede to the California goldfields. At its core are the diary and letters of 49er William Swain, who was lured from Youngstown, New York, by the promise of fortune on the western slope of the Sierra Nevada. Excerpts from an additional 500 diaries and letter collections help make this one of the best histories of the Gold Rush.

MILDRED BROOKE HOOVER, ED., *Historic Spots in California* (1932). Recently reissued, this book belongs on the shelf of every enthusiast of California, covering as it does pivotal sites from the opening up of the state by the Spanish explorers to the development of the 1930s.

NORRIS HUNDLEY JR., *The Great Thirst: Californians and Water, 1770–1990s* (1992). Californians have lied, cheated, and killed over water rights, and this new volume, which takes readers from the first settlements to the drought of the 1980s and 1990s, examines historic struggles over the precious substance, North-South conflicts over water, and the building of San Francisco's municipal water system. Hundley also touched on California's water politics in his earlier *Water and the West* (1975).

JOSEPH HENRY JACKSON, *Anybody's Gold* (1941). An anecdotal history of Mother Lode mining settlements. Half of the book is devoted to the towns as they are in modern (1941) times (illustrated by E. H. Suydam).

ROBINSON JEFFERS, *Roan Stallion* (1925), *The Women at Point Sur* (1927), *Give Your Heart to The Hawks* (1933). Poems by Jeffers can best be described as intense, brooding, and even dour, but he wrote with passion about the California landscape, particularly the rugged Big Sur country south of the Monterey Peninsula.

STEPHEN JOHNSON, GERALD HASLAM, AND ROBERT DAWSON, *The Great Central Valley: California's Heartland* (1992). Sandwiched between the Coast Range and the Sierra Nevada,

California's Great Central Valley stretches 430 miles north to south and up to 75 miles across, and encompasses nearly 15 million acres (roughly the size of England). It is the richest farming region in the world, producing more than 25 percent of America's food. This volume explores the natural and social diversity of the region as well as the contemporary perils of pollution and environmental degradation. Illustrated with 112 color and 100 duotone photographs, plus engravings and maps.

MICHELE ANNA JORDAN, *A Cook's Tour of Sonoma* (1990). Maps, a guide to wine-tasting tours, notes on food and wine, and a bit of history accompany this collection of 200 recipes focused on the region's bounty of produce.

MAXINE HONG KINGSTON, *China Men* (1977). Novelist Kingston tells the story of Chinese immigration to America through the experiences of the men of her family. Of particular interest are segments dealing with "The Father from China," who entered America via the immigration station at Angel Island, San Francisco Bay, and "The Grandfather of the Sierra Mountains," an 1860s laborer on the railroad. *The Woman Warrior* (1976) describes the painful but often hilarious experience of growing up Chinese in Stockton, California.

THEODORA KROEBER, *Ishi In Two Worlds: A Biography of the Last Wild Indian in North America* (1961). A poignant account of the life of the last member of California's Yahi tribe, who emerged from the hills near Oroville in 1911.

JAMES LAUBE, *California's Great Chardonnays* (1990). The writer surveyed 1,250 wines from 125 Chardonnay producers for this appraisal of the state's favorite white wine.

EMILY WORTIS LEIDER, *California's Daughter: Gertrude Atherton and Her Times* (1991). A biography of a San Francisco–born novelist and short-story writer (1857–1948) who, at the height of her popularity, was ranked with Edith Wharton. Atherton roamed the world, living in London, Berlin, Greece, and the West Indies, but she created California heroines Leider describes as appealing to women "seeking an identity based on their own needs and talents."

NIGEY LENNON, *Mark Twain in California* (1982). Samuel Clemens arrived in San Francisco from Virginia City, Nevada, in May 1864 and quickly fit into the lively and large literary bohemia. Lennon brings this period, when Twain produced the work that brought him his first national notice, to life.

OSCAR LEWIS, *San Francisco: Mission to Metropolis* (2nd ed., 1980). Lewis, regarded by some as the dean of San Francisco history, published this book in 1960. For this revised edition, he expanded on "The Contemporary Scene."

JACK LONDON, *The Star Rover* (1915). This fictionalized story of out-of-body and past-life experiences of turn-of-the-century California outlaw Ed Morrell is considered London's final great work. *The Valley of the Moon* (1913) focuses on the Sonoma area where London built his last home.

RUTHANNE LUM MCCUNN, *Thousand Pieces of Gold* (1981). A biographical novel about Lalu Nathoy (later Polly Bemis), a Chinese woman who was brought to San Francisco to be sold in the 1870s. Although she spent most of her American life in the Northwest, Bemis's story provides background on San Francisco's underground trade in Chinese women.

PATRICK MCGREW, *Landmarks of San Francisco* (1991). The architect and former chairman of San Francisco's Landmarks Preservation Advisory Board has compiled a helpful collection of the nearly 200 local buildings that have been granted official landmark status; not only such obvious choices as the Mission Dolores but also lesser known structures as the South San Francisco Opera House which is "not located in South San Francisco and is not an opera house."

JOHN MEYERS MEYERS, *San Francisco's Reign of Terror* (1966). A critical look at the vigilantes who took law, order, and punishment into their own hands during the city's turbulent 1850s.

LEONARD MICHAELS, ED., *West of the West: Imagining California* (1989). Fine writers such as Tom Wolfe, Joan Didion, Gore Vidal, Gertrude Stein, M.F.K. Fisher, and Simone de Beauvoir record their experiences in this novelistic journey through the Golden State.

HENRY MILLER, *Big Sur and the Oranges of Hieronymus Bosch* (1958). An insider's account of life in the literary-arts colony on the Big Sur coast in the 1940s and 1950s.

FRANCES MOFFAT, *Dancing on the Brink of the World* (1977). A longtime society editor of the *San Francisco Chronicle*, Moffat records the antics of San Francisco's rich, elite, and sometimes not-too-respectable Golden Circle. The story stretches from the city's birth to contemporary times.

KRISTIN MOORE, *Mother Lode: A Pictorial Guide to California's Gold Rush Country* (1983). Text and photographs begin with Mariposa and cover a 319-mile chain of towns to the northernmost mines.

JO MORA, *Californios* (1949). Artist-sculptor Mora wrote and illustrated this collector's piece on Old California and the men called *vaqueros,* the first American cowboys. (Readers who visit Carmel Mission will see another example of Mora's talent: He designed the ceremonial sarcophagus of Father Junípero Serra.)

DALE L. MORGAN, *Jedediah Smith and the Opening of the West* (1953). Beaver trapper Smith was the first Yankee to reach California by an overland route. He also made the first recorded trip from California to Oregon in 1828 by way of the precipitous mountains of the far North Coast.

JOHN MUIR, *My First Summer in the Sierra* (1911). Muir, walker, writer, conservationist, and founder of the Sierra Club, published this account of his 1866 Sierra Nevada summer when he was 73.

STUART NIXON, *Redwood Empire* (1966). History, geography, personality profiles, and photographs blend in a portrait of Northern California.

CHARLES NORDHOFF, *Nordhoff's West Coast: California, Oregon and Hawaii* (1987). Originally published in 1874 and 1875, Nordhoff's reports describe the extraordinary "new lifestyle" of the American West. His description of California "for health, pleasure, and residence" was both a travel guide and an inspiration for the late 19th-century migration to the state. This edition is illustrated with the original sketches.

FRANK NORRIS, *The Octopus* (1901). This heavy-handed but powerful novel focuses on the greed and ruthlessness of the builders of the Southern Pacific Railroad in Northern California's Central Valley.

JEAN-NICOLAS PERLOT, TRANS. BY HELEN HARDING BRETNOR, *Goldseeker* (1985). The first English translation of a young Belgian's adventures in Monterey, the Southern Mines, and Yosemite during the Gold Rush.

CHARLES PERRY, *Haight-Ashbury: A History* (1984). Perry's description of the world of Be-Ins, Love-Ins, flamboyance, marijuana, and LSD was garnered from participants and from the voluminous media coverage of a movement that grew from 1965 to 1966, peaked in the summer of 1967, and died in 1968.

ELIZABETH POMADA AND MICHAEL LARSEN, *The Painted Ladies Revisited* (1989). A district-by-district examination, in text and color photography, of the restoration of San Francisco's 19th-century and turn-of-the-century houses commonly called Victorians. The text sketches histories of individual houses, while Douglas Keister's photographs provide beautiful illustrations.

LAWRENCE CLARK POWELL, *California Classics: The Creative Literature of the Golden State* (1971). A compendium of good or famous efforts in California letters.

HAL ROTH, *Pathways in the Sky, The Story of the John Muir Trail* (1965). A detailed, illustrated description of the Sierra Nevada trail named after California's great conservationist.

GALEN ROWELL, *The Yosemite* (1989). One hundred color photographs by a contemporary mountaineer and master photographer celebrate Yosemite National Park's centennial. Each photograph is accompanied by excerpts from *The Yosemite* by conservationist John Muir.

WILLIAM SAROYAN, *The Human Comedy* (1943). Homer Macauly, the fastest telegram bicycle messenger in the San Joaquin Valley, is the key character in Saroyan's first novel, a story about a small-town family during World War II.

VIKRAM SETH, *The Golden Gate* (1986). This novel in verse takes the clichés and characters of contemporary life in San Francisco and the Bay Area and shapes them into a fresh, delightful story of loneliness, loss, and gentle love.

RANDY SHILTS, *The Mayor of Castro Street* (1981). A biography of Harvey Milk, the San Francisco city supervisor and gay community leader assassinated by Dan White. It also provides background on the lifestyles and politics of the nation's largest gay community in the 1970s.

REBECCA SOLNIT, *Secret Exhibition: Six California Artists* (1991). Bohemia of the 1950s and 1960s is examined through the lives and works of six artists: Wallace Berman, Jess, Bruce Conner, Jay DeFeo, Wally Hedrick, and George Herms. Chapters explore such topics as culture and counter-culture in the San Francisco of the 1950s.

KEVIN STARR, *Material Dreams: California Through the 1920s* (1990). Starr, a Northern California historian, is writing a serial history on what he calls "America and the California Dream"; this third volume is the most recent.

JOHN STEINBECK, *The Grapes of Wrath* (1939). This Pulitzer Prize–winning novel about Dust Bowl migrants—called Oakies and Arkies in California—delivers as strong a human and social message today as it did half a century ago. Steinbeck's *Cannery Row* (1945), published as Monterey's sardine fishing-and-packing industry was on its deathbed, has become California myth, shaping perceptions of Monterey for two generations.

W. A. SWANBERG, *Citizen Hearst* (1961). This biography brings to life William Randolph Hearst, the newspaper publishing tycoon, power manipulator, and builder of Hearst Castle, San Simeon, whose Northern California family roots extended to Gold Rush days.

AMY TAN, *The Joy Luck Club* (1990) and *The Kitchen God's Wife* (1991). The first of these deeply felt and superbly written novels sees the Chinese society in America through a Chinese women's mah-jongg and gossip group. The second is a search for identities through family secrets, from Shanghai in the 1920s to arrival in California in 1949. Tan's sense of the human comedy makes both hilarious; she was born in Oakland and lives in San Francisco.

GORDON THOMAS AND MAX MORGAN WITTS, *The San Francisco Earthquake* (1971). Interviews with 1906 earthquake survivors, other eyewitness accounts, and insurance, Red Cross, and military records sketch a compelling picture of an event that has passed beyond history into folklore.

MARK TWAIN, *Roughing It* (1871). In Twain's own words, this book is a "personal narrative" and a "record of several years of variegated vagabondizing" in Nevada, Northern California, and Hawaii.

JOHN VAN DER ZEE, *The Gate: The True Story of the Design and Construction of the Golden Gate Bridge* (1986). The people, politics, and technology that produced San Francisco's great bridge are thoroughly scrutinized in this volume.

STEPHEN VINCENT, ED., *O California!* (1989). California's geography is described through beautifully reproduced landscape paintings by the state's 19th-century and early 20th-century artists and words from their contemporaries.

PAUL WEBSTER, *The Mighty Sierra* (1972). An illustrated, comprehensive view of the mountain range that extends 400 miles from Tehachapi Pass to Lassen Peak.

—*Shirley Maas Fockler*

SAN FRANCISCO

By Georgia I. Hesse with Susan Shook

The port of San Francisco . . . is a marvel of nature, and might well be called the harbor of harbors, because of its great capacity, and of several small bays which it enfolds in its margins or beach and in its islands. Indeed, although in my travels I saw very good sites and beautiful country, I saw none which pleased me so much as this. And I think that if it could be well settled like Europe there would not be anything more beautiful in all the world, for it has the best advantages for founding in it a most beautiful city, with all the conveniences desired, by land as well as by sea, with that harbor so remarkable and so spacious, in which may be established shipyards, docks, and anything that might be wished. . . .

—Pedro Font, *Complete Diary of Anza's California Expeditions,* 1776

San Francisco began by being beautiful. Like Paris, its very name sings a siren song to people around the globe; but Paris owes its distinction to architecture, while San Francisco was blessed by nature.

Even philosopher Josiah Royce, who felt nature to be a poor teacher, fell under the spell of the physical place: "The high dark hills on the western shore of the Bay, the water at their feet, the Golden Gate that breaks through them and opens up to one the view of the sea beyond, the smoke-obscured city at the south of the Gate, and the barren ranges yet farther to the left, these are the permanent background

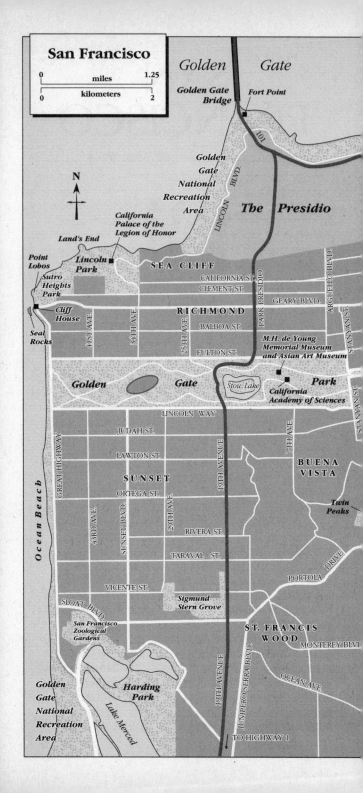

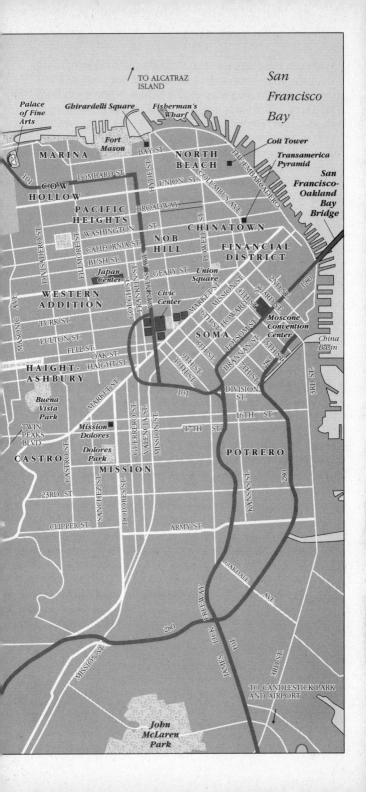

whereon many passing shapes of light and shadow, of cloud and storm, of mist and of sunset glow are projected as I watch all from my station on the hillside." (Royce was born in Grass Valley, California, of all unlikely places, went on to teach at the University of California and, later, at Harvard. His words here are from *Fugitive Essays,* 1879.)

In modern days, novelist John Steinbeck, more used to creating word-paintings of poverty than eloquent eulogies, was moved to write (in *Travels with Charley*), "I saw her across the bay, from the great road that bypasses Sausalito and enters the Golden Gate Bridge. The afternoon sun painted her white and gold—rising on her hills like a noble city in a happy dream . . . this gold-and-white acropolis rising wave on wave against the blue of the Pacific sky was a stunning thing, a painted thing like a picture of a medieval Italian city which can never have existed. . . ."

But she does exist, and twilight is perhaps her finest time, when from every hill (about six times as many as in Rome) the bay runs to meet the sea beyond the Gate, framed by the baked golden hills of Marin and the deepening blue of the sky that stretches west of the sunset toward Asia. A skinny finger of fog slips beneath the Golden Gate Bridge, and all around the darkening waters, golden dots of light wink on in salute—and one is glad to live nowhere else.

It is such moments the San Franciscan holds to himself, like inexpressible secrets, when faced with the dreary dramas of city life in the 1990s: the drugs, the homelessness, the pathetic politics. Despite inroads of urban angst, San Francisco remains a retreat for the joyous, the creative, and the civilized.

MAJOR INTEREST

Union Square area
Chinatown
Nob Hill's mansions
North Beach, for Italian atmosphere
Fisherman's Wharf
Golden Gate National Recreation Area (hikes along the bay)
Golden Gate Bridge
The Marina and the Palace of Fine Arts
Cow Hollow, for dining and shopping
Pacific Heights' Victorians
Japantown
Ethnic dining on Clement Street

Golden Gate Park (museums and nature)
Civic Center museum and performing arts area
Mission Dolores
SoMa (South of Market) café scene
Ocean Beach and Land's End
Cable cars

San Francisco (Spanish for Saint Francis, he of Assisi in Italy) derives its name from the Misión San Francisco de Asís, sixth in the series of 21 mission churches built in New Spain as outposts of the empire by the Franciscan order, largely under the direction of Father Junípero Serra. (Born in Majorca, Serra is buried within the walls of Mission San Carlos Borromeo del Río in Carmel and is being considered for sainthood by the Roman Catholic Church.)

The entrance to San Francisco Bay had been missed for more than 200 years by European explorers (perhaps it was hidden in fog) when on November 1, 1769, Sergeant José de Ortega, pathfinder for Gaspar de Portolá's expedition, marched overland in search of the "lost" bay of Monterey. Approaching from the south, he climbed a ridge and spotted the wide bay, the islands, and all the lands around. (It was a North American, however, who christened the entrance to the great inland waterway. In his *Memoirs,* General John Charles Frémont wrote, "To this gate I gave the name of *Chrysopylae,* or Golden Gate; for the same reason that the harbor of Byzantium was called Chryso-ceras, or Golden Horn.")

The site of the Presidio (fort) of San Francisco was selected by Juan Bautista de Anza on March 28, 1776 (three months to the day before Thomas Jefferson presented the Declaration of Independence to the American Congress); one wall of that fort remains as part of the Officers' Club of today's Presidio. That same year, on October 9, San Francisco's mission (missions and forts went hand in gun in early California) was dedicated at a place also picked by Anza, on the bank of a little lake and stream flowing into it (now filled). He called the stream *Arroyo de los Dolores,* having found it on the Friday of Sorrows (*dolores*). Over the years the church came by its present name, Mission Dolores. So San Francisco was born.

Some contemporary statistics: the city's population is only about 732,000, but as a metropolitan *area,* this is the nation's fourth largest; there are 14,000 surviving Victorian dwellings; the city claims the crookedest street in the world, Lombard Street; its narrowest street is DeForest Way (at four-and-a-

half feet) near the Castro district; its steepest streets are
Filbert from Leavenworth to Hyde in North Beach and 22nd
Street between Church and Vicksburg near Dolores Park,
both boasting a 31.5 degree grade.

In a day of increasing sameness and sterility, San Francisco delights in the diversity of its neighborhoods; sometimes it seems you should have a passport to go from one to
another. "Chinoiserie, chiaroscuro, chili sauce" was one
writer's description of the city's ethnic mix (forgetting the
teriyaki). Even the weather refuses homogeneity: Union
Square can be bathed in sunlight while the shoppers on
West Portal near the ocean shiver in fog.

Not all the neighborhoods are equally enticing, of course.
Here, we describe those of most interest to the traveller. We
begin at Union Square, the traditional stepping-off spot for a
tour of the town, and proceed roughly north, with detours to
the east and west, through the areas that constitute the core
of interest for visitors—the Financial District, Chinatown,
Nob Hill, and North Beach. All of these areas lie east of Van
Ness Avenue, a major north–south artery. After reaching the
shores of San Francisco Bay, we ramble west along Fisherman's Wharf to the Golden Gate Bridge, then backtrack east
through the Marina, and head roughly south, again with
detours to the east and west, particularly to Golden Gate
Park, through the neighborhoods west of Van Ness Avenue.
We then venture south to Mission Dolores and two nighttime haunts, the Civic Center and SoMa (South of Market),
the first for museums, symphony, and opera, the second for
more café-oriented culture, all three south of Union Square.
Then it's to Ocean Beach, at ocean's edge far to the west of
downtown and west of Golden Gate Park. We end with a few
of the city's specialties—cable cars, sports, and a roundup of
annual events.

UNION SQUARE

This rectangular crossroads is perhaps the single space unit-
ing the several elements and attitudes of the city. The chic
center for the "shop 'til you drop" set, it is also where pigeons
and protesters come to see and be part of the scene. This is
the stage set for such outrageous characters as Sadie, Sadie
the Rabbi Lady and the Sisters of Perpetual Indulgence (look
especially for Sister Boom-Boom), as it was for now-beloved
characters of the past such as Emperor Norton and James King
of William, and even the sandal-footed beatniks of 1958 who

marched down from North Beach on a "Squaresville Tour," following a bongo drummer and startling the stylish shoppers in Gump's, Shreve, and I. Magnin. (These blocks were made for walking; park your car at the underground Union Square Garage, the Downtown Center Garage at Mason and O'Farrell streets, or, less expensively, a block away at the Sutter-Stockton Garage.)

Union Square, bounded by Stockton, Powell, Post, and Geary streets, was originally a mighty sandbank called O'Farrell's Mountain. Presented to the city in 1850 by John W. Geary, first American mayor of San Francisco, it was leveled and turned into a green, flowery two-and-a-half-acre park. When the Civil War threatened, the square saw its first demonstrations as pro-Union rallies were staged here to protest the secession of the southern states, and the name Union Square stuck.

The square's center is the Dewey Monument, a 90-foot granite shaft that celebrates Commodore George Dewey's triumph over the Spanish navy at Manila Bay in 1898 during the Spanish-American War; should you wish to salute him, you may do so at **Dewey's**, a pub across Powell Street in the St. Francis Hotel. The face of the goddess Victory who crowns the monument is said to be a likeness of Alma de Bretteville Spreckels. (The civic benefactress, with her husband, Adolph, gave the city its California Palace of the Legion of Honor, as well as that museum's collection of Rodin sculptures; see Ocean Beach and Land's End.)

The St. Francis Hotel

Five churches and one synagogue first commanded this square, with private clubs spaced among them. Then, in 1904, Charles T. Crocker (of the banking Crockers) decided his city needed proper accommodations for the growing clutch of bonanza kings, and decreed the building of the **St. Francis Hotel** on the west side of the square. Resulting commerce eased the churches farther west in the direction of Van Ness Avenue, although the Congregational stopped only a block west at the corner of Post and Mason, where it still stands. (Concerts and other musical events are often presented here.)

Whether events have been fashionable or felonious, the St. Francis has lived on center stage. Until the wane of proper dress in the 1960s, the white-gloved (and behatted) ladies of San Francisco took Monday luncheons in the St. Francis Mural Room, and lest those gloves be allowed to

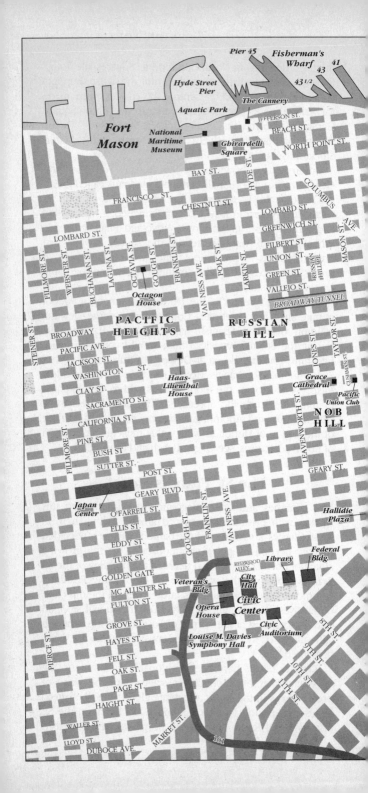

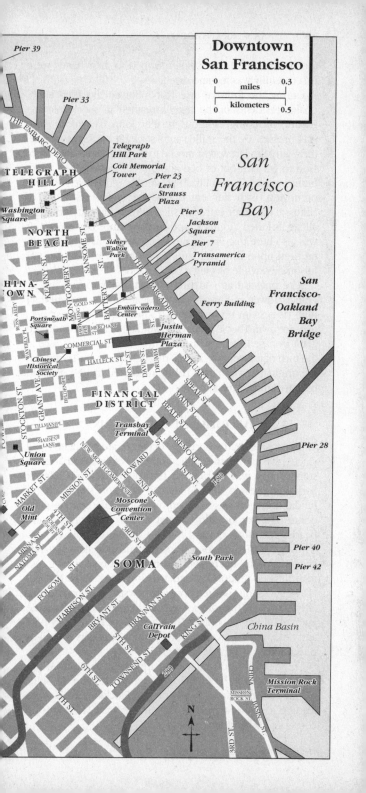

Downtown San Francisco

0   miles   0.3

0   kilometers   0.5

Pier 39

Pier 33

THE EMBARCADERO

Telegraph Hill Park

Coit Memorial Tower

Pier 23

TELEGRAPH HILL

Levi Strauss Plaza

Pier 9

San Francisco Bay

Washington Square

Jackson Square

Pier 7

NORTH BEACH

KEARNY ST.

SANSOME ST.

BATTERY ST.

Sidney Walton Park

Transamerica Pyramid

CHINA-TOWN

ROSS ALLEY

MONTGOMERY ST.

GOLD ST.

THE EMBARCADERO

San Francisco-Oakland Bay Bridge

Portsmouth Square

WAVERLY PL.

KEELING PL.

Embarcadero Center

Ferry Building

MERCHANT ST.

COMMERCIAL ST.

GRANT AVE.

Chinese Historical Society

BELDEN PL.

HALLECK ST.

FRONT ST.

DAVIS ST.

DRUMM ST.

Justin Herman Plaza

STEUART ST.

STOCKTON ST.

FINANCIAL DISTRICT

SPEAR ST.

MAIN ST.

TILLMAN PL.

MAIDEN LANE

Union Square

Transbay Terminal

BEALE ST.

FREMONT ST.

1ST ST.

I-80

MARKET ST.

NEW MONTGOMERY ST.

HOWARD ST.

2ND ST.

Pier 28

Old Mint

MISSION ST.

4TH ST.

Moscone Convention Center

3RD ST.

MINNA ST.

NATOMA ST.

SOMA

South Park

Pier 40

Pier 42

FOLSOM ST.

HARRISON ST.

BRYANT ST.

BRANNAN ST.

China Basin

5TH ST.

CalTrain Depot

KING ST.

6TH ST.

TOWNSEND ST.

280

MISSION ROCK ST.

CHINA BASIN ST.

Mission Rock Terminal

7TH ST.

3RD ST.

N

touch filthy lucre, any coins returned to their hands were first carefully washed and dried.

During the four-day fire that followed the 1906 earthquake, residents of the hotel streamed in shock into the square, including bibulous reveler John Barrymore, who was pressed by the militia into stacking bricks. His uncle, thespian John Drew, was moved to remark, "It took an act of God to get Jack out of bed and the U.S. government to get him to work." Queen Elizabeth slept here in March of 1983, occupying, with her entourage, the entire 31st floor of suites; at the other extreme, silent-screen star Fatty Arbuckle allegedly killed Virgina Rappe here on Labor Day in 1921. It was also here that President Gerald Ford walked outside to be fired upon by Sarah Jane Moore in 1975, and where Al Jolson died while playing a poker hand.

Face outward as you ride the glass elevators of the St. Francis Tower and watch Union Square and its surrounding high rises swim up into view. It's one of the best perspectives in town. The St. Francis' Tower Lobby now boasts three giant trompe l'oeil murals depicting life in San Francisco at the turn of the century. A walk through the Tower Lobby and the original Powell Street Lobby, renovated in 1991, is a trip back to a more elegant time.

Around Union Square

The opposite, southeast corner of the square had been ruled since 1896 by another relic, the City of Paris department store, until it was replaced in 1983 by controversial, almost harlequin-dressed Neiman Marcus. The store's dramatic rotunda, however, was retained, with its Belle Epoque glass dome of a barque afloat under a sky of fleur-de-lis, and bearing the motto of Paris: It Floats and Never Sinks.

Always intriguing to visitors, the curbside flower stands around Union Square sell blooms in season for a bit less than florists. Vendors owe their colorful outlets to Michael Harry de Young (of the *Chronicle* newspaper dynasty), who allowed young people to sell flowers in front of the de Young building years ago. The stands were licensed in 1904 and today are a bona fide attraction for residents as well as outsiders.

The district's most endearing artwork is the **Ruth Asawa Fountain,** created by the local sculptor to capture the spirit of the city in bronze. It sits on the Stockton Street steps leading to the entrance of the Grand Hyatt Hotel on the corner of Post and Stockton streets.

Union Square celebrates spring with April's Rhododendron Days and the Easter Flower show at Macy's at Stockton and O'Farrell streets, midsummer with the Cable Car Bell-Ringing Contest, and midwinter with the Chinese New Year Pageant.

Dining Around Union Square

Well before high noon, giving the slip to beggars, brown-baggers, do-gooders, and sidewalk traders in the tawdry, the ladies and gentlemen who frequent Union Square proper are all in their places for luncheon at **Campton Place Kempinski** (an elegant little retreat on Stockton Street with an outstanding restaurant; Tel: 781-5155), **The Rotunda** at Neiman Marcus under the glass dome (Tel: 362-4777), **Kuleto's** in the Villa Florence hotel on Powell Street (Tel: 397-7720), **Janot's** at 44 Campton Place (an alley between Sutter and Post; Tel: 392-5373), or (a few steps up on Bush) **Le Central**, where columnist Herb Caen and/or his buddy Willie Brown, speaker of the State Assembly, and/or Wilkes Bashford (clothier to the upper crust) may be spotted chatting at a windowside table; Tel: 391-2233.

Two blocks north of Union Square, Bush Street is a handy artery (one-way west to east) for drivers bound for the "back door" of the Sutter–Stockton Garage, the most moderately priced garage for those spending several hours in the Union Square vicinity. There are several worthwhile restaurants along this street, including **Café Mozart** at number 708, where French cuisine is served in a richness of parquet floors, crystal chandeliers, and red velvet curtains while the music of the master sounds gently in the background. In the block north of the St. Francis at 439 Powell, **Sears Fine Foods** has been serving delectable breakfasts for decades (lunches, too, Wednesdays through Sundays).

Shopping Around Union Square

Shopping is the sine qua non of the Union Square experience, but even strollers will appreciate an amble down **Maiden Lane**, an elegant pedestrian alley once known as Morton Street, which runs from Stockton for two blocks east to Kearny Street. (Morton Street was notable for a number of ladies of the night; hence, with the smartening-up of the area, the new name Maiden Lane.) The atmosphere is the neat streets of Paris; the one tourist sight is the **Circle Gallery** building at number 140, designed by Frank Lloyd

Wright in 1949 and a prototype for New York City's Guggenheim Museum.

At 250 Post Street between Stockton and Grant, **Gump's** is
not only the oldest but the most prestigious Asian art dealer
in the city. Founded in 1865 by the Gump brothers, two
German immigrants, it is a veritable museum as well, a
destination for anyone interested in Asian arts. The Jade
Room is fascinating.

San Francisco boasts dozens of art galleries of all persua-
sions in several districts of town; the region around Union
Square is particularly proud of its collection. On Maiden Lane,
for example, in addition to Circle Gallery, you'll find **Cona-
cher Galleries** (contemporary art, rare prints); **Hanson
Galleries** (contemporary oils, watercolors, sculpture, limited
editions); **Maiden Lane Gallery** (American masters); **Orientations** (18th- and 19th-century Oriental art and antiques); and
Richard Thompson Gallery (oils, limited-edition prints by
20th-century American Impressionists). Should gallery-hop-
ping make you hungry, you might repair to the **Iron Horse** at
19 Maiden Lane. Long a valued luncheon rendezvous for
making deals, business and otherwise, this dark retreat of
Italian flavors still plays a part in the life of the area.

Two blocks to the north of Union Square, Sutter Street—
and the streets running north and south of it—could be
called Gallery Row (see Shopping below). Shoppers and
gallery-goers alike often lunch at the **White Elephant,** a cozy
hideaway with the air of an English club (in the Holiday Inn
at 480 Sutter; Tel: 398-1331).

From Union Square, theaters and several good restaurants
are a few steps away to the west (see Theater District
Dining); burgeoning SoMa sits to the south; the shops,
restaurants, hotels, and green spaces of the Embarcadero
wait to the northeast beyond the Financial District; and Nob
Hill, Chinatown, Russian Hill, North Beach, Telegraph Hill,
and Fisherman's Wharf are to the north, reachable by foot
(for the exercise), cable car, or bus.

THE FINANCIAL DISTRICT

The Wall Street of the West, they call it: the stretch of
Montgomery Street from Market north to Washington Street.
More recently it's been dubbed San Francisco's canyon coun-
try. (Walk east from Union Square on Post Street to reach
Montgomery.)

The main Financial District stretches from Market Street north to Jackson Street and from Kearny Street and China-town on the west to Drumm Street and the Embarcadero Center buildings on the east. (A few square blocks to the south of Market are technically part of the district, but are of less interest to visitors.)

Finance and Montgomery Street have always been mated. It was on Montgomery on May 12, 1848, that Sam Brannan, a Mormon settler and publisher of San Francisco's first news-paper, the *California Star,* yelled out the news that initiated one of history's greatest runs for the riches. "Holding high a bottle full of gold dust," writes J. S. Holliday in *The World Rushed In,* "Brannan shouted: 'Gold! Gold! Gold from the American River!' By the middle of June, San Francisco stood half empty, with three-quarters of the men off to the mines, most stores closed, the *alcalde's* office shut, the newspapers suspended, outbound ships at anchor deserted by their crews. News from San Jose, Benicia, Sonoma, all the same—empty streets, abandoned businesses, fields of grain opened to roaming cattle."

Standing in front of the soaring Bank of America build-ing today at 555 California Street (perhaps near the abstract black-granite sculpture known locally as "the banker's heart"), watching dapper businesspeople bound for lunch 52 floors up at the Carnelian Room or the private Banker's Club, it's difficult to think of this as a former morass where mules mired, even drowned, in the ooze. ("This street impassable," read one street sign of the time, "not even jackassable.")

The shantytown that in 1849 sprang into being in San Francisco (a canvas tent called El Dorado was rented out to gamblers for $40,000 per year) was constructed on the car-casses of ships. All the streets we walk today east of Montgom-ery between California and Broadway began as wharves. Offshore lay an armada of ghost ships whose crews had careened off for gold; maritime historians estimate that 100 vessels were hauled into the shallows to serve as stores and warehouses, or were sunk for fill and building foundations.

The booming, naughty (some said vice-ridden) Victorian city died on April 18, 1906, when the earthquake shook the city to its shale-and-sandstone foundation. (A Los Angeles newspaper supposedly headlined the story, "San Francisco Punished!") In the following three years the town rushed to rebuild (sidewalk placards pleaded, "Don't talk earthquake, talk business"), especially in this district, with the result that it became what architectural writer Randolph Delehanty called "an up-to-date Edwardian city of remarkable architectural coherence."

The shades of some of San Francisco's illustrious literati haunt these skyscraper-shadowed streets. On the southeast corner of Montgomery and Washington, where the Transamerica Pyramid soars today, the storied Monkey Block (really Montgomery Block) first served financiers and law firms and later was occupied by the offices and/or hangouts of Ambrose Bierce, Bret Harte, William Randolph Hearst, Rudyard Kipling, Jack London, Robert Louis Stevenson, and Mark Twain. At the Washington Street corner, the Bank Exchange Saloon was a favored watering place, much frequented by the eccentric Emperor Norton; crusading newspaper editor James King of William was brought here, bleeding, after being shot by rival editor James Casey. (The approximate spot is now occupied by the Cisco Kid Cantina.)

Around in the Financial District

Walkers probably will approach this trading enclave (Randolph Delehanty has called it "... undoubtedly the most pleasant, and though costly, most efficient office core in the United States") from Union Square, most handily by walking east on Post Street to its meeting with Montgomery.

In 1982, the handsome **Crocker Galleria** at 50 Post Street joined the ranks of San Francisco's new architectural landmarks. Inspired by Milan's Galleria Vittorio Emanuele, this major shopping arena is canopied by a glass vault 70 feet high and 275 feet long. If it's lunchtime, consider the pleasant **Circolo Restaurant and Champagneria** on the Sutter Street side of the building, which serves Italian specialties and boasts a wood-burning pizza oven as well as bar murals from the Old Poodle Dog, a San Francisco institution that came to an end some years ago. On the same block, at number 191, the ▶ **Galleria Park** is a splendid place to stay at a most reasonable rate. The lively **Brasserie Chambord**, adjoining the hotel, is a friendly, attractive place serving French-Californian dishes; Tel: 434-3688.

If you have strolled down Sutter Street from Union Square, you will have passed (and should stop at) **Lascaux**, where the sizzle of the fast-track set slows down to country-French speed. It's a great cellar-level retreat at 248 Sutter; Tel: 391-1555. On the other hand, should you want to sample Old California atmosphere, plan a long lunch at **Sam's Grill**, 374 Bush Street near Kearny (really in a tiny alley named

Belden). One of the city's oldest restaurants (with waiters to match), it has served some of the best petrale sole in town from one decade into the next (Tel: 421-0594).

Nearby, at 22 Belden Place, **Café Bastille** was the first of a new generation of old-fashioned French cafés not far from the church of Notre Dame de Victoire at 500 Bush, itself once the center of a long-gone Gallic mining community known as Frenchmen's Hill. The café is simple, inexpensive, and as authentic as a Metro station. Just a few steps west at 431 Bush, the **Rendezvous du Monde** is thoroughly French with an Italian accent. Third in the tricolor trio is **Café Claude** at number 7 on tiny Claude Lane just off Bush between Grant and Kearny. It's cramped and crazily busy just like its Parisian counterparts; in fact, its furnishings were imported intact from the city of *croque monsieur,* right down to the bar. You can try to make a reservation, but you'll wait anyway; Tel: 392-3505.

It's unlikely that the traveller with limited time would spend the hours to inspect in detail all of the striking buildings on show in this district. But be sure to note the 47-story **First Interstate Center** at the corner of Sansome and California streets, a complex design that incorporates the shells of four old office buildings, a retail concourse, smart offices, and—of first importance—the elegant ▶ **Mandarin Oriental** hotel, with its highly respected restaurant **Silks**; Tel: 986-2020.

Just down the street at 240 California (between Battery and Front), the **Tadich Grill**, scarcely changed since its birth in 1849, is California's oldest restaurant, one of a distinguished clan created by Yugoslavian immigrants; fresh seafood is their claim to fame, though grilled foods are also good. No reservations are taken, and the pre-lunch line stretches down the block, so your best bet is to arrive for a late lunch (2:00 P.M. or after) or an early dinner (6:00 P.M.). One of the hottest spots in town is **Aqua**, which elbows the Tadich Grill at 252 California. The decor is beautiful, the atmosphere is fun, and the seafood is to flip over; Tel: 956-9662.

One of the most dominant structures on San Francisco's skyline is the **Bank of America** at 555 California Street, between Kearny and Montgomery. When you stare at its intriguing zigzag façade closely, you will admire it; from a distance it stands out as a black-red slab at odds with the city's generally pastel appearance. In any case it's worth the long ride to the top to the **Carnelian Room** for American cuisine and an outstanding wine cellar or to the **Pacific**

Room for cocktails, or simply to admire what their 52nd-floor position offers—the most stunning views in town.

Within the Wells Fargo Bank headquarters at 464 California Street, the **Wells Fargo History Room** (entrance at 420 Montgomery) traces the fascinating story of the Gold Rush and the famous overland stagecoaches that helped finance (if not win) the West. The bank's exhibit of photographs and antique equipment is also worth a visit. The Bank of California's **Museum of Money of the American West**, 400 California Street at Sansome, displays coins, currency, gold scales, and dueling pistols.

Tradition lives at **Jack's**, 615 Sacramento Street, a shrine in its 1864 premises. The waiters are definitely in charge, the menu is printed daily, recognized dowagers and men-about-town get the best tables, and the rex sole and sand dabs are worth writing tomes about; Tel: 986-9854. **Sol y Luna** at 475 Sacramento burst upon the scene with a contemporary version of a Spanish tradition: tapas. These bar snacks or Latin hors d'oeuvres can constitute a whole meal, especially when accompanied by lively music; full meals are also served; Tel: 296-8696.

Central, or Long, Wharf, which ran almost 3,000 feet out into the bay from between Sacramento and Clay streets, was the lively landing place for Pacific Mail steamers and, in the 1850s, "became the favorite promenade. Buildings perched on piles sprang up quickly on either side, and commission houses, groceries, saloons, mock auctions, cheap-John shops, and peddlers did a thriving business" (*Historic Spots in California*). The wharf is now landlocked Commercial Street, running between Grant and Embarcadero Center; you can look down upon it from windows in the luxurious ▶ **Park Hyatt**. The hotel's **Park Grill** reflects quiet good taste and has become a favorite site for business lunches.

North of Commercial and Clay, at 600 Montgomery Street, is the **Transamerica Pyramid**, one of the most hotly debated high rises in history when it topped out at 853 feet in 1972; now most San Franciscans have learned to like it. The observatory on the 27th floor is open to the public at no charge during business hours.

Across Montgomery Street from the Transamerica Pyramid, **Tommy Toy's Cuisine Chinoise** is one of the city's most sumptuous, even opulent, dining settings, with a collection of Chinese porcelain and artworks. The cuisine is no less refined—try the wok-charred veal in Szechwan sauce or the duckling breast smoked with camphorwood and tea leaves; Tel: 397-4888.

Jackson Square

Cross Washington Street from the Pyramid and enter the one-block alley named Hotaling that leads to Jackson Square. **Hotaling Place**, with its hitching posts and almost Dickensian air, is one of the most charm-filled footpaths in town. Its name recalls Anson Parsons Hotaling, who erected a building near here in 1866 to house his whiskey business as well as a rich collection of books and paintings; its iron shutters helped it survive the earthquake and fire of 1906. According to the chroniclers of the time, when local clergymen interpreted the quake as divine retribution for the city's notorious wickedness, a wit named Charles Field penned the question: "If, as they say, God spanked the town for being over-frisky/Why did He burn His churches down and spare Hotaling's whiskey?"

Jackson Square, which is not really a square but a district, was named a historic area in 1971; it has been much reworked and reawakened, and today lies between Washington and Pacific on the south and north and Sansome and Columbus on the west and east.

This area was the infamous Barbary Coast of the late 19th century, somewhat glorified today but part of a dramatically depraved past. Named after the pirate refuges of the Mediterranean's Barbary Coast (Morocco, Algiers, Tunis, Tripoli), it is said to have given currency to the terms "to shanghai" (to kidnap men to make up a ship's crew, especially with the help of "Mickey Finns," another local creation) and "hoodlum" (the cry of "Huddle 'em!" shouted by bullies pursuing human prey).

Today, following ingenious restoration and refurbishing, the lime-encrusted bricks have been scraped and sandblasted, the wood painted subtle colors, and the fine Federal-style façades enhanced with plane trees and shrubs. Decorators (selling mostly to the trade), followed by admen, architects, and attorneys, have moved into the landmark buildings, and refinement has replaced raffishness.

Dining Around Jackson Square

Lively **Bix** at 56 Gold Street (between Sansome and Montgomery) is called by its owner an updated supper club; certainly it recalls the era of transatlantic liners, and the nights of torch singers and wailing saxophones. The food is old-fashioned and delicious; Tel: 433-6300. A traditional favorite that had fallen on sad times has risen again, newly elegant in decor and innovative in its kitchen: For a smart evening out, try the **Blue Fox** at 659 Merchant Street (off Montgomery); Tel: 981-1177. Not far away, at 640 Sacramento Street, the Blue Fox's "little sister" **Palio d'Asti** serves pizza and antipasti in a bustling trattoria setting; Tel: 395-9800.

Ernie's, in a city of classic restaurants, just keeps getting better. From the linoleum floors of its opening in 1934, it has long metamorphosed into antiques, damask walls, and French crystal—and cuisine to match—at 847 Montgomery Street; Tel: 397-5969.

Pimm's Cup (the British cordials made of gin, whiskey, rum, or brandy) originally came to the West Coast at **India House**, the city's first Indian restaurant (it opened in 1947) and one of its most atmospheric, at 350 Jackson Street. In 1991, the **Cypress Club** opened at 500 Jackson Street with innovative dishes in an eccentric setting filled with crowds every night; Tel: 296-8555.

Because the greater Financial District and Jackson Square are spread over a rather large area between Union Square, Market Street, and North Beach–Telegraph Hill, you may want to make use of public buses from time to time. Heavy traffic runs south on Columbus Avenue, which turns into Montgomery Street, from North Point Street near Hyde Street Pier to Market Street and beyond; look for the number 15 bus. Along Sansome the best choice is number 42 (the Red Arrow Loop), which runs north from Pine up Sansome to the Embarcadero and beyond. As the Gold Arrow Loop, number 42 operates in the opposite direction from North Point Street and Fisherman's Wharf, returning down Battery Street.

EMBARCADERO CENTER AREA

From Union Square, you can wander your way northeast through the Financial District to Embarcadero Center, or walk east on Geary to its juncture with Market Street, cross Market, and take a bus numbered 8, 21, or 31 to the end of the line (signed Ferry Terminal).

You'll notice **Lotta's Fountain** at the meeting of Geary, Market, and Kearny streets. Once a watering trough for horses, then a bronze drinking fountain for human beings, this structure was presented to the city in 1875 by much-loved Lotta Crabtree, "the California Diamond," an actress of Gold Rush days. It was here on Christmas Eve in 1910 that soprano Luisa Tetrazzini sang carols to streets full of enthralled listeners.

On the next corner, at New Montgomery and Market streets, the ▶ **Sheraton Palace** reopened in 1991 after a loving $150-million restoration. It replaces the stunning Palace that opened in 1910 on the site of an even earlier marvel destroyed by the 1906 earthquake. President Warren G. Harding died in the second Palace in 1923, Hawaii's King Kalakaua in the original in 1891, and in 1906 Enrico Caruso (appearing locally in *Carmen*) was so shaken by the earthquake that he is said to have run from the hotel into the street in his nightshirt, swearing never to sing in the city again.

The hotel's once and present star is the **Garden Court**, surely one of the most opulent dining areas in the West. Several classic San Francisco dishes, such as oysters Kirkpatrick, have been reborn here; Tel: 546-5010.

Several unremarkable blocks farther east, the foot of Market Street steps into Justin Herman Plaza.

Embarcadero Center

Justin Herman Plaza, with its controversial, walk-through Vaillancourt Fountain (some think this concrete structure is a hideous modern intrusion, others find it refreshingly unorthodox), is a welcoming oasis of greenery and ease at the end of bustling, trafficky Market Street. (Its layout is now being re-thought to take advantage of the plaza's new proximity to the Ferry Building and the waterfront.) Off the plaza, the five-block complex of **Embarcadero Center** (also known as Rockefeller Center West for the developer who cooperated with architect John Portman) is considered by many city planners, and even some San Franciscans, to be the very model of an urban showpiece.

Set on three levels of open-air plazas connected by pedestrian walkways above the streets, the center is a clutch of almost 200 shops, boutiques, restaurants, cafés, galleries, and—at Building Five—the ▶ **Hyatt Regency**. A map and directory of the Center may be picked up at kiosks throughout the complex; don't try to get around without it.

At any season a shopper's fancy lightly turns to thoughts of a *truite meunière,* perhaps, or *tagliarini* with salmon and peas. The perfect dish is at hand somewhere in the Center: at splendid **Splendido's** (Building Four, Promenade Level), especially smart at lunch, **Gaylord India** (One, Promenade), **Harbor Village Restaurant** (Cantonese; Four, Lobby), **Santorini** (Four, Promenade), **Scott's Seafood Bar & Grill** (Three, Promenade), **La Brasserie Française** (Three, Promenade),

Fujiya (Japanese *shabu-shabu;* One, Lobby), or **Chevys** (Mexican; Two, Promenade).

In 1988 two new buildings were added to the Embarcadero group, Embarcadero West and the Park Hyatt Hotel (see Financial District), on either side of the Neoclassical Federal Reserve Bank.

Several attractive, interesting places for lunch and dinner in this district are just south of Market Street and Embarcadero Center: **Umberto Ristorante Italiano** at 141 Steuart Street (fine Florentine cuisine, handsome cellar rooms; Tel: 543-8021); **Harry Denton's Bar & Grill** at 161 Steuart Street next door to the new Harbor Court Hotel, with lively saloon atmosphere and dancing after 10:00 P.M. Wednesday through Sunday (Tel: 882-1333); and **Bistro Roti** in the Hotel Griffon at 155 Steuart Street (a European-style bistro from the folks who gave you Fog City Diner—more on that later—Tel: 495-6500).

At Mission and Spear streets, the site of the former Rincon Annex Post Office, a masterwork of civic design, has been reworked as a complex of shops, offices, and apartments called **Rincon Center**. The 1930s Art Deco post office lobby has been preserved, right down to the polished letter slips. The splendid murals by Anton Refregier depicting the history of San Francisco have been meticulously restored, and there's an interesting display of relics of early settlers on the site. An ambitious Italian restaurant, **Etrusca**, at the heart of the Center (121 Spear Street), is a project of the owner of the Il Fornaio chain. In a stunning setting, especially dramatic in the evening, the main courses match the pastas in excellence—not always the case elsewhere (Tel: 777-0330).

The Ferry Building

It's difficult to believe today, but the 1896 Ferry Building, at harbor's edge at the end of Market Street, was for decades the tallest structure in town. Modeled after the Giralda tower of Seville's cathedral, it stood as the symbol of the city, welcoming millions of rail travellers (who were coming across the bay from the rail terminal in Oakland) and ferry passengers. Alas, in the late 1950s, the view of its historic silhouette was marred by the ugly, mid-air, steel-and-concrete Embarcadero Freeway, which swept between the tower and the rest of the city to the west. Despite decades of argument between its defenders (who enjoyed driving above city traffic) and attackers (who hated its look), the freeway stood sturdily until it was badly shaken by the 1989 earthquake. By the end of 1991, it had been demolished in favor of water-level lanes (now under construction) that will one day run grandly along the bay toward Chinatown and Fisherman's Wharf.

Today the Ferry Building serves as headquarters for the San Francisco Port Authority and the private World Trade Center club rooms. Golden Gate Transit and the Red & White Fleet now bring more than 40 ferries each weekday to Piers 1 and 1½ at the building, and plans are under way to build five more berths for even more ferries in an attempt to relieve auto congestion and to decrease car traffic on the San Francisco–Oakland Bay Bridge.

Already, San Franciscans are coming to this long-neglected neighborhood to look in surprise upon the wide waterfront, the blue bay beyond, and the graceful leap of the Bay Bridge reaching toward Treasure Island as herring gulls soar on invisible eddies of air and lines of sailboats slap against their masts. **Gordon Biersch Brew Pub**, where you'll find most of the action, is a stylish entry in the dressed-for-success race, with superior food and brews. The high decibel level results from so many people in one place having a good time, not amplification. It's at 2 Harrison Street and the Embarcadero; Tel: 243-8246.

On the bay side of the Embarcadero (a two-way street that runs along the waterfront from Berry Street in the south to Fisherman's Wharf in the north), the Ferry Building is the marker from which piers are numbered: odd numbers to the north, even numbers to the south. The wide sidewalk serves as a track for joggers who pound along, seemingly oblivious to the fine harbor view. Several worthwhile restaurants sit at water's edge: **Sinbad's Pier 2** (seafood), the **Waterfront** at Pier 7 (seasonal local and imported seafood), and **Pier 23 Café** (California creative, funky atmosphere). **Town's End**, 2 Townsend Street at the Embarcadero, offers American dishes with a twist. Try the Basque frittata; Tel: 512-0749.

Dining at Walton Square

Abutting Embarcadero Center on the north, the Alcoa Building (a giant black box with an eerie exoskeleton) and the Golden Gateway apartment complex signal the sheltered presence of **Walton Square**, a welcome, small, green space with a fountain bordered north and south by Pacific and Jackson streets, east and west by Front and Davis streets.

In good weather, brown-baggers lunch on the grass, usually tidying up after themselves; for the visitor as well, the main interest here is in dining. **Square One** at 190 Pacific Street is one of the most innovative, excitingly eclectic restaurants in the state, with an emphasis on classic Mediterranean cooking, touched by California care for fresh ingredients (there's also a distinguished wine list); Tel: 788-1110.

On the square's south side, hidden within the Golden Gateway complex on a wide walkway called Davis Court, **l'Olivier** (465 Davis Court) remains an enclave of excellence in the French style, unknown to many San Franciscans and well worth the search; Tel: 981-7824. At 607 Front Street, **MacArthur Park** serves oak-smoked baby back ribs often voted the best in the Bay Area, as well as salads, fresh fish, and aged meats in a very pretty garden setting. Nearby, a true trattoria, glittery and high-tech **Ciao**, attracts young professionals at lunch and dinner and serves drinks to the after-business crowd at 230 Jackson Street.

Levi Strauss Plaza

Landscape architect Lawrence Halprin has achieved the essence of urban greening in Levi Strauss Plaza, which lies just west of the Embarcadero between Greenwich and Union streets (north and south) and Sansome and Battery streets (east and west). It is on the east and steepest side of Telegraph Hill. If you're driving, this is a devil of a place to get into because of the one-way streets and the strange angles cut by the Embarcadero. The easiest approach is to go north on Sansome from downtown and into the public parking lot on the corner of Sansome and Greenwich.

The firm that gave its name to this plaza, and now has its world headquarters here, was founded in 1853 as a wholesaler of dry goods and clothing, and supplied work pants made of denim material to the miners in Nevada during the Comstock bonanza days of the 1860s. (The rugged cloth was imported from Nîmes in France; hence the name denim— *de,* or from, Nîmes.)

A Reno tailor named Jacob W. Davis, finding he had to make too-frequent repairs to the pants, finally used harness-making tools to rivet the pocket corners and other areas of stress. He and Strauss applied for and received a patent on the process in 1873, and Levis took over the world. The original factory headquarters at 250 Valencia Street in the Mission district is now open for one-and-a-half-hour tours on Wednesdays at 10:30 A.M. and 1:00 P.M. Tours are for a minimum of ten people (make reservations well in advance; Tel: 565-9153).

The waterfront today is much enhanced by the low-rise headquarters building off Levi Strauss Plaza, which blends so smoothly into the site it seems always to have been here. A dramatic granite fountain makes a stunning centerpiece.

On the north of the square, a branch of the noted Italian bakery-restaurant **Il Fornaio** is a popular stop. **Fog City Diner**, across from the plaza at 1300 Battery Street, is one of the most trendsetting and delightful dining sites in the city, most fun (and most crowded) at lunch. Here, executive chef Cindy Pawlcyn created the appetizers called "small plates," inspiring the practice of "grazing" through the menu, tasting several specialties. Don't miss the crab cakes; Tel: 982-2000.

If you do not want to walk the considerable distance from Embarcadero Center to Levi Strauss Plaza, take the number 42 bus north up Sansome Street to stops on the Embarcadero (the line continues along to Bay Street, North Point, and stops just south of The Cannery, Fisherman's Wharf, and Ghirardelli Square). In the opposite direction, number 42 runs south on Battery Street to California Street, where you can pick up the cable-car line.

CHINATOWN

The Chinese capital of the Western world, Chinatown is a 24-block labyrinth of food markets selling every Asian delicacy you know of (and some you may not wish to encounter), fine restaurants in varying price ranges, temples, clan houses, souvenir stores, art and furniture shops, and banks, newspaper offices, and travel agencies where little English is spoken—all overlooked by a roofscape of arched eaves, carved cornices, and filigreed balconies.

Although it expands and shrinks as buildings rise and fall, Chinatown is generally considered to be bounded by Bush Street on the south, Broadway on the north, and Kearny and Stockton streets on the east and west. It is northeast of Union Square and west of Embarcadero Center.

Historic Chinatown

How and why did the Chinese come to settle in San Francisco in such numbers? James Benét sums it up in *A Guide to San Francisco* (now out of print): "In 1848 three Chinese, probably the first, arrived in the brigantine *Eagle* to become servants for a prominent San Francisco family. Many more came to 'Gum Sahn' (Chinese for 'golden hills'), as they called San Francisco, during the Gold Rush. Though there were reportedly only 789 Chinese men and two Chinese women in the state at the beginning of 1850, there were more than 12,000 by the end of the following year—and yet only seven were women."

During the late 1860s and early 1870s thousands of Chinese laborers were imported to do *ku li* work (Chinese meaning "bitter toil," Anglicized to coolie), especially on the construction of the Central Pacific Railway. When Rudyard Kipling visited in the 1880s he described the community as "a ward of the city of Canton set down in the most eligible business quarter of the place." In fact, the area that would become Chinatown had been the site of the first real settlement of San Francisco.

Although San Francisco was born in 1776 with the dedication of the Presidio and the foundation of Misión San Francisco de Asís, the initial settlement of the city as we know it today did not occur for another 59 years—and then under a different name.

Captain William A. Richardson arrived in San Francisco in 1822, when the Mexican flag was flying over the Presidio, and by 1825 had decided to found a port town at the best anchoring place on San Francisco Bay. He selected Yerba Buena Cove (where much of the Financial District now sits on fill), and pitched a tent for himself and his family where Grant Avenue runs today between Clay and Washington streets. Within three months he had replaced it with a wooden house, the first in the new city of Yerba Buena (meaning "good herb," the wild mint). This site is described in *Historic Spots in California* as ". . . the first habitation ever erected in Yerba Buena. At the time, Richardson's only neighbors were bears, coyotes and wolves. The nearest people lived either at the Presidio or at Mission Dolores." Richardson was also the "solitary settler" described in Richard Henry Dana's *Two Years Before the Mast*. Today the name Yerba Buena is attached to the island on which the western span of the San Francisco–Oakland Bay Bridge is anchored.

PORTSMOUTH SQUARE

Originally the central plaza of the small Spanish settlement, this square in the heart of today's Chinatown takes its name from the U.S. sloop of war *Portsmouth,* captained by one John B. Montgomery who came ashore on July 9, 1846, at what is now the corner of Clay and Leidesdorff streets to take possession of Yerba Buena and its northern frontier for the United States, raising the Stars and Stripes on the plaza.

Today, smaller than it was a century and a half ago, Portsmouth is a green park atop the Portsmouth Square Garage, an unattractive but handy place to park your car while walking in the area. (The other choice is St. Mary's Square Garage at the corner of Kearny and California streets.)

Portsmouth is ignored by many visitors to Chinatown, perhaps because they're intimidated by the happy squeals and squeaks of Asian children at play or the presence of old men bent over chess- and checkerboards. Thus they miss the Robert Louis Stevenson Monument and another corner of history. ". . . It was here Robert Louis went to observe at close range and to talk to the flotsam and jetsam of humanity drifting in from the mighty Pacific Ocean. Who knows but he found here Long John Silver and Blind Pew?" (from *Historic Spots*).

The saloons and gambling dens of Portsmouth Plaza in the 1850s have been replaced by a Holiday Inn on the east, across Kearny Street, and to the north at 720 Washington Street by **Buddha's Universal Church**, stark and white on the exterior and handsomely decorated on the interior. Tours for visitors are given on the second and fourth Sunday of each month between 1:00 and 3:00 P.M.

On the west, the square is walled off and overlooked by a business building, on the sixth floor of which is the beautiful **Empress of China** restaurant. Although more expensive than most of its neighbors, it's popular with visitors for its setting and because English is well understood by the friendly staff. Enter at 838 Grant Avenue; Tel: 434-1345.

Grant Avenue

For many travellers, Chinatown begins at the **Gateway to Chinatown** at Grant Avenue and Bush Street, a green-and-ochre doorway adorned with benevolent dragons and stone lions; this southern gateway to Chinatown first opened in 1970. (Should you want to walk here from Union Square, go east on Maiden Lane, then north on Grant past Post and Sutter streets to Bush.) Through the gate, you step onto Grant Avenue, surely the most famous street in Chinatown.

Grant Avenue is San Francisco's oldest artery (though some still claim that distinction for 16th Street along the old road to the bay from Mission Dolores). The muddy, rutted original street was *calle de la Fundación* (Street of the Founding) in the Spanish settlement of Yerba Buena. With Yankee rule, the name was changed to Dupont (to honor

naval Captain Samuel F. Du Pont, though misspelled), but by
the late 1800s, Du Pon Gai (as the Chinese called it; *gai*
means "street") had gained such an unsavory reputation as
the site of tong wars, opium dens, and slave sing-song girls
that the downtown merchants fostered an upgrading name
change to Grant (for Ulysses S., the country's 18th president).

Grant is indisputably (and successfully) commercial and
tourist oriented. At the gateway the Chinese-character street
signs, dragon-entwined lampposts, and pagoda-topped telephone booths begin. Here the Guang-zhou dialect (Cantonese) is the mother tongue, and the rash of restaurants ranges
from hole-in-the-wall bakeries selling irresistible moon cakes
and sesame cookies to the **Imperial Palace**. (The Imperial
Palace is one of the best restaurants, Oriental or Occidental,
in the city. In beautiful surroundings, order such specialties as
minced squab with plum sauce and Peking duck. It's at 919
Grant Avenue; Tel: 982-4440.)

Two blocks north of Bush Street, a most un-Chinese
structure dominates the setting: **Old St. Mary's Church** at the
Grant–California street corner. This was the first Roman
Catholic cathedral on the Pacific Coast (1854); its bricks
supposedly sailed around Cape Horn, while its granite base
is believed to have come from China.

On **St. Mary's Square**, a tiny, tidy park across California
Street from Old St. Mary's, a 12-foot rose-granite-and-stain-
less-steel statue of Sun Yat-sen, founder of the Chinese
republic, by the city's beloved sculptor Beniamino Bufano
faces a bronze screen commemorating Americans of Chinese ancestry who gave their lives for America in World Wars
I and II. Sun Yat-sen founded the city's *Young China* newspaper in the early 1900s.

A longtime favorite restaurant at 717 California Street (a
few steps west of Grant) is **Yamato**, not Chinese but Japanese, with imaginative dishes and a choice of Western or
Asian seating (low tables with leg wells). Across the street at
number 718, **Cathay House** has been a landmark since 1938.
It's quite inexpensive.

If, as tradition says, dragons are benevolent, the Bank of
America branch at 701 Grant fairly roars with good will—
golden dragons breathe fire from its front columns and
doors, and 60 dragon medallions line the façade. The
Citibank Savings branch at 845 Grant answers with grimac-
ing temple dogs.

When Johnny Kan opened nearby **Kan's** in 1953 it immediately became one of the country's best-known Chinese

restaurants. Today Johnny is gone but his welcoming tradition lingers at 708 Grant. Around the corner at 743 Washington Street, the **Old Chinese Telephone Exchange** has become the Bank of Canton, but preserves its delightful, slightly giddy Asian aspect. (Until 1949, when the dial system was installed, this exchange was staffed by operators fluent in English and in five Chinese dialects. Because Chinese ideograms are not arranged in "alphabetical" order, the directory went by streets, the ones with the most subscribers being listed first.)

At 650 Commercial Street (a bit to the east in the Financial District) between Kearny and Montgomery, the important role of Chinese immigrants in the development of the West's mining, rail, and fishing industries is delineated in the **Chinese Historical Society of America**. The collection includes artifacts, photos, and Gold Rush relics, and is open without charge noon to 4:00 P.M. Tuesdays through Saturdays.

Farther north on Grant at Jackson Street, veer west into little **Ross Alley**, a hive of jewelry shops where prices are not low but not exorbitant either, and quality is high. You can also visit the tiny **Golden Gate Fortune Cookies** factory.

Hand-carved dragons guard the entrance to **Grand Palace Restaurant**, 950 Grant Avenue, where dim sum snacking is a pleasant pastime. At Broadway, Grant leaps from Chinatown into the pasta-panettone belt of North Beach (see below).

Stockton Street

Grant Avenue is theater; Stockton Street, one block to its west, is workaday life, a hustle and bustle of Asians in a world largely untrammeled by tourism. The feel of it is very foreign to a visitor, even to a San Franciscan, who encounters here several cultures that may be very different from his own.

From Union Square, the way leads north past the handy Sutter-Stockton Garage and into the Stockton Tunnel, which runs under Nob Hill from Sutter to Sacramento Street. Immediately at its north end you plunge into a very different sea, as much today as in the 1870s, when an eastern visitor, Benjamin F. Taylor, wrote, ". . . at the turn of a corner and the breadth of a street, think of dropping with the abruptness of a shifting dream into China, beneath the standard of Hoang-ti who sits upon the dragon throne. . . ."

If you are not driving and if you do not wish to walk through the tunnel (which is rather unsavory by night), you can climb the stairway just to the north of the Stockton

Tunnel, and will find yourself atop the tunnel with Stockton Street leading ahead uphill, crossed by Bush Street. Continuing up Stockton, you'll pass the smart Ritz-Carlton hotel on your right, at the corner of Pine, and then reach California Street. From here, your choices are to walk left on California to Nob Hill or right, down to Grant Avenue and Chinatown.

If you walk or drive through Stockton Tunnel, as you exit nod your respects in a westerly direction toward the **Cameron House** at 920 Sacramento Street, where one Donaldina Cameron of the Presbyterian Church "saved" more than 2,000 slave sing-song girls who, with the connivance of U.S. officials, were imported, bought, and sold to brothels and individual owners.

At 843 Stockton Street, the gaudy headquarters of the **Chinese Six Companies** (formally, the Chinese Consolidated Benevolent Association) is a banquet of beasts (guardian lions, dragons, birds, fish) and a tempest of colors (lucky red, glaring yellow, glossy green, brilliant blue). The Six Companies organized in the 1850s to represent the six different districts of the Canton (Guang-zhou) province that operated the U.S. depot of the Chinese labor trade; political and business disputes still tend to be arbitrated here.

The **U.S. Post Office-cum-Kong Chow Temple** at the corner of Stockton and Clay streets represents the oldest family association in the United States. The temple proper, on the top floor, is open to the public daily, and its antique furnishings will remind you of Hong Kong or Singapore. The patron deity is Kuan Ti, god of those undertaking hazardous work (such as the Gold Rush's *ku li*).

On the opposite side of Stockton, the very fine **Celadon** restaurant glows with that distinctive glaze invented during the Tang dynasty. It's quieter than most Chinese restaurants (a blessing), the atmosphere is elegant, and the broiled lobster with ginger sauce may turn you into a ram (a beast of good taste). A few steps east of Stockton off Sacramento, the alley known as Hang Ah stars the **Hang Ah Tea Room**, a great place to go for dim sum.

Farther east of Stockton and of Hang Ah Alley, turn north into the second opening off Sacramento, **Waverly Place**. It's only two blocks long, but it may put you more in mind of China than any other cultural corner in town. A street of brothels before the 1906 earthquake, it's now a collection of architecturally interesting family and benevolent association offices. The one structure worth visiting is **Tin Hou Temple** at 125 Waverly. Established by one of the first three Chinese to arrive in San Francisco, it features an altar to Tin

Hou, Queen of the Heavens and Goddess of the Seven Seas, that had been installed on the ship for daily worship during the long crossing and later was moved to the temple. From the ground floor, climb the stairs to the temple, a fine place for contemplation of the cultures that make up San Francisco; open daily.

The Chinese devotion to dining becomes clear along the Stockton blocks numbered 1000 to 1200, a jumble of ginger roots and bamboo shoots, golden-glazed ducks and whole drawn pigs, lichee nuts, sharks' fins, seahorses, tankfuls of fish, and crates of cackling chickens.

Chinatown officially ends at Broadway, where North Beach begins (see below).

NOB HILL

Originally, historians say, it was Fern Hill, then Hill of Golden Promise, then California Street Hill and/or Nob Hill. Whatever. For more than a century, Nob Hill, just west of Chinatown, has been associated in travellers' imaginations with the upper crust, le beau monde.

There are two explanations for the name Nob. The more prosaic one is that it means merely "knob" or rounded hill, but the one preferred by most San Franciscans makes it a contraction of the Hindu word *nabob* or *nawab:* "a wealthy or powerful person; especially a person who has made a large fortune in India or another country of the East."

San Francisco's nobs made their fortunes in the West in the mid-1800s in gold, silver, and railroading. At the time of the 1848 gold strike, this scrub-covered hill rising 376 feet above the waterfront was virtually inaccessible; its steep grade (24.8 degrees on the south face) made the ascent difficult for even the strongest horses. Then Andrew S. Hallidie invented the cable cars, and the uphill climb became a power trip.

There already had been a handful of fine houses on the hill: Senator George Hearst (father of the founder of the newspaper empire and great-grandfather of today's publisher of the *San Francisco Examiner*) is said to have inhabited a Spanish stucco mansion; William T. Coleman seems to have built a Roman villa in a walled garden. With the advent of the cable car, though, the real rush was on.

Among the first to build their fanciful mansions on the rise (in the 1870s) were the railroad barons of the Central (then Southern) Pacific Railroad known as the Big Four:

Charles Crocker, Leland Stanford, Mark Hopkins, and Collis Huntington. Close on the barons' heels trod the Bonanza Kings of the Comstock Lode: James Flood and James G. Fair. Their creations were flights of flamboyance, outbursts of ornamentation, exuberance carried to excess, and they must have been wonderful to behold; all but one burned in 1906.

Stand today near the one survivor, an imposing brownstone erected by Flood (at 1000 California Street at Mason) in 1886. Aloof as ever behind its solid-brass filigree fence, it is now the **Pacific Union Club**, a domain of contemporary magnates currently under attack from women and minorities excluded from membership.

The Hotels of Nob Hill

From "the P-U," as it's irreverently known, you can look all around to where the palaces once stood. To the immediate east on Mason Street, the ▶ **Fairmont Hotel** occupies the block where James G. Fair ("Bonanza Jim") intended to build his home. His marriage broke up and he died while the foundations were being laid, leaving the site to his children. Daughter Theresa Alice (Tessie) had begun work on a grand hotel, but before it opened, while furniture stood crated on its lawns, came the earthquake. Novelist Gertrude Atherton left a memorable description of the fire that swept uphill on April 19, 1906: "I forgot the doomed city as I gazed at the Fairmont, a tremendous volume of white smoke pouring from where its roof had been, every window a shimmer sheet of gold; not a flame, not a spark shot forth. The Fairmont will never be as demonic in its beauty again." One year to the day later, the hotel opened, a masterwork of the architectural art of Julia Morgan.

Just across California Street to the southeast of the P-U, Mary Hopkins (wife of Mark) brought forth the most ostentatious of all the homes of the Nob-ility. As described by Randolph Delehanty, it was "a phantasmagoria of turrets, gables, pinnacles, and chimneys with a great Gothic-style conservatory." What Mark (whose interest in houses seems to have been limited to pulling garden weeds) felt about it is not known. Today's stately ▶ **Mark Hopkins Inter-Continental** opened on the site in 1926, and has a history of debuts, dinner dancing, Junior League doings, and Barbara Hutton honeymoons. It set the style for skyrooms when the **Top of the Mark** opened in 1939, just in time for the men of World War II's Pacific forces to flock up to the 537-foot-high bar in order to say good-bye to the city and their sweethearts.

The Hopkins's downhill neighbors on the east were the Stanfords. (Stanford had bought the whole block and sold the uphill portion to his partner.) Like the other barons, the Stanfords were not entirely happy in their house, an Italianate structure of truly imposing demeanor. Their beloved boy, Leland Stanford, Jr., died at age 15 on a family trip to Italy, and the bereaved parents endowed in his memory the prestigious university that bears his name (see Day Trips from San Francisco). Today the massive granite-and-basalt wall that buttresses two sides of the block is the only vestige of the Stanfords's city estate, and the ▶ **Stouffers Stanford Court Hotel** rises here above California and Powell streets where the city's three cable-car lines intersect.

Just down the slope, one of the city's best examples of Neoclassical architecture, a 17-columned building erected in 1909 for Metropolitan Life Insurance, then home to Cogswell College, became in 1991 ▶ **The Ritz-Carlton** and took its place among the city's most elegant hotels. Part of the site was occupied by Grace Episcopal Church, which was destroyed in the 1906 earthquake and succeeded by Grace Cathedral atop Nob Hill. Renowned landscape architect Thomas Church designed the ornamental garden courtyard.

To the southwest of the P-U Club, the stylish ▶ **Huntington Hotel** should, historically speaking, be called the Tobin, because the corner it dominates at California and Taylor was first graced by 1849 gold-seeker Richard Tobin's Victorian mansion. A succession of royals has slept at the Huntington (Princesses Margaret and Grace, Prince Charles) as well as a clutch of celebrities—Alistair Cooke, Luciano Pavarotti, Lauren Bacall, and Leontyne Price among them. In a little alcove near the ladies' restroom by the entrance to The Big Four restaurant there's a photographic display of San Francisco as it looked in 1877 by the renowned Eadweard Muybridge; it's a museum piece worth seeking out. The restaurant itself and its clubby bar are renowned for the power lunches that take place here. Historical art and memorabilia are showcased in this uncrowded setting; Tel: 771-1140.

Around on Nob Hill

Across a tiny lane to the west of the Pacific Union Club, lovely little **Huntington Park**, with a copy of Rome's Fountain of the Turtles in the center, is a serene spot where the David Colton abode once stood; it was purchased by Collis P. Huntington in 1892. After the 1906 fire, Huntington's widow gave the site to the city, and now it's a proper setting for perambulators, poodles, and historically minded passersby.

To the west of Huntington Park across Taylor Street rises the great, gray pile of **Grace Episcopal Cathedral**, the largest Gothic-style structure in the West. Two residences of the Charles Crocker family once stood on this block; when both homes burned in 1906 the land was donated to the church, although construction of the cathedral did not begin until 1927. Today it is visited by those in search of beauty as well as by believers; the magnificent organ and the excellent boys' choir are attractions in themselves. None of the cathedral's treasures is more arresting than its Lorenzo Ghiberti doors, casts of the gilded-bronze doors created by the 15th-century sculptor for the baptistry in Florence. Their ten rectangular reliefs depict scenes from the Old Testament; they stand at the top of the steps to the cathedral's east entrance.

Directly south of the cathedral, the **Masonic Temple** is of interest for the concerts played in its hall and for its well-located parking garage. (Other parking areas are at the Crocker Garage between Mason and Taylor, and under the Fairmont, entry from Powell.)

In addition to the restaurants within Nob Hill's hotels, several other rooms at the top are worth checking out. When **Vanessi's** was down in North Beach, it was spirited, robust, and the place to go for a good, old-fashioned Italian time. Now that it's on Nob Hill (at 1177 California Street), it's still spirited, robust, and the place to go for a good, old-fashioned Italian time; Tel: 771-2422. Just a block down the Mason Street hill from the Mark Hopkins, at 900 Pine Street, the small and pretty bistro **Rue Lepic** serves unpretentious but properly prepared French food. It's a favorite when you don't want to splurge but want things right.

RUSSIAN HILL

This hill is a fashionable residential district defined by the Russian Hill Neighbors Association as 34 blocks between Pacific Avenue on the south and Francisco on the north, Taylor on the east and Polk on the west. It is just north of Nob Hill and was named for the graves of several Russian fur trappers who were interred atop the mount; the precise sites are no longer known.

The one tourist attraction on Russian Hill is the so-called crookedest street in the world, a section of **Lombard Street** that twists eastward and downhill along the nine hairpins between Hyde and Leavenworth streets. At this writing, dwellers along Lombard are petitioning the city to ban traffic except by residents.

If you have a particular interest in San Francisco's residential architecture, take the Hyde Street cable car to its stop at Hyde and Lombard and walk around the neighborhood, or take a taxi to the intersection of Russian Hill Place (between Jones and Taylor) and Vallejo, considered the hill's summit. Several interesting houses are in the immediate area, including those on the cul-de-sac of Florence Street.

NORTH BEACH

As an observer of the local scene put it some time ago, "Naples is just across the street from Hong Kong." The split personality once so evident where Chinatown's Grant Avenue runs north into Broadway and Columbus Avenue has become less distinct in recent years, however, since Chinese families have been crowded out of their traditional home and have settled in North Beach with the Italians. Now you're likely to find tea-smoked duck next to *dindo,* lamb Szechwan edging *sacripantina.*

The first Italians arrived during the Gold Rush and were followed by thousands during the next decades, most of them from northern Italy—Genoa, Piedmont, and Tuscany. The first Sicilian fishermen came in the early 1880s, and by 1885 the community had established its own Italian Chamber of Commerce.

Cradled by Telegraph Hill on the east and Russian Hill on the west, North Beach really was a beach in the 1850s, when the shore of the bay extended far inland between the two hills. Today it remains a bohemian bastion, where the action is in cabarets, jazz clubs, galleries, inns, and several *caffès* and *ristorantes* worth a drive across town.

Washington Square

Nobody knows precisely which street marks the northern boundary of North Beach, but everybody agrees that the heart of the matter is Washington Square, with Filbert Street and the imposing **Church of Saints Peter and Paul** on the north, and by Union, Powell, Stockton, and Columbus forming the other sides of this five-sided square.

If the purpose of a park is public pleasure, Washington

Square ranks among the most successful little greenswards in the country. Children scamper and giggle, watched by their grandmothers; grandfathers stretch out under the shade trees; young people picnic; and tourists come out of the ▶ **Washington Square Inn**, smile, and stroll across the square to see what's happening at the Washington Square Bar and Grill. Unfortunately, the plight of the homeless has encroached upon this island of serenity, adding to the problems faced by the city administration and discomfiting many visitors.

On Sundays pretty young girls and handsome dandies dally in front of Saints Peter and Paul, awaiting the arrival of yet another Italian bride and groom. The church, beautifully illuminated at night, is a neo-Romanesque classic, designed in 1922 but not completed for 20 years. Known as "the church of the fishermen," it's the departure site for the annual Columbus Day Celebration parade. Inside, the church is as thronged with saints as the square is with squatters; it well repays a short visit.

The **Washington Square Bar and Grill** at 1707 Powell Street (Tel: 982-8123) is a noisy, happy institution, especially popular with members of the local and national media, who have made it their hideout. Drinks are pleasantly outsized, the menu features fresh pastas daily, and the kitchen staff has a good hand with fish. This is a fine place to introduce yourself to local petrale sole, which many San Franciscans prefer to the Dover variety.

Restaurateur/raconteur/politico Ed Moose and his wife, a cookbook author, who created the Washington Square Bar and Grill, sold it about three years ago, and are now proprietors of a new restaurant directly opposite it on the east side of the square at 1652 Stockton. **Moose's** serves Italian cuisine with a California flair, accompanied in the evenings by a jazz piano; Tel: 989-7800. On the south side of the square, **Fior d'Italia** at 601 Union Street claims to be the oldest Italian restaurant in town; it has been serving veal parmigiana for more than a century, and some of the original waiters seem still to be around; Tel: 986-1886. Also a square institution, **Coit Liquors** at 585 Columbus is a fine place to shop for picnic wines, especially some Italian favorites you can't find everywhere, and you can pick up sandwiches for that picnic at **Molinari's Delicatessen** (373 Columbus), which has been a local landmark since 1896. The deli makes its own ravioli and *tagliarini* and cures its own dry salami. On the corner at 673 Union Street, **Little City Antipasti Bar** serves drinks and antipasti all day long.

By San Francisco standards, **Amelio's** is ancient, dating to 1926, but it's as spry as ever. Try the fresh foie gras and roasted squab with star anise sauce. Amelio's is a block south of Washington Square at 1630 Powell Street; Tel: 397-4339.

Broadway

This strip, which slices east to west from the Embarcadero to Lyon Street and the Presidio, lives several lives. In North Beach from the Embarcadero to the Broadway Tunnel it's gaudy, glittering, raucous, and even rude. (In the 1960s, the devil-may-care days of Carol Doda and the Topless Mother of Eight, this stretch of the street was called, with a nod to Italy, the Bay of Nipples.) At the western end of the tunnel, Broadway blossoms with small businesses, crosses Van Ness, and matures into the conservative chic of Pacific Heights' monumental *palazzi*.

In the 1930s and 1940s Broadway was a fairly unsavory haunt of bootleggers and frequenters of brothels and pool halls. The 1950s are now considered the good old days, when Mort Sahl, Lenny Bruce, Barbra Streisand, and other soon-to-be superstars played Enrico Banducci's hungry i, and such clubs as the Purple Onion and Barnaby Conrad's El Matador, and the Jazz Workshop catered to a loud, lively, good-time crowd, watched over by the sidewalk table-sitters at Enrico's coffeehouse.

In the 1960s the scene changed again, with the arrival of more than 20 topless clubs of increasing raunchiness. It's still bawdy, but since the late 1970s it has cleaned up its act somewhat; most travellers, except the youngest and most active, may prefer to visit only during the day.

DINING AND SHOPPING ALONG BROADWAY

Nostalgia is the new trend along Broadway. **Enrico's Sidewalk Café** has reopened at number 504 to bring back the best of the old tradition and to build upon it with an upgraded Mediterranean menu at reasonable prices. The executive chef, Rick Hackett, is a veteran of such noted kitchens as Oliveto and Chez Panisse. Menus change weekly and, as in the old days, you can stay forever if you want, from 8:00 A.M. to 1:00 or 2:00 A.M. every day. Add memories to a happy mix of nightly jazz, folk, or classical music, and let the good times roll again.

Farther east, those who like it hot and hotter cannot resist

Hunan at 924 Sansome (at Broadway), where the tough
come to cry happily while cooking their tonsils. *The New
Yorker* magazine has called Hunan "the best Chinese restaurant in the world"; Tel: 956-7727.

A new taste blossoms along Broadway these days at **Helmand**, number 430, where Afghani cuisine is making a hit;
the look is civilized and the prices extremely reasonable. A
celebrated and rather new Chinese restaurant farther west at
450–52 Broadway, **Brandy Ho's** is theatrical in appearance,
rewarding in taste. The cuisine is Hunan, without the use of
MSG. Try the sweet-and-sour spareribs. (The original Brandy
Ho's is at 217 Columbus at Pacific.)

At 540 Broadway, **Columbus Books** sells both new and
used books, with a particularly good travel section. Here,
you can either continue up Columbus or take a sharp right
onto upper Grant Avenue (for which see below).

There's nothing smart or stylish about dining à la Basque
in San Francisco, but if you're in the mood for old-
fashioned, long-table, family-style food, try one of the city's
traditional Basque cafés. Two right at hand here are **Basque
Hotel and Restaurant** at 15 Romolo Place (an alley north of
Broadway between Kearny and Columbus), and **Des Alpes**,
732 Broadway. At this writing, a three-course prix-fixe dinner at Des Alpes is priced at a friendly $12, Gold Rush
atmosphere included.

At the corner of Columbus and Broadway, look south and
back into the 1950s, where two landmarks of the Beat
Generation, **Vesuvio's** and **City Lights Booksellers and Publishers**, face each other along tiny Jack Kerouac Alley (formerly Adler Place). The movement's bible was Jack Kerouac's *On the Road,* published in 1957, and the place you sat
to read it was Lawrence Ferlinghetti's City Lights, perhaps in
the company of Allen Ginsberg, Gregory Corso, Norman
Mailer, and such non-beatniks as Kenneth Patchen, Alan
Watts, and Kenneth Rexroth. It wasn't a Parisian salon, but
perhaps as close as San Francisco will get to one.

Just south, Vesuvio's lives under a sign over the entrance
that reads, "We are itching to get away from Portland, Oregon." Artists and poets, the nostalgic and the curious, come
to sip coffee and to see who else is here; the upstairs is
quieter and has a booth dedicated to Lady Psychiatrists.

If you walk south two blocks on Columbus to Jackson,
you'll find **Thomas Bros. Maps**, with an unequalled selection
of maps of every size, shape, and persuasion, as well as
atlases, guides, globes, interesting software products for
street-finding, and more.

Upper Grant Avenue

To gain a sense of North Beach, to savor it, you should walk both upper Grant and Columbus from Broadway.

Upper Grant—haunted by the ghosts of such well-known Beat Generation hangouts as The Place and the Coexistence Bagel Shop—is now a hodgepodge of garment shops, galleries, cappuccino houses, collectibles stores, and small cafés. The traffic is north, one-way, and tight. The Beatniks' Coffee Gallery at number 1353 is now the **Lost & Found Saloon**, where you may choose to be either. At 601 Vallejo, corner of Grant, **Caffè Trieste** continues through the century just as it began, serving coffee and meals in the traditional Italian manner; coffee beans are sold, retail and wholesale, at number 609.

There's a North Beach institution at 510 Green Street: the **Green Valley Restaurant**. During the Depression, Green Valley dished up five-course meals for 75 cents; they're still serving bountiful meals at very reasonable prices.

Columbus Avenue

The diagonal of Columbus cuts across the grid pattern of North Beach from Washington Street northwest to Beach Street. It's really Little Italy's Main Street. Caffès cluster along Columbus, interspersed with such finds as the classy **Pearl's** jazz club at number 256 and **Biordi Italian Imports** at number 412, where the hand-painted dinnerware and the gourmet gadgets may prove irresistible (purchases can be shipped). Follow your nose to **The Stinking Rose**, a restaurant dedicated to the glorification of garlic, at 325 Columbus.

The **Caffè Roma** coffeehouse at 414 Columbus is particularly easygoing, and no one will mind if you while an hour away with your cappuccino. There's even a curiously country-style inn here, one of the few recommendable places to stay in the area, though it can be noisy at night: the ▶ **Millefiori Inn**. The **Michelangelo Café** at 579 Columbus is tiny, but the cooking is worth the wait; Tel: 986-4058.

At 1435 Stockton Street, corner of Columbus, the Eureka Federal Savings building houses on its mezzanine the **North Beach Museum**, where the history of this whole area—Chinatown, North Beach, and Fisherman's Wharf—is illustrated in changing exhibits of photographs and relics.

On the corner where Columbus, Stockton, and Grant meet, **North Beach Restaurant** remains a favorite with local regulars despite occasional swipes by critics (usually from somewhere else) who complain it's too crowded and popular. Well? They do a superb job with calamari and other local compulsions. The zaniest show in town, *Beach Blanket Babylon,* carries on, apparently permanently, at **Club Fugazi** (see Bars and Nightlife section), 678 Green Street, in a little wedge between Columbus and Powell.

San Francisco's *Epicurean Rendezvous* magazine ranks **Buca Giovanni**, 800 Greenwich Street at Columbus, among the top 100 restaurants in Northern California, no mean achievement for this brick-walled, semi-cellar that opened in 1983 to serve Tuscan specialties. Don't miss the round raviolini stuffed with eggplant and Gorgonzola in a basil sauce; Tel: 776-7766. Across the street, the North Beach Playground saw success approach for many budding athletic stars, among them Joe DiMaggio. The only Istrian restaurant on the West Coast is **Albona Ristorante Istriano** at 545 Francisco Street between Taylor and Mason. (Istria is a peninsula on the Adriatic Sea that once was a part of the Holy Roman Empire and was added to Yugoslavia after World War II.) The cooking here reflects Venetian, Greek, Turkish, Spanish, and French influences; Tel: 441-1040.

For an offbeat treat, a beautiful view, and minuscule menu prices, try the **San Francisco Art Institute Café**, 800 Chestnut Street at Jones. It's open from 8:00 A.M. to 3:00 P.M. (closed Sundays), serves no alcohol, and takes no reservations or credit cards, but you're here to see and taste the arty future in a paper-cup, bare-bones, dress-in-black mood; stews, sandwiches, and Italian basics.

Three blocks farther north on Mason you'll reach Beach Street near Fisherman's Wharf, but first make a detour to the east along Greenwich Street to Telegraph Hill.

TELEGRAPH HILL

The first European to see San Francisco Bay, José de Ortega climbed the 275-foot hill then called La Loma Alta on November 1, 1769—and from there spotted a whole new world. In the early 1840s, Loma Alta was dubbed Windmill Hill, but in 1849 it began to be used as a station from which to observe incoming vessels, and was often called Signal Hill. Watchers within a two-story house would signal by semaphore the type of ship arriving to people concerned in the city below. On October 29, 1850, the station signaled the arrival of the steamer *Oregon,* bearing the news that California had been admitted to the Union, and it's said that huge hilltop bonfires burned all night. In 1853 Loma Alta became the first western telegraph station, and the name Telegraph Hill stuck.

The first inhabitants of the hill had been grazing goats, which were gradually displaced by little homes that rose atop the hill, populated by Italians, Spaniards, Portuguese, and French as the hill became the Latin Quarter, and later, in the 1890s, the Artists' Colony. Mark Twain lived on Telegraph Hill, as did Frank Norris, Joaquin Miller, Ambrose Bierce, Charles Warren Stoddard, and actor Edwin Booth. Bret Harte complained that goats browsed on the geraniums in his second-story windows and clattered over the roof at night "like heavy hailstones."

Today Telegraph Hill is an apartment- and cottage-covered rise with North Beach around its feet, the Embarcadero and waterfront below its steep eastern face (where sailors once dug out ballast for their ships and which was used as a quarry after 1906). It looks west toward Russian Hill, once separated from it by a swamp. Telegraph Hill remains a much-sought-after address, especially among people in newspapers, broadcasting, advertising and the like, who may hope some of the genius of the past will rub off on them.

Seeing the Hill

The steep, cement Filbert Street steps at the corner of Kearny Street lead up the west side of hill, flanked by a small slope of city-maintained grounds. An alternative to climbing the steps is the number 39 Coit bus, which can be boarded at Washington Square or along Bay Street south of Fisherman's Wharf. The hill traffic is terrible in summers, curving slowly up Telegraph Hill Boulevard; climb the steps or take the bus instead of driving.

Just east of the curve where Lombard becomes Telegraph Hill Boulevard you'll spot a bench and bas-relief memorial to Guglielmo Marconi, inventor of wireless telegraph and thus right at home on this hill.

On top, the famous monument often likened to a fire-hose nozzle is **Coit Tower**, a memorial to the volunteer firemen of early days (who well deserved it), built with a bequest from Mrs. Lillie Hitchcock Coit, who at age eight in 1851 came to the city with her family and became a fire buff (and, eventually, an honorary firefighter). The memorial, which she dedicated to "the purpose of adding beauty to the city I have always loved," was erected in 1933 after her death.

The lobby interior is covered with murals depicting the working life of 1930s California; 20 local artists were employed in a most unusual work-relief project for its time. The murals differ markedly in style and substance, but are worth seeing, especially since their refurbishing in 1990. There is a fee to take the elevator in the tower up to a platform from which 40-odd steps lead to the open loggia with a panoramic view; carry your wide-angle and telephoto lenses.

Two sets of steps lead down the eastern side: the brick Greenwich Steps and the Filbert Steps. The former begin near the light pole at the corner of the roundabout, across from the tower and near the sign marking Greenwich Street. They lead downhill past surprisingly rural-looking gardens to Montgomery Street and **Julius' Castle**, abruptly on your left at number 1541. Built in 1921 by an exuberant Italian hand, this restaurant has always been popular with visitors for its views of the bay. It has been revitalized and now presents respectable European cuisine, perhaps a bit elevated in price to match the view. There's valet parking, a necessity. To continue downhill, turn right on Montgomery, follow it to Filbert, and take the flight of steps to the left.

The Filbert Steps march precariously down from Telegraph Hill Boulevard itself from a point before you reach Coit Tower; they are an extension of the ones coming up from Kearny. (After visiting the tower you have a choice of taking the Greenwich Steps as far as Montgomery or of staying on the Filbert Steps from the start.)

From Telegraph Hill Boulevard to Montgomery, the Filbert Steps descend between cottages and gardens both tangled and manicured. Near the steps' intersection with Montgomery, at number 1349, you'll find **The Shadows**, once a rustic German restaurant, now a cozy hideaway specializing in contemporary French cuisine.

At Montgomery the descending steps become wooden and much more attractive, almost overhung by garden foliage; at Napier Lane there's a little bench where you may pause to take photos (or, you may as well admit it, to catch your breath). The wooden steps become a concrete stairway as they descend the steep banks of what was a quarry that carved away the east side of Telegraph Hill. At the bottom, at Sansome and Filbert streets, you cross into Levi Strauss Plaza (see Embarcadero Center Area above).

FISHERMAN'S WHARF AREA

The Fisherman's Wharf of history, of tourism, and of a San Franciscan's imagination are three very different entities.

Historically, the waterfront from Taylor to Leavenworth streets was set aside in 1900 by local authorities as the province of commercial fishermen, who had been catching in the bay since 1848. Since then it has stretched west to Hyde Street and east to Pier 39. To the tourist, it may mean the happy honky-tonk along Jefferson Street, loud with street musicians, clowns, and vendors of (mostly) junky jewelry, or a swirl of shops selling tee-shirts, sandals, and trinkets. There are also many "attractions" and "amusements" of doubtful value.

To the San Franciscan, however (who stays away in summer), the Wharf is a wider term that includes some of the old seafood restaurants, the historic ships, the National Maritime Museum, The Cannery complex off Leavenworth Street, Ghirardelli Square off Beach Street between Larkin and Polk, and the Golden Gate National Recreation Area. It behooves the thoughtful traveller to take the locals' view.

The Wharf area, north of North Beach and northwest of Telegraph Hill, is served by the Powell–Mason cable cars from Powell and Market streets to Taylor and Bay; by the Powell–Hyde line from the Powell/Market turntable to Victorian Park; by bus number 19 from the Civic Center up Polk; and by bus number 30 from Union Square through the heart of North Beach.

In the 1960s the Wharf was transformed for the better by the metamorphosis of the Ghirardelli Chocolate Factory and the rebuilding of the California Fruit Cannery; and in 1978 by the building of Pier 39. We look at the whole district—and its associated attractions, such as ferry excursions—from east to west.

Pier 39

Once an abandoned cargo dock, Pier 39 today is a thronging waterfront marketplace that ranks among the town's top tourist beats. Its two levels of shops and restaurants are connected by a pedestrian bridge to a 1,000-car garage on Beach Street that offers the best and easiest parking along the whole seaside sweep. (There is also a garage at Jefferson and Jones, and one underneath Ghirardelli Square.)

On the east side of Pier 39, small boats bob in a 350-berth marina (for the past few years, herds of honking sea lions have called it home, to the amusement of visitors and the vast irritation of boaters). From the west side, the craft of the Blue & Gold Fleet depart on periodic cruises around the bay (frequent daily departures, dependent on season; Tel: 781-

7877) and from the entrance of the pier, the motorized cable cars of Pier 39 Cable Car Company leave frequently for one-hour trips (Tel: 39-CABLE).

Within the complex, the **San Francisco Experience**, a theatrical trip through the city's past and present in light, sound, and special effects, offers shows daily, every half hour; Tel: 982-7550. (During the October 1989 earthquake, the audience at the Experience confused special effects with reality.)

That the architecture of Pier 39 represents Old San Francisco is a fiction; it more resembles an attempt at New England Quaint. Although this is a fast-food lover's fantasyland, it is possible to step out of the stream and into the comparative quiet of a handful of recommended restaurants, all on the second level. Spacious **Dante's** serves seafood in a casual though proper setting with smashing views at the very end of the pier; the old **Eagle Café**, a waterfront hangout for fishermen and longshoremen since 1928, was moved here from its original site and is as real and innocently raunchy as ever (breakfast and lunch only). **Swiss Louis** calls its cuisine Italian-Continental, while **Old Swiss House** offers French fare modified by Swiss-style lace curtains and beamed ceilings. **Vannelli's** serves fine seafood, and **Yet Wah**'s menu lists 200 dishes from across China; bring your appetite.

Alcatraz

The tomb-like bulk of the bastion of Alcatraz pokes up from the glistening bay in sharp contrast to the bustling, park-like scene at Pier 41, where ferry passengers waiting to board photograph the flower gardens, the high-flying balloons, and the passing cable cars and horse-drawn carriages.

Fact and fiction collide in the story of Alcatraz, *La Isla de los Alcatraces* (Isle of Pelicans). "Hellcatraz," it has been called; also, more familiarly, The Rock, a fearsome fortification since 1858 that became a maximum-security federal prison in the 1930s. In 1963 the last 27 inmates were transferred to other penal institutions, and in 1971 the Native Americans who had claimed the island were evacuated.

Alcatraz joined the Golden Gate National Recreation Area when that entity was created in 1972 and, under the custody of the National Park Service, is now one of the most popular attractions in California.

Many of the buildings on the island are ruins now, but the main block with its steel bars, claustrophobic cells, mess hall, library, and "dark holes" stands intact. It is difficult to imagine, but three inmates—Frank Lee Morris and John and Clarence Anglin—tunneled out with sharpened spoons in 1962 after years of struggle. They were never found.

Red & White ferries cast off for the 12-acre island from Pier 41 at 45-minute intervals (every half hour on weekends) until 2:15 P.M. The tour includes a self-guided trail, slide show, excellent audio-cassette tours narrated by former guards and prisoners, and special programs. Wear comfortable shoes and warm clothing whatever the season, and make reservations up to two weeks in advance during summer. For a fee, the tickets can be charged to MasterCard or VISA; Tel: (415) 546-2700.

Also from Pier 41, ferries of the Red & White Fleet depart on excursion sailings to Vallejo and the Marine World Africa USA amusement park; Pier 43½ is the departure point for Angel Island (see below), Sausalito, and Tiburon (see Day Trips from San Francisco), as well as for sightseeing boats that do a 45-minute bay circuit. Tel: (800) 229-2784 for Red & White ferry information.

The U.S.S. **Pampanito**, a World War II submarine built in 1943 at Portsmouth Naval Shipyard, New Hampshire, is open to the public daily at Pier 45. Operated by the National Maritime Museum Association, the sub offers exhibits and self-guided audio tours.

Angel Island

The largest, least-known island in the bay is Angel, christened *Nuestra Señora de los Angeles* on August 13, 1775 by Lieutenant Juan Manuel de Ayala, who probably was the first European to sail into the bay through the Golden Gate. Today it is a California State Park with a resident population of eight caretakers, four park rangers, and 200 or so deer, and serves (to those in on the secret) as a San Francisco escape hatch.

The 740-acre island is reached by Red & White ferries from Pier 43½ (Tel: 800-229-2784 for seasonal schedules), and is also accessible by short trips across Raccoon Strait from Tiburon in Marin County (see Day Trips from San Francisco). Pack a lunch, and from the dock in the island's small cove, climb a grassy rise to the picnic tables. After lunch you can amble the 12 miles of roads and hiking trails. A small museum and partially restored immigration station (almost 200,000 Chinese passed through it from 1910 to

1940) contain relics of the island's past as a military post and quarantine station. Tel: 435-1915 for information on types and locations of campsites; Tel: (800) 444-7275 for reservations only.

Seafood by the Bay

Dining, especially on seafood, is and always has been a major diversion around Fisherman's Wharf. Old Italian names reveal the fishermen's inheritance—**Alioto's No. 8** (the oldest restaurant on the wharf); **Castagnola's** (one Tomasso Castagnola seems to have invented the walkaway crab cocktail in 1916); **Pompei's Grotto** (the Pompeis, a fishing family, have been serving fresh seafood and Italian cuisine for more than 40 years); **A. Sabella's** (more than 65 years old); **Scoma's** (Pier 47, behind the fishing fleet); and **Tarantino's** (little neck clams, fettucine).

Cozy, slightly noisy, family-oriented **Caesar's** has been in business near the water at 2299 Powell Street for 36 years. **Pizzeria Uno North Point**, 2323 Powell Street, is one of the chain that pays tribute to Chicago's deep-dish pie. Across from Pier 43½, **Franciscan** serves fresh seafood with an unobstructed view of the bay; announcements are made of in- and outbound ships.

It is a sorry truism that none of San Francisco's best seafood is served at the Wharf, perhaps because the clientele of the restaurants tends to be tourists having a great time, who are less demanding than locals. We mention these for travellers who feel they must eat (not dine) at the Wharf.

Along the way, three bakeries are worth a call: **Blue Chip Cookies**, 757 Beach Street; **Boudin Bakery** at 156 Jefferson Street, for the original San Francisco sourdough French bread and sandwiches; and **Le Carrousel Patisserie** in Pier 39, for European-style tortes, croissants, pastries, and sandwiches.

Around in the Wharf Area

The Cannery, originally the Del Monte Fruit Company's peach-canning plant, was built in 1909, and for a time was the world's largest produce plant. In 1968 a new concrete building was constructed within the original brick shell, with such success that the new looks amiably old.

At 2801 Leavenworth at the foot of Columbus Avenue, The Cannery today is a spectrum of more than 50 shops, galleries, and restaurants. **Cafe Rigatoni**, a Roman-style trattoria emphasizing homemade pasta and fresh fish, offers dinner packages with next-door Cobb's Comedy Club that include reserved seats; Tel: 771-5225. **The Quiet Storm** serves Asian–Californian cuisine, with jazz on Thursdays, Fridays, and Saturdays.

The **Museum of the City of San Francisco**, the first ever to focus on the city and the Bay Area, is on The Cannery's third floor.

Hyde Street Pier

Travellers accustomed to going to the sea in comfort aboard today's ocean liners can only wonder at the courage and stamina of those sailors of the past in their cramped quarters: cold, seasick, and sometimes, surely, afraid. Across the street from The Cannery at the Hyde Street Pier (built to serve ferry traffic, which ceased after the debut of the Golden Gate Bridge), the **San Francisco Maritime National Historical Park** maintains a cache of historical nautical treasures: six old vessels, three of which may be boarded. The graceful, three-masted, deep-waterman *Balclutha* was launched in Scotland in 1886. This steel-hulled survivor of the Cape Horn fleet, a veteran of trade in spirits, salmon, hardware, coal, and wheat, is a symbol of San Francisco's seafaring heritage. *Eureka,* last of the side-wheel–powered ferries to operate in the U.S., built in 1890, hauled freight and passengers for the Northern Pacific Railroad. Built in 1895, the *C. A. Thayer* was the Pacific Coast's last commercial schooner and is now retired after service in the lumber industry and in two wars. The historic fleet also includes the scow schooner *Alma,* the oceangoing tug *Hercules,* and the side-wheel river tug *Eppleton Hall,* which cannot be boarded. The **Maritime Bookstore** at the pier's entrance sells books about ships and sailing as well as valuable regional guides.

A formal little greensward designed by renowned land-scape architect Thomas D. Church, **Victorian Park** is a pleas-ant place to sit next to the Hyde Street Pier while waiting for a cable car on the Powell–Hyde line. On the other hand, you might idle the minutes (or hours) away at the **Buena Vista Café**, 2765 Hyde Street, where Irish coffee is said to have been introduced to the United States. No credit cards and no reservations are accepted, and the squeezing for a seat is legendary. Nonetheless, it's one of the must-see cafés in the city, decade in and decade out.

Across Beach Street from Ghirardelli Square (see below) the **National Maritime Museum** at the foot of Polk Street was built in 1939 more or less in the shape of a ship. It houses meticulously executed ship models, large ship relics, and beautifully carved and painted figureheads staring into ocean space with unblinking eyes. On the second floor, a collection of photographs, models, paintings, maps, and handicrafts stands witness to the seagoing tradition of the city. The museum is open daily.

Ghirardelli Square

The first—and still among the most attractive—urban redeveloped landmarks in the country, Ghirardelli Square (pronounced GEAR-ar-deli) today boasts eye-opening views of the bay and more than 70 shops and restaurants (some of them destinations in their own right for San Franciscans). The oldest red-brick building in the complex, the Woolen Mill, dates from 1864 (Civil War uniforms were made here). Domingo Ghirardelli from Rapallo, Italy, began making chocolate here in 1893, and built a factory that produced it until the early 1960s. In 1962, fearing that the decaying Victorian complex might be destroyed, Mrs. William P. Roth and her son William Matson Roth (of the Matson Steamship Line) bought it and commissioned its metamorphosis into an environmentally enhancing mall. It occupies the block bounded by North Point, Polk, Beach, and Larkin streets.

Like an old European arcade, Ghirardelli suits amblers and oglers almost as well as shoppers and diners, especially around holiday seasons, when it becomes a fiesta of live music, entertainment, and people-watching.

Ghirardelli Chocolate Manufactory is a dieter's Waterloo—sundaes you could live on for a week and wonderful chocolate confections are served here. Some original candy-making equipment is on display.

Soothing to both the eye and the inner self is the **Mandarin**, on the top floor of the Woolen Mill, with its tiled floors, Chinese art, and an opulence surprising to those who associate Chinese food with the plainest and simplest surroundings. Founder Cecilia Chiang, who introduced a new style of Chinese cooking to the city in 1968, has now retired and turned over her cleaver (and ownership) to longtime assistant Julian Mao. It is expected that he will keep the quality of the cuisine equal to the spectacular setting; Tel: 673-8812. Because the restaurant is within a major tourist attraction, however, recipes on the regular menu are sometimes altered to suit tastes of beginners as well as experts in Chinese cooking; if you want classical seasoning or special dishes, just ask.

Gaylord India is a comfortable, restful, roomy place with a memorable view of the bay, and though purists sometimes complain, most diners leave not only satisfied but delighted. Restaurant designer Pat Kuleto is a partner in **McCormick & Kuleto's**, a classic seafood house and crabcake lounge. More than 30 fresh fish dishes are offered daily and almost every table has a stunning bay view; Tel: 929-1730.

Compadres Mexican Bar & Grill serves south-of-the-border specialties in a gleefully tropical setting and the **Boudin Bakery** has one of its four city locations here at Ghirardelli Square. Boudin, the original maker of San Francisco French sourdough, now sells bread and serves sandwiches, pizza bread, salads, and beverages.

Shops of particular interest are the **China Jade and Art Center**, the **Ghirardelli Craft Gallery**, and **Kyriakos of Hydra** (Greek handicrafts).

GOLDEN GATE NATIONAL RECREATION AREA

"It's like living in a great, gray pearl," someone once remarked about San Francisco. Indeed, often the air is opalescent, the meeting of sea and sky above the bay a clean, foggy gray sparkling, like diffused-light diamonds. A gem of a trek almost any time of year is one west from Fisherman's Wharf along the bay through the Golden Gate National Recreation Area, established in 1972, and, at 72,815 acres with 28 miles of coastline, the largest urban park in the world.

The walk may be started here and there along the area's length; the most logical starting point (especially if you are coming from Fisherman's Wharf) is to take the **Golden Gate Promenade**, a footpath three and a half miles long from the Hyde Street Pier around curving Aquatic Park, past the historic houses of Fort Mason and the Fort Mason Cultural Center, along Marina Green to Fort Point and under the south tower of the Golden Gate Bridge. (Dedicated walkers can continue west along seaside trails all the way to Land's End and Cliff House on the open ocean; see the Ocean Beach and Land's End section below.) You also could approach on foot from the northern end of Van Ness Avenue, or by bus from downtown to the GGNRA headquarters via buses numbers 42, 47, or 49 from Civic Center.

If you arrive at your starting point at Fort Mason by car, do two things: First, drive up Franklin Street off Bay, past several

historic Victorian houses (still occupied by officers and
enlisted men; the commandant's residence is an Officers'
Club), and follow the curve around to **GGNRA Headquarters**, where you may pick up a fine map and ask questions;
second, return to Bay and turn right (west), pass Gough and
Octavia, and turn right on Laguna Street and into the parking
lot for Fort Mason. This is the best starting point for the walk
if you have a car to leave.

Fort Mason Cultural Center

The bluff above Fort Mason was the site of a small battery
established in 1797 by Spanish soldiers from the Presidio,
which, under President Millard Fillmore in the 1850s, became one of three U.S. Army reservations in San Francisco.
Through stands of stately trees, the walk winds back through
the fort to Aquatic Park.

At Fort Mason's Pier 3 floats the S.S. *Jeremiah O'Brien,* last
of the unaltered Liberty ships. (These were slow cargo ships
built in large numbers for the U.S. Merchant Marine during
World War II; O'Brien himself was the first American captain
to capture a British vessel during the Revolution.) The ship
is open to the public 359 days a year, and on the third
weekend of every month (except May and December) the
steam engine is turned over at slow speed at the dock to give
visitors a look at one of the last surviving ship engines of this
type in the world. Each May two five-hour cruises are made
on the bay; Tel: 441-3101.

Fort Mason Center (entrance at the corner of Marina
Boulevard and Buchanan Street) has become a lively arts-
and-recreation community that offers more than 1,000 activities monthly and houses more than 50 resident groups; Tel:
441-5706. **Greens**, in Building A, is San Francisco's—and
maybe the country's—most creative vegetarian restaurant,
with beautiful views of anchored yachts and cooking so
good it attracts diners of every stripe. Don't be surprised if
dinners are booked a month in advance; Tel: 771-6222.
Greens also runs the **Tassajara Bakery** here, which produces
some of the finest breads in existence.

MUSEUMS AT FORT MASON
In Building A, the **San Francisco Craft and Folk Art Museum**
mounts witty and elegant exhibitions of contemporary crafts,
American folk arts, and traditional ethnic arts from home
and abroad, complemented by an enticing gift shop; Tel:
775-0990. Dedicated to the preservation, collection, and dis-

play of Italian-American and Italian art, culture, and history, the **Museo Italiano Americano** (in Building C) includes the works of prominent contemporary artists; Tel: 673-2200.

Nationally recognized exhibitions and popular field trips to black historical sites are sponsored by the **African-American Historical and Cultural Society**, a combination museum, art gallery, historical society, and resource library focusing on African-Americans and black Californians. It is also in Building C; Tel: 441-0640.

The **Mexican Museum of San Francisco**, one of only two museums in the United States to focus on Mexican art, shows works that range from the pre-Hispanic period to contemporary art. On display are many pieces by Chicano artists, folk artists, and those of the Colonial period; **La Tienda**, the museum's shop, sells Mexican arts and crafts. The museum and its shop are in Building D; Tel: 441-0404. It is scheduled to move into new headquarters on Mission Street across from the projected site of the Yerba Buena Center within five years.

The **Magic Theatre**, also in Building D, was one of the first companies in the country to devote itself exclusively to the production of new American works; its season extends year round, except for September; Tel: 441-8822. Other installations of interest to the traveller here are the **Book Bay Bookstore**, Building C; **Bayfront Gallery**, Herbst Pavilion; **Cowell Theater** (plays, dance, film, music in a 400-seat theater), Tel: 441-5706; **Golden Gate National Recreation Area Headquarters**, Building 201; **San Francisco Maritime National Historical Park**, Building E; and ▶ **San Francisco International Hostel**, Building 240, Tel: 771-7277.

Fort Point National Historical Site

In 1776, on this "extremity of the white cliff at the inner point of the entrance to the port," Colonel Juan Bautista de Anza erected a cross to mark the site of a proposed fort. **Fort Point**, a classic brick fortification completed in 1861, once housed 149 cannons—none of which was ever fired in anger. It's said the fort was copied after the design of Fort Sumter in Charleston, South Carolina. National Park Service guides in Civil War uniforms conduct daily tours of the bastion.

The Presidio

The site for the San Francisco Presidio was selected by Juan Bautista de Anza on March 28, 1776. Today it commands a spacious, spectacular site of 1,540 acres in one of the best settings in the entire city, on the heights just south of the Golden Gate. It's the headquarters of the United States Sixth Army and employs some 6,000 military and civilian person- nel, but is slowly being shut down—a victim of military cutbacks. Happily, the park-like grounds will become part of the Golden Gate National Recreation Area, although precise plans for the area are fueling intense local debate.

The only attraction within the Presidio directed toward visitors as such is the **Presidio Army Museum** at Funston and Lincoln avenues, which displays two cottages similar to the thousands that sheltered refugees from the 1906 earthquake and some interesting military memorabilia. If you have an automobile and plenty of time to explore, take a drive around the Presidio grounds, entering through the gates at Lombard and Lyon streets in the Marina or at Presidio Avenue and Pacific from Presidio Heights.

Presidio Heights

Presidio Heights, while not part of the military reservation, edges the Presidio's woody preserve to the south. Here, as on Russian Hill, the chief interest for the traveller is walking or driving up and down streets lined by very attractive houses— especially those on Jackson and Washington streets. Cruise (but quietly) around circular, prestigious Presidio Terrace, entered off the meeting of Washington and Arguello streets.

Just south of Presidio Terrace at Arguello and Lake, the **Temple Emanu-El**, a superb example of modern Byzantine architecture, is the city's major center of Reform Judaism.

Arguello Boulevard owes its name to one of the actors in a historic tragedy, as sketched by James Benét: "It concerns the wooing of Concepcion Argüello, daughter of the Pre- sidio's commander, by Count N. P. Rezanov, who visited the Bay in 1805 to seek supplies for the Russian colony at Sitka.

"Rezanov won the lady's love, and with her help and her father's also won permission to trade; then he sailed for home. For many years Concepcion faithfully awaited his return or a message, but finally entered a convent. It was 36 years later that she learned he had died before reaching Russia."

Sacramento Street

Outer Sacramento Street near Presidio Avenue has blos- somed into a shopping area similar to Union Street (see below), with clusters of shops, galleries, boutiques, coffeehouses, and cafés. At 3673 Sacramento (between Spruce and Locust), the **Magic Flute Garden Ristorante** serves Continental dishes with an Italian accent in a romantic setting. Across the street, the **Tuba Garden** at number 3634 occupies a pretty Victorian and specializes in luncheons and brunches, served outside when the weather is right. In the same block at number 3665, **Rosmarino** is a stylish newcomer with a pretty courtyard. The menu features light, simple, but tasty dishes prepared by a chef who appears to be calorie-conscious; Tel: 931-7710.

Walking east on Sacramento after a fine luncheon, you'll be diverted by several intriguing shops. In the next block from the restaurants mentioned above at number 3571 (between Locust and Laurel), **Santa Fe** shows off some of the finest Southwestern goods in the city, from fine jewelry to tableware, furniture, rugs, and specialty foods. Farther on, at 3461 Sacramento, **Cottonwood** stocks iron tables and sculptures also inspired by the Southwest, as well as tabletop accessories, glassware, ceramics, and chinaware. In the block between Walnut and Presidio, you'll find **Hawley-Bragg** (antique furniture), **Elements** (what-nots), and **Claire's Antique Linens & Gifts. Garibaldi**, 347 Presidio just north of Sacramento, is international with an Italian accent and has a full liquor license (unusual in this neighborhood); Tel: 563-8841. Returning to Sacramento, turn left (east) again toward **Forrest Jones** (a treasure trove for lovers of kitchen gadgets), **Papyrus** (stylish stationery, cards, and wrapping paper), **American Pie** (an unusual general store), **V. Breier** (ceramic fantasies), and **Sue Fisher King** (china and table linens).

If on your Sacramento stroll you walk a block south on Laurel, you'll find yourself on food-fancier's row: Laurel Village on California Street between Laurel and Locust. Here you'll find **Peet's Coffee** (fine beans to grind and teas to brew); **Laurel Super Mart & Meats** (gourmet surprises); **Wine Impression** (fine and rare wines and spirits, wine bar); **La Rocca's Oyster Bar** (small seafood café, with food to go); **Judith Ets-Hokin's Homechef Cooking School** (cookware and specialty products such as bottled herbs and vinegars); and an upscale branch of **Cal-Mart** (all you need for picnics or gifts for your hostess).

GOLDEN GATE BRIDGE

On May 24, 1987, more than 200,000 diehard bridge buffs walked, sang, and danced across the 50-year-old Golden

Gate Bridge, causing the great span, the world's longest such single-suspension, to sag in the middle by ten feet, terrifying city authorities.

One of the most durable city symbols on earth, the Golden Gate Bridge itself is not golden (that name was first applied to the natural harbor entrance), but a giant, graceful, red-orange span leaping from San Francisco north to the shores of Marin County.

It's worth mentioning that at its peak the tidal surge through the Gate is three times the flow of the Amazon and 14 times that of the Mississippi. This is a fierce place, where currents sweep through the watery slot at up to 60 miles per hour, winds whip the headlands, and fog pours over the oceanside hills like an opaque waterfall.

Engineer Joseph Strauss and his determined assistant Clifford Paine were the dynamic forces behind the dream and the completion of it: a struggle not only against the elements but against the politicians and voters who did not understand visionaries.

Finally it stood, and is best appreciated by the free walk across, which is 1¼ miles long and takes about an hour (including time out for photos). There's always wind; wear a sweater. For good views of the span, drivers should stop at the **Toll Plaza and Visitor Center** on the south (city) side and the **Vista Point** turnoff on the north (Marin County) side.

THE MARINA

Heading back from the Golden Gate Bridge, stop in the Marina district, between Fort Point and Fort Mason. This is San Francisco's Mediterranean, a low-rise, waterside, and wide-sky pastel neighborhood, where strolling is the accepted speed until you slow down and stretch out on Marina Green, and where yachts bob at their moorings on the bay.

Basically, the Marina may be said to idle between Lombard Street on the south (an extension of Van Ness Avenue/Highway 101, which runs north through the city, then west as Lombard, then north across the Golden Gate Bridge into Marin County) and the bayside greenswards of Fort Mason and Marina Green on the north, and from Van Ness west to Richardson and Doyle drives (approaches to the bridge). Up the hills to the south rise the associated worlds of Union Street and Pacific Heights (see below).

Sadly but dramatically, the Marina's most recent role on the national stage was played in October 1989, when the earthquake struck this neighborhood with particular force, the fiery results lighting up the TV sets of a nation.

Palace of Fine Arts

The Marina sits upon land reclaimed from a tidal marsh and lagoon that was filled in as the site for the Panama-Pacific International Exposition of 1915. Officially, the fair saluted the opening of the Panama Canal; in reality, it celebrated the rebuilding of the earthquake-ravaged region as a part of the City Beautiful movement.

The Exposition was nothing if not elaborate, consisting of a complex of enormous wood-and-plaster palaces dedicated to the arts, education, machinery, horticulture, transportation, agriculture, and more, all joined by landscaped courts and buttressed by colonnades. The exteriors of these eccentricities were decorated in Neoclassical fashion; on the inside, they were simple sheds.

Of these, only the Palace of the Fine Arts remains (not to be confused with the California Palace of the Legion of Honor museum, as frequently happens in print). Designed by Berkeley architect Bernard Maybeck, whose artistic contributions to American style are often compared to those of Louis Sullivan and Frank Lloyd Wright, it had curving wings, within which lay a three-acre park. Its peristyle of Corinthian columns faced a lagoon, above which rose an octagonal temple of Roman arches and columns surmounted by a 160-foot-high dome. After the fair, it was allowed to fall into disrepair as the city's very own romantic ruin.

By the late 1950s philanthropist Walter S. Johnson, who lived across the street, had become saddened by the sight of the Palace. With his funds and energy, plus a 1959 city bond issue and matching funds from the state, the building was reconstructed (one might say really built for the first time) with reinforced concrete. Today it stands as an Old World outcrop in a delightful residential setting at Baker and Beach streets, just one and a half blocks from Marina Boulevard and a harbor afloat with colorful yachts. Ducks and swans paddle on the mirror-like pond in front of the building, oblivious that women came here to do their laundry in the 1850s.

The Palace now houses the **Exploratorium**, an internationally acclaimed museum of science, art, and human perception, featuring some 650 exhibits to be manipulated, tinkered with, or activated by push buttons. (It inspired some displays in Paris's La Villette science center.) This is a museum that is particularly attractive to children and families, and, in fact, you may want to visit it even if you decide to skip the rest of the Marina. The food available here will especially appeal to children—sandwiches, ice cream, and fruit in addition to a few hot specials. To reach the Exploratorium by public transportation, take the number 30 or number 30X bus from the CalTrain depot at Fourth and Townsend streets or, more handily, from stops along Kearny in the Financial District or Columbus Avenue in North Beach; Tel: 561-0360.

Exploring the Marina

The Palace of Fine Arts and Exploratorium aside, the Marina is a thoroughly residental district sliced by Lombard (the highway, lined by restaurants, motels, and small stores, is the main feeder to the Golden Gate Bridge from the southern part of the state) and by Chestnut, the local shopping/supping/sipping street one block north of Lombard. In recent years restaurants have mushroomed on both streets, some of which lure residents from all over town. (As if that weren't enough, the shops and restaurants of Union Street in the Cow Hollow area—see below—are just a few blocks south of the Marina.)

An inspiration from the fertile imagination of Jeremiah Tower (who no longer owns it), **Balboa Café** at 3199 Fillmore Street at Greenwich is a noisy, happy watering hole serving unsurpassed and simple things: the Balboa burger, pepper steak, and seafood fettucine among them. No reservations are accepted. The prices are as pleasant as the homemade pastas at **E'Angelo**, 2234 Chestnut Street.

Cambodia has moved to San Francisco and found a home on Lombard Street. **Angkor Palace**, at number 1769 between Octavia and Laguna, offers one of the best dining experiences in the city; don't miss the crêpes, the soups, and the sizzling fresh seafood. If you can't abide sitting on pillows on the floor, call ahead for a table with a well for your legs; Tel: 931-2830.

A lighthearted informality that's not overly friendly relaxes the visitor to **La Pergola**, an oasis of northern Italian cooking at 2060 Chestnut Street. **Original Joe's #2 in the Marina**, 2001 Chestnut (at Fillmore), is a handsome wide-open, two-level space highlighted by a huge carved back bar and a loud, lively, and very Old San Francisco atmosphere; Tel: 346-4000.

When haute cuisine has become *de trop* and what you need is hearty food and generous drinks with an overlay of enthusiasm, you can't do better than to join the local gang at its neighborhood hangout, **Liverpool Lil's**, at 2492 Lyon Street across from the Presidio Gate. It feels like a pub and serves meals until midnight. Hamburgers and sandwiches of zany combinations make **Chestnut Street Grill** at 2231 Chestnut popular all hours of the day. It's particularly pleasant to sit in the garden here when it's warm.

Samui Thai is a newcomer to the Marina, specializing in southern Thai cuisine influenced by Malaysian cooking. The service here, at 2414 Lombard Street at Scott, is impeccable. **Izzy's Steak & Chop House**, reborn at 3349 Steiner near Chestnut, pays tribute to Izzy Gomez, whose saloon was the toast of the town in the 1920s and 1930s. Try a dry-aged steak, creamed spinach, or a grappa fizz.

Scott's, the seafood house at 2400 Lombard (at Scott Street, hence the name) became a star the night it opened. It's hugely popular, yet the service never seems hurried. This is a good place to order abalone properly done—if you've just come into an inheritance; Tel: 563-8988. (There are two relatives, Scott's Seafood Grill and Scott's Carriage House, both at Three Embarcadero Center.)

Lucca Delicatessen is definitely the best place in the Marina for assembling a picnic. It's at 2120 Chestnut Street, and does not accept credit cards.

Before leaving the Marina, take a drive west along Marina Boulevard from Gas House Cove (next to Fort Mason), past Marina Green to **Baker Street** (last exit before the Golden Gate Bridge). This street is flanked by proud, patrician homes of a Mediterranean persuasion, looking across the bay toward the now-green, now-golden hills of Marin County. You may even be persuaded to join the dog walkers, picnickers, and kite-fliers having a lazy afternoon in the sun on the half-mile-long Marina Green.

To take public transportation to and from the Marina (to Chestnut Street, for example), your best choice is the number 30 Stockton bus, which goes north on Kearny, through the Stockton Tunnel, up Columbus to North Point, then to Van Ness and along Chestnut Street.

COW HOLLOW

The stretch of Union Street running west of Van Ness Avenue from Russian Hill to the Presidio just south of the Marina is known as Cow Hollow to traditionalists, but just **Union Street** to shoppers and diners with no hankering for history. Only four blocks uphill (south) from Chestnut, it's frequently considered part of the Marina, and most of the restaurants mentioned in that section are just a few blocks from here.

Historic Cow Hollow

In post–Gold Rush days this was a green dale watered by small streams seeking the bay. It attracted farmers, among them one George W. Hatman who established a dairy ranch here in 1861, giving the hollow its countrified name. On the heels of Hatman came 30 or so more farmers, and soon hundreds of cows shared the grasslands with wild ducks, quail, and rabbits.

Besides supplying milk to the city, the hollow served as a communal wash basin. Fresh water was so scarce here in the 1850s that rich miners sent their laundry to Honolulu and even to China to be washed. Laguna Pequena, a little lake in the area that would now be bounded by Franklin, Octavia, Filbert, and Lombard streets, was used by the washerwomen who took in laundry from the Presidio's officers and by housewives who congregated there from the city on washdays. This was Washerwoman's Lagoon.

This bucolic era ended in the 1880s as pollution permeated the valley from sausage factories, tanneries, and slaughterhouses. When the aromas wafted uphill to the homes of the Bonanza Kings in adjacent Pacific Heights, it was all over. The cows were banished in 1891, and Washerwoman's Lagoon was filled in.

By the middle of this century Union Street was a nondescript neighborhood of hardware stores, garages, mom-and-pop groceries, and five-and-dimes. Then the decorators who had already restored Jackson Square came around for a look at the old clapboard dwellings, the converted carriage houses, and the surviving stables and barns, and began the regeneration of the late 1950s with a few stylish antique shops and home furnishings showrooms; by the mid-1960s Cow Hollow had become a faubourg with flair.

Exploring Cow Hollow

Union Street is a window-shopper's happy hunting ground for home furnishings, antiques, handicrafts, custom-made clothing, art objects and imports, books and gifts and linens, specialty foods and feminine fripperies. Handily interspersed are pubs, delis, cafés, snack spots, and restaurants representing about a dozen cuisines.

The Hollow's handsomest creations are the clusters of artfully refurbished Victorians, some metamorphosed into smart shopping compounds. Fine old façades are painted subtle shades with colorful gingerbread trims, wrought-iron fences have been retained, and, in some places, gas lights reinstalled.

At the corner of Gough and Union streets, visit the **Octagon House**. Eight-sided houses were once believed to bring good luck. This one, built in 1861 and purchased in 1952 by the National Society of Colonial Dames, is one of the few remaining local examples of the style. Furnished with colonial and Federal-period antiques, it is open to the public from noon to 3:00 P.M. on the second and fourth Thursdays and the second Sunday of each month; closed January and holidays (Tel: 441-7512).

After the Octagon House, admire the house at 1851 Union, in 1884 a stable facing Washerwoman's Lagoon. Next, amble into Charlton Court, a cul-de-sac off the south side of Union's 1900 block, believed to have been a milk-wagon loading yard. The 1873 and 1896 Victorians at numbers 2 and 4 are today ▶ **The Bed and Breakfast Inn**.

Three circa 1870 residences, including a pair of "wedding houses" (identical bungalows with a common center wall) at 1980 Union, encompass several shops and cafés, and the old Laurel Vale Dairy at number 1981 is now the home of **Earthly Goods** (women's apparel).

The three-story mansion at 2040 Union was erected around 1870 by early dairyman James W. Cudworth with lumber brought around Cape Horn. It houses several boutiques and **L'Entrecôte de Paris** (see below).

One block north, the eccentric **Vedanta Society Temple** at 2963 Webster on the corner of Filbert was built between 1905 and 1908 as a reflection of Hindu religious philosophy; the result was an amalgam of Moorish columns, lobated windows, cusped arches, crenellated towers, and onion domes. The countrified grounds of **St. Mary the Virgin Episcopal Church** at 2325 Union are often used for weddings. The Eternal Fountain here is fed by a spring that once watered the Cow Hollow herds.

Shopping and Dining on Union Street

In the block between Gough and Octavia are two ethnic art galleries on the north side of the street: **Images of the North**,

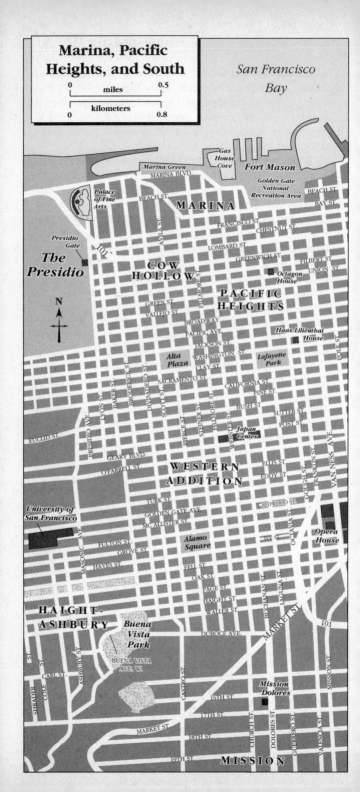

for Eskimo art and sandstone sculptures, and **A Touch of Asia** for sculptures, screens, and other wonders from several cultures. Across the street, **Margaritaville** at number 1787 is a merry Mexican spot for contemporary music, videos, traditional dishes, and great margaritas.

Between Octavia and Laguna at number 1846, **Oggetti** sells stationery and paper products, beautifully made in Florence. On the south side in the same block, **L'Escargot** is a formal, candle-lit rendezvous where many beautiful people enjoy the veal and lamb dishes; Tel: 567-0222. Pretty **Laura Ashley** creations await women and children at number 1827, and the restaurant–jazz club **Pasand** offers Madras cuisine at number 1875; Tel: 922-4498.

Perry's, at number 1944 between Laguna and Buchanan, remains a popular spot for searching singles, but everyone else seems to enjoy it, too, possibly because the American standards, hamburgers and fried chicken, are much above standard. Everybody in town has visited at least once.

Between Buchanan and Webster, **Prego** at number 2000 is the kind of pasta place you always wanted—except you wish they'd take reservations. It's sophisticated yet hip, chic yet youthful, crowded yet cool. The pasta is homemade, the pizzas from an oak-burning brick oven. **L'Entrecôte de Paris** at number 2032 is where you take your appetite when it demands French-style steak (neither so thick nor so fatty as traditional American cuts) and skinny, truly French *frites*. It's casual, and there are some outdoor tables for people-watching while munching; Tel: 931-5006. Right across the street at number 2033, **Amici's East Coast Pizzeria** caters to city dwellers who wax nostalgic for Manhattan-style pizza. The decor is virtually nonexistent, but the tastes will make your eyes glaze over anyway—from the wood-burning brick ovens come pies with any of 14 toppings. Pastas are also good and may be followed by J. M. Rosen's famous New York cheesecake. Take-out is available; Tel: 885-4500. In the same block at number 2001, **Fumiki Fine Asian Art** offers affordable, tasteful gifts and collectibles as well as fine antiques.

Between Fillmore and Steiner, consider **Doidge's Kitchen** at number 2217, a great place for breakfast (some say this is where the Social Register takes its hangovers). **Yoshida-Ya Yakitori** at 2909 Webster just north of Union makes you feel as if you've stepped out of Cow Hollow right into Kyoto. It's easy to make a whole meal out of appetizers alone here (there are more than 60), but then you'd miss *yakitori, shabu-shabu,* and vegetarian entrées. **Pane e Vino**, 3011 Steiner between Union and Filbert, opened to applause in

1991 and has played to packed tables ever since. Its unpretentious neighborhood setting, light but satisfying pastas, and ambience of happy diners should assure this newcomer a long run; Tel: 346-2111.

With almost 50 shops selling fashions for men, women, and children, Union and its cross streets are a compelling alternative to shopping downtown. Among the choice stops are **American Girl in Italy**, number 2163; bébé (buying for American babies also allowed), number 1954; **Coco's Italian Dreams**, number 2254; and **John Callahan Hats**, number 2150.

Cow Hollow, like so much of San Francisco, demands to be seen on foot, partly because of its tucked-away corners that the motorist misses, partly because the parking problem will give you ulcers or migraines. There is public parking at three garages on Union and one on Fillmore between Union and Filbert. The most convenient for ambling up and down the seven-block stretch of Union between Franklin on the east and Steiner on the west is Union Street Plaza Garage at number 2001; others are Union Garage at number 1550, Wells Fargo Garage at number 1900, and Cow Hollow Garage at 3060 Fillmore.

The best public transportation from downtown is the number 45 bus westbound on Sutter Street. From the Financial District, board number 41 westbound on Sacramento Street, or catch the number 41 along Columbus Avenue in North Beach. Get off the bus at the corner of Union and Franklin streets and walk west, or ride to the Steiner Street intersection and walk east.

POLK STREET AND VAN NESS AVENUE

Polk Street used to be referred to as *Polkstrasse,* and in some circles it still is, a reference to the city's old German population once concentrated here. Unlike some other ethnic groups, they have long since dispersed. Today Polk's two-mile march from the bay and Cow Hollow south to Market Street parallel to Van Ness offers everything from the silly to the serviceable to the sinful (both gay and straight).

In a sense, Polk has always been a commercial street, though around the turn of the century it catered to the carriage trade that rolled down from Nob Hill. Today, despite an occasional aristocratic outcrop (such as **Freed, Teller, and**

Freed for tea, coffee, and spices at number 1326 and **Mayes Oyster House** at number 1233), it's a mixed bag of small food stores, health shops, too-trendy outlets, and what-not places selling what you can't imagine anybody's wanting.

Most visitors to the city will be more comfortable on Polk the farther north they are (near the Union Street and Pacific Heights areas, there are several good restaurants; see below). South of California Street the street is known as Polk Gulch, a focus of the gay population, and becomes distinctly seedy.

When you drive along Van Ness today you strain to imagine it as what it was intended to be, and in part was, before the 1906 earthquake and fire: San Francisco's Champs-Elysées. (Of course, Paris's Champs-Elysées isn't the Champs-Elysées anymore, either.) This is the north–south axis of San Francisco, the nervous center of traffic, the throughway you try to avoid but can't. An extension of U.S. Highway 101 up from the south (linked to the Golden Gate Bridge by Lombard, which cuts from east to west at a 90 degree angle), it seems without personality or distinction to the driver speeding along.

It wasn't always this way, and civil authorities are puzzling about how to regain a bit of its erstwhile elegance. Named for then newly elected mayor James Van Ness and laid out in 1854 as a spacious boulevard to be lined by mansions set on large lots, it was described in 1892 as "our one show street, purely a residence section." Gingerbreads by the dozen, gaudy or demure, danced up and down the city's widest street.

Then came 5:13 A.M. on April 18, 1906. The earth shook and the sky burned: Some 514 blocks had gone up in flames when the army engineers decided to dynamite Van Ness as a firebreak. It worked: All the eastern side of the avenue was in ruins, but, with a few exceptions, the west side and the rest of the city were saved. Thus the richest reliquary of Victoriana remains west of Van Ness—Pacific Heights, for example.

Following the fire, commerce came to the formerly stylish street, and then in the 1920s, the heyday of automobiles as luxuries, palatial showrooms arose, many of them now turned to other uses. The northern end of Van Ness, like that of Polk, boasts a great diversity of dining spots. (For the best ones farther south, see Civic Center below.)

Around Polk and Van Ness

Acquerello ("watercolor" in Italian) is an apt name for this pretty, softly lighted room where *nuovo cucina* wonders

such as *involtini* of veal with marjoram and prosciutto are
created; the wine list is another wonder. The restaurant is at
1722 Sacramento Street between Polk and Van Ness (Tel: 567-
5432). **Maharani** has brought gracious Moghul-style dining to
1122 Post Street, corner of Van Ness. Among California's best
Indian restaurants, it specializes in tandoori and vegetarian
delicacies.

The **Café Majestic** in the Majestic Hotel, restored to its
stately splendor, is a perfect setting for rediscovered recipes
from Old California: grilled chicken Nellie Melba with wild
mushrooms, for instance. The address is 1500 Sutter Street,
two blocks west of Van Ness. Despite nay-sayers, steak is
making a comeback, and there are few better houses in
which to enjoy it than the San Francisco branch of **Ruth's
Chris**, at 1700 California, corner of Van Ness. Maine lobsters
join U.S. prime beef on the hearty menu.

If France can have haute cuisine, why not her former
colony Vietnam? Here it is, served in style in the handsome,
roomy **Golden Turtle**, 2211 Van Ness Avenue between Broadway and Vallejo; don't miss the fresh crab in ginger-and-
garlic sauce. The prices are as friendly as the staff. **Harris'**
(2100 Van Ness at Pacific) specializes in steak, and nobody
anywhere does it better. High ceilings, booth seatings, and a
man-size arrangement of space suit the prime-cut quality.

On the quieter end of Polk at number 2323 (between
Green and Union), **Casablanca** is a meeting of North Africa
and France, and a smooth one. The mood is Mediterranean
and mellow, the menu entertainingly eclectic.

About as quiet as an air-raid siren, the **Hard Rock Café** at
1699 Van Ness near Sacramento is a smash: cars crashing
through walls, waitresses dressed like 1950s carhops,
eardrum-rending rock, and, as an accent, great burgers and
fries. It's not for everybody, but everybody seems happy
lining up to get in. In distinct contrast, **Matterhorn Swiss
Restaurant** at 2323 Van Ness near Green is warm, restrained, and intimate, offering dishes from the Valais region; dinners only Wednesdays through Sundays. Try the
veal bratwurst with *rösti*.

PACIFIC HEIGHTS

You'll be permitted to live in Pacific Heights even if your last
name isn't Spreckels or Getty, even if your employer is
neither Queen Elizabeth II nor Boris Yeltsin. But such connections would help, especially in this most expensive dis-

trict in one of the most costly cities in the country. (Of the 70 consular, foreign trade, government, tourist, and development officials in San Francisco, many enjoy homes in Pacific Heights, including the consuls of England and Russia.)

This posh purlieu rises between California and Green streets on the south and north, and Van Ness and Presidio avenues on the east and west. The best way to explore it is to drive out one street and back the next, stopping to ogle at will. If you haven't the time for that, at least browse along Broadway between Webster and Lyon streets, noting particularly **Hamlin School**, 2120 Broadway, and the **Convent of the Sacred Heart**, at number 2222. Both were mansions built at different times for James L. Flood, the son of James C., one of the so-called Bonanza Kings, who rose from saloon-keeper to multimillionaire as a result of speculation in Nevada's Comstock Lode.

Also of unusual historical and architectural interest are the **Spreckels Mansion**, 2080 Washington Street, built in 1912 for Adolph and Alma de Bretteville Spreckels (patrons of the California Palace of the Legion of Honor) and the **Bourn Mansion**, 2550 Webster Street near Broadway, erected for William Bowers Bourn, whose wealth came from gold, gas, and water. The great Georgian Revival estate called Filoli in Woodside (see Day Trips from San Francisco) and Christian Brothers' Greystone Cellars in St. Helena (see Wine Country) were also built for Bourn.

Until recently, the California Historical Society made its home in the **Whittier Mansion** at 2090 Jackson Street at Laguna, a massive red-sandstone mansion built between 1894 and 1896 for the director of what has become today's Pacific Gas & Electric Company. Remarkable for having the latest in mechanical contrivances at the time, it survived the 1906 earthquake with only a few toppled chimneys. The mansion has now reverted to private ownership and the society is looking for a new home for its collections.

Victorian and Edwardian houses cluster around California and Franklin streets, and the only fully furnished Victorian in the city open to the public, the **Haas-Lilienthal House**, is nearby at 2007 Franklin Street at Jackson. Built in 1886 in the Queen Anne style, it survived the 1906 earthquake and fire intact, and sheltered successive members of the family until Alice Haas Lilienthal died in 1972. Two years later, her heirs donated the ornate home to the Foundation for San Francisco's Architectural Heritage. It may be visited from noon to 4:00 P.M. on Wednesdays and from 11:00 A.M. to 4:30 P.M. Sundays; Tel: 441-3004.

There are several eminent Victorians in the area of Lafayette Park, near Gough Street and Clay, and Washington Street between Octavia and Laguna also has a grouping of fine homes.

From Fillmore between Broadway and Vallejo there is a grand view of the Marina district, the bay, the Golden Gate Bridge, and the Marin hills beyond. Where Broderick crosses Broadway the sidewalk is so steep it's been made into a stairway; the view is an excitement in itself.

Heritage Walks, sponsored by the Foundation for San Francisco's Architectural Heritage, headquartered in the Haas-Lilienthal House, explores the stately homes of Pacific Heights and several other districts; Tel: 441-3004.

Some of the most glorious views in town, or anywhere, may be captured on film and in memory from a most elegant inn, the ▶ **Sherman House** at 2160 Green Street. ▶ **Mansions Hotel** joins the twin-towered Queen Anne built by Utah Senator Richard C. Chambers in 1887 to the Greek Revival house next door with one address, 2220 Sacramento Street (see Accommodations).

Fillmore Street

Most of the public action in Pacific Heights goes on around Fillmore Street, a once-seedy, even scary thoroughfare that's become safe and diverting. Lunch only is served at the delightful deli called **Vivande**, 2125 Fillmore between California and Sacramento. The pastas, cheeses, sandwiches, and salads on the menu (also available for takeout) lure lovers of good food from all over town.

Jackson Fillmore Trattoria, at 2506 Fillmore, is so popular it's almost maddening, but you have to say you've been there, and you're sure to have a good time. South of Lafayette Park, at 1701 Octavia Street between Bush and Pine, **La Fiammetta** has secured itself a listing among the top tables of the 1990s. Created by the clever folks who brought you nearby Jackson Fillmore, it plays a California turn on classic Roman cuisine.

The **Elite Café**'s Cajun cuisine draws crowds to this small, bright, convivial café at 2049 Fillmore at California. You'll probably have to wait for a table; no reservations accepted. **Rasselas** at 2801 California Street offers an unusual combination: American jazz joined to spicy Ethiopian cooking. Seafood of all sorts (12 to 18 varieties of oysters daily) is served at **Pacific Heights Bar & Grill**, which is really just beyond the border of that regal region at 2001 Fillmore Street between Pine and California. Try the seafood risotto.

JAPANTOWN

Only about four percent of San Francisco's approximately 12,500 citizens of Japanese descent live in Japantown (Nihonmachi), which is in great part a new town within an old city. Located south of Pacific Heights, Japantown is bounded by Geary Boulevard on the south, California Street on the north, and Octavia and Fillmore streets on the east and west.

The Japanese population of San Francisco has experienced a fragmented history, due to the destruction of their central settlement south of Market by the 1906 earthquake, the Alien Land Law of 1913 (depriving Japanese-Americans of the right to buy farm land), and the dislocations of 1941 when Japanese-Americans, both aliens and citizens, were sent to internment camps as a result of anti-Japanese hysteria during World War II.

Victims of postwar urban-renewal programs, old, Victorian, low-income houses and shops yielded to the relentless parade of modern, stern, and spare streets and structures that give Japantown its clean, redeveloped appearance, so surprising when compared to the creaky but amiable appearance of Chinatown.

The easiest way for a motorist to approach Japantown is by driving west on Geary from downtown, then parking at the city garage underneath Japan Center. The number 38 Geary bus from Union Square also brings you directly here.

Unfortunately, various housing projects in the nearby Western Addition area have experienced problems with drug-inspired rip-offs and minor violence—don't wander here alone, especially at night. This, however, has little impact on Japan Center, which is what you are really here to see.

Japan Center

For the traveller, this is the heart of the matter, a three-block showcase bounded by Post and Geary, north and south, and Laguna and Fillmore, east and west. The Center was dedicated in 1968, complete with restaurants, sushi bars, art galleries, bookstores, hotels, theaters, convention facilities, and shops specializing in Asian products and designs. The complex houses the Miyako Hotel, the East Building and Peace Plaza, the Kintetsu Center Building, and the West

Building. Many Japanese who live elsewhere in the city go to the center for shopping, dining, and such celebrations as the annual Cherry Blossom Festival.

Although architectural writer Randolph Delehanty calls the center itself "...a period piece of sterile 1960s mall design, a monument to the bad city planning and worse architecture of 1960s urban renewal," the decor of the individual shops and restaurants has done much to soften and relax the rigidity of the original plan.

American and European visitors who want to savor one of San Francisco's cosmopolitan corners by sleeping there have discovered the ▶ **Miyako Hotel** at 1625 Post Street at the eastern end of the Center. Now the hotel's restaurant lures patrons who had never visited Japantown or the Miyako. **Elka** (named for chef Elka Gilmore) takes California cuisine a step further in creativity. The room, another triumph of Pat Kuleto, is one of the handsomest in the city, but it is the cooking that elicits cheers, an exciting joining of Asian to American, with the emphasis on seafood; Tel: 922-7788.

Across Post Street from the Center, **Nihonmachi Mall** (covering a two-block area from Laguna to Webster Street), is a handsome mini-Ginza with a gardened pedestrian area, shops, and small restaurants—almost all of them inexpensive. The briny oceanside scent that floats over the area is the result of fresh seafood being prepared: tuna, albacore, salmon roe, and yellowtail.

Of the many restaurants here (in Japan Center's upper-floor West Building, there's a restaurant row that transports you immediately to a tiny passageway in Kyoto), among the best is **Sanppo** at 1702 Post Street at Buchanan (try the one-pot *yosenabe*). Accomplished, cheerful, and spotless, **Isuzu** at 1581 Webster Street may serve the best tempura in town.

At 1640 Post Street, across the street from Japan Center, **Korea House** was one of the city's first Korean restaurants, recognized especially for hearty fish and meat soup-stews. At 1620 Post, the **New Korea House** serves a smashing Korean barbecue. **Mifune** at number 1737 is notable among noodle nuts; under the same skillful management, **Iroha** at 1728 Buchanan offers traditional *yakitori,* sashimi, and tempura in exquisite surroundings. **Seoul Garden** at 22 Peace Plaza in the East Building grills unusual Korean dishes and has very friendly service.

A three- or four-block walk north from Japan Center, depending upon where you are, **Oritalia** joins the Orient to Italy, an inspired idea. Shiitake mushrooms meet sun-dried tomatoes, Chinese noodles are introduced to olive oil. All dishes are dim sum or tapas style (appetizers), leading to a great grazing experience at 1915 Fillmore Street (at Pine).

Japanese Shopping

Eating is not all there is to Japantown. Within the Center's West Building, **Kinokuniya Bookstore** is well known for an excellent stock of Japanese- and English-language books about Japan, handsome art books, and some distinctive papers. The **International Art Guild Gallery**, a shop in a very small space near the bookstore, stocks 19th-century and contemporary prints. Vintage kimonos (some wedding versions, worn once, that originally cost as much as $10,000 may be had for hundreds) and inexpensive *happi* coats are for sale at **Shige Nighiguchi Kimonos**. **Soko Hardware** at 1698 Post Street brings hardware freaks from around town for beautifully crafted Japanese tools.

If most of Japantown is new, a stony piece of history still sits at the corner of Franklin Street (just east of Japantown) and Starr King Way—a short street that runs southeast from Geary to join O'Farrell Street. This is the Romanesque-style **First Unitarian Church**, where Thomas Starr King served as pastor from 1860 to 1864. A great apostle of the Union cause, he is said to have inspired California to remain in the Union by his "matchless oratory," and now lies under the white-marble tomb facing Franklin, under the palm tree on the corner.

The glorious **St. Mary's Catholic Cathedral of the Assumption** (1111 Gough Street at Geary) rose in the shape of a Greek cross to replace the old church on Van Ness that burned in 1962. Striking as it is from the outside, its true beauty is appreciated only from within, where you'll see its great cupola and stained glass. The organ is a masterpiece; concerts are performed here occasionally throughout the year, and the experience of hearing one in such a setting is unforgettable (Tel: 567-2020).

CLEMENT STREET AND GEARY BOULEVARD

In the **Richmond District**, about 3.5 miles (6 km) west of downtown (or 1.5 miles/2 km west of Japantown), is the restaurant row of Clement Street. One block north of Geary Boulevard, Clement begins at Arguello Boulevard and runs west to Seal Rocks, within the boundaries of Fort Miley at the edge of the Pacific Ocean. Clement and the other streets are jumbled and uninteresting architecturally, but they offer some of the best restaurants in town for sampling international cuisines (especially Asian ones). California Street, one block north of Clement, has its share of worthwhile cafés, and they are included here. (See Dining for even more choices.)

Within the last six years, there has been an outburst of Thai flavors throughout town, and interest in this complex, spicy cuisine continues to grow. No newcomer, however, has replaced **Khan Toke Thai House** in popularity and handsome Thai decor. (Seating is on cushions on the floor.) At 5937 Geary Boulevard (at 24th Avenue), it's worth the trip from downtown. Don't miss the seafood with hot peppers and lemongrass.

Dishes unavailable in most regions of the United States are served at **Cambodia House**, 5625 Geary between 20th and 21st avenues, where warm service is a highlight and the food is delicious and inexpensive. **Narai** at 2229 Clement Street (between 23rd and 24th avenues) is noisy, but that's because people are enjoying the combination of Thai and Chinese cooking (crab rolls, spicy sour seafood soup).

From all around the area, diners flock to **Kabuto Sushi**, 5116 Geary Boulevard between 15th and 16th, to watch the fastest sushi slicer in town. Only the freshest fish is used.

Fountain Court devotes itself to the cuisine of Shanghai, served in a handsomely decorated setting at 354 Clement between Fourth and Fifth avenues. Experts such as food writer and chef Shirley Fong-Torres rank it among the best Asian kitchens in the city. If crab is in season, order it; Tel: 668-1100. **Ocean Restaurant** at 726 Clement Street between Eighth and Ninth avenues keeps packing them in for seafood with a Chinese flavor; freshness and fine ingredients are the guidelines. The decor is rather ordinary, but you don't eat that. In the same block at number 708, the **Clement Street Bar & Grill** uses fresh local ingredients in grills and seafood.

Classic country-French food is the lure at **Le Cyrano**, 4143 Geary Boulevard between Fifth and Sixth. The menu changes only rarely, and the fine service never varies. The menu changes all of the time, however, at **l'Avenue**, 3854 Geary at Third Avenue, a comfortably proper American bistro with a huge repertoire of recipes. Hearty, rich dishes alternate with delicate, simple ones. It's very busy, so you may have to lunch or dine early or late. Like the little café around the corner in Paris, **Le St. Tropez** is a cozy bistro with always-reliable cooking (try the wild-mushroom ravioli). Its candle-lit tables, fireplace, and antique copper pots add to the French flavors at 126 Clement at Second Avenue.

The latest rage in the Richmond district is **Mandalay**, 4348 California Street between Fifth and Sixth avenues, where unusual Burmese cuisine (such as curried beef and potato wontons with chile sauce) is pleasantly served and explained. If you're homesick for a taste of Singapore, you'll head directly for the simple, spare **Straits Café**, 3300 Geary at Parker, where the tastes, a blending of Chinese, Malaysian, Indian, Thai, and Indonesian cooking, are as cosmopolitan as that city itself.

Two non-culinary neighborhood landmarks are the Russian Orthodox **Holy Virgin Cathedral** at 6222 Geary near 26th Avenue (glorious choir singing, a tradition for music lovers on Easter) and **Temple Emanu-el** at Arguello Boulevard and Lake Street (one of the most handsome structures in the city).

Geary is a major auto thoroughfare. For public transportation, the number 38 bus runs all the way out to the ocean from the Transbay Terminal; the Geary Limited (number 38L) makes fewer stops and so is faster. For Clement, the choice is the number 2 bus, which reaches Clement from the Ferry Terminal via Sutter Street.

GOLDEN GATE PARK

Once upon a time, almost a century and a half ago, a barren land- and seaside-scape ran out from settled San Francisco toward the sea: the Outer Lands, they called it then, the domain of sand dunes and the scrubby sand oak. Then came city surveyor William Hammond Hall, who in 1870 began to reclaim San Francisco's Sahara. His successor was a creative, cranky, persevering Scot named John McLaren, who was (according to park historian Raymond Clary) "... either a martinet or a benevolent dictator ... and he loved Scotch." McLaren reigned from 1887 (when the first children's playground in a public park in the U.S. was established) until his death in 1943. When McLaren arrived, the 1,017 acres of today's park were simply "a dreary waste of shifting sand hills where a blade of grass cannot be raised without four posts to support it and keep it from blowing away." Now it is a glory, a national treasure, an unnaturally landscaped (but admirable and successful) bit of rural Victoriana in the city. It is south of Clement Street and the Richmond district, stretching west of Haight-Ashbury, which is itself southwest of Union Square and downtown.

McLaren was well-known then and is remembered now for his loathing of memorial statues: He called them "stookies," and spent his life hiding them in bushes or planting fast-growing shrubs around them when they were donated. A statue (what else?) was donated to his memory upon his death; it's in the Rhododendron Dell near one of Robert Burns by the same sculptor, M. Earl Cummings, and another of San Francisco's Civil War hero-clergyman, Thomas Starr King. If you miss all three, the ghost of McLaren will probably smile.

The drives through the park are endlessly confusing, and for successful negotiation a map is required. (The Visitor Information Center on Hallidie Plaza supplies one, as does park headquarters at McLaren Lodge, corner of Fell and Stanyan at the eastern entrance of the park; Tel: 558-3706.) In general, the east–west route in the northern part of the park is John F. Kennedy Drive; in the southern part, Martin Luther King, Jr. Drive, but there are several others. Note that Kennedy Drive is closed to cars on Sundays and holidays.

The Museums of Golden Gate Park

Within memory, it was possible for a local newspaper wag to write, "Why not put San Francisco's three museums together and have *one* bad museum?" Time, tides, and talent certainly have changed that picture. Today three museums—the M. H. de Young Memorial Museum and the Asian Art Museum in Golden Gate Park and the California Palace of the Legion of Honor at Land's End (closed until summer of 1995 for seismic upgrading and the addition of six galleries)—are linked in **San Francisco Fine Arts Museums**; a membership in the Museum Society allows admission to all three. Each is open Wednesdays through Sundays from 10:00 A.M. to 5:00 P.M.; for membership information, Tel: 750-3636. (Also, one admission charge allows entry to all three on the same day; keep your ticket stub.) A 24-hour hot line provides current information on schedules of special exhibitions for the Fine Arts Museums; Tel: 863-3330 or 750-3659 (recorded information).

Handily for the traveller, the Asian Art and the de Young museums adjoin each other, facing another winner, the California Academy of Sciences, across the Music Concourse. (For more on the California Palace of the Legion of Honor, see Ocean Beach and Land's End below.)

Five Golden Gate Park attractions may now be visited on a Culture Pass costing $10, thus giving a 30 percent discount off regular adult admission prices. In addition to the Asian Art Museum, the de Young Museum, and the California Academy of Sciences, the Japanese Tea Garden and the Conservatory of Flowers are participating in use of the pass. The Culture Pass includes descriptions of each attraction, admission coupons, and a map. It is available at each venue, at the San Francisco Visitor Information Center in Hallidie Plaza, Powell and Market streets, and at McLaren Lodge within the park. For further information, Tel: 391-2000.

CALIFORNIA ACADEMY OF SCIENCES

The oldest scientific institution on the West Coast, the California Academy of Sciences was founded in 1853 and occupied several homes before moving to Golden Gate Park in 1916. Today it comprises the **Natural History Museum**, the Morrison Planetarium with its Laserium light-and-sound show, and the Steinhart Aquarium. (Academy Bay in the Galapagos Islands was named for this museum, which sponsored one of the earliest expeditions there.)

Life Through Time, in the Natural History Museum, is the most comprehensive and up-to-date explanation of evolution in the world. Visitors journey through more than three billion years, through geological faults and sea fossils, through the lives of multicellular organisms and early land animals. They meet millipedes, dinosaurs, mammals that coexisted with dinosaurs, birds, and true mammals, rhinos, whales, and—eventually—human beings. An ingenious computer program called LIFEmap allows the visitor to select any life form and trace its genealogy through billions of years.

The Natural History complex also includes Wild California (land and marine animals and plants), Wattis Hall of Human Cultures (from the Arctic to desert Australia), African Safari (dioramas), The Far Side of Science Gallery (159 original cartoons by Gary Larson that give a weird new perspective on science and research), Hohfeld Earth and Space Hall (ride the Safe-Quake that simulates two of the city's famous tremors), and Gem and Mineral Hall (more than 1,000 specimens).

Steinhart Aquarium claims the most diverse fish collection in the world, with more than 1,000 species. The Fish Roundabout puts you in the middle of fast-swimming fish of the open ocean; there's also the largest living tropical coral reef in the country. **Morrison Planetarium** presents daily sky shows in Northern California's largest inside universe; the

Laserium presents live laser shows Thursday through Sunday evenings; Tel: 750-7141.

Within the Academy, on the lower floor of Cowell Hall, the **Jungle Café** is open for light meals until one hour before closing. The **Academy Store** offers a wide selection of books, posters, toys, and gifts.

The Academy of Sciences is open every day of the year, with extended evening hours from July 4 through Labor Day until 7:00 P.M.; the first Wednesday of each month there is no admission charge (Tel: 750-7145).

To drive to the Academy from Union Square, take Geary west to Masonic, go south on Masonic until you turn right (west) onto Fell Street and continue straight into Golden Gate Park, where you veer left at Middle Drive to the parking area.

Also from Union Square, take the number 38 Geary bus and transfer at Sixth Avenue to the number 44 O'Shaughnessy bus, which runs into the park. South of the park the number 44 connects with many bus lines, the Forest Hill MUNI Metro station, and the Glen Park BART station; for more information, Tel: 673-MUNI.

M. H. DE YOUNG MEMORIAL MUSEUM

The city's oldest, most diversified art museum evolved from vigorous backing and support of the California Midwinter International Exposition of 1894 by Michael Harry de Young who, with his older brother Charles, published the *Daily Morning and Evening Chronicle* (ancestor of today's *Chronicle*). All profits from that fair went to the construction of a major museum around the nucleus of a city collection. It opened in 1919, designed by Louis Christian Mullgardt to echo his Court of the Ages at the 1915 Panama-Pacific International Exposition, of which the Palace of Fine Arts in the Marina is the last remaining structure.

Ignored until fairly recently, the de Young's collection of American paintings is just now being recognized for its excellence, partly because in 1988 American works within the San Francisco Fine Arts Museums grouping were concentrated at the de Young, while European ones were grouped at the California Palace of the Legion of Honor. Although the American collection can't compete with that of New York's Metropolitan or Boston's Museum of Fine Arts, it ranks as the most comprehensive west of Chicago.

The de Young now has 22 galleries of American art from the 17th to the 20th century. One great strength is a most unusual group of trompe l'oeil and still-life works from the turn of the century. The most important acquisition in recent years was the gift in 1979 by the John D. Rockefeller III family of more than a hundred canvases, including the de Young's best Copley, its only Homer, two George Caleb Binghams, a Thomas Eakins portrait, and more.

Three galleries of British art lead into the primary emphasis on American art. The works date from the reign of George III and into the early 19th century, altogether an era of outstanding Neoclassical and Rococo achievements. Among the major painters represented are Constable, Reynolds, and Gainsborough. Paintings have been integrated with the furniture and decorative arts of their periods.

The museum also boasts an important textile collection, powerful exhibitions from Africa, Oceania, and the Americas, and significant holdings of ancient art. The **Archives of American Art**, a branch of the Smithsonian Institution, is housed in the de Young (open only by appointment); Tel: 861-3543.

The museum's bookstore is very well stocked and the **Café de Young** (walk through galleries 21–25 in the east wing to reach it) is a pleasant cafeteria with a tiny garden for outdoor dining; Tel: 750-3600 or 750-3659 (taped information).

ASIAN ART MUSEUM

San Francisco received the artistic distinction worthy of a Pacific Rim capital when, in the 1960s, Chicago insurance executive, international envoy, and Olympics Committee chairman Avery Brundage bequeathed his enormous collection of Asian treasures to the city. A showcase museum designed especially to house it was constructed next to the de Young Museum; it opened in 1966.

On the main floor, the recent reinstallation of the permanent Chinese galleries allows display of 135 pieces; many works are now on view for the first time. The Chinese scroll paintings and the objects in the Magnin Jade Room are extraordinary. The Korea Gallery doubles the number of Korean works that may be shown.

The second-floor galleries are devoted to the arts of India, Tibet, Japan, and Southeast Asia, in addition to the recently reinstalled Himalayan Gallery; Tel: 668-8921.

Around in the Park

There are, of course, reasons to visit the park other than the museums. From east to west (Haight-Ashbury to the ocean), main attractions include the **Conservatory of Flowers**, the oldest building in the park, a glassy Victorian glory with permanent tropical displays and seasonal exhibitions; **Stry-bing Arboretum and Botanical Gardens**, a 70-acre growing library of 6,000 species of plants, including a Cape Province Garden and a New World Cloud Forest, succulents, and California natives; and the **Music Concourse**, where Sunday concerts are held at 1:00 P.M. The Conservatory, a gift from real estate magnate James Lick in 1878, burned in 1882 and was rebuilt with funds donated by Charles Crocker. It survived the 1906 earthquake and fire intact.

Just west of the Music Concourse, the **Japanese Tea Garden** is a five-acre legacy of contemplation from the 1894 International Exposition. Amble around and under maples, magnolia, wisteria, cherries, pines, cedars, quince, bamboo, and ginkgo.

Then, on the shores of Stow Lake, appears **Kinmen Pavilion**, composed of 6,000 wooden pieces shipped from Taipei, Taiwan, a sister city. North of Stow Lake you'll find (near Rainbow Falls) **Prayerbook Cross**, a 57-foot sandstone memorial (a copy of an ancient Celtic cross) that commemorates the first North American prayer service employing the Anglican Book of Common Prayer. The service was performed by Francis Fletcher, chaplain to Sir Francis Drake, on June 24, 1579, on the shores of Marin County.

The less-frequented west end of the park is home on the range for a herd of bison; where the Pacific breaks there's the Dutch windmill, restored in 1981, and the Queen Wilhelmina Tulip Garden.

Golden Gate Park is best seen on foot or by bicycle (bicycles can be rented along Stanyan Street) but, failing that, drive in early in the morning and on a weekday, especially in summer. The parking strips around the Music Concourse are best for museum-goers; otherwise, parking all along the drives bordering the meadows is permitted.

To reach the park by public transportation from downtown, take the number 38 bus west on Geary Street out to Sixth Avenue, then transfer to the southbound number 44 O'Shaughnessy, which will let you off right at the Music Concourse, the heart of the cultural matter.

Although there's a cafeteria in the de Young Museum, picnicking is the best solution for easing hunger in the park. The corner of Lincoln Way (which runs along the south edge of the park) and Ninth Avenue (which is the closest exit from the Academy of Sciences and the museums) is an unlikely site for gastronomy, but at 1220 Ninth you'll find **Yaya Cuisine** (Tel: 566-6966), a small hideaway for an Iraqi chef who concocts masterful Middle Eastern dishes here and at Yaya in

SoMa. There's more fine dining at **Marnee Thai**, 2225 Irving between 22nd and 23rd avenues. The Thai cooking is terrific and the prices are low, a happy combination. If you leave the park at 19th Avenue and Lincoln Way, drive one block south to Irving and turn right. Take-out is available; Tel: 665-9500.

HAIGHT-ASHBURY AND ASHBURY HEIGHTS

Some people call it Holistic Haight, others just The Haight, the former flower-power haven of Haight-Ashbury that ranges irregularly from the panhandle leading into Golden Gate Park south along Clayton, Belvedere, Ashbury, and the streets climbing up the rise of Buena Vista Park. To the east is the Western Addition area and, beyond that, the Civic Center. Today, more than two decades after 1967's Summer of Love, the Haight is a gentrifying street scene mixing what one might call blue-collar yuppie with a dash of punk.

Historic Haight-Ashbury

Landscaping and cable car–line construction began in what were called the Outer Lands in the 1870s, and elaborate houses sprang up in the late 1880s and 1890s, most of them Queen Annes. Ashbury Heights was cosmopolitan, and after the earthquake of 1906 the district enjoyed a building boom. In 1924 a San Francisco *Examiner* columnist wrote, "There is a comfortable maturity about the compact little city San Francisco knows as Haight-Ashbury . . . a nice upholstered, fuchsia garden sort of grownup-ness, just weathered enough to be nice, and new enough to be looking ahead to the future instead of sighing futilely over the past."

Later came the Depression, the bohemianism of the late 1950s, and then, in 1966, Ken Kesey (author of *One Flew Over the Cuckoo's Nest*), who proclaimed a Trips Festival. As Randolph Delehanty puts it: "Thousands attended, dropped acid and spaced-out on rock music. The word 'hippie' was born. Through a new kind of music, psychedelic rock, the pacific hippie message spread around the country and the world . . . In the Haight, Victoriana came back . . . bands had names like . . . Big Brother and the Holding Company . . . Jefferson Airplane, and the enduring Grateful Dead."

Victorian houses were painted in psychedelic colors, an avalanche of publicity poured adjectives over the area, and

Gray Line briefly offered a tour (in sealed buses) called the Hippie Hop. But, sadly and predictably, drug violence followed the flowers and the Haight began its swift spiral downward, to come to a cheap death with the influx of heroin in the early 1970s.

What many San Franciscans remember of the Haight is the skid-row days of the 1970s, with boarded-up storefronts, torched Victorians, the homeless stretched in the streets, and pathetic sanitary conditions. The Summer of Love died an early, ugly death. In the 1990s, however, the Haight has, in large measure, returned to its old neighborhood status, once again a place in which residents shop, stroll, stop for coffee, and take lunch. (Although longtime residents agree it's all best done in the morning and avoided by night.)

Cole Valley and Ashbury Heights

Travellers who want to take time for an amble in the Haight can explore its micro-neighborhoods: Cole Valley, Ashbury Heights, and Buena Vista Heights. From the Powell-Market corner downtown, take the number 6 or 7 bus and get off at the corner of Haight and Masonic, right across from the Holey Bagel shop.

From there, map in hand, go west on Haight toward Stanyan, passing used and avant-garde clothing shops interspersed with small cafés. Just a block east from Masonic is the famous corner of Haight and Ashbury, the streets that gave the Summer of Love legend its home. Students of the period may want to walk one block south to Waller where, at 710 Ashbury, the Grateful Dead was born. The fine Queen Anne houses here were designed by Robert Dickie Cranston, father of Senator Alan Cranston of California. Then, returning to Haight, continue west to Stanyan, go south on Stanyan to Carl; east on Carl to Cole (this is now Cole Valley); a block south on Cole to Parnassus, and east on Parnassus to Clayton.

That's the first half of the walk. Worthwhile stops along the way are **Cha Cha Cha** (1801 Haight at Shrader), well-known for Cuban tapas, sangria, and such tastes as marinated duck breast with mango, guava, and ginger sauce; the ▶ **Stanyan Park Hotel** (across from Kezar Stadium and a corner of Golden Gate Park, a very pleasant, quiet, 36-room Victorian inn); **Real Food**, a deli-cum-health store at 1023 Stanyan; **Ironwood Café**, 901 Cole (fresh everything, especially seafood; Tel: 664-0224), and **Tassajara Bakery** at 1000 Cole, the place to pause for coffee and natural breads and pastries.

From Tassajara, go east on Parnassus to Clayton, then right on Clayton to its pointed meeting with Ashbury Street. From here, there is a good view back over the twin towers of St. Ignatius Church, part of the Golden Gate Bridge towers, part of the University of San Francisco, wooded Lone Mountain, and the Marin County headlands on the horizon.

The route climbs slightly here into **Ashbury Heights** and **Buena Vista Heights**, very quiet, pretty neighborhoods with gracious old houses along eccentrically winding streets. From Ashbury, turn right up Clifford, cross Upper Terrace, and follow Clifford Terrace down to Roosevelt Way. Off to the right, you'll spot stairs leading down to Lower Terrace. From Lower Terrace, turn a few steps left on Levant and you'll find yourself at the **Vulcan Stairway**.

In some respects, the walk down Vulcan is prettier than that down the Filbert Steps on Telegraph Hill. It is lined by "earthquake" cottages (built right after 1906) on one side, by dense and parklike plantings on the other, and is so rural that the traffic of the city seems suddenly not to exist. Too soon, you reach Ord Street and turn right (south).

From here, the choice is to go straight ahead to 17th Street and follow it a handful of blocks northeast to Market Street, at which point you enter an entirely different milieu, or to turn uphill at the nearby Saturn Stairway and to return more or less the way you came.

Saturn Stairway is more open to views than Vulcan, and on two levels there are wooden benches to sit and catch your breath while you overlook an unusual view of the inner city, studded by the rather Moorish tower of the Castro Theater. At the top of the steps, follow Lower Terrace to the right, cross Levant up to Roosevelt, and continue on to Loma Vista Terrace (you are now in Buena Vista Heights), which meets Upper Terrace and Masonic. If you follow Masonic downhill, you will return to the corner where you began. Along here, particularly between Waller and Haight, take note of the row of beautiful Queen Anne houses, again the work of Cranston in 1895–1896. One does wonder what he would have thought of their colorful paint jobs.

CIVIC CENTER

Architectural critics have called the Civic Center "the grandest in the country." Basically, it consists of a plaza flanked by eight buildings to the east and west of Van Ness Avenue between Franklin and Leavenworth streets and, north and

south, between Golden Gate Avenue and Hayes Street. It is
southwest of Union Square and just north of Market Street.

The nucleus of this composition is the French Renaissance–style **City Hall**, with a dome taller than the U.S. Capitol's. Across the street, the **Performing Arts Center**, the
second-largest such complex in the United States, after Lincoln Center in New York, comprises the War Memorial Opera
House, Louise M. Davies Symphony Hall, Veterans Building
(housing the Museum of Modern Art and Herbst Theater),
and Harold L. Zellerbach Rehearsal Hall. Tours of the Performing Arts Center are offered every Monday from 10:00 A.M. to
2:00 P.M. on the hour and the half hour; Tel: 552-8338.

To the southeast of City Hall, the Bill Graham Civic Auditorium seats more than 7,000 people for conventions and
sports or cultural events. Brooks Exhibit Hall, where giant
trade shows, computer fairs, and the like are held, was
installed in 1958 beneath Civic Center Plaza.

The **Public Library**, east across the plaza from City Hall, is a
handsome Beaux Arts building that houses some one-and-a-
half million volumes, and is home to several special collections of old maps, newspapers, and material on the 1906
earthquake and fire. Like the rest of Civic Center, the library
was badly damaged by the 1989 earthquake. By 1996 its
renovation should be complete, and the building will house
the Asian Art Museum now in Golden Gate Park. A new, $98-
million Main Library will be constructed one block south, and
should also be opened in 1996. The new library site was once
the Yerba Buena Cemetery, burial ground for citizens of the
19th-century Gold Rush era.

San Francisco Museum of Modern Art

Occupying the third and fourth floors of the Veterans Building, the Museum of Modern Art was the first museum in
California to be devoted to 20th-century works. Rotating
displays show works from the permanent collection by artists
such as Kandinsky, Matisse, Picasso, Clyfford Still, Albers,
Calder, and Noguchi, as well as contemporary California
artists. There's a lively schedule of changing exhibitions (especially creative in the field of photography), and an innovative
Department of Architecture and Design. The bookstore is
particularly well stocked with works on modern art. The
museum is closed only on Mondays; Tel: 863-8800.

In 1996 the museum will move to new quarters on Third
Street between Mission and Howard. Exhibit areas will be
twice as large as the present cramped ones.

The San Francisco Opera

The true San Franciscan is prouder of the San Francisco Opera and the splendid Beaux Arts **War Memorial Opera House** than any other institution in the city—whether or not he ever sets foot inside it. The single biggest social event of the year is September's Opening Night at the Opera, when the smart set strolls slowly up the steps, gowned, bejeweled, and tuxedoed, and everybody else who can squeeze into the street comes to gape and ogle. It's about the last scene of Old San Francisco on the town.

The opera company itself was founded in 1923 and moved into the Opera House (the first such civic house in the country) on October 15, 1932, with Lily Pons in Puccini's *Tosca*. The magnificent house seats 3,252 patrons for the fall season from September to December. Until the completion of the Symphony Hall in 1980, the opera season was followed in the Opera House by that of the symphony. Now a short opera season takes place in late spring/early summer, and a major extension of the season is being considered.

Tickets may be difficult to obtain, because the season is usually fully subscribed; Tel: 864-3330. A solution is to turn up about an hour before a performance, when unused tickets are hawked on the street.

The Opera House proudly claims to be the birthplace of the United Nations, which was founded here in 1945.

The dining area in the Opera House basement offers buffet service in a vast space that somehow suggests a retreat of the 1930s. The buffet opens 90 minutes before performances; two or three hot items are offered, as well as salads and soups. There's also a large bar serving wine and spirits. Across Van Ness and half a block south at 199 Grove, the **San Francisco Opera Gift Shop** has an extensive array of books, records, posters, gifts, tee-shirts, and other souvenirs.

The San Francisco Symphony

Founded in 1911 as the nation's first municipally supported symphony, the San Francisco Symphony played its seasons in the Opera House until 1980, when it moved into the admirable **Louise M. Davies Symphony Hall**, which manages to echo the monumental architecture of the Civic Center complex. The season in the 3,036-seat house (some seats even in a semicircle *behind* the orchestra) runs from October through June under the direction of maestro Herbert Blomstedt.

In addition, the symphony sponsors the annual Great Performers Series of soloists and visiting orchestras, the spring Mostly Mozart series, the semi-annual Beethoven Festival, and the Summer Pops performances. For the Davies box office, Tel: 431-5400.

A winning bronze sculpture by Henry Moore, *Large Four-Piece Reclining Figure,* sits before the curved glass façade of Davies Hall at Van Ness and Grove streets.

The San Francisco Ballet

Founded in 1933, the San Francisco Ballet is America's oldest professional company. In recent years, under artistic director Helgi Tomasson, former choreographer and principal dancer with the New York City Ballet, the San Francisco Ballet has attained a firm position among the leading companies of the world. The company launches its season every December with a lavish production of *The Nutcracker,* to which families have been going for generations. The regular season runs from mid-February to the end of April in the War Memorial Opera House; Tel: 621-3838.

In 1983 the Ballet Building was opened at 455 Franklin Street, directly behind the Opera House, to allow the dancers more and better space for practicing *bourrées* and *pas de deux.* Its public parking lot is very handy for those attending performances anywhere in the Civic Center.

Dining Around the Civic Center

Since the opening of Symphony Hall there has been a welcome blossoming of good-to-excellent restaurants in the immediate area. **Stars** is alive with the energy and originality of superchef-owner Jeremiah Tower at 150 Redwood Alley (between McAllister and Golden Gate); Tel: 861-7827. The prices and the noise level are high, but diners are having too much fun to notice; the main room is spacious, and the cocktail area in the middle of it is always packed. It's all dedicated to the excitement of eating well. The bright, simple decor of **Hayes Street Grill** at 324 Hayes near Franklin is seconded by the simple, tasteful treatment of seafood. Several grilled meats are also available; Tel: 863-5545.

On the streetfront of Opera Plaza at Golden Gate Avenue, **Max's Opera Café** brings New York to San Francisco in the shape of pastrami sandwiches and other deli delights. While you munch, the servers sing opera, jazz, and show tunes. At the rear of Opera Plaza's lobby, **Enoteca Lanzone** joins the art collection of restaurateur Modesto Lanzone to traditional Italian cooking in a gallery-like setting. The wine list (including many bottlings available by the glass) is outstanding; Tel: 928-0400. **Act IV** finally has the kitchen its gracious decor and atmosphere have deserved. In the Inn at the Opera, at 333 Fulton Street behind the Opera House, it serves a special after-theater supper as well as breakfast and dinner.

The **California Culinary Academy** in handsome California Hall at 625 Polk Street trains some 400 students under the tutelage of European-educated chefs. Three distinctive restaurants serve the public here (all are closed on Sundays). Cyril's serves Mediterranean fare (lunches only), the Academy Grill offers American cooking for lunch and dinner (open until 8:45 P.M.), and Câreme Room features international dishes at lunch and dinner (served until 8:00 P.M.). It's interesting to watch future chefs at work, and the prices are right.

Fish grilled over mesquite and several innovative specialties added to an informal, welcoming atmosphere have made the **Zuni Café and Grill** one of the best-liked restaurants in town. It's at 1658 Market Street near Franklin; Tel: 552-2522. In addition, three worthwhile "fast-food" cafés in the neighborhood are **Stars Café**, a tiny adjunct of Stars itself, 555 Golden Gate Avenue at Van Ness; **Spuntino**, for self-served Italian nibbling, 524 Van Ness Avenue; and **Vicolo Pizzeria**, 201 Ivy Street near Grove.

North of Civic Center, in a kind of no-visitors'-land at 601 Eddy Street (near Larkin), **Miss Pearl's Jam House** is the Caribbean re-created in both cuisine and appearance. There's even a swimming pool with tables set around it; go when you're in the mood for funky fun.

MISSION DOLORES

Simple little Mission Dolores (properly, Mission San Francisco of Assisi) is the most provocative single sight in the city, yet it is normally ignored by both San Franciscans and visitors because its neighborhood is otherwise of little interest, except to the people who live here (at Dolores and 16th streets, three blocks south of busy Market Street and southwest of Civic Center).

Yet the story of this church and its sisters is the story of the settlement of California by the Spanish, who dominated

Alta (Upper) California (as opposed to Mexican Baja—
Lower—California.)

"Spaced along the California coast a stiff day's march
apart" (to quote from Sunset Books' *The California Missions*) "stand 21 mission churches, simple and massive structures of adobe [mud] and stone ... Some ... are smothered
in the metropolitan embrace, enclosed on all sides by the
structures of a newer day. Others stand free in open valleys,
still retaining some measure of the pastoral charm that was
their original setting. Nearly all of them are merely token
survivals of once-widespreading structures that were miniature cities teeming with activity. Like shells found on the
beach, the missions that stand in varying degrees of restoration seem washed up on the shores of time, the life within
long since departed."

Originally there had been no plans to name a mission
after St. Francis of Assisi, founder of the Franciscan order, a
fact protested by Father Junípero Serra to the inspector-
general of Mexico, José de Galvez. "If St. Francis wishes a
mission," Galvez responded, "let him show you a good port,
and then let it bear his name." So in 1769, when Gaspar de
Portolá's explorers discovered San Francisco Bay, the chroniclers of the party declared, "This is the port to which
[Galvez] referred and to which the Saint has led us."

Visiting Mission Dolores

San Francisco today is so cosmopolitan, its heritage such a
cultural cocktail, that to step into Mission Dolores is to be
surprised by a sense of sadness at the lost simplicity, the
forgotten lineage from that early settlement. The interior is
beautiful in its joining of the rude tile floors and thick adobe
walls to the gilded and brightly painted Baroque altar, the
reredos (altar screens), and the stunning ceiling covered
with earth-toned chevron designs, a pattern supposed to
have been adapted from the Costanoan people. (The native
tribal groups of the region were grouped together in the
Spanish mind as Costanoans, "coastal dwellers.")

Equally interesting is the small, crowded cemetery on the
south side of the mission, where lie the famous, the infamous, and the anonymous. Among the former are Don Luis
Antonio Argüello, first governor of Mexican California, and
Francisco de Haro and José Noe, Yerba Buena's first and last
alcaldes (mayors). The infamous include James P. Casey,
murderer of crusading newspaper editor James King of
William. Most touching is a rock shrine marked "To the

neglected and forgotten who rest here"; some 5,515 Native Americans were buried in mass graves, most victims of European diseases.

The squat mission is dwarfed by its immediate neighbor on the north, the gaudy (by comparison) Mission Dolores Basilica, begun in 1913 and given its soaring towers in 1926. (The term *basilica* denotes a church that is a consecrated place of pilgrimage and of great artistic merit; this was the fourth church in the U.S. to be so honored—status was given in 1952 by Pope Pius XII—and the first west of the Mississippi.)

The services of the Mass are held in the old mission daily, except Sundays, at 7:30 A.M. Sunday Mass is celebrated in the Basilica; Tel: 621-8203. (The last mission in the 21-church chain was San Francisco Solano in Sonoma—see Wine Country.) There's now a fund-raising campaign underway to repair the damage done to the old mission by the 1989 earthquake.

To reach Mission Dolores, take the J Church streetcar from any subway stop along Market Street to Church and 16th streets, then walk a block east to Dolores. You can also take BART, which runs under Market Street, from stations at the Embarcadero, Montgomery, Powell, and Civic Center to the station at 16th Street and Mission, then walk three blocks west to Dolores.

SOMA (SOUTH OF MARKET)

Sometime in the late 1980s somebody shook San Francisco and everything loose fell south of Market into what old-timers call "south of the slot" ("slot" refers to the apertures where the cables propelling the streetcars lay) and contemporaries call SoMa (doubtless an echo of New York's SoHo). SoMa constitutes part, but far from all, of the Mission district that, as its name implies, grew up around the mission church of San Francisco de Asís. As such, the district was an early one, and predominantly home to Spanish and Mexican settlers, followed in the 1860s by German and Scandinavian immigrants. Businesses here tended to be small and rents low, and between 1950 and 1970 the Latino community doubled each decade. Today this community also grows as a result of the unrest continuing throughout Central America, and now includes large numbers of Guatemalans, Salvadorians, Costa Ricans, Nicaraguans, and Colombians, with their attendant shops and restaurants.

Randolph Delehanty has called the Mission a revolving door into American society. The casual traveller, however, will find less to interest him in the Hispanic part of this neighborhood than in most other parts of the city, unless he wants to seek out particular Latin dishes, spices, and condiments. Cafés, taquerías, Mexican bakeries, and specialty stores give 24th Street a particularly *simpático* air (see Dining for suggestions on eating out in this neighborhood). We concentrate here on the more café-oriented part of the Mission district that is known as SoMa.

Physically, SoMa is roughly a two-mile-square grid of one-way streets and narrow alleys bounded by Market Street on the north, China Basin on the south, the Embarcadero on the east, and 10th and Division streets on the west. (The whole area is geographically skewed; no streets run in precise directions.)

Essentially, SoMa is an attitude. The South of Market district metamorphosed from a smart residential area in the 1850s and 1860s (Rincon Hill and South Park are examples) to a small-business center, followed by a skid-row slum, and now to an avant-garde arts quarter. Higher rents elsewhere, combined with empty buildings and lower rents in SoMa, have attracted small cafés, galleries, experimental theaters, warehouses, studios, factory outlets, a wholesale flower mart, and nightclubs of all creative forms.

The most recent transformation began in 1981 with the building of the **George R. Moscone Center**, named for the mayor slain with Supervisor Harvey Milk in 1978; the entire project is to be completed sometime in 1994. The convention center, which covers an 11-acre site entered from Howard Street between Third and Fourth streets, is built mostly underground; its six-acre, column-free exhibit hall is one of the largest in the world.

Across the street (at 250 Fourth Street between Howard and Folsom) is the **Ansel Adams Center**. Administered by the non-profit Friends of Photography, the center houses the largest display of fine art photography on the West Coast. One of the five galleries rotates works of Adams himself, and there is a bookstore and library. Open Tuesday through Sunday from 11:00 A.M. to 6:00 P.M.; Tel: 495-7000.

Although not of interest to everyone, the **Old Mint** (opened in 1854) is one of the more curious attractions in town, housed in one of the finest examples of Federal Classical Revival architecture in the West. Some of its working rooms have been restored, and there's a Western art display and a collection of pioneer gold coins. Most dramatic is the pyramid of gold bars valued at $5 million and shown in a circular vault. The Mint is at Fifth and Mission streets, just two blocks from Moscone Center, and can be visited on weekdays free of charge; Tel: 744-6830.

Overlooking Moscone Center and a great swatch of SoMa, the **San Francisco Marriott** at 777 Market Street and Fourth opened in October 1989 to huzzahs for its convention and conference facilities and hisses for its architecture. Local critics dub it the Giant Jukebox, but everyone seems to enjoy the **View Lounge** on the 39th floor, with dramatic views through a 35-foot fan-shaped window over the Financial District to Alcatraz and the Oakland docks beyond the Bay Bridge.

Satellite restaurants have crowded into the area: the loud, cheerful, traditional Mexican **Cadillac Bar and Grill**, One Holland Court (off Howard Street between Fourth and Fifth streets); light, fresh, Mexican **Chevys**, 150 Fourth Street; and comfortable, old-fashioned, generous **Max's Diner**, 311 Third Street.

South Park

Between Brannan and Bryant streets on the south and north and Third and Second streets on the west and east, the tiny oval of South Park is for some reason difficult to find, even when you know where it is. A few years ago it was a pathetic slum, dangerous and depressing. Yet in the 1850s some of the city's most fashionable residences stood here, enjoying the town's most salubrious weather. James Benét tells the tale (in *A Guide to San Francisco*): "George Gordon, a former neighbor of the Brontë family in Yorkshire, married a barmaid and felt compelled to emigrate to California. He developed the park in 1852 in imitation of a London square and sold its 64 lots to prominent citizens. He is said to have imported English sparrows as well as roses. .

"Gordon's personal tragedy, his wife's revenge on him by making their daughter an alcoholic, was the subject of Gertrude Atherton's first novel, *A Daughter of the Vine.*"

Thinking of an old romance, an old sadness, take a seat (try to reserve one) at **South Park Café** (108 South Park), a tiny, colorful spot that's very French in feeling; Tel: 495-7275. Right at hand at 462 Bryant, you can purchase French, Californian, and German wines at **Connoisseur Wine Imports. Ristorante Ecco** at 101 South Park serves delicious Italian dishes at quite reasonable prices. Try the *lasagne al funghi* and braised short ribs; Tel: 495-3291. (Parking is very difficult in this area. You may wish to leave your car outside the park and walk in, or take a taxi.)

Jack London's birthplace is marked with a plaque on the Wells Fargo Bank at Brannan and Third streets:

Dining in SoMa

As happens with any district during revitalization, SoMa greets every new restaurant with joyful welcome, then drops it for the even newer one on the block. Here are some that show signs of lasting. (All are better choices for lunch than for dinner, partially because of the seediness of the surrounding area.)

From 1906 to 1954, the San Francisco power-lunch crowd gathered at a Sutter Street Financial District restaurant called the **Fly Trap** to eat the classic Gold Rush dish, Hangtown fry. (Ordered by miners who had struck it rich, it involved oysters, eggs, and bacon.) In 1989 the Fly Trap was reborn at 606 Folsom near Third to serve traditional San Francisco fare, including Hangtown fry. The atmosphere suggests the days of gaslights, with a tin ceiling, "strike-offs" of old botanical engravings, and old-fashioned architecture. Fly Trap is always packed at lunch; Tel: 243-0580. **Ruby's**, a woody trattoria at 489 Third Street (at Bryant), serves fine sandwiches, pastas, and pizzas; Tel: 541-0795.

At **Eddie Rickenbacker's**, nostalgia for World War I is the theme, but people who remember World War II barely or not at all make up the crowd. The mood is happy, the hamburgers terrific, and the location at 133 Second Street between Mission and Howard is handy. At 100 Brannan Street, where it meets the Embarcadero, **Embarko** looks out onto the bay from an area of hot real estate development and serves American ethnic food with nineties flair and some Japanese accents.

Two very pleasant places in the area for lunch on a sunny afternoon are around the corner from each other: Fringale at 570 Fourth Street near Brannan, and Bricks at 500 Brannan Street near Fourth. **Fringale** has a lightness to its menu as well as in its atmosphere; the dishes have a French Basque accent; Tel: 543-0573. **Bricks** is a surprise, with a refreshingly old-fashioned decor, very pleasant service, and a menu of familiar American standbys; Tel: 543-2222.

At the southern tip of SoMa, deep in the docklands of China Basin, the **Mission Rock Resort** serves some of the best hamburgers in San Francisco on outside decks that overlook slips and dry docks. It's extremely casual, even slipshod, but a great place for lunch on a sunny day. Take Third Street south, then turn east on Mission Rock Street to China Basin Street, where the restaurant sits waterside at number 817.

The **Dolph P. Rempp** is an old sailing ship that transported lumber and spices to the South Pacific and South America around the turn of the century. In her long history, as the good ship *Ellen,* she also carried troops, smuggled rum, and starred in *Mutiny on the Bounty.* Now she sits at Pier 42, near the southern end of the Embarcadero, and her galley serves a wide range of seafoods. Squint and you'll think you're back in clipper days. Parking is available alongside the ship.

OCEAN BEACH AND LAND'S END

On the far western rim of San Francisco, where rugged cliffs rise out of the sea, an immigrant once constructed a wooden fairy-tale château, a French confection seven stories high with turrets and towers and spires that perched atop a rocky outcrop at the end of a continent. This was the **Cliff House** that Adolph Sutro built.

Sutro was the kind of man who made San Francisco in the years immediately after the Gold Rush of 1849. Born in Prussia in 1830, he came with his family to the United States after the Revolution of 1848, and in 1859 joined the rush to the Comstock Lode in Nevada. After an 18-year battle against nature, politicians, and the Bank of California, he finally made his fortune—though not from silver. He engineered, financed, and constructed a great tunnel through a mountain that was being mined, making drainage and ventilation possible for the first time. When it was finished, conditions for the miners were much improved, and royalties from use of his tunnel had made Sutro rich.

Retiring to San Francisco, Sutro bought vast chunks of land, including San Miguel Rancho (where Twin Peaks and other central hills rise today); he is said to have owned one-twelfth of all the land in the city. He planted gardens, collected art, gathered a famous library (a part of which is housed near San Francisco State University), built his Cliff House château and the nearby Sutro Baths (the world's largest indoor swimming pools of both fresh- and saltwater), and served as San Francisco's mayor from 1894 to 1896.

The first Cliff House, a restaurant preceding Sutro's version, was built in 1863 and could be reached from downtown San Francisco only by carriages that plied the Point Lobos Toll Road. Sutro bought the operation in 1883, but the house was badly damaged four years later when the schooner *Parallel,* loaded with dynamite, struck and blew up on the rocks below. Then, on Christmas Day, 1894, the Cliff House burned down to its stony foundation.

Two years later, Sutro completed his fanciful château-restaurant, which became enormously fashionable, only to burn down in 1907. (There's still a brisk trade in postcards featuring that improbable palace.)

Today's Cliff House, the fifth in the series, is a squat, bland building totally unworthy of its splendid setting. It is worth visiting, however, for its site and for other attractions in the immediate area. Within the building at 1090 Point Lobos Avenue is the **Musée Méchanique**, reminiscent of an old penny arcade, that claims to have the world's largest collection of coin-operated, antique musical machines.

San Franciscans showing off their city sometimes repair with their guests to the Cliff House bar, the **Ben Butler Room**, to watch the sun set behind Seal Rocks and perhaps to raise a salute to Adolph Sutro. **Upstairs at the Cliff House**, best for a Sunday brunch or late lunch, offers an unusual menu of 30 omelettes.

The **Camera Obscura** on the seaside shelf below the building is of particular interest to children, who can't imagine a world B.C.—Before Cameras. Entering the large, darkened box-like structure, you see images of external objects received through an aperture, as with a convex lens. At the nearby visitors' center of the Golden Gate National Recreation Area, you may pick up a map of that region, as well as several helpful brochures.

Offshore Sights

About 400 feet offshore, the sea smashes up against **Seal Rocks**, where Stellar sea lions (not seals at all) loll lazily, oblivious to the army of tourists aiming at them with telephoto lenses. Of the many ships that have wrecked in the roiling waters outside the Golden Gate, one—the freighter *Ohioan*—grounded in 1936 just to the north of Seal Rocks.

On a fogless day, you may be able to spot the **Farallon Islands**, seven giant rocks rising out of the ocean about 30 miles away. They are thought to have been discovered by an expedition from New Spain in 1543. In 1579 Sir Francis Drake landed there to secure a supply of seal meat, birds, and eggs, and named the site the Islands of St. James. In 1775 Lieutenant Juan Francisco de la Bodéga (after whom Bodega Bay to the north in Sonoma County was named) called them *Farallones de los Frailes* (Friars' Cliffs), and that is still the name today.

It's not often realized that the Russians sailed as far south as this: They developed the islands as a fur station between 1809 and 1812 in their quest for sea otter pelts. The Farallons were (and are) a rich rookery, and during the Gold Rush, when a boiled egg in the city cost 75 cents, egg wars broke out among competing hunters.

The Farallons today are a bird sanctuary. **Oceanic Society Expeditions**, Building E at Fort Mason, operates the naturalist-led **Farallon Islands Excursions**. These isles form the largest seabird rookery along the Pacific Coast south of Alaska. Tours run June through November; Tel: 474-3385. (Whale-watching trips are offered December through April.)

North of Cliff House

Immediately to the north of Cliff House, the **Sutro Baths** were built in 1896, six indoor, fresh- and saltwater swimming pools that spread over three acres, complete with gardened parterres. They closed after World War II, and the building burned to the ground in 1966. Today they lie in ruins, not romantic but simply ugly.

Rising above the ruins, **Point Lobos** is the westernmost reach of the city, a rough palisade the Spanish called *Punta de los Lobos* (Point of the Sea Wolves, as they called sea lions). It's a dramatic lookout point reached by a little trail that leads from the sidewalk on the north side of Point Lobos Avenue.

Beyond, wild and usually deserted, the promontory of **Land's End** pokes above the Pacific between Seal Rocks Beach (not the same as Seal Rocks) and China Beach. It is accessible by fairly steep trails, some of which wind down to the surf. If you intend to make this hike, inquire about conditions at the aforementioned visitors' center near the Cliff House. Every year several people are swept away at Land's End, and not only during storms.

East of Cliff House, atop the bluff across Point Lobos Avenue, Sutro established his home (now long gone) and gardens on **Sutro Heights**, where he planted fir, Monterey cypress, and Norfolk pine, allowing the public free access to the grounds and gardens. When he died in 1898 his daughter Dr. Emma Sutro Meritt (one of California's pioneer women physicians) inherited his property, which she bequeathed to the city upon her death in 1938.

In recent years sadly neglected, Sutro Heights Park is a fine place for melancholy walks in early evening. Today a part of the Golden Gate National Recreation Area, it has been spruced up to include a dramatic overlook and a rock garden. A marked path leads to it from the parking lot on the south side of Point Lobos Avenue, a few yards uphill and around a bend from Cliff House.

For a dramatic hike, seek out the Land's End Trail, which leads from the Cliff House parking lot and the ruins of the Sutro Baths to the road below the California Palace of the Legion of Honor. The path is the former roadbed of the Ferries & Cliff House Railway, a narrow-gauge road along which trains ran from 1888 to 1906. The trail winds around and atop the 200-foot cliffs through wind-bent cypress trees on heights above pounding surf. Caution: In stormy weather, the hike can be challenging and even dangerous because of slippery ground and occasional small earth slides onto the rocks below. Every year somebody has to be rescued from the cliffs or, even worse, from unstable perches halfway between the trail and the sea.

In the past, at this point the hiker could walk up the rise from the trail's end and into the **California Palace of the Legion of Honor.** (The driver would take Point Lobos Avenue, continue on Geary Boulevard, and then turn left on 34th Avenue—which becomes Legion of Honor Drive—and park in front of the museum.) Unfortunately, the Legion of Honor was closed in March 1992 for seismic upgrading and remodeling and will not reopen until sometime in 1995. You may wish to visit the site in any case, to visit the moving memorial to the victims of the Holocaust created by artist George Segal and to take in a spectacular view out over the Pacific and to the hills of Marin County. Then wind east on El Camino del Mar to the superb neighborhood of **Sea Cliff.**

Sea Cliff is strictly residential and does not consider itself a thoroughfare; in fact, inhabitants of the area discourage all traffic, as would anyone privileged to live in such a quiet retreat atop such a spectacular site. The best way to admire Sea Cliff is to follow the zig-zags of the streets: McLaren Avenue, Lake Street, 30th to 25th avenues, El Camino del Mar, Sea Cliff Avenue, and Scenic Way. Below these curves, where houses turn their windows and greenswards toward the sea, breakers beat on Baker and China beaches and the view stretches west past the Marin hills to Japan.

South of Cliff House

When San Franciscans say they are going to the beach, they usually mean **Ocean Beach**, which stretches from Cliff House south to the Fort Funston part of the Golden Gate National Recreation Area and then to the oceanside golf course of the Olympic Country Club, a distance of just under five miles. The wide Great Highway runs much of that length, with parking available between the north- and south-bound lanes.

Jogging, playing ball, running with dogs, and picnicking are the pleasures at Ocean Beach; swimming is not. The undertow is as mean as a white shark along this strand; even wading is discouraged.

At the western edge of Golden Gate Park between Fulton Street and Lincoln Way there sits a small, white-pillared structure designed by Willis Polk in 1921. It hides within a stunning series of frescoes executed by locally recognized painter Lucien Labaudt in the mid-1930s. In the spirit of the day, they depict the working life of San Francisco; quotes from such writers as Bret Harte and Joaquin Miller complete the decoration. The frescoes have been freshened recently, and plans, albeit shaky, are underway to create a fine restaurant and bar in this curious corner.

Less than 3.5 miles (6 km) south of Cliff House along the Great Highway you can turn east on Sloat Boulevard to the **San Francisco Zoo**, which occupies 65 acres of a 125-acre site slated to be fully developed by the year 2000. The zoo was born in 1889 with the gift from the *San Francisco Examiner* of a single grizzly bear named Monarch. Much maligned during the last few years, the zoo has hired a new director with great plans and promises for bringing the institution up to international standards; Tel: 753-7083.

If you continue east on Sloat Boulevard to 19th Avenue, you will arrive at **Sigmund Stern Grove**, a 33-acre forest of eucalyptus and redwood trees surrounding a grassy hollow, where on summer Sunday afternoons free performances of opera, ballet, symphony, folk music, and jazz are presented. Picnicking is encouraged; Tel: 252-6252.

Drivers can reach Cliff House and Ocean Beach by taking Geary Boulevard west from downtown and veering right at 40th Avenue onto Point Lobos Avenue. In less than a mile you'll spot the Cliff House parking lot to the south of the avenue; metered parking also is available all along the road at this point, in front of Cliff House, and down the hill in the center of the Great Highway.

From the Marina, drive west on the Golden Gate Bridge approach, take the 19th Avenue (Highway 1) exit before the toll booths, proceed south to Geary, then west as above. From Golden Gate Park, drive west to one of the two beach exits and directly onto the Great Highway, then turn north. Geary bus number 38 and Geary Limited number 38L will take you all the way from Union Square to 48th Avenue at Sutro Heights Park, from which it's less than a block to Cliff House. To avoid even that walk, you can transfer to the number 18 bus at 46th Avenue, which continues to Cliff House, Golden Gate Park/Ocean Beach, and beyond.

SOUTH OF GOLDEN GATE PARK
The Sunset and South

When you come to the Sloat Boulevard–19th Avenue corner of Sigmund Stern Grove, you have arrived at the approximate center of a largely residential area little known to tourists and worth exploring only for those who have time on their hands and a wish to know San Francisco in depth. Frequently, this whole area is lumped under the designation of **The Sunset**, but the situation is more complicated than that. To the north of Sloat and east of 19th Avenue are the home-lined streets of the Sunset and Parkside areas; to the south and east are Lakeside, Stonestown (encompassing San Francisco State University), and Park Merced. North and west of the same corner are West of Twin Peaks, Forest Hill, Miraloma Park, West Portal, St. Francis Wood (which rivals Sea Cliff for fine homes), Westwood Park, and Ingleside.

Within Stonestown, **Stonestown Galleria** is a handsome shopping center, recently renovated, that claims to have been one of the first malls built. San Francisco State, adjoining it to the south, is an urban university with little of interest to non-students.

If it's mealtime and something simple will suit, continue east on Sloat to the traffic light where Sloat meets Portola Drive, and take a sharp left onto West Portal Avenue. This short commercial street serves the surrounding neighborhood with banks, small clothing stores and food markets, a post office, and a bookstore—most of the essentials of the daily routine. The best restaurant here is **Café for All Sea-**

sons at number 150, where the menu is California nouvelle and reservations are always required; Tel: 665-0900. **Anne's Kitchen**, at number 361, features simple, delicious dishes cooked with a Thai touch; Tel: 665-7920. **Il Giardino** at number 215 offers dinners of familiar, homey Italian cooking, and you'll find Japanese cuisine at **Fuji** at number 301.

The small **Spiazzo** opened at 33 West Portal in 1990 and, for an inexpensive pasta and pizza place, boasts a most innovative menu. Across the street, the little deli/bakery **Café de Leon** is a good place to order picnic lunches or a snack to eat on the premises. Old-fashioned Italian food in great portions is served in the dark, masculine, often loud **Gold Mirror** four blocks north of West Portal at 800 Taraval Street. It's probably the most authentic Old World Italian hangout this side of North Beach.

From West Portal you can take a drive past the handsome homes in **St. Francis Wood**. The easiest way to begin is by taking 14th Avenue south from West Portal, crossing Portola Drive in a southeasterly direction onto San Anselmo, and then wandering along the snaky streets. To return to downtown, take Portola Drive, which runs in a northeasterly direction to become upper Market Street. From the West Portal station, MUNI travels to major downtown stops along Market Street.

If you have time for a detour before returning downtown, however, veer left and uphill off Portola just beyond the traffic signal at Portola and Woodside Avenue, and follow winding Twin Peaks Boulevard to its meeting with Clayton Street in the Haight-Ashbury district. This is one of the most spectacular drives in the city: surprisingly wild and rural (especially when fog blows through the stands of eucalyptus trees). Views of the city, now to the west and the ocean, now to the east and the bay, will force you to stop for photos and to try to imagine the magnificence of the site as early explorers saw it.

The Castro

Where Portola Drive becomes Market Street at the corner of Castro and 17th streets, the heart of the Castro beats. Castro Street itself is quite long, running from Waller Street in the north (east of Buena Vista Park) to 30th Street in the south. The Castro proper extends only between Diamond on the west and Church on the east, 16th Street on the north and 25th on the south.

As the world knows, this is the center of gay life in San

Francisco. (Polk Street was once the center, but most of the action moved here in the late 1970s.) Not every traveller will have an interest in investigating this area, but those who do have the best chance of seeing local life on Sundays, when the streets are swarming with shoppers, diners, sightseers, and promenaders.

As you walk, or even if you are just driving through, you will notice the shops on the south side of Market between 16th and 17th streets, where men's and women's clothing designed to make statements of all kinds is displayed in shop windows. The clothing is often expensive and extravagant; as Dorothy said to Toto, "We're not in Kansas anymore." Right in the middle of this block, **The Café**, overlooking the street, caters to a mixture of residents and visitors.

Outsiders frequent the Castro particularly when film retrospectives are being held at the **Castro Theater** (429 Castro between 17th and 18th). Timothy Pflueger, a renowned regional architect of the 1920s, was responsible for this outburst of Spanish Renaissance elaboration—not to say excess. Tel: 621-6120 for program information. For a bite before or after the show try **Leticia's**, at 2223 Market between Sanchez and 15th, for Mexican cooking and good Sunday brunch.

The city is halfway through a two-year project to beautify and to install streetcar tracks on Upper Market. The tracks will extend from 17th and Castro to 11th Street near Civic Center, and Canary Island palm trees have been planted in the median strip. Traffic in the area is severely disrupted.

CABLE CARS

The only National Historical Landmarks you can ride are San Francisco's beloved cable cars, an ingenious invention of London-born Andrew S. Hallidie, who began by designing lifting machines for gold mines. The first of "Hallidie's follies" made its maiden run on August 2, 1873, from the top of Clay Street down Nob Hill's precipitous east side. It worked so well that by 1880 there were eight lines operating along 112 miles of cable.

Although there have been repeated attempts to abolish the cable cars in favor of motor coaches (in the interests of efficiency and safety), and despite the ordeal of a two-year "open-heart" surgery of the entire system (1982 to 1984), the only vehicles of their kind in the world are still in service.

Two lines run from the turntable at Powell and Market streets (near below-street-level Hallidie Plaza, where you'll find the Visitor Information Center of the San Francisco Convention and Visitors Bureau); a third line begins at California and Market streets.

There's no better way to sample the city's sweeping views than to take a cable car ride. The most spectacular ride is on the Powell–Hyde line (cars are clearly marked), with vertical and lateral zigzags from Powell/Market up over Nob and Russian hills to its turntable in Victorian Park on the northern waterfront. Stop for an Irish coffee at the **Buena Vista Café** here before the run back; nearby are the Ghirardelli Square shops and restaurants, the Maritime Museum, historic ships, the Cannery, and Fisherman's Wharf.

The Powell–Mason line runs from Powell and Market over Nob Hill (where there's a stop for Nob Hill hotels) and down to Bay Street and the hubbub of Fisherman's Wharf, three short blocks away.

The California Street line begins at the foot of that street in the Financial District (and near the Embarcadero), cuts through Chinatown's heart at Grant Avenue, crests at Nob Hill, and ends at Van Ness Avenue.

In summer the line of would-be passengers at Powell and Market is extremely discouraging; it is often better to try boarding at a stop farther along the route. Self-service ticket dispensers are located at all terminals and major stops, where a $6 all-day MUNI adult pass is also available.

The **Cable Car Museum, Powerhouse, and Car Barn** is housed in a three-level, red-brick building at Washington and Mason streets. It shows off scale models of cable cars, the original prototype car number 8, and vintage photographs. From a special viewing room visitors can watch the underground wheels playing out the cables. A 16-minute film, *The Cable Car and How It Works,* is shown continually. The Cable Car Museum is open daily; Tel: 673-6864.

SPORTING SAN FRANCISCO

As a rule, most San Franciscans wax warmly about a winning team and wail waspishly about a losing one, an attitude generally attributed to fair-weather fansmanship—and blamed in large part on the city's generally fair weather, which is enough to distract even the most ardent sports fan.

The **San Francisco 49ers**, the most consistently successful of the local professional teams, play football at windy Candlestick Park, a controversial 60,000-seat stadium 8 miles (13 km) south of town that even faithful fans love to hate. You will want to bundle up in a ski parka, wear warm socks and gloves, and carry along earmuffs. To drive to Candlestick, take Highway 101 south to the Candlestick Park exit, then follow Giants Drive and Gilman Avenue, following posted directions to the parking lots; Tel: 468-2249 (49ers ticket office). It's much easier and less expensive to take the special ballpark transportation services provided on game days. Bus number 9X (the Ballpark Express) departs from Sutter and Montgomery streets (Financial District), makes a handful of stops, then goes express to Candlestick; bus number 47 runs from Clay and Van Ness with stops on Van Ness and on Mission, then express to the park; Tel: 673-MUNI for information.

Baseball's **San Francisco Giants** were recently rescued by a group of local millionaires from being shipped off to Florida. The new owners hope to attract more local fans by improving stadium food, adding more bleacher seats, and renting out blankets to combat the wintry (even in summer) winds of Candlestick. For details on getting to Candlestick, see 49ers above; Tel: 467-8000 (tickets), 982-9400 (the Giants Dugout store, 170 Grand Avenue).

The winning **Oakland A's** are very popular in most years with San Franciscans as well as East Bay fans. They play baseball in the Oakland–Alameda County Coliseum Complex. Drive across the San Francisco–Oakland Bay Bridge, then take the Nimitz Freeway (Highway 880) south to the Hegenberger Road turnoff and head left (northeast) to the Coliseum. For public transportation, take BART's Fremont–Daly City line from Civic Center, Powell Street, Montgomery Street, or Embarcadero stations to the Coliseum/Oakland Airport station, then follow the aerial walkway into the stadium; Tel: (510) 638-0500 (tickets).

The Bay Area's **Golden State Warriors** rank among the best basketball teams in the west. They play at the Oakland–Alameda County Coliseum as well. For information and tickets, Tel: (510) 639-7700.

In October 1991, the **San Jose Sharks** hockey team made its Bay Area debut. The Sharks played their first two seasons in the Cow Palace in Daly City before moving to their permanent home in San Jose; Tel: (408) 287-4275 (tickets).

Horse races are held at Bay Meadows in San Mateo (on the Peninsula south of San Francisco; Tel: 574-7223) and at

Golden Gate Fields in Albany in the East Bay (Tel: 510-526-3020). The **San Francisco Bay Blackhawks** play soccer in Newark in the East Bay; Tel: (408) 295-4295.

Sears Point International Raceway in the rolling hills of Sonoma Valley is considered one of the finest tracks in the country, offering a wide variety of motor sports on weekends the year round; Tel: (707) 938-8448.

CITYWIDE CELEBRATIONS

You can tell a city by what it does in its spare time. San Francisco eats, drinks, and makes merry in myriad manners. The silliest of the city's episodic outbreaks is the **Examiner Bay to Breakers** race held in May, when up to 100,000 perfectly mad men, women, and children tear across town along a seven-and-a-half-mile course from near Justin Herman Plaza at the Embarcadero, through Golden Gate Park, and to the oceanside Great Highway.

Seeded runners are allowed to start in front so they don't have to fight the crowds and usually reach the finish line before the last few thousand have started. Some people make a day of it, pushing baby buggies, stopping to dance the boogaloo, or careening into other "centipedes." (A centipede is a group of runners racing together in one costume: a giant papier-mâché toothbrush from the School of Dentistry, for example, or doctors joined in a 34-vertebrae spinal column, or a jogging Golden Gate Bridge.) Then there are the individual zanies: the Medflies chasing tomatoes, and the Paleolithic cave people among them. The only elements missing are sanity, sobriety, and any sense of civic disobedience at this 82-year-old celebration of craziness.

Here are some other special events, month by month. If you need more information, contact the San Francisco Convention and Visitors Bureau; Tel: 391-2000.

January: The Dr. Martin Luther King, Jr., Birthday Celebration brings thousands of followers and enthusiasts to Bill Graham Civic Auditorium; Tel: 267-6400 (event information). The Shrine East-West All-Star Football Classic takes place at Stanford University Stadium; Tel: 661-0291.

February: The Chinese New Year Celebration, one of the biggest and best in the world, is an eight-day extravaganza of pageants, outdoor competitions, cultural programs, fireworks, and a superb parade led down Grant Avenue by a deliciously scary dragon; Tel: 982-3000. Also in February, the

Golden Kennel Club sponsors the All-Breed Dog Show at the Cow Palace (Tel: 469-6000), and the Bay Area Women's Philharmonic Orchestra, the only orchestra in the country dedicated to performances of the works of contemporary women composers, plays at the First Congregational Church at Post and Mason streets (Tel: 543-2297).

March: San Francisco's St. Patrick's Day Parade is one of the largest, loudest shows of the year, the apex of an observance that includes religious services at St. Patrick's Church, flag-raising ceremonies in the Civic Center, festivities at the United Irish Cultural Center, the Grand Marshall's Dinner, and happy hanging-out at several Irish pubs: **Harrington's**, where the brew bunch spills right out in front of 245 Front Street; **Ireland's 32**, 3920 Geary Boulevard; **Pat O'Shea's Mad Hatter**, 3848 Geary Boulevard (the awning reads, "We Cheat Tourists and Drunks"); and the **Plough & Stars**, 116 Clement Street (long, wooden tables and Irish Republic banners).

March is also the month for Tulipmania, guided tours of one of the city's largest tulip beds out of Pier 39 (Tel: 391-0850). The Grand National Junior Livestock and Horse Show is at the Cow Palace (Tel: 469-6000).

April: Every Easter Sunday, hundreds of people hike up Mount Davidson, west of Twin Peaks, for the annual Easter Sunrise Service at the base of a 103-foot-high cross. More than 2,000 Californians of Japanese descent, performers from Japan, and enthusiasts of things Japanese participate in an elaborate offering of Japanese culture and customs in the annual Cherry Blossom Festival in Japantown. The festival is held on two long weekends in April, with the big parade on the last day; Tel: 563-2313. April also brings Opening Day of the Yachting Season on San Francisco Bay (Tel: 563-6363), and the San Francisco Landscape and Garden Show at Fort Mason (Tel: 750-5105). Spring arrives with Macy's Easter Flower Show; Tel: 397-3333.

From late April into July, the San Francisco International Film Festival, the oldest cinematic festival in North America, presents more than 60 films from more than 30 countries. Screenings are held at the Kabuki 8 Theater, 1881 Post Street at Fillmore, and several other Bay Area locations. For programs, schedules, and admission costs, Tel: 931-FILM.

May: The two-day Cinco de Mayo Parade and Celebration commemorates the Mexican victory over the French army at Puebla on May 5, 1867; Tel: 826-1401. Also early in the month, the annual KQED-TV Food and Wine Festival takes place in the Concourse Exhibition Center; Tel: 553-2200. The

San Francisco Historic Trolley Festival puts vintage streetcars from around the world into commercial use along Market Street; Tel: 673-6864. Mardi Gras, San Francisco style, means *Carnaval* near the end of May, celebrated in the Mission District since 1979. Like the city itself, this event transcends traditional ethnic borders, celebrating the passions and pleasures of life in Africa, Polynesia, Asia, Europe, Central America, South America, and the Caribbean. It's a salsa ball that brings out half a million festive folks; Tel: 824-8999.

June: On the first weekend of the month, the Union Street Spring Festival Arts and Crafts Fair lures hundreds of shoppers and strollers from the neighborhood and beyond to a sidewalk display of arts, crafts, and stands selling wine and gourmet food items, with street performers and musical groups; Tel: 346-4561. The Cable Car Bell-Ringing Championships attracts hundreds of onlookers and listeners to a clanging-good party in Union Square; Tel: 391-2000. The Lesbian and Gay Freedom Day Parade attracts local and national TV attention to goings-on along Market Street; Tel: 864-3733. The Stern Grove Midsummer Musical Festival begins in June and lasts through August, bringing free outdoor Sunday performances of symphonic, operatic, jazz, and contemporary music as well as dance to the remarkable redwood grove in the West Portal/Sunset District; Tel: 252-6252.

In early June, the Free Folk Festival offers folk concerts, workshops on music, song, and dance, and children's events; Tel: 681-7966. Mid-month sees San Franciscans and visitors throng to Grant Avenue and Green Street for the North Beach Fair, an antic party of arts, crafts, food, wine, and music celebrating the city's Italian heritage; Tel: 391-2000.

July: The Fourth of July Celebration and Fireworks attracts thousands of early-evening picnickers to Crissy Field in the Marina, where the night sky glows, sparkles, and rockets against the Golden Gate Bridge backdrop; Tel: 777-7120.

August: The Nihonmachi Street Fair features live entertainment, a children's world, arts-and-crafts shows, and food stalls in Japantown; Tel: 922-8700.

September: Japantown continues buzzing with the Japantown Summer Festival, with music, food, dancing, and martial arts and flower arranging demonstrations; Tel: 922-9300.

October: The month's action begins with Fleet Week, when naval vessels and support ships are open to the public, and the Blue Angels precision jet-fighter flight team soars and roars in aerial maneuvers over the bay and city; Tel: 395-3922.

The Italian community and everybody else commemorate Columbus's arrival in the New World in the annual Columbus Day Celebration on and around the actual holiday, October 12. Queen Isabella is crowned, civic ceremonies are held, Columbus comes ashore at Fisherman's Wharf, and there's a stirring Sunday parade. The procession of the Madonna del Lume and the blessing of the fishing fleet and the animals is a perpetuation of the centuries-old Sicilian folk rite venerating the patroness of fishermen. Religious services are held at the Church of Saints Peter and Paul in North Beach, followed by a march to the Wharf for the blessings; Tel: 391-2000.

Late in October and usually into November, the San Francisco Jazz Festival features the finest in local, national, and international jazz groups and artists such as Dizzy Gillespie or Herbie Hancock. About 18 concerts are staged in venues all over town, indoors and out, from Davies Symphony Hall to cruise ships on the bay; Tel: 864-5449. Also in autumn, the San Francisco Blues Festival is held on the Great Meadow at Fort Mason; Tel: 826-6837. In October and November, the Grand National Livestock Expo Rodeo and Horse Show is staged at the Cow Palace; Tel: 469-6000.

November: The San Francisco Automobile Show is held mid-month at Moscone Convention Center; Tel: 673-2016.

December: The American Conservatory Theater gives its annual production of *A Christmas Carol*; Tel: 749-2228. Traditional Christmas-season performances of *The Messiah* by the San Francisco Symphony and *The Nutcracker* by the San Francisco Ballet are also presented.

GETTING AROUND

On Foot

An anonymous writer once opined, "When you get tired of walking around San Francisco, you can always lean against it."

The central city, with Union Square as its hub, is perfect for walking, with enticing shops, cafés and restaurants, small and stylish hotels, theaters, and more near at hand (and foot) in the Financial District, Chinatown, and Embarcadero Center. However, steep hills and long distances to Fisherman's Wharf, Golden Gate Park, the Marina, and other sights make public transportation more practical for longer excursions.

Committed strollers will want to consider a walking tour spiced with tales of the city, visits to landmarks, peeks into secret gardens and alleys, and stops at neighborhood cafés;

see our listings below or ask at the Visitor Center at Hallidie Plaza (Tel: 391-2000). A "San Francisco Biking/Walking Guide" is widely available at bookstores and newsstands.

By Car

San Francisco's celebrated hills (40 of them, of which the best-known seven are Nob, Russian, Telegraph, Rincon, Twin Peaks, Lone Mountain, and Mount Davidson) can drive an uninitiated motorist crazy. The street you travel along while trying to find a certain address is likely to bump abruptly into a park or a hill, forcing you to go back, forth, and around until you discover where it begins again. Some hills (up Divasadero Street, for example) are so steep you have the sensation of taking off or landing in a small airplane. Experienced, patient drivers may wish to rent a car; others might prefer to use public transportation in the city, picking up a rental car for trips to the countryside. If you do plan to drive in the city, rent a car with automatic transmission unless you can shift gears expertly going up a steep hill from a stop.

Limousines may be rented from any of several firms for point-to-point travel or sightseeing; for general information, call Associated Limousine Operators of San Francisco, Tel: 563-1000 or 824-2660. San Francisco's taxis are often cited as the most expensive in the country. However, they are very efficient and easily hailed on downtown streets. In residential areas you'd be wise to telephone about 15 to 20 minutes beforehand (check the Yellow Pages for phone numbers).

If you are driving, the first route to follow is the celebrated **49-Mile Drive**, an unsurpassed sweep that will give you an introduction to places you'll want to get to know better later. Marked by blue-and-white seagull signs bearing the words Scenic Drive, it begins and ends at the Civic Center. The free San Francisco Visitor Map from the Visitor Center shows it in detail.

On Land

San Francisco Municipal Railway (MUNI) operates more than 1,000 vehicles—the fabled cable cars, light-rail vehicles, electric buses, and motor coaches—to and from all major areas of the city. At this writing the fare is $1.00 for all but cable cars, which are $3; exact fare is required. The basic fare for senior citizens is 25 cents. If you intend to make extensive use of public transport, buy the Street and Transit Map showing MUNI routes (available at the Visitor Center, bookstores, and newspaper stands for $1.50).

A San Francisco Municipal Railway Passport is sold for one day ($6), three consecutive days ($10), or one week ($15) and provides unlimited rides on public transportation, including the cable cars. With the pass, discounts are also available for several museums and other sights. Passes are sold at the Hallidie Plaza Visitor Information Center at Powell and Market streets; MUNI offices at 949 Presidio, Room 239; the cable-car terminals and the ticket booth at Pier 39; the City Hall information booth; and Victorian Park; Tel: 673-6864. Monthly passes (called the Fast Pass) are available at the above outlets, at 949 Presidio Avenue, and at many local stores; the cost is $32. Monthly passes for senior citizens are $5. For route information, call 673-6864 or check the local Yellow Pages.

Cable cars run along three routes: the Powell-Hyde line from Powell and Market streets to Victorian Park, near the Maritime Museum and Aquatic Park (for the most dramatic views); the Powell-Mason line from Powell and Market to Bay Street, three blocks from Fisherman's Wharf; and the California Street line from the foot of Market Street up and across Nob Hill to Van Ness Avenue. Riders should buy tickets before boarding from the self-service machines at all terminals and major stops; the $6 all-day MUNI Passport is dispensed from the machines as well.

The 71-mile **Bay Area Rapid Transit** (BART) system links 8 San Francisco stations with Daly City to the southwest and with 25 stations in the East Bay. It's not just a transit system; it can be a road to urban adventure. Detrain at Embarcadero station for a miniworld of 140 shops, restaurants, and bars; at Berkeley in the East Bay for the University of California campus; at Lake Merritt station for the Oakland Museum and Jack London Square (a 15-minute walk). All tickets are dispensed from machines at the stations; for further assistance call 788-BART.

AC Transit operates buses out of San Francisco's Transbay Terminal at First and Mission streets to communities in the East Bay and in Alameda and Contra Costa counties, via the Bay Bridge; Tel: (510) 839-2882. **CalTrain** provides rail service to San Jose and the Peninsula from its depot at Fourth and Townsend streets; Tel: (800) 660-4287.

Golden Gate Transit, also out of the Transbay Terminal, links San Francisco to Marin and Sonoma counties by bus across the Golden Gate Bridge. Within the city, buses follow routes in the Financial District, Civic Center, and on Park Presidio and Geary boulevards. For information on city routes, schedules, and stops, Tel: 332-6600.

SamTrans, also located in the Transbay Terminal, offers service from San Francisco to SFO and to cities on the Peninsula as far south as Palo Alto; Tel: (800) 660-4287.

See Useful Facts above for details on getting to San Francisco from local airports.

On Sea

There are ferries again on San Francisco Bay. The opening of the Golden Gate Bridge in 1937 washed away the 50 white-and-orange arks that once cruised the harbor, but contemporary traffic, pollution problems, and the effects of the 1989 earthquake have signaled a sea change in the public's appreciation of water transportation.

Golden Gate Ferries depart from the south end of the Ferry Building on the Embarcadero on frequent sailings to Sausalito and to Larkspur in Marin County. Snacks and beverages of all kinds are sold on the crossings, making them minicruises. At this writing the fare on the sleek M.V. *Golden Gate* for the 30-minute trip to Sausalito is $3.75 one way for adults. Three 725-passenger ferries provide frequent daily service to Larkspur for $2.50 for adults and $1.90 for children (weekdays) or $3.25 for adults and free for children on weekends and holidays. Handicapped people and seniors receive 50 percent discounts every day; Tel: 332-6600.

Red & White Fleet vessels depart from Pier 43½ at Fisherman's Wharf for Sausalito and Tiburon (adults, $4.50; children, $2.25). In summer and on winter weekends, there's also service to Angel Island for picnicking and hiking. In addition, there are 45-minute bay cruises with daily departures from 10:45 A.M. and audio information in English, German, Japanese, and Mandarin Chinese.

Excursion cruises run daily from Pier 41 to Vallejo with bus service to Marine World Africa USA; package fare includes boat and bus trips and park admission (adults, $36; children under 12, $20.50; and seniors and youth, $30); Tel: 546-BOAT.

A bay cruise of one and one quarter hours under both the Golden Gate and Bay bridges, within yards of Alcatraz, and along the city's scenic and historical waterfront is offered by the big boats of the **Blue & Gold Fleet**, with frequent departures from Pier 39 (adults, $14; seniors and youth, $7). Sailings are fully narrated and snacks and drinks are sold; Tel: 781-7877. The ferries of the Blue & Gold Fleet also offer daily round-trip service from Pier 39 and the Ferry Building to Oakland's Jack London Square and Alameda's Gateway Center. Fares for the five morning and five evening departures are

$3.50 (adults), $2.50 (seniors), and $1.50 (children); all include AC Transit and MUNI transfers. The 277-passenger Harbor Bay Express travels between San Francisco's Ferry Plaza and Alameda's Harbor Bay Isle (in the East Bay south of Oakland). The 85-foot, double-deck ferry makes the cross-Bay trip in about 22 minutes at a one-way, weekday fare of $4 (no weekend service at this time).

You can party on the bay aboard the *California Hornblower,* the 183-foot, 1,000-passenger vessel of **Hornblower Dining Yachts**. Patterned after the classic steamers of the early 1900s, it has three enclosed decks and formally appointed dining salons. Dinner-dance cruises depart nightly from Pier 33 at the foot of Bay Street, with luncheon sailings on Fridays and brunch cruises on weekends; Tel: 394-8900.

San Francisco Spirit, the 150-foot flagship of **Pacific Marine Yachts**, makes dining cruises on some Friday and Saturday evenings and Sunday afternoons. Evening sailings include a five-course dinner, and Champagne brunches are served on Sundays. In addition, chartered cruises are available on three other vessels for groups of 10 to 700 passengers. Home port is Pier 39. For schedules and other information, Tel: 788-2221.

Several companies operate boating and sailing charters for private parties or business excursions, among them **Cass' Marina** with large sailing yachts out of Pier 39 and Sausalito (Tel: 332-6789), and **Commodore Dining Cruises** with yachts for 10 to 450 guests with boardings around the bay (Tel: 510-256-4000).

Lake Merritt Sailboat House provides various kinds of water vessels for trips around the Oakland lake; Tel: (510) 238-2196. **Let's Go Sailing** offers 1½-hour sailboat rides or private charters from Pier 39; Tel: 788-4920. **Rendezvous Charters/Spinnaker Sailing** sails the 78-foot square-rigger *Rendezvous* out of Pier 40 with individual or group departures; Tel: 543-7333.

In the Air

The jet choppers of **San Francisco Helicopter Tours** fly over San Francisco Bay, the Wine Country, and the Monterey Peninsula on completely narrated trips. The most popular is the 30-minute Vista Grande flight over the Bay Bridge and Golden Gate Bridge, Alcatraz, and past the city skyline. The heliport is easily accessible, or complimentary pick-ups will be made at San Francisco hotels. Reservations required; Tel: (510) 635-4500 or (800) 400-2404.

Relive the golden days of DC3s with the low-flying, luxurious one-hour flights of **Otis Spunkmeyer Air.** Up to 18 passengers cruise in comfort over San Francisco and the bay while enjoying Champagne and gourmet hors d'oeuvres. Call for rates and schedules; Tel: (510) 667-3800 or (800) 938-1900.

Sightseeing

More than a dozen companies operate sightseeing tours by van or bus in San Francisco and the immediate area, from three-and-a-half hour jaunts to overnight trips. Check the listings at the San Francisco Visitor Center or ask at your hotel for recommendations. The largest and best-known is **The Gray Line**, which specializes in full- and half-day excursions around the Bay Area; Tel: 558-9400. **California Parlor Car Tours** offers one- or two-night trips to Yosemite National Park, to Hearst Castle at San Simeon, and to other regional wonders. Departures are from downtown hotels; Tel: 474-7500. **Great Pacific Tour Company** employs 13-passenger minivans on four tours within San Francisco, and to Muir Woods and Sausalito, the Napa-Sonoma wine country, and the Monterey Peninsula; Tel: 626-4499.

Specialty Touring

Aardvark's Artful Adventures, 3145 Geary Boulevard near the University of San Francisco, creates excursions for adventuresome families and youth groups; Tel: 954-1296. **Artfocus**, 2616 Jackson Street between Pierce and Scott on Alta Plaza, leads tours of art galleries, museums, and art printers; Tel: 921-4111.

Cable Car Charters steers you through San Francisco in style aboard motorized cable cars that depart every half hour (9:30 A.M. to 7:30 P.M.) from Pier 41 and from A. Sabella's restaurant at Jefferson and Taylor. The one-and-a-quarter-hour tours are narrated; Tel: 922-2425.

Carriage Charters offers a leisurely horse-drawn trip from Pier 41 at Fisherman's Wharf to North Beach. Carriages roll from 1:00 P.M. to evenings daily, weather permitting; Tel: 398-0857.

An experienced naturalist leads **A Day in Nature**, half-day and full-day nature escapes in the Marin Headlands or Muir Woods that include a gourmet picnic. Door-to-door service in downtown San Francisco is available, and reservations are required; Tel: 673-0548.

Pro Photo explores scenic delights on tours conducted by a professional photographer who supplies historical and topical information, technical instruction, and composition advice. Reservations required; Tel: (510) 945-7549.

San Francisco Jewish Landmarks Tours employs qualified

historians to guide visitors to historical buildings, private art collections and homes, major synagogues, and the Holocaust Memorial; gourmet lunches included with half- and full-day programs. Group tours of Jewish pioneer history in the Gold Country are also available; Tel: 921-0461.

Visits to hotels, churches, theaters, homes, factories, and more are the purlieu of **Ticket Easy**, with lunch or dinner often included; Tel: 956-1765.

At least a dozen other firms have created unusual ways to see the city; pick up a list at the Visitor Center.

Walking Tours

A. M. Walks begin at 8:00 or 9:00 A.M. for two-hour strolls while the city is still fairly traffic-free. They highlight the frisky past of the fun-filled, often foolish town from Union Square to Chinatown and the Barbary Coast, including a *Maltese Falcon* murder site. Reservations are required; Tel: 928-5965.

Join **The City Guides** (sponsored by the Friends of the Public Library) for an anecdotal look at local history, architecture, and culture. The free tours are scheduled weekdays and weekends, and no reservations are required. For a recorded schedule and meeting points, Tel: 557-4266.

Cruisin' the Castro tells how and why San Francisco became the "gay capital" of the world and covers aspects of gay history from 1849 to the present. Groups meet at 10:00 A.M. Tuesday through Saturday on the southwest corner of Castro and Market streets (Harvey Milk Plaza) for a tour that points out interesting shops and various landmarks and ends with a visit to the Names Project, home of the AIDS memorial quilt. Reservations are required; Tel: 550-8110.

Friends of Recreation and Parks conducts free, guided walks through Golden Gate Park, examining flora, fauna, and history. Various tours are given from several points within the park on Saturdays at 11:00 A.M. and Sundays at 11:00 A.M. and 2:00 P.M. from May through October, rain or shine; Tel: 221-1311 (recorded message) or 750-5105 (more details).

Frisco Tours & Productions presents ambles through legendary San Francisco led by writers and San Francisco personalities. The three walks (each up to three hours long) are on the themes of Film and Fiction (in the footsteps of Mark Twain, Dashiell Hammett, William Saroyan), Crime/ Barbary Coast (meet scoundrels such as Black Bart), and Historic Bar Crawl (see and sip in old-time saloons). Bus tours are available for groups on subjects such as Hollywood in San Francisco or Amazing Grace, an in-depth look at the Episcopal Cathedral on Nob Hill; Tel: 681-5555.

Heritage Walks are sponsored by the Foundation for San Francisco's Architectural Heritage, headquartered in the stately Haas-Lilienthal House. Among the neighborhoods explored are Pacific Heights, Chinatown (Saturdays, June through September), and the Presidio (Saturdays, June through September 21); Tel: 441-3004.

Wok Wiz—Chinatown Walking Tours are led by Shirley Fong-Torres (television chef, cookbook writer, and restaurant critic) and her staff. Walkers meet colorful personalities and visit unusual businesses in the atmospheric back alleys and side streets of Chinatown. The tour includes a brush-paint demonstration, a private tea ceremony, a call on a Chinese rice noodle factory, and a Chinese luncheon, all accompanied by fascinating tales of the past. Evening cooking classes are also available; Tel: 355-9657.

—Georgia I. Hesse with Susan Shook

ACCOMMODATIONS

Considering its small size among the world's star cities, San Francisco can take pride in its complement of fine hotels in all price categories except that of the lowest. For rooms at the top, expect to pay $185 to $350 for doubles and twins, up to and even more than $1,000 for two-room suites. Some in this bracket are the traditional, world-recognized palaces; others are newer, smaller, less well known but equally regal hotels, also charging palatial prices. Seasonal discounts and special packages are often available; always inquire.

An encouraging trend is the burgeoning of new, small, middle-range hotels reflecting what is known locally as European style: well-managed, handsomely outfitted inns with superb service but few frills. Most of these occupy renovated old buildings that had become tired, if not seedy. Rates in these range from about $85 to $165 for doubles and twins; from $125 to $185 for suites.

There are also some inns and bed and breakfasts. The latter is an inexact and misleading term to those who think of it in the British-European sense, where it implies good, clean rooms that are also inexpensive—in San Francisco some of these charge as much as or more than the top hotels. A moderate range for doubles is $75 to $285.

A few all-suite hotels are sprouting in the city, though less vigorously than elsewhere in California and the nation.

Some are excellent value for money spent, with two-bedroom suites for a reasonable $225 or so, well-suited to families on an extended visit or to travellers combining business and pleasure. A handful of small, long-established hotels offer doubles as low as $65, but they are real finds.

With all these options available, you are unlikely to choose a motel or motor hotel in San Francisco; the best ones sit along northern Van Ness Avenue and Lombard Street in the Marina, which are segments of U.S. Highway 101 and are handy for drivers hastening through town. They charge between $65 and $110 for doubles.

San Francisco International Airport is unusually well equipped with hotels of a high standard. The best ones are listed here for travellers who, alas, must skip San Francisco proper or catch an early-morning flight.

Traditionally, hotels cluster around such centers as Nob Hill, Union Square, and the Financial District, but because the city is so compact, location may be less important than other qualities. For that reason, we cover them here by the styles set out above rather than geographically.

All of San Francisco is in area code 415; the United States code is 1. A central service number is San Francisco Reservations, which offers up to a 50 percent discount on many rates; Tel: 227-1500 or (800) 677-1550; Fax: 227-1520. Our entries give zip codes, but of course they should be preceded by "San Francisco, California."

The rate ranges given here are projections for fall 1993 through spring 1994. Unless otherwise indicated, rates are for double rooms, double occupancy.

The Palaces

▶ **Fairmont Hotel and Tower.** Sophisticated, elegant, with the showiest lobby this side of the Gold Rush, the Fairmont signals the Nob Hill of San Francisco's glory days. It was named for James G. "Bonanza Jim" Fair, one of the fabled silver Bonanza Kings, who died while the foundations for his mansion were being laid on this site. Its restaurants and bars are as unrestrained as the Neo-Renaissance pile itself: the **Squire** off the lobby for fine dining; the **Crown Restaurant** for drinking and dining while gazing off toward Japan; **Bella Voce** (informal Italian cuisine with opera-singing servers in evening, and coffee-shop style from 6:00 A.M. to 3:00 P.M.); **Mason's** for regional American cooking and supper-club piano; the **New Orleans Room** off the lobby (sipping and swing music); the **Sweet Corner** (coffee shop); the **Tonga Room** (Polynesian-campy food and drinks around a giant swimming pool complete with storms). Mr. Eckhard's men's and women's hair stylists here are among the city's most competent and chic; there is also a health spa on the premises.

950 Mason Street, 94108. Tel: 772-5000, 772-5147 (room reservations), 772-5144 (restaurant reservations), or (800) 527-4727 (general reservations); Fax: 781-3929. The Fairmont is a member of Leading Hotels of the World; in U.S. and Canada, Tel: (800) 223-6800; in Great Britain and Northern Ireland, Tel: (800) 181-123; in Australia, Tel: (008) 222-033; in Sydney, Tel: (02) 233-8422; Fax: (02) 223-5372. $180–$290.

▶ **Four Seasons Clift**. Quiet, understated, with impeccable service, the Clift was a Union Square tradition long before it entered the Four Seasons family (which did nothing, happily, except improve it). The guest rooms are tastefully furnished and unusually large. The handsome old **Redwood Room** is a restful, wood-paneled retreat highlighted by works by Gustav Klimt; the **French Room**'s cuisine is as outstanding, and expensive, as its decor.

495 Geary Street, 94102. Tel: 775-4700 or (800) 332-3442; Fax: 775-4621. $200–$340.

▶ **Hyatt Regency**. The distinctive John Portman innovations here—architectural planes, open spaces, and ceiling-soaring lobby—make you feel, entering from the street, as if you are falling up. There's a Regency Club (the Hyatt chain's VIP floor) and access to a nearby health club. The top-floor **Equinox** bar and restaurant revolves above a striking lower-city view; the **Other Trellis** is a daily showcase for local talent.

Five Embarcadero Center, 94111. Tel: 788-1234 or (800) 233-1234 (worldwide reservations); Fax: 398-2567. $149–$268.

▶ **Mark Hopkins Inter-Continental**. There can be no smarter address than 1 Nob Hill. This location was once occupied by the mansion of a member of the Big Four, who built the transcontinental railroad, but who, like James G. Fair, died before moving in. The Mark Hopkins is famous for the sky-high **Top of the Mark** cocktail lounge's magnificent views over the city and bay (the best corner is supposed to be the northeast). The **Nob Hill Restaurant** serves California-French cuisine in a prosperous, oak-paneled, 19th-century atmosphere; you can take in the pleasant garden air in an off-the-lobby lounge.

1 Nob Hill, 94108. Tel: 392-3434 or (800) 336-7070; Fax: 421-3302. $200–$305.

▶ **The Pan-Pacific**. Designed by renowned architect John

Portman and originally named the Portman, this luxurious 330-room hotel opened near Union Square in 1987. Now an elegant member of the Pan-Pacific family, owned by the Tokyu Corporation of Japan, the hotel stresses an Asian idea of service, offering personal valets on 16 of the 21 floors, chauffered Rolls-Royce service around the city, health-club facilities, and flexible check-out hours. The third-floor atrium lobby makes spectacular use of marble, sculpture, and a fireplace before which you can cozy up and read for hours. **The Pacific Grill** specializes in homey, contemporary food and **The Bar** on the third floor serves cocktails and fine hors d'oeuvres with soothing piano accompaniment.

500 Post Street, 94102. Tel: 771-8600; in U.S. and Canada, Tel: (800) 327-8585; in Great Britain, Tel: (071) 491-3812; in Australia, Tel: (02) 264-1122; in New Zealand, Tel: (9) 366-3000; Fax: 398-0267. $185–$335.

▶ **Park Hyatt.** European-style luxury arrived in Embarcadero Center when this 360-room hotel opened in 1989; many suites offer balconies. The **Park Grill** serves American specialties in a club-like setting; there are health-club privileges.

333 Battery Street, 94111. Tel: 392-1234; in U.S. and Canada, Tel: (800) 323-PARK; Fax: 421-2433. $225–$280.

▶ **The Sheraton Palace.** This grande dame of old San Francisco reopened to citywide applause in 1991 following a $150-million renovation and refurbishment. Today the 70,000 panes of glass in the **Garden Court** sparkle again, and dining under the glowing chandeliers means dining in grandeur. In **Maxfield's Pied Piper Bar,** the Maxfield Parrish mural of the Pied Piper of Hamlin is back in place above the historic bar and light American fare is served daily. There's also a new, skylit swimming pool, a health spa, and a business center. The 550 guest rooms and suites match the smartness of the public rooms.

2 New Montgomery Street at Market, 94105. Tel: 392-8600 or (800) 325-3535; Fax: 543-0671. $210–$270.

▶ **The Stouffer Stanford Court.** On the slope of Nob Hill east of the Mark Hopkins, toward the Powell Street cable-car line, this prestigious hotel occupies the mansion site of yet another Big Four member, the founder of Stanford University, Leland Stanford. It's renowned for a striking courtyard entry (for cars) with a Tiffany-style glass dome, a 1937 Maxfield Parrish painting, and its woody and paneled lobby. **Fournou's Ovens** features contemporary American cuisine in a smart Mediterranean setting; there's a lovely lounge at the entry, one floor above the restaurant.

905 California Street, 94108. Tel: 989-3500, (800) 227-

4736, or, in California, (800) 622-0957; Fax: 391-0513. $225–$325.

▶ **Westin St. Francis.** One of the old-time treasures of Union Square, this grande dame with its modern tower now caters (alas) to many tour groups. From **Victor's** on the 32nd floor there's a smashing view of the central city to accompany Continental-California cuisine; Tel: 956-7777. The lushly decorated, almost antic **Compass Rose** off the lobby is a bar and restaurant in the grand manner, where string music accompanies afternoon tea, while **Dewey's** provides drinks and sandwiches in pub-like surroundings; also available are the **St. Francis Grill** (fine dining in a comfortably old-fashioned setting), the **Dutch Kitchen** (informal), and **Oz** (a fashionable salon for drinks and dancing with a view).

335 Powell Street, 94102. Tel: 397-7000 or (800) 228-3000; Fax: 774-0124. $80–$260.

Petits Palaces

▶ **Campton Place Kempinski.** Opened in 1983 in a reworking of two turn-of-the-century buildings half a block north of Union Square, Campton quickly took its place at the very pinnacle among the country's small, luxurious hotels; it joined Europe's Kempinski group in 1991. Objets d'art, fine furnishings, and professional and caring service are among its hallmarks; many of its 126 rooms are rather small, however. The restaurant of the same name in the hotel has become one of the finest in the city.

340 Stockton Street, 94108. Tel: 781-5555. Campton Place can also be booked through Kempinski reservation centers in the U.S. and Canada, Tel: (800) 426-3135; in Great Britain, Tel: (800) 89-8588. $185–$320.

▶ **Donatello.** The restaurant in this elegant Union Square hotel is so outstanding that it gave its name to the place not long after its opening. Italian in design, craftsmanship, cuisine, and warm welcome, the 95-room hotel boasts soothing interiors of travertine, Italian marble, Venetian glass, antiques, and Fortuny fabrics. Even spoiled San Francisco diners acclaim **Donatello** the restaurant (Tel: 441-7182) for serving the best northern Italian cuisine in town; the tiny bar off the two dining rooms is fittingly quiet, a retreat in itself.

501 Post Street, 94102. Tel: 441-7100 or (800) 227-3184; Fax: 885-8842. $155–$270.

▶ **The Huntington Nob Hill.** Whatever is smart, restrained, elegant, and quietly luxurious is at home here, where the third among the Big Four (Collis P. Huntington) is remembered on Nob Hill. Rooms and suites are spacious for a small hotel. The **Big Four Restaurant and Bar** is warm, uncrowded, refined, and serves award-winning American dishes in a masculine atmosphere particularly appreciated by women who dislike "lady-finger" rooms.

1075 California Street, 94108. Tel: 474-5400, (800) 652-1539 (in California), or (800) 227-4683 (nationwide); Fax: 474-6227. The Huntington is a member of Small Luxury Hotels; in U.S., Tel: (800) 525-4800, Fax: (817) 545-1184; in Great Britain, Tel: (0800) 282-124, Fax: (081) 877-9477; in Australia, Tel: (008) 802-582, Fax: (02) 954-8123. It also belongs to Preferred Hotels and Resorts; in U.S. and Canada, Tel: (800) 323-7500; in Great Britain, Tel: (0800) 89-33-91; in Australia, Tel: (02) 247-6537. $185–$235.

▶ **Mandarin Oriental.** Perhaps nowhere else in the world can you sit in your bathtub and overlook such an eye-popping view—with no eyes popping back at you unless they are in a helicopter. This superb hotel of the Mandarin Oriental Group occupies the top 11 floors of two 48-story towers connected by sky bridges in the Financial District. The decor of guest rooms is clean, spare, and East Asian, with artistic touches reminiscent of Asian scrollwork. **Silks** is a remarkably beautiful restaurant, serving cuisine with an Asian accent. The lobby **Mandarin Lounge** is a lovely setting for breakfast, lunch, afternoon tea, and cocktails.

222 Sansome Street, 94104. Tel: 885-0999 or (800) 622-0404; in Canada, Tel: (800) 526-6566. Mandarin Oriental belongs to Leading Hotels of the World; in U.S. and Canada, Tel: (800) 223-6800; in Great Britain and Northern Ireland, Tel: (0800) 181-123; in Sydney, Tel: (008) 233-8422; elsewhere in Australia, Tel: (008) 222-033; Fax: 433-0289. $295–$410.

▶ **The Ritz-Carlton.** San Francisco's member of the distinguished chain opened in 1991 within a stately Nob Hill building that once served as Pacific Coast headquarters of the Metropolitan Life Insurance Company and later as the home of Cogswell College. Built in 1909 and one of the city's best examples of Neoclassical architecture, the massive white structure has been rehabilitated completely and its interior decorated with 18th- and 19th-century antiques and art works. **The Dining Room**, elegant and intimate, seats 84 for dinners only; **The Restaurant and Courtyard**, the city's only indoor-and-terraced café, serves all day; there's also the **Ritz Bar** and the **Lobby Lounge** serving afternoon tea and cocktails. The 336-room hotel boasts facilities for businesspeople, a fitness center with large indoor swimming pool, and conference facilities.

600 Stockton Street, 94108. Tel: 296-7465 or (800) 241-3333; in United Kingdom, Tel: (0800) 234-000; in Australia, Tel: (008) 252-888; Fax: 296-8559. $205–$400.

▶ **The Sherman House.** Its small size (eight rooms, six apartments) should classify it as an inn, but the remarkable building, the exquisite taste of its renovation, its smashing views, its Pacific Heights location, and its historic legacy qualify the Sherman as a small palace. (The Sherman House is one of only five U.S. members in Northern California of the prestigious French Relais & Châteaux group.) Leander S. Sherman arrived in 1861 with music as his passion, and he built his Sherman Clay & Co. into the leading supplier of musical instruments in the West. Luisa Tetrazzini, Madame Ernestine Schumann-Heink, and Enrico Caruso performed in what is today a small but splendid foyer. The cuisine at the Sherman's restaurant (opened to the public in 1991) is remarkable.

2160 Green Street, 94123. Tel: 563-3600; Fax: 563-1882. The Sherman is a member of Small Luxury Hotels of the World; in U.S., Tel: (800) 525-4800; in Great Britain, Tel: (0800) 282-124; in Australia, Tel: (008) 80-0896. $235–$750.

European-style Inns
▶ **The Bedford.** This 1929 building three blocks west of Union Square has been renovated to the style Lord Wedgwood appreciated when he passed through long ago. Enjoy the **Wedgwood Bar**, the **Café Champagne**, the airy decor, and the personal service.

761 Post Street, 94109. Tel: 673-6040; in U.S. and Canada, Tel: (800) 227-5642; Fax: 563-6739. $99–$109.

▶ **Diva.** In the heart of the theater district, this is a high-tech, high-profile inn where the decor glitters and the service sparkles; amenities include VCRs and mini-refrigerators.

440 Geary Street, 94102. Tel: 885-0200 or (800) 553-1900; Fax: 346-6613. $119–$129.

▶ **Galleria Park.** The Art Nouveau lobby speaks of 1911; the amenities (complete with a rooftop jogging park), of the 1990s. There has been attention to good lighting for business-oriented visitors, and meeting facilities are available. Two favorite Financial District restaurants are adjacent: **Bentley's Seafood Grill** and **Brasserie Chambord**.

191 Sutter Street, 94104. Tel: 781-3060; in U.S. and Canada, Tel: (800) 792-9639; Fax 433-4409. $109–$145.

▶ **The Griffon.** Up from the 1906 waterfront days comes a hotel with the mood of the moment, and the service of yesterday. Guests may use an adjoining athletic club; some penthouse suites have redwood terraces. The **Bistro Roti** specializes in spit-roasted entrées created by the three restaurateurs who gave the Fog City Diner to San Francisco and Mustards and Tra Vigne to the Napa Valley.

155 Steuart Street, 94105. Tel: 495-2100 or (800) 321-2201; Fax 495-3522. $125–$285.

▶ **Harbor Court.** The newest among Bill Kimpton's smart but low-key winners has a smashing waterfront view now that the earthquake-battered Embarcadero Freeway has been demolished. Guests have free use of the upscale pool and recreational facilities next door. The lively saloon-restaurant off the lobby is the popular and trendy **Harry Denton's**.

165 Steuart Street, 94105. Tel: 882-1300 or (800) 346-0555. $150–$160.

▶ **Hyatt at Fisherman's Wharf.** Larger than most European-style inns (313 guest rooms of various descriptions) but very much akin to them in ambience, this five-story hotel opened in late 1990 on the site of the old Musto Marble Works plant. Bricks from the original structure were used in the construction to maintain the historic style of the Wharf area. The lobby with its wood-burning fireplace is particularly welcoming. In addition to a heated outdoor pool, Jacuzzi, fitness center, and sauna, the hotel boasts Camp Hyatt, where guests' children can be entertained and watched over from 9:00 A.M. to 10:00 P.M. The **Marble Works** restaurant features Italian seafood and fresh pasta specialties.

555 North Point, 94133. Tel: 563-1234 or (800) 233-1234; Fax: 749-6122. $159–$189.

▶ **Inn at the Opera.** Meticulous care has been taken to transform this 1927 apartment house into an exciting retreat. Located near the Opera House, Symphony Hall, and the Museum of Modern Art in the Civic Center, it is very small and specializes in personal services for the vacationer or business traveller. The **Act IV** lounge and restaurant is like a personal discovery you might make in London or Paris.

333 Fulton Street, 94102. Tel: 863-8400; in California, Tel: (800) 423-9610; in U.S., Tel: (800) 325-2708; Fax: 861-0821. $120–$215.

▶ **Inn at Union Square.** People who have stayed here once often refuse to stay anywhere else. Most floors offer a sitting area with fireplace; the penthouse suite has a fireplace, bar, whirlpool, and sauna. Antiques abound; afternoon tea, wine, hors d'oeuvres, and breakfast are included. A meeting/conference facility, fully catered, is also available. Smoking is not permitted on the premises.

440 Post Street, 94102. Tel: 397-3510 or (800) 288-4346; Fax: 989-0529. $120–$170.

▶ **Juliana.** A historic (1903) inn near Union Square has been reborn. Reflecting the theme of art in San Francisco, the Juliana's suites are decorated with rotating collections of artwork supplied by local galleries for admiration or purchase. The lobby is intimate, with a wood-burning marble fireplace.

590 Bush Street, 94108. Tel: 392-2540; in U.S. and Canada, Tel: (800) 328-3880; Fax: 391-8447. $119–$155.

▶ **Kensington Park.** Sherry before the fireplace and a grand piano in the lobby set the civilized tone for this renovated 1924 hotel near Union Square. Updated but traditional English decor and Continental breakfast add to the soothing package.

450 Post Street, 94102. Tel: 788-6400 or (800) 553-1900; Fax: 399-9484. $115.

▶ **The King George.** Right across the street from the O'Farrell Garage (the best place to park in the Theater District) and just west of Union Square, this 143-room charmer is an unexpected haven of comfort, courtesy, and old-fashioned value. Enjoying English high tea to the accompaniment of classical piano music in the **Bread and Honey Tea Room** is a civilized pastime.

334 Mason Street, 94102-1783. Tel: 781-5050; in U.S. and Canada, Tel: (800) 288-6005; Fax: 391-6976. $107.

▶ **The Hotel Majestic.** Edwardian atmosphere, antiques, and careful attention to detail mark this restored 1902 hotel west of Van Ness Avenue; many rooms have fireplaces and refrigerators. **Café Majestic** specializes in Old San Francisco recipes and in-house pastries.

1500 Sutter Street, 94109. Tel: 441-1100 or (800) 869-8966; Fax 673-7331. $135–$250.

▶ **The Millefiori Inn.** Each of the 15 rooms has a different, stylish decor; that and sophisticated service make this a surprise in the heart of North Beach. But don't expect the quiet of a residential side-street inn.

444 Columbus Avenue, 94133. Tel: 433-9111; Fax: 362-6292. $85.

▶ **Miyako Hotel.** Traditional Japan meets California in rooms and restaurant; lovely touches abound in sunken tubs, rice-paper *shoji* screens, and a lobby garden with waterfall in the middle of Japantown. Classically designed Japanese rooms and suites are available, some with redwood saunas. **Elka** here is excellent.

1625 Post Street, 94115. Tel: 922-3200; in U.S. and Canada, Tel: (800) 533-4567; Fax: 921-0417. $129–$189.

▶ **The Monticello Inn.** To step into this colonial-style 1906 lobby, furnished in Federal-period decor with Chippendale reproductions, fireplace, and reading-and-writing parlor is to step back into a more gracious age. Early American in appearance, colors, and details, it's also old-fashioned in its welcome three blocks southwest of Union Square. The **Corona Bar & Grill**, off the lobby, has become the city's standard for judging innovative Mexican-California cuisine.

127 Ellis Street, 94102. Tel: 392-8800 or (800) 669-7777; Fax: 398-2650. $124.

▶ **The Prescott.** Urban elegance, understated *luxe*, a lobby as comfortable as a living room, Native American artifacts, suites with VCRs and whirlpools, honor bar/refrigerators, and wines in the library in the evening—such is the gracious air of this upscale inn near Union Square with one of the finest, most popular restaurants in the city, **PosTrio**. Room service by Wolfgang Puck? Believe it.

545 Post Street, 94102. Tel: 563-0303; in U.S. and Canada, Tel: (800) 283-7322; Fax: 563-6831. $155–$175.

▶ **Queen Anne.** Oak panels, a Spanish cedar staircase, antiques, and fireplaces distinguish this house built by James G. Fair (the Silver King) in 1890 as Miss Mary Lake's School for Girls. It has lived several lives in south Pacific Heights, currently a smart and stylish one with Sherry and afternoon tea in the parlor; some rooms have fireplaces.

1590 Sutter Street, 94109. Tel: 441-2828 or (800) 227-3970; Fax: 775-5212. $99–$150.

▶ **Raphael.** This was among the first of the city's European-style inns and has been refurbished recently; its location one block west of Union Square and lively café (**Mama's**) make this inn popular with theatergoers.

386 Geary Street, 94102. Tel: 986-2000; in U.S., Tel: (800) 821-5343; Fax: 397-2447. $99–$119.

▶ **Savoy.** The owners of the elegant and pricey Sherman House used all of their talent and taste to turn this old hotel, three blocks west of Union Square, into a French Provincial inn in 1990, but they kept the prices pleasantly reasonable. The informal but stylish **Brasserie Savoy** is great for theatergoers, especially its oyster bar.

580 Geary Street, 94102. Tel: 441-2700; in U.S. and Canada, Tel: (800) 227-4223. $99–$119.

▶ **Shannon Court.** In 1989 an old hotel at 550 Geary between Taylor and Jones was remodeled at great cost and metamorphosed into the warm—even elegant—Shannon

Court. There are 173 guest rooms and suites, banquet and meeting rooms, complimentary Continental breakfast, afternoon tea, nonsmoking floors, and some parking. Those who mourned the demise of La Mère Duquesne restaurant will enjoy the new **City of Paris**, reborn in the same handy location near theaters.

550 Geary Street, 94102. Tel: 775-5000; in California, (800) 228-8830; in rest of U.S., (800) 821-0493; in Canada, (800) 521-2622; Fax: 928-6813. $90–$125.

▶ **Stanyan Park Hotel.** Across the street from Golden Gate Park at the edge of the Haight-Ashbury, this 36-room inn offers neighborhood quiet, 24-hour protected parking for cars, and a welcoming atmosphere.

750 Stanyan Street, 94117. Tel: 751-1000; Fax: 668-5454. $78–$96.

▶ **The Tuscan Inn at Fisherman's Wharf.** This recent addition to Fisherman's Wharf offers European style in the heart of this touristy area. The inn's central garden court (visible from the Italianate lobby and from inner rooms) adds an elegant touch, as does the complimentary wine hour every evening in front of the Tuscan's lobby fireplace. Many rooms have sweeping bay views. **Café Pescatore** offers an Italian menu and sidewalk tables in good weather. There's complimentary limousine service to the Financial District on weekdays.

425 North Point, 94133. Tel: 561-1100; in U.S. and Canada, Tel: (800) 648-4626; Fax: 561-1199. $148–$168.

▶ **Villa Florence.** Convenient to both smart shopping and theater-going, this renovated 1908 building celebrates Tuscany, complete with a 16th-century trompe l'oeil lobby mural and a 17th-century velvet tapestry. **Kuleto's** off the lobby has become one of the most popular Italian restaurants in town, with original pastas, fresh fish, on-premises bakery, and a carved Brunswick bar brought around Cape Horn on a clipper ship.

225 Powell Street, 94102. Tel: 397-7700 or (800) 553-4411; Fax: 397-1006. $129.

▶ **Vintage Court.** A day in Wine Country is the mood in this reworked 1913 house near Union Square, with guest rooms named for California wineries and a cozy lobby in which to sit and sip before the fireplace. Adjoining, exquisite **Masa's** has been acclaimed as one of the finest French restaurants in the country.

650 Bush Street, 94108. Tel: 392-4666; in U.S. and Canada, Tel: (800) 654-1100; Fax: 433-4065. $119.

▶ **The Warwick Regis.** French and English antiques and

art meet harmoniously in this deluxe inn in the heart of the theater district. **La Scene Café & Bar** serves contemporary American-style breakfast daily and dinner Tuesday through Saturday.

490 Geary Street, 94102. Tel: 928-7900; in U.S. and Canada, Tel: (800) 827-3447; Fax 441-8788. $130–$205.

Bed and Breakfasts

▶ **Archbishops' Mansion.** Built in 1904 to house the archbishopric of San Francisco and so occupied until 1945, this Belle Epoque villa was (and is) one of the city's largest homes, overlooking a registered Historic District between the Civic Center and Golden Gate Park. The world within is an eclectic mix of European and Asian art and antiques; unusual for a bed and breakfast, laundry and cleaning are available. Unfortunately, the area, known as Alamo Square, is not recommended for after-dark ambling.

1000 Fulton Street, 94117. Tel: 563-7872 or (800) 543-5820; Fax: 885-3193. $115–$285.

▶ **The Bed and Breakfast Inn.** This is probably the place that locally fueled the fad for bed and breakfasts. In a mews off Union Street, five of the eleven rooms open to the garden; the sense is that the country has come to the city.

4 Charlton Court, 94123. Tel: 921-9784. $70–$90 (shared bath), $115–$140 (private bath), $190–$215 (penthouses).

▶ **The Mansions.** Man-about-town Robert Pritikin has joined two marvelous Pacific Heights mansions into one delightful 28-room inn. One is a gracious Greek Revival home built for Judge Charles Slack in the early 1900s, complete with seven fireplaces and polished redwood everywhere. Next door, the Queen Anne home was built for Utah Senator Richard Chambers in 1887. Concerts and magic shows are staged in the Music Room and sometimes Claudia (the resident ghost) plays the piano. Dining is excellent; the garden displays sculptures by late local genius Beniamino Bufano.

2220 Sacramento, 94115. Tel: 929-9444 or (800) 826-9398; Fax: 567-9391. $89–$350.

▶ **The Monte Cristo.** Built in Laurel Heights in 1875, this Victorian once served as a bordello, and legends linger. Rooms, unusually spacious for a bed and breakfast, have Early American and English furnishings; great breakfasts are served.

600 Presidio Avenue, 94115. Tel: 931-1875. $63–$98.

▶ **Petite Auberge.** This is a French country inn with 26

rooms right in the city, complete with some fireplaces and a super-competent concierge, sheltered from the hustle and bustle of nearby Union Square. People who've stayed here try to keep it for themselves.

863 Bush Street, 94108. Tel: 928-6000; Fax: 775-5717. $105–$155.

▶ **Washington Square Inn.** Deliciously decorated with French and English country furnishings, this 15-room inn (10 rooms with private bath) offers a restful, neighborhood setting in North Beach. Smoking is not permitted on the premises.

1660 Stockton Street, 94133. Tel: 981-4220; in California, Tel: (800) 388-0220; Fax: 397-7242. $95–$180.

▶ **White Swan.** A country-English theme is carried out with antiques, fine fabrics, and a common room near a tiny garden, where breakfast and high tea are served. All rooms have baths, fireplaces, and refrigerators. It's a surprising hideaway just three blocks north of Union Square.

845 Bush Street, 94108. Tel: 775-1755 or (800) 999-9570; Fax: 775-5717. $145–$160.

Suites and Apartments

▶ **Hyde Park Suites.** Settling down here at the foot of residential Russian Hill, you will feel like a San Franciscan, with a view of Alcatraz and the bay. There are one- and two-bedroom suites with wet bars and kitchens, extensive business facilities, and free limousine service to downtown.

2655 Hyde Street, 94109. Tel: 771-0200 or (800) 227-3608; Fax: 346-8058. $165–$220.

▶ **Nob Hill Associates.** Individually and smartly decorated, outfitted with designer kitchens and baths, these are fashionable pieds-à-terre for travellers combining business with pleasure; use of an excellent nearby health club is possible, and weekly maid service and individual phone lines are provided.

1234 Jones Street, 94109. Tel: 923-1234; Fax: 775-2441. $1,250–$2,500 per month.

▶ **Nob Hill Lambourne.** Executives staying here can be provided with fax machines, computers, and other business essentials *en suite*. Health-club memberships are available; airport limousine pickups can be arranged.

725 Pine Street, 94108. Tel: 433-2287; Fax: 433-0975. $175–$250.

▶ **Trinity Suites.** Two-bedroom/two-bath suites come equipped with color TVs, microwaves, and VCRs; some of the 18 suites are wheelchair accessible. There are kitchens and weekly maid service is available.

845 Pine Street, 94108. Tel: 433-3333. $1,995 and up, monthly.

Small Finds
▶ **Beresford**. With small, tidy rooms and friendly personnel, this is probably the most reasonably priced hotel in town; there are refrigerators and honor bars in each room. The **White Horse** café on the premises serves breakfast, lunch, and dinner; the bar is a replica of an Edinburgh pub. Sutter Street is tops for art galleries and antiques and specialty shops.

635 Sutter Street, 94102. Tel: 673-9900; in U.S. and Canada, Tel: (800) 533-6533; Fax: 474-0449. $85.

▶ **Beresford Arms**. Under the same management as the above, this is good for families, with kitchens and whirlpools in some of the junior suites.

701 Post Street, 94109. Tel: 673-2600; in U.S. and Canada, Tel: (800) 533-6533; Fax: 474-0449. $85.

Motor Hotels
▶ **Best Western Miyako Inn**. A coffee shop, some in-room Japanese-style steam baths, and balconies make this a popular motor hotel in a quiet Japantown location.

1800 Sutter Street, 94115. Tel: 921-4000; in U.S. and Canada, Tel: (800) 528-1234; Fax: 923-1064. $89–$97.

▶ **Chelsea Motor Inn**. This spot in the Marina has all the essentials, including covered parking; plenty of dining choices are nearby.

2095 Lombard Street, 94123. Tel: 563-5600. $78.

▶ **Cow Hollow Motor Inn and Suites**. Covered parking and some suites make this a good stopover spot; there's an in-house café, **First Watch**, and many fine restaurants in the immediate vicinity.

2190 Lombard Street, 94123. Tel: 921-5800; Fax: 922-8515. $78–$86.

▶ **Vagabond Inn**. A 24-hour café, a small heated pool, a meeting room, and some refrigerators and balconies make this a handy Highway 101 turnoff right in town.

2550 Van Ness Avenue, 94109. Tel: 776-7500 or (800) 522-1555; Fax: 776-5689. $85–$120.

Near the Airport
▶ **Dunfey**. Just ten minutes from SFO on Highway 101, this Tudor-style "castle" provides a soothing alternative to the often-hectic surroundings of airport lodgings. Set in a 12-

ACCOMMODATIONS   149

acre garden, the Dunfey offers a heated swimming pool, courtesy airport shuttle, free parking, **Poppies Restaurant** (California cuisine), and the Planet Lounge.

1770 S. Amphlett Boulevard, San Mateo, 94402. Tel: 573-7661 or (800) THE-OMNI; Fax: 573-0533. $100–$110.

▶ **The San Francisco Airport Hilton.** Right at the airport grounds, this is a very popular overnight stop with pool, restaurant, coffee shop, bar, exercise room, and balconies.

Box 8355, San Francisco Airport, 94128. Tel: 589-0770 or (800) HILTONS; Fax: 589-4696. $165–$181.

▶ **Hyatt Regency.** There are 791 rooms in what is nearer a resort than an airport hotel: heated pool, 24-hour room service and deli, convention facilities, exercise club, sauna, and wet bars; the luxury level is the Regency Club, with a private lounge and concierge assistance.

1333 Bayshore Highway, Burlingame, 94010. Tel: 347-1234; in U.S. and Canada, Tel: (800) 233-1234; Fax: 347-5948. $99–$200.

▶ **Marriott Airport.** An indoor pool with poolside service is an unusual amenity in this fine stopover spot with entertainment, dancing, and exercise room. The luxury floor—the Concierge Level—offers a private lounge, wet bars, and more.

1800 Old Bayshore Highway, Burlingame, 94010. Tel: 692-9100; in U.S. and Canada, Tel: (800) 228-9290; Fax: 692-8016. $179.

▶ **Oyster Point Marina Inn.** This handsome, bayside place resembles an inn rather than an airport hotel. About a seven-minute drive north of the airport off Oyster Point Boulevard from Highway 101, and a 12-minute drive south of San Francisco, it offers the hospitality you would expect from a bed and breakfast. Each guest room has an elevated fireplace and views over the Oyster Point marina. Breakfasts are complimentary, as is the shuttle to and from SFO.

425 Marina Boulevard, South San Francisco, 94080. Tel: 737-7633; Fax: 737-0795. $104–$149.

▶ **Radisson Inn.** A café, dining room, and bar are on the premises, as well as gift shop, exercise room, whirlpool, sauna, and some in-room refrigerators.

275 South Airport Boulevard, South San Francisco, 94080. Tel: 873-3550 or (800) 333-3333; Fax: 873-4524. $89–$110.

▶ **Westin.** Such luxuries as an indoor pool with service, large suites, valet parking, concierge, two restaurants, exercise room, sauna, health-club privileges, and some wet bars are available. The luxury level is the Executive Club, with private lounge and free drinks.

1 Old Bayshore Highway, Millbrae, 94030. Tel: 692-3500 or (800) 228-3000; Fax: 872-8104. $145–$170.

—Bea Pixa and Georgia I. Hesse

DINING

There are few cities more dedicated to dining out than San Francisco, where immigration and a matchless site between the Pacific Ocean and the bountiful San Joaquin Valley have combined to produce a table of astonishing diversity. Stop any two people on the street, according to a recent demographic study, and there's an 84 percent chance that they're from different ethnic groups. San Franciscans hail from every corner of the globe—and take their bread in the styles of Addis Ababa, New Delhi, Beijing, and Paris, to name just a few.

With an Asian community now reckoned at more than a third of the population, San Francisco's strongest culinary suit is the Far East. Its southern Chinese restaurants are surpassed in quality and authenticity only by their rivals in Hong Kong; they are among the more than 1,500 local establishments that represent virtually every food tradition of the Far East. But San Francisco also speaks with a decidedly Italian accent at dinner, and among the city's more notable accomplishments is that creative blending of Mediterranean and New World influences known as California cuisine.

North Beach

For more than a century this sunny enclave between Russian and Telegraph hills has been San Francisco's Little Italy, populated by generations of *emigrati* from Tuscany, Sicily, and Genoa. In the heart of the old neighborhood at 800 Greenwich Street, two blocks north of Washington Square, stands **Buca Giovanni**. The presiding genius in this cozy cellar trattoria is Lucca-born Giovanni Leoni, who makes his own pastas, roasts his own coffee, and even raises his own fresh herbs, vegetables, and rabbits on a Northern California farm. The emphasis is on the light sauces and game specialties of Tuscany; Tel: 776-7766.

When the resolutely unpretentious **Caffè Macaroni** (59 Columbus Avenue near Jackson) first opened in 1991, it served only lunch, was outfitted with only 12 seats, and had a very small kitchen. The crowd was a mix of North Beach community leaders and a few suits from the Financial District. Some months later this winsomely decorated trattoria doubled its capacity by renovating a small mezzanine and then began serving dinner, but the kitchen remains as tiny as ever. The owners hail from southern Italy, and the menu depends upon what they find in the market that morning. Come with cash: this is an old-fashioned establishment; Tel: 956-9737.

Many of North Beach's original restaurants were family-style establishments that delivered large portions of hearty Italian fare at low prices. That tradition continues at the homey **Capp's Corner**, 1600 Powell Street at Vallejo, where a five-course dinner costs less than an entrée at many restaurants. The atmospheric bar, a hangout for longtime residents of the Beach, is a friendly place to pass the time while waiting for a table; Tel: 989-2589.

In recent years thousands of Italian-descended newcomers from South America have emigrated to the Bay Area, introducing their own variations on the basic Italian themes. Among them are Argentines José and Marta Castellucci, who have won an enthusiastic following with grilled, marinated meats and poultry à la Buenos Aires. Indeed, grilled specialties are the whole story at the couple's tiny **Il Pollaio** at 555 Columbus Avenue near Green Street. Right next door in the bright, tile-lined **Castellucci Ristorante**, however, the grill is only the centerpiece of a wider menu. The homemade sausage, served on a bed of garlic-infused greens, is sensational, as are the polenta with Gorgonzola sauce and a full array of fresh pastas; Tel: 362-2774.

For decades Basque shepherds from the California and Nevada hills would spend part of each year in a string of North Beach boardinghouses near the lovely Our Lady of Guadalupe church (no longer open for regular services). Echoes of that world live on at 732 Broadway between Stockton and Powell streets in the charming turn-of-the-century **Des Alpes**, a French-Basque restaurant with a comfortable foyer bar where old gents in their berets still gather to reminisce over a *pastis*. In the adjacent dining room the tables groan under enormous five-course prix-fixe meals that vary daily. Call ahead for the choices, which range from sweetbreads *en croûte* to pan-fried sole and roast lamb; Tel: 391-4249.

In comparison with Des Alpes, **Ernie's** (847 Montgomery Street near Washington) is just a youngster at 60—but an exceptionally high-class one. It serves a contemporary French menu at both lunch and dinner in one of San Francisco's most lavish settings. A three-course bistro menu gives the patron with the slimmer pocketbook an opportunity to sample the kitchen's renowned culinary abilities; Tel: 397-5969.

Lower Broadway was all honky-tonk bars and strip joints until the mid-1980s, when adult videos consigned live burlesque to the historical ash heap. Since then a restaurant boomlet has been under way, with its unlikely leaders in two Afghan immigrants named Mahmood and Wazhma Karzai. Their **Helmand**, at 430 Broadway near Montgomery Street, offers some of the most exotic fare in town, in surroundings so elegantly appointed with Central Asian carpets and furnishings that the modesty of this restaurant's typical dinner check is remarkable; Tel: 362-0641.

Levi Strauss Plaza, a bit out of the way in the eastern shadow of Telegraph Hill, was uncertain ground for restaurants before the 1988 opening of **Il Fornaio**. Overnight this classically designed dining room at 1265 Battery Street was among the city's most popular watering holes, people-watching posts, and northern Italian restaurants. You're likely to see the luminaries of municipal politics and media rubbing shoulders here with visiting actors and corporate tycoons. What draws them is each other, of course—plus an oak-fired brick oven that turns out superb roast meats and pizzas, at surprisingly reasonable prices. There's also a bakery on the premises; Tel: 986-0100.

Across the street from Il Fornaio stands one of the hottest dining tickets in town, the streamlined, low-slung, chrome-covered **Fog City Diner** (1300 Battery at Greenwich). Launched in the mid-1980s to instant success, this stylishly casual diner, the brainstorm of proprietor Bill Higgins and celebrated proprietor-chef Cindy Pawlcyn, continues to draw patrons in numbers that are the envy of every other restaurateur. The fare here is up-to-the-minute American, and the menu of small plates—crab cakes, chili, stuffed pasilla chiles, chicken wings—makes grazing an attractive option. Finish up with a slice of fresh-fruit pie or forget your diet and try an ice cream sundae; Tel: 982-2000.

On the southern slope of Telegraph Hill, at 470 Green near Grant, the pastel quarters of **Maykadeh** are the setting for one of the West's most ambitious Iranian kitchens. Historically, a *maykadeh* was a mix of club and restaurant where the Persian intelligentsia met to enjoy fine food and wine. The tradition is respected here with exquisite shish kebabs, complex braised meats and vegetables, and sauces bound with homemade yogurt. A large Iranian clientele attests to the authenticity of the recipes; Tel: 362-8286.

In a city where seeking out offbeat regional kitchens is a serious pastime, **Albona Ristorante Istriano**, at 545 Francisco near Mason, was bound to be a hit. It serves the cuisine of the Adriatic region of Istria, where Slavic, Venetian, and Austrian recipes mingled. The name refers to the village of Albona (renamed Labin when it passed from Italian to Yugoslav control after World War II). Plump, delicious *crafi albonesi* (dumplings filled with raisins, nuts, and three cheeses) betray the imprint of both Italian raviolis and Slavic *vareniki*. The grilled cod with polenta and the sausage-and-herb-stuffed roast pork loin are also highly recommended; Tel: 441-1040.

At the easternmost end of old North Beach, at 190 Pacific Avenue, where Italian fruit wholesalers once plied their trade (since relocated to the suburbs), sits **Square One**, a handsome, upscale dining room overlooking Walton Square. At the helm of this acclaimed establishment is Joyce Goldstein, author of the celebrated *Back to Square One* and of a regularly changing menu that tends to favor the robust over the refined; Tel: 788-1110.

Notwithstanding its name, Italian classics are the mainstay of one of North Beach's most beloved neighborhood institutions, the decidedly old-fashioned **U.S. Restaurant**. The locals flock to this unpretentious establishment, at 431 Columbus Avenue near Vallejo Street, for the hearty dishes—osso buco, *coteghino* sausage with beans, pasta al pesto—that sustained their ancestors in the Old Country. But this is also the best place for an Italo-American breakfast of eggs, potatoes, and Italian sausages. No credit cards.

Nearby, at 1652 Stockton Street close to Union, is **Moose's**, whose yards of front windows face picturesque Washington Square Park. Named for its gregarious owner Ed Moose, the restaurant draws waves of customers every night, including heavy-hitting media and political types, who come for its fine California fare and self-consciously democratic atmosphere. The menu at both lunch and dinner ranges from appetizers to pastas and pizzas to such filling plates as grilled veal chops. Definitely the "in" spot in North Beach, so reservations are a must; Tel: 989-7800.

Chinatown

The 24 blocks that form the commercial heart of Chinatown are home to nearly 150 restaurants, most of them catering to the tastes of the southern Chinese who are the majority of San Francisco's Asian-descended residents. Although Cantonese is the neighborhood's predominant cuisine, it is far from the sole southern idiom. The modest **Fortune Restaurant**, at 675 Broadway near Stockton Street, features Chao Zhou cuisine, a seafood-based fare from the southern coastal city of Shantou that is regarded as true haute cuisine by the gastronomes of Hong Kong. Three classic Chao Zhou dishes at Fortune will explain why: deep-fried balls of prawn and fish meat wrapped in bean-curd skin; a thin, crisp oyster cake; and *pomfret* showered with garlic and ginger.

Chinatown boasts a vast number of Hong Kong–style barbecue houses; their hallmark is a front window full of roast ducks, poached chickens, and braised squabs. One of the best of the genre, directly across the street from the Fortune at 674 Broadway, is **Hing Lung**, a late-hours, brass-trimmed barbecue-and-noodle house favored by import-export tycoons and kung fu–crazy teens alike. In addition to the duck, they come for roast suckling pig and stir-fried rice noodles.

A clutch of restaurants serving dim sum, the small plates of savories and sweets that the Cantonese take with their midday tea, climbs Pacific Avenue between Grant and Powell. These two blocks boast such respected dim sum palaces as the **Royal Hawaii** and **New Asia**, which serve literally hundreds of plates each morning and afternoon. On weekends the crowds make waiting for a table inevitable.

The comfortable **Pearl City**, 641 Jackson Street near Kearny, harbors a southern Chinese kitchen that produces dishes to please the fussiest Cantonese critics. At noontime, the Pearl City chefs turn their attentions to preparing a full range of dim sum specialties. At the corner of Kearny and Washington is the **R & G Lounge**, which, despite a name that suggests a dimly lit suburban dance club, specializes in Cantonese seafood. You can choose between a simple, walk-down dining room and a fancier (and costlier) shoji screen–lined upstairs space.

In 1988 Shanghai-born Peter Fang decided to buck the southern Chinese tide in Chinatown when he opened the **House of Nanking** at 919 Kearny near Jackson Street. Within no time this simple diner, featuring the vinegar-spiced dishes of Jiangsu Province and neighboring Shanghai, was a smashing success. Fang turns out his Shanghai fried noodles and drunken chicken in a tiny kitchen open to the full view of his admiring diners.

The Union Square Area and Downtown

The skyline of downtown San Francisco has been reshaped dramatically in recent decades, with new hotel towers defining much of the changing picture. One of those towers is the Nikko Hotel (222 Mason near Ellis), whose crowning story houses the exquisite **Benkay** restaurant. In an elegant dining room appointed with small Zen gardens and ebony wood, kimono-clad waitresses carry trays of delicacies as refined as those found in a top Kyoto *ryokan*. The *kaiseki* dinners, elaborate set meals that vary with the season, make for a memorable splurge; Tel: 394-1111.

Among San Francisco's newest seafood restaurants is **Aqua** (252 California near Battery), a spacious dining room painted in fashionably mottled tones of ivory and beige and punctuated with spectacular bouquets. Chef George Morrone prepares a menu that blends the culinary legacies of France and Italy with those of contemporary California. The list changes seasonally, to take advantage of what is best in the market. Morrone's fans are always on the lookout for his mussel soufflé, fragrant with garlic and Chardonnay, and his repertoire of lobster dishes. Prices are consistent with the high quality of the fare; Tel: 956-9662.

Seafood is also featured at **Bentley's** (185 Sutter near Kearny), a stylishly decorated restaurant that serves everything from Hangtown fry, the California Gold Country classic, and crab cakes to fish with a choice of sauces. Oyster aficionados should take a seat at the raw-seafood bar, which serves the mollusks nonstop during the day. There is jazz on weekend evenings, and the popular brunch is sometimes accompanied by rafter-raising gospel music; Tel: 989-6895.

Some may find it too crowded and noisy, but to its legions of loyal fans, **Bistro Roti**, 155 Steuart near Howard inside the Griffon hotel, is the very best place to unwind and dine along the Embarcadero. A large rotisserie grill divides an always-hopping bar area from the quieter tables at the rear, where you can request a seat that overlooks the bay. The food is Paris bistro, but with an assertive American accent. A raw-shellfish bar offers a good selection of sea-fresh oysters; Tel: 495-6500.

When **Campton Place** (340 Stockton Street at Union Square) opened in 1983, it gave San Franciscans the opportunity to explore the considerable riches of the then-ignored American table. Appointed with Wedgwood china and crystal glassware, this smart hotel restaurant continues to be a premier dining room for American regional fare at breakfast, lunch, and dinner. Talented chef Jan Birnbaum, who embellishes traditional recipes with contemporary touches, revises the menu regularly. Campton Place also serves a prix-fixe Sunday supper; Tel: 781-5155.

The earnest exploration of Mexico's rich regional culinary nuances is possible at the **Corona Bar & Grill** at 88 Cyril Magnin Street, off the lobby of the Monticello Inn. The *paella,* loaded with chicken, spicy chorizo sausage, and seafood, is flavored with a medley of herbs and spices that authoritatively distinguishes it from all Spanish antecedents. Corona's chocolate-lined flan makes a rich finish to your meal. At lunch the tables here hum with conspiratorial conversations between editors and the better-paid reporters from the nearby *San Francisco Chronicle* and *Examiner*; Tel: 392-5500.

For months before it opened late in 1990, local restaurant mavens were buzzing about **Cypress Club** (500 Jackson Street at Montgomery). Its creator, John Cunin, who had been the maître d' at the fabled Masa's, promised a unique, no-expense-spared decor and an innovative "American brasserie" menu, and has delivered both. The dining room, with its urn-shaped columns, copper-trimmed archways, bosomlike light fixtures, and overstuffed velvet furnishings, is a decadent—some feel overpoweringly so—spectacle. The menu, similar at lunch and dinner and priced for a special occasion, lists updated regional American classics; Tel: 296-8555.

Fleur de Lys (777 Sutter Street near Jones) is also renowned for its dramatic decor. The late interior designer Michael Taylor draped the seating areas in gorgeous hand-painted fabric, so that the overall effect is of dining inside a luxurious floral tent. Acclaimed chef Hubert Keller, whose teachers included Roger Vergé and Paul Bocuse, creates contemporary French dishes that incorporate the elements of California cuisine. The pricey menu changes regularly but always includes a selection of intricate first courses, intriguing seafood entrées, and meticulously constructed desserts; Tel: 673-7779.

Near the foot of Market Street, at Four Embarcadero Center, the three-piece-suit set crowds the elegant **Harbor Village** at noon for exceptional dim sum. In the evening the cast broadens to embrace lodgers from nearby hotels and families gathered for a special celebration. The branch of a famous Hong Kong restaurant empire, Harbor Village has established an enviable reputation for serving both traditional and nouvelle interpretations of Cantonese cuisine; Tel: 781-8833.

Another popular spot for dim sum is **Yank Sing**, at 49 Stevenson near First Street. This bright, airy restaurant is operated by the Chan family, who pioneered dim sum in Chinatown more than three decades ago. In the past year the Stevenson location has expanded its menu, and today serves one of the most satisfying assortments of dim sum in the city.

Those longing for an afternoon tea break will be well

rewarded by a visit to the **Bread and Honey Tea Room** of the King George Hotel (334 Mason Street between O'Farrell and Geary), which offers traditional British service in a cozy, classically appointed setting. An array of savories and sweets accompanies an interesting selection of fine teas, brewed to meet the expectations of the fussiest British traveller. The refined, art-lined **Compass Rose** at Union Square's St. Francis Hotel also serves a respectable afternoon tea.

Famed California restaurant interior designer Pat Kuleto gave the foyer of his **Kuleto's** the look of an Old San Francisco bar, albeit with a new line of Italian appetizers to sample over drinks. At the rear of the first dining room, an open kitchen turns out northern Italian pastas and grilled meats; farther into the premises is a second, more formal dining room. Located in the Villa Florence at 221 Powell, this sunny Mediterranean restaurant, which serves breakfast, lunch, and dinner, is a great favorite of regular guests at the many hotels around Union Square; Tel: 397-7720.

The city's theater district, which lies just west of Union Square, saw the launching of two hot dining-out tickets in 1992, **City of Paris**, 101 Shannon Alley at Geary, and **La Scene Café & Bar**, 490 Geary at Taylor. The great French bistro tradition thrives at the City of Paris, where a grand cast-iron rotisserie slowly rotates a flock of roasting chickens and the menu lists such Gallic classics as celeriac salad and steak with *pommes frites*. A few steps down the street, the kitchen staff at the sleek, smart La Scene turns out a California-style menu, with strong French, Latin American, Italian, and Asian accents. Both spots are reasonably priced and both stay open to welcome playgoers after the show.

Located about midway between Union Square and the heart of the Financial District, **Le Central**, at 453 Bush Street (near Grant Avenue), presents honest, provincial French fare in a lively bistro setting. The lunchtime crowd usually includes local power brokers deep in conversation over plates of long-simmered *cassoulet,* respectable Alsatian *choucroute garni,* or lightly poached salmon crowned with hollandaise sauce. The dinner hour is less boisterous; Tel: 391-2233.

Two other nearby restaurants ripple with a constant tide of diners at lunchtime and at the dinner hour as well. **Geordy's**, at 1 Tillman Place (off Grant Avenue near Post), is the domain of Geordy Murphy, one-time manager at two celebrated establishments, Kuleto's and PosTrio, who now greets not only the folks who direct empires from the adjoining Financial District towers, but also those who claim the city's most desirable residential addresses. You can join the elite in an urbane, banquette-lined dining room and order from a Mediterranean-inspired menu that changes regularly; Tel: 362-3175. Just down the street at 1 Grant Avenue near Market Street is **Emporio Armani Express**, which occupies the mezzanine of designer Giorgio Armani's high-profile retail outlet. The chef hails from Rome and the food is guaranteed to make every Italian native—and dedicated Italophile—dream of a favorite *ristoranti* across the Atlantic; Tel: 677-9010.

Although it has been around for over a decade, **Masa's** still boasts the most sought-after reservation in San Francisco, with three weeks' advance notice necessary to garner a table. Named for its late founding chef, Masataka Kobayashi, Masa's serves sophisticated French cuisine in the formal dining room of the charming Vintage Court hotel, at 648 Bush near Powell. The kitchen staff, which carries on the highly refined style of its original master, presents exquisitely prepared portions that are as petite as the dinner checks are monumental. This restaurant is arguably the most expensive in the city—and the most highly regarded; Tel: 989-7154.

To most San Francisco natives, going out for a special Sunday brunch has always meant one thing: the buffet at the **Garden Court** of the Sheraton Palace Hotel (Market Street at New Montgomery). Now, following a major renovation that has beautifully restored the historic hotel and its famed glass-ceilinged court, San Franciscans and visitors alike are again flocking to the city's best-known—and most bountiful—Sunday brunch. Reservations are taken for three seatings; the cost reflects the high quality of everything that is served. The Garden Court is also the site of the Palace Hotel's afternoon tea; the pleasantly tart lemon curd should not be overlooked; Tel: 546-5011.

The Sheraton Palace also houses **Kyo-ya**, the outpost of a Japanese restaurant chain and one of San Francisco's finest Asian restaurants. The black-marble sushi counter holds exquisitely fresh fish, much of it flown in daily from Japan and all of it priced for a Tokyo expense account. The adjoining dining area, watched over by kimono-clad waitresses, offers an excellent variety of more moderately priced dishes, from simple fried chicken and tender grilled beef to such exotic fare as freshwater eel with cucumber and salmon roe in sake; Tel: 546-5090.

Although it did not open until 1991, the Ritz-Carlton (Stockton Street at California), like the Sheraton Palace, lays claim to a venerable gastronomic reputation through its connection to the famed Ritz of Paris. You can choose between **The Restau-**

rant and Courtyard, where the dishes marry California and French culinary conventions, and The Dining Room, a dinner-only operation that serves au courant French food. The Restaurant, which is open for breakfast, Sunday jazz brunch, lunch, and dinner, is the more casual and inexpensive of the two locations, although both are quite pricey; Tel: 296-7465.

Dining at Lascaux (248 Sutter near Kearny) is less costly than at the Ritz, and its Mediterranean menu goes perfectly with the atmospheric dining room that recalls the painted caves of Lascaux, France. In one corner a large fireplace blazes invitingly on winter evenings (securing a table near it may require a reservation made days in advance). The appetizers—stuffed squid, cheese *torta*, fried polenta—are difficult to resist, and all of the spit-roasted meats, prepared on a rotisserie open to view, make excellent entrées. Live jazz keeps the place swinging in the evenings; Tel: 391-1555.

At lunchtime, the sleekly modern Palio d'Asti (640 Sacramento near Montgomery) is filled with the suit-and-briefcase crowd closing deals between bites of Gorgonzola-sauced pasta, pizza Margherita, or a grilled veal chop. Named for the medieval bareback horse race run in the Piemontese town of Asti, owner Gianni Fassio's ancestral home, the restaurant has all of its culinary hardware on display: an imposing wood-burning pizza oven, a glassed-in pasta kitchen, a magnificent chrome pasta machine, a grill area, and carts loaded with antipasti. Come evening, Palio d'Asti attracts a more eclectic crowd to its tables and its comfortable bar area; Tel: 395-9800.

Silks, the gracious dining room of the Mandarin Oriental (222 Sansome near Pine), likewise attracts a noontime business clientele. Here they enjoy East-West cuisine created by consultant Ken Hom, a world-renowned author and chef, in concert with the hotel's executive chef, Michele Sampson. This accomplished pair has introduced such imaginative fare as spring rolls filled with chicken, bean thread noodles, and sun-dried tomatoes, and grilled prawns crowned with Asian pesto. The service at Silks is top drawer; the dinner checks reflect the high standards maintained in both the kitchen and dining room; Tel: 986-2020.

Chef Wolfgang Puck, creator of the now-legendary Spago in Los Angeles and Chinois in Santa Monica, carried his vision of California cuisine north to the Prescott Hotel in downtown San Francisco in 1989, and the city's movers and shakers immediately began lining up for breakfast, lunch, and dinner at his chic, palm-lined PosTrio at 545 Post near Mason Street. The menu matches the finest local products—

Sonoma County lamb, Dungeness crab, Sacramento Delta vegetables—with Mediterranean culinary traditions; Tel: 776-7825.

At the opposite end of the San Francisco restaurant timeline is **Tadich Grill**, the city's oldest, which was started during the Gold Rush by three southern European immigrants as a coffee stand for sailors dropping anchor in Yerba Buena Harbor. In its turn-of-the-century grill room at 240 California Street (near Battery Street), Financial District heavy hitters regularly line up for seats at the long counter or in one of the polished walnut booths. The main attraction is seafood prepared by the Buich family, who have overseen the operation since 1929. In keeping with its old-fashioned ways, Tadich takes no reservations and accepts no credit cards.

Sam's Grill, 374 Bush Street near Kearny, is another of San Francisco's legendary seafood restaurants. Like Tadich, it caters to the bankers-and-brokers set, who favor its simple preparations of local seafood and air-shipped East Coast shellfish. A no-reservations policy has Sam's loyal patrons queuing up a full 30 minutes before the noon whistle to nab a table in the comfortably clubby dining room, complete with curtained booths. Open weekdays only, the restaurant closes in the early evening.

In 1988 the owners of Wu Kong, one of the most successful restaurants in restaurant-crazy Hong Kong, opened a San Francisco branch of their **Wu Kong** in the Rincon Center (101 Spear Street near Mission Street), a beautifully renovated historical site famed for its extraordinary Art Deco murals. The menu features the regional specialties of Shanghai, the lower Yangtze Valley, and the North China plain, all served in a spacious, chandeliered dining room. Among the marvelous dishes of its Hong Kong- and Shanghai-trained chefs are a vegetarian "goose" composed of bean-curd sheets and mushrooms, velvety braised pork shoulder atop a bed of spinach, and the juicy pork-filled steamed buns called *xiao long bao* (little dragon packets); Tel: 957-9300.

At a time when many new Italian restaurants are focusing on a single Italian region, the stylish **Etrusca**, another Rincon Center tenant, is focusing on a civilization. The masterminds of this stunning two-level space spent months doing research in Italian museums to arrive at a menu featuring dishes of the ancient Etruscans, updated to meet contemporary tastes. (The culinary modernization is most evident in tomato sauces, since the love apple didn't hit the Mediterranean shores until long after the demise of Etruscan nobility.)

The large, open kitchen has at its center a monumental wood-burning oven, the walls are sheathed in yards of bird's-eye maple, mahogany, and marble, and the ceilings are painted with sublime frescoes; Tel: 777-0330.

In early 1993, chef and cookbook author Bradley Ogden, arguably the San Francisco Bay Area's most accomplished interpreter of new American cuisine, opened **One Market Restaurant** (1 Market at Steuart). It was an overnight success, with lunch and dinner reservations as hard to come by as an invitation to the White House. Part of its local allure is that it caters to nearly every hunger whim: a power lunch at noon, an afternoon snack in the bar, a relaxed dinner in the evening, a bountiful brunch on Sunday. Ogden still features American flavors, but has given some of his dishes a decidedly European spin; Tel: 777-5577.

Civic Center and the Van Ness Corridor

Brazil fever hit the Bay Area in the late 1980s in a wave of dance fads, *Carnaval* celebrations, and restaurants. At its crest is **Bahía**, ensconced in two Franklin Street buildings not far from the staid corridors of City Hall. One serves as a nightclub (Franklin at Market), the other as a dinner house (41 Franklin), and both draw large numbers of the under-35 set who have fueled the fever. Named for the city that has Brazil's liveliest Luso-African cultural scene, Bahía offers a menu full of allusions to the Creole tradition, whether you order chicken and cashews in a yucca sauce or roast pork stuffed with vegetables, bacon, and olives. The nightclub down the block may seem quiet if you pass by on your way to an early dinner; it won't if you take another look after 10:00 P.M.; Tel: 626-3306.

In 1984 Ann Harris, wife of California beef king Jack Harris, opened **Harris'**, 2100 Van Ness at Pacific Avenue, reintroducing steak-house gentility to a San Francisco that was ready for just such a traditionalist revival. In a dining room outfitted with leather booths and paneled in rich woods, a first-rate staff serves the finest dry-aged beef the state has to offer. The expertly grilled steaks can be accompanied with deep-fried onion rings, garnished baked potatoes, and creamed spinach, or with plain steamed potatoes and unadorned vegetables for waistline-watchers; Tel: 673-1888.

The **Hayes Street Grill**, at 320 Hayes, was the first upscale dining option to take root within a short stroll of the city's Performing Arts Center. Simplicity is its menu's defining characteristic. Each day about a dozen fresh-fish selections appear on the blackboard; your choice is grilled and then served with an array of sauces that may range from the classic béarnaise to an innovative Southeast Asian creation. The Grill's owners also run **Vicolo Pizzeria** at 201 Ivy Street, directly behind the restaurant, where California-style pizza and calzone are served; Tel: 863-5545.

Located at 1122 Post Street near Van Ness, half a dozen blocks north of the Civic Center proper, **Maharani** is one of the city's most popular Indian restaurants. Its Punjabi cooks are especially adept at the subcontinent's northern dishes, turning out outstanding examples of tandoori meats and breads; but, this being California, they are also more than willing to vary the tandoori formula with such distinctly un-Punjabi items as salmon and prawns. There is a conventional front room, nicely appointed to meet middlebrow tastes, and a back room done up in Mogul-style booths lined with pillows and hung with veils; Tel: 775-1988.

Miss Pearl's Jam House (601 Eddy Street at Larkin) offers West Indian food with a California-cuisine twist. The young, sometimes boisterous crowd that packs this lively bar and restaurant in the evenings is infatuated with the cross-cultural results, served in small plates that add up to a Caribbean version of Spanish tapas. The menu has some 30 choices, from Jamaican jerk chicken to deep-fried catfish. At lunch on sunny days you can eat alongside the swimming pool; Tel: 775-5267. Miss Pearl's is adjacent to ▶ **The Phoenix**, once a ticky-tacky motel that has since become a trendy downtown inn decorated in the pastel mode of Malibu; Tel: 776-1380.

The Civic Center area borders on the Tenderloin District, where thousands of Indo-Chinese refugees have settled; they're responsible for the scores of Southeast Asian restaurants that line the surrounding blocks of the Van Ness corridor. **Pacific Restaurant** (607 Larkin at Eddy) is the best of many neighborhood restaurants specializing in the Hanoi-style dish called *pho*—a fragrant broth filled with rice noodles and beef, in the form of thin, rare slices, well-cooked brisket, tripe, or meatballs. The huge bowls arrive with a plate of raw bean sprouts, coriander, green chiles, and lemon wedges, to be added as desired. It will set you back half the price of a movie ticket.

A second great spot for Asian noodles is the tiny Cambodian-run **Angkor Café**, close by at 637 Larkin. During the lunch hour, civil servants from nearby office buildings pack this bright storefront, where they fill up on soups thick with rice noodles and meats or seafood or on generous orders of stir-fried noodles. A variety of chile sauces is provided for those who want a splash of heat.

Spuntino, 524 Van Ness near McAllister Street, is a *tavola calda*—an Italian fast-food spot—the ideal place for a quick pizza, *panini,* or pasta before settling in for an evening of Verdi across the street. The routine is streamlined: Make a choice, order at the counter, and take a seat. Your brick oven–cooked pizza Margherita will be delivered in no time at all.

Jeremiah Tower, one of the granddaddies of California cuisine, wore the top toque at a number of Bay Area restaurants before opening his own phenomenally popular **Stars**, at 150 Redwood Alley (between McAllister and Golden Gate near Polk Street) in 1984. This is a place to see and to be seen, a hangout for society matrons and rising politicos, accomplished tenors and incurable foodies. You can join them in a pricey full dinner, a more proletarian house-made hot dog with sauerkraut, or a plate of raw oysters; both the food and the experience will be memorable; Tel: 861-7827.

Just next door is **Stars Café**, a sister operation where the menu is smaller and the prices are, too. The light fry—a mountain of fresh seafood and potatoes—is a favorite with City Hall bureaucrats out for an affordable lunch. The scrumptious desserts are big enough to share. Take a seat at the counter to avoid a long wait for one of the coveted tables.

Also within earshot of the Performing Arts Center is **Thepin** (298 Gough Street at Fell), named for the elaborately carved staff carried by a revered Thai deity. The small, handsome dining room, ringed with intricate Thai artworks, is the place to sample a rainbow of curries, grilled meats infused with spices, and soups built on fresh herb bouquets. For dessert, try the delicate banana leaf–wrapped custard. Thepin's large, well-selected wine list is a rare find in an Asian restaurant; Tel: 863-9335.

Zuni Café, a landmark of California cuisine, stands several blocks southwest of City Hall at 1658 Market Street near Franklin. In an inviting setting of white walls, a long copper bar, and snowy table linens, chef Judy Rodgers steers the kitchen on a creative course through Italy and southern France, using the finest fresh ingredients of Northern California. Her menu crosses the traditional culinary boundaries with great sophistication, offering assortments of the freshest shellfish, pizza topped with oil-cured olives and anchovies, and sausage with creamy polenta. You can start your day here with breakfast, or stop by at noon for a Gorgonzola-crowned hamburger and some of the best *pommes frites* in the city. Reservations are *de rigueur* for the dinner hour; Tel: 552-2522.

The Mission and South of Market

San Francisco's Hispanic soul resides in the busy, colorful streets of the Mission District. Fueled by more than a decade of unrest in Central America, the city's Salvadoran population has grown steadily through the 1980s and into the 1990s, as have the numbers of Salvadoran restaurants in this colorful neighborhood. One of the most popular of these establishments is **El Zocalo**, located at 3230 Mission Street near Valencia. This lively, plain-Jane storefront is legendary in the neighborhood for its *pupusas,* griddle-fried cornmeal rounds stuffed with cheese and/or pork that are the Salvadorean answer to the American burger. Accompany them with a platter of beans, fried plantains, and thick cream for a full meal that is surprisingly kind to the budget. No credit cards.

In recent years, the small Peruvian community in San Francisco has grown, as new immigrants have arrived from South America. The best place to sample the cuisine of these Andean natives is **Fina Estampa**, located in a small, inviting storefront at 2374 Mission near 20th Street. The country's most renowned dishes—*anticuchos, pariheula de mariscos, lomo saltado*—are all prepared with culinary finesse by the Peruvian-born chef, whose ancestors, like those of President Fujimori, hailed from Japan. Be forewarned: The chile sauce that accompanies every meal is pure dynamite.

Twenty-fourth Street, between Mission and Potrero, is not only the liveliest stretch of the barrio, but also offers some of its most serious eating. **La Victoria**, at the corner of 24th Street and Alabama, is a combination Mexican bakery and restaurant. Breads and sweets are sold inside the 24th Street entrance, and full meals are served in the dining room located at the back, reached through an Alabama Street door. Longtime customers swear by the *birria* (goat stew) and *chiles rellenos.* This is a cash-only operation.

For decades Jaliscan-born Josie Reyes and her sister Margarita ran a small diner in the Mission, where they were among the neighborhood's most popular restaurateurs. In late 1988 they launched **Los Jarritos**, 901 South Van Ness at 20th Street, decorating the cheerful dining room with hundreds of the tiny earthenware cups (*jarritos*) that Jaliscan men traditionally use for tequila. The sisters offer a full menu of Mexican classics, from *carnitas* garnished with onion, tomatoes, and fresh coriander to *carne asada* piled high on a pair of handmade corn tortillas. No credit cards.

Nicaraguans dine seven days a week at 3015 Mission near 26th Street, where the simply decorated **Nicaragua Restaurant** specializes in the dishes of their homeland. Two versions of the Mesoamerican tamale are served here: the feather-light *yoltamal* of pure cornmeal (almost a soufflé) and the *nacatamal* stuffed with seasoned shredded beef. There are fried plantains and cream, steamed yucca crowned with crisp *chiccharones,* and whole fried Pacific snapper. The menu even includes a list of traditional drinks, from *pozol* (hominy and milk) to tamarind, and the jukebox pulses with a steady Latin beat. No credit cards.

The brightly lit, practically furnished **Taquería San José**, 2830 Mission at 24th Street, turns out a true taco—not the mass-produced version found in shopping malls, but a pair of soft corn tortillas stacked with grilled beef, pork, or a variety meat—tongue, head, brains—and fresh chile-laden salsa. The package is expanded to burrito form with a large flour tortilla, beans, and rice.

The straightforward Latin food of the Mission barrio is in stark contrast to that of the adjoining SoMa (South of Market) neighborhood, where restaurant trends (and clichés) define the landscape. Attracting a mostly young, professional crowd, the low-rise district regularly sprouts new restaurants and just as regularly sees them close. One of the most dependable establishments in this constantly changing dining scene is the **South Park Café**, 108 South Park Avenue on the north side of a small square in what was once a neighborhood of stately Victorian mansions. Most of the grand homes long ago gave way to light industrial buildings, which have subsequently been converted to office space. At lunchtime and in the evenings, workers from these surrounding structures—and French-food lovers from all over town—fill South Park Café's charmingly Gallic dining room to feast on grilled *boudin* accompanied with sautéed apples and thin, crisp *pommes frites.* A rack of French newspapers and the occasional French-speaking waiter add to the overall Parisian ambience; Tel: 495-7275.

Directly across the park, **Ristorante Ecco** (101 South Park Avenue), which shares two partners with South Park Café and the same beguiling spirit, serves an array of inspired Italian dishes that draws a steady stream of regulars to its attractive, airy dining room. A window-lined façade looks out on the park and a skylit atrium brightens the often-packed bar. For dinner order the *antipasto misto* and the osso buco if they are listed on the changing menu; lunchtime brings a selection of sandwiches and pizzas in addition to more substantial fare; Tel: 495-3291.

French food is on *la carte* at **Fringale** (570 Fourth Street near Brannan), where big windows, off-white walls, and wooden wainscoting create an upbeat bistro atmosphere for a generally upmarket crowd. Chef Gerald Hirigoyen, a son of the French Basque region, prepares the classic dishes of his home, often enhanced by contemporary culinary flourishes and always pegged at moderate prices. A delicious entrée of chicken breast with an aromatic *coulis* of tomatoes and onions, which appears on both the lunch and dinner menus, and an appetizer of puff pastry encasing garlicky escargots are just two of chef Hirigoyen's kitchen masterpieces. Regulars know to leave room for dessert; the chocolate creations are irresistible; Tel: 543-0573.

SoMa diners are also flocking to **Garibaldi Goes South** (798 Brannan at Seventh Street) for grilled *ahi*–filled tacos and cheese-stuffed *pasilla* peppers. The food is Latin American with a thick north-of-the-border accent, and the prices are easy on the pocketbook. At lunchtime workers from nearby Showplace Square, the city's wholesale home-furnishings headquarters, pack the cheery dining room; at night the customers are a more diverse mix of Latin-food aficionados.

The sunny foods of the Italian and French Rivieras top the tables at the wildly popular **Lulu** (816 Folsom near Fourth Street). The stunning vaulted-ceilinged space, a renovated 1910 warehouse just south of the Moscone Convention Center, holds an outsized wood-burning *forno* that executive chef Reed Hearon fires up for everything from pizzas to Dungeness crab. Hearon's legions of fans know to order his iron skillet-roasted mussels and his rotisserie-roasted pork loin with fennel. Dishes are served family-style on large platters placed in the center of the table, so if you want the pork loin all to yourself, let the waiter know. With Lulu's success has come front-door gridlock, making reservations essential; Tel: 495-5775.

For a more modest meal of pasta or a hearty entrée of lamb shanks and white beans, head for the wonderfully offbeat **Limbo**, at the corner of Ninth and Folsom streets. This is where the heavies of the large, very active SoMa arts community sit down to lunch and dinner. Join them and contribute to a good cause at the same time: Half of the restaurant's receipts go to Artspace, a gallery featuring Bay Area talent that is located right next door. The Limbo chefs also turn out a superb burger-and-fries platter—easily one of the best in the city.

Around the corner in a handsomely restored Victorian house at 1261 Folsom stands **Appam**, an outpost of the *dum pukht* cooking of India's Mogul north. In this method, food—everything from fish curry to stuffed quail—is packed into a special clay pot with a lid, the seam is sealed with dough, the pot is placed in a wood-fired double-walled oven, and the food essentially steams in the vessel. Appam's culinary riches also include various tandoor preparations, breads, and curries. A delightful garden at the rear of the dining room is a lovely setting for lunch on sunny days; Tel: 626-2798.

Lower Haight and Japantown

Tucked away in the southern reaches of the Western Addition, in the revitalized Lower Haight neighborhood, the **Indian Oven**, 237 Fillmore near Haight Street, delivers a fresh perspective on the food of the subcontinent. Flanked by a tandoor and an ebony grand, a mostly young crowd dines on specialties from Kerala and Mysore, the Punjab and Goa. The kitchen has a real flair for contemporary interpretations, such as goat cheese–stuffed peppers. Parsi-style chicken with potato straws and apricots and a tandoor-cooked rack of lamb are just two of the superb classics offered here; Tel: 626-1628.

Just down the block at the corner of Fillmore and Waller reigns one of Thai cuisine's finest local outposts: **Thep Phanom**. Maintaining this enviable reputation almost since the day it opened in 1986, Thep Phanom's intimate, attractive dining room is full every night of the week, with a waiting line curving out the door. The *kaeng ped,* served in lovely blue-and-white bowls, combines roast duck in a rich curry enlivened with fresh Asian basil leaves. Try the flavorful coconut-based soups, barbecued meats, or banana leaf–wrapped grilled fish; Tel: 431-2526.

A cross section of Japanese dining can be enjoyed at a single site in the city, a two-story complex in Japantown (Nihonmachi). Called the Japan Center, it houses exactly the sorts of places that are found all over Japan. Located on the center's first floor, **Mifune**, a branch of a well-known Osaka restaurant, dishes up huge portions of house-made buckwheat *soba* and spaghetti-like *udon* noodles, served hot or cold in some two dozen combinations.

The bright and cheery **Izumiya**, on the second floor of the center, features *okonomiyaki,* a hearty grilled "pancake" filled with vegetables and meats or seafood that has its origins in Osaka. In Japan, customers cook their own pancakes at individual grills, but at Izumiya the chef does all the work on a large, shiny grill visible to diners. Steps away from Izumiya, at a tiny *sushi-ya* called **Kame-sushi**, a husband-and-wife team oversee an eight-seat counter topped by a glass case filled with some of the freshest, finest raw fish in town.

Fine seafood is also the draw at the Miyako Hotel's **Elka** restaurant (1611 Post at Laguna), where chef Elka Gilmore introduced a unique East–West menu in 1992. Within weeks of opening, Gilmore was flooded with accolades from even the most hardhearted restaurant mavens and there wasn't an empty chair in the brightly painted, seriously stylish dining room. Her innovative evening plates—chilled buckwheat noodles with caviar, lobsters and sweetbreads in lemon vinaigrette, deep-fried whole catfish, coriander seed–encrusted seared ahi tuna—deliver quality and flair at special-occasion prices. The kitchen serves both Japanese and Western breakfasts and a lunch menu with the same Japanese-Californian style that marks the nighttime fare; Tel: 922-7788.

North of Japantown, at 1915 Fillmore Street near Bush, is **Oritalia**, where the name says it all: one-half Orient, one-half Italy. The menu backs up the claim with such wildly innovative dishes as linguine with Japanese *unagi* (eel), and sweet potato topped with *crème fraîche* and flying-fish roe. A very contemporary decor of faux marble, abstract art, and shining brass fixtures reflects owner Nori Yoshida's experimental spirit; Tel: 346-1333.

A kindred spirit resides at **Rasselas**, 2801 California at Divisadero Street, thanks to the top-flight jazz musicians who perform in its lounge. The dining room, by contrast, is a decidedly traditional haven for the cuisine of Rasselas's Ethiopian proprietors. Spicy vegetarian dishes and braised meats arrive atop a large round of *injera,* the soft, almost spongy national bread that doubles as plate and silverware. Accompany the meal with a bottle of honey-based Ethiopian wine; Tel: 567-5010.

Tradition also rules the kitchen at **Suppers** (1800 Fillmore at Sutter), where the classics of American cuisine are prepared, including such old-fashioned plates as barbecued brisket and hominy grits, pot roast with mashed potatoes, and Virginia ham with biscuits and cream gravy. Die-hard traditionalists may find the refined food and the ascetically appointed decor too dandified to be authentically American, but everyone else will be pleased with the kitchen's culinary innovations; Tel: 474-3773.

Near Golden Gate Park

In the 1980s the broad boulevards and avenues north of Golden Gate Park—Clement, Geary, and others in the Richmond district—blossomed with scores of new restaurants, many of them serving the cuisines of the neighborhood's large and growing Asian-American population. One clear sign of this demographic trend was a mushrooming of *bulkogi-jips,* dinner houses that grill spicy Korean meat dishes right at the diners' charcoal pit–equipped tables. A fine example is the **Kyung Bok Palace** at 6314 Geary near 27th Avenue, set a mite incongruously in the shadow of the onion-domed Russian Orthodox cathedral (Soviet emigrés have also settled here in large numbers). Along with grilled meats, Kyung Bok provides an unusually ample spread of *kim chee,* the small plates of prepared vegetables and seafood that accompany every Korean meal. This is fiery stuff, not the choice for those with second thoughts about the merits of the chile pepper.

The noise that you hear coming from the kitchen of **Happy Family** (3809 Geary near Second Avenue) may well just be the chef hard at work making one of the great mysteries of China, *la mian.* These are hand-pulled noodles in which a ball of dough is slapped against a tabletop, twisted, and pulled until it magically self-separates into a perfectly uniform skein. This dish's source is the highly sophisticated Chinese school of Shandong, which sent chefs to the imperial kitchens of Beijing for centuries. The noodles are delicious in seafood soup or tossed with a variety of ingredients, from a thick, rich plum sauce to a spicy Szechwan mixture. Be sure also to order a plate of Happy Family's plump boiled dumplings—*shiu jiao*—stuffed with shrimp or pork.

Hong Kong Flower Lounge arrived in the Bay Area as the American cousin of a multibranched Hong Kong restaurant family; today, with two locations near the San Francisco International Airport and a third at 5322 Geary near 17th Avenue, the cousin is raising quite a clan of its own. Its hallmark is seafood, with great importance attached to preparations that do not disguise the natural flavors of ingredients. Its steamed fish, poached prawns, and stir-fried Dungeness crabs will transform the perspective of anyone who thinks Cantonese food means sweet-and-sour pork; Tel: 668-8998 or 878-8108.

Ten blocks farther out Geary stands the **Mayflower** (6255 Geary at 27th Avenue), yet another excellent Cantonese restaurant. It is owned in part by former employees of the celebrated Hong Kong Flower Lounge, so it comes as no surprise that the food, especially the signature seafood dishes, is strikingly similar. The dim sum lunch is popular, with a line forming even before the clock strikes noon; Tel: 387-8338.

Although the food at **La Bergerie** (4221 Geary near Sixth Avenue) is as French as the tricolor, the accomplished *chef-de-cuisine* is Cambodian-born Andy Try. The dining room looks as if it was carried whole from a provincial French town, and so does the menu: sweetbreads in Madeira sauce, entrecôte with three-peppercorn sauce, roast rack of lamb. You'll know that you are not in France when the check arrives, however; La Bergerie offers superb four-course prix-fixe dinners at truly bargain prices; Tel: 387-3573.

Before the Avenues were Asian, they were heavily Irish—and as far as the pub culture goes, they still are. **Pat O'Shea's Mad Hatter** is an immensely popular example, crammed nightly with fans of World Cup soccer and Guinness stout. The kitchen staff satisfies hearty appetites hungering for strictly American beef stew and meatloaf.

Burmese food was put on the San Francisco map by **Mandalay**, 4348 California Street near Fifth Avenue, which converted the former stage space of the Asian-American Theater into a quiet, art-lined dining room. The national dishes of Burma, *panthe kaukswe* and *mohinga* (respectively a chicken curry with rice noodles and a rich fresh-water fish soup), both come off handsomely here, as do a number of highly unusual salads that combine such ingredients as fresh ginger, tea leaves, ground nuts, dried shrimp, and tropical herbs; Tel: 386-3895.

Almost everywhere in Southeast Asia, ethnic Chinese are the chief restaurateurs, serving both indigenous and Chinese dishes. **Narai**, 2229 Clement near 23rd Avenue, is in that sense one of the most authentic Thai restaurants you'll ever patronize, because it offers both Thai and Chao Zhou Chinese dishes. In the former category, its chefs excel at a tart and chile-laden squid salad, an equally spritely noodle-and-shrimp salad, and a clay pot of fresh mussels cooked in a lemongrass-scented broth. The Chao Zhou braised duck, served at room temperature with a vinegar-and-garlic dip, is worth twice the modest price it fetches; Tel: 751-6363.

The chef at the **Straits Café** (3300 Geary near Commonwealth Avenue) is a Nonya, a scion of a fascinating culture on the Malacca Strait that blends Malay and Chinese influences. In her San Francisco kitchen, the possibilities—which in

Singapore or Penang may run to hundreds of dishes—have been narrowed to a couple of dozen, but they are executed to perfection. Highlights include *otak-otak* (fish mousse steamed in banana leaves), a searing coconut noodle soup called *laksa,* and green beans sautéed with a mixture of garlic, chiles, and shallots. The decor is also a creative mixture of California chic and Southeast Asian shophouse; Tel: 668-1783.

Of the six Chinese cuisines represented in these selections, Hakka is probably the least known outside of Asia. The term *hakka* translates as "guest" and refers to a once-nomadic people who wandered into southern China centuries ago. The Wongs, proprietors of **Ton Kiang**, wandered into the Bay Area in the late 1960s, eventually making one Hakka dish—salt-baked chicken—so popular that it has nearly become a San Francisco mainstay. The restaurant has two locations, at 3148 Geary near Spruce and a newer, fancier space at 5821 Geary nead 22nd Avenue. Both offer superb stuffed bean curd, an array of unusual wine-flavored dishes, and, at the latter location only, an exquisite assortment of dim sum.

The culinary heritage of the fertile Tigris-Euphrates river valley is showcased at the charming **Yaya Cuisine** (1220 Ninth Avenue at Lincoln south of Golden Gate Park). Iraqi-born chef Yahya Salih offers an extraordinary selection of reasonably priced dishes, each of them based on a classic preparation of his homeland and all of them influenced by his years of working in California restaurant kitchens. The dining room is done in warm sand tones with brilliant-blue details; a mural of ancient Babylon covers one wall; Tel: 566-6966.

The Marina and Cow Hollow
After a walk along the yacht-filled harbor that gives this district its name, health-conscious strollers can head right into America's best-known vegetarian restaurant. Founded and run by the San Francisco Zen Center, **Greens** is to the meatless meal what wine is to grape juice. In a spacious former army-transport pier shed at Fort Mason, diners sit before enormous windows that yield a spectacular view of the Golden Gate Bridge and Sausalito. The accent is California cuisine, and among the things that bring diners back again and again—whatever their attitudes on meat—are small pizzas from a wood-fired oven, pastas, and mesquite-grilled tofu brochettes. On weekends, five-course prix-fixe dinners are served; reserve well in advance; Tel: 771-6222.

It's entirely likely that there are as many Cambodian restaurants in the Bay Area as there are in Phnom Penh—about a dozen at last count, from Berkeley to San Jose. At **Angkor Palace**, located in the heart of the motel strip at 1769 Lombard near Laguna Street, diners can recline like royalty on pillow-strewn banquettes. Freshwater fish, caught in the great lake known as Tonle Sap, are the glory of the Cambodian table; at Angkor Palace, Sacramento Delta catfish fill the role with delicious results. Pork sautéed with banana blossoms and black mushrooms is also sensational; Tel: 931-2830.

Izzy's Steak & Chop House, 3345 Steiner near Chestnut Street, is all-American, from the vintage advertising art that covers its walls to the old-fashioned creamed spinach and scalloped potatoes that arrive on its plates. The big draw here is beefsteaks, especially thick New York strips. You can sauce them up from a choice of literally hundreds of prepared condiments. For those who don't want beef there are pork and lamb chops, plus grilled chicken breast and fish fillet. The name Izzy, by the way, refers to the famous old Pacific Street barkeep, Izzy Gomez, whose history is told in newspaper clippings displayed in the restaurant; Tel: 563-0487.

At **Pane e Vino** (3011 Steiner near Union), chef Claudio Marchesan, a native of the Veneto's Friuli region, tempts customers with half a dozen daily blackboard specials in addition to his regular menu of antipasti, pastas, and grilled dishes. This cozy trattoria attracted a loyal band of followers within weeks of opening in the spring of 1991, and the crowds haven't diminished. Such solid success can be attributed to Marchesan's commitment to hearty portions of authentic Italian fare at moderate prices served in a truly *simpatica* atmosphere; Tel: 346-2111.

Chestnut Street is the heart of the Marina, six blocks of family-run shops, markets, restaurants, and delis that evoke the Italian origins of many of the district's residents. **La Pergola**, 2060 Chestnut near Steiner Street, stakes its claim to their allegiance with a chef whose own origins lie on the shores of Lake Garda, west of Venice. His *mezza luna* (half-moon-shaped raviolis stuffed with squash and served in a butter-and-sage sauce) are cogent reminders of the traditional northern Italian menu's delicacy. A more creative touch goes into his superb risotto with smoked salmon, when it's available; the menu changes frequently; Tel: 563-4500.

Tucked away in the small, elegant Italianate-baroque **Sherman House** hotel (2160 Green Street near Fillmore) is an equally small, elegant dining room, complete with marble fireplace, fresh flowers, and candlelight. Talented chef Donia

Bijan, who blends classic France preparations with touches from her native Iran, offers a five-course prix-fixe menu and à la carte selections, all priced for a special occasion. The solarium just off the dining room is perfect for lunch on a sunny day; Tel: 563-3600.

In the mid-1980s Cow Hollow's **Balboa Café** (3199 Fillmore Street near Union Street) and **Perry's** (1944 Union Street near Buchanan) were among San Francisco's strongest magnets for the faddish singles set. On Friday and Saturday nights hundreds of young doctors, lawyers, and MBAs would squeeze into these bar/restaurants to meet and mix with their fellow professionals. Except for a highly touted hamburger served at the Balboa (created by the café's then chef, the now-famous Jeremiah Tower), little attention was paid to the American saloon–style fare turned out at either establishment. Today, although the crowds have thinned somewhat, both the Balboa Café and Perry's remain popular, albeit still more for their social opportunities than for their culinary efforts.

The Fisherman's Wharf area, which includes The Cannery and Ghirardelli Square complexes, is east along the water from the Marina. Most of the dining here is restricted to restaurants geared to visitors, although the appearance of **McCormick & Kuleto's**, a seafood house that opened in Ghirardelli Square in 1991, has improved the dining scene here somewhat. It attracts locals as well as out-of-towners partly because it boasts what is arguably one of the best views of any dining room in the city. The restaurant has the feel of Old San Francisco, and the menu, which changes daily, offers up to three dozen fish and shellfish items— from just-caught bass to the wharf's famous Dungeness crab. Stick with the simpler preparations for the best meal. Call ahead to reserve a front-row table overlooking the vast blue bay or, for a fast, light meal, take a seat in the comfortable bar area and enjoy a bowl of clam chowder or a plate of oysters on the half shell; Tel: 929-1730.

—*Sharon Silva*

BARS AND NIGHTLIFE

Ever since the gold seekers and fortune hunters rushed here to get rich in 1849, San Francisco has been a good-time, boisterous town. The combination of newfound wealth, customs from around the world, and geographical isolation created an unmatched diversity of entertainment and nightlife. What other city prohibited local police from entering gambling saloons or brothels after sunset?

But the nightlife slowed in the late 1970s, the culmination of a trend that started after World War II, which brought a new aura of respectability to the city in tandem with the pervasive influence of television. And perhaps people needed a rest from the turbulent 1960s and early 1970s. But since the SoMa (South of Market) nighttime scene began in the mid-1980s, and with the recovery of Haight-Ashbury, the San Francisco nightlife tradition has been rediscovered and is again roaring with a wide variety of entertainment—from a club where three live bands play simultaneously in different rooms to bars and restaurants resembling everything from a Caribbean jungle to Casablanca in 1941 to medieval Russia to a 1930s speakeasy.

There are five major areas of nightlife activity in San Francisco—North Beach, South of Market, Downtown, Cow Hollow, and the Haight—where you can visit a comedy or jazz club, go to the theater, check out a gay club, or have a late-night meal. And for those who want something more refined, San Francisco is dedicated to romance.

North Beach

The heart and soul of nighttime San Francisco is North Beach. For more than a decade it shook a world that for the most part only wanted it to go away. Back in the elsewhere-sanitized 1950s, the Beats (Jack Kerouac, Allen Ginsberg, Neal Cassady, Gregory Corso, Lawrence Ferlinghetti, et al.) deliberately dropped out of the success track to explore the unexplored. Donning black garments, smoking marijuana, and saying "weird" things ("Look me in the eye." "Which I?"), they sparked a cultural renaissance. Nightclubs featured Lenny Bruce and Mort Sahl, who were called Communists because they dared to say something different. Artists flocked to San Francisco, and, on October 13, 1955, when Ginsberg read his soon-to-be-famous *Howl,* San Francisco's reputation as the "Left Bank of the West" was affirmed. By the next year the authorities were punishing these same people; lawsuits proliferated, and *Howl* was judged obscene. But the movement could not be stopped; the free-thinking Beats had laid the groundwork for the Summer of Love and the student protests that eventually affected the entire world.

By the early 1960s, however, the spotlight in North Beach was on breasts, as topless dancing on the Broadway strip became the latest rage—not surprisingly, because North Beach had always had a racy past. (This is where the

Barbary Coast originated, and terms such as "to shanghai," "hoodlum," and "Mickey Finn"—named after a disreputable pharmacist—were coined.)

North Beach has mellowed a little today, but there are still plenty of cafés and some of the best bars in the city to keep it vibrant. Moreover, North Beach is alive with the aroma of fresh-ground coffee, opera singing at Caffè Trieste, street murals, and the melodic and vibrant sound of Italian being spoken.

If you're not within walking distance of North Beach take a cab (parking is very difficult) to the corner of Grant and Vallejo, where you'll find **Caffè Trieste**, a North Beach institution with an Old World spirit and a youthful feel. (Perhaps it's the patrons—artists, poets, writers, and their imitators— who manage the blend.) The café's history goes back to the Beat Era (check out the wall photos), and the place is almost always filled to capacity. The church across the street, St. Francis of Assisi, was the only building still standing on Columbus after the 1906 earthquake and fire. (It is no longer open for regular services.)

Walk downhill on Grant as far as Columbus Avenue, where you should arrive at Broadway. Make a left and walk one block to **Enrico's Sidewalk Café** at 504 Broadway. This traditional North Beach open-air café was an important meeting place for the Beat Generation. Now you can enjoy an updated Mediterranean-style menu and nightly music ranging from opera to jazz. Return to the corner of Columbus and Broadway and head south on Columbus to **Pearl's** at number 256, a mainstream jazz club with comfortable seating and good views of the stage. Halfway down the block you will find **Spec's 12 Adler Museum Café**, a colorful hangout for locals where everyone is welcome. You'll find it in tiny Jack Kerouac Alley (formerly Adler Place) at number 12; no credit cards. **Tosca** (242 Columbus), almost next door to Spec's but worlds apart in feeling, is a late-night watering hole for San Francisco's Hollywood clientele. Its jukebox is full of Italian opera.

Continue south on Columbus and make a left on Jackson to visit three of San Francisco's most intriguing restaurant/ bars. **Cypress Club** at 500 Jackson is the latest in trendy supper clubs, with an interior that has been described as a combination of Disney and Dalí. Stop here for a drink to mingle with the hippest characters in an Alice-in-Wonderland atmosphere.

Make a left at the corner of Jackson and Montgomery for the half-block walk to **Ernie's**, 847 Montgomery, a San Francisco tradition that has delightfully reinvented itself. You'll recognize the bar area from Hitchcock's *Vertigo,* where Jimmy Stewart first watched and later courted Kim Novak. For dinner, the food and service are superior. This is a special place for a romantic evening in a dressy Old World setting.

Cross to the other side of Montgomery and take a few steps to Gold Street, site of the oldest remaining buildings on the West Coast outside of the missions. This elegant area, home to many beautiful antiques shops and legal offices, is now known as Jackson Square. For more than half a century, however, it was known as the wickedest spot on earth—the Barbary Coast. Approximately 3,000 men were "shanghaied" here every year during the height of the Gold Rush, when passengers, crews, and even captains deserted their ships to head for the hills and seek riches. More than 700 ships, without the men to sail them, rotted in the San Francisco port, causing owners to refuse to send vessels here. The land on which you are now standing was, in fact, built on San Francisco's first landfill, which included the skeletons of some of those abandoned ships. On the site of San Francisco's first assay office, at 56 Gold Street, is **Bix**, a chic two-tiered restaurant/bar with a 1930s atmosphere.

After leaving Bix, return to Montgomery, walk up the incline, and go left on Pacific (an oldtime saloon/dance hall was located at 555 Pacific). At Columbus, cross to the west side of the street, and you're at the very comfortable microbrewery/bar **San Francisco Brewing Company** (155 Columbus), located almost in the shadow of the Trans-america Pyramid. This perfect example of a traditional San Francisco drinking emporium has a handsome solid mahogany bar, decor to match, and even wooden ceiling fans.

The various beers brewed here are named after historical figures or places. Try an "Emperor Norton," named for the wealthy rice merchant of the Gold Rush era who, after losing all his money and his mind, declared himself "Emperor of the United States and Protector of Mexico." He was such a likeable character that nearly every merchant in San Francisco honored the scrip he issued. When the Emperor died in 1880, just weeks before his 20 years of scrip was to be repaid, more than 10,000 cheerful mourners attended his funeral; Mark Twain wrote a commentary on his life. Even today the anniversary of his death is commemorated by hundreds of members of the jolly pioneer fraternity E Clampus Vitus, who parade out to his gravesite.

Go one block south to **Caffè Macaroni**, a cozy trattoria

with a good wine list, or backtrack north on Columbus to **Vesuvio's** (255 Columbus), a bar with a history. Since 1949 Vesuvio's has been a haunt of locals and a home away from home for many beatniks and artists. The exterior walls are worth a read and the interior ones are filled with art.

Next door is **City Lights Booksellers and Publishers**, the granddaddy of the paperback bookstores and a North Beach cultural shrine. Founded by Lawrence Ferlinghetti (he published *Howl*) in the early 1950s, the store carries books and magazines few others stock; City Lights tilts toward the arts, especially poetry, and left-wing politics. It is the spiritual center of what the Beat Generation was all about. Chairs invite you to browse, sit, and relax, and patrons mirror the diversity of San Francisco; open until midnight.

Continue in the same direction to number 401, where **Postermat** offers relics of 1960s pop culture, and then to number 411, **Caffè Puccini**, the coffeehouse where the locals hang out (especially in the early parts of the day). You might see Lawrence Ferlinghetti or former mayor Joe Alioto conferring with daughter Angela, now a local politician herself. This is a place where there is no hurry, so try the grenadine mixtures and enjoy the people-watching.

At 423 Columbus is **Caffè Greco**, the new kid on the block, where youthful energy complements a decor accented by European posters and interesting black-and-white photographs. The **Gold Spike** in the next block is reminiscent of the North Beach of the past, when a seven-course dinner could be had for 50 cents. Six courses at the Gold Spike are now $12.95, but the chance to soak up the old California atmosphere is worth the reasonable price.

Continue north on Columbus and make a left on Union to the **Little City Antipasti Bar** (673 Union), an upscale bar and restaurant where the bartenders are as friendly as the denizens. The antipasti dishes are wonderful—try the brie and garlic, heated in a cast-iron skillet, then spread on delicious bread.

Across the street to the north is the **Washington Square Bar and Grill** (1707 Powell), a sophisticated but comfortable spot for the movers and shakers of San Francisco as well as national media celebrities (Tom Brokaw and Art Buchwald have both been spotted here). It's a place to see or be seen, but also still very much a bar where people can relax. The bartenders are excellent. Across the street at the corner of Columbus and Union is the **Bohemian Cigar Store** at number 566, an old-time North Beach haunt where you can get a dose of local flavor as well as some excellent sandwiches, and the **Portofino Caffè** at number 520, a wine-and-beer bar that is home to sailors and elderly Italians. The former owner of the Washington Square Bar and Grill now presides at **Moose's**, across the square at 1652 Stockton. This is one of the hottest spots in town.

Head east on Union (you'll pass **Gelatos**, a superb Italian ice cream store) to reach **Silhouettes** at number 524, one of the first dance bars to have a 1950s motif and feature lots of memorabilia. **North Beach Pizza** at Grant and Union has the best late-night pizza around and usually an eclectic crowd to dress up a rather plain interior. There is another branch of this pizzeria two blocks away, but somehow it doesn't have the same pizzazz, so make sure you catch this one (open until 3:00 A.M. on weekends, 1:00 A.M. otherwise).

When you enter or leave the pizzeria, take a look up the hill, where you can see more than a dozen houses that were saved from the fire created by the 1906 earthquake. In a most ingenious fashion, the Italian inhabitants doused their bedding with red wine and placed it against the houses's outer walls to protect them from the flames. From here it is well worth a walk up the steep hill on Union for some marvelous bay views. When you reach Montgomery turn left onto it and continue to the apex of the hill—you'll pass a beautiful white-and-silver Art Deco apartment house that was part of the 1947 Humphrey Bogart and Lauren Bacall movie *Dark Passage*. The street ends at the next block with the approach to Julius' Castle (see Romantic San Francisco below).

Return on Union to Grant and head south to **Quantity Postcards**, a one-of-a-kind store that can get you off the hook with all those people at home you forgot to get a present for. The thousands of theme choices include the 1950s, movies, humor, antiques, and geography—including postcards from nearly every state in the Union and worldwide. Open until 11:00 P.M. every night.

Savoy Tivoli at 1434 Grant has an open-air seating area (with roof if needed) and is a good place to have a *latte* and people-watch. There's truth in advertising at **The Shlock Shop** (1418 Grant), which has a bit of everything, including a selection of men's full-brimmed hats.

Head west here on Green: At number 574 is **Caffè Sport**, which has very good Italian food if you don't mind crowds and brusque waiters. At least walk by and stick your head in to see the remarkable number of garish decorations and ornaments that have been crammed into such a tiny space.

If you're in the mood for a late-night snack, make a left on Columbus to number 430, where you will find **Calzones**, a trendy restaurant that has good food and is open late, although when it's crowded it tends to feel packed.

Caffè Roma at 414 Columbus is a fancier type of coffee-house/restaurant—in decor, atmosphere, and price. Its recently cleaned frescoes of cupids are a treat. If you're in the mood for pizza, try the pesto one.

South of Market

The area south of Market Street, also known as SoMa, is currently the site of the hottest night spots in town. Once the home of working-class Irish and of industrial San Francisco, SoMa until recently housed many artists who moved here to take advantage of the cheap rents. Now it seems a new nightclub opens every day. SoMa covers a large geographical area, but, because it is flat, it is one neighborhood in this city where you can walk comfortably (weather permitting).

Start with **Julie's Supper Club** (1123 Folsom, between Seventh and Eighth streets), an enjoyable place to down a drink and people-watch. At first you may be unimpressed by the ambience, described by one of the owners as "1950s Jetsons," but give it a few minutes. Photos of 1950s stars (Marilyn Monroe, Annette Funicello, Elizabeth Taylor, Steve Allen) line one wall, along with bowling pins and other period kitsch. The best music of the era energizes the attractive, professional crowd, few of whom wear the all-black uniform that SoMa has popularized. The appetizers are excellent—try the beer-batter catfish. Julie's is a prototypical SoMa club, where comfort, filling food and drink, and an exciting group of people mix.

Across the street is a meeting place for the 1990s—**Brain Wash**, which is a combination café/laundromat, where a spill on the shirt can be gone by dessert. There are sometimes poetry readings here, and the restrooms are labeled not by gender but for "writers" and "readers." On the next floor is Black Market Music, which lights up its storefront in an attempt at artistic statement. Just up the block is the **Up and Down Club**, a pleasant and intimate spot decorated with photos of old tap dancers and featuring live jazz upstairs on weekdays and downstairs on weekends. Keep going west up the street and you'll see Rausch Alley, where the **Half-Shell Seafood Bar and Grill** is located. The bar here, down the long entranceway to the right, has a happy hour on weekdays between 5:00 and 7:00 P.M., with complimentary appetizers and bargain-priced oysters. It's a friendly place with a tropical atmosphere.

Head back to Folsom and continue west past downscale,

minimalist **Limbo** and the relaxed **Kaffe Kreuzberg**, and head to the club hub of SoMa—11th and Folsom. **Club O**, formerly the Oasis, one of the originals of the SoMa club scene, is a lunch spot with swimming pool by day, and club haven with a dance floor that slides out over the pool by night. When the weather is good this is an open-air dance palace; when it rains a portable roof keeps the elements away.

Also at the corner of 11th and Folsom is the **Paradise Lounge**, which offers three rooms of live entertainment. The music's diversity (anything from country to punk; poetry readings on Sundays) is matched only by that of its patrons, who move freely among the rooms. The Paradise is a creative mecca on the San Francisco nightlife scene, and creativity in this case can mean something absolutely wonderful or something nearly dreadful (you can always move to the next room). The employees here are all working-to-make-it musicians, and admission is charged only on weekends or if a special act is booked.

At 333 11th Street is **Slim's**, a premier San Francisco nightclub that books big names and seats only 500. But even more important than the statistics is that the club maintains an integrity about its product—blues and roots music. This is the place where musicians go for a busman's holiday, and with good reason: It's owned by Boz Scaggs and Huey Lewis's manager. Headliners such as Elvis Costello, Laurie Anderson, Rickie Lee Jones, and Simply Red (as well as Boz and Huey) have performed here, and there's a large video screen for entertainment between live acts. Call ahead for times and roster; Tel: 621-3330.

If you want to stretch your legs, make a stop at the **DNA Lounge**, 375 11th Street. The pulse here begins at 9:00 P.M. and doesn't end till 3:30 or 4:30 in the morning, depending on the night. This is a place where black attire reigns and where the "smart, weird, and hip" play, according to the doorman. (The basic-black room with flashy art strives for a subterranean post-apocalypse feeling.) Occasionally there's live music.

If food is what you're after, there are a couple of good spots in the area to try. Across the street from Slim's at 316 11th Street is **20 Tank Brewery**, with a jukebox that blares standard rock, pub-brewed beer, and college cafeteria-style tables. Up the block from the Paradise Lounge is the **Ace Café** at 1539 Folsom. Open until 11:30 P.M. weekends, 10:30 P.M. weeknights, Ace has a stimulating, friendly environment. Across the street is **Hamburger Mary's**, a popular haunt that tends to fill up with a casual crowd. The interior is a veritable museum of pop culture, the bar is open until 2:00 A.M. most nights, and yes, there really is a Mary—she bakes the desserts.

Club DV-8 at 540 Howard is as near a theme park as any rock club in San Francisco. If you spend an evening at this club, created by a keen self-promoter now known as Dr. Winkie, you'll probably begin in the darkened downstairs room, done in basic black with seating all around the dance floor. Miniskirts are prevalent here and dress is trendy/formal. When this room fills, you'll be directed to a street-level room with Copacabana-style seating and atmosphere, including chandeliers and wall paintings created by the late Keith Haring.

But all this pales next to Dr. Winkie's latest invention: the **Caribbean Zone**, located in the back lot of the club, where an unimpressive, corrugated-sheet-metal exterior gives way to a tropical-theme bar/restaurant with reggae music. The centerpiece is a vintage airplane, displayed as if it had crashed in the jungle; its exterior holds the bar's liquor bottles, and, if it's not crowded, you can enjoy a drink inside the plane. This is definitely a place to see, but not during prime hours on Fridays or Saturdays; it's just too popular now.

If you're looking for a bit of understated elegance, try the full-sized bar at the **Fly Trap** at 606 Folsom (near Third Street). This bar and restaurant is a legend reincarnated— the original turn-of-the-century restaurant was located on Sutter Street near a horse-drawn trolley line, and the owner was forced to put a piece of fly paper on each table. Having relocated to the SoMa area in 1989, chef Craig Thomas now offers a wonderful blend of traditional fare from the original menu (try the Hangtown Fry) as well as many less-filling but equally delicious salads.

Hotel Utah (housed in a lovely Victorian at 500 Fourth Street) is the place to find local underground rock and roll and blues bands. **The Ramp** on 855 China Basin Street (along the industrial waterfront) is a friendly place to dance alfresco to a rock or jazz band. The bar itself is located indoors, so you can still have a good time if the weather is bad. **Dolph P. Rempp** is a romantic treat even if only for a drink. This exquisitely decorated ship of highly polished wood and brass, which once carried wine from France to northern Europe, has now found a resting place high on land at Pier 42 off the Embarcadero. The grounds around the ship are worth exploring in daylight.

Now that the Embarcadero Freeway has been torn down, the port is no longer cut off from the adjoining streets, and the result is stunning bay views. Taking advantage of the view bonanza is **Bistro Roti**, 155 Steuart in the Griffon hotel, a smart, rich-looking bar/restaurant with an Old World flavor. There really is a rotisserie spinning above a huge wood-burning fire. The tables with a view are on the mezzanine level; it's best to go early or late to land a table there.

Harry Denton's, located nearby at 161 Steuart adjacent to the Harbor Court Hotel, is a very popular restaurant and bar at which to see and be seen. The Financial District crowd comes here after work for excellent, reasonably priced food in a decor of dark, rich wood accented by an open kitchen surrounded in black-and-white tile. There's a dance floor in the bar area for a release of the day's tensions. **Gordon Biersch Brew Pub** at the foot of Harrison Street is a hot new pub located in the former Hills Brothers coffee processing facility. This wide-open two-story building has wonderful views of the Bay Bridge and the East Bay hills—if you can see over the young and noisy crowd at the bar.

Farther south along the Embarcadero is the aptly named **Embarko** (100 Brannan, located within the Bayside apartment complex). Embarko has cozy booths and a horseshoe bar that create an Art Deco feel with a modern twist. The menu ranges from potato *latkes* to garlicked prawns wrapped in prosciutto with polenta and peas.

For post-dinner exercise try **South Beach Billiards** less than two blocks away at 270 Brannan, a huge upscale pool hall/bar/café/bocci ball court. Formerly a licorice factory, this spot has a wide-open feeling. Food can brought to your game table; open until 2:00 A.M. **Cava 555** (559 2nd Street) announces itself with a violet neon sign. Once inside, the combination of more than 70 reasonably priced Champagnes and taped classical jazz makes this a romantic spot. Be aware that these last two spots are in a poorly-lit semi-industrial part of town.

Downtown
Downtown includes the Financial District and Union Square. The Financial District closes up early on weekdays (usually no later than 11:00 P.M.), and is just about closed altogether on weekends, but the Union Square area is geared for nightlife (see Romantic San Francisco for bars here with a view).

The **Cisco Kid Cantina** (600 Montgomery in the Financial District) is an exception to this rule and stays open late. The

Cantina is housed in the Transamerica Pyramid, which replaced the historic Monkey Block building that stood here for more than a hundred years. Mark Twain and his friend, fireman Tom Sawyer, were frequent visitors to the Monkey Block, and the father of modern China, Sun Yat-sen, drafted his country's first constitution in an office here. Today the Cantina is in the brightly lit ground floor of the Pyramid; filled with wood and stained glass, it turns into a disco at night.

Northeast of Union Square toward the waterfront, the Embarcadero Center is four skyscrapers with three levels of shops, restaurants, and bars at its base. This is a fun place to start an evening by browsing or watching the office workers stream out on their way home. If you are here after sunset, the beautifully lit Ferry Building can be seen from Building Four. **Harrington's** at 245 Front Street nearby, the **Royal Exchange** at 301 Sacramento, and **Schroeders** at 240 Front attract patrons from conservative Financial District offices. **Café Claude** (7 Claude Alley off Bush between Grant and Kearny) offers the ambience of a Parisian café. Drinks are generous and there's often live jazz.

Near Union Square, **Kuleto's** at 221 Powell, **Lascaux** at 248 Sutter, and **PosTrio** at 545 Post are all excellent restaurants where you can get a drink at the bar and watch the beautiful people. Also in this neighborhood, **The Iron Horse**, 19 Maiden Lane, is a traditional San Francisco bar frequented by local businesspeople.

The Plush Room at 940 Sutter is an intimate place to see excellent cabaret entertainment. There is a varying cover charge and two-drink minimum (call to see who's playing; Tel: 885-6800). Also on Sutter the **White Horse Taverne** at number 637 will quench your thirst for Mother England, as will the **Penny Farthing Pub** at 900 Bush. The food at both is recommended.

About seven blocks west of Union Square, **The Great American Music Hall**, 859 O'Farrell, is a great place to see a wide variety of the best talent in America, ranging from country music's Jerry Jeff Walker to jazz legend Maynard Ferguson. This old-time music hall is so small you're always close enough to really watch the performers at work. For tickets, Tel: 885-0750. Take a cab to get here, as its surrounding neighborhood is unsavory at night.

Cow Hollow

Union Street west of Van Ness is the main street in the area known as Cow Hollow. There were, in fact, dairy farms here until the 1880s, and women washed their laundry in the nearby streams and lagoon (now filled in). Now Union Street is likened to New York's Upper West Side for its boutique flavor, the plethora of upper-income single people, and the difficulty in parking. Nightlife in this area is centered on Union Street and the streets that lead off of it.

Travelling east to west along Union Street, with detours north and south along the way, you could begin with a thoroughly enjoyable time at **Pasand** (1875 Union), a sleepy Indian restaurant that is transformed into an intimate jazz spot every night until 1:00 A.M. **Perry's** at number 1944, once synonymous with Union Street nightlife, is still a popular watering hole/restaurant with a fair share of movers and shakers. The tile floor combines with a wood-and-brass bar to offer a clean but warm feeling. Across the street at number 1979, the **Blue Light Café** is a dimly lit but attractive Tex-Mex restaurant/bar created by native Texan Boz Scaggs. Open until 1:30 A.M., this is a hangout for the chic and hip of Union Street. Up the block at number 2000 is **Prego**, a stylish Italian eatery, open until midnight, that caters to a clientele similar to that of Perry's.

The **Balboa Café** (3199 Fillmore near Union) has taken over the role of hottest spot in the area; its dull-white exterior opens into a handsome wood, glass, and brass decor that is *the* place to be seen (and to make a fashion statement). Try their good hamburgers (food is served until 11:00 P.M.), but stay away on Friday and Saturday nights—Balboa is packed and the immediate area is filled with other bars catering to hundreds of college-age kids discovering drink for the first time. **Liverpool Lil's** (2942 Lyon adjacent to the Presidio) has dark wood and dim lighting, giving it the flavor of an English pub. This fun, friendly bar and restaurant serves food until midnight.

A block north of Lombard Street in the Marina district is **Windows On Chestnut** (2241 Chestnut), a friendly, casual neighborhood bar where you can strike up stimulating conversations with its varied, mostly upper-income patrons. Almost next door is the **Chestnut Street Grill**, which has a more sophisticated ambience, with garden dining in warm weather. Nearby is **The Horseshoe**, another neighborhood treasure where you can hear the best big-band jukebox in town.

Haight-Ashbury
You can see it all on Haight Street, located in the geographical center of the city: from suits to suede, from shaved heads

to Day-Glo orange-and-pink hairstyles. Home of the Summer of Love, the Haight has fallen and risen again since the
peace-and-love era of the 1960s, when it served as a refuge
for tens of thousands of hippies and their imitators. Where
once all you could see were boarded-up storefronts and
fallen, drug-laden bodies in the streets, now there is some
gentrification and prosperity, although at night the street
population is still somewhat unsavory. Window shopping
among the vintage-clothing stores, galleries, and a high-tech
furniture store is a visual treat, but even in this incarnation
Haight Street retains its wild and unpredictable nature.
Street people are prevalent at night, and only on weekends
do the rougher edges soften a bit; this is a place for the
adventurous who want to see the various permutations of
the human species.

You are invited to take a trip back in time to the era of
Casablanca at the **Persian Aub Zam Zam Room**. Through
the Moorish entrance to this bar at 1633 Haight an oasis
from the hectic street pace awaits. The near-room-size semi-
circular bar, surrounded by dim red lights, sports a local
mixed-dressed crowd, and the jukebox is filled with big-
band music. Bruno, the owner, also tends bar, dressed in
formal bartender attire. He serves the best $1.75 martini in
town and is known to throw out anyone he doesn't like, but
if he approves of your manners take a seat around the
solitary table in the main room and prepare to be over-
whelmed by the dropped circular ceiling and decorations
around the bar. **The Deluxe**, 1511 Haight, is another refuge
from the present. This spot remembers post-World War II
San Francisco in food and decor; oysters are a specialty.

Kezar (900 Cole at the corner of Carl) is a fun neighborhood bar and restaurant three blocks south of Haight Street
and worth a visit. You'll pass some beautiful Victorian mansions as you head into Cole Valley, the wealthier part of the
Haight, on your way to this bar, filled with local professionals and good conversation, ample drinks, and delectable
food (try the Mexican Pot Roast). Open until 2:00 A.M. every
day; the kitchen closes at 11:00 P.M. Across the street is the
101 Bakery Café (101 Carl), serving homemade pastries in
surroundings filled with local artists' work.

Back on Haight Street, **Rockin' Robin's** at number 1821 is
a 1950s and 1960s–style rock 'n' roll/sports bar with a good-
sized dance floor. Parts of old cars of the era protrude from
the walls, which are also covered with scores of photos—
mainly of sports and rock legends. The jukebox has a good
selection, and occasionally there's live music and dance

lessons. Farther west on Haight, **Park Bowl**, at number 1855, is the home of "Rock 'N' Bowl." This popular bowling alley displays music videos above the lanes and offers dancing between frames. It's open until 11:30 P.M. most nights, but call ahead for its weekend schedule; Tel: 752-2366.

The Lower Haight area, home of jazz joints and after-hours clubs in days past, has now become the chosen spot for the young and intellectual. This two-block strip between Fillmore and Pierce has an unusual conglomeration of clubs and coffeehouses.

Nickie's at number 460 was once a Prohibition speakeasy (nightly receipts were hauled through a hole in the ceiling to an upstairs apartment). Now its knowledgeable DJs play a different form of underground music every night (closed Mondays), from "groove" jazz to Latin and Jamaican oldies to 1970s funk. You'll find a friendly and vibrant crowd dancing and talking. Walk west and you'll pass the minimally decorated local hangout, **Café International**. At number 530 look into the wildly named **Mad Dog in the Fog**, a bar that attracts a young, semi-bohemian crowd with a slightly raw edge. Farther along the street is **Tropical Haight**, a spot filled with lush greenery and real hospitality.

Elsewhere in San Francisco

In addition to the five areas above, there are other spots in the city for nighttime fun. From hot samba to jazz and ballads, **Bahía Tropical**, 1600 Market Street at Franklin, has Brazilian music every night of the week. This large club attracts a high-energy crowd that packs the place on the weekends to hear the authentic music and to dance. Informal dress, with a cover charge that reaches up to $10 on weekends.

César's Latin Palace, for the dancing aficionado, is owned by perennial mayoral candidate César Ascarrunz and located at 3140 Mission at Army; open until 6:00 A.M. on weekends, 2:00 A.M. weekdays. Call first to see what's on; Tel: 648-6611.

The **Buena Vista Café** at 2765 Hyde (near Ghirardelli Square) began serving Irish coffee in the United States in the early 1950s. This is a very popular watering hole for both natives and visitors. **The Third Wave** (3316 24th Street) is an alcohol-free club.

The **Elite Café** (2049 Fillmore) and **Harry's on Fillmore** (2020 Fillmore) are two fine restaurants with bars where you can enjoy conversing with the urban professional folks over a good drink. Another favorite in this neighborhood is **Oritalia** (1915 Fillmore), which offers an unusual menu—

even for San Francisco: Italian and Asian influences are combined to create such dishes as fettuccine with *mabo* tofu. **La Posada** (2298 Fillmore) offers good, straightforward Mexican food.

Li Po at 916 Grant Avenue (near Washington) is a kick. For more than half a century this dimly lit room with American music on the jukebox has been a way for Westerners to experience a Chinese bar. You'll usually find a jovial crowd here. **Lou's Pier 47** is a premier music spot for those with sophisticated tastes—some of the best Bay Area musicians (Mark Naftalin, Nick Gravenites) play this very comfortable Fisherman's Wharf spot at 300 Jefferson. New Orleans Zydeco music is popular here along with the blues—or, to put it another way, any music that makes you tap your feet or moves your spirit.

Walk through the doors of the **Russian Renaissance Bar and Restaurant** (5241 Geary near 17th Avenue) to enter a world of myth and fairy tales, Russian style. Dozens of exquisite dolls stand regally, surrounded by wall and ceiling murals depicting a Russia of centuries ago; the more time you spend in this room, the more alive it becomes. For more than 30 years owner Boris Vertloogin has offered an extensive list of Russian cocktails as well as authentic Russian cuisine. (Ample drinks are a custom here, and Boris as bartender always has an appropriate story or two.) On Fridays and Saturdays a classical pianist adds even more flavor to this extraordinary place.

In the Civic Center area, the bar at the very trendy **Stars** (150 Redwood Alley) is an excellent place to people-watch the sometimes-rich and ersatz-famous in the early evening. At **Zuni Café** (1658 Market near Franklin), a restaurant/bar with Southwestern decor and a mixed crowd, much of the excellent food is mesquite grilled. Open until midnight, reservations recommended (closed Mondays); Tel: 552-2522.

Babylon (2260 Van Ness at Vallejo) is an upscale bar/restaurant where a crowd dances to piped-in music (Latin jazz on weekends). Subdued lighting and decor offer a taste of Morocco. Nearby at 1500 Broadway at Polk is **Johnny Love's**, the latest spot at which to observe the mating ritual.

Late-Night Eating
If it's late-night munchies you want, try: **International House of Pancakes** (2299 Lombard; open 24 hours), **La Rondalla**, for Mexican fare in the Mission district (901 Valencia; open until 4:00 A.M.), **Yuet-Lee**, for Chinese food (1300 Stockton;

open until 3:00 A.M.), and **Zim's** (1498 Market; open 24 hours). For Italian food try **Basta Pasta** (1268 Grant; open until 2:00 A.M.). **Clown Alley** (Columbus at Jackson), a hamburger joint, is open until 3:00 A.M.; its other location at 2499 Lombard is open 24 hours. For a sweet late-night treat, try one of **Just Desserts'** three locations (248 Church, 836 Irving, and 3735 Buchanan). All three are open until 11:00 P.M. on weekdays and midnight on weekends. **Cala**, a supermarket chain, is open 24 hours at Fifth Avenue and Geary, and also at Hyde and California.

—Mark Gordon

ENTERTAINMENT

Comedy

San Francisco and the Bay Area are considered by many to be the birthplace of modern stand-up comedy. Much of the credit should go to Enrico Banducci, who engaged Mort Sahl in the 1950s to play for months at Banducci's world-famous hungry i nightclub when few other clubs in the country would book him. Banducci was truly a point of light in the gray-flannel-suited decade, introducing to the world such unknowns as Woody Allen (who shared a double bill with Barbra Streisand), Bill Cosby, Phyllis Diller, the Smothers Brothers, Dick Gregory, and Mike Nichols and Elaine May. Lenny Bruce got his break at a North Beach lesbian club called Ann's. (A good deal of notoriety and a lawsuit followed Bruce's comedic bit here about a black hipster auditioning for "The Lawrence Welk Show.")

This tradition of ground-breaking comedy continued through the 1980s with Robin Williams, Whoopi Goldberg, and Dana Carvey, who also began their careers here. Today small clubs still exist, including **Holy City Zoo** (408 Clement in the Richmond district), the city's oldest comedy club, and the spot where Robin Williams got his first break. (Williams still drops in unannounced around town to try out his new material.) In addition to Holy City Zoo, some good places for laughs are **Cobb's** (2801 Leavenworth near Fisherman's Wharf in The Cannery), **The Improv** (401 Mason), and the **Punchline** (444A Battery).

Jazz

Some of the best jazz clubs in the country are located in San Francisco. Jazz greats such as Bobby Hutcherson and Pharaoh Sanders live in the Bay Area, so call to find out if a favorite of yours is playing, or just drop by—you won't be disappointed.

Pier 23 Café, on the waterfront at the pier of the same name near Levi Strauss Plaza, captures a taste of an era gone by. This is a comfortable, no-frills spot where longshoremen and executives come together to enjoy jazz every night. **Kimball's** (360 Grove) has returned after renovation with a near-perfect atmosphere for live jazz. **Rasselas** (2801 California at Divisadero) is an almost-elegant straight-ahead jazz joint featuring a full bar and Ethiopian food. **Pasand** at 1875 Union Street (see Cow Hollow) and **Pearl's** at 256 Columbus (see North Beach) are two more venues for excellent jazz.

Theater

When San Francisco was just a toddler of a city, it rated second only to New York as a theater town. Aside from gambling and womanizing, there was not much to do in the Gold Rush era except take in a show; from opera to burlesque, isolated San Franciscans were thirsty for nearly every form of entertainment. San Francisco maintained its edge as the theater capital of the West Coast until both Los Angeles and television grew up in the middle of this century.

Today's theaters (with several exceptions) cluster just west of Union Square, within the rectangle of Post, Geary, Powell, and Taylor streets. The **American Conservatory Theater** (ACT), one of North America's finest resident companies, presents the best of classical and modern dramatic theater. Displaced from its home in the ornate 1909 Geary Theater by the 1989 earthquake, ACT now plays out its October to May season in various venues in the theater district while rebuilding proceeds; for current venues, Tel: 749-2228. The **Cable Car Theater**, 430 Mason Street near Post, is an informal, 140-seat theater in a former speakeasy; Tel: 861-6895.

The **Curran Theater**, 445 Geary Street, was the last major theater constructed downtown, in 1922. Offerings usually fall within the Best of Broadway series that showcases musicals en route to or from Broadway; Tel: 474-3800.

Grandeur returned to the 1922 **Golden Gate Theater** (in a less-than-grand neighborhood, however) following a recent face- and body-lift. Too big for most plays, it's employed mostly for musicals (1 Taylor Street, corner of Market and Sixth streets); Tel: 474-3800. **Marines Memorial Theater**, on the second floor of the classic Marines Memorial Building at 609 Sutter Street (box office at 325 Mason), has featured one award-winning hit after another; Tel: 771-6900. At 1192 Market Street, corner of Hyde and Eighth streets (Civic Center), the **Orpheum**, inheritor of a vaudeville tradition, today relies mostly upon musicals; Tel: 474-3800.

San Francisco Mime Troupe is a sassy, smart-alecky, politically oriented company that's anything but silent on the issues or anything else. In summer they perform free shows in various regional parks; you'll find them at home in an area few travellers visit, 855 Treat Avenue at 21st Street (Mission district); Tel: 285-1717. **Theatre Rhinoceros**, 2926 16th Street at South Van Ness, founded in 1977, is the most important gay ensemble around, and produces such shows as *Gertrude Stein and a Companion;* Tel: 861-5079.

Theatre on the Square, in a lovely old building of vaguely Mediterranean persuasion at 450 Post Street, offers locally written plays as well as Off-Broadway vehicles in an elegant setting of gold leaf, wrought iron, and tile; Tel: 433-9500. In the reworked Masonic Temple at 25 Van Ness Avenue (Civic Center), the **New Conservatory Theater** presents children's plays, dance, and more; Tel: 861-6655.

San Francisco's wackiest, most endearing, zaniest, and perennial theatrical production is *Beach Blanket Babylon,* in its present incarnation as *Beach Blanket Babylon Goes Around the World,* at the **Club Fugazi**, 678 Green Street in North Beach. Now in its 18th year, it's not to be missed; Tel: 421-4222. **Frisco Productions** has re-created a musical cabaret from the Roaring Twenties era. Jake Finnegan's Rendezvous Club takes you back to a San Francisco speakeasy offering the merriment of the days when the city was the wettest dry town in the nation. Call for location; Tel: 681-5555. The **Lorraine Hansberry Theatre** at 620 Sutter Street mixes contemporary classics with new plays; Tel: 474-8800. The **Magic Theatre** in the Marina is committed to bringing new plays and playwrights to the attention of the public. Its two venues are in Building D, Fort Mason Center (Buchanan Street at Marina Boulevard); Tel: 441-8822.

The **Lamplighters Music Theatre** has entertained San Franciscans for over 40 years, mainly with performances of Gilbert and Sullivan frivolities. Its home is in the Presentation Theatre, 2350 Turk Street at Masonic in the Western Addition; Tel: 752-7755. **George Coates Performance Works'** director characterizes his company as "a hothouse of artists, designers, and performers engaged in research, development, and the evolution of large-scale live performance." The theater is housed in a renovated 1929 neo-Gothic church at 110 McAllister near Leavenworth in the Civic Center; Tel: 863-4130.

Other than the individual theaters' box offices, try **City Box Office**, Sherman Clay & Co., 141 Kearny Street, 94108 (Tel: 392-4400); and **St. Francis Theater and Sports Tickets**, Westin St. Francis Hotel, Union Square, 94102 (Tel: 362-3500).

BASS (Bay Area Seating Service) ticket centers include Supermail, Four Embarcadero; Headlines, 838 Market Street; and Tower Records, Bay Street and Columbus Avenue; Tel: (510) 762-2277 (charge by mail) or dial TELETIX (recorded calendar listings).

In addition to the above, there are about 20 smaller theatrical groups in town; for productions, see the Sunday *Examiner-Chronicle*'s Datebook section, which is a good guide to nearly all the performing arts and entertainment in the Bay Area. A section at the front of the Yellow Pages phone directory will show you the seating plan of each of the major theaters.

—Georgia I. Hesse and Mark Gordon

Theater District Dining

Grand dining and great theater do not mix well: A fine meal is theater enough in itself, and can last as long as a performance of *Les Misérables*. Some of the finest chefs in the city are within a sole's throw of the theater district but deserve to have their cuisine enjoyed without curtain pressure. Below, some rewarding compromises.

Kuleto's, in the Villa Florence Hotel at 225 Powell Street, serves continually from 11:00 A.M. to 11:00 P.M., so there's time for an early meal as well as one to last the entire evening. Plenty of delicious tastes can be enjoyed that won't put you to sleep during the second act; Tel: 397-7720. The **French Room** in the Four Seasons Clift hotel ranks among the city's best restaurants for its fine cuisine and unsurpassed service; Tel: 775-4700.

Provençal decor and European ambience enliven the **Brasserie Savoy** in the Savoy Hotel at 580 Geary; Tel: 474-8686. The brasserie opens for early dinner at 5:00 P.M. (4:00 P.M. on Sundays) and serves late suppers until 11:30 P.M. on Fridays and Saturdays. The enticing oyster bar is open all day from 11:30 A.M. to 11:30 P.M. **Donatello** at 501 Post (at Mason) is a phenomenon, a restaurant so good it gave its name to the hotel that houses it. The kitchen serves impeccable Northern Italian specialties with flair and panache; reserve well in advance to be certain of pre-theater seating. You may just decide to skip the show; Tel: 441-7182.

Trader Vic's is an institution, but, sadly, no longer to be taken seriously for its cuisine. However, it's a great people-watching place for before-theater snacks and before-bed drinks and snacks. It's at 20 Cosmo Place, off Taylor; Tel: 776-2232. **China Moon Café** at 639 Post, between Jones and Taylor, is so tiny as to give new meaning to the word cramped, but the so-called *nouvelle chinoise* dishes keep packing diners in. These are some of the best flavors—and the newest—you'll find in town, and the crowding means you won't be tempted to linger and miss the final curtain; Tel: 775-4789.

Bardelli's is one of the oldest (1909) and was one of the most prestigious restaurants downtown (243 O'Farrell Street). The beautiful stained-glass panels and cozy seating area near the bar recommend it to traditionalists. Go early and slip into your seat to be relaxed by the time warp; Tel: 982-0243.

Christophe, at 320 Mason Street, is right across the street from the Downtown Center Garage, very handy for drivers. Its French menu can be chic, light, and quick, especially when you arrive early (it opens at 5:30 P.M.) and explain that you have theater tickets; from 5:30 to 8:30 P.M., there's a very reasonable four-course prix-fixe menu; Tel: 433-7560.

Corona Bar & Grill at 88 Cyril Magnin Street (adjoining the Monticello Inn) may serve the best Mexican cooking you've ever tasted. It's open continually from 11:30 A.M., so you can arrive early or take a light meal at the bar; Tel: 392-5500. At the St. Francis Hotel, the **St. Francis Grill** opens at 6:00 P.M. and is used to serving up fresh seafood and other light specialties for its theater-bound guests; Tel: 774-0233.

If you want it quick, casual, simple, and inexpensive, choose **La Quiche**, a tiny bistro that features—what else?—quiche. It's at 550 Taylor Street; Tel: 441-2711.

Lefty O'Doul's, at 333 Geary, is a landmark as much as a restaurant. It was founded by the famous ex-Yankee ball player. Service is cafeteria style, and the laid-back sports bar attracts a nostalgic crowd; Tel: 982-8900.

Should it get really late and should you be really hungry, step into **Lori's Diner** at 336 Mason Street and back into the 1950s, where hamburgers and old-fashioned, familiar diner fare are served 24 hours a day; Tel: 392-8646.

It's cavernous, the servings gigantic, and the atmosphere nonexistent, but for filling (if nondramatic) meals there's little more satisfying than a down-to-earth, San Francisco–Italian dinner. You can put your elbows on the table at **New Joe's**, 347 Geary Street, until 1:30 A.M.; Tel: 989-6733.

For decades **David's Delicatessen-Restaurant** at 480 Geary Street, right across from the Curran and Geary theaters, has been packing them in to the only true Jewish deli in town. It's open until 1:00 A.M. for a lot of late-night noshing; Tel: 771-1600.

—*Georgia I. Hesse and Mark Gordon*

Classical Music Performances

The always-sold-out openings of the symphony and the opera seasons, held in the same week in early September, are the beginning of high society's social season—these are *the* places to be seen. Many observers of the human species hang around outside the Opera House and Symphony Hall to watch the show outside the show. Among the many cultural venues are the **San Francisco Ballet**, Tel: 621-3838, January–May season; **San Francisco Symphony**, Tel: 431-5400, September–May season; and the **San Francisco Opera**, Tel: 864-3330, September–December season. See also the Civic Center section earlier in this chapter.

The **Chamber Symphony of San Francisco** performs classical and modern chamber works at Herbst Theater in the Civic Center from January to May; Tel: 495-2919. The **Philharmonia Baroque Orchestra** also plays at Herbst Theater, with a season usually running from February to April; Tel: 391-5252. **San Francisco Contemporary Music Players** give occasional concerts in the Green Room of the Museum of Modern Art, with pre-concert discussions of new and avant-garde works; Tel: 252-6235. **San Francisco Performances** is an umbrella group for chamber music, jazz, and dance staged at Herbst Theater; Tel: 398-6449. The Herbst Theater Box Office can be reached at 392-4400.

Noted local artists and faculty as well as the Conservatory Orchestra appear at Hellman Hall, **San Francisco Conservatory of Music**, 19th Avenue and Ortega Street; Tel: 759-3475. Year-round classical concerts are presented at **Old First Presbyterian Church**, Van Ness Avenue at Sacramento Street (Tel: 474-1608); at Masonic Auditorium (Nob Hill) and Herbst Theater by **Today's Artists Concerts** (Tel: 398-1324); and in Grace Cathedral (Nob Hill) with its superb acoustics in the Cathedral Concert Series (Tel: 776-6611). Free noontime concerts are offered on Tuesdays at 12:30 P.M. at **Old St. Mary's Church**, 660 California Street in Chinatown; Tel: 986-4388.

The **Stern Grove Midsummer Music Festival** in Sigmund Stern Grove, 19th Avenue and Sloat Boulevard (Sunset district), offers free orchestral and operatic performances, recitals, dance presentations, and the annual appearance of the New Orleans Preservation Hall Jazz Band, all in a natural amphitheater set in groves of eucalyptus, redwood, and fir trees. Performances are on Sundays at 2:00 P.M. Pack a picnic and arrive very early.

Glorious music and delightful story lines are the province of the **Pocket Opera**, a small professional company supported by the eight-member Pocket Philharmonic. Works of Handel, Rossini, Offenbach, and the like are performed from early spring until midsummer at the Beale Street Theater, Market and Beale streets (Financial District); Tel: 989-1855.

The **Summer Festival of Performing Arts** presents an annual concert series in the outdoor Music Concourse in Golden Gate Park that runs the gamut from salsa to gospel choirs, big band, and swing. Performances are given from 1:30 P.M. to 3:00 P.M., usually on Thursdays in July and Saturdays in August and September, and are free. To check programs and dates, Tel: 474-3914.

Also a part of summer in the park, the **Golden Gate Park Band** has played concerts on Sundays since its founding in 1882. Pack a picnic and find a seat in the Music Concourse at 1:00 P.M. It's free; Tel: 666-7107.

—*Georgia I. Hesse and Mark Gordon*

GAY NIGHTLIFE

The central gay district is **Castro Street** between 17th and 19th streets, where restored Victorians thread their way in and around the bars, bookstores, restaurants, and a magnificent Art Deco movie theater. At 401 Castro you'll find **Twin Peaks**, a popular drinking establishment with an attractive antique bar, or stop in at **The Midnight Sun** (4067 18th Street) to check out the videos and classic television clips always playing.

Cross Market Street and head east until you reach the **Metro Bar and Restaurant** (3600 Sixteenth Street at Market); this second-floor oval-shaped bar, handsomely decorated with just a dash of violet neon, offers another view of street life. If you cross the street and continue east, you'll encounter **Café Flore** (2298 Market), a garden-like indoor/outdoor sidewalk café. The pervasive aroma of coffee here, along with marvelous desserts, makes this a pleasant place for good conversation and people-watching. **Josie's Cabaret and Juice Joint** (3583 16th Street at Market) is a great spot for comedy.

Out in Pacific Heights awaits the cozy **Lion Pub** (Sacramento and Divisadero). The *San Francisco Sentinel* and the

Bay Area Reporter are free weeklies distributed throughout the city that offer the latest information on the gay scene.

ROMANTIC SAN FRANCISCO

A century-old description of San Francisco as "the cool, gray city of love" is appropriate for the city even today, where the physical beauty serves as a stunning backdrop for a romantic evening. Modern-day skyscraper view-rooms and waterfront restaurants make it easier and more comfortable than ever for lovers to enjoy the lush hills, the water, and the necklace of lights strung across the Bay Bridge.

Start by enjoying a sunset from the **Marin Headlands**, a view guaranteed to thrill even the most hard-hearted (be sure the weather is clear, or the bridge and surrounding area could be enshrouded in fog). To get there, drive or take a cab across the Golden Gate Bridge (remember the 4:00–6:00 P.M. rush hour and keep to the right-hand lane); take the Alexander Avenue exit right off the freeway almost immediately after Vista Point on the northern side of the bridge. Turn left at the stop sign and follow the road west until you reach the Golden Gate National Recreation Area/Marin Headlands; from here follow the twisting road up the hill. You can stop at any of the numerous gravel parking areas for a magnificent view of the Golden Gate Bridge, the bay, and the city. If you want to continue, the climb eventually surpasses the height of the top of the bridge towers (746 feet above sea level). To return to the city using the same route, retrace your route back to where the road ends at the stop sign, where you should turn right onto the bridge (be aware of fast-moving oncoming traffic).

If you make a left turn here instead, you will wind your way down toward **Sausalito**, where there are many restaurants with spectacular views. The best of the bunch is the **Casa Madrona Hotel** located at 801 Bridgeway on the main street, but elevated above the hustle and bustle; Tel: 331-5888. Although the interior of the **Alta Mira Hotel**, 125 Bulkley (Tel: 332-1350), isn't as lush, the meals are more moderately priced than those at the Casa Madrona and the view is better. Reservations at either restaurant should be made well in advance.

For an even more romantic time, take a Red & White ferry from Pier 43½ across the bay to **Tiburon** (to check the time and place of departure, call 546-BOAT; a Champagne Cruise is also available, and some ferries serve drinks). After you arrive at Tiburon, you can choose to stay aboard and return directly to the city, or else disembark and have an outdoor dinner at any of a variety of local restaurants, and return on a later ferry. Situated immediately next to the ferry mooring is **Guaymas**, an upscale Mexican restaurant. Take the time to stroll through Tiburon on Main Street, which is reminiscent of Sausalito before it became a tourist mecca. You'll find **Sam's Anchor Café** along the way, an institution among locals.

If you return to the city without having eaten, try the **Mandarin** in Ghirardelli Square and request a table with a view. The Szechwan cuisine of the Mandarin, a favorite among Chinese-food fans, is expensive but worth the price, especially the crispy fried-chicken salad. Another romantic dining spot with waterfront views is **Julius' Castle** (1541 Montgomery)—it's hard to find and up a few "only in San Francisco" steep streets in the eastern part of North Beach. There's valet parking if you come by car. The panoramic view of the bay and the interior of this Continental restaurant are exquisite, although the food doesn't quite match. The same can be said for the **Waterfront** (Pier 5) and **Sinbad's Pier 2 Restaurant** along the Embarcadero. A dining room that once sailed the seas, the **Dolph P. Rempp** on Pier 42 has both good views and good food. If you visit San Francisco around Christmastime, another maritime treat is a walk around the outskirts of Pier 39 (the truck-loading areas) to see the decorated sailboats.

A very special place to catch the sunset or, better yet, to see the bright lights of the nighttime skyline from a perfect distance is **Treasure Island**. Drive or take a cab east on the Bay Bridge, exit at Yerba Buena Island (right-hand exit), then circle right toward Treasure Island, the man-made island that was the home of the 1939–1940 World's Fair. (It is now a military base.) Just before you arrive at the main gate, make a U-turn that will lead you to a parking area for a one-of-a-kind view. On the ride home, keep to the right-hand lane for the best view of the city. Turn off into the downtown area (first exit from the right-hand lanes) and head for the Westin St. Francis hotel located on Union Square, where a nightcap at the **Compass Rose** will place your feet firmly on land but put your spirit into flight. This grand room features two-story Corinthian columns, art from around the world, and a jazz trio that plays favorites from the 1930s and 1940s beginning at either 8:00 or 9:00 P.M. There is no cover charge, but the drinks and appetizers are very expensive.

If your desire for panoramas is still not sated, there are plenty of glorious skybars that can accommodate you. The

Carnelian Room atop the Bank of America building at California and Kearny has a view that softens even sophisticated San Franciscans. The lounge closes between 11:30 P.M. and midnight; a jacket and tie are required, and drinks are expensive. When the **Top of the Mark** at the Mark Hopkins Hotel opened in 1936, it was the world's pinnacle of skyrooms. Today it shares the honors with the Fairmont's **Crown Room**, across California Street, which boasts the highest elevation of any of the skyrooms.

While you're on Nob Hill, stop in at the bar of the **Big Four Restaurant** in the Huntington Hotel, where the feeling is rich and comfortable with an old-fashioned elegance, and photos and memorabilia are displayed throughout. Be sure to have a look at the area outside the restrooms: A 270-degree series of photo blowups is mounted on the circular wall showing late-19th-century San Francisco before the 1906 devastation. Especially note the single-family dwellings on Nob Hill in the foreground.

The Hyatt Regency in Embarcadero Center features the **Equinox,** a bar and restaurant revolving full-circle every hour. It has delicious vistas and is expensive, as are the public top rooms of the Sir Francis Drake, the Holiday Inn at Union Square (480 Sutter Street), and the new downtown Marriott (Fourth and Mission streets). For the best bargain "room with a view" and privacy to boot, try the **Sky Club** atop the Marines Memorial Club and Theater at 609 Sutter. When you enter the building, turn right directly to the elevators: This building is a private hotel for Marines and club members, but the theater and Sky Club are open to the public. Drinks are cheap, the employees are very informal, and there is nearly always a seat by the window as the hour nears midnight. The view, with some exceptions, is one of San Francisco of 50 years past.

At 1500 Sutter near Gough, **Café Majestic**'s horseshoe bar and surrounding tables won't win prizes for views, but they are just fine for lovers. High ceilings, stately columns, and a classical jazz pianist (often the owner's wife) make this a favorite place. Rack of lamb and mocha custard with cream are standouts on the menu. Another romantic place to dine is **l'Olivier** (465 Davis near Walton Square). The tables and lighting are arranged to contribute to the intimate atmosphere of this country French spot.

Rivaling the elegance of the St. Francis's Compass Rose is the **Redwood Room** in the Four Seasons Clift Hotel. Redwood wall panels and the tremendous height of the ceiling only serve to increase the opulent feeling associated with this traditional San Francisco room. Lighting is romantic, and chances are a pianist with the last name of Scales will be there to enhance the mood.

Hornblower Dining Yachts at Pier 33 will sweep you off your landlubber feet with a taste of the sea. A cruise offers dining, and sometimes dancing, on the bay. Seeing nighttime San Francisco from the water is perhaps the quintessential romantic San Francisco experience. Call 394-8900 (extension 7) for information and reservations. The popularity of **Fog City Diner** (1300 Battery) exploded when a credit card commercial seen nationally was filmed here. Go towards closing time (10:30 P.M.) and get a booth to experience a feeling of luxury dining as it might have been in an elegant railroad dining car.

The **Garden Court** in the Sheraton Palace hotel on Market Street is the epitome of the San Francisco class of yesteryear. A $150-million renovation has brought back to life the site where more decisions about turn-of-the-century California's political and economic future were made than anywhere else, including the State House. If you choose not to eat, there is some seating during dinner hours for casual drinks. This room soothes with its one-of-a-kind beauty, capped by its extraordinary glass ceiling. Don't miss **Maxfield's Pied Piper Bar** here with its original Maxfield Parrish mural.

A favorite outdoor spot is **Outer Broadway**, in the 2800 and 2900 blocks of Broadway in Pacific Heights. Walk along the two most expensive blocks of residential real estate in San Francisco and admire the view of the Marina district and the bay. Gorbachev slept at the Soviet consul's residence (2820 Broadway) while in San Francisco in 1990. For even more superlative views, there's always **Coit Tower** and the top of **Lombard Street**.

Finally, for outdoor vistas, anyone would have to include the ever-popular **Twin Peaks** (south of Haight-Ashbury), the second-highest site in the city at more than 900 feet. The Indians thought the two peaks were a husband and wife who were separated by lightning because of their constant bickering, while the Spanish renamed the area Breasts of the Maiden. But no matter the name or the time of day or night (as long as it's not foggy), this view will stun as you gaze past the Golden Gate over to Marin and to the East Bay, and south down the Peninsula. (Be warned: If it's windy, this is one of the coldest spots in all of San Francisco, and it's right in the middle of a fog belt.) Informational displays at the parking zone will help in getting a fix on what you're seeing.

—*Mark Gordon*

SHOPS AND SHOPPING

For dedicated consumers, San Francisco is the most important shopping destination in the northwestern United States.
The city boasts an impressive variety of boutiques, specialty
and department stores, shopping malls, and neighborhood
shops, many stocking exclusive merchandise not likely to be
found elsewhere. Most shoppers concentrate on a thriving
downtown area, a growing bargain-hunter's mecca in the
South of Market (SoMa) district, and ethnic neighborhoods
that provide shopping experiences akin to being in another
country.

In such a highly competitive market, merchants go to
great lengths to attract customers by emphasizing exceptional service (this is particularly true of the downtown
department stores). Some shops and malls offer entertainment, many stores keep evening hours, and many are open
seven days a week, although there is little consistency to the
opening and closing hours in any neighborhood. Most of the
downtown stores are open by 10:00 A.M., although some
open as early as 9:30 A.M.

North and South of Union Square

The focal point of downtown shopping is Union Square, a
pleasant oasis of greenery filled with pigeons, noontime
lunchers, sun worshippers, and more recently, the homeless
people and panhandlers found in any city's downtown. The
square is surrounded by some of the most prestigious stores
in town, as well as many boutiques with international reputa-
tions, and is bordered by Geary Street to the south, Powell to
the west, Post to the north, and Stockton to the east.

The largest store on the square is **Macy's**, next door to
I. Magnin on Geary near Stockton Street. This department
store, a West Coast branch of the famous New York Macy's,
carries a vast variety of mid-to-upper-price-range merchandise for the home and all members of the family. Fashion
lovers should head for the shop-within-a-store dedicated to
ultrachic designer clothing. Across the street, at Stockton
and O'Farrell streets, is a second Macy's, this one filled with
menswear, children's wear, electronics, and luggage. There's
also **The Plum** restaurant for table service and **The Plum
Express** for cafeteria-style dining.

In a building with a handsome white marble façade at the
corner of Geary and Stockton streets, **I. Magnin**, a long-
established store with a wide selection of upscale fashions

and one of the poshest ladies' powder rooms in town, should be your next stop. Across the street, at the corner of Geary and Stockton, is **Neiman Marcus**, the San Francisco branch of the famed Dallas specialty store. The huge stained-glass dome inside the store is all that is left of the City of Paris department store, which was demolished over many protests to accommodate the present building. Within the store is the **Rotunda** restaurant, a comfortable place to have lunch.

At number 48 Stockton, a fellow in a toy-soldier's costume greets customers as they pass **F.A.O. Schwarz**, the famous toy store that occupies three floors here. Next door is **Ghirardelli Chocolate**, a must for chocolate fanatics.

North Beach Leather (not in North Beach at all, but occupying another corner of Geary and Stockton streets) features high-style leather clothing, while **Gucci**, at 200 Stockton, offers you a luxurious wood-and-marble interior in which to make costly choices in clothing and accessories. Right next door, **Hermès of Paris**, with some of the highest prices in the city, draws an enthusiastic clientele that covets the scarves, gloves, and ties. Farther up the same side of the street at number 238, **Bally of Switzerland** carries costly, conservatively designed shoes, clothing, and leather goods for men and women. A few steps away is **Arthur Beren**, another upscale footwear shop. On the next block is **Scheuer Linens**, operated for three generations by the same family and specializing in fine accoutrements for the bedroom, bathroom, and dining room. Nearby, the **Waterford/Wedgwood Shop** stocks a complete collection of these renowned Irish and British imports. **Alfred Dunhill of London**, at the corner of Stockton and Post, is famous for its smokers' supplies and leather goods.

On the north side of the square, at 340 Post Street, is **Bullock & Jones**, with high-quality conservative menswear and a line of Aquascutum rainwear and women's apparel, and at 360 Post is Northern California's only branch of **Tiffany & Co**. At the corner of Post and Powell streets is **Saks Fifth Avenue**, a handsome branch of the reputable specialty store that dresses New York fashionables.

West of Union Square

Moving on to the west side of the square: Within the St. Francis Hotel at 335 Powell Street is **MCM**, filled with accessories and travel gear from Munich, imprinted with the manufacturers' status logo, and a **Victoria's Secret** lingerie boutique. Farther west along Post Street you'll find several interesting little shops, among them **Swaine Adeney**, at 434 Post, the only branch of this "veddy" British shop, where horsewhips, riding gear, umbrellas, and other accessories fit for royalty can be purchased. Take a few more steps and you'll come to **Bazaar Cada Dia**, which offers ethnic crafts and jewelry from around the world. At number 460 is the delightful **La Parisienne**, where French costume jewelry and vintage posters are fancifully displayed in antique French showcases.

One street north, at 522 Sutter Street, is the **Pasquale Ianetti Gallery**, which has a substantial collection of prints by Old Masters and contemporary artists. **The Forgotten Woman**, which you'll find behind a gated garden at number 550, deals in fashion in large sizes. **Boto Glass Art** is a gallery of etched and colored decorative glass; **The Bookstall**, at 570 Sutter, offers old and rare volumes. Across the street at number 563 is **La Bouquetière**, a charming shop that does custom dried-flower arrangements and sells interesting giftware and pot-pourri. Those who don't mind strolling just a little farther on will find **Obiko**, 794 Sutter, a fine little boutique specializing in unique clothing, some of which could double as works of art and most fashioned by local designers.

East of Union Square

Along Geary Street, at 1 Union Square, you will find **Joan & David**, a sleek contemporary shop selling fine footwear and leather accessories for men and women. **Kris Kelly**, 174 Geary, is a delightfully fragrant three-level shop specializing in very romantic linens and giftware, while **Betsey Johnson**, number 160, offers trendy apparel for young fashionables. **Paul Bauer**, nearby, sells fine crystal and dinnerware, and next door is the **Hanson Art Gallery**, showcasing contemporary artists. **Britex Fabrics**, at number 146, carries just about everything any seamstress would ever need on several well-stocked floors. The **East-West Gallery** at number 136 deals exclusively in contemporary Russian art. **Bottega Veneta**, at 108 Geary, sells high-status handmade Italian leather goods and accessories, and next door **N. Peal Cashmere** is the place for shoppers with a soft spot in their hearts for this very luxe knitwear, especially sweaters and socks.

At 49 Geary is the **Fraenkel Gallery**, which specializes in 19th- and 20th-century photography, the **Stephen Wirtz Gallery** of contemporary photography and artwork, and **Ebert Gallery**, specializing in regional abstract expressionism and realism. **Gallery Paule Anglim** at 14 Geary is best known for exhibiting painting, sculpture, and conceptual art.

One block north is Post Street and the chance to explore several worthwhile stores. At 272 Post is **Jaeger**, specializing in fine English sportswear. **Gump's** is nearby, a local institution founded in 1865 and known far and wide for its pearls and jade, fine Asian decorative arts, vast collection of the highest quality china and crystal, and gallery of contemporary crafts. High-status handbags, leather accessories, and luggage can be found next door at **Louis Vuitton**. Status without the high prices can be found at number 222, where **Ciro** offers faux jewelry. At number 251 is the **Allrich Gallery**, which deals mostly in contemporary California artwork, and on the same block is **Cartier**, the jewelry house. **Burberry's**, next door, carries upscale rainwear and sportswear for men and women. **Escada**, also on the same block, carries high fashion with the designer's label. Across the street is **Eddie Bauer**, for quality clothing and other gear for the well-outfitted sportsperson. **Max Mara**, 175 Post, sells well-made Italian clothing at prices that fashion mavens insist are reasonable for the styling and workmanship; not a store for the budget-minded.

At 150 Post is **Williams-Sonoma**, a premier cookware shop for serious gourmets. Next door is **Mark Cross**, purveyors of status leather accessories. **Celine**, at 155 Post, stocks apparel from the Paris designer of the same name at prices that might make you swoon, while high-quality clothing at more down-to-earth prices can be found at **Episode** nearby.

The dramatic block-long **Crocker Galleria** at 50 Post Street, modeled after Milan's elegant Galleria Vittorio Emanuele, is a handsome collection of shops on several levels, but in general the mid-price merchandise lacks real excitement. Among the more compelling of the Galleria's stores are **Gianni Versace**, **Marimekko**, and **Ralph Lauren** for label collectors.

At 353 Sutter Street **Jessica McClintock** stocks a sugary assortment of romantic clothing created by the San Francisco designer. **Wilkes Bashford**, on the same side of the street, has high-ticket, high-fashion designer apparel for men and women and a lower level full of unusual home accessories. Nearby, at number 359, is **Joan Vass**, a shop specializing in upscale sportswear made of cotton cashmere. On the same side of the street is **Michelangelo**, which carries private-label Italian clothing for high-style men, and **Bay Arts**, a gallery highlighting arts and crafts by Bay Area artists.

Just across the way **Diagonale** specializes in men's and

women's clothing, mostly by Italian designers, and **Laise Adzer**, at number 360, sells dramatic clothing with an ethnic influence. At 370 Sutter **Klaus Murer**, a former Olympic skier, designs fine jewelry for the carriage trade. **Loehmann's**, 222 Sutter, is a bargain hunter's paradise, featuring lots of deeply discounted famous-maker clothing, usually with the labels removed. Across the street is **My Favorite Clothing and Shoe Store**, another great place for discount shopping, with a particularly good shoe department. **22 Steps**, at 280 Sutter Street (down a flight of 22 steps), is a stunning store carrying upscale footwear. **Jeanne Marc**, at 262 Sutter, is named for two local designers (she's Jeanne, he's Marc) who have carved a national reputation for themselves with their colorful, whimsical clothing for women.

There are several galleries at 250 Sutter Street, among them the **Braunstein/Quay Gallery** on the third floor, specializing in contemporary works on paper, and sculpture and painting, the **Montgomery Gallery**, which shows European and American art from 1830 to 1940, and **871 Fine Arts**, which carries modern California artwork.

Maiden Lane

It's hard to believe that this charming, historic byway, running east from Union Square, parallel with Post and Geary, and bordered by pricey shops, was a seedy enclave of bordellos until the earthquake and fire of 1906. At 34 Maiden Lane is **Orientations**, a serene place to find tasteful Asian furnishings. Nearby, at number 50, is **Métier**, a new shop specializing in contemporary sportwear for men and women by up-and-coming designers. At number 60 is **Candelier**, where you can fill all of your candle needs.

The **Circle Gallery**, at 140 Maiden Lane, may attract you with its contemporary art, but it's best known because Frank Lloyd Wright designed the building, and the ramp leading to the upper floor served as a prototype for New York's Guggenheim Museum. **Pierre Deux** at number 120 offers a splendid array of French provincial fabrics and home furnishings and the mirrored and sparkling **Chanel Boutique** at number 155 is one of the most beautiful—and expensive—clothing shops in the city. Nearby, **Dreamweaver** offers hand-knit sweaters from around the globe.

Grant Avenue

One block east of Stockton Street (the eastern border of Union Square) is Grant Avenue, crammed with shops all the way down to its intersection with Market Street. Starting north of Sutter Street: **Teuscher of Switzerland**, 255 Grant, is a good place for a Swiss-chocolate break; **Jasmin**, a by-appointment-preferred boutique next door, deals very personally with fashion-conscious customers who are interested in upscale, designer clothing (Tel: 433-5550); and the **Erika Meyerovich Gallery** at number 231 carries some of the greatest names in contemporary art on its three levels. If you are ready for a rest at this point, you might appreciate the services of **La Belle Skin and Body Care Salons**, one of which is at 233 Grant Avenue, offering pedicures, facials, body massage, and other pampering services. **Malm**, a luggage-and-leather-accessories shop founded in 1856, is still run by the same family at 222 Grant.

Some of the city's best-known galleries are housed at number 228, including the **Berggruen Gallery**, dealer in some of the biggest American art names, and the **Mincher Wilcox Gallery**, which handles conceptual and minimalist work by American and European artists. For a change of pace, number 256 is **Banana Republic**, where it's always fun to poke around the safari-inspired sportswear. Across Grant Avenue is tiny Tillman Place, where you'll find the charming **Tillman Place Bookshop**.

For a bit of the delicious, head down the street to the **Candy Jar**, 210 Grant, which sells sensational egg-shaped truffles made by Joseph Schmidt, a local genius who works in chocolate. **Tom Wing & Sons**, next door, offers fine jade jewelry. **Coach Leathers**, at Post and Grant, sells fine leather goods and is one of the newest shops on the block. Across the street is San Francisco's oldest retail store, **Shreve & Co.**, a not-to-be-missed showcase of fine jewelry, silver, and crystal displayed in a historic shop full of marble columns. For conservative menswear, try **Brooks Brothers**, across from Shreve. Collectors will be charmed by the **Light Opera Gallery**, number 174, which deals in Russian lacquerware, paperweights, and kaleidoscopes. A branch of **Christofle** silversmiths of France is at 140 Grant.

At **Crate & Barrel**, 125 Grant, there are well-designed buys in home accessories, dishes, and glassware; on the next block is **Lanz**, which is famous for its flannel nightgowns and now offers daytime clothing as well. **Eileen West**, 33 Grant, is the only retail outlet for the dresses, sleepwear, and linens created by this local designer; **Overland Sheepskin**, at number 21, carries an assortment of sheepskin coats and pelts. At the foot of the street, a landmark Beaux Arts building (once a bank) is now an **Emporio Armani** boutique and trendy restaurant.

Powell and Market Streets

If you head west on Market Street from Grant, you'll find many shops of no particular distinction, but keep going. The big shopping reward is the **San Francisco Centre**, across from the intersection of Market, Fifth, and Powell streets. This shopping facility is San Francisco's first downtown mall, and most of its shops are prestigious clothing boutiques purveying labels by well-known designers and manufacturers. A distinctive element of the shopping experience here is the stacked and spiraling escalator that carries you through the oval atrium. **Nordstrom**, a famous retailer known for its service and quality merchandise, occupies the top three floors of the building and includes a beauty spa and four restaurants, where weary shoppers can refresh themselves. Nordstrom offers its customers valet parking at the Fifth Street entrance, but it's really just as easy, and cheaper, to park at the Fifth and Mission Street garage. Adjoining the San Francisco Centre is the **Emporium**, a long-established department store that carries an excellent selection of mid-priced merchandise; the store's lower level includes several snack bars and a counter for take-out food.

Bibliophiles might want to make a fast detour to 48 Turk Street (west of Hallidie Plaza at the foot of Powell) to visit the disorganized display at **McDonald's Bookstore**, which carries more than a million records, books, and magazines, many of them out-of-print editions. The block is seedy, but browsing amid the literature and erotica can be amusing. Head up Powell Street to find **Galina**, an attractive shop that deals in dramatic costume jewelry by Butler & Wilson of London.

Chinatown

Chinatown is not to be missed, although it will soon become apparent to you that while stores are plentiful, most carry the same merchandise. Nonetheless, it's a great place to find small, interesting, and inexpensive items. Stockton Street between Bush and Broadway (through a long tunnel north of Union Square) is where the day-to-day commerce of Chinatown is concentrated, and the street is usually full of housewives taking care of family shopping at bustling fish and poultry markets.

A block east, Grant Avenue caters to visitors in search of souvenirs; many shops are open until 10:00 P.M. every night. **Tai Nam Yang**, with stores at 438 and 408 Grant Avenue, carries decorative objects and rosewood furniture, and, to the north, **Dragon House**, a tiny, poorly lit shop at 455 Grant

Avenue, stocks some choice Asian antiques. As you continue north you'll find good prices on hand-embroidered Chinese linens at **Imperial Fashion**, 564 Grant Avenue, a little bit of everything at the **Canton Bazaar**, 616 Grant, and playful souvenirs at the **Chinatown Kite Shop**, at number 717. At 757 Grant is **Kee Fung Ng**, where you can get your own soapstone chop for making red ink, ideogram-like stamps.

If you're looking for an exotic cure, herb shops abound, and **Che Sun Tong Herb Shop**, 729 Washington Street (just off Grant), has the added attraction of being run by a man who speaks English. The **China Trade Center**, 838 Grant Avenue, carries a wide variety of Chinatown's wares on several shopping floors; across the street, **Man Hing Arts of China** stocks elaborate carvings and antiques. **Chew Chong Tai & Co.**, 905 Grant, deals in calligraphy supplies and claims to be Chinatown's oldest shop; **Fat Ming**, next door, is a Chinese stationery store that carries a few unusual books. The **Ten Ren Tea Co., Ltd.**, at number 949, is the place to find exotic teas and ginseng; a small factory, **Golden Gate Fortune Cookies**, 56 Ross Alley (a narrow street running from Jackson to Washington west of Grant), will supply you with some nontraditional cookies with naughty messages. **Ginn Wall**, 1016 Grant, offers all the cookware you need for a Chinese meal.

Embarcadero Center

At the eastern end of the Financial District (also east of Chinatown) is Embarcadero Center, a handsome eight-block complex with stores concentrated along Clay and Sacramento streets between Battery and Drumm, in Buildings One, Two, Three, and Four. Some, but not all, stores are open Sundays. Shops are located on the street, lobby, or podium level of these contemporary interconnected buildings; if you would like a meal you'll find plenty of places to dine or snack.

For the fashion-forward male there's **The Hound**, in the West Tower, 275 Battery Street, and nearby is **Freed, Teller, & Freed**, a branch of San Francisco's oldest coffee purveyors. In Building One is **Crabtree & Evelyn**, one of the prettiest places in town to buy toiletries, and **Game Gallery**, a shop that specializes in adult games. Building One also houses the **Pottery Barn**, which stocks attractive, affordable china and giftware. In Building Two, **Teezers** has some unusual tee-shirts and children's wear and **Papyrus** offers beautiful cards and wrapping papers. Building Three is home to **Jolin**, one of the most chic women's-wear shops in the center, and **Jest**

Jewels, featuring couture costume jewelry. In Building Three you'll also find **Bare Escentuals**, a bath and body shop full of delights, and **Cards Too**, which stocks a huge assortment of greeting cards. **The Nature Company**, in Building Four, carrying everything from books to toys, is a sheer delight for anyone with environmental interests. **Confetti**, also in Building Four, carries fine, unusual chocolates and is a good place to stop for an espresso. On the Parkway between the Hyatt Hotel and Building Four is **La Donia**, a tiny but well-stocked earring boutique.

Jackson Square and North Beach

The historic Jackson Square district, bounded by Washington, Pacific, Columbus, and Sansome streets, contains many buildings that date from the mid-1850s; thus, it is fitting that the area is now home to some of the finest antiques galleries in the city. **Robert Domergue & Co.**, 560 Jackson Street (at the corner of Columbus Avenue), carries European (especially French) furniture from the 18th and 19th centuries and high-quality architectural prints and drawings; one street north, **David Hill** (553 Pacific) deals in Asian art and fine Asian furniture. **Dillingham & Co.**, 470 Jackson, is known for its 18th-century English furniture, and, a few shops away, **Daniel Stein Antiques**, at 458 Jackson, offers a nice selection of masculine English pieces that would look right at home in an office or a den. **Challiss House**, just across the street, has a mixed stock of furniture and English porcelains, **Thomas Livingston**, at number 455, deals in American and English antiques, and **Foster-Gwin**, in nearby Hotaling Place, sells English and Continental furnishings. **W. Graham Arader**, 435 Jackson, is a fine place to shop for antique prints and maps. **Argentum—The Leopard's Head**, 414 Jackson, is well stocked with antique silver.

Prints Etc. at 494 Jackson Street carries prints and also does framing; **William Stout & Associates**, 804 Montgomery, is a marvelous store with an emphasis on architectural books; and **Arch**, 407 Jackson Street, is where you can find fanciful paper goods, art supplies, and unusual small gifts. **The Lotus Collection**, 500 Pacific, carries an impressive array of antique textiles from Europe and Asia.

North beyond the borders of downtown and Chinatown, Grant and Columbus avenues belong to North Beach, where the shops cater to offbeat and bohemian tastes. **City Lights Booksellers and Publishers**, 261 Columbus Avenue, owned by poet Lawrence Ferlinghetti, stays open until the wee hours and is a bibliophile's heaven. Works by many of San

Francisco's best-known Beat Generation writers are featured on the bookshelves. For a broad selection of new and used readables at discount prices, try **Columbus Books**, at 540 Broadway. On the next block, **Biordi Italian Imports**, 412 Columbus, stocks a good selection of ornate decorative and practical ceramics.

A few blocks east of Columbus, between Washington Square and Coit Tower, you'll find **Show Biz**, at 1318 Grant, a shop dedicated to entertainment memorabilia. **The Shlock Shop**, at 1418 Grant Avenue, is filled with all sorts of fanciful headgear to enable you to fulfill any fantasies you might harbor about dressing like a seaman, cowboy, or flying ace. A few doors away at number 1422 is the **Primal Art Center**, the place to find primitive art and sculpture, and next door is **Donna East/West**, a specialty shop dealing in up-market, contemporary clothing. Across the street are **Knitz & Leather**, specializing in one-of-a-kind knitwear and leather apparel, most of it designed by the shop's two owners; the **Kabul Afghanistan Shop**, which deals in exotic jewelry, rugs, and unusual slippers; and **Quantity Postcards**, where you'll discover thousands of collectible and current postcards, ranging in price from a few cents to big bucks. Nearby, at 478 Union Street, is a novel little shop called **Yoné**, with a connoisseur's collection of beads and buttons. Back on Grant and up the street at number 1529B is artist **Peter Macchiarini**'s jewelry and sculpture gallery; at number 1543 is **Slips**, which carries clever custom-made slipcovers suitable for folding and director's chairs, made by the shop's owner.

Fisherman's Wharf Area

In the Fisherman's Wharf neighborhood, **Cost Plus**, 2552 Taylor, is a great place to browse and purchase inexpensive decorative and practical goodies, ranging from teak trays and straw baskets to edibles. The adjacent **Cost Plus Wine Shop** has a fine selection of domestic and imported bottlings at attractive prices.

Along the water, at the intersection of Beach Street and the Embarcadero, is **Pier 39**, a wonderful place to visit with children because entertainment is regularly scheduled at several spots along the pier; shops are open from 10:30 A.M. to 8:30 P.M. Many of the businesses in this 45-acre, two-level complex are highly specialized, such as **Alamo Flags**, the place for serious flagwavers from around the world, or **Animal Country**, which stocks animal-theme toys and clothing. **Cartoon Junction** carries licensed cartoon-character merchandise; **The Disney Store** is like being in Disneyland without the rides (its stock is all licensed Disney merchandise); **Kite Flite** has a collection of kites from all over the world; and **Puppets on the Pier** deals in hand puppets and marionettes. **Wound About** is the place for a wide variety of mobile toys that get their impetus from batteries or windup keys; **Stamp-a-Teria**, filled with all manner of rubber stamps, is a budding bureaucrat's delight; Russian gift items can be found at the **Perestroika Store**. The **National Park Store**, with a tree growing up through the middle of the shop, carries maps, books, and park-related items and there are bears galore at **Ready Teddy**. On the first level, the **Cable Car Store**, with a storefront that resembles a cable car, stocks all manner of related items and the **Kids' Kottage** carries specialty children's wear and toys.

For adults the Pier offers mobiles and sculpture by local artists at **Designs in Motion**; movie memorabilia at **Hollywood U.S.A.**; and California country crafts and gifts at **Country San Francisco**. **Behind the Wheel** carries gifts for auto buffs, **Left-Hand World** deals in items for southpaws, and **Magnet P. I.** is where you can choose from thousands of refrigerator magnets.

Walk six blocks west along Jefferson Street from Pier 39 and you'll come to **The Cannery**, 2801 Leavenworth, a handsome square-block collection of shops, galleries, restaurants, and entertainment offerings in brick buildings that housed a peach-packing plant around the turn of the century. Frequently there's free entertainment in the courtyard, and always a variety of intriguing shops, including **Aerial**, with architectural books and prints as well as high-quality accessories; **Kachina** for Native American crafts and jewelry; **Peter Robins** for all manner of music boxes; **The Cannery Kid**, a colorful shop filled with kites and other toys; and **Past & Present**'s lovely assortment of home accessories, mostly handmade by local and foreign artisans. **Russian Treasure**, on the second level, offers stacking dolls, lacquerware boxes, and other giftware. On the third level is the new **Museum of the City of San Francisco**.

On the first floor is a large gourmet market full of tempting edibles and interesting wines and beers and **Best Comics**, where you'll find contemporary and collector comics, as well as posters from the psychedelic 1960s. There's a particularly good collection of art by Rick Griffin, whose posters publicized the Grateful Dead.

From The Cannery's Beach Street exit, it's just a one-block stroll west to **Ghirardelli Square**, a complex of rambling brick buildings that has National Historic Register status, and that served at various times as a woollen mill and a chocolate factory. It's a wonderful area for browsing and strolling, and you can usually find free entertainment around the patio level. In summer, shops are open 10:00 A.M. to 9:00 P.M. Monday through Saturday (until 6:00 P.M. on Sundays); in the less touristy winter months, stores are generally open until 6:00 P.M., except those on the main plaza, which stay open until 9:00 P.M.

Almost the entire second floor of the Cocoa Building is occupied by **Xanadu**, a gallery that carries Asian, African, and folk art. Also notable in the Cocoa Building is **Kilkenny Shop**, featuring Irish imports. **Goosebumps**, in the Mustard Building, is filled with amusing contemporary gifts. The **California Crafts Museum**, in the Rose Court, displays and sells work by local artists. On the Beach Street side **The Kite Shop** sells kites from many nations; **something/ANYTHING** (in the West Plaza) is a fine place to find a piece of jewelry or crafts made in California. In the Woolen Building you'll find the **White Buffalo Gallery**, which stocks mostly Native American crafts.

Cow Hollow

Named for the dairy farms that once populated this neighborhood, Cow Hollow has been transformed into a chic district that incorporates a seven-block shopping area along Union Street from Van Ness west to Steiner, and down Fillmore from Union to Lombard. Many of the shops are hidden in courtyards.

The Enchanted Crystal, 1771 Union, sells all kinds of crystal geegaws from the practical to the mystical. **Saint Eligius**, in the same complex of shops, sells gems and original jewelry designs made by the two European-trained goldsmiths who work on the premises. On the same side of the street is a delightful shingled building in which you'll find the **Lois Ehrenfeld Gallery** at number 1782, a treasure trove of Indian and Asian art. Downstairs is **Images of the North**, another gallery, but this one of Eskimo and Native American arts. At number 1784 is **A Touch of Asia**, a small shop filled with lovely Korean chests and home accessories. Across the street, at number 1749, is **Zuni Pueblo**, a tribal-owned shop specializing in jewelry, pottery, and sculpture. Nearby is **Arte Forma**, offering contemporary furnishings from local and Italian designers.

On the next block at number 1824 is **Peter Rabbit's House**, the first U.S. mainland branch of a Japanese chain of quality children's clothing shops; in the back of the store is a garden maze, where children can play while the adults shop. **Oggetti**, 1846 Union Street, carries sensational Italian paper goods. **Carol Doda**'s lingerie boutique, located next door in a courtyard, is owned by San Francisco's first topless dancer. **Bauer Antiques**, at number 1878, is the oldest antiques shop on Union Street—its specialties are French antiques from the 18th century onward, and Italian painted furniture and accessories.

The emphasis is on Art Deco–era watches and jewelry at **Paris 1925**, upstairs at 1954 Union. Across the street is **The Dolls and Bears of Charlton Court**, which stocks more than a thousand dolls and bears and runs a "hospital" to repair them. **Yankee Doodle Dandy**, on the next block, has one of the largest collections of pre-1935 quilts in the country. At number 2070 you'll find **UKO Japanese Clothing** for men, women, and children and next door **Body Time** carries its own appealing brand of toiletry products and cosmetics. **Farnoosh**, across the street at number 2001, carries dramatic women's clothing; its next-door neighbor, **Shaw**, focuses on pricey, high-fashion shoes. Innovative women's clothing by European designers is carried at **Vivo**, at 2124 Union Street. **The Lighthouse** nearby is a fine place to browse through metaphysical books. Across the street is **Enzo Valenti**, a place for seriously discounted Maude Frison shoes for women and bargain Italian shoes for men, and the **Trojanowska Gallery**, which mostly shows works by San Francisco artists. **Three Bags Full**, at number 2181, is a wonderful sweater shop, and nearby **Tampico** is part of a complex of courtyard stores. The specialty at Tampico is handmade, natural-fiber clothing, and antique and vintage jewelry.

Turn down Fillmore Street and you'll find many more interesting shops, among them **Artifacts**, for contemporary art and crafts, and **Silk Route**, with a marvelous selection of tribal rugs, clothing, carved masks, and jewelry from all over the world. If you are intrigued by hardware shops, **Fredericksen's**, 3029 Fillmore, has been pleasing do-it-yourselfers since 1896. **Mark Harrington**, a small but choice shop specializing in fine crystal and glassware, was established in 1932. A few steps along is **Warm Things**, which focuses on down bedding.

At number 3131 is **T.Z. Shiota**, a shop that has been dealing in Japanese porcelains and prints for 94 years (the last 20 in Cow Hollow). Nearby, at number 2254, is **Coco's Italian Dreams**, which carries women's one-size-fits-all, romantic, washable, handmade Italian clothing. The creations are all lacy, whipped-cream fantasies, designed by a German and manufactured in Italy.

Union Street Music Box Co., at the corner of Fillmore and Union, has a sensational collection of music boxes, from whimsical to serious. Across the street, **Carnevale** offers fashionable clothing from small designers. **PSC**, a few doors away, specializes in baseball cards and other sports memorabilia.

Haight-Ashbury

This part of San Francisco between Golden Gate Park and the Civic Center caught the public's eye during the psychedelic 1960s, and although the mood is substantially more subdued now, this remains one of the city's most intriguing shopping areas, still much favored by the counterculture. The area boasts a remarkable concentration of used-clothing stores and many shops that deal in esoterica. **Saint Adrian Company**, 1334 Haight, is one of the many used bookstores you'll find in the area, with many volumes selling for half of what they cost when new. **Mascara Club**, 1408 Haight, has an interesting assortment of Mexican, South American, and African folk art, in addition to unusual French jewelry. On the same block, the **Piedmont Boutique** almost defies description, offering the costume supplies and apparel that fit right in here in the Haight. Across the street, at number 1427, is **The New Government**, featuring vintage clothing from the 1960s and 1970s.

Living Art, 1317 Haight Street, deals in live reptiles, fish, and rodents for those eccentric visitors who would like to pick up a living souvenir of their visit. On the same block is **Bound Together**, an anarchist bookstore, and **Recycled Records**, which trades in used and rare records, tapes, and compact discs. Close by, at 1157 Masonic Street, is **Positively Haight**, where you'll discover a remarkable cache of costume jewelry, tie-dyed clothing, and collectible objects from the 1960s. Local designer clothing is the specialty at **Solo**, 1472 Haight. Art Deco pieces and vintage dresses get the spotlight next door at **Sugartit**, while those interested in magic should check out **Touch Stone**, 1601 Page Street, and **Tools of Magick**, at 1915 Page.

Artery, 1510 Haight Street, carries a striking collection of primitive art; **The Soft Touch**, 1580 Haight, displays and sells works from a Bay Area arts collective; **Dharma**, 1600 Haight, is where you'll discover the ethnic fashions favored by present-day hippies; and a former theater at number 1660 has been turned into a used-clothing shop called **The Wasteland**. **Villains**, at 1672 Haight, where "everything is a steal," sells wild clothes for the rock-and-roll set; on the next block is **American Outlaw**, a shop full of outrageous hand-painted leather clothing. Nearby is **Backseat Betty**, dealing in black-leather apparel and lingerie for female bikers. Across the street is **La Rosa**, which sells and rents vintage formal wear for men and women. On the same side of the street, **Forma** carries an intriguing selection of useful and irreverent art objects. Talismans, jewelry, rocks, and statuary are traded at **Bones of Our Ancestors**, 624 Shrader Street.

Japantown

The focal point of San Francisco's Japanese community is Japan Center, a shopping-dining-entertainment complex that covers three square blocks bordered by Post, Geary, Laguna, and Fillmore streets. The Center has never managed to be as interesting as many people had hoped it might be, so it's worth a look only if you have the time—don't make it a high priority. The **Kinokuniya Bookstore** (upper level, West Building) has books, records, and magazines about Japan; **Kinokuniya Stationery & Gifts** (Kinokuniya Building) carries imported cards and paper. In the same building, **Asakichi** has decorative items and tansu chests. **Mr. Dandy** and **O'Sha're Corner** carry small-sized clothing for women in the Kintetsu Building. Also in the Kintetsu Building is **Murata Pearls**, offering a large, high-quality selection of the precious spheres; **Gallerie Voyage**, where the owner/artist does *sumi* brush painting; **Daikoku**, featuring folk arts and crafts and antique kimonos; and the **Ikenobo Ikebana Society**, where Japanese flower arrangements are always on display. For antique tansu chests, try **Genji** in the Buchanan Mall across from the Center. **Mikado** (Kintetsu Building) stocks everything you need to properly dress in a kimono; **Mashiko** (Kinokuniya Building) is a good place to find authentic regional Japanese pottery and tansu chests; and **Ginzu Discount** (Tasamak Plaza) is a fine place for inexpensive Asian souvenirs, from judo outfits to cooking utensils.

Beyond the Center, **Soko Hardware**, 1698 Post Street, is a wonderful place for exotic cookware and gardening equipment, and if you walk over to 190B Fillmore Street you'll find **Narumi Antiques**, which has some lovely pieces—especially stained glass and 18th- and 19th-century Japanese dolls. For vintage kimonos, try **Shige's Antique Kimonos** on the Webster Street bridge.

Sacramento Street

Most visitors don't know about this shopping area, which stretches from west to east from approximately Spruce to

Baker streets south of the Presidio, but if you are interested in smart, upmarket boutique merchandise and antiques, you will find it worth a trip.

Home accessories and tableware of distinction can be found at **Sue Fisher King**, 3067 Sacramento Street. A few doors away is **V. Breier**, a gallery dedicated to whimsical American decorative pieces, and in the next block is **American Pie**, a delightful general store that sells a variety of goods suitable for impulse shoppers. **Brava Strada**, at number 3247, is a beautiful shop full of stunning leather goods and accessories at upscale prices; **The Berkeley Millwork and Furniture Company**, at number 3228, features custom-crafted Japanese, Mission, and Shaker-inspired furnishings, each piece individually crafted from fine woods. **Forrest Jones** is a fine place to shop for kitchenware; Turkish carpets are the specialty at **Return to Tradition**; and **Elements**, at number 3350, has lovely Asian-inspired lamps and decorative accessories. **Robert Hering & Associates**, 3307 Sacramento Street, is the magnet here for 18th- and 19th-century English antiques and accessories. **The Town School Clothes Closet**, at number 3325, receives donated merchandise from some very fine homes. A few doors away is **Harvest**, which offers a wonderful assortment of Shaker- and country-style furniture and household accessories.

Elaine Magnin Needlepoint, at 3310 Sacramento, has supplies for those handy with a needle; **Phoenix Gallery**, at number 3391, has a noteworthy selection of Asian artifacts; and nearby **Shiki** stocks a lovely assortment of contemporary Japanese pottery. You'll find more exotica at **Kouchak's**, number 3369, a shop filled with Persian handicrafts, and **Sondra**, 3401 Sacramento, specializes in classic and sophisticated imported sportswear. **Walker McIntyre Antiques** specializes in Georgian and French furniture and porcelain, as well as lamps made from antique vases. American handmade crafts delight shoppers at **Cottonwood** at number 3461. **Les Poisson**, on the same block, imports French antiques from Provence and Normandy. In the next block is **Udinotti**, a chic gallery specializing in figurative contemporary art. A few doors away, **Santa Fe** emphasizes Southwestern design and both antique and contemporary Native American crafts. Farther along the block is **The Sonoma Country Store**, its redwood façade and slate-tile floor creating a charming setting for home accessories, partyware, and potted plants. **Claire's Antique Linens & Gifts**, 3313 Sacramento, is a treasure trove of crystal, linen, china, and furnishings, many of them from the 18th and 19th centuries. **Vignette**, next door, carries exquisite accessories for the well-dressed home. At number 3597, **The Woodchuck** deals in oak, bronze, Victoriana, and old advertising posters. **Dottie Doolittle Shoes**, at 3681 Sacramento, stocks shoes and socks for privileged kids; across the street, another **Dottie Doolittle** shop sells up-market clothing for young fashion plates. On the same side of the street, at number 3654, is the **Silver Tulip**, a pretty shop for cards and gifts, and just a few steps away is **Button Down**, a smart shop that sells high-end European and American sportswear for men and women, as well as unusual British toiletries. **Susan**, at number 3685, stocks some of the biggest names in European designer clothing for women.

South of Market

Popularly known as SoMa, this industrialized part of town south of Market Street is a bargain hunter's heaven, chock-full of outlets selling everything from toiletries to household wares. In general it's a no-frills shopping experience—dressing rooms are often communal, and bare-bones decor is the usual rule—but savings can be substantial. Because the outlets are spread over a wide area, the shopping can be tiresome unless you're driving; otherwise, try to restrict yourself to what's offered within a few blocks.

If you have limited time you can find a number of outlets under one roof at **Yerba Buena Square**, 899 Howard at Fifth Street, where several stores are clustered (the largest is the **Burlington Coat Factory**, which sells much more than coats). Also worth a stop in this building are **Multiple Choices**, for brand-name children's wear, **Toy Liquidators**, which sells children's toys and books, and **Shoe Pavilion**, which has an impressive array of footwear at good discounts. Numerous outlets are also concentrated in one building at **660 Third Street** (at Townsend); don't miss the **Outerwear Company**, stocking leather clothing and sporty jackets, **Saratoga Sport**, for modestly priced sportwear, and **Shoe Heaven**, which sells footwear at discount prices. Next door, at 688 Third Street, you can find an amazing selection of discounted kitchen items at the **Ritch Street Outlet**. For good buys on cosmetics and fragrances there's **New York Cosmetics and Fragrances**, 318 Brannan Street and 674 Eighth Street. **Spare Changes**, at 695 Third Street, deals in local designer clothing and apparel from Harvé Benard. At 610 Third is **Simply Cotton**, specializing in bargain-priced sportswear basics. A couple of blocks away at number 308 is **Jeanne Marc Downs**, selling discounted clothing by the well-known San Francisco design duo. A **Van Heusen Factory Store** at 601 Mission Street has a great selection of shirts and other men's casual wear. The **Fritzi Factory Outlet** at 218 Fremont carries bargain-priced clothing for women and children, including larger sizes.

Those who like frilly, romantic clothing and feminine laces and fabrics sold by the yard will find a wide selection at the **Gunne Sax Outlet**, 35 Stanford (off Second Street, between Brannan and Townsend streets), with labels such as Gunne Sax, Jessica McClintock, and Scott McClintock. Nearby is **AHC Apparel**, 625 Second Street, for men's and women's washable silk sportswear with the Go Silk label. **Carole's Shoe Outlet**, 350 Brannan, is the spot for designer shoes and handbags at discount prices. For artificial flowers and plants, try **Ssilkss**, 635 Brannan Street.

The Linen Factory Outlet, 475 Ninth Street, discounts table linens, kitchen items, and bed and bath accessories. A bit out of the way, but rewarding for dedicated bargain hunters, is **Heritage House**, 2190 Palou in the southeast part of the city. Go there to find top-of-the-line flatware, crystal, china, and silver at a discount that includes a replacement warranty. One of the most attractive and largest outlets is always-crowded **Esprit**, at 16th and Illinois streets, where you'll discover a huge selection of youthfully styled unisex sportswear, and, next door, a café where shopping energies can be recharged.

—Bea Pixa

DAY TRIPS FROM SAN FRANCISCO

BERKELEY, OAKLAND, MARIN COUNTY, THE COAST, PALO ALTO

By Carole Terwilliger Meyers

Carole Terwilliger Meyers, a native Californian, lives in Berkeley. She is the author of the award-winning Weekend Adventures for City-Weary People: Overnight Trips in Northern California *and* San Francisco Family Fun. *She has also written about travel for numerous regional and national publications.*

Although San Francisco itself provides enough to see and do to last a lifetime, even natives like a change of scene once in a while, and, even more than a change of scene, they like a change of weather. Sunshine and warmer temperatures are as easy to find as a freeway out of the city.

To the north across the Golden Gate Bridge is Marin County, with its inviting beaches and natural wonders. Majestic redwood groves are just a few minutes away from spectacular rugged coastal scenery and Southern California–style beaches. The weather here is reliably sunny; it is the place to go when you've had your fill of chilly winds and foggy afternoons.

To the south are yet more rugged vistas and beaches. Inland is Stanford, the area's leading private university, and

217

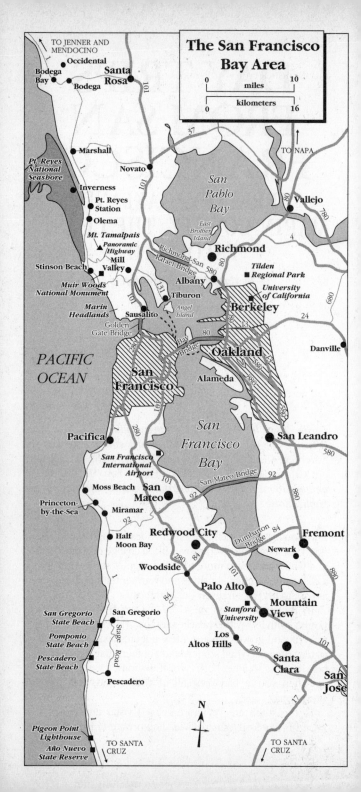

The San Francisco Bay Area

0 — miles — 10
0 — kilometers — 16

TO JENNER AND MENDOCINO

Occidental
Bodega Bay
Bodega
Santa Rosa

101

Marshall

Pt. Reyes National Seashore

Novato

TO NAPA

San Pablo Bay

Inverness
Pt. Reyes Station
Olema

37

80

Vallejo

780

East Brother Island

4

Mt. Tamalpais
Panoramic Highway
Mill Valley

Richmond-San Rafael Bridge

Richmond

580

80

Tilden Regional Park

Stinson Beach

1

University of California

Muir Woods National Monument

131

Albany

Tiburon

Marin Headlands

Sausalito

Angel Island

Berkeley

24

580

Golden Gate Bridge

101

Bay Bridge

13

580

80

Oakland

Danville

PACIFIC OCEAN

San Francisco

Alameda

880

Pacifica

101

280

San Francisco Bay

San Leandro

580

San Francisco International Airport

Moss Beach
Princeton-by-the-Sea

92

Miramar

San Mateo

92

San Mateo Bridge

880

Half Moon Bay

101

Redwood City

Dumbarton Bridge

84

Fremont

1

280

84

Newark

Woodside

101

880

84

Palo Alto

Stanford University

Mountain View

San Gregorio State Beach
Pomponio State Beach
Pescadero State Beach

San Gregorio

Stage Road

Los Altos Hills

280

Santa Clara

101

Pescadero

17

San Jose

Pigeon Point Lighthouse
Año Nuevo State Reserve

1

N

TO SANTA CRUZ

TO SANTA CRUZ

the sophisticated town of Palo Alto, which serves the needs of the university community.

To the east across the Bay Bridge is the always-fascinating community of Berkeley. Home to the University of California, the state's most prestigious public university, Berkeley is a study in contrasts, where both informal coffeehouses and acclaimed restaurants are plentiful. Nearby in Oakland you can experience the Bay Area's more conservative, Middle-America personality and east of Oakland you'll find both a fine museum and a state park.

When exploring these surrounding communities in your car, your morning trip out of San Francisco and your return later in the afternoon should be easy—commuter traffic will be going against you. But if you'd rather not drive, alternatives are the ferry to Sausalito or Tiburon in Marin County, or to Oakland's Jack London Square; CalTrain down the Peninsula to Palo Alto; and BART trains' convenient service to Berkeley and Oakland.

MAJOR INTEREST

Berkeley
University of California
Telegraph Avenue
The "Gourmet Ghetto"
Tilden Regional Park
Fourth Street

East Brother Lighthouse off Point Richmond

Oakland
Lake Merritt
Oakland Museum
Historic Paramount Theatre
Jack London Square

University of California at Berkeley Museum at Blackhawk
Mount Diablo State Park

Marin County
Sausalito
Tiburon
Mill Valley

North Coast
Muir Woods National Monument
Stinson Beach
Point Reyes National Seashore

South Coast
Princeton-by-the-Sea
Miramar Beach
Half Moon Bay
Año Nuevo State Reserve

Palo Alto and South
Stanford University
Filoli Estate
Silicon Valley
San Jose

BERKELEY

Visitors to Berkeley arrive with a variety of expectations. Some are looking for the intellectual climate associated with a community built around a great university, while others expect to see weird people and hippie communes. Those who know their food come seeking what is generally touted as the best available in the area, and those who know one of the town's nicknames, Berserkeley, expect to see a bit of that. Then there is the well-known ultraliberal political climate, in which someone who would be thought a liberal elsewhere is here considered to be a conservative, which explains another nickname—the People's Republic of Berkeley. In reality, Berkeley is all these things, and, making any stereotype impossible, it is also the place where the word "yuppie" was coined.

University of California

Because the University of California campus is the town's focal point, it is a good place to begin a visit. Reach the campus by taking the University Avenue exit off Freeway I-80 and following it east to Oxford Street, the university's western boundary. Street parking around the university can be difficult; a reasonably priced city parking lot, the Sather Gate Garage, is at 2450 Durant near Telegraph Avenue (for which see below).

The foremost attraction at the university is, of course, higher learning. Known for academic excellence, U.C. Berkeley boasts a faculty distinguished by eight Nobel Prize winners. Many noteworthy facilities on the 1,232-acre campus are open to the public, and a good way to get an overview is to take the free guided tour that leaves on Mondays, Wednes-

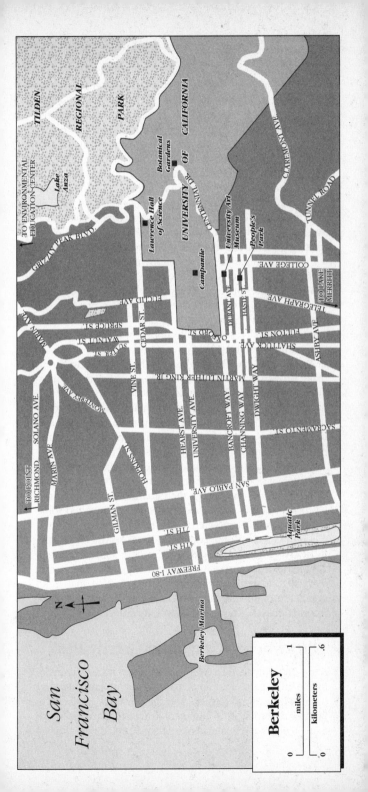

days, and Fridays at 10:00 A.M. and 1:00 P.M. from the visitors' center in University Hall, located at the intersection of Oxford Street and University Avenue. (Call for weekend schedule; Tel: 642-5215.) A self-guiding tour brochure is available here and at the Information Desk in the Student Union.

The landmark **campanile** stands approximately in the center of the campus. Rising 307 feet, it was modeled after the slightly taller campanile in St. Mark's Square in Venice. When classes are in session, ten-minute mini-concerts are hand-played on its 61-bell carillon three times each day (at 7:50 A.M., noon, and 6:00 P.M.). A 45-minute recital is given each Sunday at 2:00 P.M.—a good time to enjoy a picnic on the inviting grass surrounding the tower. You can ride an elevator to the campanile's observation platform, from which there is a 360-degree view of the area.

The **Phoebe Apperson Hearst Museum of Anthropology** (formerly the Lowie), to the south toward Bancroft Way, has been part of the campus since 1901 and houses the largest anthropological research collection in the western United States. Public exhibits change regularly.

Across from the Hearst Museum, the architecturally dramatic **University Art Museum** displays its permanent collection of modern and Asian art. It also boasts a large collection of paintings by Modernist Hans Hofmann and an attractive sculpture garden. The **Pacific Film Archive**, located in the museum's basement, is internationally known for its film exhibitions. Public programs are presented daily.

Just behind the museum, the European-style ▶ **Hotel Durant** is a good lodging choice and particularly popular with parents in town to visit their children at the university. Historic photos of the campus decorate hallways, and some of the attractively appointed rooms feature campanile views. A complimentary Continental breakfast is served downstairs in **Henry's Publick House & Grille**, where authentic Tiffany light fixtures are part of the decor. To stay in a private home, perhaps one built in the brown-shingle style that is so popular around the campus, contact ▶ **Bed & Breakfast International** (see Accommodations Reference).

Strawberry Canyon to Grizzly Peak

A trip on Centennial Drive through lush Strawberry Canyon, in the hills east of campus, takes you past fraternity and sorority houses and Memorial Stadium before you reach the **Botanical Garden**. This "library of living plants" covers more than 30 acres and contains more than 12,000 different types of plants organized into 16 collections according to geographic origin, taxonomic affinity, and economic value. Of special interest are the herb garden, rhododendron dell, redwood grove, California native-plants area, and Chinese medicinal herb garden. The Garden of Old Roses, a recent addition, is particularly beautiful in May, when it is in full bloom.

Continuing north on scenic Centennial Drive brings you to the celebrated **Lawrence Hall of Science**. Located high in the hills just below Grizzly Peak Boulevard, this participatory museum was established by the university in 1958 as a memorial to Ernest Orlando Lawrence, developer of the cyclotron and the university's first Nobel laureate. Of special interest to school-age children, this button-pusher's paradise holds educational games, an Earthquake Information Center, a seismograph, and a mini-planetarium. The snack bar provides a magnificent panoramic view of the bay and San Francisco; a computer here is keyed to the menu and allows you to score the nutritional value of your food choices.

Telegraph Avenue

This famous, or perhaps infamous, avenue runs south from the campus. Probably best known for its role as a gathering spot and point of confrontation during the 1960s Free Speech Movement, it has now slipped into a more peaceful state.

On weekdays rushing students crowd the avenue's sidewalks; on weekends visitors crowd its many boutiques. Strolling up and down Telegraph along the four blocks between Bancroft (the street forming the campus's southern boundary) and Dwight ways takes you through a street bazaar of crafts stalls where you can pick up a colorful tie-dyed tee-shirt or peace-symbol jewelry, and past **Annapurna**, a psychedelic "head shop" left over from the turbulent 1960s at number 2416. You'll also see thoroughly modern chain stores such as Mrs. Field's Cookies and The Gap here, which were controversial when they first opened because they displaced older mom-and-pop-type businesses.

In the 2400 block, bookstores include **Moe's** and **Shakespeare & Co.**, good choices for picking up unusual used editions, and **Cody's**, which holds Wednesday evening poetry readings and stocks new obscure tomes as well as the latest best-sellers. (Berkeley bookstores are said to sell more books per capita than shops in any other city in the country.) A stop for cappuccino at **The Med** makes for an atmospheric break. With a casual atmosphere and untidy decor, the coffeehouse is now an institution that seems to have been serving students forever. Don't miss their tasty chocolate layer cake with rum custard filling.

Head to **Revolution Books** (2425 Channing) to peruse a large selection of radical political reading matter. On the side of the building at the southwest corner of Haste Street, a faded mural (circa 1976) documents the turbulence on the avenue in the 1960s. Due east on this block is **People's Park**, the rallying place for many antiwar and free-speech protests in the 1960s and 1970s. Recently, in an attempt to make the park more accessible to students, the University of California cleared the site of its homeless residents and refurbished it with two sandy volleyball courts. The clearing was not accomplished without resistance and protest, but the volleyball courts remain.

For a solid meal, make a stop at **Larry Blake's** (2367 Telegraph). A campus gathering spot since 1940, it is known for its hamburgers and steaks and also serves an excellent barbecued beef sandwich. In the evening blues and jazz performances are often scheduled in its funky rathskeller. Or, if you prefer, make your way to the **Berkeley Thai House**, off Telegraph at 2511 Channing Way, where you can savor well-prepared ethnic specialties on a pleasant, sheltered upstairs deck.

At Telegraph's intersection with Bancroft Way (where Telegraph ends at the campus) you can pick up a quick, inexpensive lunch at one of the food stalls that appear here on weekdays; they dispense an assortment of international fast foods such as burritos and falafel and student favorites such as smoothies (a blended mixture of fruit and juice) and warm soft pretzels. This famous intersection also attracts all manner of performers—jugglers, musicians, revivalists. On weekends informal, free musical performances often take place in lower Sproul Plaza.

The "Gourmet Ghetto"

The area surrounding the intersection of Shattuck and Vine, northwest of campus, is not only home to the celebrated restaurant **Chez Panisse** but has sprouted a veritable garden of gourmet food shops as well.

The legendary restaurant at 1517 Shattuck Avenue, opened in 1971 by U.C. graduate Alice Waters as a hangout for her friends, is worth the trouble of making reservations. They are essential and may be made up to one month in advance; Tel:

510-548-5525. Each evening the expensive and small down-stairs dining room serves a different fixed-price menu featuring definitive California cuisine prepared with the freshest of ingredients.

An upstairs café is less expensive, though not less popular. In the café the food is simple, often bordering on bland, and could be a disappointment if you're expecting complexity or fire. A seasonal menu might offer such items as baked goat cheese salad or Spanish-style grilled chicken with lentils. Lunch reservations are only accepted for the café on the same day (Tel: 548-5049); no dinner reservations are accepted, and after 6:00 P.M. you should expect a long wait. A 15 percent service charge, which is automatically added to your bill, is divided by the entire staff.

Across the street a collective operates the **Cheese Board**, which sells freshly baked breads and hundreds of cheeses. One block north is **Saul's**, serving good deli food in a 100 percent smoke-free environment, and **Black Oak Books**, offering food for the mind. (Berkeley was the first city in the country to require restaurants to provide nonsmoking sections. Many establishments have voluntarily taken this dictate one step farther.)

East down Vine Street at the corner of Walnut, **Peet's Coffee and Tea** offers an impressive variety of coffee beans and teas. Now-retired owner Alfred Peet was the first in his trade to import specialty varieties of coffees and to dark-roast the beans. Coffee freaks still gather at this Berkeley institution in great numbers each morning, spilling right out into the street with their hot cups of deep, complex java. This is a good spot to observe the interesting mix of people that populate the city—you'll often see people in three-piece suits chatting with others in blue-collar work clothes. In Berkeley it sometimes seems that almost everyone, no matter what kind of work he or she does, has a curious, educated mind.

A few doors south of Chez Panisse on Shattuck, **Cha-Am** is the current leader in the informal ranking of the city's best Thai restaurants. Though its front dining room can be drafty in winter, many of the dishes are spicy enough to make up for it. Prices are rock bottom, keeping the restaurant jammed.

Across the street, the European-modern ▶ **French Hotel** is another popular spot to enjoy an espresso while watching the world go by. Sidewalk tables fill up fast in good weather. It is also a convenient, moderately priced place to spend the night. The hotel has only 18 rooms, each with a private patio, so the staff can treat guests to plenty of personal attention.

Next door the upscale **Andronico's** supermarket, which carries good take-out fare and local gourmet treats, has replaced the failed consumer-owned Co-op. (The Co-op operated from 1938 to 1988, and was once the country's largest urban cooperative.) South across the street is Cedar Center, a small shopping center where noteworthy shops include **Papyrus**, a branch in the chain of stationery and card stores that originated in Berkeley, and **Le Beastro**, where locals purchase trendy gifts and chow for their pets. **Café Ariel** presents yet another opportunity for a well-brewed cup of coffee. Next door to the center, ultra-casual **Smokey Joe's Café** attracts a clientele reminiscent of the Berkeley of the late 1960s. It's best at breakfast, when the unpretentious cook serves up some great meals.

GOURMET FOOD ON HOPKINS STREET

Berkeley's trendy food ghetto has an outpost on Hopkins Street, which can be reached by driving north on Shattuck Avenue, continuing on it as it becomes Sutter Street, until you come to Hopkins just before a tunnel. Turn left on Hopkins and follow it west to Monterey Avenue. Here the low-key but much-heralded **Monterey Market**, at 1550 Hopkins, caters to the sophisticated Berkeley palate with an amazing assortment of fresh produce. Locals come here to buy baby vegetables, unusual melons, and exotic wild mushrooms, and to reap the unexpected benefit of low prices. This market also supplies many of the area's finer restaurants; you might see chefs in aprons here selecting the ingredients for the day's menus.

Across the street, **Made to Order** abounds in wonderful deli fare, including freshly prepared salads and sandwiches. A coffee store, fish market, bakery, and poultry shop complete this European-style row of food shops. Plan a visit here to put together a picnic to enjoy up in the hills in magnificent Tilden Park. (To get to the park, follow Hopkins Street east to Sutter Street, turn left and then jog immediately to the right up Del Norte. Cautiously enter the traffic circle and exit up Marin, Berkeley's steepest street. Take a left at the top on Grizzly Peak Boulevard and at the second stop sign turn right onto Cañon Drive; follow it into the park to Central Park Drive.)

Tilden Regional Park

Exemplifying the wealth of natural beauty the Bay Area offers, this magnificent 740-acre regional park to the northeast of the campus is overflowing with sights to enjoy. The **Environmental Education Center,** with its informative programs and natural-history exhibits, is a good place to get oriented and obtain information about park attractions. In addition to pony rides and a 15-inch-gauge miniature train ride, the park is home to an antique carousel. Across the street from the carousel, Tilden's **Botanic Garden** features native plants and makes an ideal spot for a leisurely, quiet walk. A scenic 18-hole golf course is nearby, as is the swimming area of Lake Anza. Ten miles of hiking trails wind through the park.

Exit the park at Grizzly Peak Boulevard and head south to Claremont Avenue for a refreshing drive through less-populated areas of the city. The elegant ▶ **Claremont Resort & Spa,** a Victorian hotel built in 1915, sits where Claremont meets Ashby Avenue in the middle of an enclave of architecturally interesting homes. (Many of these homes were badly damaged or destroyed in the devastating 1991 firestorm.) The Claremont provides all the amenities of a resort in an urban setting: Olympic-size swimming pool, tennis courts, and modern spa. It also has an elegant restaurant with a good bay view (some rooms have wonderful views as well); Sunday brunch here is an extravagant buffet.

Across the street from the hotel, Domingo Square offers some interesting shopping. Of special note here is the **Bread Garden Bakery,** where superb French baguettes and baked goods are available daily. There's a branch of **Peet's Coffee and Tea** here, and cozy, informal **Rick & Ann's** serves an extensive breakfast menu until 2:30 P.M. in a completely nonsmoking environment. The menu features both the usual and the more unusual; try gingerbread waffles, hash prepared with beets, or lacy corn cakes.

Fourth Street

Surprisingly, in a city of Berkeley's size and income level, there are no department stores or traditional shopping malls here. Instead there is Whole Earth Access and Fourth Street. **Whole Earth Access** is reached by continuing west on Ashby Avenue from the Claremont until you reach Seventh Street. The sprawling store you will encounter is an offshoot of the tiny original mom-and-pop store that operated in the 1960s on Shattuck Avenue. Now under different ownership, the store encompasses three large buildings (and has five other locations) and sells everything from inexpensive imported bath soaps to pricey Sub-Zero refrigerators. You'll also find trendy clothes and comfortable shoes here. The management prides itself on offering top-of-the-line, quality products at competitive prices.

To reach **Fourth Street**, continue north on Seventh Street, turn left on Hearst, and then right on Fourth. Designed, built, and owned by a Berkeley developer/architectural firm, the 1800 block of Fourth Street features a 1920s industrial style of architecture. Buildings are kept at two stories, and the owner controls leasing of the entire block, hand-picking the approximately 20 tenants—this is a shopping mall done Berkeley-style.

Stores are unusual and oriented to the home. **The Gardener** specializes in elegant accessories for the garden, while **Builders Booksource** stocks books on architecture and design. **Elica's Paper** has an impressive selection of handmade Japanese papers, and the **Lighting Studio** displays the very best and latest in lighting fixtures. **Earthsake** stocks environmentally conscious products and donates a percentage of its profits to like-minded organizations. Other stores purvey linens, toys, and clothing. And because this shopping area is in Berkeley, where good food is never far away, you can enjoy an all American–style breakfast or lunch at **Bette's Oceanview Diner**. (There is no view of the ocean, however; the diner is named after the section of town.) Tips here are shared by all employees. If the wait is too long, you can get something to eat on the run at the adjacent **Bette's To Go**.

The newest addition to the block's dining options is the soothing and tranquil **O Chamé Restaurant & Tea Room** (Tel: 841-8783). Reminiscent of Chez Panisse in its simplicity and reliance on the freshest ingredients, the refined menu changes weekly. Upon it you might find a whimsical presentation such as a "tower" salad composed of stacked slices of daikon radish, smoked salmon, and mango, or a more traditional presentation such as a soup prepared with king salmon, mustard greens, fresh shiitake mushrooms, and soba noodles. A variety of sakes, including the Hakusan brand produced domestically in the Napa wine country, and an extensive list of teas are also available. Dessert can be simple: fresh sweet cherries served chilling amid ice cubes. Beautiful bento box lunches are available to go. Note that this is another restaurant that does not permit smoking.

On the corner of Hearst and Fourth streets, **Kona Kai Gardens** tends trendy baby lettuces on a quarter-acre plot. These are the organic baby salad greens known as mesclun that are used in many upscale restaurants, and when an excess is harvested, you can buy half-pound bags for a relative pittance. To inquire about reserving a bag, Tel: 486-0289.

One block north, outside the restrictions of the 1800 block, are several bargain-priced outlet stores. **Crate and Barrel**, the company's only outlet store in California, features clean-lined, contemporary accessories for the home and kitchen at bargain prices. Across the street, **Sweet Potatoes** carries charming cotton clothing for children.

East Brother Lighthouse

Though you'll have to detour a bit for this unusual overnight experience, the four-room ▶ **East Brother Lighthouse** offers the chance to spend the night in an operating lighthouse. Guests take a quarter-mile boat ride on the San Francisco Bay to the one-acre East Brother Island that is the site of a 120-year-old lighthouse. Then, having escaped the real world of TVs and radios, most visitors just sit around and exclaim over the magnificent views. An elegant, four-course candlelight dinner is served with thoughtfully selected wines; a full sit-down breakfast is served in the morning. Note that some rooms share bathrooms. The somewhat complicated driving instructions (the boat ramp is located in Point Richmond, just before the Richmond–San Rafael bridge north of Berkeley) are sent with lodging confirmation.

OAKLAND

Though this much-maligned city usually loses in the struggle with San Francisco for media attention, it does have a "there there." (Although Gertrude Stein, who lived here as a child, is often quoted as having said about the city, "There is no there there," in reality it seems that she was referring to what remained of her demolished childhood home.)

To reach Oakland from San Francisco, cross the Bay Bridge. Then, from Highway 580 take the Harrison Street exit and follow it west to lovely **Lake Merritt**, at the center of Lakeside Park. (From Berkeley, take Telegraph Avenue south to Grand Avenue, turn left, and follow it to the lake.)

Around Lake Merritt

On the lake's west edge near 14th Street, the 1876 Italianate-style Victorian **Camron-Stanford House**, which has been

restored and furnished in period fashion, is open for tours
on Wednesdays from 11:00 A.M. to 4:00 P.M. and on Sundays
from 1:00 to 5:00 P.M.; to tour the house at other times, Tel:
836-1976. A short film is also presented. Nearby, the Sailboat
House rents a variety of vessels, including rowboats and
sailboats, or you may want to board the replica Mississippi
sternwheeler *Merritt Queen* for a 30-minute tour of the lake.
In the park's center, near Bellevue Avenue, you'll find the
oldest wildlife refuge in the United States. Dating from 1870,
the **Lake Merritt Waterbird Refuge** is the winter home of all
kinds of migrating fowl, including brown pelicans, bay
ducks, and, occasionally, the rare tufted duck from Europe. A
highlight in the spring and early summer is a nesting colony
of egrets. The birds are fed each day at 3:30 P.M. In the
evening a lovely necklace of lights encircles the lake.

You can enjoy dinner at nearby **La Brasserie** at 542 Grand
Avenue. This restaurant serves country-style French dishes
such as *cassoulet* and sautéed sweetbreads to a loyal local
following; desserts are artistically presented in colorful
swirled sauces. La Brasserie is closed Mondays and Tuesdays;
Tel: 893-6206.

A short drive away, at 3909 Grand Avenue, **Piemonte
Ovest**, co-owned by football great Ronnie Lott, is a chic and
modestly priced spot to enjoy a weekday lunch, particularly
nice on the patio, or an informal dinner in one of the cozy
dining rooms. The menu features rustic Mediterranean-style
dishes and is particularly praised for its antipasti, pizzas, and
desserts. One delicious dessert pairs a lemon tart with silky
smooth Indian Sherry. This spot is popular with locals and is
always busy; reservations are advised; Tel: 601-0500. Next
door, **Country Home Furniture** displays quality country furniture and accessories inviting a browse, and just around the
corner and a block up on Jean Street, the **Oakland Municipal
Rose Garden** offers a quiet, contemplative stop.

Should you wish to spend the night in Oakland, the
recently restored Art Deco-style ▶ **Lake Merritt Hotel**,
which dates from 1927, is scenically positioned across from
the lake. Most of the reasonably priced rooms are spacious
suites, many with lovely views of the lake. A Continental
breakfast is included in the rates, and guests are offered
complimentary morning shuttle service to downtown Oakland. **The Terrace Room** here, which is enclosed by large
glass windows on three sides, features magnificent views of
Lake Merritt and is a good spot to enjoy lunch or an early
dinner; closed Saturday and Sunday.

Not far away, at Oak and 10th streets, the beautifully

designed tri-level **Oakland Museum** focuses on the art, natural sciences, and history of California. The museum, built in 1969, is celebrated both for its architecture and for its innovative shows. One permanent exhibit walks visitors across a miniature representation of the state, complete with appropriate plant and animal life.

A few blocks north of Lake Merritt, the grand Art Deco–style **Paramount Theatre** at Broadway and 21st Street is worth going out of your way to visit. Built in 1931, the renovated theater is at its best during an actual performance; try to come for the Organ Pops series, when silent films are accompanied live by a magnificent old Wurlitzer organ (the second largest west of the Mississippi), or for the Hollywood Movie Classics series, which features the best of the old movies. Tours are given on the first and third Saturdays of each month at 10:00 A.M.; Tel: 465-6400.

Jack London Square

Situated on the inlet of the Oakland Estuary and easily reached by following Broadway southwest from the theater to its terminus, the Jack London Square area borders the city's huge commercial shipping area. Come here to stroll the spacious, modern walkways, closed to motor traffic, and to stop in at a variety of shops. **Jack London Village**, an attractive shopping complex, is at the square's eastern end. Among the many restaurants in the area, two stand out: Upscale **Scott's Seafood Grill & Bar** (Tel: 444-3456) has an extensive menu of fresh seafood, and window tables overlooking the estuary; nearby **Il Pescatore** (Tel: 465-2188) offers a variety of Italian seafood dishes. Reservations are necessary at both.

An informal, funky bar, **Heinold's First and Last Chance Saloon** pays tribute to the area's waterfront past. Jack London, a longtime Oakland resident, was a regular customer during the period when he was an oyster fisherman here. Though somewhat menacing in appearance (it is impossible to see in through the thick windows), the saloon makes a good spot to wet your whistle. While here, you'll see still-functioning gas lamps and a clock that stopped at 5:18 A.M. in the 1906 earthquake.

If you've ever wondered what it would be like to spend the night on a luxury yacht, here's your chance to find out, although you'll never set sail. ▶ **Dockside Boat & Bed** rents out yachts anchored in the estuary that are not being used by their owners, including ones with a great view of San Francisco. A Continental breakfast is included, and arrangements can be made for dinner on board as well.

The recently opened ▶ **Waterfront Plaza Hotel**, with its glass-enclosed swimming pool deck overlooking the estuary, offers an atmosphere of casual luxury. More than half of its rooms have water views, and there are several spacious suites. The hotel restaurant, **Jack's Restaurant & Bar**, offers moderately priced meals and more splendid water views.

BLACKHAWK AND ENVIRONS

The opulent suburban housing enclave of Blackhawk, which was developed by Seattle Seahawks owner Kenneth Behring, is about an hour's drive southeast from Oakland. Take the Bay Bridge east to Highway 24, then follow 24 east to Highway 680 south. Exit from 680 in Danville at Sycamore Valley Road, follow the road east for about four miles to Camino Tassajara, then turn left and then right into the exclusive **Blackhawk Plaza**.

This shopping center, which has been landscaped with manmade rivers and waterfalls, is a soothing place. Exclusive shops here, including **Pro Image** for things sports-related and **Santa Fe Style** for home accessories in the Southwestern tradition, provide a glimpse into the upscale lifestyle of the area's residents. The **Blackhawk Market**, which once serenaded its customers with music played live on a grand piano and provided cellular phones for urgent calls to brokers, has toned down the glitz a bit but is still ultra-luxurious, with wide aisles and plenty of gourmet items. A good spot for refreshment is the elegant **Blackhawk Grille**, where refined salads and trendy pizzas share the menu with fresh fish entrées and hamburgers, and a pianist sometimes entertains. That Berkeley trend mentioned earlier has reached here, too, and no smoking is permitted. With a menu offering both sweet and savory crepes, **Café de Paris** provides less formal dining.

At the eastern end of the center are two stunning new museums built with plenty of gleaming glass and polished granite. The **University of California at Berkeley Museum** displays exhibits that have been developed from collections at the university. The Phoebe Apperson Hearst Museum of Anthropology is represented here by an exhibit using many of its early Native American artifacts, and the Department of Paleontology exhibits fossils that were found in the Blackhawk area. A selection from the University Art Museum collection is displayed in the basement. The **Behring Auto Museum** displays 100 classic and rare automobiles dating from 1897 into the 1980s, providing a complete history of automotive evolution. There are shining examples here of early Chevrolets and Fords as well as classic Bugattis and Duesenbergs. Both museums are closed on Mondays and major holidays.

Nearby **Mount Diablo State Park**, reached by taking Blackhawk Road west and continuing as it becomes Diablo Road, provides a panoramic view of the area from 3,849-foot-high Mount Diablo. On a very clear day you can see Lassen Peak, the Farallon Islands, and Yosemite's Half Dome without binoculars; it is said that only Mount Kilimanjaro in Africa has a more far-reaching view. Facilities include hiking trails, picnic tables, and a small museum at the summit.

In Danville, the **Eugene O'Neill National Historic Site (Tao House)** commemorates the playwright's contributions to American theater. O'Neill lived here while he wrote his last plays, among them *The Iceman Cometh, Long Day's Journey Into Night,* and *A Moon for the Misbegotten.* Reservations are required for the free tours of the site, which are conducted Wednesday through Sunday and include a van ride from downtown Danville; Tel: 838-0249.

MARIN COUNTY

Across the Golden Gate Bridge from San Francisco, spectacularly scenic Marin County comprises a number of prosperous bedroom communities. It is home to numerous rock stars and celebrities, including *Star Wars* filmmaker George Lucas, who built his studios in the hilly backcountry.

Books and films have poked fun at the generally upscale residents, creating a stereotype of people with an easygoing, laid-back approach to life, seeking nothing more than to tickle each other with peacock feathers while soaking in a hot tub, and emphasizing their New Age flakiness. The reality of Marin is for you to discover.

Consistently fair weather makes this area a popular destination with Bay Area locals, especially when other areas are covered by fog.

For a visit to the **Marin Headlands**, take the Alexander Avenue exit off Highway 101, just north of the Golden Gate Bridge, turn left at the stop sign, and continue west. Stop at the Visitor Center to get oriented, then enjoy a soul-soothing walk along Rodeo Beach. Ask at the Visitor Center for direc-

tions to the **California Marine Mammal Center**, where in-
jured marine mammals are nursed back to health, or to the
Bay Area Discovery Museum, a hands-on activity center for
children.

As you leave the Visitor Center, follow McCullough Road
east to Conzelman Road, which leads past some of the old
bunkers and gun batteries that attest to the area's military
past. Farther on, several twists in the road offer magnificent
views of the Golden Gate Bridge, and behind it, San Francisco; you may want to stop here to have your picture taken
on what appears to be the edge of the earth. To return to San
Francisco, continue along this road back to Highway 101,
where you can make a right turn onto the bridge; to reach
Sausalito make a left turn and follow the road under Highway 101 and downhill.

Sausalito

Sausalito is the first exit off Highway 101 after you cross the
Golden Gate Bridge and pass Vista Point and is also easily
reached by ferry from San Francisco. (Note that the exit is
marked "Alexander Avenue"; the exit three miles farther
north actually marked "Sausalito" is not as attractive or as
convenient.)

Tiny waterfront Sausalito, a former fishing village now
known as a magnet for artists and tourists, remains a pleasure for both. Set in the hilly area above **Bridgeway**, the
main shopping street, the village's charming homes and
gardens make a delightful scene. The street fronts the bay,
allowing for terrific views of San Francisco. A climb up
Princess Street (just south of the ferry terminal) will give you
an overview of both the houses and the bay.

A stroll along Bridgeway is the best way to see most of the
shops, galleries, and restaurants. Unusual among the many
boutiques is the multi-level **Village Fair** shopping enclave,
which was once a parking garage. This indoor center houses
35 shops and features a curvy, steep "Little Lombard" path to
the upper floors (there's also an elevator).

You can pick up picnic supplies in several stores along
Bridgeway. For invigorating alfresco dining, just cross the
street and find a spot to sit on the shoreline rocks, where
passing boats and seagulls provide free entertainment. The
low-profile **No Name Bar** at 757 Bridgeway is a good spot to
stop in for a drink; try a pitcher of Ramos Fizzes in the
garden-like back room. Live Dixieland jazz is performed

here every Sunday afternoon, and live jazz and blues are scheduled Wednesday through Saturday nights.

To see the less touristy side of Sausalito, go north on Bridgeway from the ferry terminal and turn left onto **Caledonia Street**, where the town's everyday business takes place. Of special interest is the spacious **Real Food Company** grocery at 200 Caledonia, which stocks an overwhelming variety of the health foods this area helped make popular.

About a half mile (1 km) north on Bridgeway, the U.S. **Army Corps of Engineers Bay Model** welcomes visitors. Located on the site of a shipyard that turned out World War II tankers and Liberty ships—built to replace cargo ships being sunk in huge numbers by enemy submarines and used to transport troops and supplies—it is a working hydraulic scale model of the Bay Area and Delta estuary systems. As big as two football fields, it was built to simulate bay water conditions for research. A computerized slide show and interpretive displays help make this complex scientific project understandable to the layman. The facility is open to visitors Tuesday through Saturday, but the model operates irregularly, so be sure to call ahead; Tel: 332-3871.

A few blocks farther north, at 400 Gate 5 Road, **Heath Ceramics** sells "seconds" of its unusual contemporary ceramic tableware at reduced prices.

STAYING AND DINING IN SAUSALITO

For fine dining and a magnificent view, try the ► **Casa Madrona Hotel**, nestled in a hill above Bridgeway. The food is California-style, the mood elegant and romantic (Tel: 331-5888). You can spend the night in one of the individually decorated rooms that are sprinkled down the hillside, each with a good view, or in one of the rooms in an older Victorian house located in back.

There is another special restaurant, the ► **Alta Mira Hotel**, in the hills above town at 125 Bulkley Avenue. Refined, reserved, and expensive, it serves traditional Continental cuisine and is a lovely spot at which to enjoy a leisurely lunch or Sunday brunch. Request a seat on the terrace, which commands an excellent bay view. Reservations are highly recommended; Tel: 332-1350. Twenty-eight quiet guest rooms and cottages, many with bay views, are available for overnight stays.

The small and quaint ► **Sausalito Hotel**, located next to the ferry landing right off Bridgeway at 16 El Portal, has 15 rooms decorated with Victorian antiques. The Marquis of

Queensberry Room holds a bed that, it is claimed, was once occupied by General Grant.

Farther north at Waldo Point is a private houseboat colony that contains both the funky and the exquisite. Visitors are not particularly welcomed by residents but are legally permitted to view the area if they respect posted no-trespassing signs. If you'd like to get a really close look by spending the night on one of the houseboats, it can be arranged through ▶ **Bed & Breakfast International**, which books guests onto several high-quality, upscale boats in the colony (see Accommodations Reference at the end of this chapter).

Across the freeway at 15 Shoreline Highway (at the Mill Valley/Stinson Beach exit off Highway 101) is the **Buckeye Roadhouse**. The latest venture by the creators of San Francisco's Fog City Diner, this popular spot is situated inside a Bavarian-style chalet dating from 1937. This unfussy restaurant features reasonable prices and generous portions; you can stop in for an impromptu snack of creative American-style food at the bar. For more serious dining, reservations are essential; Tel: 331-2600.

Tiburon

Often missed by visitors to San Francisco, Tiburon is smaller and less well known than Sausalito. Its tiny Main Street is sprinkled with a variety of boutiques and galleries, but locals usually visit with a restaurant in mind. Two of the most popular are the casual **Sam's Anchor Café**, which attracts a singles crowd for hamburgers and Sam's celebrated Ramos gin fizz, and **Guaymas**, which serves unusual regional Mexican fare and attracts a somewhat trendier crowd. A few doors down, the inexpensive **Sweden House Bakery** is the place to go for a delightful dessert pastry. You can enjoy more sedate dining upstairs at **Christopher's**, where the specialties are innovative fresh seafood dishes and extraordinary views of the bay and San Francisco. Especially recommended are the crab-and-lobster wontons and scampi. Dinner is served daily, lunch on weekends, and reservations are suggested; Tel: 435-4600.

Around the corner from the restaurants, still on Main Street, a series of shops occupy a strip known as Ark Row. These landbound houseboats are more than 100 years old. Stop in at the **Windsor Vineyards** tasting room for samplings of wines available only here. Wines bearing custom-made labels with your message of choice make unusual gifts and souvenirs. ▶ **Tiburon Lodge**, the only overnight accommodation in town, is just one block from Main Street. Amenities include a heated outdoor pool and whirlpool spas in some rooms. One whirlpool sits atop a platform right in the room with the bed; another room's spa is in an alcove of a black-tiled bathroom with piped-in stereo music and underwater mood lights. Across the street, the tiny, casual **New Morning Café** is a cheery place to squeeze in for a well-prepared breakfast.

If a picnic with a view sounds appealing, hasten to **McKegney Green**. Located on the outskirts of town on Greenwood Beach Road off Paradise Drive, this flat expanse of grass overlooks the bay and San Francisco. Pick up your picnic fare from **Let's Eat**, nearby at 1 Blackfield Drive in the Cove Shopping Center, where delicious salads and made-to-order sandwiches are packed to go. And you won't want to miss the fine desserts available almost next door at **Sweet Things**.

Not far away, at 376 Greenwood Beach Road, the 11-acre **Richardson Bay Audubon Center and Sanctuary** shelters a variety of birds and animals and offers a self-guided nature trail leading to a rocky beach and lookout spot with sweeping views of San Francisco. The oldest Victorian home in Marin County, the 1876 **Lyford House**, is located here, and is open for tours on Sunday afternoons; Tel: 388-2524.

The ferry to **Angel Island State Park** leaves from a dock located behind Main Street's restaurants (for schedule information, call 435-2131), or you can take the Red & White Fleet from San Francisco (see that chapter). This 740-acre island in the middle of San Francisco Bay is perfect for a picnic or a hike—it has about 12 miles of well-marked trails and paved roads so you can completely circle it. Some paths lead to old military ruins, reminders of the island's past: It has been a prison for Native Americans, a holding camp for quarantined immigrants (the island was once called the Ellis Island of the West), a prisoner-of-war camp, and a missile defense base.

To reach Tiburon by car from San Francisco, cross the Golden Gate Bridge and continue on Highway 101 to the Tiburon Boulevard exit; follow it east into town. (From Sausalito, take Highway 101 north and follow the same route.) See Getting Around for ferry information.

Mill Valley

Thought of by many as the quintessential Marin, the tiny laid-back town of Mill Valley originated as an enclave of vacation cabins built by San Franciscans eager to escape the city's notoriously cool summers. It rests in the shadow of Mount

Tamalpais, the county's principal landmark (see North Coast below). The center of town is Lytton Square, and the main shopping streets are Miller and Throckmorton avenues, which run off of the square. Use the charming **El Paseo** courtyard—where the shops and restaurants are housed in attractive buildings made with Mexican adobe bricks, hand-hewn railroad ties, and handmade tiles—as a shortcut from Throckmorton to Sunnyside Avenue.

For a walking tour of this tiny town, begin with a cup of coffee or a light snack at the **Depot Bookstore and Café** at 87 Throckmorton Avenue. Once the town's Northwestern Pacific Railroad depot, the café now seems to be its unofficial center and features both indoor and outdoor seating and, as the name suggests, plenty of books.

Continuing up Throckmorton, at number 59, you'll see the site of the original **Banana Republic** store—now a chain selling comfortable travel clothing all over the country. Around the corner at 44 East Blithedale Avenue, **The Avenue Grill** features a noisy, yet cozy, open dining room and an eclectic dinner menu; it's usually packed. Among the winners on the interesting menu are a superb corn griddle cake and a wonderful light crème brûlée that is perfect with coffee served in one of the restaurant's oversized cups. A large selection of unusual beers is also available in this 100 percent smoke-free restaurant; Tel: 388-6003.

For picnic supplies, stop in at the **Mill Valley Market** at 12 Corte Madera Avenue. Family-owned since 1929, it is well stocked with gourmet edibles; try the deli in the back for prepared salads and baked goods, among them an exquisite oatmeal-prune muffin. (A few blocks west on Throckmorton Avenue, **Old Mill Park**, sheltered by an old-growth redwood grove, offers idyllic stream-side picnicking. The park holds the town's namesake sawmill, which dates from 1834 and was recently restored, minus its waterwheel.) Continue up Corte Madera Avenue to number 35, where you can shop in the modest original location of the **Smith & Hawken** garden-supply store.

Back on Throckmorton, a branch of Berkeley's **Peet's Coffee and Tea** is at number 88. A little farther on, **Capricorn** stocks both kitchen accessories and an impressive collection of antique pine furniture. A block farther, at number 154, is **Footwear First**, which showcases an inspiring collection of imported shoes. Across the street at number 153, the almost legendary **Sweetwater** night club schedules intimate evening performances by an array of noteworthy rock and blues musicians. Bay Area residents Robert Cray and John Lee

Hooker have been known to drop in here. Call for the current lineup and show times; Tel: 388-2820. Down at the corner, the **Mill Valley Coffee Roastery** offers yet another opportunity to relax over coffee, with the added enticement of perching on a bag full of coffee beans while you sip.

Then turn down Miller Avenue: the **Susan Cummins Gallery** displays striking modern art and jewelry, while next door the **Summer House** purveys an unusual collection of home accessories. A few doors down, **Staccato** stocks a dazzling selection of fine women's clothing and accessories and a noteworthy hat collection.

This block is also home to two good restaurants. **Piazza D'Angelo** presents a menu of grilled meats and a large variety of pastas in an attractive setting. At casual **Jennie Low's Chinese Cuisine**, where all items are prepared without MSG, co-owner Jennie Low has designed a menu making use of her own sauces, which are also available bottled to take home. In the same building, **Roots & Legends** purveys Chinese medicinal herbal preparations that promise to cure what ails you.

To reach Mill Valley, take Highway 101 to the East Blithedale Avenue exit. Follow East Blithedale approximately 2 miles (3 km) west to Throckmorton Avenue, turn left, and follow Throckmorton into town. Note that on Saturdays you can park at meters free for two hours.

NORTH COAST

Head north from San Francisco to the west coast of Marin County for an escape into a quieter, less-populated area. Take the Highway 1 exit 5 miles (8 km) after you cross the Golden Gate Bridge. Highway 1, a two-lane road, winds through fragrant eucalyptus groves, then rustic countryside rife with wildflowers in spring, and for long stretches hugs oceanside cliffs. Good beaches add to the appeal, as does a spectacular national seashore.

Note, however, that this road can become quite congested on those sunny summer days when San Franciscans, like everyone else in the area, want to head to a spot where they can soak up some of that famous California sunshine that can be so elusive in the city.

A few miles before you arrive at Muir Woods the ▶ **Green Gulch Farm** Zen retreat is reached by a sharp downhill turnoff from the highway. The retreat offers public meditation programs on Sundays, when participants are also welcome for lunch. Visitors are welcome to walk through its organic garden any time (the garden supplies the herbs and vegetables for Green's Restaurant in San Francisco). Lodging is available in a peaceful Japanese-style guesthouse, and meals (included in the rates) may be taken with the residents.

About 1 mile (1½ km) farther on, the Muir Beach Overlook offers panoramic coastline views and is a good spot from which to watch the winter whale migration. From here the winding road drops like a rollercoaster into **Muir Beach**, left off the highway down a leafy, blackberry-lined lane just before the Pelican Inn. Swimming is unsafe, but sunning and people-watching are excellent, and picnic tables are available.

If you're looking for a pleasant stop for afternoon tea, try the ▶ **Pelican Inn.** Sheltered by towering pines and alders, it is a persuasive reconstruction of a 16th-century English Tudor inn. It has a cozy, wood-paneled bar area, and lunch and dinner are served every day but Monday. Several snug rooms, complete with canopied beds, are rented out upstairs. It was in this area (the exact spot is still disputed) more than 400 years ago that Sir Francis Drake beached the *Golden Hinde,* formerly known as the *Pelican,* and claimed California for Queen Elizabeth I. After the Pelican, fantastic views begin to loom ahead as you approach the turnoff for Muir Woods.

Muir Woods National Monument

Coast Redwood trees have a normal life span of 400 to 800 years, but some have been known to live for more than 2,000 years. They are found only in a 540-mile-long by 30-mile-wide strip of the Northern California coast. Located just off Highway 1, Muir Woods National Monument, a fragrant redwood forest, is a convenient way to see these majestic trees. Among its six miles of walking trails in 560 acres is an easy, paved Main Trail with interpretive exhibits; there are also seven unpaved trails, which are more challenging and lead away from the crowds. (This is an exception to the area's promise of escape from the masses—almost two million people visit Muir Woods each year. Only a visit early or late in the day, preferably midweek, offers the hope of some solitude.)

Naturalist John Muir, for whom the forest was named, said of it, "This is the best tree-lover's monument that could be found in all the forests of all the world." No matter what time of year, bring along warm wraps; the dense forest lets in very little sunlight, and the weather is usually damp, foggy, and cold.

From here you can either continue north to Stinson Beach on Highway 1 or backtrack a few miles to pick up the steep, winding, but very attractive Panoramic Highway over **Mount Tamalpais State Park** (or "Mount Tam" as the mountain is affectionately nicknamed). This two-lane road passes the ▶ **Mountain Home Inn**, a rustically attractive inn and restaurant, and continues on to Pan Toll Ranger Station (Tel: 388-2070), where you can park your car and get a trail map to the 200-plus miles of trails leading past creeks, waterfalls, and spectacular views.

If you are lucky enough to be in the area in May or June, save time for the **Mountain Play**. Presented annually since 1913 in the natural outdoor amphitheater atop Mount Tamalpais, the plays have run the gamut from the obscure to Shakespeare to well-known Broadway musicals; for ticket and parking information, call 383-1100. In the old days people came on burros, by stagecoach, or on the old Mount Tamalpais Scenic Railway, also known as the Crookedest Railroad in the World. Now many audience members ride the free shuttle buses up the mountain, and after the performance hike four miles down to an area where they can board a shuttle bus for the rest of the journey back to the parking area.

Stinson Beach

Among locals this seems to be everyone's favorite beach. This magnificent stretch of sand, at the end of the Panoramic Highway west of Muir Woods and north of Muir Beach on Highway 1, offers a small taste of the Southern California type of beach scene immortalized in song by the Beach Boys. Unlike at most Bay Area beaches, summer visitors may actually swim here, although the water is still quite cold and lifeguards are not always on duty. When the rest of the Bay Area is lost in fog, this small hamlet can be warm with sunshine. To check the weather at Stinson before setting out, call for a report; Tel: 868-1922.

Spending the night in one of the beach houses fronting the ocean here is a fantasy most people indulge in while sunbathing on the sand. The ▶ **Stinson Beach House** is a privately owned, million-dollar mansion that can be rented for two or more nights. It is claimed that the four windows in its dramatic front room cover such a wide horizon that you can actually see the curvature of the earth.

For people who prefer to spend just one night in Stinson Beach, with some pampering included, the lodging of choice is the relatively new Mediterranean-style ▶ **Casa del Mar**, where a full breakfast is served to guests each morning. Perched on a hill above town, it has six rooms, some of which have gorgeous ocean views. In fact, with balcony doors ajar, the sound of the breaking surf can be heard quite clearly. The inn's garden, dating back to the 1930s and obviously loved by the owner, was used as a teaching garden by the University of California's School of Landscape Architecture in the 1970s. Now guests are welcome to pinch and prune, should the mood strike them.

There is little commercial lodging in town, so spending the night here is a pleasure few enjoy. Bulging with tourists during the day, the town quiets significantly by sunset, when the busy, congested highway becomes calm and empty. Best of all, spending the night allows early access to the beach, so you can stroll the ocean's edge in search of shells in peace.

At night there isn't much to do for entertainment except dine at the casual, comfortable **Stinson Beach Grill**; that's enough because the food here is quite good. The eclectic menu includes a well-executed Greek salad and fresh fish, and the chef isn't afraid of spices. The bar dispenses a large variety of beers from Northern California microbreweries, plus many more from around the world. On sunny days you can enjoy lunch on a roadside deck. Reservations are suggested on weekends; Tel: 868-2002. Note that there is no gas station in town. According to a local resident, "It disappeared one night and didn't come back."

Point Reyes
National Seashore

About 15 miles (24 km) north of Stinson Beach on Highway 1 is the entrance to Point Reyes National Seashore, which stretches over approximately 25 miles of spectacular coastal land. Known for its beaches and hiking trails, the park has a wealth of interesting things for visitors to do.

Many activities are clustered around the park headquarters, a half mile west of Olema (Tel: 663-1092). A visitors' center houses a working seismograph and a variety of nature displays. A short walk away is **Kule Loklo**, a replica Miwok Indian village that was re-created using the same tools and materials that the Miwok used. Demonstrations of weaving, arrowhead-making, and other crafts are sometimes scheduled. At the adjacent Morgan Horse Ranch, pack and trail animals for the national parks are raised and trained.

Numerous hiking trails begin near the headquarters, including the self-guided Woodpecker Nature Trail; the mile-long, self-guided Earthquake Trail, which follows the infamous San Andreas fault; and the popular 4½-mile Bear Valley Trail, which winds through meadows, fern grottoes, and forests before ending at the ocean. Point Reyes also has more than 70 miles of equestrian trails, and horses may be rented at Five Brooks Stables, 3 miles (5 km) south of the park headquarters on Highway 1.

Twenty-three miles (37 km) northwest of the park headquarters is the **Point Reyes Lighthouse**, where, it is claimed, winds have been recorded blowing at 133 miles per hour—the highest rate in the continental U.S. The bottom line is that it gets very windy, cold, and wet at this scenic spot. The lighthouse, reached by hiking 300 steps down the side of a steep, rocky cliff, is a strategic spot in winter for viewing migrating gray whales; open Thursday through Monday, 10:00 A.M. to 4:30 P.M., weather permitting.

At the northern end of Point Reyes, wide, flat **Drake's Beach** is a good spot for taking a walk. An informal café here serves inexpensive fare such as home-style soups, hamburgers, and barbecued oysters. In the style of California cuisine, most items are prepared using fresh ingredients, many of which are obtained locally. The exceptional quality is a surprise in such rustic surroundings.

Within the park area you can view the various stages of the commercial oyster-farming process at the scenically situated **Johnson's Drakes Bay Oyster Company.** (Oysters are also available for purchase.) There are more oysters several miles north on Highway 1 in the rustic town of Marshall, where the house specialty at informal **Tony's Seafood** is oysters barbecued in their shells. Deep-fried oysters and fresh fish entrées are also good here.

STAYING AND DINING IN THE POINT REYES AREA

Many day-trippers end their excursions to this area with a casual dinner at the **Station House Café** in the town of Point Reyes Station on Highway 1. Moderately priced fare includes fresh fish, local oysters, and beef from organically fed cattle raised at the nearby Niman-Schell ranch. Breakfast and lunch are also served daily. Reservations are suggested on weekends; Tel: 663-1515.

Should you wish to spend the night, ▶ **Manka's Inverness Lodge** provides a romantic setting. This rustic old hunting lodge has both cozy lodge rooms and larger cabin units.

Room 1 boasts a large deck overlooking Tomales Bay, a clawfoot tub, and a large four-poster bed built from whole logs. You must climb up a step stool to reach the bed, which is made up with a featherbed and a fluffy down comforter. Local game is often on the dinner menu at the inn, served in the lodge's small dining room. An inexpensive but outstanding breakfast is served fireside in the lobby. One gustatory extravaganza featured eggs, scrambled with both local goat cheese and hand-gathered local mushrooms, served with a side of toasted herb bread with homemade rhubarb purée and blood-orange marmalade.

There are many charming little bed and breakfasts in this area; ▶ **Inns of Point Reyes** can provide information on them (P.O. Box 145, Inverness, CA 94937; Tel: 415-663-1420), as can ▶ **Coastal Lodging–Point Reyes National Seashore** (P.O. Box 1162, Point Reyes Station, CA 94956; Tel: 415-485-2678). One standout is the ▶ **Holly Tree Inn**. Located just beneath the Inverness Ridge in its own valley complete with a picturesque stream running through, the inn offers lots of space in attractively appointed rooms and two cottages. The rustic Sea Star cottage, situated on Tomales Bay, features a fireplace and a hot tub overlooking the bay.

On the return drive from Point Reyes, sometimes-crowded Sir Francis Drake Boulevard east from Olema takes you through different terrain; winding east through the coastal hills, it passes through several tiny hamlets and Samuel P. Taylor State Park, ending at busy Highway 101. Then it's a 12-mile (20-km) drive back down the highway to the Golden Gate Bridge and San Francisco. Another route back to 101 is east from Marshall over Marshall-Petaluma Road and Novato Boulevard, which leads you to Novato, a little more than 20 miles (32 km) north of San Francisco.

Or you can continue north on Highway 1 to the fishing village of **Bodega Bay**, where Alfred Hitchcock filmed *The Birds,* to watch local fishermen bring in their catch at the wharf. **The Tides Wharf Restaurant** offers moderately priced seafood and casual bay-view dining. A good place to spend the night here is the ▶ **Bodega Bay Lodge**, situated on the southern end of town overlooking the wetlands marsh and sand dunes of Doran Park. Most rooms in this rustically attractive modern motel have stunning ocean views, and a glass-enclosed whirlpool spa overlooks the marsh and ocean. Use of bicycles and an elaborate buffet breakfast are included in the rates.

About 10 miles (16 km) farther north, the tiny town of **Jenner** occupies the scenic site where the Russian River empties into the Pacific Ocean. Here you can begin your journey back to San Francisco by taking Highway 116 east. Plan a stop at **Duncans Mills**, about 10 miles (16 km) inland. Once a lumber town, this tiny village is now home to a number of small shops and several inexpensive restaurants. Continue on Highway 116 through Sebastopol and back to Highway 101 for your return to San Francisco.

SOUTH COAST

Like the north coast area, the coast south of San Francisco along Highway 1 is strikingly scenic. Leave San Francisco via 19th Avenue, then take the exit marked John Daly Boulevard south of the city toward Pacifica and Highway 1. After passing ridges of boxy houses in pastel tones (called "ticky-tacky" by folk singer Malvina Reynolds in her 1960s song "Little Boxes") and the beach town of Pacifica, Highway 1 winds to the ocean through a eucalyptus-lined gap in the coastal foothills.

Beginning about 2 miles (3 km) south of Pacifica, a 4-mile (6½-km) section of the narrow two-lane road known as **Devil's Slide** hugs cliffs that drop steeply into the sea. In fact, part of the road itself occasionally drops off. Though many people make informal stops here to take pictures, it can be unsafe, and restraint is in order until you find an obvious parking zone. This is one of the most dangerous stretches of road along the coast. Once the road passes through these hills, it turns inland a bit and becomes flatter and straighter.

This area is often covered by morning fog, which tends to burn off by noon. In fact, on many late summer and early fall days, when San Francisco is completely fogged in, this area is at its most beautiful. The spectacular unspoiled beaches are a popular destination any time, but especially then, when the weather is usually warm and clear. Be cautious, though, about going in the surf, as tides can be dangerous. Check with a ranger station or lifeguard before swimming or even wading.

Princeton-by-the-Sea

About 25 miles (40 km) south of San Francisco on Highway 1, the scenic fishing village of Princeton-by-the-Sea makes an inviting stop. Famed as a haven for bootleggers during Prohibition, it is now known more for its appeal to surfers and for its seafood restaurants.

Situated inside a Cape Cod–style structure built on the site where a speakeasy once stood, the **Shore Bird** specializes in serving fresh local fish in a refined atmosphere. Steaks, ribs, and pasta dishes are also on the menu, and the restaurant takes pride in its dressings, chowders, and desserts. Across the street the more modest **Fish Trap** beckons with a moderately priced fresh fish menu and casual dining on a glassed-in deck overlooking the harbor.

Fishing charters leave from Princeton harbor, and weekend whale-watching boat trips are scheduled December through April. These latter are sponsored by the nonprofit Oceanic Society Expeditions (Tel: 474-3385 or 800-326-7491) and cost from $27 to $32. (Advance reservations are necessary; call weekdays.)

Located about 5 miles (8 km) north of Princeton, the **James Fitzgerald Marine Reserve** in Moss Beach is considered one of the best spots on the West Coast to explore tidepools. Call ahead (Tel: 728-3584) to check the tide schedule; low tides provide the best opportunity for seeing unusual specimens, and free walks led by naturalists are scheduled then.

Miramar Beach

Two miles (3 km) south of Princeton, a turn toward the sea on Magellan Avenue brings you to peaceful Miramar Beach. Off the beaten path, it provides a chance to view the area as the lucky local residents do. The beach, reached by climbing down a breakwater constructed with large boulders, is a pleasant place to watch brown pelicans and scurrying sandpipers.

You can stay the night in the comfortable and attractive ▶ **Cypress Inn**. Located on a quiet frontage road, it claims to be the only beachfront inn for 50 miles in either direction, with magnificent ocean views from every room. Delicious afternoon snacks and a complete breakfast are included in the rates.

Just a few doors away, at 307 Mirada Road, the **Bach Dancing and Dynamite Society** presents jazz and classical concerts on Sunday afternoons at 4:30; the doors open at 3:00. Reservations are not accepted, but it is a good idea to call ahead for the lineup and performance times; Tel: 726-4143.

A few doors farther down, the **Miramar Beach Inn** serves fresh seafood and steak dinners. Though the menu is on the pricey side, dinner on a Friday or Saturday night includes free admission to the 10:00 P.M. live rock show. Reservations are recommended; Tel: 726-9053.

Half Moon Bay

The oldest of the coastal towns in this area, Half Moon Bay has an interesting Main Street that looks much as it has for a century. Two shops are noteworthy: **Feed & Fuel**, an old-time farm supply store, sells farm, pet, and garden supplies to locals, and has plenty of chicks, ducklings, bunnies, and other small farm animals for petting; the other, the **Cavanaugh Gallery**, displays a large selection of spare Amish-style furnishings and country art.

Good use is made of local seafood and produce in the kitchen of the attractively appointed ► **San Benito House**. Dinner is served Thursday through Sunday, or stay for Sunday brunch. Reservations are advised; Tel: 726-3425. Guest rooms upstairs feature solid walls, high ceilings, and bathrooms (some shared) with old-fashioned tubs. There's a formal English garden and a croquet lawn, as well as a deli for picnic fare and a lively Western-style saloon.

You also can put a picnic together at the quaint **Cunha Country Store**, which has been in the same building for more than 50 years, and the **Half Moon Bay Bakery**, which still uses its original brick ovens and is known for its French bread and Portuguese sweet bread. To enjoy all this good food, head west to Dunes Beach, a pleasant spot for picnicking.

South of Half Moon Bay

South of Half Moon Bay Highway 1 passes through bucolic, rich farmland, and there is a string of special beaches. Picturesque and popular, **San Gregorio State Beach** often has sunshine when there is none elsewhere along this stretch of coast. An "unofficial" nude beach is located just to the north. Pomponio State Beach and Pescadero State Beach are also good choices; the latter has large sand dunes and a 210-acre waterfowl refuge with hiking trails.

In the town of San Gregorio, a half-mile drive inland via La Honda Road to Stage Road, you'll find the **Peterson and Alsford General Store**. Built in 1899, this old-fashioned country emporium stocks rural wares and picnic supplies, and locals gather around its long bar to chew the fat. Take Stage Road south for a 7-mile (11-km) drive through the quiet coastal back country that ends almost in front of family-run **Duarte's Tavern**—a favored spot for a casual home-cooked meal—in the tiny agricultural town of Pescadero. Of special note are the restaurant's grilled fresh local fish and artichoke dishes, prepared using produce fresh from the local fields. (Artichokes are so plentiful in this area that a local high school has a cheer, "Artichokes to the left, artichokes to the right, stand up, sit down, fight, fight, fight!")

Eight miles (13 km) south from Pescadero on Highway 1 is the ▶ **Pigeon Point Lighthouse**. Named after the first big ship that crashed on the rocks here, the lighthouse now houses a hostel, where inexpensive rooms are available to anyone willing to put up with the inconveniences associated with hosteling. Rooms for couples are available by reservation. Built in 1871, this is the second-tallest (115 feet) free-standing lighthouse in the U.S. Public tours are usually given on weekends; for reservations, Tel: 879-0633.

Año Nuevo State Reserve

Continuing south a few more miles brings you to Año Nuevo State Reserve, one of only two mainland breeding colonies in the world for the northern elephant seal. The huge seals return to this beach each year to bear their young and to mate again. The season runs something like this: The males arrive in early December (this is when battles often occur), the females arrive in January, and the pups begin to arrive in late January. (Births can sometimes be observed.) Mating occurs in February, when the population peaks, and then the seals begin to leave.

Docent-guided tours, lasting two and a half hours and covering three miles, take visitors close enough to observe the seals basking in the sun or sleeping. Usually that is the extent of the activity to be seen, but occasionally one of the two-ton bulls roars into battle with a challenging male. Though the seals look fairly harmless, they are unpredictable and can be dangerous—males are especially irritable— so the law dictates that visitors may get no closer than 20 feet. Reservations are required for the tour and must be made at least ten days in advance; Tel: (800) 444-7275.

About 15 miles (24 km) south of the reserve is Santa Cruz (see The Central Coast chapter).

PALO ALTO AND SOUTH

Stanford, California's premier private university, stretches into the foothills at the edge of the sophisticated town of Palo Alto. With wide tree-lined streets and impressive mansions on its outlying boulevards, the city historically has been home to upper-class residents, many of whom are affiliated with the university. More recently it has become known for being a part of that nebulous area known as Silicon Valley.

Stanford University

Founded by Leland Stanford in 1885 on what had been his family's horse farm, Stanford University is dedicated to the memory of Stanford's son, who died of typhoid fever at the age of 15. It is now home to approximately 13,000 students.

Entry to the campus off busy El Camino Real (from San Francisco take Highway 101 and exit at the University Avenue exit) is down aptly named Palm Drive, at the end of which you'll find the main quadrangle. The oldest part of the 8,180-acre university, this area features buildings of mission-style architecture, with thick stucco or sandstone walls and red-tile roofs. Free hour-long campus tours, led by students, leave from the Visitor Information Booth daily at 11:00 A.M. and 3:15 P.M. (call to confirm; Tel: 723-2560). Tours of the two-mile-long linear accelerator are available by appointment (Tel: 926-2204).

Hoover Tower, Stanford's shorter version of the University of California's campanile, rises east of the main quadrangle. Standing 285 feet tall, the tower affords a panoramic view of the area and a visual orientation to the campus from its observation platform, which you can reach by elevator. A museum at the tower's base, part of the Hoover Institution on War, Revolution, and Peace, honors Stanford graduate Herbert Hoover.

Back down Palm Drive and to the west on Museum Way you'll find the **Stanford University Museum of Art**. Built in 1892, it is the oldest museum west of the Mississippi and the first building to be built of structurally reinforced concrete. It suffered severe damage in the 1989 earthquake and has been closed indefinitely for repairs. (To check the status, call before visiting; Tel: 723-4177.) When open, the museum offers extraordinary jades, Asian and Egyptian treasures, Stanford family memorabilia, and interesting California Native American exhibits, among them a canoe carved by the Yuroks from a single redwood log. Its eclectic collection also holds the gold spike that marked the meeting of the two sections of the transcontinental railroad in 1869.

An adjacent one-acre **Rodin Sculpture Garden** remains accessible. Tours are given at 2:00 P.M. on Wednesdays, Saturdays, and Sundays. Together the museum and garden hold the world's second-largest collection of Rodin sculpture. (The largest is in Paris.) The **Thomas Welton Art Gallery**, located between the tower and the quadrangle, is home to revolving exhibitions of international and regional artists' works.

The campus **Stanford Bookstore**, one of the largest bookstores in the country, carries both general-interest and scholarly tomes. A separate branch at 135 University Avenue specializes in medical, technical, and business books.

STANFORD SHOPPING CENTER

The fashionable Stanford Shopping Center, the only shopping center in the world owned by a university, is located north of the main campus, just west of El Camino Real. Among its 150 shops are a branch of the Wine Country's **Oakville Grocery**, filled with esoteric foods; **Smith & Hawken**, the innovative Mill Valley–based garden store; **Gleim Jewelers**, where the world's largest emerald is sometimes on display; a branch of Berkeley's **Monterey Market**; and **Schaub's Meat, Fish, and Poultry**, where a unique "black steak" is available. Don't miss the open-air **Polo/Ralph Lauren Home Collection**, located in the Inner Circle section. The unusual **Tribal Eye** offers African antiquities and handicrafts (its only other branch is in Nairobi, Kenya), and six major department stores are also represented. Several restaurants here (located in the Street Market section) attract crowds even when the stores are closed. **Babbo's Pizzeria Restaurant** serves up pizzas baked in wood-burning ovens at courtyard tables, and a branch of San Francisco's **Max's Opera Café** dishes up deli sandwiches ("ham" is provided by the servers, who double as opera-singing entertainers).

Beyond the shopping possibilities, the architectural design and landscaping of the center itself is of interest, as is the art on display, which reflects the center's philosophy of making art accessible, easy to understand, and fun for visitors.

Downtown Palo Alto

Follow Palm Drive east out of the campus and cross El Camino Real (where Palm Drive becomes University Avenue) to the center of the charming town of Palo Alto. Park your car and walk up one side of University Avenue, the main drag, and down the other along the brick-inlaid sidewalk. Most spots of interest are located on University in the six blocks between High and Webster streets. The side streets running off University also hold pleasant surprises.

As would be expected in a university town, bookstores are plentiful. **Stacey's** has an extraordinary collection of technical computer books, from esoteric computer-science subjects to personal computer programming books. **Bell's Bookstore,** 536 Emerson, has a good selection of general-interest titles but is best known for its extensive stock of new and used gardening books.

One of the most unusual sights here is the **Barbie Hall of Fame** at 460 Waverly Street. Opened in 1984 on the Barbie doll's 25th birthday, it is packed with more than 16,000 dolls and accessories. Open Tuesday through Saturday 1:30 to 4:30 P.M. and Saturday mornings from 10:00 A.M. to noon.

Restaurants on this busy street are varied and casual. **The Good Earth** is a popular natural-foods coffee shop open daily for breakfast, lunch, and dinner. Specialty coffees and pastries can be found at **Il Fornaio Café**, where sidewalk seating is available in good weather. A few doors away, **Suzanne's Muffins** offers a different selection each day from more than 100 breakfast, dessert, and savory varieties. Nearby **Liddicoat's Market** houses a variety of ethnic food stalls and is home to the very first Mrs. Field's Cookies stand.

Trendy Italian food is available for breakfast, lunch, and dinner daily at always-jammed **Il Fornaio Restaurant**, just off University at 520 Cowper, cousin to the aforementioned café. Rustic pizzas are served here either in the elegant interior or the sunny, peaceful courtyard in back. Reservations are recommended; Tel: 853-3888. For an overnight stay, the attractive ▶ **Garden Court Hotel** operates on the two floors above the restaurant (which prepares the room-service menu) and matches it in quality. Down another side street, **The London House** serves traditional pub fare and afternoon tea at 630 Ramona Street.

Several movie theaters on University are also worth a visit. The 1,200-seat **Stanford Theater** has been meticulously restored to its 1925-era grandeur by former classics professor David Packard, Jr., son of computer tycoon David Packard. Plush red mohair seats, elaborate ceiling paintings, and magnificent tile work in the lobby help take audiences back in time as they view pre-1950 Hollywood films. Silent films are often accompanied by an organist on the theater's Wurlitzer. Proceeds from the theater are used for film restoration (for information, Tel: 324-3700). Another old-time movie palace, the unrestored mission-style **Varsity Theatre**, operates a few blocks away and features foreign movies (Tel: 323-6411).

Convenient lodging can be found at the ▶ **Palo Alto Holiday Inn**, centrally located and offering the amenities typical of the chain. In addition to a large pool, which is particularly enjoyable here because of the generally good weather, it has an attractively landscaped garden area with a large *koi* pond.

little farther away, just north of the Stanford Shopping Center, the sedate ▶ **Stanford Park Hotel** offers spacious rooms, some with fireplaces and balconies. Each room is furnished with custom-made English yew wood furniture, including a full-sized desk with computer and fax hookups. Rooms also have an innovative computer-operated video system that allows guests to watch any of approximately 60 movies starting at any time around the clock. Facilities also include a pleasant pool area with a whirlpool spa and an adjacent fitness room and sauna. Complimentary treats served in the comfortable lobby include wine between 5:00 and 6:00 P.M., cookies at 10:00 P.M., and coffee and newspapers in the morning. There's also a full-service restaurant and bar here.

For a relaxed dining experience reserve a table for lunch or dinner at popular **MacArthur Park**. Situated a bit off the beaten path at 27 University Avenue near El Camino Real, the restaurant operates within a designated Historical Landmark. Designed for the U.S. War Department in 1918 by Julia Morgan, the architect of Hearst Castle, the building is now divided into several dining areas, including indoor balconies and a great barn-like room on the main floor. The kitchen is particularly celebrated for its baby back ribs, cooked here in an oakwood smoker; dry-aged steaks, live Maine lobster, and California game are other specialties. You can select a dessert from a menu fronted with a mouth-watering color reproduction of Wayne Thiebaud's *Two Meringues.* Parking is limited, but free valet service is provided; Tel: 321-9990.

When you return to Highway 101, or when you exit it into town, **Ming's** at 1700 Embarcadero Road is a convenient stop for a meal. The restaurant has existed in Palo Alto since the 1950s, when it opened on El Camino Real, and has been at its new location for several years. Ming's Beef, a somewhat sweet dish prepared with tender wok-charred beef that is a generic dish on many Chinese menus, was the restaurant's invention, as was its delicately flavored chicken salad. Made with shredded, deep-fried chicken, the salad is in such heavy demand that the restaurant employs one chef to prepare just that. Another chef prepares just dim sum delicacies; they are made fresh every morning and are available daily from 11:00 A.M. to 5:00 P.M.; Tel: 856-7700.

Filoli Estate

West of Palo Alto, in the wealthy suburban village of Wood-side, is the Filoli Estate. Under the protection of the National Trust for Historic Preservation, this 654-acre country king-dom features a 43-room modified Georgian mansion. Built in 1917 by architect Willis Polk, its ballroom is gilded with 200 pounds of gold extracted from the original owner's Empire Mine in Grass Valley (see The Gold Country chap-ter). The mansion is now best known as the exterior of the Carrington home shown at the beginning of TV's "Dynasty."

Tours of the 16 landscaped acres of mature formal gardens include such delights as two herbal gardens, a garden de-signed to resemble a stained-glass window at Chartres cathe-dral in France, and a practical cutting garden. Tours are scheduled Tuesday through Saturday, February through early November. Reservations are required (Tel: 364-2880); chil-dren under 12 are permitted only on Fridays.

Silicon Valley

Ever since the silicon chip was invented in a warehouse in nearby Mountain View, people have wanted to see the Sili-con Valley named after the chip. This isn't easy to do because the valley is an amorphous place. Unless you are extremely determined to see something in particular, you are better off not venturing into the morass of traffic jams that occurs in the heart of the area, around Santa Clara—this rapidly grow-ing area has been unable to keep its population as neatly laid-out and bug-free as a good computer program.

For an easy and representative view of the area's many computer firms, drive along Page Mill Road at the southern perimeter of the Stanford campus. There you will see the boxy low-rise architecture and expansive lawn landscaping typical of these big-name, world-famous electronics firms. Stretched out along this road are Alza, Varian, IBM, and Hewlett-Packard. Because of the secretive and competitive nature of the electronics business, none offers public tours.

San Jose

Farther south on Highway 280 is the sprawling metropolis of **San Jose**. Currently touting itself as the "capital of Silicon Valley" (24 of the area's largest computer companies have headquarters or divisions here), San Jose, although Califor-nia's third-largest city, has received little attention for its attractions. But that seems to be changing as the city concentrates on revitalizing its downtown area. Now visitors to the city center can enjoy its reliably mild climate as well as its many cultural offerings.

The following three facilities are all located along an impressive two-block stretch of West San Carlos Street. You'll find performances of ballet, symphony, and popular theater at the **San Jose Center for the Performing Arts**, and children ages 3 through 13 are sure to be entertained inside the striking **Children's Discovery Museum**. Designed by Mexico City architect Ricardo Legorreta, the lavender building houses the largest children's museum in the West.

It seems fitting that the capital of Silicon Valley should have a museum dedicated to documenting the valley's virtues. The compact **Museum of Innovation** acts as an interim facility until a more elaborate building, also to be designed by architect Legorreta, is constructed next to the Children's Discovery Museum. Focusing on what is currently being done at local computer companies, exhibits allow visitors to view how silicon chips are produced, to design a bicycle, and to meet Vanna the spelling robot. Most displays were designed and donated by local high-tech companies. A guided tour is highly recommended; they are scheduled regularly or you may request one on the spot. Volunteers are also on hand to answer questions, and video and newspaper clippings provide enlightening background information. Both museums are closed Mondays.

The **Rosicrucian Egyptian Museum**, at Park Avenue and Naglee, holds a collection highlighted by mummies, fine jewelry, and a full-size reproduction of a 4,000-year-old rock tomb—the only such tomb in the United States. Also here is the **Rosicrucian Science Museum and Planetarium**, which presents daily space-oriented programs. The grounds that surround the two museums are stunning, perfect for a stroll.

The **Winchester Mystery House**, at 525 South Winchester Boulevard, seems to have grown in sympathy with its city. Sarah Winchester, heir to the Winchester rifle fortune, believed that to make amends for a past wrongdoing she had to build additions to her home continuously, 24 hours a day. Her eccentric ideas resulted in some unusual features: asymmetrical rooms, narrow passageways, zigzag staircases, and doors opening into empty shafts. The tour takes in 110 rooms, climbs more than 200 steps, and covers almost a mile.

For luxury lodging in San Jose, try the high-rise ▶ **Fairmont Hotel**. Located conveniently within walking distance of all the downtown attractions, the hotel has an attractive pool and several restaurants. Best of all, it is next door to the **San Jose Museum of Art** and its collection of contemporary American art. The museum's unusual combination of 1892 Romanesque and 1991 stark sandstone styles is meant to serve as a metaphor for contemporary art's ties to tradition.

Within walking distance of the hotel at 33 East San Fernando, the upscale **Gordon Biersch Brewery and Restaurant** offers pleasant patio dining as well as seating in a spacious, airy dining room featuring views of stainless-steel brewing tanks. April through October live jazz is performed outdoors on Sunday afternoons from 2:00 to 5:00 P.M., and a variety of music is presented on Monday through Saturday evenings. There is a cover charge for music, and reservations are recommended on Sundays; Tel: 294-6785. The eclectic menu changes regularly and features salads, sandwiches, and individual pizzas as well as more substantial entrées and desserts. In addition to three styles of house-made German-style lager beers, the menu offers a selection of varietal wines and coffees; a wonderful sourdough pumpernickel bread is served gratis.

For a taste of this area's wine country, take a freeway ride into the suburbs. South of San Jose, take the Capitol Expressway exit east off Highway 101 and follow it about a mile to Aborn Road. Turn right and continue several miles through dense housing tracts until you reach what appears to be the area's last agricultural expanse, where grapevines tip you off to the entrance for **Mirassou Winery**. The winery, which has been at this location since 1937, is operated by the fifth generation of the Mirassou family, who started making wine in 1854. The spacious tasting room provides samples of a broad selection of the winery's premium wines. Tours are available, although the schedule is irregular. Special events are offered frequently, among them cooking classes, Sunday brunches, and sunset dinners featuring refined, elegant menus. Call ahead for details; Tel: 274-4000.

GETTING AROUND

The East Bay is across the Bay Bridge from San Francisco. It is served by BART (Tel: 510-465-2278), with stations in Oakland near Lake Merritt (19th Street, 12th Street, and Lake Merritt stations) and in Berkeley near the University (Berkeley/downtown station). AC Transit buses run here (Tel: 510-839-2882) and a Red & White Fleet ferry (Tel: 546-BOAT) operates from the Ferry Building to Jack London Square.

From San Francisco you can reach Marin County by car by crossing the Golden Gate Bridge. This area is also served by

Golden Gate Transit ferries from the Ferry Building at the foot of Market Street to Larkspur and Sausalito (Tel: 332-6600), and Red & White Fleet ferries from Pier 43½ near Fisherman's Wharf to Sausalito, Tiburon, and (with bus connection) Muir Woods (Tel: 546-BOAT). Gray Line offers bus tours to Sausalito and Muir Woods (Tel: 558-9400), and Golden Gate Transit (Tel: 453-2100) provides public bus service.

You can reach the Peninsula south of San Francisco by car by taking Highway 1 from 19th Avenue for the South Coast; take Highway 101 for Palo Alto, San Jose, and the Filoli Estate. Palo Alto is also served by CalTrain (Tel: 557-8661), with a stop in Palo Alto at the eastern end of University Avenue, and SamTrans (San Mateo Transit System) buses (Tel: 800-660-4287), with a stop at the Stanford Shopping Center.

ACCOMMODATIONS REFERENCE

The rate ranges given here are projections for fall 1993 through spring 1994. Unless otherwise indicated, rates are for double room, double occupancy.

▶ **Alta Mira Hotel**. 125 Bulkley Avenue (P.O. Box 706), Sausalito, CA 94966. Tel: (415) 332-1350; Fax: 331-3862. $80–$170.

▶ **Bed & Breakfast International**. P.O. Box 282910, San Francisco, CA 94128. Tel: (415) 696-1690 or (800) 872-4500; Fax: 696-1699. $58–$95.

▶ **Bodega Bay Lodge**. 103 Coast Highway One, Bodega Bay, CA 94923. Tel: (707) 875-3525 or (800) 368-2468; Fax: 875-2428. $120–$210.

▶ **Casa Madrona Hotel**. 801 Bridgeway, Sausalito, CA 94965. Tel: (415) 332-0502 or (800) 288-0502; Fax: 332-2537. $105–$225.

▶ **Casa del Mar**. P.O. Box 238 (37 Belvedere Avenue), Stinson Beach, CA 94970. Tel: (415) 868-2124. $100–$225.

▶ **Claremont Resort & Spa**. Ashby & Domingo avenues, Oakland, CA 94623. Tel: (510) 843-3000 or (800) 551-7266; Fax: 843-6239. $175–$215.

▶ **Cypress Inn**. 407 Mirada Road, Half Moon Bay, CA 94019. Tel: (415) 726-6002 or (800) 83-BEACH; Fax: 712-0380. $150–$275.

▶ **Dockside Boat & Bed**. 77 Jack London Square, Oakland, CA 94607. Tel: (510) 444-5858; Fax: 444-0420. $95–$275.

▶ **East Brother Lighthouse**. 117 Park Place, Point Richmond, CA 94801. Tel: (510) 820-9133. $295.

► **Fairmont Hotel.** 170 South Market Street, **San Jose**, CA 95113. Tel: (408) 998-1900 or (800) 527-4727; Fax: 287-1648. $155–$195.

► **French Hotel.** 1538 Shattuck Avenue, **Berkeley**, CA 94709. Tel: (510) 548-9930. $68–$125.

► **Garden Court Hotel.** 520 Cowper Street, **Palo Alto**, CA 94301. Tel: (415) 322-9000 or (800) 824-9028; Fax: 324-3609 or (800) 826-8059. $175–$180.

► **Green Gulch Farm.** 1601 Shoreline Drive, **Muir Beach**, CA 94965. Tel: (415) 383-3134; Fax: 383-3128. $90–$120.

► **Holly Tree Inn.** P.O. Box 642, **Point Reyes**, CA 94956. Tel: (415) 663-1554 or (800) 286-4655. $100–$175.

► **Hotel Durant.** 2600 Durant Avenue, **Berkeley**, CA 94704. Tel: (510) 845-8981; in California, (800) 2-DURANT; Fax: 486-8336. $95–$180.

► **Lake Merritt Hotel.** 1800 Madison, **Oakland**, CA 94612. Tel: (510) 832-2300 or (800) 933-HOTEL; Fax: 832-7150. $89–$169.

► **Manka's Inverness Lodge.** Argyle Street, P.O. Box 1110, **Inverness**, CA 94937. Tel: (415) 669-1034. $95–$160.

► **Mountain Home Inn.** 810 Panoramic Highway, **Mill Valley**, CA 94941. Tel: (415) 381-9000; Fax: 381-3615. $131–$215.

► **Palo Alto Holiday Inn.** 625 El Camino Real, **Palo Alto**, CA 94301. Tel: (415) 328-2800, (800) 874-3516, or (800) HOLIDAY; Fax: 327-7362. $126–$150.

► **Pelican Inn.** 10 Pacific Way, **Muir Beach**, CA 94965. Tel: (415) 383-6000. $140–$150.

► **Pigeon Point Lighthouse Hostel.** Pigeon Point Road, **Pescadero**, CA 94060. Tel: (415) 879-0633. $9–$15 (per person).

► **San Benito House.** 356 Main Street, **Half Moon Bay**, CA 94019. Tel: (415) 726-3425. $60–$117.

► **Sausalito Hotel.** 16 El Portal, **Sausalito**, CA 94965. Tel: (415) 332-4155; Fax: 332-3542. $75–$175.

► **Stanford Park Hotel.** 100 El Camino Real, **Menlo Park**, CA 94025. Tel: (415) 322-1234 or (800) 368-2468; Fax: 322-0975. $180–$290.

► **Stinson Beach House.** P.O. Box 162, **Forest Knolls**, CA 94933. Tel: (415) 488-9721. $195.

► **Tiburon Lodge.** 1651 Tiburon Boulevard, **Tiburon**, CA 94920. Tel: (415) 435-3133; in California, (800) TIBURON; in rest of U.S., (800) 762-7770; Fax: 435-2451. $110–$250.

► **Waterfront Plaza Hotel.** 10 Washington Street, **Oakland**, CA 94607. Tel: (510) 836-3800 or (800) 729-3638; Fax: 832-5695. $85–$145.

THE WINE COUNTRY
NAPA AND SONOMA

By David W. Toll

David W. Toll, author of The Compleat Nevada Traveler, *is a publisher and journalist. He divides his time between Healdsburg, California, and Gold Hill, Nevada.*

Wine has been an indispensable part of California's social environment ever since Father Junípero Serra planted vines at the Mission San Diego in 1769; today, wine grapes are produced in almost every part of the state. The beautiful Napa-Sonoma region, an hour's drive north of the Golden Gate Bridge, has led California in wine production since the Gold Rush. Today it is one of the most important wine regions of the world, as well as one of the most visited. Despite health concerns (and warning labels), stirrings of neo-Prohibitionism, and the gloom of economic recession, fine wines are still as strongly identified with California as beaches, sunshine, and movie stars.

People who don't know Champagne from Chardonnay can enjoy the Wine Country just as much as wine enthusiasts do. For one thing, they can educate themselves by sampling the wines. For another, there are many attractions besides wine in this beautiful area. The countryside is so colorful and charming, the air so soft and sensuous, the two-lane roads so inviting, the food so delicious, and the accommodations so comfortable, that it's not necessary to take even one sip to have an unforgettable visit.

MAJOR INTEREST

Winery tours and tastings
Fine dining
Early California history

Napa Valley
Carneros region wineries
Towns of Yountville and St. Helena for dining
Highway 29 wineries
Silverado Trail wineries
Calistoga mineral and mud baths
The Wine Train
Hot-air balloon rides

Sonoma County
Sonoma Plaza for mission and other historic
   buildings
Sonoma Valley wineries
Luther Burbank Home and Gardens in Santa Rosa
Russian River Valley wineries
Jack London State Park
Healdsburg and nearby Alexander Valley wineries

Touring the Wineries

To reach the Wine Country from San Francisco take Highway 101 north across the Golden Gate Bridge through Marin County. You have three options: to continue north on 101 to enter the wine country of northern Sonoma County; to turn east on Highway 37 and then follow Highway 12 to the wine country of the Sonoma Valley; or to follow 37 farther east to Highway 29, which will take you north through the Napa Valley. Any of these three choices will lead you into an enchanting region of small towns, country roads, and wineries, with a strong emphasis on accommodating visitors.

   The Wine Country is less like a pair of counties than a little kingdom, the wineries scattered across its rich green valleys and over its oak-dappled hills appearing to be dukedoms, châteaux, and country manors. A network of two-lane roads laces through this little kingdom, and a wine tour may be a random affair, governed by caprice, or a carefully planned excursion with specific destinations in mind. Either way, you are likely to stray off the main routes of travel and proceed by roundabout routes. This is just as it should be, and a definite part of the pleasure, because the best wines aren't necessarily from the biggest and best-known wineries, and these little lanes will lead you to special discoveries of your own.

The rationale for the wine-tasting tour is that it allows you to select the wines that suit you best. Some who make these tours, however, forget that tasting is a prelude to buying and have led some wineries to not offer tastings at all. Of those that do, some make a small charge, and others require that you purchase a souvenir glass (for two or three dollars), which they are then happy to fill and refill. The majority of wineries, though, do offer free tastings. Perhaps surprisingly, the price of the wine at the winery may be somewhat higher than in retail stores, but the surroundings are charming, discounts are usually available for quantity purchases, all necessary shipping arrangements are effortlessly made, and there is something special about a wine you buy yourself at the winery that made it, so that the small difference in price is only one consideration out of many.

Most often, the winery lists the wines available for tasting on the day of your visit (usually from three to six varieties) and provides bottle and case price information for you to refer to as you taste the wine. Often, especially at the smaller wineries, the person pouring the tastes is a member of the family that produced it and knows its history intimately. But even employees of the corporate wineries know their wines well, and you may ask almost any question without hesitation.

A long day in the Wine Country begins at 10:00 A.M. when most of the tasting rooms open to the public. You can choose a few wineries to visit, take a tour of the facilities at one of the larger ones (one tour is plenty for one day, and maybe for a lifetime), have a leisurely late afternoon lunch or early dinner at one of the fine restaurants along the way, and still return to your San Francisco hotel at a reasonable hour.

The recommended route to the Napa Valley from San Francisco is across the Golden Gate Bridge on northbound Highway 101 through Marin County. Eight miles (13 km) past the town of San Rafael, take the Vallejo-Napa exit and drive east on Highway 37 for 7 miles (11 km) to the Sonoma-Napa turnoff at Highway 121. Turn north here, and you are in the Carneros district, which is the newest formally estab-lished viticultural region of the state, and one of its earliest grape-growing regions as well.

Carneros

This district was known for generations as Los Carneros, after the huge sheep ranch that embraced it during the Mexican period. It lies far south of the better-known sections of the Wine Country, extending south almost to San Pablo Bay, and the migration of cool air from the bay into the warm Napa and Sonoma valleys on summer days provides the Carneros grapes with a longer, cooler growing season than the valleys provide.

The first small vineyard was planted here in 1830, and by the early 1870s a substantial grape harvest supported the Winter Winery. Carneros wines won prizes in the 1880s, but phylloxera in the 19th century and Prohibition in the 20th combined to destroy the wine business here. A new winery was built in 1935, and in the 1940s Louis M. Martini, a leading Napa Valley producer, began experimenting with Pinot Noir and Chardonnay clones. In the 1960s more Carneros pastures were converted to vineyards, and in the 1970s a genteel land rush ensued.

Today there are more than a dozen wineries in Carneros, which overlaps the southern reaches of both Sonoma and Napa counties, and three or four times that number of vineyards. The Carneros Viticultural Area was officially recognized in 1983—the first to transcend political boundaries— and the designation is now highly regarded in the world of wine.

From the south, Highway 121 brings you immediately to **Roche Winery**, which overlooks green pastures spackled with wetlands and dotted with plump cattle. The emphasis here is on carefully made and moderately priced estate-bottled varietals. Tasting is offered, some without charge, some with. A few hundred yards farther on, **Viansa Winery and Italian Market** is a cheerful and inviting indoor market-place selling gourmet deli foods (many prepared here in the Viansa kitchens) and wines to enjoy at a shaded table out-side. The bread is baked fresh every day, and many of the herbs and vegetables come from gardens on the winery grounds. The attractive non-restaurant presentation of food and wine together is unique in the Wine Country, but it sets such a good example that others are bound to follow. Viansa is owned by Sam Sebastiani, an estranged member of the family that owns the well-known Sebastiani Vineyards in Sonoma.

A short distance farther north, **Cline Cellars** is one of the newest of the many newcomers to the Carneros region. While new vines are being established, Cline Cellars makes its wine from grapes grown on the family properties in Contra Costa County, producing Rhône-style varietals, including the unfiltered Côtes d'Oakley, and reds made with the relatively unfamiliar Carignane and Mourvedre grapes. The winery occupies a part of what was once General M. G. Vallejo's ranching empire, and includes a historic bathhouse decorated inside with carved graffiti dating back to the 1860s. The extensive stone walls lining the parking lot, pathways, and ponds are made with the rocks cleared from the hillsides for new Zinfandel plantings.

Also on Highway 121 in this area, **Gloria Ferrer Champagne Caves** is a part of the international enterprise that includes the Cava Freixenet outside Barcelona, and reflects the generations of winemaking heritage of the Ferrer family. Hourly tours are given of the winery and the great cavern in which the wine, made by the traditional *méthode champenoise,* reposes in its racks. The sparkling wines aren't available for free tasting, but may be purchased for three to four dollars per glass and enjoyed in pleasing surroundings.

Not far beyond Gloria Ferrer, Highway 121 turns east. A short distance ahead on the left is Highway 12. Take it north to the historic town of Sonoma and to the wineries—some of them sources of California's great wine reputation—in the soft hills around the old town. If your destination is the Napa Valley, continue east on Highway 121 as it meanders through dairy farms and pasture lands for several miles. Just when you think you've somehow strayed out of the Wine Country altogether, you'll round a bend and see **Domaine Carneros** commanding a hillside bursting with grapevines at the intersection of Duhig Road. This is the Wine Country at its most French, from the classic château inspired by the Taittinger family home in Champagne to the 110 acres of Pinot Noir and Chardonnay grapes surrounding it. Even the shears used to harvest the grapes are French. The interior is just as grand and, with a portrait of Madame de Pompadour at the entrance, just as French. The sparkling wine is made by the traditional *méthode champenoise,* of course, and available at four dollars per glass. Tours are offered hourly 11:00 A.M. to 4:00 P.M. every day, except November through May, when the winery is closed on Tuesdays and Wednesdays.

Mont St. John, a short distance farther east at the corner of Dealy Lane, stems from an altogether different but equally flavorful tradition of winemaking. In the 1920s Andrea Bartolucci, an Italian immigrant, established a 24-acre vineyard and winery at Oakville in the Napa Valley to produce sacramental wines and sell grapes to home winemakers. His son Louis took over in 1946 and built Mont St. John Cellars into one of the largest wineries in California. The family enterprise was sold in 1970, and Louis's son Buck bought 160 unplanted acres in the farthest southern reaches of the Napa Valley, named them the Madonna Vineyards after his grandfather's winery, and planted them with Pinot Noir and Chardonnay grapes. The wines reflect the traditional philosophies of wine making, and are made to express the character of the vineyard.

Go north a short distance on Dealy Road to **Carneros Creek Winery**. Los Carneros was still mostly grazing land for cattle and sheep when Francis Mahoney established a 10-acre vineyard of Pinot Noir, Cabernet Sauvignon, and Chardonnay grapes here in 1972. He began producing wine while undertaking a major 15-year research project to determine which Pinot Noir clones would produce wines to match the best of Burgundy. He eventually settled on six, and the current release features three different Pinot Noirs, each made to a different recipe of clones and plantings. For all its achievements, this is a modest operation, without even a picnic table. The wine itself is the great attraction, and the tasting room is open daily.

Cordoniu Napa can be seen to the north of Highway 121 if you're sharp-eyed, and it is clearly visible on the approach along Dealy Lane and Henry Road as you proceed north: The stepped and grass-covered "pyramid" bunkered into the lip of an 800-foot prominence is an architectural tour de force almost impossible to describe. The many steps up from the parking lot are set off by fountains and by stripes of gushing water; the only visible part of the structure itself is a wedge of black glass protruding through the grass from within the sculpted mound. The architecture is defined as minimalist, but the visual impact is maximal, and it grows as you draw nearer. The interior is spare, beautifully appointed, and decorated with paintings and with a set of massive antique wine casks. The structure is so wonderful that all by itself it would draw visitors, but the excellent sparkling wine (four dollars a glass) is also quite fine.

Backtrack to the highway and continue east from Dealy Lane (or take Old Sonoma Road) to Highway 29 and turn north into the Napa Valley.

NAPA VALLEY

The Napa Valley extends a little over 30 miles (48 km) north from the large and, for our purposes, irrelevant town of Napa. The valley is a little paradise of brilliant green vineyards spreading across the valley floor and into the surrounding hills, ornamented with fine restaurants and comfortable inns and resorts. It contains as dense a concentration of wineries as any region of the world, and it is a widely accepted claim—or criticism—that the Napa Valley is second only to Disneyland as a California tourist attraction. The valley itself is astonishingly beautiful and peaceful in any season except summer, when the beauty remains but the peace is gone, at least on Highway 29, which connects the towns of the valley and is lined by wineries on both sides for most of its length. The California Wine Country is most highly evolved, technically and commercially, here in the Napa Valley, and because the area is an easy one-hour drive from San Francisco it is a popular day trip for visitors based there. Although the valley is more crowded in the summer, this is still the next-best time, after spring and fall during daylight saving time, for a wine-tasting day trip because of the extra hours of sunlight.

Half a dozen roads run east–west to connect Highway 29 and the parallel Silverado Trail, both of which run south–north from Napa to Calistoga through the heart of the Napa Valley (the Trail is on the valley's eastern side.) These connecting roads are lined with wineries and vineyards as well; there are more than 150 wineries in the Napa Valley now. It is obvious that no day trip can do more than begin to explore even this one valley—the ideal Wine Country visit would be for two weeks, with a car and no itinerary, and the minimum to get a full taste of this pleasing place is three days. But even a day trip can produce a lifelong memory.

Entering the Valley

The **Hess Collection Winery** is located at 4411 Redwood Road, which takes off to the west from Highway 29 at the northern outskirts of Napa and winds for several miles up the slopes of Mount Veeder. Here mineral-water tycoon Donald Hess bought the 1903 Christian Brothers' jug-wine facility and transformed it not only to produce quality varietal wines, but also to exhibit a part of his storied collection of contemporary art, ranging from enormous can

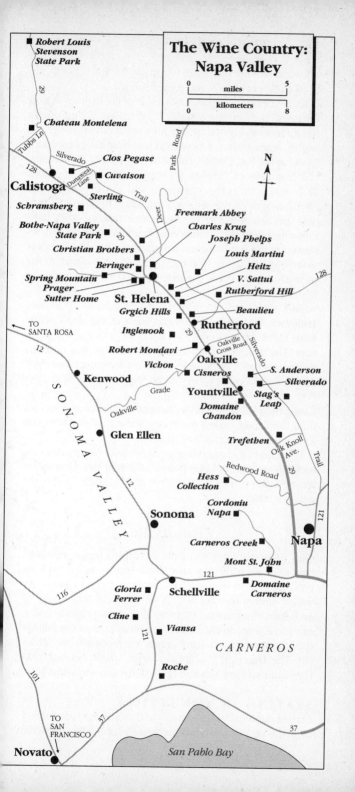

The Wine Country: Napa Valley

0 —— miles —— 5

0 —— kilometers —— 8

N

Robert Louis Stevenson State Park

Chateau Montelena

Silverado

Clos Pegase

Cuvaison

Park Road

Calistoga

Dunaweal Lane

Sterling

Deer

Trail

Schramsberg

Bothe-Napa Valley State Park

Freemark Abbey

Charles Krug

Joseph Phelps

Christian Brothers

Louis Martini

Heitz

Beringer

V. Sattui

Spring Mountain

Rutherford Hill

Prager

Sutter Home

St. Helena

Grgich Hills

Beaulieu

Inglenook

Rutherford

Robert Mondavi

Oakville Cross Road

Silverado

TO SANTA ROSA

Vichon

Oakville

Cisneros

S. Anderson

Kenwood

Grade

Yountville

Silverado

Stag's Leap

Oakville

Domaine Chandon

Glen Ellen

Trefethen

Oak Knoll Ave.

Redwood Road

Hess Collection

Cordoniu Napa

Sonoma

Carneros Creek

Napa

Mont St. John

Gloria Ferrer

Schellville

Domaine Carneros

Cline

Viansa

CARNEROS

Roche

TO SAN FRANCISCO

Novato

San Pablo Bay

S O N O M A   V A L L E Y

Tubbs Ln.

vases and striking sculptures to a magical construction made of 60 eucalyptus leaves and some fishline.

A mile or two north on the east side of the highway is **Don Giovanni,** the latest in a series of ambitious Wine Country restaurants established by Bay Area restaurateurs. Over the last 15 years, in fact, a new food tradition has been established in the Napa Valley that nearly equals that of the wine. The hallmarks of the style are imagination and scrupulous freshness, both in the ingredients and in the presentation (which begins on the plate and extends to the decor). Chefs here are almost as famous as the wine makers—they have followings, and their achievements are written up and reviewed in the San Francisco newspapers. This dining spot is an airy, rather spare, high-energy bistro, with a new menu each day, a fashionable clientele, and 260 wines in the cellar (Tel: 707-224-3300).

Take Oak Knoll Avenue east from Highway 29 to visit **Trefethen Vineyards,** one of the finest of the small family wineries and best known for its award-winning Chardonnays. The immense salmon-colored building that contains the tasting room is the oldest (1886) remaining three-story gravity-flow wooden winery in the Napa Valley. (The gravity-flow system works by crushing the grapes on the top floor, letting the juice flow into fermentation tanks on the second floor, and then letting the young wine flow down to the lowest level for storage and aging.)

From here, you can return to Highway 29 or continue east to the Silverado Trail (see below). The **Red Hen Cantina** on the west side of the highway offers good Mexican food on an outdoor patio.

Yountville

Only a few years ago Yountville was a dusty farm community best known for the Veterans Home that occupies spacious grounds on the west side of town, and a good hamburger wasn't always easy to find. Now the town, just north of Trefethen Vineyards on Highway 29, is crowded with American and European chefs operating restaurants of the highest quality, and even the hamburgers are modest works of art (try **The Diner** on Washington Street, where hearty breakfasts and excellent Mexican dinners are also specialties).

STAYING IN YOUNTVILLE

One of the Napa Valley's largest and most luxurious country inns, the ▶ **Vintage Inn** is an example of the trend toward blending modern comforts into a country environment. There are 80 guest rooms, including two-story villas clustered amidst three acres of gardens and man-made babbling brooks fed by numerous fountains. All the rooms have wood-burning fireplaces as well as air conditioning, antique-style ceiling fans, color cable television, and mini-refrigerators. There are also tennis courts, a heated lap pool, a limousine, cruises, and rides at dawn in the inn's own hot-air balloon.

The ▶ **Magnolia Hotel**, built in 1873, is a fashionable stone-and-brick bed and breakfast in the center of town that has been modernized with a pool and Jacuzzi. You can also find intimate bed-and-breakfast accommodations inside the brick walls of the ▶ **Bordeaux House** and ▶ **Burgundy House**, both of which are downtown as well.

Choices away from the center of town include the comfortable ▶ **Napa Valley Lodge**, a modern, well-managed motel with nice rooms, a comfortable lobby with a fireplace and piano, and a large pool area near Highway 29 at the north end of town; ▶ **The Webber Place**, a red farmhouse with a homey atmosphere; and the ▶ **Oak Knoll Inn**, 3 miles (5 km) south of town, one of the valley's most elegant bed-and-breakfast inns.

DINING IN YOUNTVILLE

All of Yountville's esteemed restaurants are in the same few blocks of Washington Street. Garlic lovers are directed to **Piatti**, a trendy trattoria with an open kitchen serving distinctive meals of pasta, grilled meats and fish, oven-baked breads and pizzas, and daily risotto specials; Tel: 944-2070. The **Maison Rouge** serves French dinners in classical country style (Tel: 944-2521), and **Aneste's Grille Rotisserie**, a few doors away, is a dinner house serving steaks and a few Greek entrées as well (Tel: 944-1500). The **French Laundry** is a local favorite that's every bit as unusual as its name: An old French laundry in a tiny stone-and-redwood structure has been converted to a family restaurant serving the kind of French country food that keeps the place packed; Tel: 944-2380. **California Café**, a Bay Area chain of super-slick bar-and-grills, specializes in California cuisine served in a neon-bright dining room or at outdoor tables; Tel: 944-2330. **Compadres** provides a refreshing break from the relentless wine and California cuisine by serving Mexican food, beer, and margaritas in festive indoor and outdoor surroundings.

Vintage 1870, which was the landmark Groezinger Winery until 1954, is now a fashionable shopping mall, with two floors of gift shops and restaurants as upscale and trendy as anything on San Francisco's Union Street. **Café Kinyon** here serves a delightful lunch of imaginative soups, salads, and sandwiches. Nearby, the **Red Rock Café** occupies the brick depot built in 1868 by Sam Brannan for his Napa Valley Railroad. The old Groezinger Winery is out of production for good, but the **Groezinger Wine Company** across the street is now a wine seller of merit. You can create a magnificent picnic lunch from their offerings and from specialties you'll find at **Gerhard's Sausage Kitchen** and the **Yountville Bakery** in Vintage 1870.

The culinary distinction that is now characteristic of Yountville, and of the entire Napa Valley for that matter, dates from 1977, when **Domaine Chandon**, at the southwest corner of Yountville on Highway 29, opened the first fine restaurant in the valley and began serving nouvelle cuisine. **Domaine Chandon Restaurant** is still one of the loveliest and most satisfying places to dine in the valley, with an open-air view of the vineyards and parklike grounds that make lunch a delight. The superb service goes well with the refined dinner atmosphere. Reservations are essential; Tel: 944-2892. Owned by Möet-Hennessy of France, producers of some of the world's finest Champagnes, Domaine Chandon first produced its own "sparkling wine" (which is how the French insist we refer to any bubbly wine made outside the province of Champagne, even when it's made by the *méthode champenoise*) in 1977. Möet-Hennessey made an initial investment of $12 million in this 900-acre vineyard; millions more have been spent expanding production capacity since. Tastings are not free here, but you can purchase flutes of Chandon and sip them on a sunny patio—just don't call it Champagne.

About a mile north of Yountville and easy to spot on the west side of the highway, **Mustards Grill** (Tel: 944-2424) is one of the valley's most popular eating places. Another of the new wave of California bistros, Mustards is part of the distinguished group that operates the equally popular Fog City Diner in San Francisco, Tra Vigne (a few miles up the valley in St. Helena), and a number of other small but dazzling culinary jewels. The food here is local and delectable, the atmosphere convivial, and the pairing of food with wine emphasized. A few steps north of Mustards is the **Cisneros Winery**, a newcomer to the Napa Valley and the first Meritage producer in the United States. Cisneros has a collection of gold medals from its past years in the San Joaquin Valley; the winery is especially noted for its Bourdeaux and Chardonnay wines.

From Yountville
to St. Helena

A few miles farther north on Highway 29 you can purchase the ultimate in picnic supplies at the increasingly famous **Oakville Grocery**. This 19th-century crossroads general store and valley landmark is country on the outside, foie gras and quail eggs on the inside. Dusty pickup trucks and shiny Mercedes park side by side here while their drivers equip themselves with the finest French pâtés, Sonoma cheeses and sausages, crusty loaves of French bread, and an astonishing assortment of fine foods from nearby farms and faraway places.

Vichon Winery is a short drive west of Highway 29 along Oakville Grade Road. This top-quality small winery is high enough to give you a grand view of the valley below; picnic tables under shady oaks are a perfect place to share the view with a bottle of Vichon's trademark wine, Chevrignon.

From Oakville north to Rutherford and on to St. Helena you will pass winery after winery on both sides of Highway 29, including some very famous names. Among the most popular for tours and free tastings is **Robert Mondavi**, a powerful draw for the name as well as for the excellence of the tour and the architectural merits of the winery. **Inglenook**, a major producer of mass-marketed wines, is located in a high, handsome, ivy-covered winery built in 1879 by Finnish sea captain Gustave Niebaum. Casks of wine are still aged in the caves he dug into the sides of the Mayacamas foothills. **Beaulieu** has been making renowned Cabernet Sauvignons since 1900 and provides one of the most informative of all the winery tours. At **Grgich Hills**, French owner–wine maker Mike Grgich is famous for his Chardonnays and is now working to bring his Cabernets to the same exalted level, and **Louis Martini** also merits a stop, if only to toast the family that has been making fine Napa Valley wines since 1933 without losing sight of the Martini philosophy of wine making: good wine that pairs well with food, that is made so you can drink it right away, and that is priced so you can afford it.

V. Sattui produces a wide range of varietal wines in a wonderful stone winery that resembles a cross between a Spanish Mission and a German Schloss (and is fairly new despite its timeless appearance). In addition to the wine, a deli shop provides a variety of picnic fixings, including almost 200 varieties of cheese, and more than two acres for picnicking.

The **Heitz Cellars** tasting room on the east side of the highway, just south of St. Helena, is a small building with a small gravel parking area, befitting a small family winery, which this is, but belying its exalted reputation. Now in its second generation and heading into a third, the Heitz family has for many years produced a landmark Cabernet Sauvignon from the grapes grown on the vineyard of Tom and Martha May in Oakville. New releases of the famed Martha's Vineyard Cabernet draw lines of customers before dawn to buy limited quantities at $50 a bottle. (The 1985 is still available—limit two bottles per customer—but the price is now $100.) Other wines carry more affordable prices, and the contrast with the more imposing corporate wineries all around is part of the appeal.

Farther north toward the outskirts of St. Helena and on the west side of the highway, the contrast between large and small wineries is emphasized by tiny **Prager Winery & Port Works**, tucked behind the huge complex producing **Sutter Home** wines. Both are family operations, but the Prager wines are sold only by the bottle or by the case at the winery, by winemaker Jim Prager himself or one of his sons, while next door at Sutter Home 4.5 million cases a year rumble out by the truckload for national distribution from the winery developed over nearly 50 years by the Trinchero family.

St. Helena

This stalwart town of handsome stone and brick buildings (with an occasional fanciful structure like the spectacular 1892 Ritchie Building that astonishes the eye on Main Street) serves the everyday needs of a large part of the Napa Valley, as well as the special interests of visitors. Main Street is thus a pleasing mix: here a hardware store, there a boutique, here an auto parts store, there a gallery. The ▶ **Hotel St. Helena**, a classic small-town hotel refurbished in the grand Victorian style, looms above a collection of shops and galleries, and there is enough variety on Main Street to provide an hour's promenade and an attractive assortment of places to eat. **Gillwood's** serves espresso, salads, sandwiches, and breakfasts all day. At **Rissa's Oriental Café** the all-Asian specialties—Thai salad, *donburi,* chow mein—are offered with sake, wine, and beer. The **Green Valley Café** is a trattoria serving hearty Italian lunches and dinners, and **Ana's Cantina** serves authentic and delicious Mexican food in an attractive brick building. The **Model Bakery** provides pizza specials and loaves of fresh-baked bread, some as big as watermelons. You can make a tasty picnic with sandwiches from **Giuli's Deli** down the street and pick up the wine to accompany it at **The Bottle Shop**.

If you are more ambitious about your lunch, or if you are ready for dinner, try **Trilogy** (the address is 1234 Main Street, but the entrance is a dozen steps east on Hunt Street; Tel: 963-5507). Here the atmosphere is quiet and restrained, but not formal. Chef Diane Pariseau produces classic French cuisine with a light touch, and maître d' Don Pariseau superintends a stunning wine list with 500 available selections. **Showley's**, a neighbor just around the corner at 1327 Railroad Avenue (Tel: 963-1200), serves lunches and dinners, and the well-rounded menu—lamb shanks, sweetbreads, halibut, duck breast—is meticulously prepared and served. At **Terra** (Tel: 963-8931) a few steps away, the dinner menu reflects the East-meets-West relationship of co-proprietors Lissa Doumani, a Napa Valley native, and Hiroyoshi Sone, a graduate of the Tsuji Cooking School of Osaka and alumnus of Wolfgang Puck's Spago restaurants. The imaginative and thoroughly modern blending of European and Asian traditions results in appetizers like grilled rare tuna with Calistoga field greens and Tahini sauce, and entrées like grilled Wolf Ranch quails with Kabocha pumpkin and Pecorino cheese ravioli. The 1884 stone building that houses Terra's deli adds another pleasing touch.

Tra Vigne (Tel: 963-4444), in another historic stone building, this one alongside Highway 29 on the southern edge of town, is one of the valley's most popular restaurants, serving daily lunches and dinners of fresh local meats and vegetables prepared in a bold and exuberant Italian style. The neo-Gothic interior, with its high ceilings and huge windows, is graced with both high-tech and rustic touches, and the busy kitchen is completely open to the noisy roomful of customers. **The Cantinetta** next door offers delectables to take out, including some of the items on the restaurant menu.

There are two more fine restaurants a short distance north of St. Helena at the **Freemark Abbey Winery**, where the tasting room is open from 10:00 A.M. to 4:30 P.M., with one daily winery tour at 2:00 P.M. The **Abbey Restaurant** (Tel: 963-2706) is open for dinners of nouvelle and classic cuisine, with a mesquite grill, a full bar, and a grand atmosphere in the original stone winery building. **Brava Terrace** (Tel: 963-9300) is less formal—the waiters wear blue jeans under their white linen aprons—and more like a country French bistro, with an open kitchen where chef Fred Halpert devotes himself to the cuisine of his native Provence (such as the "Cassoulet from Puy," which combines lentils, turkey sausage, pork, and lamb in a long-simmered stew). Lunch or dinner may be enjoyed inside or on the terraces overlooking the serene valley and its bright green quilt-patterned vineyards, bordered here and there by narrow lanes, and scalloped at the edges by gently rising hills, shaggy with trees.

STAYING IN ST. HELENA

A nice place to stay the night in St. Helena is the ▶ **Ambrose Bierce House**, a luxurious bed and breakfast built within strolling distance of the center of town in 1872. This was the author's occasional residence until 1913, when he vanished into Mexico in search of Pancho Villa and the revolution. And although the ▶ **Creekside Inn** is in the heart of town, its three guest rooms are sheltered by large oaks, and White Sulfur Creek meanders past the garden patio.

Some of the best St. Helena lodging choices are just outside town. ▶ **Harvest Inn**, built among vineyards off Highway 29, is a sprawling, lavish hostelry with an antique English Tudor look and all the modern conveniences of luxury-sized rooms, fireplaces, televisions, a pool, and a Jacuzzi. ▶ **Villa St. Helena** has only three guest rooms, but they are elegant, as are the wood-paneled library and parlor, the manicured lawn, the large pool, and the orchid solarium. Verandahs offer special views of the grounds, the flower gardens, and the valley. The larger ▶ **Wine Country Inn** offers 25 antiques-decorated rooms with country views, some with fireplaces, private balconies, and patios. The beds even have quilts.

▶ **Bartel's Ranch**, secluded in a quiet valley, has the natural charm of country surroundings and offers three guest rooms, which have the comforts of private baths and views, and share a pool and a Jacuzzi. ▶ **Zinfandel Inn**, an English Tudor–style home surrounded by vineyards, serves sparkling wine to you in three rooms with private baths and antique touches such as brass and four-poster beds. And in a Victorian vein, ▶ **The Farmhouse** is a bed and breakfast in the Joseph Phelps Vineyards featuring a spring-fed swimming pool and the chance to jog, hike, or stroll through the vineyards.

Two miles east of St. Helena is the ▶ **Meadowood Resort**, the ultimate in deluxe Napa Valley lodging, set in a forest of 256 heavily wooded acres. The 58 luxurious guest rooms and suites are well distributed among several small lodges nestled among the trees; you can choose a view of the nine-hole golf course, the tennis courts, the pool, or the croquet courts. This is the site of the Napa Valley Wine Auction each June. The serenity of the surroundings is complemented by the California cuisine in the resort's romantic **Restaurant at Meadowood**, where you would be well-advised to book a dinner reservation regardless of where you spend the night; Tel: 963-3646.

St. Helena's public library houses the **Napa Valley Wine Library**, and the **Silverado Museum** exhibits Robert Louis Stevenson memorabilia. If you would like to shop, visit the **Dansk** and **Gorham** factory outlets at 801 Main Street (on the southern edge of St. Helena) or the **London Fog** outlet north of town in Vintner's Village.

St. Helena Wineries

Some of the valley's most historic wineries are located in and around St. Helena. **Beringer**, built north of town in 1876 by German immigrants Charles and Frederick Beringer, is the oldest continually operated winery in Napa Valley—and is always crowded with visitors. Tours are led through the wine caves tunneled deep into the limestone hillside, then welcomed to the spectacular Rhine House, Frederick's gorgeous gingerbread mansion now serving the multitudes as the Beringer tasting room and gift emporium. **Charles Krug** was the valley's first winery, established here in 1861 by the Frenchman for whom it was named, a friend and colleague of the pioneering Haraszthy in Sonoma. Krug died in 1902 and the winery closed, but it was revived in 1943 when Cesare Mondavi bought it to make wine with his two sons, Peter and Robert. Twenty years later the Mondavis erupted in one of the valley's nastiest family feuds, and Robert Mondavi left the family business to acquire his own property near Oakville, where he quickly became one of the biggest names and most dominant personalities in California wine. His two sons now help run the Robert Mondavi Winery. Peter Mondavi and his two sons, meanwhile, still own and operate Charles Krug, now one of the valley's largest producers.

Spring Mountain Winery and Vineyards is a pleasing destination for a short drive along Spring Mountain Road west from Highway 29 at the north side of St. Helena. The road meanders to an impressive new winery built out from the old hillside tunnels. The wines are first rate, and the original 1885 home has been faithfully restored; if you experience a slight case of déjà vu at the sight of it, that's because this is the house used in the television series "Falcon Crest." **Christian Brothers** began making wine in the Napa Valley in the 19th century, and since 1888 its Greystone Cellars on Highway 29 has been one of the valley's most impressive monuments. Built as the largest stone cellar in the world, Greystone was recently purchased by the Culinary Institute of America to serve as its West Coast campus. The great building is being remodeled to accommodate the high-tech kitchens in which chefs from around the country will perfect their skills. Their "class work" will be available in a soon-to-be-opened restaurant.

Farther north, **Schramsberg**'s location atop Diamond Mountain overlooking the valley from the west dates from 1862 and was given lasting literary fame in 1880 when Robert Louis Stevenson wrote romantically of Jacob Schram's "cellars dug far into the hillside, and resting on pillars like a bandit's cave—all trimness, varnish, flowers, and sunshine among the tangled wildwood." Stevenson, who was honeymooning at the time, characterized the Napa Valley wine as "bottled poetry." Jack Davies revived the defunct historical landmark in 1965 and for several years has made one of California's best sparkling wines here. The natural charms that enthralled Stevenson have been carefully protected, and although Schramsberg is not usually open to the public, guided tours can be arranged by appointment; Tel: 942-4558.

Dunaweal Lane is the northernmost of the crossroads that connect Highway 29 with the Silverado Trail, and it is home to two of the most impressive of the valley's wineries. **Clos Pegase** is a majestic structure reminiscent of the Valley of the Nile and the Las Vegas Strip, a combination that has no peer among even the most architecturally ambitious wineries in the valley. A self-guided tour is available, and the tasting room is open daily.

Across the road, **Sterling Vineyards** is another architectural marvel, situated on top of a 300-foot knoll you reach by aerial tram. There is a five-dollar fee for the ride, and a large tasting room awaits you at the end of a self-guided tour, where you can relax at tables indoors and out and enjoy the view while you sample the wine. Established in 1969, Sterling was sold to Coca-Cola in 1977, and in 1983 became a part of the Seagram's empire.

Calistoga

Calistoga was a popular destination for visitors long before wine became a lure to the Napa Valley. Established in the early 1860s on a square-mile parcel of land at the northernmost part of the valley by the colorful Sam Brannan, San Francisco's first Gold Rush millionaire, Calistoga developed around the natural hot springs into a spa of wide reputation. Today Calistoga is a pleasant community of fewer than 5,000 people, with Mount St. Helena and the surrounding hills rising up to the north. The hot baths are still the principal attraction, but they have been augmented by restaurants and lodgings of considerable distinction. And, of course, there is the wine.

You'll find the spas in and around town, most of them with overnight lodgings similar to motel accommodations. You can also just drop in for a mineral or mud bath, facial, or invigorating body rub. Notable are ▶ **Dr. Wilkinson's Hot Springs,** ▶ **Calistoga Spa Hot Springs,** ▶ **Golden Haven Hot Springs** (two-night minimum stay), and ▶ **Nance's Hot Springs.** Northern California's two top producers of bottled mineral waters also do business here: Calistoga Mineral Water is bottled at a plant on the Silverado Trail, which leads south from Calistoga's east side, and Crystal Geyser's plant is in town (at 501 Washington Street) and open to visitors for tours.

STAYING AND DINING IN CALISTOGA

You can find deluxe accommodations without the hot springs in two splendid Calistoga hotels that are antique in appearance but thoroughly modern in amenities. The ▶ **Mount View Hotel** at the center of town—Lincoln Avenue is Calistoga's main business street—has a nice pool area, and its restaurant, **Valeriano's,** is white-linen Italian. The 17-room ▶ **Calistoga Inn** a few blocks west also offers fine rooms and a top dinner house. A small brewery on the property produces a variety of delicious ales and lagers to accompany meals served on the garden patio. Another good place to eat on Lincoln Avenue is the **All Seasons Café,** where the food is California-French and the wine list is superb, for both its breadth of selection and its pricing, which is never more than five dollars over retail. Entrées on the lunch menu are grouped according to the wine suggested as accompaniment. Moreover, a storeroom adjoining the café is packed to the ceiling with wine for sale, so that if something wonderful crosses your palate at dinner, you can take a bottle or two home with you. The same enlightened wine-pricing policy applies at the **Silverado Restaurant and Tavern** across the street, a spirited gathering place for locals not seeking the culinary distinction of the All Seasons.

Seed Time & Harvest, on Washington Street a half block north of Lincoln, serves egg-, salt-, and oil-free entrées (except by special request) with fresh-baked breads. There's a vegetarian buffet from 11:30 A.M. to 2:30 P.M.; dinners are served in a courtyard on summer evenings. Its culinary opposite must be **Alex's**, around the corner on Lincoln, where prime rib is the main attraction. **Bosko's Ristorante**, in an attractive brick building at the corner of Lincoln and Washington, offers inexpensive pasta specialties, along with espresso, gelato, and wine, and **Las Brasas** and **Café Pacifico** are enjoyable Mexican restaurants. Most of the rest of Lincoln Avenue is devoted to spas, galleries, shops, and ice cream parlors. You can find espresso and cappuccino at **Caffè Marco**, which is down a narrow passageway on the south side of Lincoln.

▶ **Brannan Cottage Inn**, an easy walk from the center of town, is an award-winning restoration of one of Sam Brannan's 1862 Greek Revival guesthouses, with six air-conditioned rooms, gourmet breakfasts, and private baths. ▶ **Calistoga Wayside Inn** and ▶ **Wine Way Inn**, both close to downtown, are among the numerous bed-and-breakfast choices. ▶ **Calistoga Country Lodge** is a restful haven in the hills north of town, and ▶ **Larkmead Country Inn**, south of Calistoga, is another quiet retreat.

▶ **Christopher's Inn**, a new arrival in Calistoga, is just south of the intersection of Highway 29 with Lincoln Street. The inn embraces three former vacation cottages and is decorated with a floral Country English motif. Five of the ten rooms offer the warmth, romance, and elegance of fireplaces, all of the rooms are bright with sunlight during the day, and none of them has a telephone.

Chateau Montelena, about 2 miles (3 km) north of Calistoga off Highway 29 at 1429 Tubbs Lane, is rich in history and graced by a little lake ideal for picnics (available by arrangement). This well-preserved 1882 winery is a small French-designed stone castle built into the slope of a hill, where it overlooks a tranquil setting of Chinese inspiration— Jade Lake, the legacy of a former owner who built bright red bridges in zigzag patterns (to confuse evil spirits) to two small islands adorned with teahouse pagodas.

Right where the Silverado Trail intersects with Lincoln Street/Highway 29, the **Lord Derby Arms** offers a little island of English ale and shepherd's pie in this sea of wine and brie. Service in the dining room, at the bar, or on the large shaded outside deck comes complete with an English accent.

The Silverado Trail

The Silverado Trail begins at the east corner of Calistoga and winds back south along the lower mountain slopes to the southern end of the Napa Valley, offering a peaceful alternative to more-or-less parallel Highway 29. Commercialism is not as intrusive along the Trail, and interesting wineries are tucked here and there along this road, parts of which are high enough to provide panoramic views of the valley. The Trail is the link to a new wave of wineries that have taken to higher ground in the last 20 years as land on the valley floor became prohibitively expensive or unavailable at any price.

Cuvaison, just south of Calistoga, was built in 1970 and has become recognized as one of the Napa Valley's finest labels. This Spanish Mission–style winery of bright white walls and red-tile roof is a striking centerpiece in a panorama of vineyards, and its landscaped grounds provide a perfect place to picnic.

Joseph Phelps, a winery on Taplin Road, occupies the lower slope of the hills to the east above the Silverado Trail. Founded in 1974, this small winery is a consistent producer of fine wines and is the site of the farmhouse bed and breakfast described earlier. Farther south along the Trail, on Rutherford Hill Road, the **Rutherford Hill Winery** gives interesting tours of the more than 30,000 square feet of caves bored into the hillside and now filled with wine aging in French oak barrels.

Just south of Rutherford Hill Winery on the same road, you will see the rustic elegance of ▶ **Auberge du Soleil**, one of the valley's most fashionable retreats for dining or lodging. Built at considerable cost on the side of the mountain to give guests spectacular views of the valley, the Auberge has 48 pricey rooms and suites, where natural wood is matched with leather furniture, and terra-cotta floors lead to private decks. The showpiece restaurant, designed by an architect and an interior designer from the ranks of San Francisco society, gives a Southwestern effect with earth-tone colors and striking architectural flourishes. Chef Udo Nechutnys, who inaugurated fine dining in the Napa Valley some 15 years ago at Domaine Chandon, restored the restaurant here to preeminence by adhering less to the tenets of nouvelle cuisine and adopting a somewhat more familiar menu. Now the kitchen is in the hands of Nechutnys's former sous chef, David Hale. Reservations are essential; Tel: 963-1211. Even without a dinner waiting, a visit here is always a pleasure, if only for a drink on the terrace or at the bar, or just to gaze briefly at the magnificent view.

A few miles farther south, turn west on the Yountville Crossroad to **S. Anderson Vineyard**, a sparkling-wine maker par excellence—when Gorbachev dined at the White House, it was S. Anderson's wine in the glasses he and President Bush clinked together—that is yet another Napa Valley family affair. The tasting room is in the small stone building that originally housed the entire winery. The winery now produces 10,000 cases a year (still very small by industry standards) and has expanded into a larger, less interesting building next door. Tours are offered, and if you telephone ahead you can be sure someone from the family will be available (otherwise you may have to wait until someone can break away); Tel: 944-8642. The tour features the caves dug into the hillside to store wines; they were the first new caves to be dug in the Napa Valley in 100 years. The natural stone walls rising 18 feet to the vaulted ceiling, the cool, still vastness, and the sight of 400,000 Champagne-style bottles awaiting their celebratory moments—it all evokes an awed religious feeling in some visitors. "It's like being in church," is a regular comment.

Back on the Silverado Trail, you'll find **Silverado Vineyards**, well-signposted and easily accessible on the west, where it occupies a high piece of ground. Owned by Walt Disney's widow (see if you can find the portrait of Mickey Mouse hidden in the stained glass), this ultramodern winery was built in 1981. The early California–style structure in which outstanding Cabernets, Merlots, and Chardonnays are produced also houses a tasting room where the reception is most pleasant; the views from the sunny verandah are delightful.

Two miles south of the Yountville Cross Road, **Stag's Leap Wine Cellars** is a sight to make Cabernet lovers' hearts beat faster. Its vineyards planted in 1970 and its winery completed two years later, Stag's Leap has been a benchmark of great Napa Valley Cabernet ever since. Indeed, we're crossing serious red-wine country now.

▶ **Silverado Resort and Country Club**, at the southern end of the Trail, is a toney resort that uses the Napa Valley as its backdrop, but caters more to serious golfers than to wine tasters. The accommodations are deluxe and contained in modern condominium-style units, from studios to three bedrooms.

The Napa Valley Wine Train

The controversial Napa Valley Wine Train was universally damned by the valley's old guard from inception, but it has received rave reviews from paying passengers since it finally overcame legal roadblocks and began service in the fall of 1989. The train tour was the brainstorm of determined San Francisco millionaire Vincent DeDomenico, who also gave America Rice-A-Roni. He took some of the millions Quaker Oats paid him for his company and bought the Southern Pacific's near-defunct Napa Valley line, originally built by Sam Brannan to haul passengers to the Calistoga mineral spas. DeDomenico improved the roadbed, bought turn-of-the-century Pullman cars and 1950s diesel locomotives, and stood his ground against detractors who said diesel fumes would pollute the air and foul the vineyards, trains crossing country roads would cause traffic jams and accidents, and, worst of all, the train would bring more tourists into a valley already overcrowded with them. Protestors succeeded in derailing the original plan for the train to make scheduled stops at selected wineries, but the train is still a great ride.

Prices range from $59 per person for a lunch excursion to $68 for a dinner ride. Wines from the vineyards the train glides through are also available at additional cost. You board at the Main Depot, 1275 McKinstrey Street in Napa, and then spend two and a half to three and a half hours, depending on whether you've chosen lunch or dinner, riding the rails in bygone luxury. The Pullman cars are plushly carpeted and lavishly decorated with velvet curtains, etched glass, and chandeliers; food and wine is served at linen-covered tables set with fine china, Sheffield silver, and crystal stemware. But all this soon takes a back seat to the panorama of the Napa Valley passing in review outside your window. The train rolls gently (never faster than 20 miles per hour) to St. Helena while half the passengers dine and the other half gaze out the windows of the lounge car and daydream or wine-taste. At St. Helena the locomotive lets go, chugs around to the other end of the train, and the passengers change places for the pleasant return ride. The Wine Train is usually heavily booked during the summer and on weekends throughout the year, and reservations should be made well in advance; Tel: 253-2111 or (800) 427-4124.

Other Napa Valley
Activities

Hot-air balloons have long been a popular way to see the Napa Valley from a different perspective. Strong afternoon winds—and a proper sense of drama—require that balloon launches be made at dawn. The gondola holds as many as seven passengers and drifts for about an hour here and there through the silent sky above the valley; the landing is traditionally accompanied by the pop of a sparkling wine cork. Balloon companies are numerous, so the most convenient way to go is with the company that launches nearest to where you will be at dawn. Adventures Aloft is at Yountville's Vintage 1870 shopping plaza (Tel: 255-8688); Napa Valley Balloons launches from Domaine Chandon (Tel: 253-2224); Once in a Lifetime, Inc. is at 1546 Lincoln Avenue in Calistoga (Tel: 942-6541). Be sure to call ahead for reservations, as they launch from different sites depending on conditions. Glider and biplane rides are a popular valley thrill offered by Calistoga Gliders (Tel: 942-5592) at the Calistoga airport on Lincoln Avenue.

Dolphin Charters offers weekend wine-tasting cruises from San Francisco on the Napa and Petaluma rivers every summer; each vessel carries a chef, wine steward, and 40 passengers. Tickets are $79; for reservations, Tel: (510) 527-9622.

The valley's meandering country lanes are excellent for bicycling, and rentals are available throughout the valley. And while the whole Napa Valley seems to resemble one giant picnic ground, two state parks also offer facilities. **Bothe–Napa Valley State Park**, in the western hills between St. Helena and Calistoga, has picnicking, camping, swimming, and hiking trails, one of which leads to the Old Bale Grist Mill, an 1846 flour mill with a spectacular water wheel, now restored to original working condition. **Robert Louis Stevenson State Park** is north of Calistoga via Highway 29, near the summit of Mount St. Helena, and offers panoramic views of the Napa Valley and the mountains surrounding it.

A growing number of special events crowd the Napa Valley calendar throughout the year. The themes of music, art, food, and wine dominate these events with the Napa Valley Wine Auction at the Meadowood Resort being the premiere occasion of the year each June; Tel: (707) 963-5246. Other annual events include the Concourse d'Elegance vintage motorcar show in June at the Silverado Resort and Country Club, June music concerts at Domaine Chandon, the Summer Jazz Festival at Robert Mondavi during July and August, and the Charles Krug Winery Harvest Festival in September. The Napa Valley Conference and Visitors Bureau can supply information on these and other special events; Tel: (707) 226-7459.

SONOMA COUNTY

Sonoma County, in contrast to the compact Napa Valley almost entirely devoted to vineyards and wine making, is a large, sprawling, agriculturally diversified county to the west of the Napa Valley. It extends from the Sonoma Valley north to Mendocino County and west to the Pacific Ocean. There are actually two primary wine regions here, the Sonoma Valley and the Russian River Valley (northwest of the Sonoma Valley), but neither has the exclusive concentration of vineyards, wineries, and wine-related pleasures aligned in the tight, convenient order of neighboring Napa Valley.

There is far more territory here than can be covered in any single tour of Sonoma Wine Country, but it is a rewarding journey for anyone who can enjoy a leisurely drive through lovely countryside with an occasional stop at a winery or a shrine of early California history. Most of Sonoma County retains a strong, unvarnished country atmosphere. Here, the ever-increasing number of vineyards still must share the land with fruit orchards, beef and dairy cattle, sheep, and poultry.

The recommended route to Sonoma County from San Francisco is across the Golden Gate Bridge, continuing north on U.S. 101 through Marin County. Eight miles (13 km) past the town of San Rafael, take the Vallejo-Napa exit east to State Highway 37, and continue on Highway 37 for 7 miles (11 km) to the Sonoma turnoff north onto State Highway 121. Follow Highway 121 through the Carneros region to its junction with Highway 12 at Schellville, just south of Sonoma. Continue north on Highway 12 for 4 more miles (6 km) and you're at the historic Sonoma Plaza.

Sonoma Plaza

The central plaza at Sonoma is a natural starting point for any trip through Sonoma County, and an attraction of considerable appeal in its own right. The eight-acre plaza is pleasantly tree-shaded, and decorated with a pair of stone municipal buildings—the city hall and the library, now a visitor information center—from the turn of the century. All around, the buildings that face the square date from the early 19th to middle 20th century, embodying a century and a half of California history.

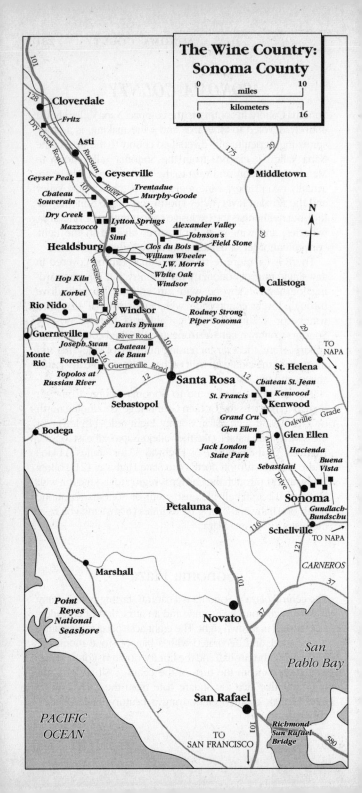

The Wine Country:
Sonoma County

miles 0 — 10

kilometers 0 — 16

Cloverdale

Fritz

Asti

Geyser Peak

Geyserville

Chateau Souverain

Trentadue Murphy-Goode

Dry Creek

Mazzocco

Lytton Springs

Simi

Healdsburg

Alexander Valley

Johnson's

Field Stone

Clos du Bois

William Wheeler

J.W. Morris

White Oak

Windsor

Hop Kiln

Korbel

Rio Nido

Foppiano

Windsor

Rodney Strong Piper Sonoma

Davis Bynum

Guerneville

Joseph Swan

Monte Rio

Forestville

Chateau de Baun

Topolos at Russian River

Santa Rosa

Sebastopol

Bodega

Chateau St. Jean

Kenwood

St. Helena

St. Francis

Kenwood

Grand Cru

Glen Ellen

Glen Ellen

Hacienda

Jack London State Park

Buena Vista

Sebastiani

Sonoma

Petaluma

Gundlach-Bundschu

Schellville

TO NAPA

Marshall

CARNEROS

Point Reyes National Seashore

Novato

San Pablo Bay

San Rafael

PACIFIC OCEAN

TO SAN FRANCISCO

Richmond-San Rafael Bridge

Middletown

Calistoga

TO NAPA

N

HISTORIC SONOMA

Misión San Francisco Solano, last of the California missions to be built, was established here by Father José Altimira in 1823, two years after Mexico won its independence from Spain. For ten years Father Altimira and his successor, Father Fortuny, built the mission into a thriving center of agriculture. With Native American labor, the missionaries built adobe walls and buildings, established hayfields, planted vegetable gardens and grapevines, and produced the first wine in the Sonoma Valley.

This first bottling took place too late to be included in the first world-wide compendium of wine published in Paris in 1824, but California wines generally—all of them mission wines—were summarily dismissed as being "of the third class." This judgment lived on well past its day and influenced popular (and even informed) opinion long after those first rough reds had been supplanted by subtler and more ambitious wines.

In 1833 the Mexican government secularized the missions and sent Lieutenant Mariano G. Vallejo to establish a settlement at Sonoma. The town was garrisoned with soldiers to protect against the Russian intrusions at Ross and Bodega Bay (see the Redwood Country chapter) and to police the Yankees who were trespassing everywhere on this far northern Mexican frontier.

General Vallejo (as he came to be) created the Sonoma Plaza as a parade ground for his soldiers and built his own 20-room adobe home, Casa Grande, facing its north side. His brother Salvador also erected a large adobe residence facing the plaza, and other adobe structures were built to house the soldiers and the Native American slaves.

Sonoma was a sleepy, sunny, out-of-the-way Mexican outpost until 1846, when American rebels forced their way into Casa Grande at gunpoint and seized Vallejo and his family. They ran up their homemade Bear Flag in the plaza, and declared California a republic. The life of this bold republic was short—25 days—and ended when Commodore Robert Stockton captured Monterey and claimed California for the United States.

California's Mexican era ended with the Bear Flag Revolt, and the Gold Rush buried the Mexican heritage under the huge migration from the East Coast and Midwest. Statehood came in 1850, and brick-and-board Anglo-style architecture began to appear on the plaza among the tile-roofed adobes.

SONOMA PLAZA TODAY

Today both types of structures still stand around the old plaza, thick-walled adobes side by side with high-shouldered Victorians, and here and there a few modest buildings from more recent years. You can spend a pleasant hour making your way around the plaza and visiting the art galleries, gift shops, and clothing boutiques that now occupy many of the old buildings.

Any visit to the plaza should begin at the mission—now a California State Park—with its luminous collection of California mission paintings by Chris Jorgensen. These watercolors are exhibited in the priests' quarters, which date from 1825 and are the oldest original structures remaining in Sonoma. The interior gardens are also striking. A stroll west from the mission leads along the old Colonial façades of the soldiers' barracks on Spain Street, and past the old Toscano Hotel museum exhibit, also a part of the state park.

The grandly refurbished ▶ **El Dorado Hotel**, a plaza landmark originally built by Salvador Vallejo, is now one of Sonoma's most deluxe places to eat and sleep. The elaborate remodeling undertaken by Claude Rouas, of Napa Valley's Auberge du Soleil, has gracefully highlighted El Dorado's Spanish heritage, and each of the 27 tastefully decorated rooms comes with a four-poster bed and private bath, some with a private balcony. The hotel's **Ristorante Piatti** has an attractive dining room and a flower-filled courtyard dominated by a lovely old fig tree; its regional Italian menu features pasta, risotto, grilled meats, seafood, and memorable pizzas; Tel: 996-2351.

Across the street is the three-story ▶ **Sonoma Hotel**, a classic Victorian with an easygoing atmosphere. Seventeen rooms and suites offer private or shared baths, views of the plaza, brass beds, and claw-foot bathtubs. The hotel bar and dining room have the same unpretentious style, serving good regional wines and foods at pleasing prices. Bed-and-breakfast accommodations are available nearby, notably at the ▶ **Hidden Oak**, where three rooms are available to travellers a block and a half from the plaza. The ▶ **Thistle Dew Inn** is cozy and comfortable, and the ▶ **Victorian Garden Inn** offers an unusually outfitted Woodcutter's Cottage, three rooms in a former water tower, or a room in the main house, all of which open onto a glorious garden.

Dining Around the Plaza

In the course of a promenade around the plaza, you can settle in at an inviting restaurant for a light snack or a full meal. For Italian food, **Della Santino's**, **Pasta Nostra**, and **Zino's on the Plaza** are all good. **L'Espérance** resembles a Parisian bistro, nicely mixed with Mexican California, and turns out characteristically hearty meals; at the **Bonito Oyster Bar**, at 133 East Napa, the menu is appropriately maritime. It's especially nice to eat in the outdoor patio. Around the corner from the plaza, **Peterberry's Espresso Café and Aviation Gallery** is a coffeehouse with a lot of variety to its coffees, salads, sandwiches, and clientele.

A long block from the plaza at 241 First Street West is the **Depot 1870 Restaurant**. Former San Francisco chef Michael Ghilarducci serves northern Italian cuisine in this restored railroad hotel in two dining rooms or poolside on the garden terrace. Ghilarducci has assembled a strong Sonoma Valley wine list to offer in a country-inn atmosphere.

You also might choose to gather the makings for a magnificent picnic lunch to enjoy later at a winery from the inviting food shops around the plaza that give old Sonoma so much of its contemporary flavor. At the **Old Sonoma Creamery** you'll find locally made mustards and a generous deli assortment; the **Sonoma Sausage Company** offers 60 kinds of local sausage and provides tastes to help you make your selection; the **Sonoma Cheese Company** is arranged so that you can watch the fat wheels of Sonoma Jack cheese being made and taste the cheeses on sale along with wines and deli items. The venerable **Vella Cheese Company** is a longtime producer of Sonoma Jack, cheddar, and magnificent specialty cheeses a block off the plaza at 315 Second Street East. You can buy fresh-baked bread in loaves long and slender or plump and round at the **Sonoma French Bakery** and fine wine to complement your picnic at half a dozen of the food shops around the plaza; one of the best selections and most knowledgeable staffs in the Wine Country is at the **Sonoma Wine Exchange**. Their selection of unusual domestic and imported beers is also excellent.

Wineries Near Sonoma

In 1851, as if to emphasize the cultural dislocation (and his own astonishing powers of assimilation), General Vallejo moved with his large family from his famous Casa Grande into a two-story Yankee-style Gothic Revival house a half-mile from the plaza. The new house (now a part of the state park that comprises the mission and other buildings) was located among 500 acres of citrus trees and grapevines, and Vallejo's wines were soon well known throughout California. Six years later a colorful Hungarian exile, Agoston Haraszthy, joined General Vallejo in the wine-making business by establishing Buena Vista Vineyards on the eastern fringes of Sonoma. Haraszthy, a bright and energetic pioneer who introduced many thousands of European grapevines into Sonoma County vineyards, is honored today as the father of the California wine industry.

Vineyards and wineries proliferated throughout the Sonoma Valley in the 1860s and 1870s, and more French, Italian, and German vines were introduced. Increasingly, however, the vines were attacked and ultimately devastated by a deadly pest, phylloxera. It was not until 1879 that it was found that European vines were safe from attack when they were grafted onto the old mission rootstock. Sonoma County then became by far the biggest wine producer in California, and dozens of Sonoma Valley wineries flourished through the turn of the century making table wines for San Francisco and the other towns of post–Gold Rush California. Some wineries shipped their wines worldwide, but in 1920 Prohibition put most of the wineries out of business. The repeal of Prohibition in 1933 brought some of the old firms back, mostly in bulk production, but the business was nothing like the lively affair it had been at the turn of the century. The beginnings of a Wine Country revival could be seen in the mid-1960s, but as recently as 1968 only five wineries were operating in the Sonoma Valley.

Today, however, it is possible to visit several historic Sonoma wineries just a short distance from the plaza. Take Napa Street east and follow the signs to **Buena Vista**, Haraszthy's pioneer winery. Born in European splendor, it survived fires, phylloxera, and high taxes, only to have its stone cellar collapse during the 1906 earthquake. A gradual revival of its fortunes began after World War II, and today Buena Vista is owned and operated by a German company. You can enjoy self-guided tours of the limestone caves, free tastings inside one of the original stone winery buildings, and spacious, shaded picnic grounds.

Hacienda Wine Cellars, established by Frank Bartholomew in 1973, incorporates some of the original Haraszthy acreage and uses a former hospital as its tasting room and offices. Vines of several wine grape varieties grow in front of the building as a living exhibit. On the short drive west from Buena Vista to Hacienda you'll pass a jewel-box house standing alone. This is the reconstructed residence of the legendary Haraszthy, built as a memorial to Bartholomew by his widow. Mrs. Bartholomew died on the day it was dedicated, and the house has stood carefully maintained and protected, but virtually unused, ever since.

Gundlach-Bundschu, the easternmost winery on Napa Street, is an old-line Sonoma winery dating from the 1850s. By the turn of the century hundreds of cases of wine produced at "Rhinefarm" were being warehoused in San Francisco for shipment to the domestic and world markets, so the company was devastated when the warehouse was destroyed in the earthquake and fire of 1906. Prohibition closed the winery altogether. Restored to life by fifth-generation Jim Bundschu in 1976, the old winery has tucked its informal tasting counter into a corner of one of the old stone buildings, with a good close view of the bottling machinery.

The **Sebastiani Vineyards,** a mile northeast of the plaza on Napa Street, has been one of Sonoma County's major producers and a colorful mainstay of town history since Samuele Sebastiani arrived from Italy in the 1890s and purchased some of the vineyards originally planted by General Vallejo in 1835. Samuele started his winery in 1904, but it was his son, August Sebastiani, who took the family winery to national prominence by expanding production beyond a million cases a year. The antithesis of today's self-important set who cloak wine in a mystic aura, August wore striped overalls, smoked cigarettes while sipping his Cabernet, and insisted he was just a simple farmer growing grapes to make everyday wine. In fact, he was a very astute businessman and one of the great characters in the history of the California wine industry.

After August's death in 1980, command passed to his son, Sam Sebastiani, an outstanding wine maker who successfully strived for a higher level of premium vintages as well as a higher profile for himself. But in another of those family bloodlettings that play out like a TV soap opera, Sam lost a power struggle with his younger brother Don and was unceremoniously fired from the family winery by his mother Sylvia Sebastiani, August's widow and, not incidentally, the majority stockholder in Sebastiani Vineyards. Don managed to become a controversial state legislator for a short term and remains in charge of the family winery, while Sam has built Viansa, an impressive new estate winery of his own, in the Carneros region to the south described earlier. Only selected parts of this provocative family history are related on the otherwise excellent tour that includes Sebastiani's famed collection of original wine-barrel carvings done by a local artisan in the Old World tradition.

Sonoma Valley

From the Sonoma Plaza, continue north on Highway 12 into the Sonoma Valley, a 17-mile greenbelt extending to within a few miles of Santa Rosa, the Sonoma County seat and its largest city. Rapid population growth in Santa Rosa and in the Sonoma Valley occasionally makes for heavy traffic on Highway 12, the main artery through the valley. But for the most part, the gentleness of the country still fills the air.

The ▶ **Sonoma Mission Inn and Spa**, only 2 miles (3 km) northwest of the plaza, is the region's premier luxury resort, a pink temple of healthful indulgence and supreme relaxation isolated from its jumbled neighborhood of ugly suburban clutter. In the tradition of the Native Americans who once enjoyed the therapeutic waters of the local hot springs, this serene resort provides its jet-set clientele with indoor and outdoor Jacuzzis and a heated pool, part of a spa that offers a number of rejuvenating treatments, including an herbal wrap. You can register for the full spa program or simply spend a night or more as a pampered guest with access to tennis courts and an Olympic-sized pool. **The Grille Room** at the inn is one of the valley's finest restaurants, a health-oriented spot serving grilled fish and chicken, pasta with vegetables, crisp crab cakes, and regional specialties; Tel: 938-9000.

More of a country atmosphere can be found in Sonoma Valley's bed-and-breakfast inns and ranch-style guest houses such as ▶ **Beltrane Ranch**, which has tennis courts, and ▶ **Gaige House Inn**, in the town of Glen Ellen, a few minutes' drive northwest of Sonoma on Arnold Drive west off Highway 12. At the Gaige House Inn rates include a full breakfast and wine and cheese every afternoon. The 1916 ▶ **Glenelly Inn** has eight rooms opening onto a verandah or garden, each decorated in a different style but featuring antiques. All rooms have private bath (most with a claw-foot bathtub) and most have queen-sized beds. The centerpiece of the grounds is an outdoor spa.

GLEN ELLEN ENVIRONS

Jack London State Park, on London Ranch Road west of Glen Ellen, is on the ranch property where the popular writer settled in 1904 to live out his dream life in what the Indians had named the Valley of the Moon. In 1913 he and his wife, Charmian, built their dream castle, Wolf House, with huge chunks of native stone, concrete, and timbers, but the house burned just as they were about to move in, and its massive rock-and-concrete ruins still stand as a silent monument to their dreams of grandeur. Also preserved is the modest ranch house where they lived after the fire, and where London wrote some of his most popular books before his death in 1916. The House of Happy Walls, in which Charmian lived after Jack died, is the visitors' center, and displays memorabilia from their life together and from Charmian's long life afterward. You can also visit Jack London's grave on a nearby knoll, beneath one of the stones from Wolf House, a few feet away from the graves of two children from a family of early settlers.

Glen Ellen Winery, on the same road as the state park, is another pioneer winery, dating from the 1860s and revived in 1980 by the Bruno Benzinger family. Their inexpensive Glen Ellen wines have been quite successful, and the family has added an upgraded line carrying the Benzinger name. There's a self-guided tour of this friendly winery that is a throwback to the 19th-century days of family wine making, and odds are good that some member of the large Benzinger clan (or Goober the dog) will be present to introduce you to their wines.

NORTH OF GLEN ELLEN

Grand Cru Vineyards is tucked away on a country lane (Vintage Road, behind Dunbar School) a short distance off Highway 12 northwest of Glen Ellen. It was built in 1970, making use of 1886 cellars and stone-and-concrete fermenting tanks. The vineyard has a tasting room and a scenic picnic area under large oak trees. **Kenwood Vineyards**, operating northeast of the tiny town of Kenwood, opened in 1970 in a converted 1906 winery. The harvest from each vineyard is handled separately within the winery to preserve its individuality, and literary sippers might want to taste the wine made solely from the grapes grown on Jack London's Beauty Ranch. The tasting room occupies a refurbished barn, which is, appropriately enough, the first stop on the horse-drawn tour offered by **Wine Country Wagons** (Tel: 833-2724) for $40 per person, including a magnificent picnic buffet; reservations are required 48 hours in advance. The wagons are new models with rubber tires that take the jolt out of the three-hour trip, and the horses are magnificent Clydesdales driven by an expert teamster. You can clip-clop along to wineries, vineyards, and tasting rooms from the first weekend in May through the end of October.

St. Francis Winery stands directly across the highway from **Chateau St. Jean**, and both of them are highly re-

garded, St. Francis for Merlot and St. Jean for Chardonnay.
Chateau St. Jean looks and seems French, but was actually
established by a group of California businessmen on a 1920s
country estate, and named for the wife of one of the men;
thus its American pronunciation. Suntory International, Ltd.
operates the winery now, and you can take a self-guided tour
of the state-of-the-art wine-making technology and sample
the wine in the handsome tasting room. There's a beautifully
maintained picnic area available for use; St. Francis also
offers picnic tables and lovely surroundings.

The **Kenwood Restaurant**, one of the best eating stops
along Highway 12, is an airy, city-style bistro with contemporary art and views of the countryside. The regularly changing
menu may feature roast duck, Sonoma rabbit, venison, sweetbreads, and summer salads, with an emphasis on locally
grown foods; Tel: 833-6326. **Café Citti**, an Italian trattoria on
the west side of the highway, has an agreeably informal style
and a menu of hearty Italian specialties; Tel: 833-2690
(closed Sundays). **Oreste's Golden Bear Lodge** is a delightful hideaway for a leisurely lunch in an enchanting setting.
Dating from the 1920s, the Golden Bear presents a modest
front alongside the winding Adobe Canyon Road, but there's
a cozy dining room and, behind that, the main attraction:
outdoor tree-shaded tables overlooking a meandering country stream. The Italian menu features pizzas, pastas, seafood
ravioli, and Sonoma sausage with grilled polenta; Tel: 833-
2327. The **Vineyards Inn** restaurant (at 8445 Highway 12 in
Kenwood) has been highly praised for its Mexican cuisine.
The restaurant is closed on Tuesdays; Tel: 833-4500.

Northern Sonoma

You can reach the northern Sonoma County region and the
Russian River Valley either directly from San Francisco on
Highway 101 to Santa Rosa or by continuing north from
Kenwood in the Sonoma Valley on Highway 12. From the
Napa Valley, drive north on Highway 128 from Calistoga to
Geyserville or Healdsburg.

The Russian River flows south into Sonoma County as a
fast-splashing stream through a spectacular landscape of
gorges, mountainsides, and cliffs. It slows and calms as it
enters Cloverdale, the lumber town at the northern frontier
of the Wine Country, and proceeds in a leisurely fashion
until it loops around Fitch Mountain near Healdsburg and
turns west, away from the valley into the redwood forests
and toward the sea. By the time it enters the Pacific Ocean at

Jenner, the Russian River has grown large and slow, its sun-flashed surface and cool depths pushing slowly through the timbered hills.

Although a few wineries in this region have been in production for many years, most wine grape production in the Russian River Valley dates from the repeal of Prohibition, and it wasn't until the wine boom of the late 1960s that full-scale investment in new vineyards and wineries gained serious momentum in this part of Sonoma County. Now you will find wineries up and down the Russian River watershed, and some of California's finest wines of every variety are identified with this region's distinct viticultural areas, such as Alexander Valley, Chalk Hill, and Dry Creek. More than 60 wineries operate in the Russian River Valley now, and most of them can only be found by deciphering the maze of narrow roads twisting well back into the countryside. As everywhere throughout the Napa-Sonoma wine country, the searching is sometimes as memorable as the finding.

Santa Rosa

You'll have no trouble finding Santa Rosa, which is at the junction of Highway 12 (the Sonoma Valley highway) and Highway 101. This attractive modern city is the Sonoma County seat, but is of little interest to the wine tourist except for its lively downtown district. Prime among the undeniable attractions here is the monument to Santa Rosa's most famous pioneer, the **Luther Burbank Home and Gardens** at Sonoma and Santa Rosa avenues. The famed plant breeder and experimenter established himself here in 1875 and began introducing more than 800 varieties of plants, including more than 200 kinds of fruit, to California agriculture. Admission is free and tours are available from April to mid-October.

From here it is only a short walk to Old Courthouse Square, at the flourishing center of the city. **La Cucina** serves sandwiches, salads, and light entrées in the courtyard, with a wide selection of wines. **Piazza Uno**, next door, is a dinner house in the high Italian style, and the brand-new **Cantina**, on Fourth Street, features a modern Mexican menu.

A dozen more inviting eating and drinking places await the wanderer within a block or two in any direction, and if you walk west on Fourth Street you will encounter the great brick structure of the Santa Rosa Mall. Enter, go left past Mervyn's, and exit the west side, proceeding along the promenade through the parking lot and under the freeway to **Railroad Square**. This is the old downtown district that grew up around the railroad station. Much of this area was rebuilt after the great earthquake of 1906, which was as destructive here as it was in San Francisco. Today the district has been transformed into a shopping district of considerable variety. Antiques shops predominate, but there are also art galleries, clothing shops, even a store devoted to environmentally conscious products from shower nozzle restrictors to electric automobiles. There is also an interesting combination of restaurants at the Square. You can dine at the **Hotel La Rose Restaurant** (see below); at **Mixx** on combinations of new cooking traditions with old such as pumpkin cannelloni and a smoked mozzarella quesadilla at lunch and dinner; or enjoy traditional French dinners (and the extensive wine list) at **La Gare**. **Aroma's**, across the street from the hotel and built of the same black granite as the hotel and the depot, is a popular coffeehouse serving cappuccinos, mochas, espressos, and more at tables on the sidewalk in good weather.

If sheer luxury is your goal, try the ▶ **Fountain Grove Inn** on Mendocino Avenue at the northern edge of the city. Not only are the rooms luxurious, but the inn's **Equus** restaurant is Santa Rosa's most recommended destination for haute cuisine. The less formal but no less elegant **Sonoma Grill** serves innovative dishes made with fresh local foods.

Santa Rosa offers visitors some other interesting places to stay. ▶ **The Gables**, on three and a half acres on the south side of town, is a symphony of claw-foot tubs, marble fireplaces, six guest rooms, and fifteen gabled windows. ▶ **Pygmalion House** is a porched and steepled Victorian offering five guest rooms at the end of a quiet residential street a short walk from the Railroad Square historic district. The imposing ▶ **Hotel La Rose** is a full-service hotel in the English style, and occupies a massive gray stone building adjoining Railroad Square.

Across the freeway and to the left on Barnes Road (take the River Road exit from Highway 101) is the deluxe ▶ **Vintner's Inn**, surrounded by 50 acres of vineyards. This inn is in the elegant European style, with unusually large guest rooms in two-story town houses separated by piazzas and generous landscaping. Also at the inn is **John Ash & Co.**, which built a reputation as one of the most creative and satisfying restaurants in all the Wine Country when it was originally established in a Santa Rosa shopping center. Here you can enjoy a more appropriate setting, viewed through huge windows from the two-tiered dining area or from the terrace, as John Ash continues his devotion to cooking with the freshest fish, fowl, and produce available from the surrounding areas; Tel: 527-7687.

Chateau de Baun is located at the Fulton turnoff from Highway 101. This recently established winery uses the Symphony grape—a new variety developed at the University of California at Davis from Grenache Gris and Muscat of Alexandria—to produce several white wines with unexpectedly spicy overtones.

Russian River Valley

River Road is an easy-to-follow and extremely scenic route leading west out of the valley and into the forest. It intersects the Russian River at the east end of the resort area, a favorite summer destination for Bay Area families since before the turn of the century. The little towns of Rio Nido, Monte Rio, and Guerneville (pronounced GURN-vil) offer inexpensive rental cabins and motels and provide everything necessary for boating, rafting, canoeing, and kayaking on the river.

In recent years the Russian River resort area has also become known as a popular gathering spot for gays, who own and operate many of the area's lodges, bars, and restaurants. This area is an inexpensive alternative to the higher-priced attractions of the Napa Valley, but it is showing its age and cannot quite match the level of the restaurants, accommodations, and other amenities available elsewhere in the Wine Country.

One of the most prominent of California wineries, both historically and architecturally, is located on the stretch of River Road that traverses this resort area. **F. Korbel and Bros.** is one of California's leading producers of sparkling wines using the *méthode champenoise,* and of estate-bottled varietals and brandy. Francis Korbel moved from San Francisco with his brothers Anton and Joseph and acquired this forested acreage in the 1870s. They logged the redwoods, used the proceeds to plant vineyards that are still producing today, and released their first vintage in 1881. Owned by the Heck Family since 1954, the Korbel Champagne Cellars have been developed into a prime visitor destination. Guided tours are provided every day, ending in the elegant tasting rooms in the former brandy barrel warehouse; the spectacular rose gardens and the carefully groomed grounds provide another feast for the senses. On a sunny day in the off season, nothing could be more inviting, but the combination of attractions at Korbel sometimes makes for summertime crowds.

Another route to the river resorts and Korbel is the Guerneville Road/Steele Lane exit west from Highway 101 at Santa Rosa, then north on Highway 116 (the Gravenstein Highway). A pleasant stop along the way is **Topolos at Russian River Vineyard** just south of Forestville on Highway 116. The attraction here, in addition to the wine, is the cuisine, served indoors and on the outdoor terrace on sunny days. The Greek specialties that appear on the menu along with more customary Continental/California fare reflect the ethnic heritage of the proprietors, although their wines are Italian in character. Guitar music adds a special dimension to the dining experience at Topolos; Tel: 887-1575. From here you can continue north on the Gravenstein Highway to Guerneville, and then turn east on River Road to Korbel and back into the heart of Wine Country.

BACK ROADS OF THE VALLEY

Numerous wineries are scattered along the back roads of the Russian River Valley. Westside Road, which you can pick up between Korbel and the river, is an especially rewarding route that will take you past a dozen inviting entrances on your way north to Healdsburg. **Davis Bynum**, notable for the quality of its wines rather than the historic or architectural interest of its facilities, is on Westside Road, as is **Hop Kiln Winery**, one of the most-photographed of the wineries— Hollywood has even used the dramatic three-towered hops barn as a setting in several movies. Both wineries produce exceptional red table wines.

One very small winery that has only recently opened its tasting room to visitors (and only on weekends) is **Joseph Swan Vineyards**, which is just south of River Road on Vine Hill Road. Joseph Swan Zinfandel is available in stores, but most of their other bottlings are experiments with old-growth vines and unusual varieties that can be tasted and purchased only at the vineyard.

Eastside Road, north of River Road, will take you back to Highway 101. Just before you reach the highway, **Piper Sonoma Cellars**, **Rodney Strong**, and the **Foppiano Vineyards** are all lined up along the two-lane Old Redwood Highway that parallels Highway 101. Piper Sonoma began as a 1980 partnership between the prestigious French Champagne maker Piper Heidsieck and the Sonoma winery that featured the highly regarded Rodney Strong as wine maker. Now operated separately, Piper Sonoma concentrates on sparkling wines, while Rodney Strong produces a full line of varietal wines. Both complexes are worth visiting for their distinctive architecture. Piper Sonoma also provides one of the most elaborate tours imaginable of the sparkling wine–making process, while the Rodney Strong tasting room overlooks the enormous wine cellar far below.

You can take either Westside Road or Eastside Road and Highway 101 a few miles north to Healdsburg.

Healdsburg

Until the wine renaissance of the mid-1960s, Healdsburg had been for nearly a century "the buckle in California's prune belt," a sleepy, dusty farm town surrounded by fruit orchards and hay ranches. In the last generation, though, thousands of acres of plums, cherries, peaches, apples, and pears have been replaced by Zinfandel, Cabernet, Grenache, Merlot, and other varieties of wine grapes. The growing areas surrounding the town have become well known for the quality of their wines and the diverse character of their wine makers, and in the process Healdsburg has developed into a regional wine center of considerable distinction.

The town of Healdsburg itself is plain downtown (except for the central plaza and the old Carnegie Library, now the local museum), and pretty in its neighborhoods, where handsome Victorians, Georgians, Edwardians, and Queen Annes rise up above luxuriant gardens along the pleasantly tree-shaded streets. The downtown plaza is much smaller than Sonoma's—it never had to serve as a parade ground—but it offers a pleasant stroll and a variety of enticements to visitors along the streets that mark its perimeter. The plaza itself is a small sunny park with a permanent bandstand, sometimes crowded with people at a concert, an antiques fair, or the annual wine festival, but more often available for a few minutes rest on your perambulations around town.

DINING IN HEALDSBURG

Jacob Horner is a calm, cool, high-ceilinged restaurant on the plaza that serves stylish lunches and dinners (and drinks at a brass-railed bar) in a carefully maintained old-fashioned way; Tel: 433-3939. Across the grassy expanse is **Samba Java**, a bright and lively café that takes a light approach to ambience, but a serious and adventurous tone in its menu; Tel: 433-5282. **Bistro Ralph**, next door, is cool, classy, and comfortable, the type of place (and the kind of calamari) that gives California cuisine a good name.

Bakeries abound in Healdsburg, where even the Safeway

turns out an exemplary baguette, but the old favorites are the **Downtown Creamery** on the plaza, where bread is made according to the Italian tradition, and **Costeaux**, on Healdsburg Avenue half a block north of the plaza, which represents the French. Both offer coffee, and Costeaux serves a modest lunch menu as well. A local favorite for lunch or a light dinner is a block north of the plaza next to the Raven Theater: **Ravenous** with a menu of pastas, salads, and house specialties. **Giorgio's**, on Healdsburg Avenue south of the bridge, is a celebrated San Francisco pizza restaurant reborn here as a dinner house, still featuring the spectacular pizzas but with a wider Italian menu as well.

There are two great stars of Healdsburg cuisine. The rising star is **Tre Scalini**, less than a block south of the plaza on Healdsburg Avenue, offering modern Italian cuisine with an informal flair, a taste for the adventurous, and an outstanding wine list; Tel: 433-1772. The **Madrona Manor** restaurant, a mile west of town on Westside Road, has consistently received the highest praise from restaurant reviewers since it opened. Chef Todd Muir prepares a different menu each night featuring fresh Sonoma County produce, poultry and meats, fish from the nearby ocean waters, pizza from wood-burning brick ovens, delectable trout, duck, and other wonders from the smokehouse out back, and fresh herbs and vegetables from the garden. Reservations should be made as far in advance as possible; Tel: 433-4231.

STAYING IN HEALDSBURG

The ▶ **Madrona Manor** also provides luxurious accommodations in a magnificent three-story Victorian mansion with pool, terrace, and gardens. Guests here slip into the world of the wealthy a century ago by gathering around the rosewood piano in the music room, sipping the finest of wine in front of the roaring fire, and retiring to canopied beds in one of the eighteen rooms and three suites.

There are other notable bed-and-breakfast inns in Healdsburg. At ▶ **Belle du Jour** guests stay in four attractive farmhouse cottages (one with a steam bath) at the northern outskirts of town; the ▶ **Grape Leaf Inn** is a graceful Queen Anne restoration in the heart of the old residential district. The ▶ **Healdsburg Inn on the Plaza** offers nine rooms, each with a private bath, and breakfast is served in the rooftop solarium. The ▶ **Raford House** offers seven comfortable rooms in a registered landmark Victorian farmhouse set in the midst of vineyards; the six-room 1912 ▶ **Haydon House** has added a two-story Gothic cottage next door, with two bedrooms on the upper floor, and offers complimentary wine to guests. The ▶ **George Alexander House** is one of Matheson Street's long row of splendid residences, and one of its most elaborately ornamented. It was built in 1905 for the tenth child of Cyrus Alexander, for whom Alexander Valley was named. George and Nellie's stately bedroom is now one of three devoted to guests.

WINE TASTING IN HEALDSBURG

If you stay at one of the downtown inns you can walk to the plaza (and everywhere else in town, for that matter) and to the increasing number of tasting rooms in town representing some of Sonoma County's most- and least-famous wineries. **Clos du Bois**, at 5 Fitch Street, is building a tasting room north of town in the Alexander Valley. Its red and white varietal wines are highly regarded. **White Oak**, at 204 Haydon Street, is a small winery with a very low public profile, but a very high level of acclaim in the industry and the Gold Medal wines to prove it. **J. W. Morris**, at 101 Grant Avenue off Healdsburg Avenue on the far south side of town, produces a distinctive Port-type wine in addition to its red and white table wines. The whimsically decorated tasting rooms of the **William Wheeler Winery** are right downtown at 130 Plaza Street, and the **Windsor** tasting room is nearby at 239A Center Street.

A recent addition to the local wine scene is the **Kendall-Jackson** tasting room and store on Healdsburg Avenue a few steps north of the plaza. In addition to the many vintages and varieties of this popular brand, the shop offers Wine Country specialties, souvenirs, and books. Also new in Healdsburg: a tasting room for **Royce** and **Hidden Cellars**, wines produced by two winemakers sharing a single winery—an innovation that is a lifeline to small, independent winemakers such as these. It is another way in which the wine business is constantly changing.

Simi, on Healdsburg Avenue at the north end of town, is the only winery still offering regular daily tours in northern Sonoma County (at 11:00 A.M., 1:00 P.M., and 3:00 P.M.). Simi's handsome stone buildings date from its founding in 1876, but the equipment inside is state of the art, and its wine is made from the grapes grown on 300 acres of nearby vineyards. Like many other prime California wineries, Simi is now operating under foreign ownership, in this case the prestigious French firm Moët-Hennessy.

Healdsburg Environs

Healdsburg's surroundings are largely given over to wine production now, but there are still many farms and ranches in the rumpled hills, some of them offering produce to the public. There is a Saturday morning and Tuesday afternoon Farmer's Market in the parking area between Matheson and North streets a block west of the plaza; fresh vegetables, fruits, and flowers are sold out of the backs of trucks just in from the farms. You can also visit some of these farms, if you wish, and sample the harvest on the premises. On Westside Road you'll find **Middleton Gardens**, where you can get fresh strawberries, peaches, apples, pears, persimmons, and more, and **Westside Farms**, where you'll find gourmet popcorn and fertile free-range chicken eggs. **The Hoskins Ranch** at 15101 Kinley Drive, to the west of the freeway, sells peaches, apples, and pears in season, and **Timbercrest Farms** at 4791 Dry Creek Road sells dried fruits and other organically grown California produce in bulk, in gift packs, and by mail order.

DRY CREEK VALLEY

Dry Creek Road leads northwest from Healdsburg to meander through hundreds of acres of vivid green vineyards and past more than a dozen wineries in Dry Creek Valley, some heavy with history, others newer and less traditional in presentation, but all devoted to making the best possible wines. **Dry Creek Winery**, west on Lambert Bridge Road, is especially noted for its Zinfandel and other reds, including a Cabernet Franc, which is usually used as a blending wine to add strength to a faltering Cabernet Sauvignon. Lake Sonoma is at the northern end of Dry Creek Road, and the recreation facilities there provide a pleasant resting place.

ALEXANDER VALLEY

To reach the Alexander Valley, take Lytton Springs Road east from Dry Creek Road past **Mazzocco Vineyards**, best known for its Chardonnay, and **Lytton Springs Winery**, where award-winning Zinfandels are produced. This road becomes Lytton Station Road and then Alexander Valley Road before intersecting Highway 128, which runs for several miles north and south through the Alexander Valley. Or, from Healdsburg, proceed north on Healdsburg Boulevard past Simi Winery and then go east on the Alexander Valley Road to Highway 128. Along the way you'll pass one of California's finest roadside stores: the **Jimtown Store**. A fixture of the neighborhood on and off since 1893, the store had been drowsing here for years until it was revitalized recently by new proprietors from New York. They have startled the place wide awake with their energy and their flair for the decorative and the delicious. Antiques, memorabilia, and regional products are sold, but the main attraction for the Wine Country traveller is the food. Boxed lunches and picnic dinners may be ordered ahead by telephone (Tel: 433-1212), or you can create a hot or cold picnic lunch and eat it on the back patio at sturdy red school desks patterned after Mexican originals. The list of possible sandwiches includes marinated shrimp with green olives, roast pork with honey onion marmalade, lamb with fig *tapenade,* and peanut butter with Jimtown Jam.

To tour the entire Alexander Valley, turn right (south) onto Highway 128 and proceed to Chalk Hill Road. Along the way you'll see **Alexander Valley Vineyards, Johnson's Alexander Valley Winery** (where an antique organ is now operated by computer), and **Field Stone Winery**, where summertime concerts are performed.

If you turn left (north) where Alexander Valley Road intersects Highway 128, you will see the **Alexander Valley Fruit & Trading Company**, which offers local food products—olive, honey-ginger, and garlic-tomato sauces among them—separately or in gift packs along with their varietal wines. **Murphy-Goode**, a relative newcomer to the valley, is a near neighbor producing delicious dessert wines as well as more common varietals. Across the Russian River from Murphy-Goode on Geyserville Road is **Trentadue**, a small family operation with an attractive picnic area. If you cross over to the west side of Highway 101 south of Geyserville you will find **Chateau Souverain**, a majestic presence on the west side of the valley overlooking the vineyards and the hills beyond.

North of the little town of Geyserville on Chianti Avenue to the west of Highway 101 is the **Geyser Peak Winery**, an impressive modern stone castle-like building overlooking the valley. Established in 1880, this was Geyserville's first winery. It is now co-owned by the Trione family of Santa Rosa and Penfolds Wine of Australia, so you can sample both the local vintages and the Australian Sea View wines here. To the east of the highway, the **Hoffman House** on Geyserville Avenue offers a California country menu that changes daily but always showcases hearty dishes made with the fresh market produce of the district, augmented with herbs and spices grown in its gardens; Tel: 857-3264.

Continue north on Geyserville Avenue, which becomes Asti Road. To the west you can see hundreds of acres of new vineyards planted on hillsides that were stripped of soil, sculpted to the proper grade for optimal drainage, and then resoiled with extra nourishment for the young vines. This is the **Asti Ranch**, where the Gallo family is entering the estate winery business with more than 1,500 acres of Sonoma County vineyards.

Cloverdale, the northernmost outpost of Sonoma County Wine Country, is a pleasant and scenic town, rooted in the timber industry and graced with some fine examples of historic architecture. The spectacular ▶ **Vintage Towers** bed-and-breakfast inn at 302 North Main offers seven guest rooms, including three in the namesake towers. Just a few steps away is the ▶ **Abrams House Inn**, with four rooms, where the rates include a full breakfast. In Geyserville, the impeccably restored ▶ **Hope-Bosworth House** and ▶ **Hope-Merrill House** across the street offer gourmet picnic lunches to wine-touring guests in addition to breakfast feasts. The Hope-Merrill House was selected from among more than 200 nominees as the "Outstanding Bed-and-Breakfast Inn Restoration" in the United States in 1990 by the National Trust for Historic Preservation.

From Cloverdale you can return south directly to San Francisco via Highway 101 or detour through either the Dry Creek or Geyser Peak areas on the way. Dutcher Creek Road leads southwest off Highway 101 to the Dry Creek district, passing the **Fritz Winery**, an unusual arched structure recessed into the hillside, along the way. Geysers Road, which will return you eventually to the Alexander Valley, climbs east from Cloverdale into the near wilderness of Big Sulfur Creek, clings to cliffs (safe, but definitely dramatic), and winds around Geyser Peak. Once you have left civilization far behind, you'll see huge geothermal developments on the mountainsides, with bunkers and Keep Out signs, and pipelines zigzagging up and down the steep slopes. You'll think you have travelled to Mars or happened onto the set of a James Bond movie. Once past the geothermal strangeness, the road climbs westward and then drops down into the Alexander Valley, which is a luscious sight in the rich golden light of the setting sun.

GETTING AROUND

The best way to tour the Wine Country is by private car, giving you the flexibility to set your own schedule. However, there are some options for non-drivers. Gray Line offers bus tours from San Francisco (Tel: 415-558-9400 or 800-556-5660), and Viviani Touring Company in Sonoma offers customized wine-oriented touring (Tel: 707-938-2100). Two invaluable sources of information are the Napa Valley Conference and Visitors Bureau (1310 Napa Town Center, Napa, CA 94559; Tel: 707-226-7459) and the Sonoma County Convention and Visitors Bureau (10 Fourth Street, Suite 100, Santa Rosa, CA 95401; Tel: 707-575-1191).

ACCOMMODATIONS REFERENCE

Weekends and warm-weather months, from about April to the end of the crushing season in October, are naturally the most difficult times for reservations. Lower rates for midweek and winter reservations often apply. Travellers should be aware that many of the bed-and-breakfast establishments do not allow children and have strict no-smoking policies. The area code for the Wine Country is 707.

The rate ranges given here are projections for fall 1993 through spring 1994. Unless otherwise indicated, rates are for double room, double occupancy.

▶ **Abrams House Inn.** 314 North Main Street, **Cloverdale**, CA 95425. Tel: 894-2412. $75–$115.

▶ **Ambrose Bierce House.** 1515 Main Street, **St. Helena**, CA 94574. Tel: 963-3003; Fax: 963-5036. $99–$139.

▶ **Auberge du Soleil.** 180 Rutherford Hill Road, **Rutherford**, CA 94573. Tel: 963-1211 or (800) 348-5406; Fax: 963-8764. $295–$315.

▶ **Bartel's Ranch.** 1200 Conn Valley Road, **St. Helena**, CA 94574. Tel: 963-4001. $135–$275.

▶ **Belle du Jour.** 16276 Healdsburg Avenue, **Healdsburg**, CA 95448. Tel: 433-7892; Fax: 431-7412. $115–$185.

▶ **Beltrane Ranch.** P.O. Box 395, 11775 Sonoma Highway 12, **Glen Ellen**, CA 95442. Tel: 996-6501. $95–$120.

▶ **Bordeaux House.** 6600 Washington Street, **Yountville**, CA 94599. Tel: 944-2855 or (800) 677-8370. $90–$110.

▶ **Brannan Cottage Inn.** 109 Wapoo Avenue, **Calistoga**, CA 94515. Tel: 942-4200. $95–$155.

▶ **Burgundy House.** P.O. Box 3156, 6711 Washington Street, **Yountville**, CA 94599. Tel: 944-0889. $121.

▶ **Calistoga Country Lodge.** 2883 Foothill Boulevard, **Calistoga**, CA 94515. Tel: 942-5555. $95–$125.

▶ **Calistoga Inn.** 1250 Lincoln Avenue, **Calistoga**, CA 94515. Tel: 942-4101; Fax: 942-4914. $50–$60.

▶ **Calistoga Spa Hot Springs.** 1006 Washington Street, **Calistoga**, CA 94515. Tel: 942-6269. $68–$79.

▶ **Calistoga Wayside Inn**. 1523 Foothill Boulevard, **Calistoga**, CA 94515. Tel: 942-0645 or (800) 845-3632. $105–$125.

▶ **Christopher's Inn**. 1010 Foothill Boulevard, **Calistoga**, CA 94515. Tel: 942-5755. $105–$165.

▶ **Creekside Inn**. 945 Main Street, **St. Helena**, CA 94574. Tel: 963-7244; Fax: 963-7220. $95.

▶ **Dr. Wilkinson's Hot Springs**. 1507 Lincoln Avenue, **Calistoga**, CA 94515. Tel: 942-4102. $49–$99.

▶ **El Dorado Hotel**. 405 First Street West, **Sonoma**, CA 95476. Tel: 996-3030 or (800) 289-3031; Fax: 996-3148. $80–$140.

▶ **The Farmhouse**. 300 Taplin Road, **St. Helena**, CA 94574. Tel: 963-3431. $125–$135.

▶ **Fountain Grove Inn**. 101 Fountain Grove Parkway, **Santa Rosa**, CA 95403. Tel: 578-6101; in California, Tel: (800) 222-6101; Fax: 544-3126. $99.

▶ **The Gables**. 4257 Petaluma Hill Road, **Santa Rosa**, CA 95404. Tel: 585-7777. $95–$175.

▶ **Gaige House Inn**. 13540 Arnold Drive, **Glen Ellen**, CA 95442. Tel: 935-0237. $90–$160.

▶ **George Alexander House**. 423 Matheson Street, **Healdsburg**, CA 95448. Tel: 433-1358. $80–$130.

▶ **Glenelly Inn**. 5131 Warm Springs Road, **Glen Ellen**, CA 95442. Tel: 996-6720. $80–$125.

▶ **Golden Haven Hot Springs**. 1713 Lake Street, **Calistoga**, CA 94515. Tel: 942-6793; Fax: 942-0485. $49–$105.

▶ **Grape Leaf Inn**. 539 Johnson Street, **Healdsburg**, CA 95448. Tel: 433-8140. $85–$130.

▶ **Harvest Inn**. 1 Main Street, **St. Helena**, CA 94574. Tel: 963-9463 or (800) 950-8466; Fax: 963-4402. $110–$325.

▶ **Haydon House**. 321 Haydon Street, **Healdsburg**, CA 95448. Tel: 433-5228. $85–$115.

▶ **Healdsburg Inn on the Plaza**. 110 Matheson Street, **Healdsburg**, CA 95448. Tel: 433-6991. $75–$160.

▶ **Hidden Oak**. 214 East Napa Street, **Sonoma**, CA 95476. Tel: 996-9863. $95–$130.

▶ **Hope-Bosworth House**. P.O. Box 42, 21253 Geyserville Avenue, **Geyserville**, CA 95441. Tel: 857-3356 or (800) 825-4BED. $65–$95.

▶ **Hope-Merrill House**. P.O. Box 42, 21238 Geyserville Avenue, **Geyserville**, CA 95441. Tel: 857-3356 or (800) 825-4BED. $95–$125.

▶ **Hotel La Rose**. 308 Wilson Street, **Santa Rosa**, CA 95401. Tel: 579-3200; Fax: 579-3247. $37–$85.

▶ **Hotel St. Helena.** 1309 Main Street, **St. Helena**, CA 94574. Tel: 963-4388. $100–$190.

▶ **Larkmead Country Inn.** 1103 Larkmead Lane, **Calistoga**, CA 94515. Tel: 942-5360. $195–$210.

▶ **Madrona Manor.** 1001 Westside Road, **Healdsburg**, CA 95448. Tel: 433-4231 or (800) 258-4003; Fax: 433-0703. $135–$225.

▶ **Magnolia Hotel.** 6529 Yount Street, **Yountville**, CA 94599. Tel: 944-2056 or (800) 788-0369. $99–$169.

▶ **Meadowood Resort.** 900 Meadowood Lane, **St. Helena**, CA 94574. Tel: 963-3646; in California, (800) 458-8080; Fax: 963-3532. $175–$425.

▶ **Mount View Hotel.** 1457 Lincoln Avenue, **Calistoga**, CA 94515. Tel: 942-6877. $100–$165.

▶ **Nance's Hot Springs.** 1614 Lincoln Avenue, **Calistoga**, CA 94515. Tel: 942-6211. $66–$83.

▶ **Napa Valley Lodge.** P.O. Box L, Highway 29 and Madison Avenue, **Yountville**, CA 94599. Tel: 944-2468 or (800) 368-2468; Fax: 944-9362. $132–$195.

▶ **Oak Knoll Inn.** 2200 East Oak Knoll Avenue, **Napa**, CA 94558. Tel: 255-2200. $175–$225.

▶ **Pygmalion House.** 331 Orange Street, **Santa Rosa**, CA 95401. Tel: 526-3407. $50–$70.

▶ **Raford House.** 10630 Wohler Road, **Healdsburg**, CA 94558. Tel: 887-9573. $85–$130.

▶ **Silverado Resort and Country Club.** 1600 Atlas Peak Road, **Napa**, CA 94558. Tel: 257-0200 or (800) 532-0500; Fax: 257-5400. $130–$450.

▶ **Sonoma Hotel.** 110 West Spain Street, **Sonoma**, CA 95476. Tel: 996-2996. $70–$115.

▶ **Sonoma Mission Inn and Spa.** P.O. Box 1447, **Sonoma**, CA 95476. Tel: 938-9000 or (800) 862-4945; Fax: 938-4250. $160–$340.

▶ **Thistle Dew Inn.** 171 West Spain Street, **Sonoma**, CA 95476. Tel: 938-2909. $80–$120.

▶ **Victorian Garden Inn.** 316 East Napa Street, **Sonoma**, CA 95476. Tel: 996-5339. $79–$139.

▶ **Villa St. Helena.** 2727 Sulphur Springs Avenue, **St. Helena**, CA 94574. Tel: 963-0262. $145–$225.

▶ **Vintage Inn.** 6541 Washington Street, **Yountville**, CA 94599. Tel: 944-1112 or (800) 351-1133; Fax: 944-1617. $139–$199.

▶ **Vintage Towers.** 302 North Main Street, **Cloverdale**, CA 95425. Tel: 894-4535; Fax: 894-5827. $80–$125.

▶ **Vintner's Inn.** 4350 Barnes Road, **Santa Rosa**, CA 95403.

Tel: 575-7350; in California, (800) 421-2584; Fax: 575-1426. $108–$185.

► **The Webber Place**. 6610 Webber, **Yountville**, CA 94599. Tel: 944-8384. $69–$119.

► **Wine Country Inn**. 1152 Lodi Lane, **St. Helena**, CA 94574. Tel: 963-7077 or (800) 473-3463. $97–$211.

► **Wine Way Inn**. 1019 Foothill Boulevard, **Calistoga**, CA 94515. Tel: 942-0680. $72–$110.

► **Zinfandel Inn**. 800 Zinfandel Lane, **St. Helena**, CA 94574. Tel: 963-3512; Fax: 963-5310. $125–$225.

THE REDWOOD COUNTRY

By Georgia I. Hesse and Jean Pierce

Jean Pierce is Editor of Chevron Odyssey, *the magazine of the Chevron Travel Club. While Senior Editor at Rand McNally, her* National Parks Recreation Directory *for Northern California won a Lowell Thomas Award for Excellence in Journalism. A member of the Society of American Travel Writers and a third-generation Californian, she resides in the Napa Valley.*

In the deep, still shade of old-growth groves in Redwood National Park, north of Eureka, you can't hear a pin drop; even your own footfalls are silenced, buried in the duff of the forest floor. The ticks of time and life themselves are muted: Water drips, somewhere beyond your sight, through beds of moss and sprays of giant ferns; little winds wail high in the thick, green vault; you start at the sudden, sharp staccato of a woodpecker.

The drama that began in prehistory can give the thoughtful traveller chills.

In the Jurassic period, about 160 million years ago, when dinosaurs ruled the earth and mammals were just being born, a sturdy plant sprouted and began its steady growth into giant forests, the ancestors of the redwoods. Eras passed, flying reptiles became extinct, insects and flowering plants and primates appeared, and by about 20 million years ago, redwoods as we know them today stood in tall parade around the globe, from western Canada to the Atlantic, from France to Japan.

Then came the great glacial ages. Arctic ice sheets crept inexorably south over lands and seas. When eventually they retreated, the tall trees had vanished almost everywhere— except in a slice of Northern California and in a remote region of China (where they were identified only in 1946).

Today's redwoods have been classified by botanists into three species: *Sequoia sempervirens* (the Coast Redwood; sempervirens means "evergreen"), *Sequoiadendron giganteum* (Giant Sequoia), and *Metasequoia glyptostroboides* (China's Dawn Redwood). The redwoods were baptized *sequoia* by Hungarian botanist Stephen Endlicher, who wished to honor a Cherokee Indian named Sequoyah who had invented an alphabet for his people.

The Coast Redwood is the titan, towering over all other living things: One overachiever in Redwood National Park is the tallest tree in the world, topping out at 367.8 feet. Exceptional giants may reach a height of 350 feet, a diameter of 20 feet, and an age of about 2,000 years. The Founders' Tree in Humboldt Redwoods State Park, already a sprout when Christ was born, is 346 feet high, almost 13 feet in diameter, and 40 feet in circumference.

When Europeans first arrived in California, the coastal redwood belt stretched about 450 miles from a pinch of southern Oregon to the south tip of Monterey County and the Santa Lucia Mountains, and into the hills behind what is today Oakland. Forests blanketed much of today's San Mateo, Santa Cruz, and Marin counties, but now most of those old trees have been cut except the ones preserved in the Big Basin, Portola, Butano, Cowell, Mount Tamalpais, and Samuel P. Taylor state parks, and much-visited Muir Woods National Monument north of San Francisco. The most dramatic stands today are found in Humboldt and Del Norte counties farther north, part of what we call the Redwood Country.

The redwoods are rulers of a varied empire: a few towns that serve as toeholds of civilization; fine, burgeoning vineyards; sunny uplands; a wave-battered, now brilliant, now fog-shrouded coast; and still enough wilderness to soothe the city-strangled soul.

Like the traveller who starts in San Francisco, we will wander the Redwood Country from south to north (on the major inland highway) and back (on the scenic coastal highway).

MAJOR INTEREST

The Redwood Highway
Anderson Valley wineries
Small-town flavor of Ukiah, Willits, and Garberville

Humboldt Redwoods State Park
Avenue of the Giants
Founders' Grove Nature Trail
Rockefeller Forest

Eureka and Region
Eureka's Old Town, Carson Mansion
Ferndale and the Lost Coast
Coastal towns from Arcata to Orick

Redwood National Park
Tall Trees Trail
Lady Bird Johnson Grove
Prairie Creek Redwoods State Park (Fern Canyon)

Del Norte County
Alder Basin Trail
Damnation Creek Trail
Crescent City
Jedediah Smith Redwoods State Park

Coastal Highway 1, Mendocino Coast
Fort Bragg (Skunk Train, Jug Handle State Park)
Mendocino (art colony, coastal activities)
Coastal towns of Little River, Albion, Elk, Gualala
Sonoma County Coast

THE REDWOOD HIGHWAY

It is physically possible to drive north from San Francisco to
Eureka (or perhaps even to Crescent City on the Oregon
border) and back in two or three days—but all you will
experience is exhaustion. At least a week or ten days are
demanded if you wish to appreciate the natural majesty and
the cultural quirks of this compelling country.

The best plan is to follow an itinerary that runs north of
San Francisco on the Redwood Highway (U.S. 101), through
Leggett to Eureka and beyond to Crescent City (359 miles/
574 km from the Golden Gate Bridge), returns to Leggett,
then winds south on coastal State Highway 1. A dozen
satisfying detours may be made along the way.

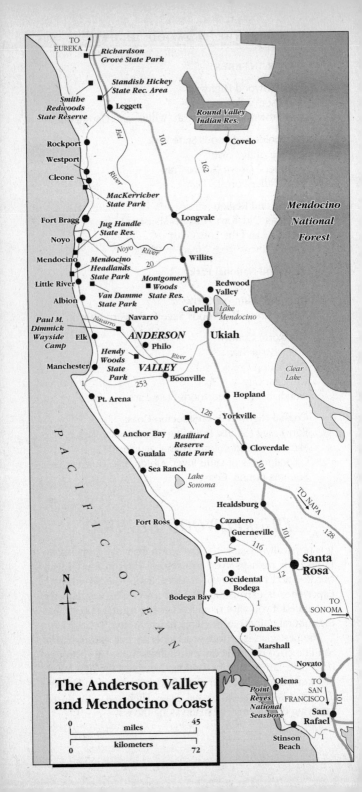

TO
EUREKA

*Richardson
Grove State Park*

*Standish Hickey
State Rec. Area*

Leggett

*Smithe
Redwoods
State Reserve*

Rockport

Westport

Cleone

*MacKerricher
State Park*

Fort Bragg

*Jug Handle
State Res.*

Noyo

Mendocino

*Mendocino
Headlands
State Park*

Little River

*Van Damme
State Park*

Albion

*Paul M.
Dimmick
Wayside
Camp*

Navarro

ANDERSON

Philo

Elk

*Hendy
Woods
State Park*

VALLEY

Manchester

253

Boonville

Pt. Arena

128

Yorkville

Anchor Bay

*Mailliard
Reserve
State Park*

Gualala

Sea Ranch

*Lake
Sonoma*

Healdsburg

Cazadero

Fort Ross

Guerneville

116

Jenner

Occidental

Bodega

Bodega Bay

Tomales

Marshall

Novato

Olema

TO
SAN
FRANCISCO

*Point
Reyes
National
Seashore*

San
Rafael

Stinson
Beach

Eel

River

*Round Valley
Indian Res.*

Covelo

162

101

Longvale

**Mendocino
National
Forest**

Noyo River

20

Willits

Redwood
Valley

*Montgomery
Woods State Res.*

Calpella

*Lake
Mendocino*

Navarro

Ukiah

River

*Clear
Lake*

Hopland

128

Cloverdale

101

TO NAPA

128

**Santa
Rosa**

12

TO
SONOMA

PACIFIC OCEAN

N

101

The Anderson Valley
and Mendocino Coast

0	miles	45

0	kilometers	72

A first stop might be made in Santa Rosa or Healdsburg (about 70 miles/112 km north of San Francisco) in Sonoma County, both with rewarding inns, restaurants, vineyards, and other attractions (see the Wine Country chapter).

Beyond Cloverdale, north of Healdsburg, commuter communities yield to farmland and vineyards; just north of town, State Highway 128 leaves 101 to snake northwest into Mendocino County and Anderson Valley.

Anderson Valley

Traditionally remote, isolated, self-sufficient, and unfriendly to outsiders, the wide-spot towns of the valley—Yorkville, Boonville, Philo, and Navarro—are stirring in their afternoon naps these days, with wineries springing up like California poppies, and with one restaurant that alone is worth the drive from San Francisco, the Boonville Hotel.

San Franciscans heading for long weekends on the Mendocino Coast often take Highway 128, the rural road that runs northwest from its junction with U.S. 101 at Cloverdale, easing in an unconcerned manner past the stately redwoods of **Mailliard Reserve** and **Hendy Woods State Park** (pleasant ambles in redwood groves interspersed with the twisted red-gold madrones that echo the shades of the sun, and with Douglas firs, California laurels, and deer ferns), on through the shady silence of **Navarro River Redwoods State Park,** to emerge suddenly at the sea south of Albion (for which see South of Mendocino later in this chapter). Navarro is mainly for day use (hiking, swimming, fishing, and picnicking); a few primitive camping sites are available, though limited in off-seasons; for the latest information, call (707) 937-5804.

BOONVILLE

In Boonville, about 25 miles (40 km) northwest of Cloverdale, you should plan for dinner (Wednesday through Sunday) at the ▶ **Boonville Hotel**, a creaky-looking wooden structure on the wide main street. The emphasis here is on California cuisine, featuring fresh herbs and vegetables and regional wines. There's open-air dining in good weather; Tel: 895-2210. The hotel now features eight Shaker-style rooms for overnight guests.

If you're lucky, you may hear someone "harping Boont," otherwise known as speaking the private local language called Boontling, a dialect preserved in a handy guide to the town and its native tongue entitled *A Slib of Lorey* (A Bit of Folklore). Try this example: "The shoveltooth was at a sharking match when the telef rang, calling all kimmies to help dreek a jeffer" (The doctor was playing cards when the phone rang, calling all men to help put out a fire). The 700-plus "kimmies," "dames," and "tweeds" (men, women, and children) of Boonville don't all harp Boont perfectly, but they're all proud of it. Boontling originated in the 1880s, it is said, so that tweeds could converse without their parents' understanding, and it delighted the backcountry folk to harp unintelligibly in front of the occasional "bright light" (city dude).

There's not total joy in Boonville these days, even though since the Boonville Hotel arrived you can "gorm a bahl gorm" (eat a good meal). The "posy tweeds" (hippies) have gone, sure, but they have been succeeded by the environmentalists and "Gold Dome kimmies" (men from the state capital), who are irritating the "croppy kimmies" (sheepmen) with too many regulations.

One place where the good times always roll is the **Buckhorn Saloon**, home of the Anderson Valley Brewing Company and its brews: Poleeko Gold, a light ale; High Rollers, a wheat beer; Boont Amber, a medium-bodied pale ale; Deep Enders Dark, a full-bodied porter, and Barney Flats, an oatmeal stout. The brew pub serves such fare as nachos, spicy chicken wings, sausages, soups and salads, sandwiches, and even beef ribs, fettucine Alfredo, and fish and chips. Lunch and dinner are served daily except Wednesdays and some Tuesdays.

Despite its determined rusticity, Anderson Valley stands ready to soothe the slowed-down driver with two retreats: the small, fashionable ▶ **Toll House Restaurant and Inn**, just east of Boonville on Highway 253, and the neat, seven-room ▶ **Anderson Valley Inn** in Philo, a few miles north on Highway 128.

Toll House was built in 1912 to serve as the headquarters of the vast Miller family ranch, where tolls were charged the mule-skinners who hauled redwood logs to the inland lumber mills. Today it's a four-room escape commanding 360 acres, with hiking, riding, and fishing available. The restaurant serves its own organically grown vegetables and locally produced veal, lamb, beef, and free-range chicken. Room rates are moderate by city standards.

Should you be in the neighborhood in late April, plan to attend the colorful Annual Wildflower Show at the Boonville Fairgrounds. The Mendocino County Fair & Apple Show is held late in September at the same arena.

Anderson Valley wineries are sparking statewide nods, even from tasters who've never heard of Boonville. They are clustered around Philo: try Husch Vineyards (tours are available), Scharffenberger, Navarro, Greenwood Ridge, Christine Wood, and Handley. (In 1991 the French Champagne producer added Roederer Estate to the valley's attractions.) Each offers daily tastings and is just a few yards off Highway 128 to the left or right, clearly signposted.

Hopland

Wine enthusiasts who don't detour into Anderson Valley may want to stop around Hopland, about 15 miles up Highway 101 from Cloverdale, especially at the **Fetzer** winery, which has been producing since the 1960s at 1150 Bel Arbes Road (tours by appointment only; Tel: 744-1737). Fetzer's organic acres, Valley Oaks Garden, produce apples, vegetables, and herbs (Tel: 744-1250).

Fans of cheesecake who have discovered Robin Collier's compelling creations in Bay Area restaurants have been known to go all the way to Hopland just to taste the desserts fresh from their home oven. Stop in at the **Cheesecake Lady** at 13325 Highway 101 on the east side of the highway. **Milano Winery**, just south of town, is a good place to buy a picnic-suitable Zinfandel.

Enthusiasts of California history often stop in Hopland to see the ▶ **Thatcher Inn**, a smart 1890 Victorian. They may also sip in the lobby bar, where 48 varieties of single-malt Scotches wait to be savored, and peek into the wainscoted Fireside Library, where good reading awaits in more than 4,000 volumes. Even better to stay the night in one of 20 rooms, outfitted with period pieces but renovated with modern plumbing. The restaurant (California-Continental cuisine) serves regional specialties, such as Sonoma goat cheese, whenever possible.

The **Hopland Brewery** opened its doors to the public in August 1983, the first brew pub to open in the state since Prohibition. Located at 13351 South Highway 101 it produces four brews: Peregrine (pale ale), Blue Heron (pale ale tending toward the English bitter style), Red Tail Ale, (most popular), and Black Hawk (full-bodied stout). The pub occupies one of Hopland's century-old buildings and operates daily from 11:00 A.M. There are picnic tables and a store with brew-oriented gifts and souvenirs.

Ukiah

Drivers who detoured into Anderson Valley can return to the freeway north of Hopland via Highway 253. Highway 101 then hurtles past Ukiah, a pleasant wide-street town with a vaguely Midwest air suggestive of the thwack of Saturday afternoon Little League baseball games. At 431 South Main Street here, the **Grace Hudson Museum** (open daily except Mondays and Tuesdays) is installed in Sun House, home of John Hudson and his wife, Grace Carpenter Hudson, a painter of the primitive, little-known Pomo Indians. "My desire is that the world shall know them as I know them, and before they vanish . . . before the opportunity is no more," the artist wrote in 1934. In Hudson's day her work was considered sentimental and trivial, but today it is recognized as a genuine record of a day and people long since gone.

Late in May and into June, Ukiah stages the Hometown Festival, a combination regatta, marathon, and food show spiced with tours of local Victorian homes; the Redwood Empire Fair comes to town in late August.

If you tire of the road about here, you might detour west of Ukiah on Vichy Springs Road to ► **Vichy Mineral Springs Resort/Bed & Breakfast**, where 19th-century cottages and rooms occupy private, 700-acre resort grounds. Relax in Champagne baths, a mineral hot tub, or a mineral pool; hike or mountain bike on uncrowded trails, visit an old cinnabar mine, picnic under the redwoods, or enjoy a massage. (The springs were used by the Native Americans before the Europeans arrived.)

On the other hand, near downtown Ukiah, across from the Crossroads Shopping Center, the ► **Discovery Inn**'s 154 units have been redecorated, and you'll find a heated swimming pool, sauna, tennis court, and all the essentials. Just off Highway 101 at 950 North State Street, the ► **Manor Inn Motel** has 57 well-decorated rooms and Continental breakfast along with an Olympic-sized swimming pool; no pets allowed.

If you're in the mood for wine, **Parducci Cellars**, a long-time producer of premium wines, offers tastings and tours a few minutes north of Ukiah; Tel: 462-3828. Beyond Calpella in the town of Redwood Valley, **Weibel Vineyards** also has a tasting room; the winery's headquarters in Mission San Jose south of Oakland were established by Leland Stanford, a California governor and founder of Stanford University. Five miles (8 km) northeast of Ukiah is **Lake Mendocino**, which provides sports facilities especially suited to families—swimming, waterskiing, boating, fishing, hiking, picnicking, and camping; Tel: (707) 462-7582. For information and regional maps, stop by or write to the Ukiah Chamber of Commerce, 495 "E" East Perkins Street, Ukiah, CA 95482; Tel: (707) 462-4705.

North of Ukiah, about 10 miles (16 km) south of Willits, is Black Bart Rock, a large stone outcrop dedicated to one of Northern California's favorite rogues, who practiced in this area a century ago. Black Bart didn't drink or smoke, he fussed about his personal linen, his breast pocket held a silk handkerchief, and his head bore a proper topper. When he robbed Wells Fargo stagecoaches (almost 30 of them), he donned a flour-sack mask and a linen duster and spoke politely as he demanded (in resonant tones, they said) the strongbox. Then he left behind delightful doggerel: "I've labored long and hard for bread—/For honor and for riches—/But on my corns too long you've tread,/You fine-haired sons of bitches."

Black Bart's colorful career came to an end in the autumn of 1883, when, following a holdup, he dropped a silk handkerchief that was traced by its San Francisco laundry mark to one Charles Bolton, a mining engineer and, some histories say, a former Wells Fargo clerk. Released after a five-year stay in San Quentin prison, Black Bart soon vanished. It is not known whether he ever returned to his faithful wife in Illinois, who claimed he was a good and tidy man.

Willits to Leggett

Willits, 23 miles (37 km) north of Ukiah, was until recently a town in search of instant identity; it lacked a Golden Gate Bridge or an Eiffel Tower. In 1990 though, the town gained a landmark—the famous old arch that once identified Reno, Nevada, as "the Biggest Little City in the World." It now proclaims "Gateway to the Redwoods."

Willits is known by most visitors solely as the eastern terminus of the famous **Skunk Train**, which chugs for 40 miles through ranch country and redwood groves from Fort Bragg on the coast to its depot here (off Main and Commercial streets) and back again (see Fort Bragg below). This little town of 5,000 is worth a stop in itself, however, chiefly for the **Mendocino County Museum** on East Commercial Street (open Wednesday through Sunday), a repository of artifacts and crafts from the regional Pomo Indian culture and items illustrative of pioneer history. Willits's **July 4 Frontier Days Rodeo** is the oldest continuous annual rodeo in the state, a fine occasion for countrified whoop-de-doo.

Drivers who have decided not to make the trek to the really big trees farther north can take Highway 20 west from Willits across the Coast Range to Noyo, through scenery similar to that seen aboard the Skunk; the drive is about 42 miles (67 km). (For Noyo, see The Mendocino Coast below.)

"Covelo . . . is the gathering place for a rude population which rides in on mustang ponies whenever it gets out of whiskey." So a traveller wrote in *Harper's* in 1873. That particular pastime may have changed, but **Covelo** and the Round Valley Indian Reservation (50,000 acres) echo the Old West (or, more properly, Hollywood's classic Westerns) along State Highway 162, which cuts east off 101 around Longvale, north of Willits. Few travellers will take the time to poke around here, but you may like to ponder its history as you continue north to Leggett and the Smithe Redwoods State Reserve.

In the mid-1880s some 20,000 Yuka Indians lived in Round Valley. As Stuart Nixon describes its aspect today in *Redwood Empire:* "The great white oaks and lush green pastures of Round Valley's big ranches suggest the manorial estates of Surrey or Shropshire, but Covelo, all dusty streets and false fronts, proposes Dodge City or Deadwood. In time, the last hunted Yuka would tell an Army agent: 'We have lost faith in everything but death.' "

If you do take time for a detour to Covelo, visit the **Tribal Center** with displays of Native American crafts and jewelry; the All-Indian Rodeo is held in September.

The Big Trees Begin

Leggett, where Highway 101 meets the northern end of Highway 1 running inland from the coast, is really the entryway to the northern redwoods, just south of Humboldt County, and a natural spot in which to take a break. There are camping sites for hikers, bikers, those who seek developed sites, and wheelchair travellers. **Standish-Hickey State Recreation Area** on the south fork of the Eel River here is a handy place for a picnic; a comfortable hiking trail leads to the Captain Miles Standish Tree, 225 feet tall, and the rugged five-mile Mill Creek Loop leads south to a superb overlook.

Two miles (3 km) north of Leggett, the ▶ **Bell Glen Resorts** (closed mid-December to mid-April) encourages an overnight stop with six redwood-decked cottages overlook-

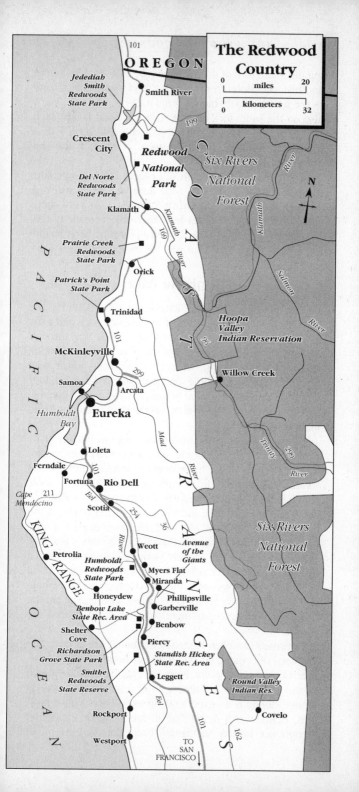

The Redwood Country

| 0 | miles | 20 |
| 0 | kilometers | 32 |

OREGON

Jedediah Smith Redwoods State Park

Smith River

Crescent City

Redwood National Park

Six Rivers National Forest

Del Norte Redwoods State Park

Klamath

Prairie Creek Redwoods State Park

Orick

Patrick's Point State Park

Hoopa Valley Indian Reservation

Trinidad

McKinleyville

PACIFIC

Samoa

Arcata

Willow Creek

Humboldt Bay

Eureka

Loleta

Ferndale

Fortuna

Rio Dell

Cape Mendocino

Scotia

KING RANGE

Weott

Avenue of the Giants

Petrolia

Humboldt Redwoods State Park

Myers Flat

Miranda

Honeydew

Phillipsville

Garberville

Benbow Lake State Rec. Area

Six Rivers National Forest

Benbow

Shelter Cove

Piercy

Richardson Grove State Park

Standish Hickey State Rec. Area

Smithe Redwoods State Reserve

Leggett

Round Valley Indian Res.

OCEAN

Rockport

Covelo

Westport

TO SAN FRANCISCO

COAST

RANGES

Klamath River

Salmon River

Trinity River

Mad River

Eel River

ing the south fork of the meandering Eel River. A restaurant and historic saloon from stagecoach days are right at hand, as are a river beach, bicycles, and a 24-hour sauna. Nearby, also on the south fork of the Eel, ▶ **Big Bend Lodge** offers housekeeping cottages with gas or fireplace heating. Fish or hike, relax or bike, kayak or swim, or read in the sun: Tranquility is the password.

Four miles (7 km) north of Leggett, the highway slips through Smithe Redwoods State Reserve (old-growth redwoods) and Richardson Grove State Park. Touristy shops (many selling coffee tables and other objects made of redwood burl) and diversions abound all through here, including a Drive-Thru Tree (but wait for the one at Myers Flat).

Benbow Lake

Five miles (8 km) north of Richardson Grove, Benbow Lake State Recreation Area consists of 786 forested acres and a six-mile lake created by a seasonal dam from May through September. In season there are campfire programs, hiking and horse-riding trails, outdoor theater, non–power boat rentals, swimming, fishing, and camping. A huge outdoor Arts and Crafts Fair is staged in June, and the annual Benbow Lake Shakespearean Festival brings the Bard to the Big Trees in August.

Motels abound in the immediate region, but for style, atmosphere, warm welcome, and good food the grateful traveller settles down in ▶ **Benbow Inn**, 2 miles (3 km) south of Garberville. In partially timbered Tudor, Benbow commands a bow in the south fork of the Eel; it is a place for deep, relaxed breathing and a sense of having arrived at the proper place at the end of a long day (particularly if it's the first overnight stop from San Francisco). The lobby is a cozy, eclectic sitting area of vaguely Victorian persuasion, with a fire blazing whenever possible; on pleasant afternoons and evenings you can retreat to the outdoor terrace. A nine-hole golf course, putting green, lawn games, and reading are the diversions of choice; at night wonderful old movies are shown.

Gourmets from San Francisco frequently are critical (and justly so) of cooking beyond their city limits. Benbow, however, does not disappoint. From the eggs Benedict at brunch to the roast duck *à l'abricot* or shrimp scampi sauté at dinner, dining is an experience in excellence. Unlike most inns, Benbow is a destination in itself; slightly expensive, though not by city standards. (Unfortunately, Benbow is closed from December through mid-April except for one week at Christmas.)

Benbow should serve as headquarters for a day-long meander through Humboldt Redwoods State Park (see below), the largest of its kind in California and one very likely to make you trip over your own adjectives. Although there are informal cafés and snack spots along the route, those who choose to match dining to scenery should ask Benbow to prepare a picnic luncheon with suitable beverages.

Directly east off Highway 101 from the Benbow Inn is ▶ **Benbow Valley Resort**, a recreational-vehicle park with a vaguely country-clubbish atmosphere and its own nine-hole golf course, coffee shop, grocery, and boat rental.

Little Garberville, just north of Benbow, is mainly a jumping-off and provisioning point for redwood park visitors and for excursions west to Shelter Cove, nearby fishing streams, wilderness camping, and the like. Although the aforementioned Benbow Inn is the clear choice in this region, a few motels are available in Garberville: ▶ **Best Western Humboldt House Inn** has 75 modestly priced units, Continental breakfast, and a swimming pool; ▶ **Garberville Motel**, with restaurant, provides special facilities for winter salmon/steelhead fishermen at reasonable prices. Yet another choice can be found 8 miles (14 km) south of Garberville at Piercy, where the 62 cabins of the ▶ **Hartsook Inn** sit on 30 redwood-shaded acres along the Eel River, next to Richardson Grove State Park. Diversions include river swimming, lawn games, and hiking. The well-regarded dining room (eclectic cuisine) serves only beer and wine.

HUMBOLDT REDWOODS STATE PARK

Through fog of summer and rain of winter, with bursts of sun searing through, the forests of Humboldt have stood (with trillium and sorrel and ferns at their feet) since the bubonic plagues ravaged Europe; winds have whispered in their crowns since Charlemagne and the Vikings and the birth of Cairo. Sounds are muffled; time appears a permanent twilight; hoary age rules.

Take the signposted turnoff south of Phillipsville to slip into the shadows of the 31-mile (50-km) **Avenue of the Giants** (Scenic Route 254). This route parallels 101, returning to that raceway just south of Scotia.

Your first stop should be at **Chimney Tree**, where hunters who had camped near a great redwood in 1914 left their fire unextinguished. For days, perhaps weeks, it burned inside the giant trunk and when the tree's top was sheared off in a mighty windstorm, a living chimney was created. This is a superb example of the redwoods' regenerative powers, as new growth continues to seal old cracks and hundreds of shoots sprout from the old tree.

Just a hop north of Phillipsville on this route at Miranda, the Avenue of the Giants Association supplies information on redwoods, camping, lodging, dining, biking, and summer recreation. At Miranda the 16 cottages of the ▶ **Miranda Gardens Resort** are sheltered in the forest; some have fireplaces and whirlpools. There's a heated pool, and campfires are held nightly in summer; rates range widely according to the size of and facilities in the cabins.

A little farther on at Myers Flat the **Shrine Drive-Thru Tree** was struck by lightning centuries ago, creating a fire that ate away at its base for years. Today visitors drive their cars through the resulting hole in the 2,000-year-old trunk and photograph each other doing it. You also can park your car on a log that weighs 100 tons.

Along the winding way, visitors will note signs that identify more than 570 memorial groves, such as the Garden Club of America Grove or the Franklin K. Lane Grove, which are a result of the Save-the-Redwoods League's efforts (begun in 1918) to purchase redwood lands from local owners in order to create the park.

South of Weott, near Burlington Campground, the **Humboldt Redwoods State Park Visitor Center** houses worthwhile exhibits on natural history and sells publications about the big trees and the various parks. Inquire about the summer campfire interpretive programs, ranger-guided walks, children's Junior Ranger program, and more.

Just north of Weott there's a parking lot for the **Founders' Grove Nature Trail**, a gentle, short, and level walk that begins at the foot of magnificent Founders' Tree, 40 feet in circumference and 346 feet high. (It was thought to be the world's tallest tree until the Libbey Tree in Redwood National Park—see below—was measured.) Pick up a self-guiding brochure and follow the trail past the fallen Dyerville Giant, toppled by a fierce storm in March 1991. Although it stood 362 feet tall, the tree is even more impressive today, its upended root system several times the height of a man. Early in May some 2,000 runners from the United States and Canada join in the

Avenue of the Giants Marathon, cruising a course beneath the soaring redwoods; it begins at the wide spot named Dyerville.

Directly opposite Founders' Grove, a marked turnoff under Highway 101 leads into **Rockefeller Forest** (named for the signature on the check), often called the world's finest forest. Turn off your car's engine at Bull Creek Flat, about five miles from Dyerville Bridge, and listen to the silence. Superb specimens in the woods include the Tall Tree (359 feet high) and the strangely shaped Flatiron Tree.

When you can bear to move on, turn back the way you came and then continue north along the Avenue of the Giants to Redcrest, north of which you may wish to make short stops at the Eternal Tree and the Immortal Tree. Both are ancient (Eternal is 70 feet in circumference) and demonstrate the redwoods' resistance to fire and disease.

To sleep in the deep dark of Humboldt is a special experience available at three family campgrounds. Reservations should be made eight weeks in advance; Tel: (800) 444-PARK.

The Avenue of the Giants rejoins Highway 101 just south of Rio Dell and Scotia, which face each other across the Eel River. (Early settlers and lumbermen imported the name of their home, Nova Scotia, for the town.) The **Pacific Lumber Company** of Scotia, the world's largest processor of redwood, offers interesting self-guided mill and museum tours from 7:30 A.M. to 10:30 A.M. and noon to 2:30 P.M. Monday through Friday. Pacific Lumber's **Demonstration Forest**, 4½ miles (7 km) south of Scotia, offers a short walk, a longer trail, and picnic tables. It's open on weekdays from Memorial Day to Labor Day at no charge. A traditional spot for a meal in town is the **Scotia Inn**, which opened in 1888 and serves dinners Wednesday through Sunday.

FERNDALE AND
CAPE MENDOCINO

Several miles north of Scotia, Highway 211 takes an abrupt swing southwest off 101 and makes a short run through dairy farms to **Ferndale**, the self-proclaimed Victorian Village, a State Historical Landmark, and the prettiest little cow town in Northern California.

The rich agricultural community of Ferndale was settled in the 1860s by prosperous Swiss-Italian and Portuguese farmers. Later a welcome was extended to Danes forced to leave Denmark during the battles with Prussia over Schleswig-Holstein, adding to the human cultural cocktail. The village seems to have stepped intact out of the 19th century, smart and sparkling with freshly painted façades, outstanding examples of ornately decorated gimcrack and gingerbread Victoriana. The local architectural styles—Italianate, Roman-Renaissance, Carpenter Gothic, Gothic Revival, Stick, Queen Anne, Eastlake—demand an extensive walking tour, chiefly along Main and Ocean streets, camera in hand.

After you have ogled the houses, a natural stop is the **Ferndale Museum and Gift Shop** at Third and Shaw streets, where the town's heritage is displayed in cameo settings, exhibits of antique farm and logging equipment, and more. If you want to stock up on the past, stop by **Golden Gait Mercantile** at 421 Main Street to buy such latter-day essentials as Dr. Kilmer's Swamp-Root, red suspenders, long johns, straight razors, fish-eye tapioca, and even horehounds.

Of the several galleries in Ferndale, the most curious and compelling is **Hobart Galleries**, also on Main Street; it was Hobart Brown who fathered the local madness known as the Great Arcata-to-Ferndale Cross-Country Kinetic Sculpture Race, staged annually on Memorial Day weekend. The point is to drive, push, or otherwise encourage an engineless, wheeled artwork over land, water, beaches, and highways for 35 miles south from Arcata to the finish line in Ferndale. Other less loony local celebrations include June's Portuguese-inspired Holy Ghost Festival; the Humboldt County Fair, early to mid-August; and the unusual Scandinavian Mid-Summer Festival in mid-June. This last celebrates Scandinavia's midnight sun and the settlement of Scandinavians on the Humboldt County coast; you'll find dancing, food stalls, arts, crafts, soccer matches, and parades.

The area's bucolic landscape and peaceful atmosphere belie the fact that this is one of the most active earthquake zones in California. In early spring 1992 the ground shook, trembled, rocked, and rolled in two separate shocks a day apart. When it was over, the towns of Petrolia and Honeydew, south of Ferndale, lay in devastation (see The Lost Coast, below). Ferndale itself was badly shaken by the experience: Many of its old houses slid right off their insufficient foundations, and one hostelry, the Ferndale Inn, was so badly damaged it has not reopened. Heroism and hard work have prevailed, however; today Ferndale shows few signs of its recent, near-fatal attack by nature.

Some travellers choose to settle down here for two or three days to explore the countryside at a measured pace.

Others headquarter in Eureka (see below) and visit Ferndale on a day trip. In town on Berding Street, ▶ **The Gingerbread Mansion,** an 1898 mansion with nine guest rooms, is an unusually attractive hideaway with lavish baths, antique furnishings, parlors, an English garden, and bicycles for loan; the quality justifies the room rates. Another stylish place is the six-bedroom ▶ **Shaw House Inn,** a gabled, Gothic Carpenter house built in 1854 by Ferndale's founder on Main Street.

Most restaurants are located on Main Street as well: Try **Fern Café** (for lunch), a deli sandwich at **Ferndale Meat Company,** bistro-style lunch or dinner at **Bibo and Bear,** or elegant dining at the **Victorian Inn.**

A wilderness area of 105 acres, **Russ Park,** in the southeast corner of town off Bluff Road, is a refuge and breeding place for more than 60 types of birds. It's open daily for walking, horseback riding, and picnicking.

A delightful, hand-drawn brochure, "Visitors' Guide and Walking Tour," is available at most inns and shops in town or call the Ferndale Chamber of Commerce (Tel: 707-786-4477).

Cape Mendocino

To wander magnificent country rarely traversed even by seasoned California travellers, take Mattole Road (Highway 211), which meanders southwest from Ferndale toward Cape Mendocino, passes through wide spots called Petrolia and Honeydew, then continues inland and eastward back into Rockefeller Forest and Dyerville (Founders' Grove). From there it's possible to make a speedy return to Ferndale on 101 or to continue on to Eureka.

On this and similar backcountry outings throughout Northern California, check your gasoline gauge before setting out, and stop by a deli for picnic supplies; you won't find any charming country inns or service stations along many of these routes.

Mattole Road runs almost into the sea at Cape Mendocino, the most westerly point of the continental United States, named to honor Don Antonio de Mendoza, a 16th-century viceroy of New Spain. The name Mendocino later was given to the county immediately to the south and to the town there that has become a popular weekend retreat for San Franciscans (see The Mendocino Coast below).

It remains uncertain which Spanish explorer first spotted the monumental point, but surely it was around the mid-16th century, when the Manila galleons plied the wild sea lanes from Asia across the Pacific to Acapulco and New Spain. The annual Manila-to-Mexico crossing was called "the longest and most dreadful of any in the world," taking six to eight months and sometimes ending in disaster: Between 1565 and 1815, thirty Manila treasure ships were lost on the crossing, many pounded into pieces on these rocks.

For 250 years the Spaniards sailed the route, and many a famous explorer marked his course by the rocky tip: Sir Francis Drake in 1579 on his voyage around the world; Sebastián Rodríguez Cermeño in 1595, while hunting a port for the galleons; Sebastián Vizcaíno in 1602 and 1603, while charting the coast; and Captain George Vancouver, sent by England in 1792 to report on the Spanish possessions along the Pacific coast.

The wind shrieks, the sea swells, on inland pastures the sheep huddle into their woollen coats as you strain to imagine the galleons, blown in from the Far East with their luxurious cargoes of gold and spices and silks bound for the Old World via the New.

The Lost Coast

The only place that can claim the title of town in this country is skimpy **Petrolia**, near the banks of the Mattole River where oil was discovered in the 1860s. Originally the land had been called, rather pompously, New Jerusalem, but on the occasion of California's pioneer oil strike by Governor Leland Stanford's Mattole Petroleum Company in 1865 it became Petrolia. Trivia collectors will pause to photograph the commemorative marker. Mattole Road bends sharply inland at Honeydew, where the post office/general store has not been rebuilt since the aforementioned earthquake.

Much of this unknown land is known as California's Lost Coast; part of it is officially the **King Range National Conservation Area**, a riot of peaks, valleys, and shoreline barely scratched by logging roads. The first inhabitants in this wilderness were the Whilkut, Sinkyone, and Mattole Indians, who used the land for hunting and gathering for more than 2,000 years; they have been gone for more than a century. Two major trails, the King Crest and the Chemise Mountain, may be hiked, but walkers should carry drinking water, tell friends where they are going, and be aware that rattlesnakes abound in driftwood and rocky areas. For maps and information on hunting, camping, and other activities, call the U.S. Bureau of Land Management's office in Ukiah; Tel: (707) 462-3873.

Few people make a living along this isolated, forbidding

coast except those who farm marijuana. Tourist authorities don't like it, but marijuana is, at this writing, the leading cash crop in Humboldt County. If you're hiking, be careful to stay on marked paths and trails and off private property.

If you return to Ferndale and then back to 101 and continue north toward Eureka, stop in the small town of Loleta (off 101) for a visit to the family-run **Loleta Cheese Factory**, which produces 14 types of cheeses, from creamy Monterey Jack to smoked salmon Cheddar.

EUREKA
Humboldt Bay

Humboldt Bay, the only fine large harbor between San Francisco and Puget Sound, escaped discovery even longer than did San Francisco Bay, having eluded the eyes of Juan Rodríguez Cabrillo, Bruno Heçeta, Sir Francis Drake, and George Vancouver, all of whom sailed by without spotting it.

Named for the great German naturalist and traveller Baron Alexander von Humboldt, the bay was finally found in 1806 by Captain Jonathan Winship, an American hired by the Russian-American Fur Company to hunt seals along the coast. He named it the Bay of the Indians because of the many villages around its shore, and it was christened for Von Humboldt in 1850. (The explorer would have been pleased; he once remarked, "There are three stages in the popular attitude toward a great discovery: First, men doubt its existence, next they deny its importance, and finally they give the credit to someone else.")

It was 1850 when one James Talbot Ryan, a descendant of the earls of Shrewsbury and at the time a surveyor in the employ of the Mendocino Exploring Company, came to the shores of Humboldt Bay in search of the proper site for a lumber-shipping port. "Eureka!" he is supposed to have cried, hence the name of the major town on the bay. At first the settlement waged small struggles for "top town" with Humboldt City and Uniontown (now Arcata), but Eureka soon proved to have the finest site, not too far from the bay's entrance and unimpeded by mud flats. By 1853 a post at Fort Humboldt had been built within the city limits as defense against the surrounding tribes.

Surely the most notable man to serve at Fort Humboldt (though no one would have believed it at the time) was Captain Ulysses S. Grant, who arrived in 1854 to find the foggy bay a dreary duty. Soon he discovered the whiskey barrel at Ryan's Store; not long after he was requested to resign. The day he departed Eureka for Ohio and civilian life, the future president told post surgeon Jonathan Clark, "My day will come, they will hear from me yet."

"By 1854," writes Stuart Nixon in *Redwood Empire,* "nine mills were sawing fir and pine on Humboldt Bay. But not redwood. Everyone suspected profits lay in the big trees, but nobody cared to tackle 400 tons of tree. Finally in 1856 a New Brunswicker, William Carson, took the plunge. Using a leased mill, Carson sawed and shipped the first redwood lumber across Humboldt Bay. In no time, redwood was the rage in San Francisco. Its elegant color and its rot-resistance commanded premium prices."

The days of "mining" red gold had begun. By 1881, twenty-two sawmills were at work in Humboldt County alone. Spans of oxen, as many as seven at a time, towed the enormous logs over a slip of lesser logs laid crossways: From this arrangement the term "Skid Road" evolved (now corrupted to Skid Row). Then came steam "donkey" engines that snaked logs out of the forests with a manila line; they were faster and complained less than oxen. Rails were laid for logging locomotives.

The 200-foot-tall redwoods didn't give up easily: Every one that fell with a thunderous crash cost five days' exhausting labor for two "choppers." Even the Paul Bunyans who leveled the monarchs respected them. As one old logger sighed, gazing at the green tangle high above his head (quoted by Stuart Nixon): "She sure makes a big hole in the sky."

Today debates rage between the preservation-minded environmentalists and the remaining lumber companies, their employees, and adherents who see no economic future in Northern California without such industry. Offshore oil drilling comes into the arguments, too. Anyone who doubts the tenacity with which the two sides stick to their guns should start a discussion some night in a Eureka saloon.

Old Town

Eureka, with a population of almost 27,000, is one of the largest cities in the state north of Sacramento, and its fishing fleet is second only to San Francisco's. Along Highway 101 (which becomes Broadway in town), traffic seethes in summer, but elsewhere there's a wide-street, low-rise tranquillity reminiscent of an old Midwestern town.

As in so much of the state, tourism is the real growth

industry. Sensing its importance a few years ago, city fathers encouraged restoration in and around Old Town, which had been allowed to slip into seediness. The result is a remarkably attractive (and not too cute) collection of specialty shops, promenades, art galleries, antiques nooks, restaurants, and saloons in exuberant Victorian settings.

Just in back of the Humboldt waterfront, Old Town proper extends from 1st to 4th streets, running east and west, and C to M streets, running north and south. This historic heart is a spruced-up, partially pedestrian area with a waterfall, gazebo, and sculptured benches. There are even horse-and-buggy tours of Old Town. A first stop might be at the Eureka/Humboldt County Convention & Visitors Bureau at 1034 2nd Street, which can supply information on the entire region; Tel: (707) 443-5097 or (800) 338-7352; outside California, Tel: (800) 346-3482.

SHOPPING IN OLD TOWN
There are several art galleries and museums worth visiting in Old Town. At 3rd and E streets, regional history, antique firearms, Victorian relics, and a superb collection of Karuk, Huma, and Yurok Indian baskets are lures to the **Clarke Memorial Museum**, housed in the former Bank of Eureka building, which is an example of what's locally called Roman Renaissance Revival style. Nearby on 2nd Street the **Romano Gabriel Wooden Sculpture Garden** displays a whimsical collection of sculptures created over a period of 30 years from wooden discards and scraps by Gabriel, a local carpenter-artist. About a block away at 422 1st Street, the **Humboldt Cultural Center** occupies an 1875 loft-style brick building with a cast-iron storefront; delights include changing exhibitions as well as pottery, jewelry, and gift shops. The **Indian Art Gallery** at 241 F Street was established by the Northern California Indian Development Council to provide artists an opportunity to show and market their works in a gallery setting; there's also a gift shop here featuring handcrafted items. A few doors away, the **Old Town Art Guild** is a cooperative venture of many North Coast artists, with one-person shows held monthly. At 123 F Street, **Strictly for the Birds** is a shop dedicated to the appreciation of wildlife.

DINING AND STAYING IN OLD TOWN
When hunger strikes in Old Town, seek solace at **Lazio's**, 327 2nd Street (between D and E streets), renowned for seafood, some of which has just swum in. All that noise you hear is

the happy sound of gregariousness. Should a Mexican mood strike, try **Luna's** at 1134 5th Street.

A three-block walk from Old Town, ▶ **The Eureka Inn** adds another traditional style to the cityscape: English Tudor. Eureka's major hotel, the inn offers 105 rooms in a 1922 structure that's now a National Historic Landmark, complete with heated pool, whirlpool, and saunas. This is the kind of place for reading in a deep chair before the fireplace. A local clientele, which includes everyone from loggers to attorneys, breakfasts and lunches in the **Bristol Rose Café**; the **Rathskeller** is a German-style pub, and the **Rib Room** serves international cuisine, local seafood, and, of course, prime rib.

At Broadway and 5th streets, the ▶ **Best Western Thunderbird Lodge** has been remodeled and caters to families with a swimming pool, coffee shop, and family-plan rates. Half a dozen blocks in the other direction, on the corner of 4th and V streets, the ▶ **Red Lion Inn** is another leading hotel, with 180 reasonably priced rooms, a pool, and the well-regarded **Smoke House Grill**. The ▶ **Carson House Inn** (not to be confused with the landmark Carson Mansion, below) brings contemporary luxury to an old name with 60 motel rooms (some with whirlpool tubs), a heated pool, and an indoor spa and sauna. The inn is near the mansion at 4th and M streets.

Victoriana in Eureka

Gingerbread Gothic sweeps to its glorious pinnacle in the **Carson Mansion** at 143 M Street, one of the most photographed homes in California. Completed in 1886 to the order of aforementioned redwood king William Carson, it employed a hundred carpenters and artisans to create a fantasy in three stories and eighteen rooms, with spacious porches and balconies, arched recesses, soaring staircases, carved panels, stained glass, and outbursts of onyx in the fireplaces.

Unfortunately Carson Mansion must be enjoyed—and photographed—only from the outside, since it is now the very private property of the select Ingomar Club. Still, you won't want to miss this joyful explosion of creamy spinach-colored finials, gables, friezes, parapets, and roofs as pointed as witches' hats.

The Eureka Chamber of Commerce, 2112 Broadway (Tel: 442-3738 or 800-356-6381) issues a brochure on a self-guided "Victorian Architectural Tour of Eureka," which will direct you to 26 of the most interesting houses; there are almost 100 others. Prominent among the styles are Eastlake, Queen Anne, Carpenter Gothic, and French Empire.

VICTORIAN INNS IN EUREKA

As you might expect, it's possible to sleep in a Victorian mansion here. The ▶ **Old Town Bed-and-Breakfast Inn**, dating from 1871, was Carson's original home; it offers seven rooms, an afternoon snack, and full breakfast to guests. The ▶ **Carter House Inn**, near the entrance to Old Town, is a splendid 1982 re-creation of an ornate San Francisco Victorian, vintage 1884. Furnished with antiques, Oriental rugs, marble fireplaces (one suite boasts its own whirlpool), and exuding an air of old-fashioned hospitality, Carter House is as winning as Eureka itself. Catty-corner from Carter House, the 20-room ▶ **Hotel Carter** is owned by the same family and offers the same warm welcome; it was modeled after Old Town's classic Cairo Hotel, now vanished. Both inns have a no-smoking policy.

Ambling distance from Old Town, on a rise overlooking the town, Humboldt Bay, and the Samoa Peninsula, ▶ **An Elegant Victorian Mansion** is a restored 1888 Victorian, a prize example of the Eastlake style. Of its four bedrooms, one has a private bath; the other three share three baths. For 50 years the mansion was home to William S. Clark, twice Eureka's mayor, who entertained such guests as Lillie Langtry and Ulysses S. Grant. It has been designated a California State Historic Site and is on the National Register of Historic Places. All rooms boast period furnishings and queen-sized beds; a strict no-smoking policy is followed.

A few blocks from Old Town, the restored Queen Anne Victorian home now called the ▶ **Iris Inn** joins antiques to contemporary art in happy proximity. Guests of the four rooms enjoy a full breakfast, afternoon tea, use of the library, and a nightcap in the parlor.

Sights and Tours in Eureka

For a special long-lasting memento of Redwood Country, stop by **North Coast Concepts** at 233 Manzanita Street; this timber nursery sells Coast and Sierra (Giant Sequoia) Redwood seedlings in an Adopt-a-Redwood plan. If ships and sailors are more to your fancy, you'll find the seafaring tradition of the North Coast beautifully displayed at the **Humboldt Bay Maritime Museum**, 1410 2nd Street.

Fort Humboldt State Historic Park sits just off Broadway

(Highway 101) and Highland Avenue southwest of downtown. Within the complex (much of it under restoration), the walk-through **Logging Museum** is regarded by knowledgeable enthusiasts as one of the best in the country. Tours and picnicking are available, but it's wise to check on details; Tel: 445-6567.

Forty-six acres of redwoods surround **Sequoia Park and Zoo** at Glatt and W streets in the south of town, near Sequoia Park. A duck pond, gardens, trails, children's playground, snack bar, and picnic facilities make it popular with families.

In a most unusual circumstance, a historic local lumbering operation doubles as a dining experience that's all but a requirement for travellers in Eureka. The **Samoa Cookhouse** is the last surviving lumberjack cookhouse in the West, operating in the small company town of Samoa, near the Louisiana-Pacific plywood mill.

To reach this relic of the 1885 rough-and-ready lumberjacks and millhands, take the Samoa Bridge off R Street, in northern Eureka, and follow the signs to the Cookhouse. Be prepared for Paul Bunyan–size flapjacks, soups served in tub-size tureens, beef roasts King Henry VIII would have envied, and plates of potatoes that could serve a whole squad of ravenous loggers. The decor might be called Early Oilcloth, and the prices are about that old-fashioned, too. Adjoining, the Cookhouse Historical Museum of Lumbering is open daily.

Enterprises Tours offers four- to six-hour coach trips and walking tours around the city that include visits to Fort Humboldt, Sequoia Park and Zoo, and Victorian neighborhoods, a Humboldt Bay cruise, and lunch at the Samoa Cookhouse. Reservations are necessary; Tel: 445-2117 or (800) 400-1849. Informative tours of Old Town are conducted by the **Old Town Carriage Co.** Percheron horses pull Victorian-era carriages starting at the Old Town Gazebo at 2nd and F streets; rates are $16 for 25 minutes per carriage, $34 for 45 minutes.

Humboldt Bay Harbor Cruise operates 75-minute sailings aboard the M.V. *Madaket,* once the Eureka–Samoa ferry, from the foot of C Street. They run daily from May through mid-October; Tel: 445-1910.

Sport fishing, especially for salmon and rockfish, is available through **King Salmon Charters**, 3458 Utah Street (Tel: 442-FISH), and through **Celtic Charter Service**, Woodley Island Marina (Tel: 442-7580).

Major celebrations in Eureka include the Rhododendron Festival and Parade during the last week of April and first week of May; Fourth of July Celebrations; and the Redwood Art Fall Exhibit.

Late in November and throughout December, Eureka and its neighbors celebrate A Coastal Christmas, an unparalleled celebration of the season with repertory theater productions, concerts, boutique and craft shows, invitational art exhibitions, museum open houses, art shows in bed-and-breakfast inns, tree-lighting ceremonies, carolers, parades, and ballets. Everybody has a riotously good time, especially guests at the Eureka Inn, a center for many of the festivities. The most unusual event is the annual Holiday Trucker's Convoy. Imagine (it's difficult) the sound and sight of 150 18-wheel big rigs festooned with thousands of lights, wildly colored bunting, and decorations, all moving in slow procession and blasting their air horns. One year, a standout was a flatbed rig outfitted with a complete manger scene and a working carousel. It's certainly worth a detour; ask the Eureka/Humboldt County Convention and Visitors Bureau (1034 Second Street, Eureka, CA 95501-0541) for this year's dates and details; Tel: (707) 443-5097, (800) 338-7352 (in California), or (800) 346-3482 (in U.S.).

Eureka's Backcountry

Back roads wiggle and twist around the vast, little-populated country to the east of Eureka. This is empty, rugged land where, in the shadows of Douglas fir trees, you may stumble across the path of Big Foot, the huge, hairy humanoid occasionally seen in the deep woods, particularly within Six Rivers National Forest. Big Foot is known as Sasquatch along Canada's west coast and invites comparison with the Himalayan yeti (the Abominable Snowman). From time to time, spottings of Big Foot are reported in newspapers from Eureka to San Francisco and even Los Angeles. In 1958 a tractor driver in the wilderness beyond Bluff Creek found a series of sixteen-inch, human-looking footprints that indicated a creature weighing from six hundred to eight hundred pounds with an average stride of four feet. Since then seven people claim to have glimpsed Big Foot, and thirty-eight findings of footprints have been recorded, all of which have been judged not to have been made by an animal. Skeptics should join the debates in the hamlets along the Trinity and Klamath river valleys.

Following Highway 101 north from Eureka for 10 miles (16 km) and then turning eastward on State Highway 299, you will drive 40 winding miles (64 km) to reach **Willow**

Creek, nestled in the heart of the world's largest virgin stand of Douglas firs. In Gold Rush days this was a distribution point for mining supplies; today Willow Creek introduces visitors to the wonders of the great outdoors with white-water trips, rafting and tubing, horseback riding, fishing, hunting, camping, hiking, cross-country skiing, and even golf.

Trinity River Rafting on State Highway 299 in Big Flat offers half-day, full-day, and multi-day raft and kayak trips on the upper Trinity River. Trips are geared for beginners and inter-mediates (Class I to III). Contact them at P.O. Box 572, Big Bar, CA 96010; Tel: (916) 623-3033. At least five motels operate in Willow Creek; ask for details at the local Chamber of Commerce, P.O. Box 704, Willow Creek, CA 95573; Tel: (916) 629-2693.

About a 20-minute drive north of Willow Creek via State Highway 96, the settlement at the **Hoopa Valley Indian Reservation** on the Trinity River is worth a call for the excellent Native American basketry, weaponry, and arts on display at the **Hoopa Tribal Museum**. Tours of nearby Hoopa villages can be arranged ($5 charge); Tel: (916) 625-4110.

Watered by the Klamath, Smith, Eel, Trinity, Van Duzen, and Mad rivers, the more than a million acres of **Six Rivers National Forest** provide excellent fishing, hunting, camping, and picnicking north of Hoopa. For information on camp-ing, hiking, fees, licenses, and the like, check with the Rangers Districts (Tel: 916-627-3291 or 629-2118).

HUMBOLDT COUNTY

You face a dilemma here: whether to remain headquartered in Eureka, to stop at one of the neighboring towns or coastal resorts, or to roar onward to the north to Orick and Red-wood National Park. Although it's only 41 miles (66 km) from Eureka to Orick, that means an 82-mile (132-km) round trip, and it's impossible to see much of the park in one day. That dilemma will probably be solved by the time at your disposal and which of the following attractions prove intriguing to you.

Arcata

In 1850 a party of 30 men from San Francisco founded a city-site on Humboldt Bay and called it Uniontown, which in 1853 became the seat of newly organized Humboldt County and eventually the busy center of mule pack trains that carried goods over mountain trails to the mines. As mining faded and lumbering took the spotlight, Eureka, with its deep-water site, became county seat in 1856 and Uniontown substituted the Native American name for its spot, Arcata.

In 1857 the frontier poet Francis Bret Harte, out of pocket after a stay in the Sierra mines and in San Francisco, stepped ashore to stay with his sister Maggie and her husband while looking for a paying job. A year later Harte became editor of the local weekly, *Northern Californian,* an entry into the literary world to which he would eventually contribute some of pioneer America's best stories, such as "The Outcasts of Poker Flat."

Today Arcata's Victorian homes, wide streets, green lawns, and flower gardens center around Town Plaza, which is watched over by a stern memorial to President William McKinley. The best way to gain a sense of Arcata is by taking a self-driven **Architectural Homes Tour,** a 45-minute swing past 21 structures of note. A driving map and other information is given out by the Arcata Chamber of Commerce, 1062 G Street, Arcata, CA 95521; Tel: (707) 822-3619.

In 1857 Augustus Jacoby built the first sturdy business building in Arcata at 8th and H streets off the plaza. It's still here, as **Jacoby's Storehouse**, today housing 16 shops and restaurants.

Enthusiastic bird-watchers enjoy a literal field day within the 154 acres of the **Arcata Marsh and Wildlife Sanctuary,** headquartered at the foot of I Street. It's an outstanding achievement in the use of treated waste water, with aquaculture projects including a fish hatchery, salt marshes, and sloughs, frequented today by more than 200 species of birds. The Audubon Society conducts nature walks on Saturdays at 8:30 A.M., and the park is open daily from sunrise to sunset.

In addition to parks open to the public for all kinds of sports, the Activities Center at **Humboldt State University** offers year-round classes and outings that take participants rafting, canoeing, windsurfing, and sailing; Tel: 826-3357.

Arcata has lured several accomplished new restaurateurs, and one of the best has opened **Abruzzi**, at 791 8th Street. Breads and pastas are fresh daily, as is locally caught seafood, and the prices are moderate; Tel: 826-2345. Healthful and heart-conscious Mexican cuisine may seem an oxymoron, but it exists at **Casa de Que Pasa**, 854 9th Street, where flavors riot, servings are the size of a hacienda, and prices are reasonable. Musicians appear from time to time; Tel: 822-3441.

Not long ago, anything other than steak and potatoes was considered international, even exotic, cuisine in Arcata. Now there's a mix of Greek, Hungarian, Italian, French, Thai, and Chinese cooking with refreshing prices at **Ottavio's**, 686 F Street; Tel: 822-4021.

In the north of town on Valley West Boulevard, the ▶ **North Coast Inn** maintains 78 modern rooms, a pool, spa, coffee shop, restaurant, and lounge.

McKinleyville

McKinleyville, about 4 miles (7 km) north of Arcata on Highway 101, was one of many towns across the United States renamed for President William McKinley following his assassination in 1901. Its main attraction, aside from the Hammond Trail, which follows the route of an historic railroad now used by hikers, bikers, and equestrians, is the **Azalea State Reserve**. Here some 30 acres glow pinkish-white from April into summer; turn off 101 on North Bank Road. At 1100 Griffith Road, the **Fairyland Begonia and Lily Garden** hybridizes and develops new lilies and begonias; visitors are welcome to tour the nursery and greenhouses year round and to purchase the unique varieties.

McKinleyville is highly residential in nature, though the ▶ **Bella Vista Motel** does offer 16 modest and informal family units in a pretty rural setting overlooking the Pacific. Dining above the ocean is the lure at **Merryman's Dinner House**, north of town on Moonstone Beach. Seafood and steaks are the specialties, and reservations are accepted only for banquets; open only Friday through Sunday between October 1 and April 1. No credit cards are accepted; Tel: 677-3111.

Trinidad

It was Holy Trinity Sunday, June 9, 1775, when explorers Juan Francisco de la Bodéga and Bruno Heçeta sailed into Humboldt Bay and named the site in honor of the day (*La Santisima Trinidad* in Spanish). Its foggy, rocky headland then rested undisturbed for 18 years until Captain George Vancouver landed here and found the rough-hewn cross erected by the Spaniards.

Trinidad is the oldest town along the northern coast, founded in 1850 as a trading post for the mining camps. By the following year it had boomed to a population of perhaps 3,000 residents; today it has fewer than 400.

The glory days of gold have gone now, but the rugged meeting of waves and wooded headlands creates another kind of riches. **Trinidad Head Trail** is one of the most spectacular scenic walks on the entire California coast, allowing you views of migrating whales (February through April) as you amble from redwood-topped cliffs to coves filled with lacy ferns. Sea lions sun on offshore rocks, hummingbirds pirouette in garden ballets, and hawks swoop and soar on coastal waves of air. Most visitors whiz right by on Highway 101. Instead, take the Westhaven Drive exit and follow along Main Street to Trinity, then turn right on Edwards and follow the signs to the trail parking lot. Keep on the trails and roads here, as everywhere, because poison oak is omnipresent.

Anyone with an interest in marine life will be fascinated by the **Humboldt State University Marine Biology Lab** south of town; take College Cove Beach Access. There's a good self-guided tour. Right at the Trinidad Bay Pier, the **Seascape Restaurant**, an informal family-owned place, serves simple, well-prepared seafood and sandwiches.

A restaurant that's pulling in diners from all around the area, **Larrupin Café** at 1658 Patrick's Point Drive, is small and elegant with cuisine to match: barbecued cracked coastal crab with mustard-dill sauce, and chicken breast in phyllo with artichokes, just for starters; Tel: 677-0230.

Nearby on Patrick's Point Drive one mile off the Redwood Highway, ▶ **The Lost Whale Bed and Breakfast** is a cozy Cape Cod–style inn with four spacious suites overlooking the ocean. When sea lions bark and fog blankets the Pacific, shrug into a sweater and stroll into Patrick's Point. On a sunny morning, breakfast on the inn's deck (home-baked goods and locally smoked salmon, for instance) before hunting for agate and jade on the beach. A two-night minimum stay is required from June to October and on weekends the year round.

Also on Patrick's Point Drive is the ▶ **Trinidad Inn**, a recently remodeled nine-unit motel set within a grove of redwoods and a mile from beaches and fishing. ▶ **Trinidad Bed and Breakfast** is another Cape Cod home (with four rooms overlooking the ocean) above Trinidad Bay on Edwards Street, within strolling distance of shops, restaurants, beaches, parks, and trails.

A rustic cluster of cottages, the ▶ **Bishop Pine Lodge** is a longtime favorite of wanderers along the North Coast who appreciate quiet and seclusion. The thirteen cottages have one, two, or three rooms; ten are equipped with kitchens. Picnic tables, grills, and a children's playground are available; a café is nearby. Take the Trinidad exit northbound or the Seawood Drive exit southbound to Patrick's Point Drive.

Patrick's Point State Park

Five miles north of Trinidad, Patrick's Point State Park is a splendid introduction to stands other than redwoods: Waves may batter offshore rocks, but here you are sheltered in forests of pine and hemlock, Sitka spruce, red alder, and cypress. The floor is as intricate as an Oriental carpet: azaleas, blackberry, fairy bells, huckleberry, false lily-of-the-valley, salmonberry, rhododendrons, thimbleberry, and trilliums. Rim Trail is a comfortable walk from the Agate Beach parking area to Palmer's Point, from which six other steep, short trails lead to the shoreline. For information on camping, call 677-3570.

North of Patrick's Point, Highway 101 enters dramatically diverse **Humboldt Lagoons State Park**. Fifteen miles of sandy beaches, lagoons, and rocky headlands are backed by an eye-popping parade of rolling farmlands, mountainous outcrops, and cool, shaded, old-growth forests where rays of sun filter down to illuminate outbursts of shrubs and wildflowers. Unfortunately, in midsummer the beaches are almost obscured from view by campers and RVs parked tailgate-to-tailgate along the edges of the road.

REDWOOD NATIONAL PARK

On a glorious autumn day in 1967, President Lyndon B. Johnson signed into being a richness of 50,000 acres north of Eureka to form the Redwood National Park, and Lady Bird Johnson dedicated the handsome nature trail that today bears her name. Ten years later, following a decade of struggle between conservationist forces led by the Save-the-Redwoods League on one side and lumbering interests on the other, President Jimmy Carter signed the Redwood National Park Expansion Act, increasing the size of the park to 106,000 acres. In a curious geographical amalgamation, Redwood National encloses three *state* parks: Prairie Creek Redwoods, Del Norte Redwoods, and Jedediah Smith Redwoods. These 28,000 acres are administered by the California Department of Parks and Recreation. The state's battles of the budget can be heard today even in the dense forests of old-growth redwoods, however. ("Old-growth" redwoods are those in areas that have never been logged.) California is exploring the idea (some say it's a fait accompli) of transfering the administration of the three state parks from the California State Park system to the National Park system, in this case, Redwood National Park. There are heated arguments on both sides of the issue; one can only hope for an enlightened decision.

The original inhabitants of these great reaches were, among the major regional tribes, the Karok (meaning "up-river people"), the Yurok ("down-river"), and the Hoopa, who lived around the confluence of the Klamath and Trinity rivers. The tribes kept their cultures distinct: Stuart Nixon writes that a man could wander from one tribal region to the next and never come upon the same language twice.

It is said that the Spanish explorers were regarded as strange gods. In most ways they left the natives alone, but the Yankee arrivals were less respectful. By 1851 the so-called Indian Wars had begun, and raged sporadically until about 1870. (The fiercest of these encounters was the Bridge Gulch Massacre of 1852, which took place near Weaverville in northeastern California.)

Seeing the Forest

Surrounded by an army of soaring giant-trunked redwoods, you come upon a mysterious gathering: trees of respectable size and age in a ring around—what? Sometimes it's a mere circular slump in the forest floor; less often, it may be a ragged stump, broken apart like a bad tooth.

This is a "family circle," a grouping of three or even four generations, paying court to their ancestral tree. When it was toppled, by nature or loggers, and its stump returned to the earth from which it had arisen, a second generation sprouted from the still-living root crown. Members of the second generation that were logged produced a third, and if you peer closely you may see the sprout of yet another generation. The latest young have to fight to survive, since their still-mighty elders shut out the life-giving sun. (Most conifers reproduce only by seeds and cones, not by sprouting, thus giving the Coast Redwood a family advantage.)

Look for the "goose pen," the hollowed-out stump or trunk resulting from natural or man-made fires. (The Chimney Tree near Phillipsville is a prominent example.) The name results from the pioneers' practice of penning poultry within the hollows. Another phenomenon is the "penthouse," a clutch of new growth taking root far up in a tall trunk, its top having been sliced off by lightning or a big wind.

Trees that would be giants anywhere else are merely tall here: the massive Oregon white oak, the regal California black oak, the coast hemlock, the stately Douglas fir, and the noble Sitka spruce, in addition to big-leaf maples and cedars. Note also the shorter, twisted madrone and the California laurel (also known as bay, myrtlewood, or pepperwood), popular for its leaf used in cooking.

Sadly, a recent import in the woods is the invisible protozoan called giardiasis, which inhabits streams and lakes. Even the clearest waters may swarm with these microscopic creatures that when ingested produce chronic diarrhea, abdominal cramps, bloating, fatigue, and loss of weight in human victims. Only treatment by a physician who recognizes the symptoms can effect a cure. Walkers, hikers, and campers should always carry water canteens or flasks in addition to canned or bottled beverages to avoid drinking from potentially contaminated waters.

Even in summer, coastal areas and high altitudes can be cool; you would be wise to carry coats, jackets, or sweaters in your car. Breaking storm waves and high tides can sweep away not only swimmers but also beach and cliff walkers. Never turn your back on the ocean. Also, poison oak (similar to poison ivy) abounds. Stay on trails and/or wear high-topped sneakers or boots, and do not pluck strange foliage.

No lodging is available in Redwood National Park proper (a version of Yosemite's Ahwahnee Hotel would be much appreciated), and there are no federally developed campsites, although nearly 400 sites exist within the three state parks. Thus you should decide well in advance where you wish to headquarter, depending on whether you are choosy about accommodations or, on the other hand, want to avoid long daily round trips. The choices are those described above in Trinidad, about 21 miles south of Orick and the park entrance; in Orick itself (modest accommodations); or in Klamath, 20 miles north of the park's entrance in Del Norte County (see below).

Orick

Little Orick is an essential stop for the **Redwood Information Center,** near Redwood Creek at Freshwater Lagoon just west of Highway 101. It's the headquarters for all national park information, state park camping, maps, nature walks, and special summer programs. Some horseback-trail rides begin here, and ocean-facing decks allow whale watching in season. The center is open daily except on Thanksgiving, Christmas, and New Year's Day; Tel: (707) 488-3461. Horseback rides in Redwood National Park, ranging from one hour to all-day or overnight trips, can be arranged in summer through **Lane's Pack Station**. For information and reservations, write P.O. Box 31, Orick, CA 95555; Tel: (707) 488-5785; Fax: 488-5225.

Aside from the center, the only attraction south of town is **Stone Lagoon Schoolhouse Museum**, a one-room structure built of redwood in 1893 that houses Native American artifacts and regional memorabilia.

Orick has standard motels, modest to moderate in facilities and prices, each with kitchens in some units: try ▶ **Park Woods Motel**, ▶ **Green Valley Motel**, or ▶ **Prairie Creek Motel** (ten units and a café). They are mentioned here only for the convenience of those who may not want to make round trips each day from Klamath or Trinidad or the Eureka area to the park.

An unassuming stop remarkable for the high quality of its food and the diversity of its menu is **Rolf's Park Café** two miles north of Orick just west of the highway near the road into Fern Canyon. Breakfast, lunch, and dinner are served Wednesday through Sunday, featuring such rarities as elk steak, buffalo steak, and wild-boar roast. German dishes are a specialty; chef-owner Rolf Rheinschmidt has a fine hand with sauerbraten and wienerschnitzel. Crab cioppino and deviled oysters are among the seafood specialties, and breakfast enthusiasts can feast on a giant German Farmer's Omelette. For reservations, Tel: 488-3841.

Exploring the Park

From Tall Trees trailhead in Redwood National Park you gaze down and into the past where, just over a mile away and 680 feet below, the world's tallest tree (so far as is known) lofts its head high into the sky above Redwood Creek. Howard Libbey Tree, reaching 367.8 feet, is only one in a family of giants, born about the time the Magna Carta was signed, before the days of Joan of Arc. As the Tall Trees Trail (with interesting signposts en route) twists toward the river, plants enlarge, as if you were entering a primordial universe and peregrine falcons might become winged reptiles. (It is best to be alone with your imagination on this trail, or at least with companions not compelled to be chatty.) Giant, feathery ferns bow gently over sorrel (like fat, outsized clover), trillium holds out its three leaves, here each about the size of a human hand. The trail abuts a large earth bank—but it isn't a bank. It is the body of a sleeping giant, a redwood returning to the soil from which it arose, in a slow decaying process that may last for centuries.

Eventually you stand at the foot of the **Libbey Tree,** but its top eludes your view, closed in as it is by those of other titans. The sign at its base reads, simply and cautiously, "Tall Tree." (Tall Trees Grove was "discovered" and measured by a joint expedition of the National Geographic Society and the National Park Service in 1964. There is reason to believe some even taller tree might be found some day.)

Approximate hiking time on Tall Trees Trail is four hours (contemplation time unknown). It's rated as a Class 5 hike on a scale running from Class 1 (the easiest) to Class 6 (most difficult, steep grades with switchbacks). In high season the Tall Trees Shuttle Bus transfers hikers between the Redwood Information Center on the beach west of Orick and the trailhead, with sprightly, educational commentary by the driver. From May 25 through June 14 it runs on weekends only; June 15 to September 2, twice daily; and September 3 to 15, once daily. A seven-dollar donation is requested; private vehicles must obtain a permit, which are issued without change.

Even the least athletic explorer will be stirred by the stroll (Class 1) along the **Lady Bird Johnson Grove Nature-Loop Trail,** a one-mile circle near Little Lost Man Creek that can be ambled in 30 minutes. The well-marked turnoff from 101, slightly north of Tall Trees Trail, leads two miles inland on Bald Hills Road to a parking area. From there you cross a footbridge and follow an old logging trail through mature forest. This is a fine experience (with self-guided brochure) for those who because of health, age, or lack of time, cannot negotiate a longer, more difficult trail. Be on the lookout for "widow-makers" (lower branches the size of small trees that can come striking down as a result of winter storms), and keep your eyes peeled for sprouts at the base of a mother tree, "goose-pens," delicate forest lace, toothy tan oak, and showy, wild rhododendron (California Rose Bays).

In May 1982, Redwood National Park was dedicated as a World Heritage Site. It's a park undergoing restoration, some 39,000 of its acres having been clear cut by loggers before they were added to the park in 1978. Some 200 to 300 miles of abandoned logging roads and 2,000 to 3,000 miles of crisscrossing tractor trails remain to be rehabilitated as the natural forest land recovers. A century or more may pass before the land and streams fully return to their natural state.

Prairie Creek Redwoods State Park

About 10 miles north of Orick, a grassy meadow spreads out along U.S. 101 in which wild iris blooms, herds of Roosevelt elk roam, and a sign alerts you to turn the car's radio dial to A.M. station 1610 for recorded information. You have arrived in Prairie Creek Redwoods State Park. At the northern edge of the meadow, follow the marked road left toward the small visitors' center and museum that serve the 12,544-acre park, where hiking on more than 55 miles of trails, camping, fishing, and picnicking may be enjoyed among redwood groves or on broad, sandy beaches. (Avoid the elk!)

One of the most fascinating trails in all of Redwood Country begins near the visitors' center: the circular, 1-mile **Revelation Trail** (Class 1). It's a self-guided nature walk for the blind and handicapped, dedicated to the proposition that many senses other than sight may contribute to an understanding of the woods. Superbly designed, it is lined by a guide rope on which knots have been placed, indicating where to stop, smell, listen, and turn on the tape player to hear the message (players and cassettes loaned free of charge at the visitors' center.)

Revelation comes even to the sighted, calling attention at 17 stops to the textures of tree barks, the pungent odor of bay leaf, the splash of Prairie Creek roiling in its bed through the woods. The walk takes about 45 minutes.

Too many travellers skip **Fern Canyon** on the west side of the park because the narrow, winding, 8-mile (13-km) dirt Davison Road into it is a half-hour's drive each way. The route runs west from U.S. 101 at a well-marked point about halfway between Orick and the Prairie Creek headquarters.

En route to the canyon you'll pass Gold Bluff's Beach, a name recalling the 1850s, when gullible fortune-seekers swarmed to sands said to be glittering with gold and panned themselves into penury. Today a beach campground nestles into the sand dunes, and the only gold that twinkles is in the sky at twilight. The road ends at a wooded picnic area near Home Creek, which bubbles out of Fern Canyon. The canyon itself is a gash more than a mile long through the coastal bluffs, its 50-foot walls draped with ferns that seem to be dense, green waterfalls.

Fern Canyon Trail, a loop of less than a mile (Class 2), wiggles up the creek to a prairie where a small mining town once sat. Whether or not you know a fern from a *fritillaria,* you'll be enchanted by the intricate intertwinings of five-fingered ferns (used to create those black designs in Native

American baskets), sword ferns (complete with hilts), feathery lady ferns (they might fit on Sunday bonnets), and giant horsetails, looking today exactly like their fossils, millions of years old. Fern Canyon is a fine place for a pensive picnic.

If you want to hike into Fern Canyon rather than drive, you can do so from the Prairie Creek Visitors' Center along James Irvine Trail (Class 3), which takes about three hours one way.

DEL NORTE COUNTY

The saying "Redwoods follow the fog" is nowhere better proven than in Del Norte County, where nature often mimics the rain forests of Washington's jungle-like Olympic Peninsula. Rhododendrons in this blooming land grow to 30 feet in height.

Klamath Country

For about 10 miles (16 km) north of Prairie Creek Park, U.S. 101 runs through memorial groves, crosses the Del Norte County line, then debouches onto the flood plain of the Klamath River, across a bridge guarded by the statues of four golden grizzly bears, symbols of the state. (If you haven't stopped to drive through a redwood before, there's another chance here at the northern end of the bridge. The **Tour-Thru Tree**, some 700 years old, was damaged by fire about 300 years ago. Most cars, vans, and even pickups can negotiate the passage.)

The Klamath area was long a wild mystery, its vastness all but impenetrable. The diary of explorer Peter Skene Ogden (for whom Ogden, Utah, was named) is the earliest account of the visits of Europeans into the country north of Mount Shasta. It was the course followed by Jedediah Smith (see Jedediah Smith Redwoods State Park below) and his band of trappers in the spring of 1828 when he blazed the trail down the Klamath River from the Sacramento Valley into Oregon.

Klamath

Klamath is a phoenix, having been wiped out and rebuilt twice. Established near the mouth of the Klamath River in 1851 by miners with great expectations, it was shortly deserted because of the ocean's shifting sandbars. Later, with the rise of farming and small, regional industries, it came back into existence, only to be erased by devastating floods in 1964.

Repositioned to higher ground today, Klamath is a burgeoning town that bills itself as "the Steelhead [trout] Capital of the World" and makes its living off outdoor activities, camping, and retirement-vacation homes. In summer the pilots of **Jet-Boat Cruises** take thrill seekers on a sixty-four-mile, six-hour escape up the Klamath River from ocean to wilderness; Tel: (707) 482-4191.

Four miles north of town, **Trees of Mystery**, announced by a winking, forty-nine-foot figure of Paul Bunyan flanked by faithful Babe the Blue Ox, appears at first to be a garish tourist trap. Not so: Its **End-of-the-Trail Indian Museum** houses one of the West's most outstanding collections of Native American artifacts, basketry, costumes, masks, and jewelry. The items offered for sale are choice, not souvenirs. Trees of Mystery itself is a theme park featuring the story of Bunyan, as carved from redwood by chainsaw sculptor Kenyon Kaiser, as well as a natural reserve of Douglas firs, cedars, spruces, and redwoods.

One mile (1½ km) west of U.S. 101 on Requa Road, historic ► **Requa Inn** offers 16 pleasant guest rooms from April to October; its dining room is geared to steaks and seafood for the public as well as guests and full breakfasts are included in the rates; Tel: 482-8205. Across 101 from Trees of Mystery, ► **Motel Trees** has 23 units with cable TV, tennis courts, lounge, and restaurant; rates are moderate.

Del Norte Redwoods State Park

Much of Del Norte Redwoods State Park, the northern part of Redwood National Park, is dense, virgin forest; it's certainly the least developed of the redwood parks. There's splendid, scenic hiking along about 28 miles of trails.

The short, easy walk known as **Alder Basin Trail** exemplifies the care that has been taken to make the redwoods accessible to visitors of all ages. It's a Class 1, two-mile round trip that takes about forty-five minutes through alder forest and maple and willow groves and is especially pretty in autumn. The unmarked trailhead is at Mill Creek Campground across the road from the Mill Creek trailhead.

On the distinctly opposite hand, **Damnation Creek Trail** (only 2½ miles but it consumes at least three hours) is a trek for serious walkers, taking you from old-growth trees and a hidden sea cove at the bottom of a steep trail through an oceanside spruce forest. The trailhead is on U.S. 101, north of False Klamath Cove, a wide turnout on the oceanside near U.S. 101 marker 16.0.

Crescent City

Just north of Del Norte Park and about 18 miles (29 km) south of the Oregon line, Crescent City tends to think of itself as the little metropolis of the northern redwoods, which is overstating the case a bit. Its first settlers arrived in 1853 from San Francisco aboard the schooner *Pomona* and by the summer of 1854 had set up 300 buildings and a supply center for the gold miners of southern Oregon and Siskiyou and Trinity counties.

Those were heady days. The first newspaper made its debut in 1854, and two years later the first drama appeared on the local boards: "The Toodles and Paddy Miles, the Limerick Boy." Crescent City, small, chilly, and inaccessible during winter, was nonetheless proposed as the new capital of California. A county history regales us today: "What an immense amount of ignorance must have been concentrated in that legislative body of the days of '55! But the Crescentarians were buoyant with life and energy, and the news of the failure was but a passing cloud across their bright hopes and expectations. No doubt, as the principal men of the place discussed the matter over their wine and cigars, new speculations and day-dreams of future greatness served to 'solace the hopes that ended in smoke.'"

Diggings and diggers came and went, along with the occasional tragedy. On July 30, 1865, the side-wheeler *Brother Jonathan,* plying offshore toward Oregon during a severe storm, struck St. George's Reef with (according to A. J. Bledsoe, author of *Indian Wars of the Northwest*) "such force that her foremast went through the hull, her foreyards resting across the rails . . . the ship was fast sinking in the embrace of the hungry waves, and short time was left to prepare for death." Today **Brother Jonathan Cemetery**, at Pebble Beach Drive and 9th Street, shelters 203 of the 232 people aboard who drowned.

On Good Friday of 1964 a tsunami created by the gigantic Alaskan earthquake smashed Crescent City's business district to bits. Crescent has since called itself Comeback City, U.S.A.

Chiefly a research center, **Del Norte County Historical**

Society Main Museum at 577 H Street displays exhibits of local pioneer history and artifacts of the Yurok and Tolowa tribes. The northernmost Redwood Information Center is located at 1111 2nd Street. Like the center at Orick, it offers informational brochures and maps and sells books, post-cards, and souvenirs.

Battery Point Lighthouse, constructed in 1856, now houses a small museum of seafaring. Visitors are admitted several hours a day at low tide, when you can approach on foot across the ocean floor. In town you might stop at Rumiano Cheese Company, the largest producer of Dry Monterey Jack in California, at 9th and E streets, to see the cheese being made and to sample their imported and domestic cheeses.

Of the handful of motels available in the area, the ► Best Western Ship Ashore Resort should be considered first. It's 16 miles (25 km) north on the Redwood Highway in Smith River and offers 50 units, suites, and a penthouse (some rooms with kitchens). Also on hand are a hairdressing salon, a whirlpool, fishing guides, and a museum in a converted yacht—rather eclectic accommodations, at reasonable prices. Across Highway 101 from the harbor and half a mile south of Crescent City, the ► Curly Redwood Lodge was built entirely from one redwood tree. The 36 motel units have queen-size beds and color TVs.

On Highway 101 immediately north of Crescent City, two lodging choices are the ► Pacific Motor Hotel and the ► Crescent Travelodge. The ► Best Western Northwoods Inn is just south of town, across the highway from the ocean. The best restaurant in Crescent City is the Harbor View Grotto, specializing in—what else?—seafood.

If you're in Smith River in July, be sure to enjoy the annual Easter-in-July Festival, a celebration of the midsummer harvest of blooming lily plants. Smith River is the Easter lily capital of the country, supplying 90 percent of the nation's lily bulbs.

Jedediah Smith
Redwoods State Park

The 9,560 acres of Jedediah Smith Redwoods State Park stand as a memorial to one of the sturdiest pathfinders in California's history, Jedediah Strong Smith. Mountain man and fur trader driven out of California by the Mexican authorities, Smith completed an arduous journey down the

Klamath River to the Pacific, which is detailed in his comrades' journals. As quoted by Stuart Nixon: "Sometimes the party made only a mile a day. Animals tumbled into the wild gorges. Armed Indians harassed the party constantly, shooting the horses which they mistook for a new kind of elk."

This was not easy country. As reported in *Historic Spots in California,* "Trails had to be blazed over steep and rugged mountains, while progress was often impeded by heavy fogs. The scarcity of wild game, which was almost their only food, added to their hardships." Handily, en route to Crescent City, 10 to 15 Native Americans visited the Smith camp, "bringing with them a few Muscles [*sic*] and Lemprey [*sic*] Eels and some raspberries." Camped in the vicinity of Crescent City on June 19, 1828, Smith discovered the river that today bears his name. As Smith's party pushed north from Crescent City into Oregon, the Umpqua Indians massacred all except Smith and three companions; Smith was killed three years later by Comanches on the Cimarron River. His remarkable coastal trail north was followed in later years by trappers of the Hudson's Bay Company.

EXPLORING THE PARK

To enter Jedediah Smith Park, take 101 north from Crescent City to its junction with Highway 199, and follow 199 9 miles (15 km) east to the park entrance. Or look for Elk Valley Road south of Crescent City, which then branches off onto unpaved but scenic Howland Hill Road.

Howland Hill is a beautiful introduction to the park, paralleling the old stagecoach road for part of its length. Pull off at the indicated parking area for Stout Memorial Grove, a sanctuary presented to the state in 1929 as the first of the park's memorial groves. It preserves the park's largest measured redwood, 340 feet high and 22 feet in diameter.

The Stout Grove Trail (Class 1), about a circular mile, shows off several other spectacular sights along Mill Creek, including the upturned base of a giant tree that reveals its surprisingly shallow root system.

Off the Highway 199 entrance, the Hiouchi Ranger Station (closed in winter) hands out trail maps, offers interpretive programs, presents exhibits, and stocks informative publications.

You can emerge from the mystery of the redwoods and travel south to the beauty and tranquillity of the Mendocino Coast by following Highway 101 south from the park through Eureka to Leggett, then turning west onto Highway 1 all the way to the coast.

THE MENDOCINO COAST

In 1913 J. Smeaton Chase described the decaying settlement of Navarro, in a deep valley at the river mouth that opened upon the sea: "Most of the buildings were out of plumb; the church leaned at an alarming angle; and a loon, swimming leisurely in the middle of the stream, seemed to certify the solitude of the place." That Navarro has vanished, but its name lives in the little town 14 miles (22 km) up the Navarro River in Anderson Valley.

"The solitude of the place": It is that, almost as much as the dramatic meeting of land and sea, that lures today's traveller to the Mendocino Coast. Only in the very small town of Mendocino itself has tourism made real inroads, and they are relatively tasteful. North and south, and east into forest stands and along narrow riverbeds where no roads run, there remains that rare commodity in the United States of the 1990s: room to be alone.

On a clear day sun glitters golden on the blue Pacific and you look west toward the horizon of Asia, half a world away. On other days, when fog swaddles the sharp, black, offshore rocks, the coast turns in on itself like a cat, sheltering in its own warmth, aloof. The lone walker braves the beaches and knows that nature is indifferent.

Nature aside, there are no demanding sights along this compelling coast: no cathedrals, no great museums, no antique monuments. Laziness soon seduces the wanderer; there is time and space for stretching in the grass, for picnicking on a rock-ribbed headland, for sipping wine in the sun and reading before the fireplace.

A corollary is that accommodations take on an unusual importance here. A hotel-motel room must be more than a respite from the business and the busyness of the day. It should serve as retreat, be it an aerie above the sea or a snuggery beneath the trees. Hence the many country inns that have arisen during the last decade and the space we devote to them here.

If you wish to drive directly from San Francisco's Golden Gate Bridge to Mendocino, you have several choices. You may follow Highway 101 to the Russian River turnoff at Cotati (Highway 116), emerging at the sea at Jenner; take 101 farther north to the Cloverdale turnoff, then continue on Highway 128 through Anderson Valley and Boonville to the sea south of Albion; or travel north as far as Willits on 101, turning west onto Highway 20 and following it west to meet the sea at Noyo. The distance will be 150 to 200 miles (240 to 320 km).

On the other hand, if time is not of the essence, cut off Highway 101 just north of Sausalito and follow Shoreline Highway west as it climbs and falls over the coastal hills. Jack London, who made the drive with a four-horse team, wrote of "the poppy-blown cliffs with the sea thundering in the sheer depths hundreds of feet below." It remains as exciting an experience today as you skirt the entrance to Muir Woods National Monument, climb to the heights of windy crags, and then glide down to Muir Beach. Much of the 6-mile (10-km) stretch between Muir Beach and Stinson Beach to the north was shaken and slid toward the sea in the 1989 earthquake. Rebuilding was undertaken in late 1990, however, and gloriously winding Highway 1 is once again open to traffic. (See Day Trips from San Francisco for more stops along the way.)

Rockport, Westport, and Cleone

In 1851 a vessel loaded with silk and tea bound for San Francisco was battered onto the Mendocino beaches at Caspar, just north of Mendocino. Men sent to salvage the freight first saw the timber along this coast and reported to mill owner, lumberman, and alderman of San Francisco, Harry Meiggs. The trees were so tall they hid the sky, Meiggs was told, and they were so broad 20 men with outstretched arms couldn't span one.

By the following year, Meiggs had arrived with heavy machinery and set up a sawmill to mine the "red gold." During the height of the felling fury a mill could be found up every creek or river. Ships were loaded by chutes on which lumber plummeted down from the cliffs; early photographs show wharfs and wire networks that look as if Rube Goldberg had invented them.

Today's Rockport, Westport, and Cleone, the northernmost towns of the Mendocino Coast, were all but abandoned by the end of World War I. Now they are small scatters of wooden houses, waiting patiently for the gods (or perhaps tourism) to push them into prosperity once again. All share the wild seascape and the mountainous sand dunes built up during winter storms.

In his *Northern California,* Jack Newcombe reports that in 1881 Westport boasted "three hotels, six saloons, two blacksmith shops, three stores, and two livery stables," and that 50 schooners had docked in town between April and December.

Today's visitors make their own action: surf fishing, picnicking, hiking, and more. **Westport–Union Landing Beach**, south of Rockport, has opened five new access trails and offers restrooms and camping. The **Westport Community Store** sells groceries and gas and houses the post office.

Those who mean it when they say they want to be alone can hide out in atmospheric comfort up here, far from city chic. The ▶ **Howard Creek Ranch**, 3 miles (5 km) north of Westport on Highway 1, named for the rancher who established it in the 1870s, comprises an inn and cabins in a pleasant valley near the beach. An unheated swimming pool, hillside hot tub, and sauna add to the welcome.

Most historic of the hostelries is Westport's former Cobweb Palace, built of redwood in the 1890s and one of a dozen or so inns where lumbermen once bellied up to the bar and the table. It has metamorphosed into the ▶ **Pelican Lodge and Inn**, now spruced up so much you'd like to call it home. There are six rooms in the inn and a house completely outfitted for families that can sleep six. The full restaurant and bar are open daily, except Mondays and Tuesdays, to the public as well as guests; vegetables are homegrown. Rooms are quite reasonably priced, as is the house.

Ten miles north of Fort Bragg, the ▶ **Orca Inn and Cottages by the Sea** command 850 acres of rugged Pacific coastline. The cottages, some only 10 feet from the sea, are equipped with kitchens and fireplaces, and the farmhouse-style inn, vintage 1876, is furnished with period antiques.

▶ **Cleone Lodge**, on five and a half acres near the beach in Cleone, offers 11 rooms, including Aslan House, a cottage with two suites available. (Some units have kitchens, fireplaces, private deck, and balconies.) Picnic tables and a grill are available for the use of guests, and prices are moderate (even for suites, considering their facilities).

South of Cleone and 3 miles (5 km) north of Fort Bragg, ▶ **MacKerricher State Park** offers campsites, biking, fishing, and trails for hikers and horseback riders; for information, Tel: (707) 937-5804.

Fort Bragg

The metropolis of the Mendocino coast, relatively speaking, Fort Bragg was born not as a lumber town (though it soon became one) but, in 1857, as a military post on the Mendocino Indian Reservation. It was named to honor General Braxton

Bragg, a hero of the Mexican War. Both reservation and fort were abandoned in 1867 when the Indians were moved to Covelo, and the town settled down to decay.

A history of the place, written in 1880 (and quoted by Mendocino's Barbara Dorr Mullen) said, "Long years ago the paint and whitewash had been washed off the buildings by the fogs of summer and the rains of winter, and their places had been taken by a coat of green moss . . . The plaza, once so smooth and nicely kept, is now overgrown with a heavy crop of dog fennel and chickweed."

But in 1885 Charles Russell "C.R." Johnson raised money in his native Michigan for the construction of a wharf and a mill at Fort Bragg and founded what became the Union Lumber Company, now owned by the Georgia-Pacific Corporation (tours given weekdays in July and August). Fort Bragg bounced back. The mill and much of the town were leveled by the San Francisco earthquake of 1906, but demand for lumber to rebuild San Francisco restored business. The little city has prospered since as a lumber, agricultural, recreational, and fishing center.

The driver who accelerates along Fort Bragg's Main Street (Highway 1), probably late for lunch in Mendocino, sees an unexceptional town with the usual complement of grocery stores, banks, gas stations, drug stores, general merchandise outlets, and the like. But along the back streets, away from the through traffic, you find a quieter, prettier Fort Bragg, where houses and even barns and fences have been handsomely restored, where beautiful gardens (wild and man-made) and several nurseries glow with fuchsias, rhododendrons, trillium, ceanothus, broom, lupine, and other lovely blooms. A pamphlet illustrating the self-guided **Historic Outdoor Fort Bragg Walking Tour** is available from motels, inns, or the Chamber of Commerce at 322 North Main Street. It begins at the Skunk Railroad Depot.

In summer old coast hands often prefer staying in unpretentious, accommodating Fort Bragg to dealing with the increasing tourist trauma of Mendocino. Even a few artists have left that scene to settle here in what one called "a more honest atmosphere." In fact, there's now a **Fort Bragg Center for the Arts**, with changing exhibits on the mezzanine of Daly's Department Store. **Guatemalan for Now**, an unusual shop at 120 Laurel, sells affordable, one-of-a-kind clothing items.

The three-story Victorian home of the aforementioned lumber baron C.R. Johnson became the Union Lumber Company's guest house from 1912 to 1969. Today it's the **Guest House Museum** at 343 North Main Street, open Wednesday through Sunday to display photographs of old-time logging operations, artifacts, and some donkey engines and locomotives. The house itself is worth the visit, with its 12-foot ceilings, stained-glass windows, marble-top bathroom basins, and other luxuries rare on the frontier.

Whale-watching is a major diversion for locals and visitors alike from December to April as the pods of California grays migrate north and south just off the coast. A **Whale Festival**, with watch-tours and cruises, films, and other activities is staged in late March (call Mendocino Chamber of Commerce for what's available; Tel: 707-961-6300). Other annual events include the Rhododendron Show in May; the Salmon Barbecue at Noyo Harbor in early July; and Paul Bunyan Days, with logging competitions, a parade, and a fuchsia show over the Labor Day weekend.

The Skunk Train

It was busy lumber titan C.R. Johnson who in 1885 pushed a logging railroad line from Fort Bragg through the dark, dense woods for 40 miles east to Willits. Steam passenger service began in 1904 and was extended to Willits in 1925, when the self-powered, yellow Skunk rail cars were inaugurated. (They were nicknamed for their original gas engines; the saying was, "You can smell 'em before you can see 'em.") Now, as then, travel on the line is casual, with frequent stops en route for deliveries of mail and groceries in areas inaccessible by car. (For Willits, see above in the Redwood Highway section.)

Over today's tracks, California Western Railroad also operates **Super Skunks**, a line powered by historic diesel and steam logging locomotives featuring open observation cars. Two kinds of trips operate in each direction: full-day trips between Fort Bragg and Willits, starting at either point, and half-day round trips from either terminus to Northspur, the halfway point on the line. In either case, a snack or outdoor luncheon is served at Northspur.

Going east, the route passes along Pudding Creek from Fort Bragg, then along sleepy Noyo River in the redwood shadows. If you want to make the all-day trip and stay over at one terminus, assign one of your group to follow Highway 20 through Jackson Demonstration State Forest (firs, redwoods, hemlocks, bishop pines) to meet you at the terminus. The

Fort Bragg depot is just off Main Street and Laurel Avenue, and reservations are advised; Tel: (707) 964-6371.

Fort Bragg's best restaurant, **The Restaurant**, at 418 North Main Street opposite the Skunk depot, is chef-owned, specializing in seasonal dishes, fresh salmon, and in-house baked goods. There is no smoking in the dining room, and the house is closed on Wednesdays; Tel: 964-9800.

Staying In Fort Bragg

A most unusual bed and breakfast is the ▶ Grey Whale Inn, a weathered redwood structure that once served as the Redwood Coast Hospital, built in 1915. Because of their medical past, most of the 13 rooms are unusually spacious for a bed and breakfast. The Campbell Suite is particularly choice; the Sunrise Suite has its own deck and whirlpool. Travellers who dislike the forced friendliness of many such inns can find privacy here; the rates are moderate, considering the amenities.

Near the Skunk Train depot at 700 North Main Street, the ▶ Pudding Creek Inn consists of two Victorian homes built in 1884 and connected by a garden court. Of the ten rooms, two have working fireplaces; rates are reasonable. The ▶ Glass Beach Inn, just down the road, has nine rooms, some with fireplaces, and a hot tub.

Old-fashioned windows, wainscoting, wallpapers, and sloping ceilings accent the restored redwood warmth of the ▶ Country Inn Bed and Breakfast, with eight rooms, appointed throughout with watercolors and photographs by the owner. The ▶ Colonial Inn occupies a 1912 house on quiet, residential East Fir Street. One of the eight guest rooms boasts a fireplace. No credit cards are accepted, no pets allowed; open all year except two to three weeks in October and two weeks in spring.

For details on other local inns, call the Chamber of Commerce for its helpful visitor Information Guide; Tel: (707) 961-6300.

Visitors who prefer motels to bed and breakfasts have several choices: Try the ▶ Best Western Vista Manor with beach access, fireplaces in suites, indoor pool, and a variety of rooms, suites, and cottages; the ▶ Harbor Lite Lodge with 79 rooms, most with a harbor view; the ▶ Pine Beach Inn, 51 rooms and suites, a café, tennis courts, and some private patios; or the ▶ Seabird Lodge, with some balconies, private patios and kitchens, just a block north of Noyo Bridge. All rates are eminently reasonable.

Around Fort Bragg

Two miles (3 km) south of Fort Bragg, in a coastal pine forest and on sea-cresting headlands, the **Mendocino Coast Botanical Gardens** show off 47 acres of native and planted species—rhododendrons, azaleas, fuchsias, heather, hydrangeas, daisies, ferns, and trees. Even if you are completely ignorant of botany you'll find a stroll along these paths and trails spectacular. Picnicking is allowed on coastal meadows or in the fern canyons. There's also a pleasant café, a nursery, and a shop near the parking lot just west of Highway 1. Restrooms and main trails are now accessible by wheelchair, and two electric wheelchairs are available to the handicapped at no charge; Tel: 964-4352.

On weekdays from April through November, Georgia-Pacific's **Forest Tree Nursery** in town welcomes visitors to its miniature woods, with three million redwood and Douglas fir seedlings destined for reforestation projects on regional timberlands. Facilities on Walnut Street include a visitors' center, a nature trail, and picnic tables; Tel: 964-5651.

One of the early lumber towns, Noyo today is a photogenic fishing village called **Noyo Harbor**, immediately south of and contiguous with Fort Bragg. It's a center for charter sport-fishing boats as well as commercial ones, and a pleasant spot for lunching with a view of the dock action. The ▶ **Noyo River Lodge**, under the cypress trees along short Casa del Noyo Drive, is an 1868 craftsman-style building overlooking the Noyo River, with a pleasant library-sitting room. **The Wharf** at 780 North Harbor Drive prides itself on its fresh seafood, great prime-rib sandwiches, clam chowder, and a superb view; Tel: 964-4283.

Noyo Harbor is the site of the roasting facility of **Thanksgiving Coffee Company**, producers of one of America's finest coffees, well recognized in wine and redwood country but little known elsewhere. Top bed and breakfasts in Mendocino County serve Thanksgiving; specialty packages make good gifts and may be found locally in groceries, supermarkets, and delis.

JUG HANDLE STATE RESERVE
You can see one of the most remarkable natural phenomena in the state, or the nation, at Jug Handle State Reserve, 5 miles (8 km) south of Fort Bragg and slightly north of Mendocino. Here, over half a million years, the forces of climate and geology have created five seaside terraces—the Ecological Staircase—climbing out of the sea and back from the ocean at

a remarkably even rate, each approximately 100 feet lower and 100,000 years younger than the one above it. Five terraces and 500,000 years: The newest terrace is forming under the roiling waters of the Pacific.

Walk half a million years back in time. The trees of the first terrace are the Bishop pine and the Monterey pine. On the second terrace, 200,000 years old, Bishop pines are joined by grand fir, Sitka spruce, western hemlock, and plants that love the redwood shade.

By the third terrace, and the fourth and fifth, you have reached the strange world of the pygmy forest, where the podzolization process (well explained in the self-guiding brochure) has reduced a cypress (which might reach 100 feet elsewhere) to a stunted dwarf; you are a giant. The sand on the third terrace is half-a-million-year-old beach that has washed down from the fifth terrace.

The Ecological Staircase may be climbed year round, although it's not recommended on stormy days. The self-guided round-trip hike to the third terrace (the fourth and fifth are similar) takes about three hours.

Just south of Jug Handle, Highway 1 skirts Caspar, a clutch of creaky frame houses as yet unawakened by tourism, and enters Mendocino.

MENDOCINO

A straggle of Victorian houses and water towers set back from wave-battered cliffs, Mendocino is the very model of an antique eastern coastal town, set on a stern (at least in winter) and rockbound coast as rugged as any in Maine. So close is the resemblance, indeed, that the little city has long been the stand-in for the New England hamlet of Cabot Cove in the television series "Murder, She Wrote."

The town began, like her coastal sisters, as a lumber port at the mouth of Big River (the Pomo Indians' Booldam), just to the south. Settlers began to arrive in the 1850s: State-of-Mainers and other Yankees, Nova Scotians, and New Yorkers. Surely they wanted to build a town that looked as much as possible like those they left and expected never to see again, and so they did. (Chinese, Portuguese, and representatives of many other peoples followed, but they had little effect on the look of the place.) There was no architectural restraint. The styles here have been classified as Gothic Revival, Saltbox, Gingerbread, Rustic, Pointed Cottage, Carpenter's Gothic—an overall description might be Redwood Rampant.

These are the houses of the 1840s to 1860s; in distinct contrast is the town's sentinel, the Presbyterian Church, which is pristine, stiff, almost accusing in its whiteness.

As Dorothy Bear and Beth Stebbins put it in their *Mendocino,* "There was formed a definite social structure based on the mores of the 19th century. The elite . . . kept within their own groups. They owned the mill, the banks, the mercantile stores. The others worked for them.

" 'Fast houses,' pool halls and saloons seem to have been plentiful. During the height of the lumber industry it is reported there were 19 saloons . . . So-called Fury Town was a district in east Mendocino . . . When the loggers came to town from the logging camps, the idea was to have a good time; and according to their tastes they did. . . "

Even before World War I, however, the lumber business was moving from boom to dust. The *W.P.A. Guide to California* tells how the town appeared in the depressed 1930s: ". . . a jumble of weathered, gabled wooden buildings fronting dirt streets, edged by the gloomy pine woods of encircling hills."

It was poverty that preserved Mendocino, kept old buildings from being "improved," and tempted no tract developers. Looking at photographs of 19th-century Main Street, you can identify many houses as they stand today: Bever's Temperance House (1878), for instance (no liquor served to boarders), which became the Central Hotel and is today the smart Mendocino Hotel (definitely not a temperance house).

In the 1960s artists (some said hippies) and their celebrators, fleeing what they felt was the confinement and commercialization of Carmel, Sausalito, and San Francisco's North Beach, found Mendocino. Fortunately they liked it just as it was (though local loggers and fishermen didn't like *them* much) and proceeded with paint, nails, plumbing, and elbow grease to bring the old beauty back to life.

One can't help but notice today a creeping cuteness, a hint of the quaint. Still, Mendocino is small by California art-colony standards (population about 2,000), and her spectacular setting remains untrammeled.

Downtown Mendocino

A helpful first stop in town is the **Ford House Visitor Center** at 735 Main Street, built by Jerome Bursley Ford in 1854, which offers exhibits and information on natural and cultural history of the coast.

The town's major hostelry is the aforementioned

▶ **Mendocino Hotel**, right across the way, a landmark with 51 rooms (38 with bath), some with balconies, fireplaces, and ocean views; the **Garden Café and Bar** is particularly pleasant for lunch. The rates will remind you of the expensive antiques around.

On the corner of Main and Evergreen, the ▶ **Mendocino Village Inn** offers 12 rooms in an 1882 Queen Anne Victorian, built by town physician W. A. McCornack. It's locally called the House of the Doctors, having been occupied successively by four village doctors. The breakfasts are particularly notable (blue-cornmeal banana pancakes), and the rates moderate. Yet another place to sleep on Main Street is the ▶ **Sears House Inn**, an 1870 Victorian "main house" with cottages and a water tower behind it. Some of the eight guest rooms boast fireplaces and kitchens.

One of the most highly acclaimed chefs in Northern California is Margaret Fox, whose **Café Beaujolais** at 961 Ukiah Street is highly praised for the originality and imagination devoted to the use of local produce in dishes of American, French, and Californian inclination. Breakfast and lunch are served daily, dinners May through November (but closed January 4 to March 10). Reservations are always advised; Tel: 937-5614.

The menu at **Bay View Restaurant**, in a water tower on Main Street, is nothing if not eclectic, featuring fresh seafood, crab, clam chowder, but also stir-fries, nachos, and escargots. Everything's good; Tel: 937-4197.

After you're sated, cross the street to snap the signature picture every traveller takes before leaving, that of the Mendocino Masonic Temple. The lodge was formed by the hardy pioneers of the country in 1866 and crowned by the landmark sculpture of Father Time and the Maiden, carved from a single redwood log by the lodge's builder, Eric Albertson.

Little Lake and Albion Streets

The practice of crafts and instruction in them goes on at the **Mendocino Art Center and Gallery**, 45200 Little Lake Street, four blocks north from Main. For show and for sale are examples of glass-staining, painting, photography, pottery- and print-making, and more. The gallery is open daily year round (except Christmas and New Year's) and exhibits the works of some 180 artist-members. In addition drama, dance, and musical performances are presented and fairs staged here in midsummer and at Thanksgiving; Tel: 937-5818. The

Mendocino Performing Arts Company is on the grounds of the center and presents six plays a year.

The Art Center occupies the site of the Denslow-Morgan-Preston mansion where Elia Kazan shot *East of Eden* in 1954; it burned in 1956. (Angela Lansbury's house in "Murder, She Wrote" is nearby on the corner of Little Lake and Ford streets.) Farther east on Little Lake, where there's a turnoff from Highway 1, Joshua Grindle from Maine built a handsome Italianate home in 1879. Today it's the ten-room ▶ **Joshua Grindle Inn**, one of the finest along the coast. There is also one cottage, as well as three rooms in the water tower. Despite the impeccable taste in decoration, rates are moderate.

The **Kelley House Historical Museum & Library**, at 45007 Albion Street, occupies a home constructed in 1861 for William H. Kelley, a native of Prince Edward Island and one of the original men who arrived aboard the brig *Ontario* in 1852. Intriguing old photos of the town and coast, historical shows, and gardens with century-old plantings are open to the public daily, afternoons only.

Just across the street, the ▶ **MacCallum House Inn** ranks among the top bed and breakfasts in the area, especially respected for its fine dinners. One of the prettiest houses in town, it was built by Kelley for his daughter Daisy MacCallum in 1882. Some of the 20 rooms are located in the grounds' Carriage House and Water Tower, Greenhouse, and Gazebo Playhouse and Barn. Rates range from reasonable to expensive; some rooms have fireplaces. Nearby, at the corner of Howard and Albion, is the ▶ **Headlands Inn**, an 1868 Victorian built to be the town's barbershop. The five-room inn (one room in a separate cottage) overlooks an English garden and the ocean; smoking is not allowed on the premises. All rooms have wood-burning fireplaces and queen- or king-size beds. Included in rates are a gourmet breakfast and afternoon tea.

Several blocks west on Albion, the 1882 **Temple of Kwan Tia** is one of two remaining joss houses (Chinese temple for a cult figure) in Northern California. It may be visited by appointment only; Tel: 937-4506 (evenings).

Around Mendocino

Yet another bed and breakfast, the ▶ **Whitegate Inn** on Howard Street, occupies an elegant 19th-century house overlooking the **Mendocino Headlands State Park**, which partially surrounds the town. The inn's five moderately priced guest rooms, all nonsmoking, are handsomely appointed. The ▶ **Hill House Inn** offers forty-four rooms, four suites, a café and bar, a library, and some private patios and balconies. It overlooks the ocean and soothes with privacy those who find a bed and breakfast slightly confining. Another good inn to try is the ▶ **Agate Cove Inn** on Lansing Street, a grouping of ten cottages in gardens surrounding an 1860s inn. There are private baths, four-poster beds, Franklin fireplaces, and some balconies and oceanfront views; complimentary country breakfasts are cooked on an antique wood stove.

The ▶ **John Dougherty House**, vintage 1867, sits in the center of the village and speaks of the past with antiques, large verandahs, and peaceful evenings. Just north of Mendocino is Larkin Road, a loop off the highway to the east. Here you'll find a 13-room lodge, spread out with units that resemble old Western storefronts. This is the ▶ **Blackberry Inn**, in a serene setting where an old inn was demolished and a new one built in 1981. The result is larger rooms, bathrooms superior to those found in the traditional bed and breakfast, many fireplaces, and ocean views throughout.

Just to the south of town across Big River is an unusually attractive resort on ten acres of private grounds. ▶ **Stanford Inn by the Sea (Big River Lodge)** offers 25 rooms in a redwood lodge that stretches out above the sea to offer luxurious, spacious units with ocean views, wood-burning fireplaces, large decks, cable color TVs, and bicycles on loan. A greenhouse complex houses a huge swimming pool, spa, and sauna. It's rather expensive, and worth it. The **Catch a Canoe & Bicycles Too!** operation, under the same management, can arrange canoeing along Big River through a narrow canyon forested with redwoods and firs; it's the habitat of great blue herons, ospreys, wood ducks, and beavers, to name a few of the living treasures that abound here. High-tech cycles are available for mountain biking; Tel: 937-0273 or (800) 439-5245.

Also right at hand near Stanford Inn, the Comptche-Ukiah Road is a wonderfully rugged run east through the woods that eventually winds back to Highway 101 at Ukiah. At a point on the upper Big River, it splits into Low Gap Road and Orr Springs Road; the latter passes through Montgomery Woods State Reserve.

SOUTH OF MENDOCINO

Little River, Albion, Elk, and several other settlements along this coast are called "dog hole" ports, from the complaint of an early lumber schooner captain that "the ports are so narrow and tight only a dog could turn around in them."

Little River

Among these ports was Little River (just south of Big River), a pleasant, rural hamlet described in 1912 by equestrian author J. Smeaton Chase as "a pretty, straggling village of high-gabled houses with quaint dormer windows, and red roses clambering all about." Today it's just as pretty, not much busier, but a prosperous little hub of inns and restaurants.

Just north of the village, Van Damme State Park is a pleasant detour inland. Stop at a marked parking area for the Pygmy Forest, especially if you missed Jug Handle.

The ▶ **Little River Inn** has sat here, just off the highway and near the sea, for nearly a century and a half, famous for its cozy cottages and dining room; many people drive down for dinner from Mendocino. There are 56 moderate-to-rather-expensive units in the inn, annex, and 26 cottages, as well as lighted tennis courts, a nine-hole golf course, many fireplaces, some refrigerators, and patios and balconies. The welcome is warm, the style rustic. Note that personal checks and credit cards are not accepted.

Queen of all the coastal resorts and a pacesetter among country inns, ▶ **Heritage House**, west of the highway on the coastal cliffs, was built in 1877 for the lumber-rich Pullen family, when the cove below was called Pullen's Landing. In 1949 Loren Dennen, the builder's grandson, opened the original farmhouse as an inn. It was an immediate hit, perhaps because of Dennen's refusal to regiment his guests: "No one is going to hound you to play games," he proclaimed.

Today Heritage has 80 rooms in cottages, some perched high on cliffs over the pounding Pacific. The inn operates exclusively on the Modified American Plan (includes breakfast and dinner), and has no telephones. It's closed in January, and reservations are required for dinner and for lodging; Tel: 937-5885.

Inns and bed and breakfasts have sprung up along this route like California poppies, and this area is so compact that you can easily find any of them. Among the most splendid is ▶ **Stevens Wood** on the Shoreline Highway, where spacious ocean-view suites are outfitted with wood-burning fireplaces, cable TVs, and stocked honor bars. There's even a fine art gallery. The ▶ Victorian Farmhouse was built in 1877, by the John Dennen of Heritage House, with six rooms, private baths, and complimentary breakfast delivered to each room; ▶ Glendeven Inn, an 1867 farmhouse, has decor from antique to abstract modern; and ▶ Rachel's Inn features etchings and tapestries created by the inn's owner. Twelve comfortable cottages and rooms, all with ocean views, constitute the ▶ Inn at Schoolhouse Creek. The inn's ten acres of garden, meadow, and forest are on the southern edge of Little River. There are fireplaces and some kitchens; the central lodge dates from 1862.

Little River Restaurant (not to be confused with the Little River Inn) is a tiny place squeezed next to the Little River Post Office. You'll be surprised by the high quality of the California-French cuisine served at the seven tables Friday through Tuesday in high season, Friday through Monday in winter. Reserve for seatings at 6:00 and 8:30 P.M. It's fairly expensive and well worth it; Tel: 937-4945.

The Ledford House at 3000 North Highway One serves what might be called California Current cuisine—ravioli stuffed with ricotta cheese, say, or duck-liver pâté with Granny Smith apples, capers, roasted garlic, and goat cheese. There's a little straining for elegance; Tel: 937-0282.

Travellers who want the independence and hands-off attitude of motels should enjoy the ▶ S.S. Seafoam Lodge, three miles south of Little River. It has 29 reasonably priced rooms, some with fireplaces, decks, refrigerators, or porches, and offers fine ocean views over a grassy lawn.

Albion

Named for ancient Britain, Albion, just a skip south of Little River, grew up around a lumber mill started in 1853. The aforementioned J. Smeaton Chase in his *California Coast Trails* (1912) wrote, "The piece of coast between Albion and Little River seemed to me almost the finest I had seen. Such headlands, black and wooded, such purple seas, such vivid blaze of spray, such fiords and islets, a painter would be ravished by it."

Not much has happened in Albion since the last "lokey" (a Baldwin locomotive) hauled the last logs out of the forest and loaded them by wire chutes onto bobbing schooners—and that's just the way the whale-watching weekenders like it. What has happened is that the ▶ Albion River Inn, long recognized for fine dining (seafood, pasta, veal, and wines from nearby Anderson Valley vineyards), now offers 20 lodge rooms in addition to oceanfront bedroom suites and cottages (rather expensive). Breakfast is included. You should reserve for dinner; Tel: 937-1919.

Elk

Even by Highway 1 standards, Elk (once Greenwood) is little more than a wide spot on the coast—but what a photogenic one. Offshore, the ocean beats itself white against great black sea stacks, pointed as broken teeth. A wooden fence decays, wildflowers growing over its body. The wind seems to whistle with the curses of mule skinners, the creaks of the lumber chutes. There is nothing to do in Elk but stroll the surf-scalloped shore and the wind-whipped headlands, sip Scotch or wine before a fireplace, speak softly with friends, or read a big book.

Fortunately, there are inns in this tiny spot that allow you to do all that. A traditional old place is the ► **Harbor House**, an inn built in 1916 as an executive residence and guest lodging by the Goodyear Redwood Lumber Company. Rates for the ten units and four cottages include breakfast and dinner. Lawn games, a library, and a private beach add to the sense of cosseted privacy.

The first bed and breakfast along the North Coast is believed to have been the ► **Elk Cove Inn**, the property of German-born Hildrun-Uta Triebess, with four cabins with sweeping views, some fireplaces, gardens, and a library; no smoking, pets, or credit cards.

The ► **Greenwood Pier Inn** is gaining in popularity with San Franciscans and others in the region for its outstanding service and excellent cooking. The 11 rooms occupy contemporary cottages with views of the ocean, fireplaces, gardens, and decks. You can even be served breakfast in bed.

Two other tranquil escapes are the 1920s cottages at the ► **Griffin House at Greenwood Cove**, with ocean and garden views, and the redwood interior and lovely garden of the ► **Sandpiper House Inn**.

Point Arena

About 15 miles (24 km) south of Elk, Punta de Arenas (Sandy Point) was once the most thriving town between San Francisco and Eureka, with gardens and houses sheltered from the wind behind inland-curved cypresses. In 1870 a lighthouse was erected on the point in reaction to the many shipwrecks along this stormy coast; on the one night of November 20, 1865, ten vessels were blown ashore within a few miles of the point. The early lighthouse was ruined by the 1906 shaker in San Francisco, but was rebuilt and still functions as the **Point Arena Light Station**. It is open to the public from about 11:30 A.M. to 3:00 P.M. except on Thanksgiving and Christmas, and gives sensational views of the coastline to those who climb the almost 150 steps. The Fog Signal Building (1869) houses historical artifacts. Point Arena today is only a drive-through town otherwise, not worth an overnight stay with so many good inns to the north and south of it.

Anchor Bay

Off tiny Anchor Bay in September of 1938, the S.S. *Dorothy Wintermote* smashed up on the rocks, bringing a pleasant bounty to the Depression-downed town south of Point Arena. The town mostly subsisted for a decade on the ship's 1,400 tons of coffee, shortening, and soap. Today a clutch of mobile homes sullies the wooded valley at the northern edge of town, which supports a general store and a couple of cafés.

Also north of Anchor Bay, however, you will round a curve to come upon a surprising sight, a dramatically contemporary clutch of buildings radiating out from a central, hexagonal house, built in the 1970s by an architectural designer to be his second home. It seems every bit as suited to its blufftop spot as the aging Victorian up the road, the 18-room ▶ **Whale Watch Inn**, on a protected inlet with sandy beaches. Adults and nonsmokers only are admitted to this seaside sanctuary to enjoy spacious decks, fireplaces, four rooms with kitchens, some with spas, all with private patios. Full breakfast is included and served in the rooms. It looks expensive, and it is.

Gualala

This is where the road ends (or begins) in Mendocino County. South lie the seductions of Sonoma County (see below and Wine Country chapter) and the return to San Francisco.

Gualala, where a curving beach at the mouth of the Gualala River meets the sea (super for driftwood collecting), boomed in the 1860s and 1870s, but by the 1930s apparently had a population of only 15. Only a decade ago, when you rented a cottage or house at nearby Sea Ranch (just south in Sonoma County), you had to ice and carry your own meat with you in order to have edible supplies for the weekend. No more. Gualala (pronounced "wah-la-la," probably Pomo Indian for "water coming down place") is today's boom town, with 600 residents—hundreds of second-home part-time citizens, a Surf Supermarket, delis, inns, ye olde gifte shoppes—all the comforts of home away from home. It's not spoiled; it has merely come of age.

The locals and their visitors go fishing for steelhead and silver salmon, canoe, swim, and camp. In town, the ▶ **Gualala Hotel**, which used to look (and probably smell) exactly like the hotel in "Gunsmoke," now has nineteen rooms (but only five with private bath; tradition lives); its Italian dining room has always been popular. Prices are exceedingly and befittingly modest. The ▶ **North Coast Country Inn** on Highway One has only four kitchen units, but they feature hot tub, refrigerators, fireplaces, and private decks (nonsmokers only).

When someone says "you can't miss it," you know you can—except for ▶ **St. Orres**, 2½ miles (4 km) north of Gualala, which appears to be a fantasy Russian dacha with an onion dome. It has eight tiny rooms (shared baths) and eleven cottages. For pure luxury, request the Tree House. The restaurant is highly regarded throughout the area; Tel: 884-3335.

SONOMA COUNTY COAST

Sonoma County's rugged shoreline, backing up against the mountains of the Coast Range, presents a very different aspect from bucolic, inland Sonoma (see the Wine Country chapter). Highway 1 curls and weaves south from Gualala through Sonoma County (said to have been the name of an Indian chief baptized by the mission fathers in 1824), occasionally straying inland into wooded coves and out along windy promontories, followed by sheep and grass and the smell of the sea.

South of Gualala, you will begin to notice homes of a distinctive style, cresting the hills and sitting in the meadows, of non-intrusive, weathering wood suited to the play of wind and wave. This is **Sea Ranch**, a second-home community designed not to look like a single cohesive complex that commands 5,500 acres of a former Mexican land grant, although that is what it is. About 12 miles (20 km) south of the river's mouth, the ▶ **Sea Ranch Lodge** sits on a seaside bluff to the east of Highway 1, a two-story inn with eighteen rooms (some fireplaces) and smashing views of the sea, a good restaurant, and a bar. Guests have the use of the Ranch's two heated swimming pools with saunas, nine-hole golf course, and tennis courts; not inexpensive but a worthwhile escape. Some of the Sea Ranch houses can be rented; see Vacation Rentals at the end of this chapter.

From Stewarts Point, a couple of miles south of Sea Ranch, the fairly rough but beautiful Stewarts Point-Skaggs Springs Road crawls up and over the ridges east to Highway 101, affording a freeway return for those in a hurry to reach San Francisco.

If you take it, however, you'll miss a coastline studded with natural and historic diversions. Just south of that turnoff, for example, **Kruse Rhododendron State Reserve** is a 317-acre glory of the tall, pink plants, in bloom usually from early April into June; Tel: 847-3221. Slightly farther south, two dramatic coastal areas are open to the public: Salt Point State Park (miles of wave-sculpted shoreline, hiking, riding, fishing, and campsites) and Stillwater Cove Regional Park (redwood trails to the beach, fishing, hiking, and beachcombing).

Fort Ross

Ten miles (16 km) south of the Kruse Reserve, you round a curve and drive into old Russia. In 1741, Russian Admiral Vitus Bering, tracking the fur seal, discovered the white wastes of Alaska and the sea now named after him. Following his lead, the Russian-American Fur Company was firmly established in the north by the close of the 18th century, but came to require more fertile soil and a warmer growing climate in order to supply its colonists with food.

Pushing down the coast, the fur-seekers found this site in 1811, where they negotiated with the Native Americans for 1,000 acres, began building a log fort, and by the next year dedicated their settlement, complete with cannon, blockhouses, Orthodox chapel, officers' quarters, and other buildings inside a palisade, and 50 buildings outside the enclosure. They called it Fort Ross, an ancient name for Russia.

The community flourished, not only shipping supplies to the Alaskan colonies, but also trading with its Spanish neighbors, which was officially forbidden but winked at in practice. Then, in December 1823, came the promulgation of the Monroe Doctrine, which brought an end to any ambition of

Russia's to acquire California. The colony at Ross, however, continued to prosper until 1840, when the sea otter had become almost extinct. In 1841 Czar Nicholas I ordered the return of his people from California, and the whole property was sold (for an estimated $30,000) to Captain John A. Sutter.

After World War II, the state park system began constructing **Fort Ross State Historic Park**, which today—despite two fires—is an intriguing grouping of redwood structures closely copying the originals: stockade, blockhouses, Orthodox chapel, officers' barracks, water well, and two houses. The Visitors' Information Center near the highway offers interpretive displays, meeting rooms, a library, and book and souvenir sales. There's also a picnic area; Tel: 847-3286. "Living history" events are staged throughout the year, and a Russian Orthodox Easter service is held in the chapel.

Staying Along the
Sonoma County Coast

Two miles (3 km) north of Fort Ross (albeit with a mailing address in Jenner, to the south), ► **Fort Ross Lodge** has 24 motel-type units with ocean views, fireplaces, TVs and VCRs, a hot tub, and sauna; rates range from moderate to expensive, with special midweek prices.

Hardly anyone, even Californians, knows **Cazadero**, a wide, wooded spot at the juncture of Fort Ross Road and King Ridge Road inland from Fort Ross. In these days of intensive escapism, however, the town is coming into its own with three secluded hideaways worth mentioning. Chief among them is ► **Timberhill Ranch**, one of the most stylish country resorts in the state, set on 80 acres of woods atop a 1,100-foot ridge. Opened in 1984, it was awarded membership in France's prestigious Relais & Châteaux group in 1990, one of only 22 such inns in the United States. Rustic outside, luxurious inside, it consists of a ranch house reworked into a splendid lodge, and ten cottages, swimming pool, Jacuzzi spa, lawn games, and tennis courts. Gourmet breakfasts and dinners are included in the understandably rather expensive rates.

► **Cazanoma Lodge** looks and feels like an Old World retreat, overlooking streams, a small waterfall, and a trout pond. There are rooms in the lodge and some cabins with fireplaces on the 147-acre site shaded by redwood and fir forests. Sunday brunch and American- and German-style dinners are served; the lodge is open March through mid-

December. On a bluff overlooking the Russian River and Duncans Mills Valley, the ▶ **House of a Thousand Flowers** offers two guest rooms with private entrances, full breakfast, and use of a deck spa and living room; no pets allowed.

Until the late 1980s, **Jenner**, about 12 miles (20 km) south of Fort Ross, where the Russian River flows into the Pacific, was a somnolent village of peak-roofed white and green cottages hugging the riverside slopes. Its inhabitants were outnumbered by a colony of 200 harbor seals that gathered near Goat Rock to bark their contentment, and drivers bound north on Highway 1 to Mendocino or south to San Francisco usually swerved speedily around the river's mouth, stopping only to refill the gas tank or to take a libation at Murphy's.

Today, though, the little fishing town has awakened and blinks its eyes seductively at visitors. ▶ **Murphy's Jenner Inn** offers nine in-house rooms and a clutch of cottages, billing itself as a "Bed & Breakfast & Retreat Center." In addition, the owners of the inn can arrange for stays in five nearby homes. (The two-story, two-bedroom Taylor House, set on a cliff above the beach, is a good choice.) Where the highway swings out to sea again, about a quarter-mile north of greater downtown Jenner, the ▶ **River's End Resort** offers seven units on the cliff with private decks and seemingly private sunsets; a separate house can sleep several people. Sixteen miles north of Jenner, ▶ **Stillwater Cove Ranch** joins solitude to intimacy with six units and a "bunkhouse" on 50 acres between a sea cove and redwood forests.

Jenner is also a gateway for the inland Russian River resorts (see the Wine Country chapter); here we keep to the coast road.

Bodega Bay and South

It was October 3, 1775, when explorer Juan Francisco de la Bodéga sailed his schooner *Sonora* into the bay and protected harbor today bearing his name, about 10 miles (16 km) south of Jenner. Nothing much happened for years after, except that an expedition led by Captain George Vancouver came ashore in 1793, and a small Russian fur station was set up in 1809.

Today, the 300-plus residents of Bodega Bay watch for migrating gray whales (in season), catch crab and fish commercially, operate charter fishing boats, and enjoy a slow but steady increase in tourism. The contemporary-style **Lucas Wharf Restaurant and Bar**, right on the water, emphasizes seafood, caught fresh almost every day. A most attractive place to spend a night or two is the ▶ **Inn at the Tides**, which attracts some San Franciscans who don't want to drive farther to spend a weekend by the sea. It is a smart place with 86 rooms (some with fireplaces and/or patios), an indoor-outdoor pool, sauna, good restaurant, and lounge; a golf course is nearby. Directly across the highway, the creaky, old-fashioned **Tides Restaurant** is now under the same management as the inn, and while the casual atmosphere has not changed, the cooking has definitely improved. The fresh seafood has an Italian accent now, and don't miss the crab cakes.

On a handsome bluff-top setting, the ▶ **Bodega Bay Lodge** offers 78 units, exercise area, some refrigerators and fireplaces in rooms, and a heated pool. There's complimentary buffet breakfast and evening dining at the **Ocean Club** next to an 18-hole golf course. The lodge is more informal than Inn at the Tides; neither one could be called inexpensive. The 45 rooms of the ▶ **Bodega Coast Inn** overlook the harbor and bay; some have fireplaces, whirlpool tubs, and VCRs. There's a restaurant on the premises; golfing and beaches are nearby.

If you visit between February and April, drive to the **Bodega Head State Park** on the north edge of town and descend the three-mile trail to Salmon Creek Beach at Sonoma Coast State Beach for the chance to spot the annual migration of California gray whales.

From Bodega Bay, detour inland to tiny Bodega, a village still snoozing in the 19th century, where Victoriana lives in St. Teresa's Catholic Church (1861) and a schoolhouse that played a role in Alfred Hitchcock's *The Birds*. **Bodega Landmark Studio Collection** at 17255 Bodega Highway (slow down or you'll miss it) is a worthwhile regional gallery displaying landscape painting, photography, sculpture, ceramics, and folk arts and crafts. The gallery is closed on Tuesday and Wednesday.

A town devoted almost solely to the consumption of Italian cuisine is **Occidental**, inland and slightly north of Bodega Bay about 9 miles (15 km) via Bodega and Bohemian highways. In the late 1880s this town was established as a rail terminus, but nothing much came of that, and the population flowed away, leaving in its ebb three loud, lively restaurants dedicated to serving the crowds who haven't had a good family-style meal since they left San Francisco's North Beach. **The Union Hotel** and **Negri's** (both on five-block Main Street) serve up enough spaghetti, ravioli, tagliarini, and other temptations to make a Neopolitan weep.

▶ **The Inn at Occidental** occupies an 1867 Victorian home on Church Street. Its eight rooms are the ultimate in coziness, with antique furnishings, goose-down comforters, and fresh flowers, and the breakfasts are sumptuous.

South of Bodega, Highway 1 turns out to the coast again, running through hamlets such as Tomales and Marshall, across Tomales Bay from Point Reyes National Seashore (see Day Trips From San Francisco).

As an alternative to driving congested Sir Francis Drake Boulevard between Olema and San Rafael to Highway 101, you might consider returning to San Francisco from Marshall over Marshall-Petaluma Road and Novato Boulevard, a pleasantly rural route that puts you back on Highway 101 near Novato, 20-some miles (32 km) north of the Golden Gate Bridge. Another choice is to follow Highway 1 all the way along the coast to where it turns inland at Muir Beach and goes east to leave you 5 miles (8 km) north of San Francisco on Highway 101.

GETTING AROUND
The most practical as well as the most enjoyable way to explore Redwood Country is by private car. From San Francisco's Golden Gate Bridge, Highway 101 (the Redwood Highway) is the most direct route north to points of interest in Marin, Sonoma, Mendocino, Humboldt, and Del Norte counties. Via Highway 101 it's 359 miles (574 km) to Crescent City, just south of the Oregon state line.

On one leg of the round trip, we recommend you drive coastal Highway 1, a slower, narrower, and more scenic road. If you can afford the time for them, several routes across the high country of the Coast Range are recommended: State Highway 128 from north of Cloverdale (on 101) to Navarro Point south of Albion (on 1); similarly, State Highway 20 from Willits to Noyo, and State Highway 211 from 2 miles (3 km) north of Fortuna to Cape Mendocino and beyond.

If a fly-drive itinerary suits your schedule better, there is service out of San Francisco International Airport to various cities to the north. American Eagle flies from SFO to Santa Rosa and Eureka (Tel: 800-433-7300), while United Express serves Santa Rosa, Eureka, and Crescent City (Tel: 800-241-6522). All the airport facilities include rental-car pickup.

All major towns along the route are served by Greyhound/ Trailways Bus Lines; for information, Tel: (415) 558-6789.

Several companies offer regional bus and/or van services

in both Mendocino and Humboldt counties. For details and current schedules, call Mendocino Transit Authority, Coast Van, Tel: (707) 884-3723; Mendocino Stage, Tel: (707) 964-0167; Arcata-Mad River Transit System, Tel: (707) 822-3775; Redwood Transit Eureka Service, Tel: (707) 443-0826; Redwood Transit, Orick-Scotia service, Tel: (707) 443-0826; Redwood Empire Lines, Eureka-Redding service, Tel: (707) 443-9923.

For details on the Skunk Train of California Western Railroad, Tel: (707) 964-6371; for trips on the North Coast Daylight Railroad, Tel: (707) 442-7705.

Backroads, in Berkeley, arranges weekend or week-long vacations (camping or inns) along the coast and in the redwoods; Tel: (510) 527-1555.

For further information: A map of Marin, Sonoma, and Mendocino counties with listings of motels, bed and breakfasts, and other lodgings, recreation and real estate firms, and more, is published in Gualala; it's extremely helpful. Send $2 for the packet to The Porters, P.O. Box 999, Gualala, CA 95445; Tel: (800) 726-9997.

ACCOMMODATIONS REFERENCE

Most of the following hotels and inns have a small number of rooms, so it's always wise to make reservations. You should also check on smoking policies, whether children (and/or pets) are accepted, whether credit cards may be used, seniors' rates, AAA discounts, and if weekend stays must be for more than one night.

In some areas, particularly along the Pacific coastline, vacation home rentals are a popular alternative to hotel accommodations. The best of them are listed at the end of the Accommodations Reference.

The rate ranges given here are projections for fall 1993 through spring 1994. Unless otherwise indicated, rates are for double room, double occupancy. The area code for Redwood Country is 707.

▶ **Agate Cove Inn.** Box 1150, 11201 Lansing Street, **Mendocino**, CA 95460. Tel: 937-0551; in Northern California, (800) 527-3111. $79–$175.

▶ **Albion River Inn.** 3790 North Highway One, **Albion**, CA 95410. Tel: 937-1919. $85–$225.

▶ **Anderson Valley Inn.** P.O. Box 147, **Philo**, CA 95466. Tel: 895-3325. $35–$45.

▶ **Bella Vista Motel.** 1225 Central Avenue, **McKinleyville,** CA 95521. Tel: 839-1073. $48–$60.

▶ **Bell Glen Resorts.** 70400 Highway 101, **Leggett,** CA 95585. Tel: 925-6425. $85–$120.

▶ **Benbow Inn.** 445 Lake Benbow Drive, **Garberville,** CA 95542. Tel: 923-2124. $98–$260.

▶ **Benbow Valley Resort.** 7000 Benbow Drive, **Garberville,** CA 95542. Tel: 923-2777. $15–$25.

▶ **Best Western Humboldt House Inn.** 701 Redwood Drive, **Garberville,** CA 95542. Tel: 923-2771 or (800) 528-1234. $66–$84.

▶ **Best Western Northwoods Inn.** 655 U.S. 101 South, **Crescent City,** CA 95531. Tel: 464-9771 or (800) 528-1234; Fax: 464-9461. $66–$95.

▶ **Best Western Ship Ashore Resort.** 12370 Highway 101 North, **Smith River,** CA 95567. Tel: 487-3141 or (800) 528-1234. $50–$120.

▶ **Best Western Thunderbird Lodge.** 232 West Fifth, **Eureka,** CA 95501. Tel: 443-2234 or (800) 521-6996. $56–$88.

▶ **Best Western Vista Manor.** 1100 North Main Street, **Fort Bragg,** CA 95437. Tel: 964-4776 or (800) 821-9498. $50–$90.

▶ **Big Bend Lodge.** P.O. Box 111, **Leggett,** CA 95585. Tel: 984-6321. $60.

▶ **Bishop Pine Lodge.** 1481 Patrick's Point Drive, **Trinidad,** CA 95570. Tel: 677-3314. $60–$90.

▶ **Blackberry Inn.** 44951 Larkin Road, **Mendocino,** CA 95460. Tel: 937-5281. $75–$125.

▶ **Bodega Bay Lodge.** 103 Coast Highway One, **Bodega Bay,** CA 94923. Tel: 875-3525 or (800) 368-2468; Fax: 875-2428. $108–$188.

▶ **Bodega Coast Inn.** 521 Coast Highway One, **Bodega Bay,** CA 94923. Tel: 875-2217 or (800) 346-6999; Fax: 875-2964. $78–$175.

▶ **Boonville Hotel.** 14050 Highway 28, **Boonville,** CA 95415. Tel: 895-2210. $70–$150.

▶ **Carson House Inn.** 1209 4th Street, **Eureka,** CA 95501. Tel: 443-1601 or (800) 772-1622; Fax: 444-8365. $55–$90.

▶ **Carter House Inn.** 1033 Third Street, **Eureka,** CA 95501. Tel: 445-1390; Fax: 444-8062. $95–$225.

▶ **Cazanoma Lodge.** 1000 Kidd Creek Road, **Cazadero,** CA 95421. Tel: 632-5255. $75–$105.

▶ **Cleone Lodge.** 24600 North Highway 1, **Fort Bragg,** CA 95437. Tel: 964-2788. $68–$116.

▶ **Colonial Inn.** 533 East Fir Street, **Fort Bragg,** CA 95437. Tel: 964-9979 or (800) 831-5327. $56–$90.

▶ **Country Inn Bed and Breakfast.** 632 North Main Street, **Fort Bragg,** CA 95437. Tel: 964-3737. $75–$125.

▶ **Crescent Travelodge.** 725 Highway 101 North, **Crescent City,** CA 95531. Tel: 464-6106 or (800) 255-3050. $57–$67.

▶ **Curly Redwood Lodge.** 701 Redwood Highway South, **Crescent City,** CA 95531. Tel: 464-2137. $50–$73.

▶ **Discovery Inn.** 1340 North State Street, **Ukiah,** CA 95482. Tel: 462-8873; Fax: 462-1249. $50–$60.

▶ **An Elegant Victorian Mansion.** 1406 C Street, **Eureka,** CA 95501. Tel: 444-5594. $75–$110.

▶ **Elk Cove Inn.** P.O. Box 367, **Elk,** CA 95432. Tel: 877-3321. $108–$138.

▶ **The Eureka Inn.** 518 7th Street, **Eureka,** CA 95501. Tel: 442-6441 or (800) 862-4906; Fax: 442-0637. $115–$175.

▶ **Fort Ross Lodge.** 20705 Coast Highway One, **Jenner,** CA 95450. Tel: 847-3333. $60–$175.

▶ **Garberville Motel.** 948 Redwood Drive, **Garberville,** CA 95542. Tel: 923-2422. $40–$69.

▶ **The Gingerbread Mansion.** 400 Berding Street, **Ferndale,** CA 95536. Tel: 786-4000 or (800) 952-4136. $110–$185.

▶ **Glendeven Inn.** 8221 North Highway 1, **Little River,** CA 95456. Tel: 937-0083 or (800) 822-4536. $80–$200.

▶ **Glass Beach Inn.** 726 North Main Street, **Fort Bragg,** CA 95437. Tel: 964-6774. $62–$95.

▶ **Green Valley Motel.** P.O. Box 67, **Orick,** CA 95555. Tel: 488-2341. $32–$45.

▶ **Greenwood Pier Inn.** 5928 South Highway One, Box 36, **Elk,** CA 95432. Tel: 877-9997. $90–$195.

▶ **Grey Whale Inn.** 615 North Main Street, **Fort Bragg,** CA 95437. Tel: 964-0640 or (800) 382-7244. $80–$150.

▶ **Griffin House at Greenwood Cove.** 5910 South Highway One, **Elk,** CA 95432. Tel: 877-3422. $80–$140.

▶ **Gualala Hotel.** Box 675, **Gualala,** CA 95445. Tel: 884-3441; Fax: 785-2146. $44–$55.

▶ **Harbor House.** Box 369, **Elk,** CA 95432. Tel: 877-3203. $160–$240.

▶ **Harbor Lite Lodge.** 120 North Harbor Drive, **Fort Bragg,** CA 95437. Tel: 964-0221 or (800) 643-2700. $58–$94.

▶ **Hartsook Inn.** 900 Highway 101, **Piercy,** CA 95587. Tel: 247-3305. $39–$100.

▶ **Headlands Inn.** Box 132, **Mendocino,** CA 95460. Tel: 937-4431. $103–$172.

▶ **Heritage House.** 5200 North Highway 1, **Little River,** CA 95456. Tel: 937-5885 or (800) 235-5885; Fax: 937-0318. $125–$335.

▶ **Hill House Inn.** 10701 Palette Drive, **Mendocino,** CA 95460. Tel: 937-0554 or (800) 422-0554; Fax: 937-1123. $110–$175.

▶ **Hotel Carter.** 301 L Street, **Eureka,** CA 95501. Tel: 444-8062. $69–$159.

▶ **House of a Thousand Flowers.** 11 Mosswood Circle, **Cazadero,** CA 95421. Tel: 632-5571. $80.

▶ **Howard Creek Ranch.** 40501 North Highway 1, **West-port,** CA 95488. Tel: 964-6725. $50–$110.

▶ **The Inn at Occidental.** 3657 Church Street, **Occidental,** CA 95465-0857. Tel: 874-1311. $125–$225.

▶ **Inn at Schoolhouse Creek.** 7051 North Highway One, **Little River,** CA 95456. Tel: 937-5525. $65–$120.

▶ **Inn at the Tides.** 800 Coast Highway One, **Bodega Bay,** CA 94923. Tel: 875-2751 or (800) 541-7788; Fax: 875-3023. $110–$160.

▶ **Iris Inn.** 1134 H Street, **Eureka,** CA 95501. Tel: 445-0307. $60–$90.

▶ **John Dougherty House.** 571 Ukiah Street, P.O. Box 817, **Mendocino,** CA 95460. Tel: 937-5266. $85–$165.

▶ **Joshua Grindle Inn.** 44800 Little Lake Road, **Mendocino,** CA 95460. Tel: 937-4143. $90–$135.

▶ **Little River Inn.** Box B, **Little River,** CA 95456. Tel: 937-5942; Fax: 937-3944. $75–$255.

▶ **The Lost Whale Bed and Breakfast.** 3452 Patrick's Point Drive, **Trinidad,** CA 95570. Tel: 677-3425. $100–$130.

▶ **MacCallum House Inn.** 45020 Albion Street, Box 206, **Mendocino,** CA 95460. Tel: 937-0289. $75–$180.

▶ **Manor Inn Motel.** 950 North State Street, **Ukiah,** CA 95482. Tel: 462-7584 or (800) 922-3388. $40–$60.

▶ **Mendocino Hotel.** 45080 Main Street, **Mendocino,** CA 95460. Tel: 937-0511 or (800) 548-0513; Fax: 937-0513. $55–$225.

▶ **Mendocino Village Inn.** 44860 Main Street, **Mendocino,** CA 95460. Tel: 937-0246 or (800) 882-7029. $65–$190.

▶ **Miranda Gardens Resort.** P.O. Box 186, **Miranda,** CA 95553. Tel: 943-3011. $45–$155.

▶ **Motel Trees.** P.O. Box 309, **Klamath,** CA 95548. Tel: 482-3152 or (800) 848-2982. $43–$73.

▶ **Murphy's Jenner Inn.** 10400 Coast Highway One, **Jenner,** CA 95450. Tel: 865-2377 or (800) 732-2377. $65–$150.

▶ **North Coast Country Inn.** 34591 South Highway One, **Gualala,** CA 95445. Tel: 884-4537 or (800) 959-4537. $135.

▶ **North Coast Inn.** 4975 Valley West Boulevard, **Arcata,** CA 95521. Tel: 822-4861 or (800) 233-0903; Fax: 822-2036. $56–$78.

▶ **Noyo River Lodge.** 500 Casa del Noyo Drive, **Fort Bragg**, CA 95437. Tel: 964-8045 or (800) 628-1126. $80–$140.

▶ **Old Town Bed-and-Breakfast Inn.** 1521 Third Street, **Eureka**, CA 95501. Tel: 445-3951; Fax: 445-8346. $75–$150.

▶ **Orca Inn and Cottages by the Sea.** 31502 Highway One North, **Fort Bragg**, CA 95437. Tel: 964-5585. $45–$55 (inn rooms), $65–$175 (cottages).

▶ **Pacific Motor Hotel.** Box 595, **Crescent City**, CA 95531. Tel: 464-4141 or (800) 323-7917; Fax: 465-3274. $47–$65.

▶ **Park Woods Motel.** P.O. Box 61, **Orick**, CA 95555. Tel: 488-5175. $28–$48.

▶ **Pelican Lodge and Inn.** 38921 North Highway One, **Westport**, CA 95488. Tel: 964-5588. $45–$75.

▶ **Pine Beach Inn.** P.O. Box 1173, **Fort Bragg**, CA 95437. Tel: 964-5603. $65–$90.

▶ **Prairie Creek Motel.** P.O. Box 265, **Orick**, CA 95555. Tel: 488-3841. $25–$35.

▶ **Pudding Creek Inn.** 700 North Main Street, **Fort Bragg**, CA 95437. Tel: 964-9529 or (800) 227-9529; Fax: 961-0282. $65–$125.

▶ **Rachel's Inn.** 8200 North Highway One, Box 134, **Mendocino**, CA 95460. Tel: 937-0088. $96–$165.

▶ **Red Lion Inn.** 1929 Fourth Street, **Eureka**, CA 95501. Tel: 445-0844 or (800) 547-8010; Fax: 445-2752. $110–$125.

▶ **Requa Inn.** 451 Requa Road, **Klamath**, CA 95548. Tel: 482-8205. $60–$80.

▶ **River's End Resort.** Coast Highway One, **Jenner**, CA 95446. Tel: 865-2484. $98–$150.

▶ **St. Orres.** 36601 South Highway One, **Gualala**, CA 95445. Tel: 884-3303. $60–$180.

▶ **Sandpiper House Inn.** P.O. Box 49, **Elk**, CA 95432. Tel: 877-3587. $110–$165.

▶ **Seabird Lodge.** 191 South Street, **Fort Bragg**, CA 95437. Tel: 964-4731 or (800) 345-0022. $70–$80.

▶ **Sea Ranch Lodge.** Box 44, **The Sea Ranch**, CA 95497. Tel: 785-2371 or (800) 732-7262; Fax: 785-2243. $125–$180.

▶ **Sears House Inn.** 44840 Main Street, **Mendocino**, CA 95460. Tel: 937-4076. $60–$110.

▶ **Shaw House Inn.** 703 Main Street, Box 1125, **Ferndale**, CA 95536. Tel: 786-9958. $75–$125.

▶ **S.S. Seafoam Lodge.** 6751 North Highway One, **Little River**, CA 95456 (mailing address: Box 68, Mendocino, CA 95460). Tel: 937-2011. $85–$150.

▶ **Stanford Inn by the Sea** (Big River Lodge). P.O. Box 487, **Mendocino**, CA 95460. Tel: 937-5615 or (800) 331-8884. $160–$245.

▶ **Stevens Wood.** 8211 Shoreline Highway, **Little River**, CA 95456. Tel: 937-2810 or (800) 421-2810. $95–$195.

▶ **Stillwater Cove Ranch.** 22555 Coast Highway One, **Jenner**, CA 95450. Tel: 847-3227. $38–$75.

▶ **Thatcher Inn.** 13401 South Highway 101, **Hopland**, CA 95449. Tel: 744-1890 or (800) 266-1891; Fax: 744-1239. $85–$140.

▶ **Timberhill Ranch.** 35755 Hauser Bridge Road, **Cazadero**, CA 95421. Tel: 847-3258; Fax: 847-3342. $296–$350.

▶ **Toll House Restaurant and Inn.** P.O. Box 268, **Boonville**, CA 95415. Tel: 895-3630. $115–$150.

▶ **Trinidad Bed and Breakfast.** P.O. Box 849, **Trinidad**, CA 95570. Tel: 677-0840. $105–$145.

▶ **Trinidad Inn.** 1170 Patrick's Point Drive, **Trinidad**, CA 95570. Tel: 677-3349. $50–$75.

▶ **Vichy Mineral Springs Resort/Bed & Breakfast.** 2605 Vichy Springs Road, **Ukiah**, CA 95482. Tel: 462-9515; Fax: 462-9516. $80–$155.

▶ **Victorian Farmhouse.** 7001 North Highway One, **Little River**, CA 95456. Tel: 937-0697. $80–$125.

▶ **Whale Watch Inn.** 35100 Highway One, **Gualala**, CA 95445. Tel: 884-3667 or (800) WHALE-42. $160–$250.

▶ **Whitegate Inn.** 499 Howard Street, **Mendocino**, CA 95460. Tel: 937-4892 or (800) 531-7282. $95–$155.

Vacation Rentals

In recent years, vacation home rentals have become increasingly popular with travellers in Northern California, particularly in the coastal counties of Mendocino and Sonoma. Following are some select agencies with whom to make arrangements for stays by the week or longer. (In some cases even two- or three-night rentals may be arranged.)

Mendocino County

In Manchester, a tiny fishing village 10 miles (16 km) north of Point Arena, the ▶ **Irish Beach Rental Agency** handles 35 seaside homes with full kitchens, fireplaces, some hot tubs; guests furnish their own towels and linens. Daily charges (two-night minimum) are $65–$165 Sunday through Thursday, $80–$200 on weekends; weekly rates are available. Meadow and forest sites are also available; Tel: 882-2467 or (800) 882-8007.

▶ **Mendocino Coast Reservations** in Mendocino arranges rentals of homes, cottages, and studios, from romantic hideaways to family retreats. Inquire about hot tubs, fireplaces, oceanfront or ocean-view sites; rates vary widely. For information, Tel: 937-5033 or (800) 262-7801. Also in Mendocino, ▶ **1021 Main Street Vacation Rentals** maintains two houses for a minimum two-night rental, each at $135 for two people. One house can accommodate three people for $145. Breakfasts and maid service are not included; Tel: 937-5150.

In Point Arena, restored lighthouse keepers' homes may be rented through ▶ **Point Arena Lighthouse Vacation Homes**. The three-bedroom, two-bath homes are fully furnished except for towels and linens and accommodate from two to six people for two-night-minimum stays. Rates range from $80 to $110 per night for three to six guests. The site is that of the historic Point Arena Lighthouse, with ocean views, whale-watching in season, and restaurants, shops, and fishing piers nearby; Tel: 882-2777.

In Gualala, ▶ **Serenisea** rents housekeeping cottages and vacation homes on the oceanfront or with ocean views. Most houses have fireplaces, hot tubs, and private beach access, some have original artworks, libraries, or antiques. Prices range from $65 to $160 nightly, and no credit cards are accepted; Tel: 884-3836 or (800) 331-3836.

▶ **Shoreline Properties** of Mendocino provides vacations in homes to suit any lifestyle and budget: dramatic houses, cottages, or suites in locations by the ocean, with ocean views amid sand dunes, or with ocean views on the rocky coast. Accommodations are offered for from 2 to 20 guests at nightly rates of $100 and up; discounts for extended stays. Linens, towels, and kitchen utensils are provided. Options include beach access, decks, fireplaces, hot tubs/spas, and barbecues; children and pets are welcome in some of the houses. Tel: 964-1444 or (800) 942-8288.

Sonoma County
There are many beautiful homes available for rental in the coastal Sea Ranch area. ▶ **Don Berard Sea Ranch Rentals** offers 54 architecturally interesting homes. Rates range from $170 to $400 for a minimum two-night stay; Tel: 884-3211 or (800) 643-8899. ▶ **Ram's Head Realty** offers 120 homes ranging from $174 to $625 for a two-night stay; Tel: 785-2427. The 55 homes of ▶ **Sea Ranch Rentals** range from $167 to $420 for a two-night stay; Tel: 785-2579.

NORTH-EASTERN CALIFORNIA

By Barry Anderson

A third-generation Californian, Barry Anderson has written about California for more than 30 years, first as a Sunset Magazine *editor, then as a free-lance writer of magazine and newspaper articles and guidebooks. He has contributed to many publications, including the* Los Angeles Times *and the* World of Travel *series.*

Head northeast out of the San Francisco Bay Area on Interstate 80 and pick up Interstate 505, then I-5, through the broad, agricultural Sacramento Valley. Somewhere beyond the town of Willows you begin to notice the snowcapped tip of a large mountain poking above the intervening foothills. By the time you reach Red Bluff, 198 miles (317 km) north of San Francisco, 14,162-foot Mount Shasta, the signature landmark of north-central and northeastern California, dominates the horizon.

If you could perch atop Shasta for a bird's-eye view in every direction, you'd see some of the loveliest and least-visited country in California. To the west the heavily forested mountains of the Coast Range stand between the hot, dry interior and the cool, moist coast. To the southeast the rugged Sierra Nevada punctuates the horizon and, in the foreground, rocky volcanic landscapes and the cone of 10,457-foot Mount Lassen spread at your feet. To the east and northeast, jumbled hills and valleys, studded with manzanita and pine and cut by clear rushing streams, gradually give way to the high sagebrush desert of the Great Basin that seems to stretch away forever.

You'd also notice that there are few signs of civilization in this vast mountain and desert corner of the state—few towns, few barns and ranches, and, beyond the interstate, only a handful of roads.

Californians call this last part of northeastern California the Lonely Corner. As the state and its visitor attractions become more crowded, this area is becoming increasingly attractive as a destination that offers plenty of untrammeled nature as well as a measure of solitude that is increasingly rare.

Among the trade-offs you must make to savor all this quietude and natural beauty are elegant accommodations and gourmet dining. With some exceptions, accommodations are conventional motels. The term "resort" is used rather broadly in this region and usually means rustic cabins or housekeeping accommodations, sometimes bordering on the primitive—you select them for their location, not their amenities. Where accommodations choices are unremarkable, we've included a range for various budgets. As for dining, with the exception of ethnic specialties, restaurant menus typically include several beef entrées, chicken, and fish or shellfish, but usually nothing to write home about.

MAJOR INTEREST

Unspoiled natural beauty
Mount Shasta for skiing and hiking
Shasta Lake for houseboating and camping
Lassen Volcanic National Park
Fall River Mills for fly fishing
Lava Beds National Monument
Klamath Basin bird-watching

THE I-5 CORRIDOR
Red Bluff

Red Bluff is the smaller, but historically more interesting, of these two small cities at the top end of the Sacramento Valley, about 136 miles (218 km) north of Sacramento. Detour off the interstate at Red Bluff to **William B. Ide Adobe State Park**, the restored homestead of a leader of the Bear Flag Revolt that briefly made California an independent republic in 1846.

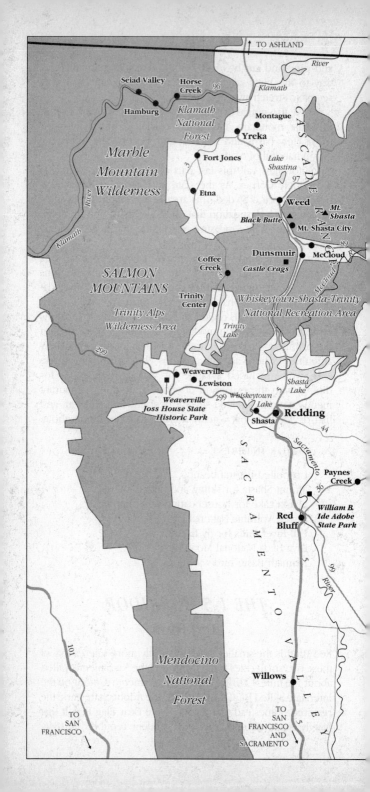

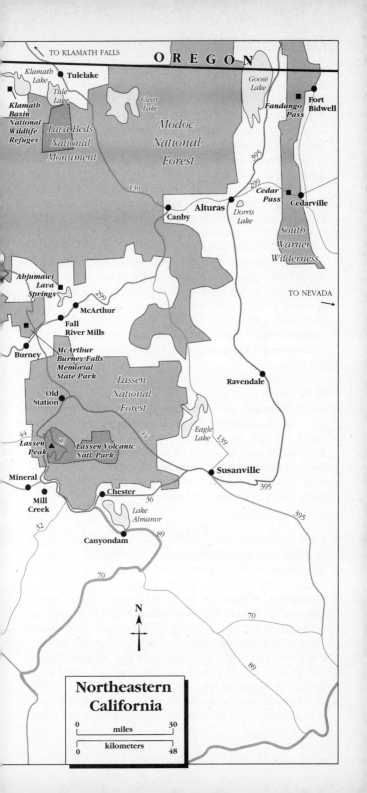

With big shade trees beside the Sacramento River, it's a lovely spot for a picnic, especially on those summer days when the thermometer exceeds 100 degrees F, as it frequently does in July and August. Red Bluff is also a treasure house of Victorian architecture, with dozens of ornate residences and business and public buildings dating from 1870 to 1890 scattered around downtown; the chamber of commerce distributes driving maps that identify many of them. **The Kelly-Griggs House Museum**, a classical Victorian gingerbread design, is open to the public. ▶ **The Faulkner House** offers bed-and-breakfast rooms in an 1890s Victorian home, and ▶ **Valu Inn** is a good 61-unit motel with a central location.

The Sacramento River, lifeblood of the valley, is also the focus of recreation in these river towns. Red Bluff's **City River Park** offers broad lawns sloping down to the river, picnic tables beneath big shade trees, and band concerts on summer weekends. A couple of miles south a diversion dam provides a salmon-viewing plaza where you can watch salmon climbing fish ladders on their way upstream to spawn. The **Riverside Restaurant** has outdoor dining overlooking the river.

Once you get beyond the interstate more than a few miles to the east or west, accommodations and restaurants are few and far between, yet the essence of this region is precisely the splendid scenery, historical sightseeing, and outdoor recreation that are remote from I-5. Both Red Bluff and Redding have a wide choice of facilities, so consider basing yourself in either city and making day trips to Lassen Volcanic National Park, to the three big lakes, and to the backcountry to the west and northeast.

Redding

Redding, 30 miles (48 km) north of Red Bluff, has a population of about 70,000 and is the commercial hub of the region. A string of quality chain lodgings— ▶ **Best Western Hilltop Inn,** ▶ **Days Inn,** ▶ **Holiday Inn-Redding,** ▶ **Motel Orleans,** ▶ **Motel 6,** ▶ **Oxford Suites,** ▶ **Red Lion Inn** —is conveniently located on Hilltop Drive, just off the freeway. (The Hilltop, Oxford Suites, and Red Lion are the best of these choices.) Some other options are the ▶ **Grand Manor Inn**, an all-suites hotel on a quiet side street in the same area and the ▶ **Vagabond Inn,** offering 71 motel units west of the freeway and close to downtown Redding. ▶ **Tiffany House** is a delightful Victorian bed and breakfast with hilltop views and the ▶ **Cabral House** bed and breakfast looks back to the era of the 1920s–1940s.

The Shasta-Cascade Wonderland Association (1250 Parkview Avenue, Redding, CA 96001; Tel: 916-243-2643 or 800-326-6944) and the Redding Convention and Visitors Bureau (777 Auditorium Drive, Redding, CA 96001; Tel: 916-225-4100 or 800-874-7562) are good sources of information on the city and all of the surrounding area. (Take the Highway 299 West exit from I-5 to the convention bureau.) The bureau offers a map detailing three driving tours of the city that include such historic architecture as the 1879 **James McCormick Residence** and the classic Mission Revival–style **Hotel Redding**. Other stops of interest include Caldwell Park, adjacent to the river, with its **Carter House Science Museum** (children's exhibits), and the **Redding Museum of Art and History** (Native American, pre-Columbian, and local art). The newly opened **Sacramento River Trail** is a paved loop of nearly five miles on both sides of the river through park-like surroundings. This walk is especially appealing in the early morning when the riverbanks are alive with birds.

You can make an unusual excursion from Redding to **Lake Shasta Caverns**, limestone caves high on a hillside above Shasta Lake. The three-hour round trip includes a boat-crossing of the lake and a guided walking tour of the lighted caverns, where you view flowstone, bacon rind, popcorn, and other formations typical of limestone caves via a route that is somewhat steep and rough. (Take the Lake Shasta Caverns exit from I-5 about 15 miles/24 km north of Redding.)

Redding has a delightful variety of restaurants, including Chinese, Japanese, French, Italian, and Mexican establishments. Recommended are **El Papagayo** (Mexican) at 460 North Market, **Nello's Place** (Italian) at 355 Bechelli Lane, **River City Bar and Grill** (Cajun/Creole) at 2151 Market, **Maxwell's** (upscale American/Continental), also on Market, and **The Hatch Cover** (American) at 202 Hemstead Drive. Two good choices for seafood are **Kenny's Seafood Grill** at 2705 Churn Creek Road and **Red Lobster** at 1345 Dana Drive.

Mount Shasta

North of Redding I-5 crosses an arm of Shasta Lake (see Big Lake Country below) and begins to climb; the broad highway swings wide on curves and winds its way through the mountains. Far below, the Sacramento River cuts a steep brush-covered canyon, and the Southern Pacific Railroad, route of

Amtrak's Coast Starlight, crisscrosses the river on spindly bridges and plunges into tunnels through the mountains.

Three stops on this stretch of highway are worth considering if you have the time. **Castle Crags State Park** features dramatic granite spires towering more than 4,000 feet above the river. The park has picnic spots and campsites, hiking trails, naturalist programs, and good views of the crags and Mount Shasta. The historic California-Oregon Toll Road passes through the park.

For train fans it just doesn't get much better than ▶ **Railroad Park Resort,** just beyond the state park. Twenty-three cabooses from various railroads are scattered around the resort's fifty landscaped acres. The cabooses have been completely refurbished as bedrooms and are comfortable and private; all have a private bath. The resort has splendid views of Castle Crags and includes a swimming pool, hot tub, wooded campground with RV hookups, and a 1920s dining car complete with arched ceiling and overhead fans. Dinner entrées range from pasta primavera to prime rib.

A few miles farther north on Interstate 5 is **Dunsmuir,** a ramshackle old railroad town squeezed in stair-step fashion into the narrow river canyon; its venerable downtown is in the National Register of Historic Places. Dunsmuir advertises itself as "The Home of the Purest Water on Earth," since the city water system gets its supply from nearby mountain springs. The **Dunsmuir Museum** has displays featuring railroad history. The ▶ **Dunsmuir Inn,** a delightful bed-and-breakfast establishment on the main street, provides a free ice cream cone to each guest from a shop in the same building.

Until the summer of 1991, the Sacramento River in the vicinity of Dunsmuir had a reputation as one of the great trout-fishing streams in California. On July 14 a toxic spill from a derailed railroad tank car killed everything in the river (including all the fish and shellfish and the insects on which they live) for a stretch of 40 miles from Box Canyon Dam to Shasta Lake. The river still remains closed to fishing.

From Dunsmuir I-5 climbs steeply out of the Sacramento River Canyon and comes face-to-face with the massive white bulk of Mount Shasta. Depending on the time of year you're here, the mountain may be glittering in sunshine or truncated, with its summit lost in the clouds.

EXPLORING MOUNT SHASTA

Shasta is a major recreation area, with skiing and snowmobiling in the winter and climbing, hiking, and mountain biking the rest of the year. **Mount Shasta Ski Park** is modest, with just two high-speed triple chairlifts serving 22 runs that drop from the 6,600-foot elevation to 5,500 feet at the day lodge, but what it lacks in sophisticated facilities, Mount Shasta makes up for as a low-key, uncrowded, and affordable family winter-sports area. Here you can cross-country ski, snowboard, sled, snowshoe, or toboggan, and not have to fight the crowds. In summer, ski runs become mountain-bike trails and the lifts take cyclists and sightseers up the mountain.

In **Mount Shasta City**, stop at the **Sisson Museum**, a combination of the oldest trout hatchery in the country and displays covering wildflowers, geology, weather, and other natural history. Another way to explore the Shasta area is to join the llama-packing trips that travel Shasta's trails from June through September. You walk, and your docile llama follows closely behind carrying your pack. Try **Rainbow Ridge Ranch** (P.O. Box 1079, Mount Shasta City, CA 96067; Tel: 916-926-5794) or **Shasta Llamas** (P.O. Box 1088, Mount Shasta City, CA 96067; Tel: 916-926-1146). **Shasta Mountain Guides** (1938 Hill Road, Mount Shasta City, CA 96067; Tel: 916-926-3117) leads climbs of Mount Shasta and Castle Crags as well as glacier seminars, photography workshops, and cross-country ski treks.

A short distance to the west, Lake Siskiyou, a dammed section of the Sacramento River, has swimming beaches, camping, and water sports. **Sisson-Callahan National Recreation Trail** here follows the river for nine miles to Deadfall Summit and ranks high for its spectacular views of Mount Shasta, Castle Crags, and the Trinity Alps.

STAYING NEAR MOUNT SHASTA

There are no accommodations at the ski area itself, but Mount Shasta City, on the west flank of the mountain, has a cluster of motels. Among the best are the ► **Swiss Holiday Lodge**, with just 21 units and fine views of the mountain, the ► **Best Western Tree House**, a large establishment with landscaped grounds, indoor pool, and restaurant, and the ► **Mountain Air Lodge**, with 38 units on shaded grounds.

McCloud

From Mount Shasta detour 10 miles (16 km) east on Highway 89 to McCloud. Once a wholly owned lumber company mill town (massive log buildings on the side streets once housed lumber company offices), it's now doing a thriving business as a recreation center. The original home of the company president now serves as ▶ **The McCloud Guest House**, an elegant 1907 country inn and upscale restaurant that lists among its guest activities, "mountain and cloud gazing." ▶ **Stoney Brook Inn**, another country bed and breakfast on the south shoulder of Mount Shasta, nestles among the pines. The McCloud River and nearby Lake McCloud are noted for their fine trout fishing; three modest waterfalls on the river plunge into a sheer-walled gorge south of town. **Ah-Di-Na Campground**, south of McCloud, is the remains of an Indian settlement and the ruins of a homestead of the William Randolph Hearst family.

As you continue north on I-5 from Mount Shasta City, you'll pass the nearly perfect volcanic cinder cone of **Black Butte**, a fairly young (about 10,000 years old) crater. The two-and-a-half-mile trail to the summit, built by the Civilian Conservation Corps in the 1930s, makes a nice respite from driving, and the view from the 6,325-foot summit is spectacular. You can see all the way to Mount McLaughlin in Oregon on a clear day.

Weed

In addition to enjoying breathtaking views of Mount Shasta to the southeast, **Weed**, a few miles north of Black Butte on I-5, lies at the junction of two of the three major routes to the Pacific Northwest (the third is the Redwood Country's U.S. 101). Interstate 5 continues north on the west side of the Cascade Mountains via Oregon's Rogue and Willamette river valleys to Portland and Seattle. This route is faster and generally enjoys better winter driving conditions, although it also tends to be wetter, cloudier, and cooler in the summertime. U.S. 97 takes the eastern path alongside the Cascades, passing through ranch and recreation country around Bend, Oregon, crossing the Columbia River east of Mount Hood, and transiting Washington's Yakima Valley wine country. Access to Portland is via the Columbia Gorge and to Seattle via the Cascade mountain passes. This route is warmer and drier in summer, colder in winter.

Weed offers a cluster of standard motels and restaurants close to the freeway. The ▶ **Sis-Q-Inn Motel** has splendid views of the mountain from most units. Nearby **Lake Shastina** has a full-fledged golf resort, with fairways flanked by pines and dominated by Mount Shasta, less than a dozen miles away. Lakeside houses and condominiums can be rented through ▶ **Lake Shastina Accommodations** (see Accommodations Reference).

Yreka

North of Weed, I-5 crosses a lovely high valley dotted with ranches, where cattle graze beside the road. Yreka (why-REE-ka) is worth considering for your overnight stop. This historic little town at the foot of the Siskiyou Mountains has good, conventional accommodations, several restaurants, and some intriguing things to see and do. The only serious barrier to north-south travel in winter is the crossing of the Siskiyou Mountains between Yreka and Ashland, Oregon. Several times each winter, snowstorms close 4,466-foot Siskiyou Summit for several hours or more—enough to make Yreka a welcome haven.

Shortly after the discovery of gold at Coloma, the much-sought-after element was found near Yreka in 1851, and enough prospectors had gathered by 1857 to justify giving the settlement a name: Thompson's Dry Diggings. Begin your exploration of Yreka at the **Siskiyou County Museum** (910 South Main Street), a small but outstanding collection of Gold Rush exhibits, Native American displays, a stagecoach and other pioneer vehicles, and a typical miner's cabin. At 311 Fourth Street, the county courthouse displays a dazzling array of gold nuggets taken in the area. Much of 19th-century downtown Yreka is preserved in a historic district bounded by Lane, Lennox, Third, and Gold streets; the old business blocks on Miner Street are especially photogenic. The **Miner Street Deli** features wall murals painted in 1910 by a local Russian immigrant and is said to be the oldest meat market in California.

From Memorial Day through Labor Day the **Blue Goose Short-Line Railroad**, featuring a 1915 Baldwin steam engine, provides passenger excursions on a three-hour round trip to the old railroad town of Montague, where there's time to stroll the single main street. For more information, Tel: (916) 842-4146.

Good choices among Yreka's lodgings are ▶ **Klamath Motor Lodge,** ▶ **Best Western Miner's Inn,** ▶ **Thunderbird Lodge**, or ▶ **Motel Orleans**—all conveniently located just off the freeway and with swimming pools. Most of Yreka's dining establishments are within walking distance of the city's motels: **Ming's** serves a variety of Chinese dishes in a dimly lit atmosphere; **Grandma's House** has an American menu served in an 1890s home; and **The Boston Shaft** offers a wide-ranging American menu.

The Klamath River

The Klamath River leaves Upper Klamath Lake in Oregon, swings southwestward into California, and cuts through Klamath National Forest, northwest of Yreka, to the sea. One of California's premier recreational rivers, the Klamath plunges in white-water cataracts through rocky canyons and dense forest, offering superb rafting and canoeing, kayaking, excellent fishing for steelhead and trout, and a pristine environment for hiking, camping, and wildlife viewing. Just north of Yreka, Highway 96 leaves I-5 to follow the river's north bank, then crosses over and hugs the south bank for most of the way west to the coast, where the river empties into the sea at Klamath (see the Redwood Country chapter).

Several recreational vehicle parks and rustic resorts are scattered along the river, including ▶ The Sportsman's Lodge, ▶ Oaks RV Park, ▶ Beaver Creek Lodge, and ▶ Young's Ranch Resort. Accommodations are simple and typically include housekeeping facilities with grocery, laundromat, gasoline, and fishing-tackle shops nearby. The emphasis here on river activities—fishing, rafting, boating, swimming—makes this a good choice for families who want a vacation strong on outdoor recreation. The Sportsman's Lodge has the only restaurant in the area. **Orange Torpedo Trips** (P.O. Box 1111, Grants Pass, OR 97526; Tel: 503-479-5061) and **Wilderness Adventures** (19504 Statton Acres Road, Lakehead, CA 96051; Tel: 800-323-RAFT) schedule rafting trips down the river. There are dozens of other rafting companies in the area; for information contact the Siskiyou County Visitor's Bureau, Tel: (916) 842-7857.

BIG LAKE COUNTRY

Drive north through the Sacramento Valley on any warm-weather weekend and you'll follow a procession of trailer-mounted boats—sleek racing boats, elegant cabin cruisers, modest fishing craft, and an occasional sailboat. They're heading for the Shasta country north and northwest of Redding.

Water—lots of it—is the reason most Californians come to this region. You'll find more recreational water here than any place north of San Francisco Bay, and, with the exception of Lake Tahoe, more than anywhere else in the state.

Shasta Lake

In the late 1930s, toward the end of the Great Depression, President Franklin Roosevelt's administration embarked on a series of vast hydro projects. In Northern California a huge concrete dam—Shasta—plugged the Sacramento River as it emerged from its river canyon just above Redding. Shasta Dam, completed in 1945, is the centerpiece of the Central Valley Project, a massive complex of dams, canals, and power and pumping plants that irrigates more than five million acres of the state's Sacramento and San Joaquin valleys and has made this region the richest farmland in the country. However, recreational demands on Shasta Lake, the lake created by the dam, are so great that they compete with hydroelectric and irrigation needs during periods of low water, when there's not enough for everybody.

Shasta Lake, the largest man-made lake in the state, is surrounded by steep red-clay hills covered with pine, manzanita, and chaparral. Lake waters back up into the Sacramento, McCloud, and Pitt rivers, plus Squaw Creek and dozens of smaller tributaries; the result is a many-armed lake with 365 miles of shoreline, ideal for houseboating, exploring by boat, and waterside camping at scores of secluded coves, inlets, and beaches. The steep hills and labyrinthine waterways have another benevolent effect for boaters: They tend to break up any wind, making the lake unusually calm for its size.

Shasta and its neighbors, Whiskeytown and Trinity lakes (see below), constitute the **Whiskeytown-Shasta-Trinity National Recreation Area.** The U.S. Forest Service maintains several waterside campsites around the lake, most of them accessible by road, as well as boat-launching ramps. Shasta has an open season year-round for fishing the 19 species that inhabit the lake, including rainbow and brown trout; silver salmon (landlocked); largemouth, smallmouth, and spotted bass; bluegill; crappie; and catfish. **Shasta Dam Visitor Center** (just off I-5) has displays depicting the construction of the dam and its hydroelectric generating plant as well as the Central Valley Project. Guided tours of the galleries inside the dam and the powerhouse at the base of the spillway are sometimes available; inquire at the visitors' center.

HOUSEBOATING ON SHASTA LAKE

Houseboating and power boating are the favorite activities on this lake, and at least ten firms rent boats (both the Shasta-Cascade Wonderland Association and the Redding

Convention and Visitors Bureau furnish lists). Houseboating veterans wax enthusiastic about mooring in a remote cove that you have all to yourself, jumping over the side to swim in the cool waters of the lake, and cooking up a barbecue on an evening when a big full moon climbs above the ridge and lights a path on the lake.

The popular houseboats sleep five to eighteen people and come fully equipped with kitchen, toilet and shower, and utensils. Most have a gas barbecue, rooftop sunning deck, and covered bow deck, while some even come with television, VCR, and stereo tape deck. Prices between mid-May and mid-September range anywhere from $1,200 to $2,000 per week, somewhat less in other seasons. Among the largest firms renting houseboats are ▶ **Seven Crown Resorts**, located at Bridge Bay Marina (P.O. Box 1409, Boulder City, NV 89005; Tel: 800-PLAY-NOW); ▶ **Lakeshore Resort and Marina** (Star Route Box 760, Lakehead, CA 96051; Tel: 916-238-2301); ▶ **Holiday Floatels**, at Packers Bay Marina (16814 Packers Bay Road, Lakehead, CA 96051; Tel: 916-245-1002); ▶ **Holiday Harbor** (P.O. Box 112, O'Brien, CA 96070; Tel: 800-776-BOAT); and ▶ **Jones Valley Resort** (22300 Jones Valley Marina Drive, Redding, CA 96003; Tel: 916-275-7950). All of these marinas also rent power boats for fishing or cruising. The single motel on the lake is ▶ **Bridge Bay Resort**, located just off I-5 about 12 miles (19 km) north of Redding. Seven other marina-resorts around the lake offer cabins, and eight lakeside resorts have full-hookup recreational vehicle camping.

Whiskeytown Lake

Spreading over 3,200 acres in the brush-covered hills 8 miles (13 km) west of Redding, Whiskeytown is the smallest of the three lakes in the recreation area, and, unlike the other two, remains nearly full during the heavily used summer months. For the visitor Whiskeytown is quieter than Shasta and is best suited for swimming, sailing, canoeing, windsurfing, and fishing for trout, bass, and kokanee (landlocked sockeye salmon). A visitors' center perches on a bluff overlooking the lake; ranger-guided walks, gold-panning demonstrations, and illustrated evening programs are scheduled at Oak Bottom Amphitheater during the summer months. There are two campgrounds beside the lake and two in the hills to the south, as well as several picnic sites and sandy beaches ideal for sunning or swimming.

President John F. Kennedy dedicated Whiskeytown Dam in 1963, and if you're a Kennedy admirer you will want to detour the mile from the visitors' center to the dam to hear tape-recorded excerpts from his speech and view the bas-relief plaque that details the accomplishments of his administration. Just beyond the western end of the lake, **Tower House Historic District** consists of abandoned Gold Rush–era mine workings, the 1852 Camden House, and the site of an early hotel. Detour three miles north to **French Gulch**, a photogenic, ramshackle old settlement from the 1850s, situated on the original California-Oregon Trail. (The historic French Gulch Hotel is scheduled to open as a bed-and-breakfast inn.)

Shasta

The 47-mile (75-km) drive west from Redding to Weaverville, via Highway 299, is loaded with historical sightseeing of the Gold Rush era. Barely 6 miles (10 km) beyond Redding, the red-brick walls and iron-shuttered doors of Shasta (also called "Old Shasta" to avoid confusion with Mt. Shasta City) flank both sides of the highway. There isn't much left of the old town, but what's there is well worth stopping to explore. If you're a photographer, try to arrive early in the morning or late in the afternoon, when long shadows throw the rugged old walls into bold relief.

Now preserved as a State Historic Park, Shasta began as a boomtown named Reading Springs after the discovery of gold nearby in 1848 by Major Pierson B. Reading. Because it lay astride the main wagon-and-stage route north to Oregon, it thrived until the railroad bypassed it with a route through Redding in the 1870s.

Many of the dozen or so buildings are roofless relics but have signs to identify them. Litsch Store still operates as a museum store, its shelves stocked with vintage top hats, axe handles, stove pipes, barrels of whiskey, and patent medicine. Across the street the Masonic Hall, California's oldest lodge, chartered in 1852, still holds meetings. The highlight of the old town is the 1855 Shasta County Courthouse, a well-preserved building operated as a museum by the state parks department. In addition to the completely furnished courtroom and basement jail, the museum displays one of the best collections of California landscape paintings in the state, including works by Frederick Shaefer, Charles Hittell, and Charles Christian Dahlgren. One curiosity is a pistol used by abolitionist John Brown in his raid on the Harper's Ferry Arsenal in 1859.

Beyond Shasta the highway passes Whiskeytown Lake, then climbs its way over Buckhorn Summit. Twisting and turning as it ascends, the road provides splendid views of the surrounding countryside. You can almost hear teamsters cracking whips and urging on the teams of horses and mules that struggled over these hills carrying supplies to the gold miners. After driving this route to Weaverville, you shouldn't be surprised that Trinity County boasts it has no freeways and no traffic signals.

Weaverville

Weaverville has a bit more bustle than it did a century ago, and the strip of brightly signed businesses south of town is beginning to change the look of the place. Still, the false-front buildings and covered sidewalks in the heart of town look very similar to those in California's Gold Country. The town was founded in 1849, the year after gold was discovered on the Trinity River by the same Reading after whom Reading Springs (Shasta) was named. More than four dozen homes and public and business buildings date from the 19th century. You can pick up a free walking-tour map at the Trinity County Chamber of Commerce, 317 Main Street; Tel: (916) 623-6101.

Weaverville Joss House State Historic Park is the most unusual and most popular attraction in town. Set in the trees just off Main Street, this ornate wooden structure is typical of many Chinese houses of worship built last century to serve Chinese miners in the Gold Rush country. It's the oldest continually used Chinese temple in California and is considered the finest historic temple remaining in North America. A ranger-guided tour leads you into the dimly lit interior for an explanation of the shrines, banners, and symbols. One of the extremely rare "dogs of foo" (small idols in the shape of lion-like dogs), stolen from the joss house many years ago, was recently returned anonymously.

Just down the street, the **J. J. Jackson Memorial Museum** features pioneer and gold-mining displays, a large collection of old bottles, a miner's cabin, and a restored, steam-operated stamp mill. Other attractions include the High-lands Art Center; Trinity County Courthouse, dating from 1857, the oldest courthouse in continual use in the state; and the ornate Weaverville Bandstand, built in 1902 and still used on the Fourth of July and other civic occasions. The

Weaverville Drugstore, established in 1851, is the oldest drugstore still operating in California.

If you're a fan of old-fashioned ice-cream concoctions (especially ice-cream sodas), stop in **The Confectionery** on Main Street, which has operated continually since 1891. Among their specialties are the sinfully rich, multilayered Weaver Bally and Bully Choop.

If it's lunchtime, consider the **Pacific Brewery Café**, serving salads and sandwiches in an 1855 brick brewery, **The Mustard Seed**'s eclectic breakfast and lunch menu that ranges from quiche to Mexican dishes, or, adjacent to the bandstand, **The Village Station**, which offers soup and sandwiches.

The best among the town's handful of conventional motels are ▶ **The 49er** and the newly constructed ▶ **Weaverville Victorian Inn**. For bed and breakfast in a 19th-century house, try ▶ **Granny's House**.

Trinity Lake and the Trinity Alps

North of Weaverville, California Route 3 runs for about 100 miles (160 km) through some of the most rugged and wildly beautiful country in the state to return you to I-5 at Yreka. This is a scenically rewarding route, but the road is two lanes all the way, narrow and steep in spots; plan to spend the better part of a day en route. **Trinity Alps Wilderness Area**, the third largest in California, flanks the road to the west and is a destination for hiking and horse- and llama-packing trips that depart from the tiny towns of Trinity Center and Coffee Creek. Etna and Fort Jones are departure points for trips into nearby **Marble Mountain Wilderness**. No motorized vehicles are permitted in this vast mountain and forest region.

Recommended packers and guides in this area include:

- Bryan/Sherman. 4125 Eastside Road, Etna, CA 96027; Tel: (916) 467-3261.
- Heart D Guide and Pack Service. 356 Bridge Street, Fort Jones, CA 96032; Tel: (916) 468-5548.
- Kleaver Pack Station. 8033 Big Springs Road, Montague, CA 96064; Tel: (916) 459-5426.
- McBroom & Co. Packers and Guides. 28904 Sawyers Bar Road, Etna, CA 96027; Tel: (916) 462-4617.
- Meamber Creek Pack Station. 9317 Scott River Road, Fort Jones, CA 96032; Tel: (916) 468-5488.
- Quartz Valley Pack Outfit. 12712 Quartz Valley Road, Fort Jones, CA 96032; Tel: (916) 468-2592.

- Six Pak Packers. P.O. Box 301, Weaverville, CA 96093; Tel: (916) 623-6314.
- Steve Riede's Fishing Adventures. P.O. Box 29, Horse Creek, CA 96045; Tel: (916) 496-3652.
- Trinity Outfitters. P.O. Box 1973, Weaverville, CA 96093; Tel: (916) 623-2476.
- Wilderness Packers. P.O. Box 405, Happy Camp, CA 96039; Tel: (916) 493-2793.

Trinity Lake, the third lake in the national recreation area, is actually two adjoining lakes—Clair Engle (usually referred to as Trinity) and Lewiston. Both lakes are even prettier and quieter than either Shasta or Whiskeytown. Deep, cold, and ringed by steep, conifer-clad hillsides, Lewiston is a bit chilly for swimming, but trout love it. Trinity is warmer and an outstanding smallmouth bass fishery. Lewiston's western shore has four Forest Service campgrounds, rustic resorts, and an RV park. Houseboat-rental firms are scattered along the lake. The town of Lewiston dates from the mid-1800s and still has several historic wooden buildings standing, including antiques shops and a general store.

Trinity Center, the small community at the northern end of Trinity Lake, features the Scott Museum, with small but excellent pioneer, Native American, and barbed-wire collections. ▶ **Wyntoon Resort**, on the lake, has housekeeping cottages, RV campsites, and rental boats. ▶ **Trinity Alps Resort** also has cabins on the lake. Other rustic resorts nearby include ▶ **Bonanza King Resort,** ▶ **Coffee Creek Chalet**, and ▶ **Coffee Creek Guest Ranch** (where rates include all meals), all on Coffee Creek to the north of Trinity Lake, and ▶ **Ripple Creek Cabins,** on Ripple Creek overlooking Trinity River. All are the kind of quiet, cozy places you might build for yourself as a vacation cabin in these mountains.

Scott Valley, a lovely 28-mile-long valley of pastures full of fat cattle, big barns, and stacks of newly mown hay, lies at the northern end of California Route 3. **Etna**, originally called Rough and Ready, is the largest town in the valley and seems frozen somewhere in the early part of this century. The town is loaded with venerable architecture to tempt your camera; pick up a free guide pamphlet at Scott Valley Drug, 511 Main Street.

At Fort Jones stop at the Fort Jones Museum for its excellent collections of Native American basketry and stone mortars and pestles. Nearby, the Doll Museum displays more than 6,000 dolls from many different countries. Yreka and the intersection with I-5 are a few miles north of Fort Jones.

LASSEN VOLCANIC NATIONAL PARK

When Washington's Mount St. Helens blew its top on May 18, 1980, it shocked the nation. The awesome spectacle of nature beyond control unnerved many because of where it happened—in the continental United States. Mainland Americans are comfortable with volcanic eruptions in Hawaii, which seems distant and exotic—not in their backyards. Yet, for some people, the memory of another mainland volcano eruption is still alive—one that blasted the skies of Northern California. Between 1914 and 1921 Lassen Peak erupted almost continually, first in flows of hot lava and mud that washed down its flanks into the valleys below, then, on May 22, 1915, in air blasts preceding avalanches that leveled trees and sent a towering mushroom cloud of ash more than 20,000 feet aloft. Today Lassen and the national volcanic park that surrounds it are quiet; the volcano is not extinct, just dormant, as the dozens of hot springs, steam vents, and boiling mud pots in the park testify.

Lassen is a gentle park, the mountain's scarred slopes covered with brush and trees, its meadows deep with grass and wildflowers, its streams running clear. The rehabilitation that has taken place over the past three-quarters of a century is really quite remarkable and provides a preview of what may eventually happen at Mount St. Helens.

There are a number of reasons to schedule a trip to Lassen. The park offers excellent outdoor recreation—fishing, horseback riding (for Drakesbad Ranch guests), hiking, camping—and its volcanic features make for fascinating sightseeing. But one of the strongest incentives is its relative serenity compared to other Western national parks. In 1988, for example, just half a million people visited Lassen compared to the more than three million who visited Yosemite.

EXPLORING LASSEN VOLCANIC NATIONAL PARK

Two state highways lead to the park's north and south entrances. From Red Bluff it's 47 miles (75 km) east via Highway 36 to Mineral and park headquarters. It's exactly the same distance to the north entrance from Redding east via Highway 44. There are no conventional accommodations in the park itself (other than Drakesbad Guest Ranch in a remote eastern valley; see below), and motel facilities near the entrances are somewhat limited. Still, if you find everything booked up on a busy summer weekend you can easily base yourself in Red Bluff or Redding and make the park a day trip. Both approaches from the west climb gradually into the foothills through stands of pine and hillsides covered with manzanita and past ruins of mining operations.

California 89, the Lassen Park Road, loops through the western third of the park from both the north and south entrances, encircling all but the western side of this 10,457-foot mountain. Pick up a copy of the road guide at either entrance station; it provides mile-by-mile driving information keyed to 67 numbered roadside markers (numbered from the south entrance). Some caution is required: The road is wide but steep and winding in places with sharp drop-offs, and you can encounter patches of ice in the shady places as late as June. It's 30 miles (48 km) through the park and 34 miles (54 km) between Route 89's junctions with routes 36 and 44. Allow a minimum of one and a half hours for this drive with no stops, a bit more if the road is busy with sightseers on a midsummer weekend. But, as with most national parks, the key to enjoying Lassen is to get out of your car and walk or hike the trails to its attractions.

From the southwest entrance, the road climbs more than 1,400 feet in the first 6 miles (10 km). You'll have barely shifted out of first gear before you reach the first attraction, **Sulphur Works**. Filling the air with the smell of rotten eggs, a sulphur-laden mist emerges from dozens of vents in the ground. A short signed nature trail leads to bubbling hot springs, gaseous fumaroles, and plopping mud pots. In the next several miles the road twists and turns to give you fine views of the landscape to the south, west, and northwest; this stretch is one of the best in the park for photos. In addition to Lassen, you'll see 9,235-foot Brokeoff Mountain, Little Hot Springs Valley, and Mill Creek Canyon. Pristine Emerald Lake and Lake Helen, at 8,000 feet and 8,162 feet respectively, lie right beside the road.

One of the park's most popular sights is **Bumpass Hell**, the largest area of geothermal activity in the park. From the parking lot a 1½-mile self-guiding nature trail leads to a Dante-esque scene of hot springs, steam vents, and mud pots. The trail is an easy one, climbing about 500 feet and descending about 250 feet en route, crossing the flank of ancient Mount Tehama for excellent views westward.

About 7½ miles (12 km) from the south entrance you will reach the parking lot and trailhead for the **Lassen Peak Trail**. This 2.3-mile trail to the top, one of the best hikes in the park, is not difficult, but it does climb about 2,000 feet on a steady grade; you should allow half a day if you're going to take it. Once on top you have sweeping views of the vast volcanic landscape stretching away on all sides. During the summer rangers are often on hand at the peak and at Bumpass Hell to explain the geologic features you are viewing. In this case you can see an example of each of the four types of volcanoes found in the world from Lassen Peak's summit. The park's newspaper, available free at entrance stations, lists the schedule of talks at various locations.

As you continue driving toward the summit of the park road you encounter more and more vegetation, especially red fir, lodgepole pine, and western pine. At several places the road opens out for top-of-the-world views of Warner Valley and Lake Almanor to the east. Dersch Meadows is bright with wildflowers in July and August and is one of the best places in the park to spot deer, in contrast to the Devastated Area, the most visible evidence of the 1915 eruption, where you can still see some of the old tree trunks felled by the avalanches and mud flows (all pointing away from the crater). Just beyond, at Hot Rock, rests a huge boulder, measuring 10 by 15 feet and weighing 300 tons, that was carried by a mud flow five miles down the mountain by the 1915 blast and was still scalding hot 40 hours later. The road descends the last few miles to the north entrance, through stands of white fir, Jeffrey pine, incense cedar, ponderosa pine, and manzanita, to Manzanita Lake, a favorite destination for anglers and canoeists. Manzanita and Reflection lakes are excellent vantage points from which to photograph the mountain's reflection in the lakes' waters.

The Backcountry

The eastern two-thirds of the park is wilderness, studded with a lovely chain of lakes and laced with good hiking trails. No matter when you go, you're likely to have this backcountry mainly to yourself. One of the best overnight routes begins at Summit Lake, proceeds to Twin Lake, and ends at Echo Lake, for eight miles filled with beautiful wildflowers, terrific views, and excellent lakeside stopping spots. A dirt spur road enters the park at the southeastern corner and reaches Juniper Lake, largest and deepest of the park's lakes at an elevation of 6,792 feet. At the northeast corner, Butte Lake, reached via a dirt road from Highway 44, is noted for rainbow trout fishing.

Lassen offers eight developed campgrounds, none with recreational-vehicle hookups. The campgrounds at Manzanita and Summit lakes are the most popular and often fill up early in the day in summer. There's fast-food service at Lassen Summer Chalet, at the southwest entrance, and fast food, groceries, and camping supplies available at the store at Manzanita Lake near the northwest entrance.

Other than campgrounds, ▶ **Drakesbad Guest Ranch**, in Warner Valley at the southeastern edge of the park, is the only overnight accommodation in Lassen. The venerable ranch, which, with its galvanized-roof ranch house and pole fences, looks as if it belongs in a Western movie, has been in operation for more than a century and offers horseback riding, a swimming pool filled from hot springs, and hearty meals served on the American Plan. Rooms are modest, some without electricity, but the ranch is quite popular; reservations, as much as a year in advance, are advised (the ranch operates only from mid-June to mid-October). Warner Valley itself, with its timber-lined trails, soft meadows, and Boiling Springs Lake, is a bit of a Shangri-la in this park; it's also accessible to campers.

Lassen Off Season

Lassen operates year round, but the main park road is closed by snow from November until snowplows can finish clearing it, usually by Memorial Day. Park nature programs, which include hikes, campfire talks, star-gazing programs, children's activities, and nature and cultural demonstrations, get into full swing in mid-June and continue through Labor Day weekend.

For seekers of solitude, September and October are delightful, with their warm sunny days and cool crisp nights, when park trails are nearly empty and fall foliage, especially at lower elevations, provides a bright backdrop. On winter weekends, **Lassen Park Ski Area**, at the southwest entrance, operates a chairlift and surface tows; facilities include a rental shop, instruction, and a cafeteria. For the adventurous, the park's snow-covered roads and trails offer ideal cross-country skiing conditions. Several signed routes begin from Manzanita Lake and from Lassen Summer Chalet and wind through stunning park scenery mantled in white. On weekends rangers lead snowshoe walks and programs on winter wildlife and survival techniques.

South of Lassen

A good choice for overnight accommodations on Highway 36 southwest of the park entrance is ▶ **Lassen Mineral Lodge**, a motel with pool, restaurant, store, and tennis courts.

Follow Highway 36 6 miles (10 km) east from Mineral, south of the park's southern entrance, to reach Mill Creek and the best choice of lodging near the park: the fine meadow and forest views of ▶ **Mill Creek Resort**, cozy and rustic ▶ **Deer Creek Lodge**, ▶ **Black Forest Lodge** (offering 14 rooms and excellent views), and ▶ **St. Bernard Lodge** (a seven-room chalet that has been operating since 1929). Good choices for dining include St. Bernard Lodge (locally famous for its three-quarter-pound hamburger on a homemade bun), Fire Mountain Lodge, and Black Forest Lodge, which specializes in German cuisine.

Lake Almanor, and its little resort town of **Chester**, is the most significant water-recreation area east of Lake Shasta. Situated at a summer-cool 4,500 feet, fringed with pine forest, and dotted with rustic resorts and vacation homes, Lake Almanor is a popular summer destination for fishing and boating. It's close enough to Lassen National Park to make it a good choice for a base from which to combine aquatic recreation and park sightseeing. The 52-square-mile lake boasts a summertime surface temperature in the mid-70 degrees F, making it comfortable for swimming, and local fishing tackle shops will tell you where to rent a boat and give you advice on the best techniques for catching the lake's trout, kokanee, bass, catfish, and perch. In Chester, ▶ **Antlers Motel**, ▶ **Seneca Motel**, and ▶ **Cinnamon Teal Bed and Breakfast** are modest but good choices for lodging. Lakeshore accommodations (suitable for families) include ▶ **Plumas Pines Resort**, ▶ **Lassen View Resort**, and ▶ **Almanor Lakeside Lodge**—all tucked away in the woods on the east and west shores. For unusual surroundings for dinner, try the **Timber House**, constructed of huge wooden blocks; beef and seafood entrées are featured. **The Old Mill Café**, in nearby Westwood, features hearty meals, especially breakfast.

From here it's about 35 miles (56 km) east on Highway 36 to Susanville, the gateway to the Lonely Corner (see below).

NORTH OF LASSEN
Burney and Old Station

About 50 miles (82 km) east of Redding, Highway 299 crests at 4,368-foot Hatchet Mountain Pass, revealing a lovely mountain valley below, and the little town of Burney. Burney's focus has always been the lumber industry, but because it lies near the intersection of east-west Highway 299 and north-south Highway 89 from Lassen, it thrives on vacationers, both those just passing through and those who use it as a base for the superb fishing and hiking country in Burney Basin that surrounds it, especially in Lassen National Forest and the Thousand Lakes Wilderness to the south. The Chamber of Commerce (37477 Main Street in Burney) distributes a walking-and-driving tour guide that describes nine tours in the area. **McArthur-Burney Falls Memorial State Park** features a 129-foot waterfall along Burney Creek that plunges over a mossy rim into a narrow, rocky gorge below. Theodore Roosevelt, never at a loss for superlatives, called the falls one of the wonders of the world—a bit of an overstatement, but they are lovely. A mile-long, signed nature trail takes you down to the base of the falls, which are often enveloped in mist and rainbows. They face northward and are shaded most of the day, making photography difficult except on overcast days, but try for early-morning light.

The site of the California Stage Company's Hat Creek Station in the 1850s, **Old Station** (south of Burney on Highway 89) is the location of the University of California Radio Astronomy Observatory, whose dish antennas you can see on a nearby hill. Other points of interest at hand include Subway Cave, an underground lava tube, common in these parts, but noteworthy for its "lavacicles," pendants of lava that dripped from the ceiling and solidified (it's not illuminated, so take a flashlight or lantern), and Spattercone Trail, which departs from Hat Creek Campground north of town and leads for two miles through scenes of fairly recent volcanic activity. The **Hat Creek Playhouse** (on Highway 89) presents little theater on summer weekends. You can stay overnight at the ▶ **Mount Lassen Inn**, a bed and breakfast well known for the quality of its home-cooked meals (for inn guests only). The inn is closed January through March.

Fall River Mills

Not much more than a wide spot in the road northeast of Burney on 299, Fall River Mills takes the honors as the fly-fishing capital of this part of California—the fishing here is legendary, drawing eager anglers from all over the West. Not surprisingly, the town boasts several fly shops where you can hire a local guide to take you to the best spots and recommend what flies to use. The four buildings of Fort Crook Museum display Native American artifacts, antique furniture, a blacksmith's shop, and an old jail. **Ahjumawi Lava Springs State Park**, 3 miles (5 km) north of McArthur (just up the road from Fall River Mills), is a most unusual state park: It can only be reached by boat (available at Rick's Lodge and the Fall River Hotel—see below). The park's 6,000 acres of wilderness encompass Big Lake, Ja-She Creek, and the Tule, Fall, and Pit rivers. As you'd expect of a park that is so well protected, the wildlife is abundant and is one of the primary reasons visitors make the extra effort to get here. Birds include bald eagles, ospreys, and herons, and large herds of deer forage along the lake shoreline.

▶ **Rick's Lodge**, a rustic getaway nine miles northwest of Fall River Mills on County Road A-19, specializes in fishing vacations, offering a fly shop, guide service, boat rentals, fly-fishing school, and a fly-tying bench in each of the 12 rooms. To get to Rick's, take A-20 5½ miles (9 km) north of town to reach A-19. In town you can stay overnight at the ▶ **Fall River Hotel**; the dining room serves hearty meals and hotel staff will make arrangements for licensed fishing guides and boats.

The climatic and topographic changes in this part of California can be abrupt. Within a score of miles east of the cool, forested country around Fall River Mills you enter open, rolling sagebrush rangeland and near-desert, where summertime temperatures are scorchers. The gateway to this area, however, is not Burney/Fall River Mills, but Susanville, to the area's south, about 35 miles (56 km) east of Chester and Lake Almanor on Highway 36.

THE LONELY CORNER

Once a rough-and-tumble town of the 19th century, **Susanville** is now devoted to the cattle and sheep industries, and is becoming increasingly popular as an outfitting and jumping-off spot for fishing, hunting, hiking, horse packing, and backcountry exploring in nearby Lassen National Forest and Caribou Peak Wilderness, adjacent to Lassen Volcanic National Park. It is also the gateway to the so-called Lonely Corner, the far northeastern part of the state.

Eagle Lake, one of the largest natural lakes in California, is 16 miles (26 km) north of Susanville; situated at the 5,000-foot level in an isolated valley, it's a favorite destination for anglers, who come to catch the native trout that thrive in its alkaline waters and can weigh up to 11 pounds. The lake is also a paradise for wildlife viewing, with mule deer, antelope, porcupine, and small animals often observed along the shore, and for bird-watching, including grebe, pelicans, gulls, Canada geese, and ospreys, which perch high in the trees and swoop down to the lake surface to grab a glistening trout in their talons.

In Susanville, **Roop Fort and Lassen Museum** has pioneer, Native American, and logging exhibits housed in a small wooden fort constructed during local skirmishes in 1854. For hikers there's the **Bizz Johnson Trail**, which follows the old grade of the Fernley and Lassen Railroad through tall timber to the little mill town of Westwood, 21 miles west. **Historic Uptown Susanville** (36 South Lassen Street) provides free maps for self-guided walking tours of the old town.

Adequate motels in Susanville include ▶ **Best Western Trailside Inn**, ▶ **River Inn Motel**, and ▶ **Super Budget Motel**. The ▶ **Hotel Mt. Lassen** dates from 1927, was restored in 1950, and includes an old-fashioned Western saloon with stained-glass windows and a restaurant specializing in Italian cuisine. ▶ **Roseberry House Bed and Breakfast** offers three guest rooms in a 1902 residence.

▶ **Spanish Springs Ranch**, northeast of Susanville off Highway 395, is about as close to the Old West as you're likely to get in the 1990s. Sprawling over sagebrush and juniper country, this working ranch offers guests an authentic Western experience that includes cattle and horse drives, a buffalo herd, rodeos, hayrides, cookouts (all meals are included), horsepacking trips into the backcountry, and trout fishing. Guests can also participate in rounding up cattle, branding, and other ranch chores. You can choose from accommodations in a big log lodge, cabins, a bunkhouse for children, or satellite ranches that are several miles from the main facility.

Exploring the Lonely Corner

At Susanville the demarcation line between forested mountain environment and sagebrush desert is sharply drawn.

Within a half-dozen miles you descend from cool pine forest, pass through Susanville heading east, and emerge onto bunchgrass rangeland that soon gives way to less hospitable sagebrush country. If you squint your eyes against the sun and look east, you'll see the terrain flattening out into the Great Basin. Those white patches you see 20 or more miles away are alkali flats backdropped by a haze of purple mountains on the horizon. This is mind-expanding country, the kind of wide-open spaces where you can drive for hours and seldom encounter a town worthy of the classification. Drive north on U.S. 395 from Susanville to Alturas, for example, and you'll find the traffic so sparse you can ease up to within 50 yards of a herd of pronghorn antelope standing beside the road without startling them.

This is also cowboy country, with vast ranches sprawling across thousands of acres of rangeland. If you're lucky you may encounter one on horseback following a fence line or herding cattle, but don't be disappointed if the cowboys you see are driving pickup trucks instead of riding horses. Still, they're plying their outdoor trade on these ranches with the same skills they've used for more than a century.

The other figure indigenous to this landscape is the sheepherder, for this is also sheep-ranching country. As you travel along, you may encounter bands of woollies grazing along a hillside followed by a solitary man and a black-and-white dog. The man is probably Basque; the dog, a Border collie.

The Basques came to the West from their native home in the Pyrénées in search of gold, but most came after the great bonanzas were over and instead turned to the vocation they knew best, sheepherding. For generations they lived in curious canvas-covered wagons while on the range (you can see one preserved in the Klamath County Museum in Klamath Falls, Oregon), but these days they're likely to live in small travel trailers pulled behind battered pickup trucks. You're most likely to see them and their herds along U.S. 395, in the 110 miles (176 km) between Susanville and Alturas, and along California Route 139, southeast of the town of Tulelake (see below).

Alturas and Surprise Valley

Modoc County has lots of elbow room. Northeasternmost of the 58 California counties, it covers a land area of a little more than 4,373 square miles—with a county population of about 9,500. That makes a population density of about two people per square mile; Alturas, the county seat, accounts for about 3,400 of those residents.

Situated in the broad valley of the Pit River, Alturas, 110 miles (176 km) north of Susanville via U.S. 395, is a town with a Western flavor. Saturday mornings the curbs are lined with pickup trucks as ranchers come to town to shop, and restaurants tend to serve extra-large portions, heavy on the beef. Focusing on that Western heritage, the **Modoc County Historical Museum** features a large collection of firearms and cattle brands in addition to a steam locomotive and memorabilia from the Modoc War (discussed below).

Basque cuisine covers a broad range but typically includes lamb (sometimes boiled, sometimes barbecued), soups, stews, sausages, beans, and the traditional sheepherder's bread. You can try Basque food—and the spicy Basque Picon punch—served family style at the **Brass Rail** in Alturas. The frontier-style **Niles Hotel** includes a traditional cowboy saloon, historic photos on the walls, an arcaded sidewalk outside, and prime rib and steak. Alturas is not big enough to have a wide variety of accommodations, but the ▶ **Best Western Trailside Inn** and the ▶ **Dunes** offer reasonably priced, conventional motel accommodations. ▶ **Dorris House** has bed-and-breakfast rooms in a 1912 ranch house on the shore of nearby Dorris Lake.

From downtown Alturas you can look east and see the snow-capped peaks of the Warner Mountains, at the extreme eastern edge of the state. Just beyond the mountains lies **Surprise Valley**, named by westward-bound pioneers because its lushness came as such a pleasant surprise after crossing the trackless miles of Nevada desert. If you have a day to spend exploring, consider driving a 98-mile (157-km) round trip from Alturas east over 6,350-foot Cedar Pass to Surprise Valley, returning west via 6,250-foot Fandango Pass (14 of the 19 miles between Fort Bidwell and Highway 395 are unpaved but usually in good condition; inquire locally).

Cedarville, the largest settlement in Surprise Valley, looks as though it hasn't changed much in this century; several of its well-maintained residences date from the 1880s. Stop at the Cressler and Bonner Trading Post, the 1865 log cabin that housed the first mercantile store in the county, then head north 25 miles (40 km) to Fort Bidwell, a former cavalry post established in 1862. The ▶ **Fort Bidwell Hotel and Restaurant**, circa 1906, operates as a bed-and-breakfast inn, with a restaurant open to non-guests. A portion of the Warner Mountains is protected as the South Warner Wilderness, an alpine area studded with mountains over 8,000 feet high and laced with trails. **Modoc Wildlife Adventures** (P.O. Box 1882, Alturas, CA 96101; Tel: 916-233-3777) leads backcountry horse-packing trips into the wilderness.

Lava Beds National Monument

One of the most tragic stories in Western history was played out in the 1870s in what is now Lava Beds National Monument. A band of Modoc Indians, under a leader named Kientpoos (also called Captain Jack), unable to live with their traditional enemies, the Klamaths and the Paiutes, on the Klamath Indian Reservation, fled to the jumbled terrain of Lava Beds. In the ensuing negotiations with the U.S. Army for their surrender, the Modocs killed two of the negotiators, General Canby and Reverend Thomas. For nearly five months the Modoc band, which never numbered more than 51 warriors, plus women and children, managed to hold off an army of more than 1,000 troopers equipped with modern weapons and artillery, but the end result was inevitable. The Modocs managed to escape from Lava Beds, only to be caught two months later; Captain Jack and three of his lieutenants were hanged, while other survivors were sent to a reservation in Oklahoma where their identity as a tribe ceased to exist. As one old Modoc chief said, "Once my people were as the sand along the shore. Now I call to them and only the wind answers."

The National Monument combines the history of the Modoc War with the unusual geology of vulcanism in a primeval and dramatic landscape that brings to mind the earth's beginnings. Located on the northern flank of a shield volcano known as Medicine Lake Volcano, the monument is significant geologically for the many different volcanic phenomena you can see in such a small area (only about 47,000 acres).

EXPLORING LAVA BEDS
NATIONAL MONUMENT

Follow Highway 299 west from Alturas 19 miles (30 km) to its junction with Highway 139 at Canby, then take 139 northwest about 50 miles (80 km) to the entrance of the park. Driving the main park road is the easiest way to get an overview of the monument in the space of about two hours, but if you have more time, stop and walk the short trails to natural attractions that interest you. Beginning at the northeast entrance off Highway 139 south of the town of Tulelake, follow the paved route 22 miles (35 km) to the north

entrance, then cut across the lava fields to exit at the southeast entrance, where the visitors' center is located. Signs
along the way describe the historical and geological highlights.

The first (northern) stretch of road concerns Native American history and connects the main sites of the Modoc War.
About a mile before the entrance, a graded dirt road leads to
a large group of prehistoric Indian petroglyphs—stick figures, circles with rays, and squiggly lines—carved in rock
over an area of about two city blocks. At Captain Jack's
Stronghold you can follow trails leading into the lava beds to
reach what was the Modoc vantage point in the conflict.
Canby's Cross marks the spot where the two negotiators
were killed.

As the road swings south, you pass beneath steep lava
bluffs, then climb to a viewpoint above Devil's Homestead
Lava Flow, where you can see the great river of molten rock
that poured downhill toward Tule Lake. The road continues
to wind through lava beds, climbing for a while, then descending to cross prominent lava flows before climbing
again. Among the most remarkable of the monument's features are the lava tubes, caves that lie beneath much of this
surface-of-the-moon landscape. Formed when the surface of
a molten lava flow cooled more rapidly than the still-liquid
interior, these caves are sometimes a quarter-mile in length.
There are more than 200 in the monument, 25 of which are
easily accessible to the public. Cave Loop Road takes you
past the only electrically lighted cave, Mushpot, plus at least
a dozen others; rangers conduct cave walks as well as orientation and evening interpretive programs from mid-June
through Labor Day.

At first encounter, Lava Beds may seem like an empty desert
of rocks, uninhabited and uninhabitable, but stay a while and
this harsh environment will begin to intrigue you. Rocky
Mountain mule deer, pronghorn antelope, coyote, fox, wea-
sel, skunk, and badger inhabit the monument, and yellow-
bellied marmots are ubiquitous. They're especially plentiful
along the north boundary road, and you may first encounter
one as a large, blond ball of fur scurrying in front of your car
or as a fat lump sunning on a flat rock. Several varieties of
squirrels, chipmunks, cottontail, and jackrabbits are also common. Large colonies of bats inhabit some of the caves in
summer, emerging at dusk to feed at nearby Tule Lake. There
are 225 species of birds in the monument; some are residents,
some come as visitors. You can pick up a checklist at the
visitors' center.

Klamath Basin Birding

For bird watchers the **Klamath Basin National Wildlife Refuges** are prime destinations. Straddling the California-Oregon border north of Lava Beds, lakes and marshes scattered across the basin host one of the largest concentrations of migrating waterfowl in North America. In November, when the greatest concentrations occur, thousands of ducks and geese make brief rest and feed stops here before continuing south along the Pacific Flyway. It can send shivers of delight up your spine to watch skeins of high-flying geese dotting the sky from horizon to horizon, the leaders honking their distinctive calls to keep their flocks together.

The best place to start is the refuge headquarters, 5 miles (8 km) west of Tulelake, where you can view interpretive exhibits that will help you understand what to look for. The refuge provides free checklists to the more than 254 species that regularly stop here, as well as maps to help you find your way around the various ponds and marshes.

If you're visiting Lava Beds and the wildlife refuges, you'll probably want to find accommodations and a place to dine a few miles north in Klamath Falls, Oregon, as motels and restaurants close to the California attractions are virtually nonexistent. ▶ **Best Western Klamath Inn,** ▶ **Comfort Inn,** ▶ **Klamath Falls Motor Inn,** ▶ **Thunderbird Motel,** and ▶ **Molatore's Motel** all offer good, standard motel facilities. ▶ **Thompson's Bed-and-Breakfast Inn by the Lake** has three bed-and-breakfast rooms with spectacular views of Upper Klamath Lake and visiting waterfowl. In the dining department at Klamath Falls, **Fiorella's** features northern Italian fare, **Chez Nous** serves excellent Continental cuisine in a former residence, and **The Stockman's Social Club** concentrates on beef and seafood, Western decor, and country-and-western music.

GETTING AROUND

The most practical means of exploring northeastern California is with your own vehicle or a rented car; Redding is about a four-hour drive from San Francisco via Interstates 80, 505, and 5. Public transportation systems serving the entire region do not exist. United Express (Tel: 800-241-6522) and American Eagle (Tel: 800-433-7300) feeder airlines have frequent service from San Francisco International Airport to Redding Airport. Hertz, Avis, and National rental-car systems have offices in the Redding airport.

ACCOMMODATIONS REFERENCE

The rate ranges given here are projections for fall 1993 through spring 1994. Unless otherwise indicated, rates are for double room, double occupancy.

▶ **Almanor Lakeside Lodge.** 3747 Highway 147, **Lake Almanor,** CA 96137. Tel: (916) 284-7376. $65.

▶ **Antlers Motel.** P.O. Box 538, **Chester,** CA 96020. Tel: (916) 258-2722. $32–$45.

▶ **Beaver Creek Lodge.** 16606 Highway 96, **Klamath River,** CA 96050. Tel: (916) 465-2331. $54.

▶ **Best Western Hilltop Inn.** 2300 Hilltop Drive, **Redding,** CA 96002. Tel: (916) 221-6100 or (800) 528-1234. $85–$94.

▶ **Best Western Klamath Inn.** 4061 South Sixth Street, **Klamath Falls,** OR 97603. Tel: (503) 882-1200 or (800) 528-1234. $60–$68.

▶ **Best Western Miner's Inn.** 122 East Miner Street, **Yreka,** CA 96097. Tel: (916) 842-4355. $53.

▶ **Best Western Trailside Inn.** 343 North Main Street, **Alturas,** CA 96101. Tel: (916) 233-4111 or (800) 528-1234. $44–$46.

▶ **Best Western Trailside Inn.** 2785 Main Street, **Susanville,** CA 96130. Tel: (916) 257-4123 or (800) 528-1234. $46–$48.

▶ **Best Western Tree House.** I-5 and Lake Street, **Mount Shasta City,** CA 96067. Tel: (916) 926-3101. $68–$77.

▶ **Black Forest Lodge.** Route 5, Box 5000, **Mill Creek,** CA 96061. Tel: (916) 258-2941. $38.

▶ **Bonanza King Resort.** Route 2, Box 4790, **Trinity Center,** CA 96091. Tel: (916) 266-3305. $465–$490 (week).

▶ **Bridge Bay Resort.** 10300 Bridge Bay Road, **Redding,** CA 96003. Tel: (916) 275-3021 or (800) 752-9669. $89.

▶ **Cabral House.** 1752 Chestnut Street, **Redding,** CA 96001. Tel: (916) 244-3766. $70–$125.

▶ **Cinnamon Teal Bed and Breakfast.** Highway 36 and Feather River Drive, **Chester,** CA 96020. Tel: (916) 258-3993. $65–$95.

▶ **Coffee Creek Chalet.** Star Route 2, Box 3969, **Trinity Center,** CA 96091. Tel: (916) 266-3235. $80.

▶ **Coffee Creek Guest Ranch.** Star Route HC 2, Box 4940, **Trinity Center,** CA 96091. Tel: (916) 266-3343. $100 (two-day minimum).

▶ **Comfort Inn.** 2500 South 6th Street, **Klamath Falls,** OR 97601. Tel: (503) 884-9999 or (800) 221-2222. $60.

▶ **Days Inn.** 2180 Hilltop Drive, **Redding,** CA 96002. Tel: (916) 221-8200 or (800) 325-2525. $79.

▶ **Deer Creek Lodge**. Route 5, Box 4000, **Mill Creek**, CA 96061. Tel: (916) 258-2939. $44.

▶ **Dorris House**. P.O. Box 1655, **Alturas**, CA 96101. Tel: (916) 233-3786. $45.

▶ **Drakesbad Guest Ranch**. California Guest Services, Inc., Adobe Plaza, 2150 Main Street, Suite 5, **Red Bluff**, CA 96080. Tel: for reservations, ask long-distance operator for Drakesbad Toll Station #2, operator route 028-181 in Susanville; for information, Tel: (916) 529-1512. $178–$211.

▶ **Dunes**. 511 North Main Street, **Alturas**, CA 96101. Tel: (916) 233-3545. $50.

▶ **Dunsmuir Inn**. 5423 Dunsmuir Avenue, **Dunsmuir**, CA 96025. Tel: (916) 235-4543. $50–$60.

▶ **Fall River Hotel**. P.O. Box 718, **Fall River Mills**, CA 96028. Tel: (916) 336-5550. $33–$38.50.

▶ **The Faulkner House**. 1029 Jefferson Street, **Red Bluff**, CA 96080. Tel: (916) 529-0520. $55–$80.

▶ **Fort Bidwell Hotel and Restaurant**. P.O. Box 100, **Fort Bidwell**, CA 96112. Tel: (916) 279-6199. $50.

▶ **The 49er**. P.O. Box 1608, **Weaverville**, CA 96093. Tel: (916) 623-49ER. $36–$38.

▶ **Grand Manor Inn**. 850 Mistletoe Lane, **Redding**, CA 96002. Tel: (916) 221-4472. $63.

▶ **Granny's House**. P.O. Box 31, 313 Taylor Street, **Weaverville**, CA 96093. Tel: (916) 623-2756. $65–$75.

▶ **Holiday Inn-Redding**. 1900 Hilltop Drive, **Redding**, CA 96002. Tel: (916) 221-7500. $75–$89.

▶ **Hotel Mt. Lassen**. 28 South Lassen Street, **Susanville**, CA 96130. Tel: (916) 257-6609. $40.

▶ **Klamath Falls Motor Inn**. 2627 South 6th Street, **Klamath Falls**, OR 97603. Tel: (503) 882-9665. $65–$75.

▶ **Klamath Motor Lodge**. 1111 South Main Street, **Yreka**, CA 96097. Tel: (916) 842-2751. $40–$42.

▶ **Lake Shastina Accommodations**. 6030 Lake Shastina Drive, **Weed**, CA 96094. Tel: (916) 938-4111. $70.

▶ **Lassen Mineral Lodge**. **Mineral**, CA 96063. Tel: (916) 595-4422. $42.

▶ **Lassen View Resort**. 7457 Highway 147, **Lake Almanor**, CA 96137. Tel: (916) 596-3437. $49.

▶ **The McCloud Guest House**. 606 West Colombero Drive, **McCloud**, CA 96057. Tel: (916) 964-3160. $75–$90.

▶ **Mill Creek Resort**. **Mill Creek**, CA 96061. Tel: (916) 595-4449. $40.

▶ **Molatore's Motel**. 100 Main Street, **Klamath Falls**, OR 97603. Tel: (503) 882-4666. $42–$46.

▶ **Motel Orleans**. 2240 Hilltop Drive, **Redding**, CA 96002. Tel: (916) 221-5432. $38.

▶ **Motel Orleans**. 1804 B Fort Jones Road, **Yreka**, CA 96097. Tel: (916) 842-1612. $37.

▶ **Motel 6**. 1640 Hilltop Drive, **Redding**, CA 96097. Tel: (916) 221-1800. $36.

▶ **Mountain Air Lodge**. 1121 South Mount Shasta Boulevard, **Mount Shasta City**, CA 96067. Tel: (916) 926-3411. $44–$48.

▶ **Mount Lassen Inn**. P.O. Box 86, **Old Station**, CA 96071. Tel: (916) 335-7006. $70–$80.

▶ **Oaks RV Park**. **Klamath River**, CA 96050. Tel: (916) 465-2323. $30–$40.

▶ **Oxford Suites**. 1967 Hilltop Drive, **Redding**, CA 96002. Tel: (916) 221-0100 or (800) 762-0133. $68–$78.

▶ **Plumas Pines Resort**. 3000 Almanor Drive West, **Canyon Dam**, CA 95923. Tel: (916) 259-4343. $50.

▶ **Railroad Park Resort**. 100 Railroad Park Road, **Dunsmuir**, CA 96025. Tel: (916) 235-4440 or (800) 974-RAIL. $65.

▶ **Red Lion Inn**. 1830 Hilltop Drive, **Redding**, CA 96002. Tel: (916) 221-8700 or (800) 547-8010. $97–$112.

▶ **Rick's Lodge**. Glenburn Star Route, **Fall River Mills**, CA 96028. Tel: (916) 336-5300 (April–November); (916) 336-6618 (November–April). $95 (two-day minimum).

▶ **Ripple Creek Cabins**. Star Route 2, Box 3899, **Trinity Center**, CA 96091. Tel: (916) 266-3505. $60.

▶ **River Inn Motel**. 1710 Main Street, **Susanville**, CA 96130. Tel: (916) 257-6051. $38–$42.

▶ **Roseberry House Bed and Breakfast**. 609 North Street, **Susanville**, CA 96130. Tel: (916) 257-5675. $50–$70.

▶ **St. Bernard Lodge**. Route 5, Box 5500, **Mill Creek**, CA 96061. Tel: (916) 258-3382. $57.50.

▶ **Seneca Motel**. P.O. Box 504, **Chester**, CA 96020. Tel: (916) 258-2815. $34.

▶ **Sis-Q-Inn Motel**. 1825 Shastina Drive, **Weed**, CA 96094. Tel: (916) 938-4194. $40–$44.

▶ **Spanish Springs Ranch**. P.O. Box 70, **Ravendale**, CA 96123. In California, Tel: (800) 272-8282; in rest of U.S., (800) 282-0279. $100–$150.

▶ **The Sportsman's Lodge**. 20502 Highway 96, **Klamath River**, CA 96050. Tel: (916) 465-2366. $30–$40.

▶ **Stoney Brook Inn**. 309 West Colombero, **McCloud**, CA 96057. Tel: (916) 964-2300. $45.

▶ **Super Budget Motel**. 2975 Johnstonville Road, **Susanville**, CA 96130. Tel: (916) 257-2782. $34–$44.

▶ **Swiss Holiday Lodge**. 2400 South Mount Shasta Boule

vard, **Mount Shasta City,** CA 96097. Tel: (916) 926-3446. $37–$43.

▶ **Thompson's Bed-and-Breakfast Inn by the Lake.** 1420 Wild Plum Court, **Klamath Falls,** OR 97601. Tel: (503) 882-7938. $60–$65.

▶ **Thunderbird Lodge.** 526 South Main Street, **Yreka,** CA 96097. Tel: (916) 842-4404. $34–$38.

▶ **Thunderbird Motel.** 3612 South Sixth Street, **Klamath Falls,** OR 97603. Tel: (503) 882-8864. $70–$78.

▶ **Tiffany House.** 1510 Barbara Road, **Redding,** CA 96003. Tel: (916) 244-3225. $75–$105.

▶ **Trinity Alps Resort.** Star Route, Box 490, **Lewiston,** CA 96052. Tel: (916) 286-2205. $350–$575 (week).

▶ **Vagabond Inn.** 536 East Cypress Drive, **Redding,** CA 96001. Tel: (916) 223-1600. $48–$70.

▶ **Valu Inn.** 30 Gilmore Road, **Red Bluff,** CA 96080. Tel: (916) 529-2028. $37–$41.

▶ **Weaverville Victorian Inn.** 1709 Main Street, **Weaverville,** CA 96093. Tel: (916) 623-4432. $58.

▶ **Wyntoon Resort.** P.O. Box 70, **Trinity Center,** CA 96091. Tel: (916) 266-3337. $70.

▶ **Young's Ranch Resort. Somes Bar,** CA 95568. Tel: (916) 469-3322 or (800) 552-6284. $50–$56.

THE GOLD COUNTRY

AND YOSEMITE

By Eloise Snyder

Eloise Snyder, formerly a reporter at the San Francisco Examiner, *is a free-lance writer based in Jackson, California.*

Linking the unspoiled villages, the ghost towns that survive only with a marker, and the neon-lit main streets of thriving county seats is the highway that courses through the history of the Gold Rush and marks the way to Yosemite National Park. It is, appropriately, Highway 49. For 318 miles (509 km) it climbs from 200 to 6,000 feet in altitude up roller-coaster hills, through pine forests and oak stands, and into plunging canyons. It is the route from the Northern to the Southern Mines once travelled by the legendary grizzled prospector by jackass, by stagecoach, or on foot.

For the fast-track traveller, one day devoted to a couple of Gold Rush sites is possible—but superficial. Searching for the offbeat, learning to pan for gold, and listening to some tall tales will take three days to a week.

In communities that recognize the extraordinary value of tourism, chambers of commerce outdo each other with comprehensive maps, carefully designed self-guided walking tours, schedules of seasonal events, and volumes on colorful local history.

While the name Mother Lode is applied generously along the Highway 49 Golden Chain, it was first used in 1851 to designate a vein of enormous richness that stretched for about 100 miles midway between the Northern and South-

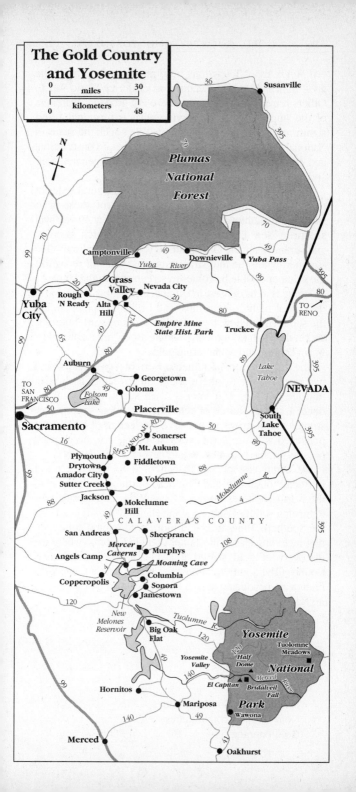

The Gold Country and Yosemite

0   miles   30

0   kilometers   48

N

Susanville

36

395

70

Plumas National Forest

70

70

99

70

49

Camptonville

49

Downieville

Yuba Pass

Yuba River

89

20

Grass Valley

Nevada City

Rough 'N Ready

Alta Hill

Yuba City

80

TO RENO

99

65

49

20

80

Empire Mine State Hist. Park

80

Truckee

89

395

Auburn

80

Georgetown

Lake Tahoe

NEVADA

TO SAN FRANCISCO

49

Coloma

Folsom Lake

Placerville

Sacramento

50

50

89

South Lake Tahoe

395

16

SHENANDOAH RD.

Somerset

Mt. Aukum

395

Plymouth

Drytown

Fiddletown

88

Amador City

Sutter Creek

Volcano

Mokelumne R.

88

Jackson

Mokelumne Hill

4

60

49

C A L A V E R A S   C O U N T Y

San Andreas

Sheepranch

Mercer Caverns

Murphys

108

Angels Camp

Moaning Cave

Columbia

Copperopolis

Sonora

Jamestown

120

New Melones Reservoir

Tuolumne R.

Big Oak Flat

120

Yosemite

Tuolumne Meadows

Half Dome

Yosemite Valley

140

El Capitan

Merced River

National

Hornitos

Bridalveil Fall

Park

99

Mariposa

49

Wawona

140

Merced

140

41

Oakhurst

ern Mines areas. Today lofty headframes mark some of the great mines closed by executive order during World War II. Others remain unmarked, but there is a growing awareness of the importance of preserving what is meaningful and significant from the Gold Rush era: Cities seek the status of National Historic Landmarks as a measure of conservation, and communities unite to save the old stone general store and its massive iron shutters.

Those iron shutters, integral to the architectural styles of the Gold Country, speak of the origins of those who swarmed to California in 1849. Along Highway 49 you will see prim New England cottages, soaring church steeples, and verandahs of the Old South. (If you travel Highway 49 in summer, when the temperature climbs, you will recognize the value of double balconies to screen against the sun.)

Traffic is at its densest in summer. Spring promises warm days, cool nights, green hills, and brilliant poppies. In fall the sun turns mellow, toyon bushes produce scarlet berries, and in the High Country of Yosemite aspen and maples glow warm bronze and shimmering gold.

The distance from Sacramento, born of the Gold Rush and two rivers, to the Northern and Southern Mines is short in mileage but long in contrasts. Each surviving community, once a ragtag cluster of tents and wooden shacks, now struggles as it grows to preserve the feeling of a time that produced an aura of romance—a feeling that the grizzled prospector, the true 49er, would never have understood.

We begin east of San Francisco in Sacramento, travel northeast to Auburn, and then head north on Highway 49 to the Northern Mines towns of Grass Valley and Nevada City. Returning south of Auburn along Highway 49, we head into the Southern Mines area and more gold-mining communities, including Placerville, Sutter's Mill in Coloma (where the discovery of gold started it all), Jackson, and Calaveras County. (The Southern Mines area is also one of California's finer wine-producing areas.) Finally, we turn east to Yosemite National Park.

MAJOR INTEREST

Sacramento
Historic buildings
River cruises

Northern and Southern Mines
Gold Country communities
Gold panning

Exploring caves
Wine tasting
Western architecture
Museums
Steam-train trips

Yosemite National Park
Hiking
Yosemite Valley's beauty
Natural splendor of the High Country
Seasonal sports activities
Photography

SACRAMENTO

The grand dome of the state capitol building, which once dominated the skyline of Sacramento, is hedged today by tall buildings that speak eloquently of the city's surge toward major metropolitan status. Comfortable little "River City" is up-tempo and making a statement of its own to get out from under the shadow of San Francisco, a 90-minute drive to the west on Highway 80.

There is still small-town pride in California's capital city, where urban dwellers can thank early settlers for planting protective shade trees along every street to combat the torrid summers. Sacramento today says it has more trees than Paris (nobody is challenging the claim). Another source of pride is its designation as "Camellia City." More than a million camellia bushes transform the city into a veritable garden every March, when the city celebrates its blossoms with a formal ball and a parade.

Exploring Historic Sacramento

A good place to get acquainted with the city is in the historic **Old Sacramento** section on the east bank of the Sacramento River, now a State Historical Park, west from the capitol building. Before the truck and the automobile quelled river travel, the Sacramento River was famous for its luxurious steamboats, and had an enormously profitable river trade. Today a paddle wheeler takes passengers up the river for a few miles, from Raley's Landing across from Old Sacramento. You can purchase tickets at the Old Sacramento Schoolhouse.

In addition to browsing in shops that sell everything from

cotton candy to leather boots to quality paintings, you may be interested in exploring the many carefully renovated buildings here, just north of Capitol Mall. The **History Center**, at Front and I streets, is a re-creation of the town's first city hall and waterworks building of 1854; exhibits tell the story of how the city survived the tumultuous growth brought on by the Gold Rush, as well as getting through two devastating floods and a depression.

The showplace of Old Sacramento for both train buffs and those who have never ridden the rails is the extraordinary **Railroad Museum**, an impressive collection of railroad memorabilia displayed as fine art. Sounds and mirrors give the sensation of rumbling through the night on one of the vintage locomotive, passenger, and freight cars that have been polished and lovingly restored. A visit is highly recommended.

Along with revolving contemporary exhibits, the **Crocker Art Gallery**, on the other side of Capitol Mall at Second and O streets, evokes nostalgia with its splendid collection of classic Old West paintings. The oldest art gallery and museum west of the Mississippi, it is an expansion of the architecturally distinguished home of railroad magnate Charles Crocker, who founded the gallery in 1873 after the Crockers returned from a trip to Europe.

THE STATE CAPITOL BUILDING

You can't miss the **Capitol dome** at the end of Capitol Mall, which leads east from Old Sacramento and the river. The recently restored building, which dates from 1874, stands in a cherished park with hundreds of species of trees, each carefully designated, and platoons of friendly squirrels. The real show is inside the Capitol building, where the glorious rotunda dome has been painted in pastels and trimmed with plaster decoration and sparkling lights on a gold background. The first floor has museum rooms complete with original furnishings looking much as they did in 1906; stop by the office of then-Governor Pardee, maintained as it was left the day after the San Francisco earthquake. Free guided tours are offered daily on the hour, or you can wander on your own. Be sure to peek in on the senate and assembly chambers if the legislature is in session.

VICTORIAN ARCHITECTURE
IN SACRAMENTO

The streets around the Capitol building are a veritable outdoor museum of Victoriana. Take a few minutes to walk or drive among the three blocks closest to the back of the Capitol building.

Another Victorian-era site is the **Governor's Mansion** at 16th and H streets. This 1877 mansion was built by hardware magnate Albert Gallatin and later bought by Joseph Steffens (father of writer Lincoln Steffens) before becoming the first official residence for California's chief executive. Unused since Ronald Reagan's term, the mansion is now open to the public. Gingerbread details, high ceilings, and a graceful staircase are typical of the mansion's architecture; sideboards, settees, and small marble-faced fireplaces add decorative flavor. You can visit the mansion 10:00 A.M. to 5:00 P.M. daily; there are hourly tours.

SUTTER'S FORT

Drive or take J Street bus number 30 or 31 east several blocks to Sutter's Fort, at 26th and L streets, site of the fort built by John Augustus Sutter, owner of the Coloma mill where gold was discovered. Sutter's dream of building a city named Sutterville at the site of the fort was crushed in the wake of the Gold Rush, but it's all been put back together here—carpenter, cooper, and blacksmith shops ring the courtyard; inside are guest quarters, guards' quarters, and Captain Sutter's office. An Indian Museum around the corner from the fort entrance displays an impressive basket collection.

Staying and Dining in Sacramento

For overnighters the ▶ **Best Western Ponderosa Motor Inn**, three blocks from the capitol on H Street, is convenient for city sightseeing and dining. The ▶ **Holiday Inn Capitol Plaza** is only a minute from Old Sacramento on J Street, and top-floor dining here provides a fine view of the city and its surroundings. Or, if new and grand is your style, the ▶ **Hyatt Regency**, on L Street directly across from the capitol, is a good bet.

Small and elegant, with Italian-marble Jacuzzis in each of its 12 guest rooms, the ▶ **Sterling Hotel** at 1300 H Street is a restored Victorian. Smoking is not permitted in the traditionally furnished rooms. Jacuzzis are also available in many of the nine rooms at ▶ **Vizcaya**, where furnishings are contemporary and accents are Victorian. Just off Highway 80 on the fast track east to the Gold Country is ▶ **Red Lion Inn**, on Point West Way. It's about ten minutes from downtown and has two pools, two restaurants, and a shuttle service to the airport.

Sacramento's reputation for attractive restaurants and good dining reflects a growing demand for ethnic variety. You don't have to stray from the downtown area to find a price and a menu to suit your tastes. On the moderate end, **Capitol Grill**, 28th and N streets, offers such delights as grilled pork loin, Mexican chicken soup, and fine desserts. Upscale **Biba**, 2801 Capitol Avenue at 28th Street, is where regulars relish tortellini and green lasagna, and **Chanterelle**, in the Sterling Hotel at 13th and H streets, serves California cuisine from seafood sausage to Frangelico soufflé.

LOCKE

For a 30-minute side trip southwest of "River City," take Highway 160 to the village of Locke. Although its appearance is that of a Western movie set, this town is an entirely Chinese community built 77 years ago when fire wiped out a nearby Chinatown. Two-story wooden buildings with balconies shade Main Street sidewalks, where cats may outnumber inhabitants of the riverside village. A few miles farther south on Highway 160, which rambles alongside the Sacramento River, a stay at the ▶ **Grand Island Mansion** at Ryde will introduce you to the Delta region and its pleasure-boating scene.

THE NORTHERN MINES

Less than an hour's drive northeast of Sacramento on Interstate 80 is **Auburn**, a Gold Rush town experiencing the clutches of urbanization. Between Auburn and rugged little Downieville, about 72 winding miles (115 km) north on Highway 49, are the Northern Mines. This is a region of contrasts: bustling communities determined to preserve some of the flavor of a romantic past, and, beyond them, unspoiled miles of pine forests, oak woodlands, and streams that invite gold panning.

How much time you have available will determine how far up Highway 49 you go, but Auburn, where Highway 49 intersects with I-80, is a convenient starting place. At the gateway to Old Auburn, you'll find a stone sculpture of Claude Chana, the man who discovered the first three nuggets and stayed to found the city in 1848. Auburn's Old Town and all of its Gold Rush structures have been designated collectively as a National Historic Landmark. Don't miss the four-story red-and-white firehouse; it's irresistible to photographers.

Nevada City

For fast relief from high-speed I-80, take the turnoff to the west for Highway 174, north of Auburn, to Grass Valley and Nevada City. Plunge deep into the past on gravel U-Bet Road, which makes a loop east off of Highway 49 and passes You Bet and Red Dog, historic hydraulic mining towns. (All that's left in Red Dog now are a few old frame buildings and a small cemetery.) Curving west, U-Bet Road rejoins Highway 49 in Nevada City, restoration gem of the Gold Country, with white church steeples and turreted Victorians sparkling on its seven pine-clad hills.

Today's primly charming homes and public buildings cloak Nevada City's boisterous past. From a primitive camp in 1849, the city grew to challenge San Francisco and Sacramento in the 1850s as third-largest city in the state. What lured a peak population of 10,000 were accounts of miners pulling a pound of gold a day—gold for gambling, whiskey, bawdy ladies, and an occasional pipe of opium—from Old Coyote Ravine. Murders over claim-jumping were routine.

As gold-seeking gave way to commerce, conservative easterners brought their families and built the gingerbread Victorians that are the primary tourist attractions more than a century later. Queen Anne, Italianate, and Gothic Revival styles, most dating from the 1870s, stand behind white picket fences and boast steep roofs, turned posts, and stained-glass windows. Some have been classified as historic landmarks but are still private residences. Walking-tour brochures leading you to these gems are available from the Chamber of Commerce at 132 Main Street in the downtown section (a designated Historical Preservation District).

Nevada City's twisting streets glow with gaslights in the evenings, and horse-drawn-carriage tours add the appropriate flavor. Old-timers still tell tall tales in city saloons, where the spirit of Madame Moustache lurks. A fashionably turned-out young woman who stepped off the stagecoach in Nevada City in 1854, Madame Eleanor Dumont opened a *vingt-et-un* parlor that became famous the length of the Mother Lode. She dealt games for a couple of years, becoming famous as "Madame Moustache," a reference to the dark line on her upper lip, but as gold discoveries dwindled she moved on. Where she went from Nevada City is unknown, but the guess is that she combed the West for boomtowns and gambling parlors open to the game of Twenty-One and a female dealer.

To tour the town, start a block from the Chamber of Commerce at the splendidly face-lifted Nevada Hose Company No. 1 firehouse. Built in 1861 of whitewashed brick and capped with a highly embellished bell tower, the building serves as the **Firehouse Museum** and is operated by the Nevada County Historical Society. Inside you'll find relics from the tragic Donner Party and an altar from a Chinese joss house (temple). Along Broad Street a restoration standout is the state's oldest theater building, the 1865 Nevada Theater, site of historic stage presentations by Mark Twain and Jack London, as well as current community events.

Nearby, the ▶ **National Hotel** is resplendent with Victorian antiques, red plush, and dark rosewood in every room. The hotel opened its doors nine years before the theater and is the oldest continually operating inn west of the Rockies. Where government currency buys refreshments today, nuggets and gold dust were once exchanged for beer and whiskey at the polished bar that was shipped here via Cape Horn and San Francisco.

Up the street is the 1880 New York Hotel, now a collection of shops and galleries and home to the Museum of Ancient and Modern Art (actually a gallery of local art). At **Main Street Antiques**, old and rare books, old toys, and primitives draw collectors. **Mountain Pastimes**, on Spring Street, specializes in toys for "thinking grown-ups" and in puzzles for fanciers of all ages.

Across the street is the **Nevada City Winery**, located only a few blocks from its original site of a century ago and center of the northernmost of the Sierra foothills' wine-producing regions. Call (916) 265-WINE for tasting times, when you can sample Chardonnays and Zinfandels bearing the Nevada City Winery label.

The pioneer cemetery is out on West Broad Street, as is a big boulder considered by Native Americans to have healing powers. On top of the Indian Medicine Stone are hollows where the ill sought cures and took the sun in ancient times.

Restaurants and cafés in Nevada City reflect the historic ethnic mix of the Gold Rush. A short stroll from the winery at 211 Spring Street, **Bit of England** serves crumpets, scones, sandwiches, and Devonshire cream; there's also a pub here with a long list of British beers. **Country Rose**, at 300 Commercial Street, features patio dining on French country fare; **Coach House** is a longtime favorite with a conventional

Continental menu; family-oriented **Northridge Inn** can be found at the Nevada Street exit off of Highway 49.

The Gold Country is witnessing a boom in bed-and-breakfast inns at popular traveller destinations, and in Nevada City the mood is frequently Victorian. Century-old ▶ **Downey House**, on West Broad Street, has a lovely garden with a lily pond, and ▶ **Grandmère's** is a three-story Colonial Revival with an inviting garden. ▶ **Piety Hill** offers cottages and a shaded courtyard. The ▶ **Northern Queen Inn**, on Railroad Avenue, is a comfortable motel with a café.

Grass Valley

Although the Gold Rush was the genesis of both Nevada City and Grass Valley, the two cities, four miles apart on Highway 49, are more cousins than twins. Where Nevada City was able to preserve its architectural treasures despite a disastrous fire, Grass Valley burned to the ground in 1855 in a blaze that consumed 300 buildings in 90 minutes. It was probably the most calamitous of the many fires that roared through the tent camps and collections of wooden shacks all over the Mother Lode.

Historians say the rebuilding of the city, using heavy masonry walls and ponderous iron shutters, influenced the character of Mother Lode architecture. Downtown Grass Valley has a decidedly contemporary air today, but the winding back streets tell a different story.

Probably the most famous of the surviving residences of the great fire is the **cottage of Lola Montez**, at 248 Mill Street. Authentically restored, the cottage is now the headquarters of the Nevada County and Grass Valley Chamber of Commerce; walking-tour brochures are available here.

The names of singer-dancer Montez and her young student Lotta Crabtree, once famous throughout the mining camps, are a part of the history of the Northern Mines. Sensational Lola (born Eliza Gilbert in Ireland) and her husband bought the Grass Valley cottage in 1852 as a retirement haven after a disappointing national tour. She brought to the Gold Rush town a penchant for big parties and a scandalous reputation as an ex-mistress of King Ludwig I of Bavaria and as an intimate of Franz Liszt and Victor Hugo, but what titillated the mining townspeople most was that Lola installed her own bathtub. Visitors can see it on the front porch today (although you can only imagine the grizzly bears and monkeys Lola kept as pets).

Restless Montez became acquainted with her neighbor

Lotta Crabtree when the seven-year-old girl stopped by for a visit. Soon Montez was tutoring her in singing and dancing, thus beginning Crabtree's lifelong theatrical career; she made her debut at age eight at a local tavern and left an estate of $4 million when she died in 1924. Lola Montez was not so fortunate. After a disappointing attempt to revive her career, she went on the lecture circuit, never to return to Grass Valley. She died in New York at the age of 43.

Grass Valley's main street since 1849 has been Mill Street, a fragment of a trail that led to a nearby mine site. Little remains of that exciting past on the main street today except for the long wooden awnings over the sidewalks. Over on South Church Street, built on land donated by a mining company, you can visit the oldest Episcopal house of worship in California. First opened for services in 1858, Emmanuel Episcopal Church is one of only two area churches that date from the Gold Rush days. At Church and Chapel streets, early Irish settlers are buried in St. Patrick's Cemetery, marked by towering cedar trees. Gravestones date from 1853, many girdled by ornate iron fences.

STAYING AND DINING
IN GRASS VALLEY

Back in town the ▶ Holbrooke Hotel on West Main Street, now into its second century, was rebuilt in 1862 after the fire; its guest register bears the names of Mark Twain, presidents Ulysses S. Grant and Grover Cleveland, and stagecoach robber Black Bart. Rooms at the hotel today are furnished with original period pieces and named after Gold Rush personalities of fame or notoriety.

Within walking distance of central Grass Valley is one of several bed-and-breakfast inns: Lovingly decorated ▶ Murphy's Inn, on Neal Street, was built in 1866 by a railroad and mine magnate. Downtown is the ▶ Swan-Levine House, on Church Street, a three-story restored Victorian that caters to artistic guests by offering studio space and art instruction. ▶ Annie Horan's, on West Main, is elegantly Victorian, with breakfast on the patio. Two other choices are the ▶ Alta Sierra Resort, a contemporary-style inn with pool, golf, and tennis, and the ▶ Golden Chain Resort, on Highway 49, away from the town center in a park-like setting with picnic facilities.

If you're feeling hungry and want to sample some local cooking, Cornish pasties are staples on more than one menu in town. Pasties are special favorites, along with scones, at the annual Cornish Christmas celebrations, when gas-lit streets are closed to vehicle traffic and cars are replaced by horse-drawn carriages and wagons. There has long been a strong Cornish influence in Grass Valley; in 1910, people with ties to Cornwall were estimated to make up two-thirds of the city's population, bringing with them the hard-rock mining skills of their native England (and the introduction of the invaluable pump that kept the mines dry and boosted the city's output). The miners back then carried pasties in their lunch pails, and today the meat pies make splendid picnic fare for a gold-panning expedition or a side-road foray to a nearby creek. **Marshall's**, at 203 Mill Street, produces authentic vegetable- and meat-filled varieties for the enjoyment of all.

At the **Empire House**, 535 Mill Street, Swiss chef Karl Resch offers an extensive menu that ranges from game and fresh seafood in season to standard prime rib and steaks. The osso buco is temptingly Italian, the sauerbraten is zippy with spices, and the wine list includes selections from Napa and Sonoma vintners. In an earlier life the restaurant was the site of a boarding house for miners employed at the nearby Empire Mine; photographs on the dining room walls are reminders of that era.

The **Main Street Café**, at 213 West Main, features wild game in season and fresh seafood for lunch and dinner. **Tofanelli's** is "family friendly," at 302 West Main. Most local markets operate delicatessens for picnic-minded travellers; try the **Whistle Stop Deli**, 408D Colfax Avenue.

Look into **Something Different** on Mill Street if you are interested in handiwork by local artisans; here you'll find footstools and pine-needle baskets in addition to more conventional crafts.

Around Grass Valley

Where the charm of neighboring Nevada City lies in its dedication to maintaining a strong historical presence today, Grass Valley's significance in Gold Rush history lies in its gold. Here gold mining developed into a major industry, not with picks and panning, but with heavy machinery that set a precedent for other Mother Lode mining operations. A visit to the Northstar Mining Museum and the showplace Empire Mine State Park clearly illustrates Grass Valley's place in Mother Lode history.

It all started modestly, so the story goes, and by accident. Local historians say the big hard-rock mining boom was sparked when George McKnight stubbed his toe on a rock while pursuing an errant cow one night. The rock gleamed in the moonlight, and when McKnight crushed it he found gold flecks. A discovery marker on Jenkins Street memorializes this occasion.

Beyond lower Mill Street at the **Northstar Mining Museum** is one of the finest collections of hard-rock mining equipment and artifacts in the nation. The star attraction here is the giant 1896 Pelton wheel, which—at 30 feet in diameter and weighing 10 tons, the largest Pelton wheel in the world when installed—still awes visitors. This waterwheel used turbine principles to produce power and was invented by Lester Pelton of nearby Camptonville. There is a creekside picnic area near the museum.

EMPIRE MINE STATE PARK

About a mile and a half east of the museum on East Empire Street is the Empire Mine State Park, site of the oldest and most profitable hard-rock gold mine in California. More than $960 million in gold was removed over a period of 107 years from shafts that plunge 11,000 feet and tunnels that burrow for 360 miles underground. Scattered over the large park area are restored buildings, including the baronial home of the mine owners, the Bourn Cottage, flanked by formal gardens. (William Bourn inherited the mine, and his love for gardens lives on at the estate he built, Filoli, south of San Francisco.)

The Empire Mine State Park is open daily, with programming and hours governed by the season. Check the schedule for the movies and slide shows as well as the self-guided and docent tours of the cottage, grounds, and mine yard. The antique rose garden is a draw when it's at its peak in color and fragrance; June is a fairly safe bet, but nevertheless it depends on the weather; Tel: (916) 273-8522.

Rough 'N Ready

West of Grass Valley a few minutes off Highway 49, along the Rough 'N Ready Highway (also known as Highway 20), is the town of Rough 'N Ready, a thriving little village named during the Gold Rush by a band of Mexican War veterans in honor of their ex-commander, General Zachary Taylor, and his nickname. Rough 'N Ready seceded from the Union in 1850 when a mining tax outraged the locals. Then, after having elected its own president and having adopted a constitution, the new republic reversed its engines and saluted the Union flag at a Fourth of July celebration. It was not until 1948, however, that the secession was officially ended and the federal government gave its blessing to a local post office. Send a postcard, because collectors prize the unusual postmark.

Surviving buildings of interest from the 1850s include the Fippin blacksmith shop, the Grange Hall, and the Old Toll House, which charged 25 cents for passage for a man on horseback and $3 for a flock of geese. For browsing or shopping, **Bertie's Nest** is the antiques haven in Rough 'N Ready.

On the way back to Highway 49, take time to scan the wall mural at Lyman Gilmore School, on the stretch of the Rough 'N Ready Highway before it becomes West Main Street in Grass Valley. It honors the colorful local for whom the school is named—reputedly California's first aviator. The present school site, covering 20 acres, is located on the first commercial airfield in the United States. There is evidence that Gilmore built and flew his own aircraft a year before the Wright Brothers became celebrated at Kitty Hawk in 1903. Gilmore, little known to the world at large, was a Grass Valley celebrity until he died in 1951.

North to Downieville

From Grass Valley and Nevada City, Highway 49 curls and curves up toward the Yuba Pass. This stretch is not heavily travelled, and, except in winter, supplies another kind of Gold Rush flavor to a flexible itinerary.

If you're going to be in this region in spring, you'll find yourself surrounded by dogwood blossoms and cascading waterfalls. Autumn, on the other hand, is mellow, with clear skies and colors like slashes of gold and bronze against a wall of evergreens.

It is about 45 miles (72 km) to **Downieville**, a true survivor of 49er days with crooked streets and 1860s brick-and-frame buildings. The town sprawls on both sides of the rushing Yuba River and climbs pine-thick hills. You may want to stop at the Sierra County Museum, housed in a building with walls of schist, on Main Street, or ask at the store for the best gold-panning locations.

A few blocks from the museum is the site of the original town gallows, where the hanging of a woman named Juanita brought notoriety to this Sierra outpost. Many historians agree it was self-defense when the dance hall girl killed a miner with a knife, but frontier "justice" prevailed.

Follow Highway 49 as it wanders south from Downieville

through Camptonville and North San Juan, skirting Nevada City and Grass Valley on the road to the Southern Mines, and you'll pass through communities whose populations once numbered in the thousands but now are sparsely populated.

Camptonville has two monuments at the west end of town. One is in memory of Lester Pelton, inventor of the Pelton wheel that brought prosperity to Grass Valley, and the other is dedicated to William "Bull" Meek, who was, as the monument says, a stagecoach driver, Wells Fargo agent, teamster, and merchant. Meek deserves attention because he was allegedly the only regular stage driver in the area to escape holdups. Locals say it was because he carried supplies to a Downieville bawdy house, and the influence of those fancy ladies produced a pact with the robbers that protected him.

THE SOUTHERN MINES

Mother Lode is the name attached to much of the California Gold Country, but the precious primary vein the Mexican miners called *Veta Madre* extends from Auburn south about 100 miles along the Highway 49 corridor to Melones. Melones is now only a memory beneath a reservoir, but thriving communities that were once scattered tents—and the region's silent ghost towns—draw most travellers to the Southern Mines. Not only visitors, but retirees and young families are flocking to the Sierra foothills here to settle where restless miners sought their fortune before moving on to the next glory hole, as they called any profitable concentration of the precious mineral.

From Auburn's Old Town to Coloma, the original glory hole, the highway winds and twists south through pastures and rolling hills, green year round with ponderosa pine and live oak, then plunges a thousand feet into the American River canyon. Before you encounter the early history of the Gold Rush at Coloma, detour to Georgetown, 20 miles (32 km) east of Auburn. Once known as "Growlersburg" for the nuggets that growled in miners' pans, this tiny community boasts homes and old-fashioned gardens from the Victorian past. The ▶ **American River Inn** is a restored survivor of the Gold Rush with more than an acre of gardens and the region's only croquet field.

Take Greenwood Road southwest from Georgetown to Coloma, where a bronze statue of James Marshall marks the site of the discovery that brought the world to California. A stop at ▶ **Sierra Nevada House** on Highway 49 will be an appropriate mood setter. It is the third inn built on this location since the Gold Rush, and offers a restaurant, bed-and-breakfast accommodations that operate seasonally, and a soda parlor that is a cool haven on hot summer days.

Coloma

Just a mile farther south of Sierra Nevada House on the highway is Coloma, on the bank of the American River. Here John Augustus Sutter naively instructed his lumber-mill construction workers to keep secret James Marshall's discovery of gold in the mill tailrace on January 24, 1848. The news was out in days.

The entire town of Coloma is now James Marshall Gold Discovery State Historic Park. Rangers have detailed maps, and you'll find plenty of comfortable picnicking areas in shady groves. Authentically restored interiors of picturesque stone buildings include a Chinese store and a blacksmith shop. You can also wander through a reproduction of a mine tunnel and poke into a meticulously equipped assay office. A reconstruction of the rough cabin where Marshall lived after he discovered gold illustrates the Spartan lifestyle of the 49er.

Marshall himself became a miserable recluse, living on handouts and sales of his autograph after a $100-a-month state pension was cut off in 1876. The man who sounded "Eureka" died in tiny nearby Kelsey in 1885. Miner friends packed the body in ice and transported it to Coloma for a wake and burial near his old cabin.

Sutter's Mill has been reconstructed on the river using the original techniques of hand-hewn beams and mortise-and-tenon joints. The sawmill operates seasonally on weekends, and there is an ore-crushing stamp mill nearby.

Once a rowdy collection of 10,000 souls, Coloma has experienced violence in its history. A bizarre double hanging, which occurred in 1855 after most miners had moved on, was the occasion for entertainment by a brass band from nearby Placerville, but it was the two convicted murderers who were center stage. A school teacher named Crane marked his final exit by singing a song of his own composition that ended abruptly with "here I come," and badman Mickey Free danced a jig. His gravestone is in the Coloma cemetery.

If you want to try your luck, gold panning is permitted in a recreation area of the American River across from the bronze statue of Marshall. For an overnight stay, Victorian-style guest rooms, a restaurant, and a reputation for being haunted distinguish historic ▶ **Vineyard House**. The ▶ **Coloma Country Inn**, a restored 1852 country home, is two blocks from Sutter's Mill. The inn can arrange hot-air ballooning and white-water rafting.

Placerville

Jagged cliffs ripped by hydraulic mining mark the approach to Placerville, about 10 miles (16 km) south of Coloma. The second-largest of all Gold Rush cities, it is a high-growth area with burgeoning residential developments serving commuters to fast-growing Sacramento.

Once just a branched-out version of Coloma called Dry Diggin's, Placerville was also known as Hangtown after a series of lynchings in 1849. One was a triple hanging; the usual plaque on Main Street marks the site of the tree. The city was also a stop on the pony express and overland mail routes and commemorates this every June with an abbreviated memorial run.

One person who took advantage of Placerville's Gold Rush prosperity to "build a poke" (build up a bank account) and go on to better things was J. M. Studebaker, who reaped profits from building wheelbarrows for the miners. He returned to the Midwest and founded the wagon factory that became the Studebaker Corporation. Meat packer Phillip Armour once ran a butcher shop in Placerville, and financier and railroad builder Mark Hopkins was a grocer here.

City-owned **Goldbug Mine** is 1 mile (1½ km) east of town off busy Highway 50. There are scheduled tours of the historic park, a real gold mine, which, with its special lighting, is worth exploring. Or check out a gold pan and try your luck in the sands of a nearby creek. Picnic facilities and hiking trails make it likely you will want to spend an entire day here.

Browsers for antiques will find old post office boxes and pie safes, sepia portraits of early settlers, and potbellied stoves in downtown Placerville shops.

La Casa Grande at 251 Main Street is well known for its informality and good food. It's worth the 3-mile (5-km) drive east of Placerville to Smith Flat Road for the linen-and-crystal hospitality and the extensive menu at the **Historic Smith Flat House Carriage Room**, situated in a beautiful country setting. It's wise to reserve, especially on weekends; Tel: 621-0667. For local flavor, try **Zachary Jacques** at 1821 Pleasant

Valley Road. For an overnight stay, the ▶ **Gold Trail Motor Lodge** is located in downtown Placerville.

Seasonal cultural events in Placerville include "Celebrate the Arts," a county-wide festival featuring local artists (third week in May), and the Annual Hangtown Jazz Jubilee in October. Little-theater fans will enjoy the spring and winter productions at Discovery Playhouse on the county fairgrounds. Ask about the schedule at the Chamber of Commerce; Tel: 621-5885.

WINERIES IN THE PLACERVILLE AREA

Wine making in the Sierra foothills has been a tradition ever since some of the early settlers opted for grapes over gold. Small family-owned-and-operated vineyards and wineries are producing award-winning vintages 150 years later. Most wineries here are north and southeast of Placerville, off Highway 50 along Carson Road and off Mt. Aukum Road. A few are open daily, most on weekends. An informative brochure with a map is available at the Placerville Chamber of Commerce, 542 Main Street.

The tasting room at **Boeger Winery**, on Carson Road, is housed in a stone cellar built in 1872 and listed on the National Register of Historic Places. You can picnic under ancient fig trees on the rambling grounds. **Fitzpatrick Winery**, on Fairplay Road in Somerset, about 20 miles (32 km) east of Placerville, offers bed and breakfast in ▶ **Fitzpatrick Lodge**, a replica of a hand-peeled log lodge. The rooms are upstairs, a country kitchen and tasting room downstairs.

Amador County

About 25 miles (40 km) south of Placerville, in neighboring Amador County's sensuous hills, are the mines where half the prodigious wealth of Mother Lode gold was extracted. In this region, about midway along the 318-mile stretch of Highway 49, are the mines that helped Leland Stanford finance the Central Pacific Railroad, Stanford University, and a political career. Millions of dollars from this area amplified the resources of Wall Street's Hetty Green, who was known as "the richest woman in the world" in her day and who, for a time, owned the Old Eureka Mine near Sutter Creek.

Landmarks along Highway 49 in Amador County include the headframes of the Keystone Mine at Amador City and the Argonaut and Kennedy mines at Jackson. The latter had some of the deepest vertical shafts in the world—at 5,000 feet—before closing in 1942.

WINERIES IN AMADOR COUNTY

In Jackson pack your picnic basket at the **Mother Lode** deli on Main Street and head for a tour of local wineries and tasting rooms in the Shenandoah Valley (take Shenandoah Road east off Highway 49 at the Plymouth intersection). Local wine makers, many of them students of enology who moved to the area in the early 1970s, have made vineyards and the fruits of the vine an important economic asset to the county.

More than a dozen wineries have opened in the last 20 years, and the traditional, robust, local Zinfandel now shares the tasting roster with Sauvignon Blanc, Chardonnay, Chenin Blanc, and Cabernet Sauvignon. Most wineries schedule tastings on weekends; ask the Chamber of Commerce just west of the intersection of Highways 49 and 88 for a brochure and a map.

FIDDLETOWN

A reminder of the importance the Chinese have had in the history of the region can be found in a dozing village called Fiddletown, 6 miles (10 km) east of the Highway 49–Plymouth junction on Fiddletown Road. Here remains one of the few rammed-earth adobe buildings in the state from the 1850s. Once the shop of an herb doctor, **Chew Kee Store** has been restored by state and private funding. Now a museum, its interior and the amazing collection of items from the past constitute a visible time capsule: There are tiny pots of herbs, medicines, an abacus, cooking implements, tools, and stamps, all of which have been catalogued and returned to their original places.

Why the name Fiddletown? Elder Missourians, who settled here in 1849 to farm, found younger men "always fiddling." Later this name offended a dignified local judge who prevailed on the legislature in 1878 to change Fiddletown to Oleta. But the "damage" was already done: He had become known as "the man from Fiddletown," and Bret Harte's "An Episode in Fiddletown" had fixed the name firmly. Cooler heads officially restored it in the 1920s. There's a post office in town, if you collect postmarks.

DRYTOWN AND AMADOR CITY

"Founded in 1849," announces more than one community in this Mother Lode region, but tiny Drytown is a year older. It possesses no famous mine but is the first village you'll encounter after Highway 49 curves sharply west past Plymouth in Amador County. Once a tent camp with a raucous collection of 26 saloons and 10,000 miners, Drytown today is down to a solitary saloon, pegged "the only wet spot in Drytown." In a small cluster of buildings on the west side of the highway as it climbs up from Dry Creek is the store where publisher William Randolph Hearst's father, George Hearst, operated a printing press in his mine office.

A few minutes beyond is Amador City, which once laid claim to being the smallest incorporated city in the United States; its population now hovers around 200. Snacks, antiques, quilts, and period fashions are tucked along the abbreviated main street, Highway 49.

Recently restored, the tasteful ▶ **Imperial Hotel**, situated where the road curves, is operated as a bed-and-breakfast inn. It has a mellow bar and an excellent restaurant where Amador residents come to catch up on local gossip. Also popular with Gold Country regulars is the ▶ **Mine House Inn**, complete with pool and framed against a hillside just above the city looking across at the headframe of the Keystone Mine.

Rambling stone walls (most often constructed by Chinese laborers on their day off from mining), classic barns with sagging roofs, fat grazing cattle, and spreading California oaks provide special photo opportunities on this section of Highway 49.

Sutter Creek to Jackson

The contrast to this purely Western landscape makes your first glimpse of **Sutter Creek** at the end of a sweeping curve even more surprising—it has the appearance of a New England village, with trim white cottages, green shutters, church steeples, and cherished gardens.

Spring in Sutter Creek is an extravagance of azalea and camellia blossoms and flowering fruit trees, but gardening is not of historical significance in the founding of this city—it was a pine and cedar forest on a nearby ridge that in 1846 sparked a tent city in the pleasant little valley straddling what is now Sutter Creek.

Before long, seven mines were operating within two miles of Main Street (Highway 49), one of which was the Lincoln Mine, partly owned by Leland Stanford. A major mining company is now preparing to mine the land adjacent to the old Lincoln, and with new technology, both new and old gold mines are opening and reopening in more than one Mother Lode community. Engineers believe the Gold Rush only hinted at the wealth of minerals that still exists.

A walking tour of Sutter Creek's winding, shaded back streets is included in a useful Visitor's Guide put out by the Amador County Chamber of Commerce; the brochure can be obtained from most merchants. Sutter Creek has an abundance of antiques; everything from four-poster beds to stained-glass art to funky old postcards are displayed in the shops.

One of the first bed-and-breakfast inns in the West, the ▶ **Sutter Creek Inn** on Main Street is a carefully preserved New England–style 1859 home that retains the classic white picket fence. Shaded by towering trees and cooled by green lawns, the inn supplies hammocks, and there are cottage accommodations as well as lovingly furnished guest rooms in the main building. Some rooms have fireplaces, others swinging beds. A lavish sit-down breakfast is served in the big country kitchen or outdoors in the garden. Next door is ▶ **Foxes**, which boasts individually designed rooms, carefully chosen furnishings, and a Victorian flavor. It also offers a splendid breakfast.

VOLCANO

Nothing could be farther from prim and proper Victorian than rugged and unspoiled little Volcano, a half-hour side trip east off Highway 49 from Sutter Creek on Sutter Creek–Volcano Road. The miners thought this spot looked like a crater dwarfed by pine-covered circling hills, so "Volcano" it was. Some old-timers say it is the torrid summer weather that inspired the name, and there is probably truth in both stories.

There are more tales to be told at the tiny bar in Volcano's ▶ **St. George Hotel**. Built in 1862, this simple, comfortable lodging (with shared baths) still retains its traditional second-story balconies and vine-shaded verandah. Dinners in the restaurant are hearty prime rib, steak, or chicken, depending on the day of the week. It's strictly home-style cooking—and highly recommended. Reservations are necessary; Tel: (209) 296-4458.

Photographers find Volcano worth the film for its sleepy Main Street stone buildings and for "Old Abe," one of the oldest bronze cannons in the United States, used by the Volcano Blues in the Civil War. In addition to the 40 saloons, three breweries, and fandango halls it once supported, Volcano claims some California "firsts": a public library, private law school, and little-theater group. The Volcano Theatre Company carries on the thespian tradition with weekend performances from mid-April through mid-October in the charming Cobblestone Theatre.

For a longer look back in the history of the region, plan to spend some time at **Chaw Se**, a few minutes south of Volcano on the Pine Grove–Volcano Road. This 40-acre state park is a showcase for a limestone outcropping covered with more than 300 Native American petroglyphs and more than a thousand mortar holes. It was here that the Miwok Indians pulverized acorns and other nuts, seeds, and berries. Among the authentically reproduced structures in the park are a roundhouse for religious gatherings, a conical bark dwelling, and an Indian "football" field. There is also a museum with artifacts and Miwok crafts; for tours call (209) 296-7488.

JACKSON

From Volcano take Highway 88 southwest to return to Highway 49 and a stop at the busy county seat of Jackson, where you'll find the **Amador County Museum**, dedicated to another era; it's located two blocks up from Main Street in one of the oldest houses in the community. Mother Lode memorabilia is the attraction in this 1859 building centered among lawns with scattered picnic tables. There is an extraordinary scale model of a stamp mill, the towering Kennedy Mine tailings wheels and headframe, and an amusing collection of household appliances used by homemakers more than a century ago.

Just below the museum is a full-scale replica of a narrow-gauge railroad locomotive, a model of the kind of machine that opened the West that has appeared in movie and television productions.

Almost as much a landmark for Jackson as the Kennedy tailings wheels is **St. Sava Serbian Orthodox Church**, mother church of the denomination in North America and a gem of pristine design. Lit at night, it is visible from many parts of the city and to the east from Highway 49 as the highway curves down into the city.

If you wander by St. Patrick's Catholic Church, a block south of the museum, you will discover that the founder of Columbus Day was a Jackson native named Angelo Noce. A monument in front of the 1868 church building honors him.

In recognition of Jackson's ribald past, there is a sidewalk plaque on Main Street in front of a venerable bar memorializing the ladies of the evening once headquartered in the "female boarding houses" on Jackson Creek, the city's lively recreation area of those bygone days.

Rinky-tink piano and community singing often erupt from the commodious bar in the old ▶ **National Hotel** at the end of Main Street. An early stage stop, the hotel is still in operation. There are also motels along busy Highway 49 as it borders the city. In the bed-and-breakfast category are the ▶ **Court Street Inn**, two blocks up from Main Street, a tastefully restored 1870 Victorian listed on the National Register of Historic Places, and the quiet ▶ **Gate House Inn**, on Jackson Gate Road, a stately home with a pool and Victorian antiques.

Calaveras County

Bret Harte and Mark Twain celebrated the Mother Lode in chronicles and fiction as they drifted in and out of Calaveras County, where Highway 49 bends south from Jackson to continue through the Southern Mines corridor. The haunts of the two writers extend from the Mokelumne River in the north to the Tuolumne River in the south, where tall tales of badmen and big nuggets in the Gold Country still find an avid audience.

If you take a jog off Highway 49 a few minutes south of Jackson, you'll come upon small but spirited **Mokelumne Hill**. This city, whose population ballooned after 1849 to the point where claims were limited to 16 square feet, is proud of its I.O.O.F. Hall, the first three-story building in the Mother Lode.

A chance encounter with a local historian sipping beer under the high ceiling fans of the old **Hotel Leger** bar in Mokelumne Hill will verify an account of the Perkins Nugget, which reportedly was taken from a mine a few miles to the south in 1854 and assayed at 190 pounds. At the time its $40,000 value was a fortune—and no larger single nugget has since been found in the United States. Another beer may prompt the tale of the ghost of George Leger, allegedly a regular visitor to the saloon, who was assassinated at the hotel in 1879.

A few doors down on Main Street, **Rod Hanchett** hand-throws and fires stoneware and porcelain pottery for both decorative and kitchen use in a kiln on the premises.

SAN ANDREAS

In San Andreas, south of Mokelumne Hill, drop in at the local museum, which maintains a broad collection of minerals, Native American handicrafts, and Gold Rush treasures. And walk on over to the old jail behind the courthouse to see the cell marked "Black Bart Slept Here." This most famous stage robber of them all postdated the peak of the Gold Rush but remains associated with the era because of the 28 robberies he staged between 1877 and 1883. Always polite, wearing a flour sack over his head with holes cut for eyes, his invariable request to stagecoach drivers was: "Throw down the treasure box, *please*," backed by a menacing shotgun. Bart's career ended when a handkerchief he dropped near Copperopolis was traced by a laundry mark to a San Francisco location: Black Bart turned out to be Charles Bolton, respected citizen and prominent socialite. He was tried in San Andreas and served less than six years in San Quentin. History loses him after his release.

The ► **Black Bart Inn** in San Andreas has modern hotel accommodations and a comfortable Victorian-style dining room (the Friday night seafood buffets here are legendary). For bed and breakfast try the ► **Robin's Nest**, a Gold Rush–era mansion restored to its original Victorian charm.

Nothing much happens today in Altaville, where Highways 49 and 4 intersect south of San Andreas, but the town is remembered as the birthplace of a mammoth hoax in the Gold Country involving a skull found in a mine at Bald Mountain. The find was proclaimed in 1866 to be the "Pliocene skull," the remains of a prehistoric man, but 50 years later it was discovered to be the skull of an Indian, and the whole episode was dismissed as a practical joke. Bret Harte wrote a poem "To the Pliocene Skull"—a fraud nobody ever admitted to masterminding.

For a round of local wine tasting, take Murphys Grade Road east from Highway 49, before Angels Camp, to **Stevenot Winery**, the largest producer in the Sierra foothills, 3 miles (5 km) beyond the community of Murphys. You'll also find other wineries open weekends for tasting; check for the schedules at ► **Murphys Historic Hotel**. Said to have been described by Bret Harte in "A Night in Wingdam," the hotel retains its old iron shutters and second-story balcony with iron railing, not to mention the bullet hole in the doorframe. The hotel, which has hosted such notables as J. Pierpont Morgan and Mark Twain, has a restaurant and saloon along with lodgings. A walking-tour map of small, well-preserved Murphys has an astonishing 55 listings.

If you prefer bed and breakfast to a hotel, try ► **Dunbar House 1880**, an Italianate-style Victorian establishment in century-old gardens. They've got air-conditioning for hot summers and wood stoves for crisp fall weather.

EXPLORING CAVERNS AND CAVES

For a different perspective of the Mother Lode, go underground for exploring instead of mining at **Mercer Caverns**,
one mile north of Murphys up Highway 4 on Sheep Ranch
Road. A tour of this subterranean setting with its dazzling
crystalline formations and "curtains" takes 45 minutes. The
maze of passageways is still being explored more than 100
years after prospector Walter Mercer discovered the caverns.

If one cavern is not enough for you, there are two more in
the vicinity. **California Caverns Park**, a few miles north of
Murphys, offers Wild Cave expedition tours lasting two to
four hours, led by experienced guides. You can explore,
crawl, and climb with ropes and ladders, or take a tour that
crosses crystal lakes on rafts. There are also family tours that
follow in the footsteps of naturalist John Muir and, of course,
Harte and Twain. Reservations are recommended; Tel: (209)
736-2708.

Moaning Cave is California's largest public cave, off Highway 104 as it turns south toward Columbia State Park from
Highway 4. At Moaning Cave visitors can rappel almost 200
feet into the huge main chamber, which is vast enough to
hold the entire Statue of Liberty and more. Studies show that
the cave was a burial place 13,000 years ago, and bones
preserved here by mineral-rich waters are considered possibly the oldest human remains found in North America.

Where Highway 4 joins Highway 49, **Angels Camp** (memo-
rialized by Bret Harte in "Luck of Roaring Camp") straddles a
creek and climbs wooded hills. Near the creek is Angels
Hotel, where Mark Twain reportedly heard the jumping-frog
story. The city remembers both celebrities with a monument
to the frog on Main Street and a statue to Mark Twain in a
park alongside Highway 49. There's an annual Frog Jump
competition in May.

Columbia

A short distance to the south, just over the border into
Tuolumne County and a jog north off Highway 49, is a truly
living Gold Rush town. **Columbia** was once the "gem of the
Southern Mines" and is now Columbia State Historic Park. A
clamorous community of 5,000 within a month of gold discovery in 1850, Columbia missed being the state capital by a scant
two votes in the legislature. After $87 million in gold was
shipped out by 1858, things quieted down, but Columbia
never became a ghost town. Since 1945 its park status has
preserved the historic buildings as a living museum, some-

what like Virginia's Colonial Williamsburg. When you stroll the shaded streets the only traffic will be an occasional horseman or a stagecoach.

Don't be turned off by the veneer of commercialism: The people costumed in the style of the Gold Rush era here do make their living in Columbia and live inside the park. The sweet shop and the harness shop, the blacksmithy, the saloon, and the trading post operate today as they did more than a century ago.

There are opportunities here to pan for gold, taste wine, take a stagecoach ride, or visit a mine—or you may prefer to find a shady spot and settle for a moment to envision 15,000 obstreperous miners, slick gamblers, men of commerce, camp followers, and the ubiquitous fancy ladies. The ▶ Columbia City Hotel is a salute to them all. The nine upstairs rooms are remarkably restored and open to overnight visitors. The **City Hotel Restaurant** is tucked into the main floor of the hotel in a comfortable setting with crystal and flowers on every table. The award-winning restaurant changes specials daily, putting a Continental accent on the veal piccata and juicy rack of lamb. There are fluffy soufflé desserts and a flaming baked Alaska. The **What Cheer** bar adjacent offers an adequate California wine list and cocktails. Luncheon and dinner are served daily, with Sunday brunch a traditional feast.

For bed and breakfast, the ▶ **Fallon Hotel** in Columbia is a Victorian jewel with flocked wallpaper, tall ceilings, and lace-trimmed lampshades. The nearby Fallon House Theater is the setting for Columbia Actors' Repertory productions September through May.

Sonora

What was once a main street of adobe, rough plank, canvas, and tin shacks is now heavily trafficked Washington Street in Sonora, just south of Columbia on Highway 49. The Queen of the Southern Mines now claims the busiest main street in the Mother Lode and is in the grasp of phenomenal growth. Where horse races and bull-and-bear fights were once on the entertainment agenda, today you'll find gift shops and commerce and the seat of county government. But a block or so off Washington Street there are strong echoes of earlier times.

Beside proudly restored Victorian homes stands the **St. James Episcopal Church**, a landmark since 1860 and one of the most photographed of Gold Rush churches because of its impressive steeple and fine stained-glass windows. If you are looking for the Tuolumne County Museum, at 158 Bradford Avenue, you'll find it in the Old County Jail, listed on the National Register of Historic Places. Walking-tour maps and information are available weekdays in the same building from the Chamber of Commerce.

To satisfy your hunger, **Hemingway's Café and Restaurant** on Stewart Street serves up California cuisine with an emphasis on fresh produce, innovative sauces, and creative presentations, and offers a good wine list. For pastas and other Italian specialties, **La Torre** is downtown on Washington Street. **Kyoto House** is a well-established Japanese restaurant also on Washington Street.

▶ **Barretta Gardens Inn**, within walking distance of downtown Sonora, is a bed-and-breakfast accommodation in a restored Victorian farmhouse with an assortment of elegantly furnished parlors. Also near the town center, ▶ **Gunn House** is a local historic hotel filled with antiques. Country English is the theme at ▶ **La Casa Inglesa**, 2 miles (3 km) out of town on a tree-shaded gold-mine site. ▶ **Llamahall Guest Ranch** is in a wooded setting on a creek and surrounded by a llama-breeding farm. At this comfortable inn 5 miles (8 km) east of Sonora, guests can relax in a hot tub or sauna and settle into the library and music room with a fireplace. Outdoorsy types can fish, pan for gold, visit Indian grinding rocks, or jog on a mile-long trail beside the creek. There's even a barbecue grill for travelling chefs.

Jamestown

Serious gold seekers and steam-train buffs will find **Jamestown** a welcome stopover. West of Sonora and just off Highway 49, "Jimtown" is the spot where gold was discovered by a prospector searching for his lost jackass. (He found gold nuggets and a thousand ounces of gold in Jackass Gulch.) In those days the amount of gold dust you could hold between thumb and finger was valued at a dollar, a wineglass full was $100, and a tumbler $1,000. In 1985, when a couple entered a Jamestown shop carrying 11 pounds of gold nuggets in a shopping bag, their value was placed at $140,000. The couple refused to say where they discovered the gold and refused to give their names, but you can see it all as it happened on a videotape shown at the Old Livery Stable on Main Street.

Jimtown offers opportunities for gold-prospecting expeditions and for polishing up gold-panning, sluicing, and other prospector techniques on trips that can last anywhere from two hours to five days. You can get information about these trips and about helicopter and white-water raft runs at the Old Livery Stable on Main Street, where **Gold Prospecting Expeditions** is headquartered; Tel: (209) 984-4653.

Nostalgia is the draw for the **Railstown steam-train rides** offered weekends from the Sierra Railway Depot on Fifth Avenue. A five-acre California State Historic Park and launching spot for a variety of theme trips, Railstown schedules train rides on weekends March through November. There are also roundhouse tours and picnic grounds. A full run-down on steam-train rides is available at the park; Tel: (209) 984-3953.

Jamestown's historic ▶ **National Hotel**, operating since 1859, has beautifully restored guest rooms with shiny brass beds and patchwork quilts, and a saloon with a glossy, 19th-century redwood bar. Fresh seafood, veal, and pasta are turned out with skill from the hotel's kitchen, and dinners are served under a cool grape arbor in warm weather. Reservations for dining are advised; Tel: 984-3446. ▶ **Jamestown Hotel**, a bed-and-breakfast inn on Main Street, is elegantly restored in Victorian fashion and serves a Continental breakfast.

Bear and Coyote Gallery, behind the Jamestown Hotel, displays and sells the work of 20 artists, mostly California Native Americans. Graphic arts focus on dance, religion, stories, and traditions; baskets, jewelry, and weavings are also exhibited. In addition to local artists, the galleries include samplings from Native American communities throughout the United States.

South to Mariposa

From San Andreas to Sonora to the most southern of the Southern Mines (near Mariposa), you'll find historical markers and plaques memorializing the legendary Joaquin Murieta. A bandit hero of the "take from the rich and give to the poor" school, he was the Gold Rush Robin Hood, and whether or not he actually existed, Murieta is the subject of books, paintings, and innumerable tall tales. He adopted his lifestyle, the story goes, to avenge the killing of his family and the rape of his wife by Yankee marauders. In some quiet San Andreas saloon, you may hear the anecdote of the man who fashioned a bulletproof vest for Murieta and took a shot from the bandit to prove its worth.

In tiny Hornitos, west of Highway 49 toward Mariposa, is

an underground tunnel that was reputedly used more than once by Murieta as an escape route from the self-styled "wildest and most wicked city of the Southern Mines." The entrance is marked on a corner of this sleepy little town.

Was it the real Murieta who was hunted down by a lawman who cut off his head for proof and claimed a $5,000 reward? That's questionable. Some historians believe Murieta is more myth than legend, but he remains a romantic figure of a romantic time.

As Highway 49 continues on the home stretch toward its terminus in Oakhurst, it passes through Mariposa. A suitable final stop for a Gold Country tour is the **Mariposa County Fairgrounds**, where an expansive collection of precious minerals, which for years was in the Ferry Building in San Francisco, is now on exhibit. Much of what is on display is pure gold.

YOSEMITE NATIONAL PARK

Yosemite is a magnet for three million visitors a year from around the world. Its unparalleled natural beauties have lured solitude-seekers and gregarious summer campers for more than a century.

The park is an easy three-hour drive south from Sacramento (via Highways 16 and 49 through Sonora to Moccasin, then Highway 120 to the park; via Highway 49 to Mariposa and then Highway 140; or on Highway 49 to Oakhurst, where you can pick up Highway 41). It is a four-hour drive east from San Francisco (take the Bay Bridge to Highway 580, south to Highway 50, then east to Manteca; from there take Highway 120 to Yosemite). The park's approaches converge from three entrances when they reach **Yosemite Valley**. The valley is a preeminent example of a canyon carved by a primordial river of ice. The seven-mile, U-shaped valley floor area, dominated by shouldering masses of granite, is both goal and gateway point for rock climbers and wilderness backpackers, anglers and horseback riders, skiers and ice skaters in winter, day-trippers and vacation campers spring through autumn.

Narrowing your choice to a season and its unique attractions is the key to a rewarding visit. One day to explore Yosemite's wonders would be only a tantalizing introduction to granite monoliths, towering waterfalls, and giant Sequoias. A stay of three days or more is not overdoing it. Yosemite's 1,200-mile sprawl comprises altitudes that climb from 2,000 to 13,000 feet. In the High Country you will find the serenity of open meadows and pine forests, solitary lakes and challenging peaks; in the valley there are easily accessible waterfalls and rewarding hiking trails. Whatever your destination, you can reach it via more than 800 miles of marked trails or 360 miles of paved roads. Reservations are strongly advised for all park accommodations, from the valley's venerable and luxurious Ahwahnee Hotel to the Curry Village cabins and High Country dormitory-style housing.

The Yosemite Valley

Whether you are travelling in a private car or by public transportation, abandon the wheels once you arrive in the valley. Plan to walk or take the free shuttle buses to shops and trailheads. Open-air trams operate seasonally, and there are commercially guided tours of Yosemite Valley and beyond that range from two to four hours. During full-moon weeks spring through fall, the enchanting mystery of the valley at night can be experienced on open-air moonlight tours.

Even a one-day excursion is a dramatic revelation of 500 million years of evolutionary process that began when the Sierra Nevada lay beneath an ancient sea. As sediment merged with molten rock, granite was formed and then exposed by erosion. Where summer visitors today picnic and sun on Merced River's beaches in the park, an ancient Alpine glacier cut through weaker granite and enlarged the canyon. What remains are the stunning monoliths—El Capitan, Half Dome, Cathedral Rocks, and their sisters.

Rare for most travellers is the opportunity to learn basic rock-climbing techniques as beginners or to polish up advanced skills. The prestigious **Yosemite Mountaineering School** teaches classes daily from May through September at Tuolumne Meadows, 55 miles (88 km) by road north of Yosemite Valley. You will learn hand- and footholds and the use of belays and rappels. Classes move back to the valley in the fall.

Climbers come to Yosemite from around the world to scale the face of **El Capitan**, guardian of the valley entrance and the largest single granite rock in the world. More than three times as high as Australia's Ayers Rock, it is almost 4,000 feet from summit to base. From a turnout along El Capitan Meadow in summer, climbers can be glimpsed as tiny moving dots on the sheer surface. These great brooding blocks of stone generated superlatives in a newspaper article as early as 1855, from one of the park's early visitors nine years before Abraham Lincoln signed the Yosemite Grant— an act that laid the foundation for all succeeding national and state parks.

Unlike many of the nation's parks, Yosemite's activity agenda is controlled by changing seasons. At two visitors' centers in mid-valley, maps and backcountry information are available. A video program illustrating "One Day in Yosemite" and a helpful staff will help to plan an itinerary. The invaluable, free, fact-packed Yosemite Guide lists every scheduled program and activity in the park. Write Yosemite Association, P.O. Box 230, El Portal, CA 95318, or call general information for the park at (209) 379-2646.

Summer is predictably the peak-activity and peak-crowd period. Last-minute accommodations can be limited or nonexistent on holiday weekends, so be sure to plan ahead. Summertime is for swimming in the beautiful but chilly Merced River at the eastern end of the valley, and river rafts, life jackets, and paddles are available for rent in early summer at Curry Village in the valley. Hazardous rapids put a limit on the safe rafting area, but rafting here is an exciting adventure nonetheless.

Gear up for a guided saddle ride if you're in the park any time from early spring through November (weather permitting). At a leisurely pace, savor valley meadows carpeted with spring wildflowers and flowering shrubs, and ride through lush oak woodlands and cedar forests. With luck you can spy a mule deer, a black bear, or a glorious orange-and-black monarch butterfly in a field of lupine. Look for the pale-gold mariposa lily and the pink-crimson shooting star. Your horse has the right-of-way on all trails, something to remember as well if you are a hiker. Parents of small children can rent gentle ponies to take along on walks. Horses are rented at Yosemite Valley Stables at the upper end of the valley. Reservations are necessary; Tel: (209) 372-1248.

Hiking and climbing shoes and sports gear are the practical merchandise offered by Yosemite Valley shops. For the browser as well as the collector with an interest in Native American jewelry and handicrafts, visit the Ahwahnee Hotel shop and the Indian Shop at Yosemite Lodge (see below for both). Original photographs by Ansel Adams, who glorified Yosemite for almost 70 years, are on display at the **Ansel Adams Gallery**, where staff photographers conduct free workshops and lead camera walks in spring and fall.

The Yosemite Guide's rating and timing chart of hikes to almost a dozen popular Yosemite attractions is a valuable planning tool for the novice as well as the dedicated mountaineer. The scale ranges from easy to very strenuous, and the times range from 20 minutes to 12 hours. Half Dome and Bridalveil Fall are two popular hikes.

Incomparable **Half Dome**, perhaps the most photographed and easily identified of the ice-carved giant granites, is rated very strenuous—a 10- to 12-hour 17-mile round trip. If you opt for a view from the base, look for the profile of an Ahwahnee Indian princess on the vertical surface.

Much less taxing is a 20-minute round-trip walk to Lower Yosemite Falls from a valley-floor start at a shuttle-bus stop. Upper Yosemite Falls is more demanding, with a trail climb of 2,700 feet in 3½ miles, and is a six- to eight-hour round trip. The reward is a memorable view of the highest of North America's falls (most dramatic in May and June). Linked by an intermediate cascade, the Yosemite Falls plunge 2,425 feet.

Bridalveil Fall, in the western part of the valley, was *Pohono* (spirit of the puffing wind) to the Yosemite Indians, because swirling drafts often force the frothy water sideways in billowy surprise. But after mid-August the falls are a disappointment because they become nearly or completely dry.

How the falls and Half Dome were formed during the half a billion years of Yosemite's existence is the subject of a film shown evenings in the theater at the visitors' center. Check the Yosemite Guide for this and other nature films.

Little changed in the wondrous valley that became the heart of the park between the time the first people arrived 10,000 years ago and the 1868 arrival of famed naturalist John Muir, whose indefatigable efforts set the tone for preservation awareness that has endured in the succeeding years. An introduction to the descendants of the land's first inhabitants, the Miwok and Paiute tribes, is the centerpiece of the **Yosemite Museum** and the **Indian Cultural Exhibit** at the visitors' center. Displays and a re-created Ahwahnee Indian village show aspects of the life of a people who gathered and ground acorns, hunted with bows and arrows, and developed basketry to a high art.

It was an expedition aimed at subduing Indian hostility to gold miners in the early 1850s that brought the volunteer Mariposa Battalion of soldiers face to face with the magnificence of the valley, and began the revelation of its wonders to outsiders. Later two Native Americans served as guides for the first tourist, James Hutchings, whose impassioned adjectives in a newspaper article encouraged 42 tourists to make their way to Yosemite Valley in 1855. That was the beginning.

The High Country

In a park bigger than the state of Rhode Island, there is still escape from high-season crowds: in the High Country, reached by daily bus service or private car. The summer-only Tioga Road has turnouts for sublime views of lakes, domes, and crags that were under glacial ice 10,000 years ago. (The road branches off Highway 120, which leads east from Big Oak Flat, a tiny town about an hour east of Sonora.) Tenaya, one of the most beautiful of the Sierra lakes, is in this area and deserves a stop.

As you continue east you will come to Tuolumne Meadows Visitor Center, just south of Tioga Road a few miles before the Tioga Pass crests at 9,900 feet. Tioga is the highest of California's vehicle passes through the Sierra and is closed in winter.

From **Tuolumne Meadows**, trails branch off in all directions into the wilderness. Maps at the visitors' center will direct day-hikers toward Lembert Dome and Elizabeth Lake, both splendid treks for becoming acquainted with the largest subalpine meadow in the entire Sierra Nevada range. Information is also at hand about four-day guided hiking trips offered by both the Yosemite Mountaineering School and the Yosemite Association.

Early summer promises an abundance of wildflowers and wildlife activity in that brief, warm, growing season at 8,500 feet. Follow John Muir, who said, "Climb the mountains and get their good tidings. Nature's peace will flow into you as sunshine flows into trees." Icy lakes and ponds reflect emerald meadow borders or chains of granite crags, and attract the mule deer, the wily black bear, and the elusive coyote. More elusive still are the California bighorn sheep. Once facing extinction in Yosemite National Park, herds of the sheep are being reintroduced and can be sighted occasionally along the eastern park edge beyond Tuolumne Meadows. During mating season in late October the aggressive rams, bearing magnificent antlers that can weigh up to 30 pounds, butt heads with crashes audible almost a mile away. Celebrated for its song and its eccentricities is the Sierra ouzel; the fortunate hiker should be alert to this gray, wren-like bird that walks on pool and stream bottoms to search for food. It is capable of underwater flight when the current is swift.

Staying in Yosemite

If your focus in Yosemite is on the High Country, you can rent tent cabins at ► **Tuolumne Meadows Lodge** from summer to fall. Breakfast and dinner are served in a rustic tent within sight and sound of the Tuolumne River. Reservations for dinner are required; Tel: 372-1313. Backpackers have their pick of five High Sierra camps, each in an area selected for its nature interests and mountain grandeur. Accommodations are dormitory style, and morning and evening meals are included in the price.

► **White Wolf Lodge** is just north of Tioga Road, about halfway between Yosemite Valley and Tuolumne Meadows; day-hikers value its proximity to Lukens and Harden lakes. If you are planning a longer stop, tent cabins are available. Dinner reservations are advised; Tel: 372-1316.

Summer-camp simplicity is not a hallmark of the ► **Ahwahnee Hotel** in Yosemite Valley. A National Historic Landmark, this recently refurbished luxury hotel opened in 1927 and has maintained its reputation for elegance, comfort, and fine cuisine through the succeeding years. Framed by nature with the granite Royal Arches at the north end of the valley, the hotel has rooms with TVs, mini-bars, and hairdryers, as well as vistas of thick forests and of the meadow. Towering dining room windows set the stage for meals served with distinctive china, silver, and crystal. Casual is acceptable for breakfast and lunch, but dinner is dressy—no jeans or shorts. Dinner reservations are required; Tel: 372-1489.

In mid-valley the ► **Yosemite Lodge** occupies the site where Fort Yosemite, headquarters of the U.S. Army Cavalry, once stood. The Army was responsible for the administration and protection of the park from 1906 to 1914 (the National Park Service took over two years later). Rooms are scaled from deluxe-with-balcony to bath-down-the-hall to rustic cabins. The lodge is open all year and offers three choices of dining: a cafeteria, which serves three meals daily; the **Four Seasons Restaurant**, where family dining is the key; and the **Mountain Room Broiler**, where broiled steak and chicken are popular.

Glacier Point overshadows ► **Curry Village** on torrid summer days in the valley. At this, the oldest establishment in the park, cabins and hotel rooms are available from spring to fall.

An hour's drive south of Yosemite Valley on the way to the Mariposa Grove, the largest of the three giant Sequoia stands in the park, is the charming Victorian ► **Wawona Hotel**. Like the Ahwahnee, it is a National Historic Landmark and is also recognized by the California Trust for its meticulously restored interior. The rambling, white-balconied Wawona (a Native American word thought to mean "big tree") is circled by lawns and a nine-hole golf course, where players share the greens with grazing deer herds. Time your evening meal for sunset in the hotel dining room, memorable for its views as well as its cuisine. Dinner reservations are required; Tel: 375-6556.

South of Yosemite itself via Highway 41 in the town of Fish Camp, the new ▶ **Marriott Tenaya Lodge** joins resort amenities (indoor-outdoor pools, saunas, programs for children) to a rustic atmosphere. It's also handy for drivers who want to pick up Highway 49 at its beginning in Oakhurst.

Other Sights in Yosemite

From the Wawona Hotel a historic covered bridge leads to the **Pioneer Yosemite History Center**, a collection of relocated historic buildings and horse-drawn carriages. Ranger-led walks, stagecoach rides, and living history programs focus on the people who shaped Yosemite's history.

Another 15-minute drive farther south from Wawona is the **Mariposa Grove**. The history of the giants here parallels that of the Western world. The average mature *Sequoiadendron giganteum* is 20 feet in diameter; the largest, 35 to nearly 40 feet. As you stand beneath their crowns, towering 200 to 300 feet above, you can't help feeling not only dwarfed, but also awed and uplifted.

Private vehicles are not allowed beyond the grove parking area; walk or take the tram ride May through October. It is less than a mile from the lot to the foot of dominating Grizzly Giant, thought to be the oldest of the Sequoias at 2,700 years. These trees are cousins of the taller Coast Redwoods (*Sequoia sempervirens*), which tower up to 367 feet but whose girth is only 20 to 22 feet.

One of the oddities of the Sequoias' survival mechanism is a need for fire to assure reproduction, so the National Park Service sets prescribed fires to simulate natural ones and encourage growth. You'll find smaller groves at the Tuolumne stand near Crane Flat and at Merced Grove, off Big Oak Flat Road near the northwest entrance to the park.

Winter in Yosemite

Winter is a different world in Yosemite. The Merced River flows along snowy banks decorated with icicles then, and the snow-covered valley floor is stark against the circles of deep-hued evergreens and bare-branched trees. Weather is generally mild here, when the visitor count dwindles along with the rates.

You can ski at **Badger Pass**, 40 minutes southwest of the valley, with 90 miles worth of trailheads and roads for cross-country and downhill skiing, or you can ice skate—at the only outdoor rink in California—at the Curry Village complex in the valley against the spectacular backdrop of snow-blanketed Half Dome and Glacier Point. Snow may close most valley hiking trails in winter, but there are other activities. Park Service naturalists lead a daily snowshoe interpretive walk on a moderate 3-mile course in the Badger Pass Ski Area. No experience is necessary, and you can rent snowshoes. If you'd like to see an animal in the wild, your chance of spotting a bobcat or coyote multiply in winter, when wildlife tracks are easier to pick out in the snow. Or head for the snow-play area on Southside Drive in the valley.

Gourmets and wine connoisseurs find the winter season here attractive for its annual Vintners' Weekends and Chefs' Holidays at the Ahwahnee Hotel. These events are pricey but worth the indulgence. The Yosemite Winterfest is a traditional winter carnival at Badger Pass, complete with slalom racing and other forms of ski competition. The Winter Hotline has all the information for these events and takes reservations for them; Tel: (209) 454-2000.

No description of the glories and delights of Yosemite is complete without mention of the ten-year planning effort by the National Park Service to return Yosemite Valley to its natural state in the face of an overwhelming surge of visitors. Progress has been made in backcountry cleanup and in restoring one of the park's meadows—and there's still more on the agenda. Some critics, though, call the plan unrealistic for including proposals to remove primitive tent cabins and, eventually, prohibit all private vehicles. Budget constraints are blamed for the lag in "de-urbanizing" the Incomparable Valley.

Although millions who visit every year glow with memories, there are some to whom nature is not benevolent. Tragedy can result unless hikers stick to marked trails and roads and realize that rivers, streams, and waterfalls can look inviting but may prove treacherous. Feeding wild animals is not only inadvisable, it will subject you to a Park Service fine. Fines also apply to any failure to store food properly in designated lockers provided to outwit black bears—they look brown, but they are indeed black bears—and they are no fools. Bears know the connection between ice chests and food and may break into containers whether food is present or not. Canny Yosemite bears figured out long ago the tenderfoot backpacker technique of hanging food in one tree and tying it with a rope to another tree; chewing through the rope and waiting for the food to drop is no puzzle to the bears. So far, a counterbalance method has been bear-proof, but no one is taking any bets.

GETTING AROUND

Sacramento Metropolitan Airport is only 20 minutes from downtown Sacramento by cab or shuttle bus. Rental cars are available from the airport or at downtown locations, and some hotels have courtesy transportation. Most points of interest are within easy walking distance from Old Town. Sacramento has an efficient bus and light rail system; there is also a Sacramento Sightseeing Service with daily tours of one or three hours; Tel: (916) 486-9262.

Once outside the metropolitan area, driving yourself is the only real option, because public transit systems in the Gold Country are purely local and limited. Driving distances are manageable; driving times will depend on the byways you want to follow.

While "rush hour" in the Gold Country may seem mild to the average urban dweller, there are areas where the traffic light is still unknown. Plan your long hauls between the morning and evening traffic crunch.

The Golden Chain map of Highway 49 is a detailed guide geared to Gold Rush history and interests. Any Chamber of Commerce in the area should be able to supply you with one. County maps may also be helpful, because road signs do not crop up on every corner, and you could find yourself with a picnic basket and no park table.

Ask for activities schedules wherever you plan a stopover. Art and little-theater festivals are popular the length of Highway 49, with many taking place during summer or in early fall.

Few gas stations in small Gold Rush towns are open 24 hours a day, so plan your purchases accordingly. If you venture north to Downieville, go with a full tank.

Dress for comfort in the Gold Country. Tank tops and

shorts are acceptable in summer, jeans and shirts when it's cooler. Remember, the first Levi's were made here during the Gold Rush from tent material—that is one fashion that hasn't changed.

Yosemite National Park can be reached from Oakland (across San Francisco's Bay Bridge) by daily Amtrak service, which stops in Merced and connects there to the Yosemite Gray Line tour (daily from Merced year round); for Amtrak information, Tel: (800) 872-7245; for Gray Line information, Tel: (209) 383-1563. (Merced is about 40 miles/64 km west of Mariposa, one of the last Highway 49 Gold Rush communities in the Southern Mines area.)

ACCOMMODATIONS REFERENCE
The rate ranges given here are projections for fall 1993 through spring 1994. Unless otherwise indicated, rates are for double room, double occupancy.

▶ **Ahwahnee Hotel.** Yosemite Park & Curry Company, **Yosemite National Park**, CA 95389. Tel: (209) 252-4848. $188–$208.

▶ **Alta Sierra Resort.** 135 Tammy Way, **Grass Valley**, CA 95945. Tel: (916) 273-9102 or (800) 992-5300. $69–$145.

▶ **American River Inn.** Orleans and Main streets, **Georgetown**, CA 95634. Tel: (916) 333-4499 or (800) 245-6566; Fax: 333-9253. $80–$100.

▶ **Annie Horan's.** 415 West Main Street, **Grass Valley**, CA 95945. Tel: (916) 272-2418. $75–$105.

▶ **Barretta Gardens Inn.** 700 South Barretta Street, **Sonora**, CA 95370. Tel: (209) 532-6039. $80–$95.

▶ **Best Western Ponderosa Motor Inn.** 1100 H Street, **Sacramento**, CA 95814. Tel: (916) 441-1314 or (800) 528-1234; Fax: 441-5961. $80.

▶ **Black Bart Inn.** 55 West Saint Charles Street, **San Andreas**, CA 95249. Tel: (209) 754-3808. $49–$58.

▶ **Coloma Country Inn.** 2 High Street, **Coloma**, CA 95613. Tel: (916) 622-6919. $89–$99.

▶ **Columbia City Hotel.** Main Street, **Columbia**, CA 95310. Tel: (209) 532-1479. $65–$90.

▶ **Court Street Inn.** 215 Court Street, **Jackson**, CA 95642. Tel: (209) 223-0416. $90–$135.

▶ **Curry Village.** Yosemite Park & Curry Company, **Yosemite National Park**, CA 95389. Tel: (209) 252-4848. $72.25.

▶ **Downey House.** 517 West Broad Street, **Nevada City**, CA 95959. Tel: (916) 265-2815 or (800) 258-2815. $70–$90.

▶ **Dunbar House 1880**. 271 Jones Street, **Murphys**, CA 95247. Tel: (209) 728-2897. $105–$145.

▶ **Fallon Hotel**. Main Street, **Columbia**, CA 95310. Tel: (209) 532-1470. $50–$90.

▶ **Fitzpatrick Lodge**. 7740 Fairplay Road, **Somerset**, CA 95684. Tel: (209) 245-3248; Fax: 245-6838. $79.

▶ **Foxes**. 77 Main Street, **Sutter Creek**, CA 95685. Tel: (209) 267-5882; Fax: 267-0712. $95–$135.

▶ **Gate House Inn**. 1330 Jackson Gate Road, **Jackson**, CA 95642. Tel: (209) 223-3500. $75–$105.

▶ **Gold Trail Motor Lodge**. 1970 Broadway, **Placerville**, CA 95667. Tel: (916) 622-2906. $39–$40.

▶ **Golden Chain Resort**. 13363 Highway 49, **Grass Valley**, CA 95945. Tel: (916) 273-7279. $42–$68.

▶ **Grand Island Mansion**. 14340 Highway 160, P.O. Box 43, **Ryde**, CA 95680. Tel: (916) 775-1705. $55–$90.

▶ **Grandmère's**. 449 Broad Street, **Nevada City**, CA 95959. Tel: (916) 265-4660. $95–$145.

▶ **Gunn House**. 286 South Washington Street, **Sonora**, CA 95370. Tel: (209) 532-3421. $40–$75.

▶ **Holbrooke Hotel**. 212 West Main Street, **Grass Valley**, CA 95945. Tel: (916) 273-1353 or (800) 933-7077; Fax: 273-0434. $55–$140.

▶ **Holiday Inn Capitol Plaza**. 300 J Street, **Sacramento**, CA 95814. Tel: (916) 446-0100 or (800) 465-4329. $96.

▶ **Hyatt Regency**. 1209 L Street, **Sacramento**, CA 95814. Tel: (916) 443-1234 or (800) 233-1234. $99–$175.

▶ **Imperial Hotel**. Highway 49, **Amador City**, CA 95601. Tel: (209) 267-9172. $60–$90.

▶ **Jamestown Hotel**. 18153 Main Street, **Jamestown**, CA 95327. Tel: (209) 984-3902. $59–$118.

▶ **La Casa Inglesa**. 18047 Lime Kiln Road, **Sonora**, CA 95370. Tel: (209) 532-5822; in California, (800) 870-5057. $75–$100.

▶ **Llamahall Guest Ranch**. 18170 Wards Ferry Road, **Sonora**, CA 95370. Tel: (209) 532-7264. $85–$105.

▶ **Marriott Tenaya Lodge**. 1122 Highway 41, **Fish Camp**, CA 93623. Tel: (209) 683-6555 or (800) 635-5807. $139–$215.

▶ **Mine House Inn**. 14125 Highway 49, **Amador City**, CA 95601. Tel: (209) 267-5900. $55–$65.

▶ **Murphys Historic Hotel**. 457 Main Street, **Murphys**, CA 95247. Tel: (209) 728-3444. $70–$80.

▶ **Murphy's Inn**. 318 Neal Street, **Grass Valley**, CA 95945. Tel: (916) 273-6873. $77–$131.

▶ **National Hotel**. 2 Water Street, **Jackson**, CA 95642. Tel: (209) 223-0500. $45.

▶ **National Hotel.** Main Street, **Jamestown**, CA 95327. Tel: (209) 984-3446. $45–$80.

▶ **National Hotel.** 211 Broad Street, **Nevada City**, CA 95959. Tel: (916) 265-4551. $42–$68.

▶ **Northern Queen Inn.** 400 Railroad Avenue, **Nevada City**, CA 95959. Tel: (916) 265-5824. $54–$90.

▶ **Piety Hill.** 523 Sacramento Street, **Nevada City**, CA 95959. Tel: (916) 265-2245 or (800) 443-2245. $79–$125.

▶ **Red Lion Inn.** 2001 Point West Way, **Sacramento**, CA 95815. Tel: (916) 929-8855. $76–$114.

▶ **Robin's Nest.** 247 West Saint Charles Street, **San Andreas**, CA 95249. Tel: (209) 754-1076. $55–$95.

▶ **St. George Hotel.** 16104 Pine Grove Volcano Road, **Volcano**, CA 95689. Tel: (209) 296-4458. $110.

▶ **Sierra Nevada House.** P.O. Box 496, Highway 49 and Lotus Road, **Coloma**, CA 95613. Tel: (916) 621-1649. $65–$75.

▶ **Sterling Hotel.** 1300 H Street, **Sacramento**, CA 95814. Tel: (916) 448-1300 or (800) 365-7660; Fax: 448-8066. $110–$225.

▶ **Sutter Creek Inn.** P.O. Box 385, 75 Main Street, **Sutter Creek**, CA 95685. Tel: (209) 267-5606. $50–$135.

▶ **Swan-Levine House.** 328 South Church Street, **Grass Valley**, CA 95945. Tel: (916) 272-1873. $55–$85.

▶ **Tuolumne Meadows Lodge.** Yosemite Park & Curry Company, **Yosemite National Park**, CA 95389. Tel: (209) 252-4848. $36.75.

▶ **Vineyard House.** 530 Cold Springs Road, **Coloma**, CA 95613. Tel: (916) 622-2217; Fax: 933-1031. $70–$89.

▶ **Vizcaya.** 2019 21st Street, **Sacramento**, CA 95818. Tel: (916) 455-5243 or (800) 456-2019; Fax: 455-6102. $79–$225.

▶ **Wawona Hotel.** Yosemite Park & Curry Company, **Yosemite National Park**, CA 95389. Tel: (209) 252-4848. $63.25–$86.25.

▶ **White Wolf Lodge.** Yosemite Park & Curry Company, **Yosemite National Park**, CA 95389. Tel: (209) 252-4848. $31.75–$56.

▶ **Yosemite Lodge.** Yosemite Park & Curry Company, **Yosemite National Park**, CA 95389. Tel: (209) 252-4848. $33.50–$89.25.

LAKE TAHOE AND FAR WESTERN NEVADA

By David W. Toll

Nevada is not like California. Despite being next-door neighbors, with interwoven social and economic ties, these two very Western states are quite distinct from each other. To oversimplify: California is the leading edge of the 21st century, and Nevada is the last remnant of the 19th.

California, with the seventh-largest economy in the world, is the tip of the United States arrow, a world leader in social and political innovation. Nevada is the seventh-largest state in the nation, more than half a million square miles of mostly undeveloped scrub-forested mountains and broad brushy valleys. Its two urban areas, Reno and environs in the north and Las Vegas in the south, contain 80 percent of the state's population.

You will experience a subtle sense of dislocation as you travel from California into Nevada when the pine forests of California's High Sierra suddenly drop away and you rocket down 3,000 feet into the desert vastness of Nevada, land of hidden treasures.

Lake Tahoe buttons these two unlikely neighbors together at the border. The magnificent natural landscapes of Tahoe and far western Nevada combine with their hell-raising histories and with the luxuries and comforts of modern resort hotels and gambling casinos to form a beguiling mix that attracts more than seven million visitors each year.

Nevada's northern metropolitan area—the other, larger one is based in Las Vegas nearly 500 miles to the south, and we do not cover it in this guidebook—is centered on the adjacent cities of Reno and Sparks, with a western lobe at Tahoe and a southern lobe containing Virginia City, Carson City, and the Carson Valley.

Reno, once a rambunctious little railroad town at Lake's Crossing, has outgrown its naughty youth and begun at last to live up to its Roaring Twenties brag as the Biggest Little City in the World. Sparks, Reno's near neighbor on the east side of the Truckee Meadows, has developed an energetic reputation of its own as an industrial city. Carson City, the old Territorial capital, has lately become a manufacturing center, and the smaller towns of the region, almost all of them dating from the pioneer period, reflect their adventurous beginnings on the Western frontier.

Base yourself in Lake Tahoe's High Country if you can, and make day trips down to Reno, Carson City, Virginia City, and the other nearby communities. They have much to offer, but none of them can match Tahoe for sheer physical beauty.

MAJOR INTEREST

Lake Tahoe
Casinos
Ski resorts
Truckee

Carson City
Carson Valley
Historic Virginia City

Reno and Sparks
Casinos
Pyramid Lake
Washoe Valley

LAKE TAHOE

Mark Twain called Lake Tahoe "the fairest picture the whole earth affords." He visited Lake Tahoe in 1863, just 19 years after the first visit to Tahoe from the East Coast, by John C. Frémont in 1844. Twain set up camp at what is now Marla

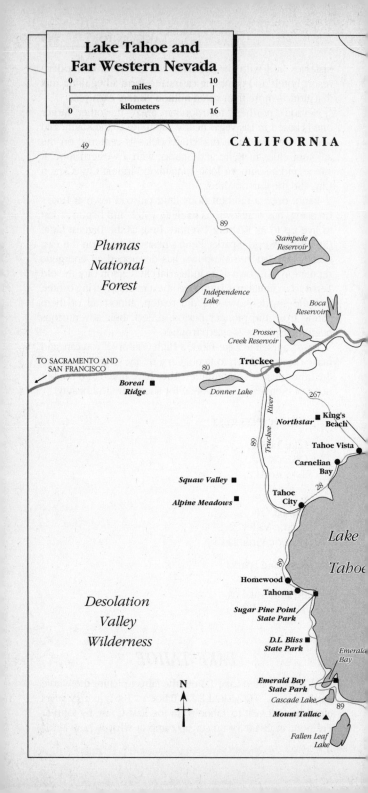

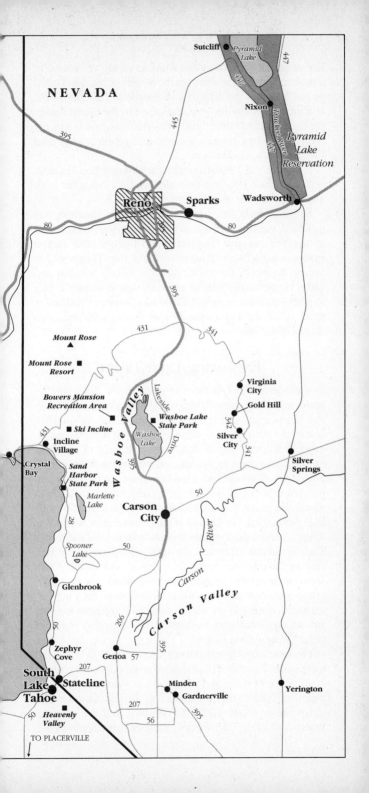

Bay in an attempt to establish a timber ranch; unfortunately, a mishap with his campfire set the forest on fire, and he had to row out into the lake to save his life as his camp—and half the mountainside—was consumed by the raging flames. He then pursued other career opportunities, first as a quartz miner at Aurora, then as a newspaper reporter at Virginia City, but that's another story.

It was also in 1863 that stagecoach tycoon Ben Holladay built a vacation retreat at Emerald Bay. Lake Tahoe has been a favorite vacation getaway ever since.

In those early times and in the dreamy summers that followed, vacationers came to Tahoe by stagecoach and later aboard the train that chugged up the Truckee River canyon from the main line at Truckee to Tahoe City. They rested in luxury at enormous resorts like the Glenbrook Inn and Tallac House and glided out across the lake from pier to pier in graceful steamers named *Tahoe* and *Governor Stanford*. A string of small communities grew up on the north and south shores of the lake.

Exploring Lake Tahoe

As a modern visitor to Tahoe, you can fly or drive into the basin, most likely from Northern California, to stay in a high-rise hotel-casino, in a less expensive motel, or—if you have reserved your campsite ahead of time—in a public camp-ground. You can choose from among dozens of excellent eating places, take to the lake on everything from boogie boards to many-decked glass-bottomed excursion boats, play tennis and golf, and lounge around swimming pools in which the water is considerably warmer than in the chilly lake. Ski resorts, unheard of at Tahoe until after World War II, attract enthusiastic winter visitors from around the world. Through all this expansion, the small settlements of the 19th century have grown larger and denser, and, at the South Shore in particular, peak summer weekends are positively urban with crowds and traffic jams. Still, even on a hot July weekend, once you are off the main thoroughfares the lake and its surrounding mountains provide a perfect vision of beauty, majesty, and peace.

The best ways to experience the lake are to make the spectacular 72-mile (115-km) drive around its perimeter, to hike the forest trails, and to take to the water. Lake cruisers maintain regular schedules from May through October. The sternwheeler **Dixie** (Tel: 702-588-3508) and the trimaran **Woodwind** (Tel: 702-588-3000) embark from Zephyr Cove

Marina on the Nevada shore, the **Tahoe Queen** (Tel: 916-541-3364) from Ski Run Marina at the South Shore, and the smaller **Sunrunner** (Tel: 916-583-0141) from Tahoe City on California's North Shore. (The *Dixie* and the *Tahoe Queen* also offer dinner cruises.) Small boats can be rented for fishing, water-skiing, or cruising at many of the marinas around the lake, and there is even a seaplane to take passengers for an air-and-water tour at **Cal Vada Aircraft, Inc.** (Tel: 916-525-7143) in Homewood, on the west shore.

The surface of Lake Tahoe is officially designated at 6,226.95 feet above sea level, although actual elevation varies according to the season and the amount of water allowed to flow out into the Truckee River for the use of the Nevada communities and agriculture downstream. Tahoe, about 12 miles wide and about 22 miles long, with nearly 200 square miles of surface area, is the largest Alpine lake on the North American continent, 1,645 feet deep at its deepest point. Its pure (99.9 percent) water would cover the entire state of California 14 inches deep. While the surface layer of the lake warms to 68 degrees F by the end of summer, allowing swimming and water-skiing in relative comfort, the winter temperature of the water drops to a chilly 39 degrees. (It gets so chilled because it's mostly snow-pack runoff that lies motionless in the depths at this high elevation.) Five consecutive drought years have lowered the level of water in the lake to well below normal.

Statistical data aside, the Lake Tahoe Basin is one of the most beautiful places on the face of the earth, with a thriving economy based on pleasing visitors. A drive around the perimeter leads to so many different possibilities for enjoyment that it's best to devote the whole day to it. It's possible (but not recommended) to make the drive in less than three hours, assuming you're resolute enough to avoid stopping, but by making it a day's outing you'll give yourself the freedom to stop for food, drink, and to take walks through the pine forests as your mood and inspiration dictate.

Although you will probably enter the Lake Tahoe region via Interstate 80 at Truckee, to the northwest of the lake, our circular tour begins and ends on the South Shore, where you are most likely to be staying.

The South Shore

The blaze of bright lights at the Nevada-California borderline provides the focal point for the communities at the south end of Lake Tahoe collectively known as South Shore, particularly

South Lake Tahoe, on the California side of the border, and Stateline, on the Nevada side. The enormous resort hotel-casinos here, all on the Nevada side of the line (casino gambling is legal in Nevada and not in California), provide employment for many of Tahoe's full-time residents. To the customers who patronize them and play the gambling games, they provide entertainment (often featuring major stars), comfortable accommodations, and food varying from a cup of snack bar coffee to a lavish gourmet feast. ▶ Harrah's, for example, has, in addition to its 535 guest rooms and its casino, a snack bar, a deli sandwich shop, a 24-hour coffee shop and restaurant, a steak and seafood restaurant, a brunch and dinner buffet, a gourmet dining room, and a showroom where meals are served as a part of the first show of the evening. ▶ Caesars Tahoe, ▶ Harvey's, and the ▶ Horizon offer accommodations and dining on a similar scale. Their best is among the very best at the lake.

In contrast to the international style of the casinos, a variety of local and regional cuisines are represented on the South Shore. In the town of South Lake Tahoe the **Dory's Oar** (Tel: 916-541-6603) offers a New England seafood menu; at **Nepheles** (Tel: 916-544-8130) it is California cuisine, complete with hot tubs for after-dinner relaxation. At **Evan's American Gourmet Café** (Tel: 916-542-1990) on Highway 89, the name says it all, while at the **Tahoe House** at 625 Tahoe Boulevard (Highway 50) half a mile south of Highway 89, the menu is Swiss, with French, German, and Italian accents. The wine list is good and desserts are a specialty (Tel: 916-583-1377).

There are many other dining places worth considering. For the views and the ascent—getting there is half the fun—dine at the **Top of the Tram** at the Heavenly Valley ski area (Tel: 916-541-1330; in summer, 544-6263). The dinner cruises aboard the *Tahoe Queen* from Ski Run Marina and the *Dixie* from Zephyr Cove (see above) make a most glamorous experience on a silky summer's night, with dance bands that play after dinner.

And that's just the beginning. The care and feeding of visitors is the leading local industry, with more opportunities around the lake than even most residents have tried yet, and even the least pretentious of them is good. **Izzy's Burger Spa**, for example, is just a little hamburger stand beside the lake in South Lake Tahoe, but the burgers it serves are memorable.

The **Lake Tahoe Historical Society Museum** (Tel: 916-541-5458), adjacent to the Chamber of Commerce on Highway

50 in South Lake Tahoe, provides a brief glimpse into Tahoe's past and includes a small exhibit of Native American artifacts.

The six miles of lakefront on the California side of the state line are heavily built up with small businesses of every description, but from the junction where Highway 89 turns north along the lake's western shore (U.S. 50 continues west to Placerville and Sacramento), the bustling traffic of town is left behind.

The West Shore

Tahoe's west shore is what remains of the old classic era of Lake Tahoe's gilded age. Most of the area is still relatively unchanged from that earlier era when only a favored few could afford lodges, chalets, and cabins for the summer, and only two or three dozen people toughed it out through the long, deep winters.

A few miles past the junction with Highway 50, just north of the Fallen Leaf Lake turnoff on Highway 89, is the U. S. **Forest Service Visitor Center** (Tel: 916-573-2674). Camping and hiking information is available here for the entire Tahoe Basin; guided walks and boat tours are also offered. One of the highlights of the visitors' center is the stream-profile chamber on Taylor Creek, an underground room built so that its "windows" provide a trout's-eye view of the stream and its aquatic life. Fascinating at any season, the chamber is especially colorful when the kokanee salmon are spawning in the autumn. Rangers also conduct campfire programs at the Lake of the Sky Amphitheater near the center.

Not far away is the **Tallac Historic Site**, where the mansion-size stone-and-log "cabins" of the Pope and Baldwin estates hark back to long Sunday afternoon picnics with parasols and boater hats. They are now maintained by the forest service, which offers tours during the summer months; also in the warm months, events such as August's Great Gatsby Festival, a Roaring Twenties celebration with Dixieland music and classic cars and boats, and the Starlight Jazz and Blues Festival (in August and September) are offered.

NATIVE AMERICANS AT LAKE TAHOE
Along with an exhibit devoted to pioneer tycoon-gambler Elias "Lucky" Baldwin, a Native American museum is open Saturday and Sunday on the grounds of the adjacent **McGonagle Estate**. Indians inhabited the Tahoe Basin for some 10,000 years before the arrival of the white man, and

you will see evidence of their activities—grinding stones, for example, where they crushed and pulverized the seeds they gathered—all around the lake.

The Washoe tribe were the dominant people to live here in the 19th century, coming up from the valleys to the east in spring and departing again with the onset of the snows; they spoke Hokan, a language unrelated to the Uto-Aztecan languages spoken by the Nevada Shoshone and Paiute tribes to the east. The name Tahoe is derived from the Washoe words *Da ow* (meaning "big water"—not "grasshopper soup," as Mark Twain explained it).

Barely 20 years after Frémont's sighting of Tahoe, the Washoe were being written off by these newcomers. In 1866 the superintendent of Indian Affairs reported, "There is no suitable place for a reservation in the bounds of their territory, and in view of their rapidly diminishing numbers and the diseases to which they are subject, none is required." By 1870 the Washoe population had diminished to about 500 people. One of them, a young woman named Dat-So-La-Lee, learned the traditional survival skills of her tribe and excelled in basket making. In the 1890s, the baskets she made attracted the attention of Abe Cohn, a Carson City merchant and trader, whose promotion and sponsorship of Dat-So-La-Lee brought recognition to the beauty and artistry of her baskets; today the examples of her handiwork are considered priceless works of art. The Washoe tribe is now based near Gardnerville in the Carson Valley, their traditional homeland.

EMERALD BAY AND HOMEWOOD

Highway 89 continues north from the museum through thick pine forests with meadows and glades and leads to D. L. Bliss and Emerald Bay state parks. Mount Tallac, the lake rim's tallest peak, bears a snowy cross—an X-shaped feature that can be seen from all around Tahoe Basin until the last of the snow melts in the spring. The mountain towers over the pine-forested western shore of Tahoe and Cascade and Fallen Leaf lakes.

The lovely and much-photographed Emerald Bay is a few miles farther north. Emerald Bay encloses Tahoe's only island, Fanette Island, sometimes known as Dead Man's Island because Ben Holladay's caretaker drowned here while rowing back from Tahoe Tavern during a storm. Emerald Bay is also the site of the mighty 38-room Scandinavian-style stone castle called **Vikingsholm**, which you can reach by a one-mile walk down from the parking lot on the highway. Vikingsholm, a replica of a 1,200-year-old Viking castle, was owned by a millionaire who had the home built in one summer by a crew of 200 craftsmen and furnished it with exact copies of antique Scandinavian furniture. Estimated cost of construction in 1928: $500,000 (not including the wildflowers growing in the sod roof). Tours are conducted during the summer months.

At Sugar Pine Point State Park, about 5 miles (8 km) farther north, the 1902 **Ehrman Mansion** provides another glimpse of vanished glories. It's open for touring in summer and has a park for swimming and picnicking. The ▶ **Captain's Alpenhaus** (Tel: 916-525-5000) at nearby Tahoma is an Old World country inn where breakfast, lunch, and dinner are served in a relaxed atmosphere. Meals are Alpine/Italian except for Wednesday dinners, which feature Basque cuisine served family style. The inn also functions as a bed and breakfast.

For an adventure off the beaten track on the quiet western shore at Tahoma, try **Uncle Fudd's Fabulous 50s Diner**. This popular spot serves breakfast and lunch Tuesday through Sunday and dinner Wednesday through Sunday. Call ahead to find out what's being served that night (there's no menu to choose from; just one dinner served to all) and to make dinner reservations (Tel: 916-525-6644); seating is limited in the tiny knotty-pine dining room. To find Uncle Fudd's, turn off Highway 89 on West Lake Boulevard a quarter-mile south of the "Pop. 200" sign and proceed to number 6821.

Homewood, a few meandering miles farther along, is one of Tahoe's venerable resort areas. ▶ **Sunnyside Lodge** is a very contemporary resort serving a modern clientele with the lake's traditional stock in trade: comfortable accommodations, fine food and drink, and natural splendor all around. The pleasing view from the deck looks across the lake to the sparkling lights of the casinos at South Shore, and the bar and restaurant are open to all (reservations are essential). The **Firesign Café** (Tel: 916-583-0871) across the highway serves breakfast and lunch with an emphasis on natural foods and home-style cooking. Mountain Bob's **Old Tahoe Café** on West Lake Boulevard (Tel: 916-525-5437) represents the rustic Tahoe tradition, while the **West Shore Café** (Tel: 916-525-5200) maintains a somewhat more contemporary ambience with outside tables at lakeside.

TAHOE CITY

At Tahoe City, 2 miles (3 km) farther north, the lake spills over its banks to form the Truckee River, which you will cross on the famous Fanny Bridge, so named because of the way folks like to rest their elbows on the rails along each side, peering out over the edge and down into the river at the schools of enormous trout undulating in the current. The Gatekeeper's Cabin, a recently built replica of the structure that stood here from 1909 until 1978, when it burned, is now maintained as a museum by the local historical society and is open to visitors without charge in the summer months.

You'll see a big roadside sign here advertising horses for trail riding, or, when there's enough water in the Truckee, you can rent a raft at Fanny Bridge to float down the more than four miles (about a two-and-a-half-hour cruise) to the **River Ranch** (Tel: 916-583-4264). Partying boaters fill the sunny riverside deck here by day, and diners sample the casual Continental menu by night (for more nearby dining choices see The North Shore, below). Mountain bikes can be rented at Tahoe City, and the bicycle trail along the Truckee River has been paved from the city to River Ranch.

Highway 89 leaves the Lake Tahoe shore at Tahoe City and continues north along the banks of the Truckee to join I-80 just west of Truckee. Both **Alpine Meadows** and **Squaw Valley** ski areas are to the west off this twisting canyon road. Alpine Meadows, 3 miles (5 km) west into the mountains from River Ranch, is the starting point for hiking trails into Sherwood Forest. A few miles farther north, Squaw Valley, which made Tahoe synonymous with the best of skiing, is transformed into a self-contained summer resort when the ski season ends in the spring. The 150-passenger cable cars and six-passenger gondolas carry sightseers up the sheer mountain face for walking and dining at the top of the runs. The views are unforgettable. (See Lake Tahoe Ski Areas below for details on ski-season facilities.)

Truckee

Fewer than 20 miles (32 km) north of Tahoe City on Highway 89 is Truckee, once the ugly duckling of the Sierra, built to accommodate the logging industry's need for railroad access, now an attractive community of considerable distinction and charm. Truckee's architecture ranges the whole spectrum of 19th-century aesthetic, from the brooding, heavy-shouldered Truckee Hotel, bulked up against the deep and heavy snows of winter, to the lightest and airiest of filigreed Victorian mansion houses, all framed by the pine forest and Sierra summits.

The railroad still passes through Truckee, but it is no

longer the crucial link with the rest of the country that it once was. After World War II, U.S. 40 took over the importance the railroad once had, eventually becoming Interstate 80, which passes Truckee on the north and provides the town's main connection with the outside world.

Travellers from the East first passed through here in 1844. Led by Elisha Stevens, they came upon a Paiute Indian, Truckee (later Captain Truckee and then Chief Truckee), who agreed to show them the way over the summits. The grateful pioneers named the river, as well as the trout that swam in it, in his honor. The town of Truckee was called Gray's Station when it was a log-cabin trading post in 1863; renamed Coburn's Station a while later, it was finally named Truckee in the chief's honor when the rails were spiked down here in 1868.

The building of the railroad attracted many people to the area, including a large Chinese population to fill the labor force. All through the 1870s gangs of railroaders, loggers, and others raided the Chinatown that grew when the railroad came through. It was burned four times, and in 1886 all the Chinese residents were forced out of their homes and out of Truckee for good. Truckee's tough reputation persisted into the 1920s as economic stagnation and its relative isolation preserved its frontier character.

The 1960 Winter Olympics, held nearby at Squaw Valley, sparked a reawakening for the town, and now Commercial Row, the little city's main street, is an attractive collection of shops and restaurants serving an all-season clientele of highway travellers, Tahoe visitors, and local folks.

DONNER LAKE

One of the great tragedies of the Western frontier occurred just 3 miles (5 km) west of town, on the shores of Donner Lake. In 1846, as the great national migration westward was just beginning to stir, an "uncohesive assemblage of individuals" (as one historian describes them) set out from Illinois, bound for a better life in California. The Donner Party, as it is now forever known (named for one of its leaders, George Donner), got this far after weeks of wandering in the Nevada desert and suffering six deaths. Here 37 more men, women, and children died, starved and frozen, held captive in this foodless place by the freezing temperatures and the deep snows.

Some who survived reportedly ate some of those who didn't, and some of the dead may have been killed for meat. The horror of cannibalism hung over the lake for many years afterward as other wagon trains crossed the Sierra for the more hospitable regions of California. Thus there is a special irony in the 154-site campground operated here by the state park system.

Staying and Dining in Truckee

Nightlife and dining out are almost synonymous in Truckee, and despite the town's modern attitudes the sidewalks tend to roll up early, even in summer. The **Bar of America**, the **Capitol Saloon**, and a few other drinking houses provide such after-dinner excitement as Truckee offers, except on special occasions. Dinner itself is another matter. Several excellent restaurants cater to local customers as well as to the skiers and summer vacationers who make Truckee a stopping place on their Lake Tahoe vacations.

The **Passage Restaurant** (Tel: 916-587-7619) in the Truckee Hotel offers an ambitious California-cuisine menu in tasteful surroundings. **The Left Bank** on Commercial Row (Tel: 916-587-4694) specializes in seafood in relaxed French style with lots of garlic. (The emphasis on garlic in the Truckee culinary tradition stems from a now-departed French chef who attracted an international clientele from visitors to Lake Tahoe; his legacy lives on at **Pop's**, where the garlic-chip pizza is a highlight.)

The **Cottonwood**, decorated with railroad ties and heavy timbers harking back to Truckee's youth, offers an intriguing menu featuring Cajun and Italian specialties, as well as a welcoming view of downtown from the dining room of the spacious deck.

At the **Truckee Brewing Company** at the junction of Highway 89 and Donner Pass Road the attraction is less the pizzas and submarine sandwiches than the beer brewed on the premises. The Company's boast that it is "the highest brewery in the U.S." is probably safe from contradiction. The **Coffee And** is a classic coffee shop seemingly frozen in time about 40 years back, with delectable homemade fruit pies; cappuccino and espresso are served at **The Cookery Deli** on Commercial Row. **O.B.'s** is a Truckee landmark, with an eclectic menu and cozy surroundings done in lace curtains and antiques—a look known here as Tahoe Rustic.

Several motels serve travellers in Truckee, as does the ► **Truckee Hotel** at the corner of Bridge Street and Commercial Row. This is the largest residential structure in Truckee, built in 1868, the year of Truckee's founding. Rates, which include a full breakfast, are moderate for the renovated rooms. Bed-and-breakfast accommodations are also available in Truckee at ▶ Richardson House on Spring Street and on weekends (two-night minimum) at the ▶ Donner Country Inn on the west shore of Donner Lake. Rates at the Richardson House include evening wine and hors d'oeuvres.

You can return to the shores of Lake Tahoe from Truckee via two all-weather highways. Highway 267 runs southeast to King's Beach and serves the Northstar ski area. Highway 89 follows the course of the Truckee River and provides access to Squaw Valley and Alpine Meadows on the way to Tahoe City. Both cross beautiful forested highlands.

The North Shore

Tahoe City is at the southwestern end of the 15-mile string of small California and Nevada communities collectively called the North Shore. These small towns, extending north-eastward across the state line as far as Incline Village, Nevada, are noticeably quieter and slower-paced than the bright band of lights far across the lake at the South Shore. But for all their calmer qualities, these towns provide numerous enticements to visitors, from lodgings to boat rentals to good food. And while there are many activities available, such as hiking, tennis, and golf, the greatest attraction is still the mountain lake itself. Parks, recreation areas, and public beaches are accessible from the highway at many places along the way—Commons Beach in Tahoe City is right beside the highway—and no matter which way you turn a delightful experience awaits you.

DINING ON THE NORTH SHORE

The North Shore offers a wide variety of dining places, from the cozy and colorful to the most sophisticated, often with evening entertainment.

Sunday brunch is a tradition at Lake Tahoe, and there are any number of wonderful places to serve you. Pick from **Gar Wood's Grill & Pier** (Tel: 916-546-3366) at Carnelian Bay, where the classic wood-boating era at Tahoe is commemorated with oversized photographs and mahogany beams; the **Tahoe Biltmore** (Tel: 702-831-0660) and the **Cal Neva Lodge Resort** (Tel: 702-832-4000) at Crystal Bay; and in Incline Village, **Hugo's Rotisserie** (Tel: 702-831-1111, ext. 4280) at the Hyatt Regency or **Spatz** (Tel: 702-831-8999) on Ski Way Boulevard. All of these brunches include Champagne. The hotel-casinos in Crystal Bay also serve splendid Friday night seafood buffets.

For breakfast on the other days of the week, the **Wildflower Restaurant** (Tel: 702-831-8072) and light-hearted and imaginative **Bobby's Uptown Café** (Tel: 702-831-0404) in Incline Village and the **Log Cabin Caffè** (Tel: 916-546-7109) in King's Beach are local favorites. In Tahoe City the indoor/outdoor **Café Cobblestone** (Tel: 916-583-2111) and friendly **Rosie's Café** (Tel: 916-583-8504) start the morning off right within a few blocks of each other on North Lake Boulevard. You'll find moderate prices, informal atmosphere, and California casual cuisine at all of these cafés.

For French cuisine try **Le Petit Pier** (Tel: 916-546-4464) overlooking the lake at Tahoe Vista, **Soule Domaine** (Tel: 916-546-7529) in King's Beach for relaxed gourmet dining in an elegant log cabin, and **La Fondue** (Tel: 702-831-6104) in Incline Village. **Marie France**, at 907 Tahoe Boulevard in Incline Village (Tel: 702-832-3007), is a dinner house reflecting the personal approach and culinary mastery of its namesake owner-chef. Marie is a graduate of the Cordon Bleu in Paris, and her "filet mignon" of pork with pears and red wine sauce, sweetbreads in lemon sauce, roasted duck with rhubarb sauce, and other favorite entrées are French and creative. There is piano music nightly.

Mexican food is the delight at the long-established **Cantina de los Tres Hombres** (Tel: 916-546-4052) in King's Beach and **Las Panchitas** (Tel: 702-831-4048) in Incline Village, which is unpretentious and homey with friendly service. Italian entrées are featured at **Azzara's** (Tel: 702-831-0346) and **Ferrari's Testarosa** (Tel: 702-831-8878), both in Incline Village.

STAYING ON THE NORTH SHORE

Highway 267 connects the town of King's Beach here on the North Shore with Truckee and leads to **Northstar**, a modern ski resort that provides a variety of amenities and temptations in warmer seasons as well. Take advantage of their shops, 18-hole golf course, tennis courts, swimming pool, horse and mountain-bike rentals, hiking trails, and a restaurant serving lunch at the **Day Creek Lodge**, reached by gondola. (See Lake Tahoe Ski Areas below.)

If you are a golfer, the venerable nine-hole Brockway golf course, now called **Wood Vista**, is at the junction of highways 28 and 267 near Tahoe Vista, and there's another nine-hole course at Tahoe City right on North Lake Boulevard. At Incline Village the Robert Trent Jones–designed **Champion-**

ship course overlooks the lake, as does the shorter Executive Course; both are 18 holes.

A bright cluster of small casinos is gathered at the state line, which actually bisects the venerable ▶ Cal Neva Lodge Resort at the great fireplace in the old lobby, continues across the floor, and outside through the swimming pool. This is the hotel-casino that Frank Sinatra owned a share of in the 1960s until his gambling license was rescinded by the Nevada Gaming Commission for having unsavory playmates; now under new ownership, the Lady of the Lake has been restored to her original elegance and charm and offers cabins, chalets, and lakeview hotel rooms. The **Tahoe Biltmore** and the **Crystal Bay Club**, both lined up on the Nevada side of the state line, also offer gambling, as does **Jim Kelly's Tahoe Nugget**, a small casino that still maintains the local tradition of closing for the winter.

Also east of the state line is the community of **Incline Village**, which has long since outgrown its roots in 19th-century logging and is now a modern, attractive settlement of homes and small businesses set off by the ▶ **Hyatt Regency Lake Tahoe**, a larger hotel-casino than most of its North Shore neighbors. Even the Hyatt, despite its relative size, maintains a quieter presence than any of its South Shore relatives. The ▶ **Inn at Incline** offers a range of accommodations, including 38 deluxe rooms; ▶ **Haus Bavaria**, high on the mountainside above Tahoe, is a bed-and-breakfast inn with five comfortable rooms and an idyllic forest setting.

Highway 431, the Mount Rose Highway, departs Lake Tahoe at Incline Village and heads northeast for Reno and Virginia City. A short distance up this road, stop to take in the stunning view, and if you're hungry head over the summit to the **Christmas Tree** (Tel: 702-849-0127), a steak house about halfway to Reno.

EXPLORING THE NORTH SHORE

The **Ponderosa Ranch**, an amusement park devoted to television's "Bonanza," is located at the east end of Incline Village. From Memorial Day to Labor Day, one-and-a-half-hour hayrides are offered every morning at 8:00 A.M., with a pancake breakfast served afterward. The area beyond the Ponderosa around the east side of the lake to Glenbrook is largely undeveloped. **Lake Tahoe State Park** is the principal exception, with swimming beaches and a boat-launching ramp at Sand Harbor as well as picnic sites and parking. In August the annual **Shakespeare at Sand Harbor** (Tel: 916-583-9048) is presented in a natural lakeside amphitheater. Spectators bring their own picnic dinners and spread blankets on the sand for performances of *Twelfth Night, A Midsummer Night's Dream, The Tempest,* and other Shakespeare plays, as well as plays by other authors, such as *Cyrano de Bergerac* or *A Lion in Winter.* You can find other swimming beaches along the east shore, some difficult to reach, with very limited roadside parking.

Highway 28 follows the east shore of the lake past the former Whittell Estate, at one time the home of an extensive private zoo (and not open to the public), to its junction with Highway 50 at Spooner Lake. This little lake was once a stagecoach station and sawmill site and is now a small park and trailhead for the beautiful 10-mile round-trip hike (with spectacular views) to Marlette Lake, perched high above Lake Tahoe.

Glenbrook, south of Spooner Lake, was once a bustling lumber town graced by an exclusive lakeside resort and served by daily steamers; now it is a modern, developed community with a nine-hole golf course open to the public. Highway 50, which leads north to Carson City, continues south past Zephyr Cove to Round Hill and the par-72 **Edgewood Tahoe Golf Course** (Tel: 702-588-3566).

From Edgewood it's only a short distance to the South Shore casinos at Stateline, where we started. The turnoff for the Kingsbury Grade (Highway 207), which connects Lake Tahoe with the Carson Valley (see below), is along the way, and a detour here will give you a wonderful bird's-eye view of the valley below. This road approximates the route once taken by the Pony Express (1860 to 1861), which served Tahoe at Friday's Station, not far from the modern-day Harrah's, where the station is commemorated by a larger-than-life bronze sculpture of a rider dashing westward. Friday's was the home station for Pony Bob Haslem, who made the greatest ride in the history of that spectacular organization—380 miles through hostile Indian country, where stations were burned and relief riders and horses were run off into the desert. His heroism, and the cruel events of the frontier that prompted it, now seem very long ago and far away when compared to the comforts and conveniences of this vacation paradise.

Lake Tahoe Ski Areas

In the 1850s a Norwegian gold seeker changed his occupation by agreeing to carry the mail between Placerville and the small settlement at Genoa, Nevada. "Snowshoe" Thompson, as he came to be known, used long oak skis to make the winter crossing of the Sierra and created a legend in the process. His example was unique, however, and he was regarded as something of a curiosity, virtually the only skier in the West until the 1860s, when the residents of a few isolated mountain communities turned to skiing as a winter diversion. Settlements such as La Porte and Whiskey Flat challenged one another to downhill ski races between town teams, and local champions developed new techniques and secret concoctions of wax to speed them down the slopes.

Their activities did not attract others to the sport, however. Just the opposite: Skiing was considered a sport for hillbillies and was scorned by the swells who vacationed at the mountain resorts in summer and abandoned them when the snow began to fall. In the 1930s a few students at the University of Nevada were making ski trips to Mount Rose, but it wasn't until World War II, when U.S. combat units were trained to fight in the deep snows of winter here, that skiing began to take on a wider appeal. After 1945 a few small ski areas were developed in the Sierra, and in 1960 resort developer Alex Cushing made an almost impertinent bid to hold the Winter Olympics at Squaw Valley. When the bid was accepted, winter sports began to be taken seriously in the Sierra.

Today the Lake Tahoe region has the greatest concentration of ski areas in the United States, with 15 major resorts offering alpine (downhill) and nordic (cross-country) skiing, as well as snow-play areas and all the amenities associated with winter recreation. Most years the ski season extends from Thanksgiving through Easter and is enhanced by an average 350-inch snowfall (double that of the Swiss Alps), pleasant temperatures (25 to 45 degrees F), and frequent sunny days. The terrain varies from gently sloping meadows to the most challenging expert runs. Some resorts offer a limited number of lifts and modest base facilities, while others operate a wide array of lifts including gondolas and cable cars, with entire self-contained communities at the base. Most resorts run shuttles from hotel-casinos to the base lodges, with exact routes and schedules changing each year. Here are the leading Tahoe ski areas:

- **Alpine Meadows** (Tel: 916-583-4232 or 800-TAHOE-4-U), on Highway 89 6 miles (10 km) north of Tahoe City, prides itself on maintaining the longest ski season in the Tahoe region and on the family orientation of its slopes and services. The area covers 2,000 acres and is served by 13 lifts, with top elevation at the 8,637-foot summit of Ward Peak. The longest run is 2½ miles. Terrain is rated 25 percent beginner, 40 percent intermediate, and 35 percent advanced. There are daily lessons, private and group, for skiers ages three and up and for handicapped skiers. All base facilities are available, including one of California's largest rental shops. Ski shuttle service is available daily to the North Shore and midweek to the South Shore.

- **Boreal Ridge** (Tel: 916-426-3668), on I-80 at the Castle Peak exit, offers night skiing until 10:00 P.M. every night except Christmas Eve. This long-established resort operates ten lifts to a 7,800-foot summit, with a 600-foot drop to the base lodge. Terrain is rated 30 percent beginner, 55 percent intermediate, and 15 percent advanced.

- **Diamond Peak** (Tel: 702-832-1177 or 800-GO-TAHOE; 24-hour Ski Line: 831-3211) is at Ski Incline on Tahoe's North Shore. The 8,540-foot summit of Diamond Peak is served by seven lifts, has an 1,840-foot drop, and offers exquisite views of Lake Tahoe. Terrain is rated 19 percent beginner, 48 percent intermediate, and 33 percent advanced. There's a Child Ski Center here, and most of the terrain is served by a computerized snowmaking system. A free shuttle operates to the North and South shores.

- **Heavenly Valley** (Tel: 916-541-1330 or 800-2-HEAVEN) is the largest ski area in the United States, with nine summits in 20 square miles of ski slopes straddling the California-Nevada state line above the South Shore of Lake Tahoe. Twenty-four lifts take skiers to summit elevations of over 10,000 feet, some with drops of 3,600 feet, and the longest run is 5½ miles. Six day lodges provide amenities, including the Top of the Tram restaurant. Instruction is available. Terrain is rated 25 percent beginner, 50 percent intermediate, and 25 percent advanced. Free shuttle service is provided to the South Shore. Access to the Nevada slopes is via Highway 207 (Kingsbury Grade) and Benjamin Road; on the California side, Ski Run Boulevard leads to the base lodge from South Lake Tahoe.

- **Kirkwood Meadows** (Tel: 209-258-7000) is a little

off the beaten track, about 30 miles (48 km) south of Lake Tahoe on Highway 88 (closed from the east during the winter, when you must approach from the west via Stockton). Kirkwood's 65 runs traverse 2,000 acres. Eleven lifts carry skiers 2,000 feet to the 9,800-foot summit from the highest base elevation of any California ski resort. With five bars and restaurants and 104 condominium units, Kirkwood has been developed as a self-contained destination resort. A cross-country ski area with groomed meadow and mountain trails provides for all experience levels. Terrain is rated 15 percent beginner, 50 percent intermediate, and 35 percent advanced.

- **Mount Rose** (Tel: 702-849-0704) is on the east slope of the Sierra overlooking Washoe Valley, about 11 miles (18 km) northeast of Incline Village via Highway 431 and 22 miles (35 km) southeast of Reno, via U.S. 395 to Highway 431. Its base elevation of 8,260 feet is the highest in the Lake Tahoe region, and snowfall averages 400 inches a year. Five lifts serve 900 acres with drops of 1,450 feet, and the longest run is 2 miles. Terrain is rated 30 percent beginner, 35 percent intermediate, and 35 percent advanced. A daily shuttle serves Reno.

- **Northstar** (Tel: 916-562-1113) is another self-contained community development centered around skiing in the winter but with a variety of recreational opportunities in other seasons. It is located on Highway 267 about midway between King's Beach and Truckee. Eleven lifts, including a six-passenger gondola, carry skiers 2,200 feet to the summits of Mount Pluto and Lookout Mountain. The longest run on the 1,700 acres is 2.9 miles, and in addition to the downhill skiing, sleigh rides and more than 25 miles of cross-country ski trails are offered. Terrain is rated 25 percent beginner, 50 percent intermediate, and 25 percent advanced.

- **Sierra Ski Ranch** (Tel: 916-659-7453, 800-AT-TAHOE, or 916-659-7475 for ski information) is on the west slope of the Sierra, southwest of the Tahoe Basin at Twin Bridges on U.S. 50, about 15 miles (24 km) southwest of its junction with Highway 89. The area contains three mountainsides in its 2,000 acres, with a top elevation of 8,852 feet. Nine lifts carry skiers from the 6,640-foot base lodge. Terrain is rated 20 percent beginner, 60 percent intermediate, and 20 percent advanced. Shuttles operate to the South Shore.

- **Squaw Valley** (Tel: 916-583-6985 for the resort; 583-5585 or 800-545-4350 for accommodations) was the site of the 1960 Winter Olympics and is one of the world's leading ski areas. Thirty-two lifts, including a 150-passenger cable car and a six-passenger gondola lift, carry skiers to a summit elevation of 9,050 feet. Base and upper-mountain facilities at the 8,300-acre resort are highly developed, with a variety of restaurants, bars, and shops. The longest run is three miles, and a cross-country area is adjacent to the alpine runs. Terrain is rated 25 percent beginner, 45 percent intermediate, and 30 percent advanced.

CARSON CITY

Carson City, about 15 miles (24 km) east of Lake Tahoe's Glenbrook on Highway 50, no longer announces itself as the nation's smallest state capital—in fact, there are nine others that are smaller now. But much of the simplicity and charm of its frontier past are still very evident in this pleasant community, where the Sierra Nevada towers against the western horizon.

Carson City was a rough settlement of a few dozen small structures when it was proclaimed capital of the Nevada Territory in 1861. By the time statehood was achieved three years later—Lincoln so urgently needed Republican votes and Comstock silver that population standards were ignored—Carson City had begun to exhibit some of the charm that characterizes its large downtown historic district today.

Historic Carson City

Much of this mostly residential district at the center of town west of Carson Street remains unchanged from a century ago, when the homes were built to house prosperous frontier merchants, politicians, lawyers, and bankers. Begin a half-hour stroll through the tree-shaded Victorian streets at the 1870 silver-domed Capitol building, meander westward as far as the Governor's Mansion on Mountain Street— Robinson Street between Mountain and Division streets is especially rich in architectural treasures—and then continue northeast to conclude at the **Nevada State Museum**, which occupies the imposing stone building that once housed the U.S. Mint. The stamps that transformed gold and silver bullion from the mines of the Comstock Lode into coins of the realm are still here and are still used to produce commemorative coins from time to time. Exhibits from the animal, vegetable, and mineral kingdoms complement the historical artifacts displayed, and the basement has been transformed to replicate the underground workings of a silver mine.

The **Carson City Nugget**, a long-established casino in the center of town on Carson Street, displays an extraordinary collection of gold specimens amassed from around the world. In addition to large nuggets discovered in streambeds, you'll see ribbons, wires, threads, and crystals of native gold formed in the cracks and crevices of the quartz veins. There are even twigs and leaves of gold, created when the original organic materials decomposed and left voids in the rock in which gold was later deposited.

On the south side of town, the **State Railroad Museum** occupies a complex of modern and historic structures beside the highway. Some of the buildings housed the collection of rolling stock rescued from the scrap pile and from the Hollywood movie studios, others are former depots and section houses moved here from original sites elsewhere in the state. Trains are fired up for display and to move around the short sections of track, and plans are in place for extending the rails to carry passengers into Carson City's historic district and back. The small gift shop is devoted entirely to railroad memorabilia and may be the best place in the state to shop for children or grandchildren back home.

The **Roberts House** museum on Carson Street is a residence from pioneer days restored to give a glimpse of the mundane realities of frontier home life. There is a small **Firefighting Museum** on the second floor of the stone firehouse at Musser and Curry streets, where the Warren Engine Company No. 1 (Carson City's venerable fire department) still maintains a roster of volunteers in addition to the paid staff. The museum is open to visitors in the afternoons and displays historical firefighting tools, gear, clothing, and other unusual artifacts—even segments of the redwood water mains that once served the city.

An **Indian Museum** occupies the former superintendent's residence at the Stewart Indian School on Snyder Road, east of U.S. 395, once a boarding school for children from Western tribes. When the school closed in 1980 after 83 years of operation, students from 20 tribes were enrolled. The stone school buildings, built by Native American craftsmen, are enrolled on the National Register of Historic Places, and the exhibits of tribal arts and crafts are exceptional. A small store stocks Native American art, jewelry, pottery, rugs, basketry, and beadwork, and the school grounds—now devoted to a variety of state uses—are the site of an annual powwow in June that brings together Native Americans from around the Western states, many of them alumni and descendants of alumni. You will see many craftspeople at their traditional work.

Staying and Dining in Carson City

Since the frontier period when shootings and stabbings were common, nightlife has not been much of a priority in Carson City, which was, with very few exceptions, a charming community of homebodies. Today, though, the situation is considerably improved, with quite a variety of first-class restaurants catering to visitors and residents alike.

On Carson Street, the **Carson City Nugget** and the **Ormsby House**, the city's principal casinos, each offer 24-hour coffee shops and dining rooms much patronized by the local residents, and the Nugget has a small oyster bar as well. The **Best Western Carson Station**, the **Senator**, and a small handful of other gambling houses also provide simple fare. The elegance of Carson City's Victorian past is represented at **Adele's**, perhaps the city's most refined dinner house, in a bandbox Victorian home on Carson Street. **Valentino's**, in a shopping center on the north side of town, serves Italian specialties; **Stanley's**, a little farther north, is another local favorite that offers a Continental menu. **Silvana's** occupies an odd basement-only building on North Carson Street. The menu is Italian, and the wine list is the best in town.

Bodine's, at the junction of Highways 50 and 395 south of town, is a nostalgic visit to the 1950s with its barnwood decor and steak-lovers' menu. A half-dozen Chinese restaurants maintain the Nevada tradition; **Genghis Khan** serves Mongolian sautés at 260 East Winnie Lane just east of Carson Street. **Tarantino's Black Tie Deli**, Carson City's hidden treasure, is located on South Loop Street behind K-Mart. This San Francisco–style sandwich bar and deli counter offers gourmet treats of every description.

El Charro Avitia on Carson Street at the south end of town is a popular Mexican restaurant, as are **Mi Casa Too** on Carson Street at the north end of the city, **Tito's** two blocks east of Carson Street on U.S. 50, and **La Raza** a few miles farther east on U.S. 50, just across the line in Lyon County. **Miramar House**, also on Carson at the south end of town, is Carson City's first Thai restaurant, and **Amimoto**, in the nearby Silver City mall, serves Japanese food.

Two hotel-casinos, the ▶ **Ormsby House** and ▶ **Best Western Carson Station**, are next-door neighbors on South Carson Street, and a large number of motels also provide accommodations.

Carson City is especially lively during the summer and fall months, when a series of public events take place. The very best of them is the Nevada Day Parade that celebrates Abraham Lincoln's creation of the state—a brilliant show every October 31. Another colorful interlude is provided by the Kit Carson Rendezvous, a three-day gathering of mountain men, Native Americans, and enthusiasts of the 18th and 19th centuries portraying cavalry soldiers and traders. A farrier's contest, amateur boxing matches, and food and arts and crafts booths are all free to the public (more than 35,000 people attend each year). The event takes place in the great park on the east side of town in June.

CARSON VALLEY

After a grueling trip west by mail wagon, Horace Greeley entered the Carson Valley in July 1859. "I had previously seen some beautiful valleys," he wrote in a dispatch to his newspaper in New York, "but I place none of them ahead of the Carson. . . . This valley, originally a grand meadow, the home of the deer and the antelope, is nearly inclosed by high mountains, down which, especially from the north and west, come innumerable rivulets, leaping and dancing on their way to join or form the Carson [River] . . . producing an abundance of the sweetest grass, and insuring bounteous harvests also of vegetables, barley, oats, etc. . . . I may never see this lovely valley again—it is hardly probable that I ever shall—but its beauty, its seclusion, its quiet, the brightness of its abundant rivulets, the grandeur of its inclosing mountains, the grace and emerald verdure of their vesture of pines, have graven themselves on my memory. . . ."

The splendor of the towering peaks of the Sierra Nevada rising steeply up out of the lush valley pasturelands makes a profound impression, even if you haven't bounced and bumped across Nevada in a mail wagon. The valley lies just south of Carson City (which is itself situated in Eagle Valley) on Highway 395. It can also be reached by way of Highway 207 (the Kingsbury Grade) from the southeast corner of Lake Tahoe. This is the route that Greeley followed when he continued west, and it provides a breathtaking view of the valley as you descend.

Each of the Carson Valley's three communities has its distinctive character, and all three are growing rapidly as population spills over the summits from Lake Tahoe and south from Reno in search of affordable housing.

Genoa

About 10 miles (16 km) south of Carson City is Genoa (Juh-NO-uh), established at the base of the Sierra Nevada as a trading post by Mormon pioneers from Salt Lake City in 1851, two years after California achieved statehood (it was Nevada's first permanently settled community). Take Highway 57 west off Highway 395 to reach the town, which comprised 40 or 50 houses when Horace Greeley passed through and became the seat of government for Carson County, Utah Territory. The reconstructed Mormon Fort is now the centerpiece of a small state park, and the former Douglas County Courthouse (Genoa lost the county seat to Minden in 1916) is now a historical museum.

Several of the town's pleasantly rambling old residences have been converted to restaurants. The **Inn Cognito**, a block east of the center of town, is a former private club now open to the public as a dinner house. The facilities occupy what once was a barn, with the bar in the hayloft and the comfortable dining room in the space that once housed milk cows. The menu is Continental, with the addition of at least one wild-game entrée, ranging from bear to alligator, on any given evening; Tel: (702) 782-8898. The **Pink House** is a celebrated dinner house, and Nevada's first saloon, **The Genoa Bar**, still slakes the thirst of travellers here.

Genoa's stunning setting—the Sierra rises steeply up behind the town—and Victorian charm have attracted movie-makers in recent years, and the Candy Dance, an autumn fundraiser for the local volunteer fire department, attracts many visitors.

A few miles south of Genoa, ▶ **Walley's Hot Springs** caters to visitors as it has for more than a century—with hot-water pools and baths and overnight accommodations. The resort was a favorite among the wealthy residents of Carson City and Virginia City when it was located on the main line of travel; then, after some years of decline, the original resort burned to the ground. The modern Walley's was built a few years ago, a 20th-century version of the original available for a brief swim or a week's indulgence.

Gardnerville and Minden

Gardnerville, a few miles southeast of the Genoa turnoff on Highway 395, was established as the farming and ranching center of the valley, growing to prominence as Genoa declined after the 1860s. It is best known to visitors for the family-style Basque restaurants that have served generations of diners: the **J T**, the **Overland Hotel**, and the **Carson Valley Country Club** south of town, where the restaurant (you can select steaks, shrimp scampi, or lamb chops as your entrée) adjoins the golf course. Each of the Basque restaurants has a bar where, along with the usual fare, you can order the traditional Basque cocktail, Picon Punch (Amer Picon and brandy are the principal ingredients). Check out the **Buckaroo Sub Shop** in the Adaren Hotel, not just for the food and drink but also for the fine bluegrass music offered Friday and Saturday nights.

Every Nevada town has at least one local casino, and **Sharkey's** in Gardnerville is famous for its huge prime rib dinners, the boxing and cowboy memorabilia displayed on the walls, and the lavish Eastern Orthodox feast given to the community at Easter by proprietor Sharkey Begovich.

Minden, one mile north of Gardnerville, is the youngest of the Carson Valley's three communities. In 1905 the Virginia & Truckee (V&T) Railroad was deprived of its main revenues by the depletion of the Comstock mines and the construction of a new Southern Pacific spur line that severed the V&T's connection to the Tonopah and Goldfield mines far to the south; the railroad turned to the vegetable kingdom to make up the income by shipping the harvest from the Carson Valley. The V&T made its last run in 1950—its brick depot is a café now—but Minden's pleasant downtown area still reflects a turn-of-the-century small-town atmosphere, with a park at its center, complete with velvety lawn, charming gazebo, and shade trees all around. The Minden Inn, where Clark Gable once married, is closed now, but the new ▶ **Carson Valley Inn** at the center of town beside the highway provides accommodations, dining, and a casino. In an unusual and welcome variation, the inn's dinner house, **Fiona's**, is located in its own building away from the frenetic casino environment.

VIRGINIA CITY AND THE
COMSTOCK LODE

In the 1860s and 1870s, Virginia City was the gaudiest and brawniest city in the West, rivaling San Francisco with its wealth and abandon. Today most of the wealth of the gold and silver mines of the Comstock Lode has been depleted and spent, but Virginia City, although its population has dwindled and many of its fine mansions now stand empty, is still the dowager queen of the Old West, an open-air, three-dimensional museum a little more than a half-hour's drive southeast of Reno and an even shorter drive northeast of Carson City.

From Carson City take Highway 50 east about 7 miles (11 km), then turn left (north) onto Highway 341. Four miles (6 km) farther along you'll reach Silver City, once a bustling mining town, now a venerable collection of homes and a post office. The highway continues north through Devil's Gate, an eroded volcanic flow that once plugged the narrow canyon, and climbs the steep old wagon road through Gold Hill to Virginia City.

The highway from Reno climbs the pinyon- and juniper-stippled Virginia Range to an 8,000-foot summit, providing panoramic views of the cities in the Truckee Meadows below and of the Sierra Nevada on the western horizon.

The Comstock Lode was discovered at Gold Hill, a settlement just south of Virginia City, in February 1859, when the famous Red Ledge was uncovered by prospectors from a camp a few miles down in the canyon. A second discovery of astonishing richness followed in June at what is now the northwest corner of Virginia City, and for 20 years the drama of discovery and development was unceasing.

In October 1875, when Virginia City had swollen from the primitive tents and shanties of its beginnings to a major city of more than 20,000, it burned in a catastrophic fire. Two-thirds of the city was destroyed, including much of the business district on B and C streets. So rich were the ores being brought out of the seemingly inexhaustible mines, however, that rebuilding began immediately, and as a consequence the city stands today as a showplace of Western Victorian architecture. As tourism has replaced mining as the economic mainstay, most of the important buildings—particularly those on C Street, the main commercial center—have been opened to visitors.

The V&T Railroad, once one of the richest (and crooked-est) short lines in the world, has been restored as far as Gold Hill and takes passengers back and forth daily from Memorial Day through the end of October. The depot car is parked on a siding on F Street in Virginia City or you can purchase tickets at the Gold Hill Hotel to make the 10-minute train trip from there. Either way you'll have time to explore both towns.

Historic Virginia City

Saint Mary-in-the-Mountains, on D Street, is a celebrated monument to the Victorian period, a spired and steepled Gothic-style brick Roman Catholic church still in everyday use. Its interior reflects the richness of its origins, with soaring ceilings above the altar and choir loft, and a baptismal font brought from Paris more than a century ago.

Similarly, the **Storey County Courthouse**, with its unusual unblindfolded Justice over the entrance, offers a rare opportunity to step into the past. County business is conducted here in the same offices as in the glory years and in the long decline that followed.

Piper's Opera House, a block north of the courthouse, is intriguing for its raked stage (slanted downward toward the footlights so that the audience has unobstructed views from the level-floored hall) and for its distinguished roster of players, including the incomparable Jenny Lind.

The **Fourth Ward School**, at the south end of C Street, is the only schoolhouse remaining from the bonanza period (there were four others this size, and another in Gold Hill). It was preserved as much by inertia and neglect—the signatures of its last graduating class (1936) are still scribbled in chalk on the blackboards—as by more recent restoration financed by a whiskey distiller and by the owner of the county's brothel. It is now maintained as a museum.

Some of the palatial private homes are also open to visitors. **The Castle**, on D Street, was built with silver doorknobs for a mining superintendent before serving as the residence of a leading banker for many decades. It is still furnished and appointed exactly as it was in the glory days—even the lace curtains that flutter in the vagrant breeze are original.

Other bonanza-era mansions—the Mackay Mansion and the Chollar Mansion on D Street—are open for tours, and some have been converted to bed and breakfasts (see below).

Virginia City clings to the eastern flank of Sun Mountain,

and on its rumpled northeastern outskirts the old cemeteries—nine of them—combine to make a substantial burying ground. Celebrities such as Indian fighter Edward
Storey and Fire Chief K. B. "Kettle Belly" Brown lie beside
paupers and babies in such a confusion of headstones and
plot enclosures that the burying ground almost seems
lively. Virginia City's most famous murder victim, Julia
Bulette, was a prostitute so beloved by the community that
her strangled body was conducted to its grave by a civic
parade led by the Volunteer Fire Department. She was not
permitted to spend eternity within the regular cemeteries,
however, and her lonely gravesite is barely visible on a
hillside far to the south.

EXPLORING C STREET

C Street is Virginia City's lone remaining commercial district,
two lively rows of saloons, cafés, shops, and restaurants
facing each other across their wooden sidewalks (a good
reason to wear flat shoes). These buildings are a fascinating
collection of authentic Victorian commercial architecture,
with some of the original signs still weathering across their
fronts: B.S. Dwyer was an early-day merchant in the building
that houses the **Crystal Bar** today, and the legend "Hardware,
Stoves & Metals" still appears across the top of the **Red
Garter Saloon**. The shops themselves reflect a higher level of
enterprise than in the recent past, when the cheap, the
tawdry, and the plastic predominated. These days a more
elevated taste is represented, with gift shops offering the real
goods, including an astonishing variety of brilliant stones
and gems, Native American jewelry, and other western items
appropriate to the Comstock Lode. Museums include an
eclectic collection at the **Mark Twain Museum**, elaborate
mining displays at **The Way It Was**, and gleaming slot machines, photographs, and gambling memorabilia—dating
from the stick and bone games of the Paiute Indians—at the
Gaming Museum. Another interesting visit is to the basement workrooms of the **Territorial Enterprise Building**,
where the old presses and type library gather dust, and Mark
Twain's desk sits like a shrine.

And just as in Mark Twain's days, on C Street saloons
predominate. The **Bucket of Blood** and the **Delta** saloons at
the center of town once feuded over the patronage of Lucius
Beebe (the newspaper columnist and railroad writer who,
for a time, published the weekly *Territorial Enterprise*) and
his St. Bernard, T-Bone Towser. Like most of the drinking
emporia along the street, their walls bristle with memora-

bilia. Photographs of the mines, the railroad, and the city decorate every interior surface along C Street, so that even a pause for refreshment is a museum visit.

There's a banjo-strumming jazz band at the Bucket of Blood, and the **Silver Stope** maintains a long-standing tradition of jazz jam sessions on Sunday afternoons. At the **Union Brewery** the beer is brewed fresh in the basement, where a small Nevada beer museum has also been installed.

Virginia City tends to be quite crowded in the summer, far from the ghost town you might expect, and if swarms of tourists are not your preferred milieu, come in the late afternoons and evenings when the family vacationers have swept their school-age offspring back down to Reno and Carson City. Crowds are thinner in spring and fall, and in the winter you're apt to have the saloon to yourself at any given moment and actually experience the ghostliness.

There are some interesting events in Virginia City each year, most notably the exciting spectacle of the Camel Races held in September (with real camels). A Dixieland Band festival and a John Philip Sousa festival fill the city with sound on August weekends, and St. Patrick's Day is celebrated here with special vigor in tribute to the thousands of Irish miners who labored underground. August's Fireman's Muster is a major spectacle, as firefighters and their gleaming antique trucks and pumpers come from several states to congregate and compete in uproarious contests.

Closed in 1942 as nonessential to the war effort, few of the great mines of the Comstock Lode ever reopened. Most mining since then has been the open-pit variety at odds with the historic nature of the district, and only one company is now at work underground with a small-scale operation. The played-out Chollar Mine is at the south end of D Street, and the back door of the Ponderosa Saloon on C Street opens into an extension of the underground workings that honeycomb the mountain beneath Virginia City. Tours are available at both.

Staying and Dining in Virginia City

You'll find snacks and light lunches easily available up and down C Street during the day. An Italian menu is served at the **Sharon House** (Tel: 702-847-7023), and steaks are the enticement at the **Silver Stope** (Tel: 702-847-9011). Gold Hill, a mile down the canyon toward Carson City, is one of the most cosmopolitan towns its size (population less than 100) in the West. A prime reason is **The Gold Hill Hotel** (Tel: 702-847-

0111), a pioneer hostelry recently restored, enlarged, and now operated in the grand manner of the bonanza era. The hotel's dining room offers a French menu. **Joe Conforte's Cabin in the Sky**, a half-mile down the canyon, features steaks and Italian dishes.

Because so many of its summer visitors are day-trippers, Virginia City's long summer evenings belong to those who take motel accommodations or stay at one of the handful of bed-and-breakfast inns— ▶ **Edith Palmer's Country Inn** on Virginia City's B Street, the bonanza-era ▶ **Chollar Mansion** (where rates include Sherry in your room and an afternoon snack), and ▶ **The Hardwicke House** in Silver City. This last is a monumental stone structure on Main Street that has been a general store and (downstairs) a stable. Now it caters to overnight visitors as a cordial bed-and-breakfast inn. The ▶ **Gold Hill Hotel** takes guests in both older and modern rooms, all decorated with antiques, and the ▶ **Comstock Lodge** in Virginia City offers six comfortable rooms, all furnished with antiques as well. (These accommodations are all easily visible from the highway.)

WASHOE VALLEY

This valley at the eastern foot of the Sierras between Reno and Carson City, parallel to the Virginia City area, is traversed by Highway 395, a modern freeway that bypasses the attractions that make the valley more than just a beautiful drive. The **Bowers Mansion** is accessible via the Franktown Road exit on the west side of the valley; Washoe Lake State Park is accessible only from Lakeside Drive on the east.

When Sandy Bowers struck it rich as one of the original discoverers of the Red Ledge in Gold Hill he married his landlady, Eilly Orrum, and the two of them set out to live as grandly as Sandy's newfound fortune permitted, building this grand cut-stone mansion at the edge of the pine forest and travelling to Europe to furnish it. They had money enough "to throw at the birds," in Sandy's memorable phrase, and they spent it lavishly, shipping furniture around Cape Horn for their new home.

But Sandy died within a few years of striking it rich, and Eilly lived on long after the money had all been spent. She progressively closed off more and more of the great stone house until at last she could not afford to live there even on the most meager scale. So she sold this monument to grandeur and moved back to Virginia City, where she eked out a slender living as the Washoe Seeress, telling fortunes to a gullible clientele until she died, broke.

The house she and Sandy built passed through a number of hands—it acquired a steamy reputation as a roadhouse during Prohibition—before being acquired and restored to something like its original splendor by the Washoe County Park District. Tours are conducted, and the grounds are available for picnics.

A few miles south along Franktown Road you can see what is left of the town of that name, which was settled as a sawmill site, developed as an ore-milling center, and served by the V&T Railroad—the old water tank marks the depot site—when its fruit and vegetable farms fed the miners in Virginia City. A little farther south stands a log cabin, barely visible through the pine trees from the road, in which Will James wrote "Smoky" and other stories that established his reputation as a Western storyteller.

Washoe Lake State Park is on the other side of the valley. Its main attraction is usually to boaters, but a succession of drought years has completely dried it out. The **Cattlemen's Restaurant**, with a menu strong on beef, is located beside Highway 395 near the center of the valley at the old settlement of Ophir.

RENO

Reno, 30 miles (48 km) north of Carson City on Highway 395 or 25 miles (40 km) northeast of Truckee via Interstate 80, was a child of the railroad, a patch of lots in the sagebrush bottom of the Truckee Meadows sold at auction when the Central Pacific pushed through in 1868. A homely little burg, it prospered as the shipping point for the rich Comstock mines, as well as for other nearby mining districts and for Carson City. With the slowing of production from the gold and silver mines in Tonopah and Goldfield after 1910, Reno transformed itself into the commercial and financial center of Nevada. As prosperity overtook the roughneck little railroad town, trees were planted to give the city an inviting and charming air, and gambling was made illegal.

But in 1931, when four successive drought years combined with the Depression to devastate the Nevada agricultural and mining economy, the state legislature relegalized gambling, the purpose being to put the licensing fees into the public treasury, instead of the pockets of "cooperative" sheriffs and district attorneys who allowed gambling to continue underground. It succeeded, and in the process created a mechanism for regulating what had until then been outlaw enterprises. The statute has succeeded so well that "gaming" (as gamblers call gambling when it becomes an industry) has far overshadowed ranching and mining in Nevada, both economically and politically, for most of two generations now.

Since the recession of the early 1980s, the state government has earnestly promoted industrial development to mitigate the overwhelming reliance on casino slot machines and on other forms of tourism for jobs and tax revenues. The success of this program can be seen in the prospering new industrial parks east and south of the Reno airport and in Sparks, where increasing numbers of businesspeople, engineers, and managers have joined the population of card dealers, cowboys, and other colorful folks who give Reno its flavor.

Exploring Reno

Most of Reno's casinos are centered in the heart of the city, which is bisected by the Truckee River, flowing from west to east, and by Virginia Street, the main north-south boulevard. Fourth Street (once U.S. 40) is the main east-west artery connecting Reno and Sparks, but most crosstown drivers use the freeways (I-80 east to west and U.S. 395 north to south).

Reno's history reflects the individualism of the Western frontier and a moment when independence and self-sufficiency were highly prized qualities. The frontier has lingered longer in Nevada than elsewhere, and as a consequence men like Harold "Pappy" Smith and Bill Harrah who came here in the 1930s to operate storefront bingo parlors stayed to create the gambling industry that now leads the state's economy.

THE NATIONAL AUTOMOBILE MUSEUM

The high-rise Harrah's is a fitting monument to Bill Harrah's business sense, but this highly individualistic man left a legacy on his personal side as well. At his death, Harrah, an eager collector of antique and classic automobiles, left three warehouses stuffed with 1,400 cars, plus a $3 million research library and a fully staffed and equipped restoration garage.

When the Harrah's casinos were acquired by the Holiday Inn chain of hotels in 1978, the collection was whittled down to the crème de la crème, and these 175 cars were donated to the National Automobile Museum, at Lake and Mill streets. Other cars have since been acquired by the museum, and now more than 200 painstakingly restored antiques and classics are displayed in showroom condition in exhibit space designed to emphasize the automobile's impact on American life and culture, both as artifact and as icon. Video presentations, a handful of small shops, and the Roadhouse Café supplement the automotive displays, where you can also view the restoration workshop. Make sure you stop by to see the Thomas Flyer that won the 1908 New York-to-Paris race, the 1948 Tucker Sedan, Buckminster Fuller's 1934 Dymaxion, the one-of-a-kind 1938 Phantom Corsair, and James Dean's 1949 Mercury from *Rebel Without A Cause*. Other delectable celebrity cars include Al Jolson's 1933 Cadillac phaeton and Elvis Presley's 1973 custom white-on-white Eldorado coupe.

WEST ALONG THE TRUCKEE RIVER

The Truckee River is Reno's primary landmark, and a walk west along its banks from the auto museum is a good way to make the city's acquaintance. Follow a path that has been created along the riverbank to connect Wingfield Park downtown, with its free summertime band concerts, to Idlewild Park, about one and a half miles west, with its nationally acclaimed rose gardens and broad green lawns. The 20-minute walk leads through the Reno of the 1920s and 1930s, the "city of trembling leaves" that Walter Van Tilburg Clark wrote about in his novel of that name: gracefully porched Victorian and Edwardian mansions (some of them serving in earlier years as boardinghouses for six-week divorcées—women taking advantage of Nevada's lenient law requiring only a six-week residence in the state to file for divorce) on quiet, tree-shaded streets.

THE MUSEUMS OF RENO

The **Sierra Nevada Museum of Art** occupies two near-downtown locations. The E. L. Weigand Museum at 160 West Liberty Street offers an array of travelling exhibits from modern works to paintings of the 16th and 17th centuries; the Hawkins House, a Neo-Georgian mansion at 549 Court Street, on the south side of the river, has exhibits of 19th- and 20th-century American art.

North of the city center, the University of Nevada campus maintains a busy schedule of art exhibits at the **Sheppard Galleries** in the Church Fine Arts complex on Virginia Street, and you can walk through the campus to view the Gutzon

Borglum sculpture of Comstock Lode mining magnate John Mackay. The university also offers an active schedule of theater and music performances throughout the year. On the north side of the campus, the **Nevada State Historical Society** maintains an archive for research and a museum, part of which is devoted to a historical overview of Nevada and part to changing exhibits on various themes and topics.

Across from the Historical Society is another monument left by one of Nevada's supreme individualists, Major Max Fleischmann. A prime incentive for wealthy outsiders to settle in Nevada has been its low tax rate, particularly the absence of state income and inheritance taxes. Of the many monied men and women who settled here to take advantage of this benign climate was the scion of the Fleischmann's Yeast family fortune, who came here in the 1930s. Max Fleischmann fell in love with Nevada—not uncommon among people who live here—and in the years before his death he established the Fleischmann Foundation to contribute funds to many community projects around the state. The **Fleischmann Planetarium** (Tel: 702-784-4811 for recorded show information; 784-4812 for reservations), a part of this legacy, plays a 60- to 70-minute double feature that combines a planetarium star show (such as one on UFOs) with a hemispheric wraparound movie (such as one on arctic light) in the Cinema-360 film format. A small museum presents exhibits about the solar system and outer space, and free public sky-gazing sessions are offered regularly throughout the year.

At the **Rancho San Rafael**, a few blocks west of the campus, is yet another memorial to a wealthy Nevada transplant—Wilbur D. May, a member of the May department store family. Before going on a year-long safari in 1929, May, a devoted big-game hunter, sold his stock portfolio and invested in government bonds. When he returned—with some of the wildlife trophies exhibited here—he had escaped the catastrophe of the stock market crash and emerged with his wealth intact. He used it to travel around the world and to support a leisurely lifestyle on the Double Diamond Ranch a few miles south of Reno. Since May's death in 1980, the Wilbur D. May Museum has displayed the eclectic collections of this charmed life—T'ang dynasty horses, West African musical instruments, and Lalique vases among them—with a major emphasis on big-game trophies. Spacious grounds and ponds with geese make this a pleasant spot for a picnic lunch.

A big part of Reno's appeal to visitors is the series of major public events that take place throughout the year. The September Reno Air Races attract visitors from all over the world, the Reno Rodeo in June is a big-league cowboy show, and Hot August Nights is a romp that may fill you with nostalgia for the 1950s and 1960s.

As enjoyable as Reno's parks and public places can be, the main attraction for visitors is the hotel-casinos, most of which are clustered at the center of the city. This is where Pappy Smith, Bill Harrah, and other pioneers built little bingo parlors into the huge casinos known around the world. Today the casinos are bigger and brighter than ever, but few of them are operated by single owners any longer; most have corporate owners now and reflect a smoother, less idiosyncratic management style.

Sparks

Sparks, like Reno, was originally created by the railroad. When the Central Pacific came through in 1868, the division point for this section of the road was located at Wadsworth, about 30 miles (48 km) east. Shortly after the turn of the century, however, the repair shops and crew facilities were moved to a new community at Harriman (named for the railroad tycoon), just east of Reno in the Truckee Meadows. Once the railroad was established, Harriman changed its name to Sparks, in honor of Nevada's governor John Sparks, and the town began amassing a long and uneventful history as a slowly growing one-industry town. By the 1950s, when the railroad's influence and economic importance began to wane, Sparks had grown westward and Reno eastward so that the two communities intertwined.

Despite their interconnections, Reno and Sparks have maintained quite separate identities, with Sparks developing as a city of light industry in contrast to Reno's casino- and tourism-based economy. Recently, however, the old downtown district on B Street has been transformed, first by the expansion of **John Ascuaga's Nugget**, a major hotel-casino with more than 600 rooms and suites in its new tower, then by the construction of the Disneyesque **Silver Club** across the street, and finally by the transformation of B Street itself into **Victorian Square**. The 90-year-old business houses of Harriman, refurbished with Victorian motifs, have achieved a splendor they never actually had when new, and the square, with its fountain and bandstand gazebo, serves as a focal point for community celebrations throughout the year.

Besides the attractions of its downtown core, Sparks also offers a refreshing respite from the summer heat at **Wild**

Waters Water Fun Resort, on Sparks Boulevard just north of the I-80 freeway. Open from May through September, the recreation area offers thrilling descents, daredevil plunges, lazy floats, and plenty of sunshine, with food and drink available into the evening.

Staying in Reno and Sparks

All of the hotel-casinos in Reno and Sparks are alike in offering comfortable accommodations, dining that is exceptional in quality or price or both, and more or less identical gambling games. But there are differences too. The ▶ **Reno Hilton** was the largest hotel-casino in Nevada when it opened in 1979 (as the MGM Grand) about a mile east of downtown via either Mill or Second streets. Its size and splendor made it one of the favored destinations for high-rolling gamblers, who have since become something of an endangered species, but the ambience lingers on for ordinary mortals to enjoy. The gambling floor is the size of two football fields, an arcade of shops offers items ranging from simple souvenirs to Native American art and artifacts to clown paintings by Red Skelton, and seven restaurants cater to every dining mood. Accommodations range from generic upscale hotel rooms to the most lavish celebrity suites.

▶ **Harrah's** and the ▶ **Flamingo Hilton**, both downtown, and the ▶ **Peppermill Hotel Casino** on South Virginia Street also cater to the public in the high style that was once reserved only for elite players. The food and the amenities reflect the highest standards. At ▶ **John Ascuaga's Nugget** in Sparks the hotel tower is a relatively recent addition to this long-established casino famous for its food. Trader Dick's, a Polynesian restaurant, was once the Nugget's most exotic offering, but now it is only one of several excellent restaurants in the casino complex. The Nugget is also the last word in accessibility: The I-80 freeway is built through the property, right across the roof of the casino, with two offramps giving onto immense parking lots. At Fourth and Virginia streets in downtown Reno, the ▶ **Eldorado Hotel & Casino** has also established a reputation for fine food, and its restaurants are popular with local people as well as with visitors (see Dining in Reno and Sparks, below).

The ▶ **Comstock Hotel & Casino** is interesting as one of the first "theme" hotels in Reno, modeling its decor after the famous Comstock Lode and the mines beneath Virginia City. It caters to a mixed clientele of visitors and locals who appreciate its down-home Nevada atmosphere and modest prices.   ▶ **The Virginian**, the   ▶ **Sundowner**, the   ▶ **Sands**, the   ▶ **Riverboat**, and   ▶ **Fitzgerald's** all project their own distinct styles and offer moderately priced accommodations. The   ▶ **Ponderosa Hotel & Casino** proclaims itself the world's first non-smoker's hotel-casino, and the   ▶ **Holiday Hotel**, on Center Street beside the river, originally opened as Reno's premiere non-gaming hotel, although it has a small casino now. The most unusual of Reno's hotel-casinos is   ▶ **Circus Circus Hotel & Casino**, an extraordinary combination of gambling house and carnival midway, with aerialists, performing dogs, jugglers, high-wire artists, and other traditional circus acts doing their routines above the crowded carnival games. This is one hotel-casino where you are likely to see infants in strollers at the registration desk and teenagers in the elevators.

Standing like monuments to the pioneer past are two of the most wonderful of Reno's casinos: the Mapes and the Riverside. Both have lively histories—the Riverside dates back almost to Reno's 19th-century beginnings. The great brick building opened as the first hotel in the state during the dark period in the 1920s when gambling was illegal, and in the 1930s served as home base to a generation of divorcées who found the out-of-town dude ranches too rustic or confining. It is now closed, as is the Mapes, which was the first hotel-casino built after World War II and one of the last Art Deco structures built in the U.S.—the plans had been drawn up in 1938, but construction was delayed by the war. Today they loom like ghosts in the glare of the bright lights on Virginia Street.

The term "one-armed bandit," once a jocular synonym for the slot machine that helped build Reno's reputation, is obsolete now. Some slot machines have no arms at all but are operated by pushbuttons; others are not traditional slot machines with spinning reels, but video poker and keno games. There are some slots that have handles but then have video displays instead of reels. And even the machines that combine the traditional handle on the right side with spinning reels are actually computer-driven—the handle is painstakingly designed to give the impression that it operates mechanically, resisting the pull as if an internal spring were tensing, but the flexing is just for effect. The handle simply engages a switch to activate a tiny computer that commands an electric motor to spin the reels and display a result randomly chosen by the computer.

That may not sound like a lot of fun, but the popularity of the machines proves that many still enjoy them. Increasingly, casinos devote expensive floor space to slot machines and less to table games such as craps and blackjack. The clubs still serve free drinks to active players, and entertainment is still a mainstay of the casino experience, although not quite on the lavish scale as in the past. Today some of the spectacle that was once supplied by big-name stars is provided by the architecture and the food.

Dining in Reno and Sparks

Typically each hotel-casino offers a wide variety of dining options under its roof, from a snack bar serving coffee and hot dogs to a gourmet restaurant priding itself on lavish cuisine and service. Thus, as you might expect, some of Reno's finest dining is found at the casinos.

Spectacular buffets have become a staple of the Nevada casino, almost an indigenous art form, and they are well represented in Reno. The breakfast buffet at the **Eldorado**, at Fourth and Virginia streets, is especially highly regarded and often has a line of eager locals waiting when it opens at 8:00 A.M. For lunch or dinner the buffet at the **Peppermill**, 2707 South Virginia Street, provides a tropical decor as exotic as the food, and the mountain of shrimps may be worth the entire price. The **Rotisserie Restaurant & Buffet** at John Ascuaga's Nugget in Sparks provides another impressive spread, and the brunch at **Bally's** is a Sunday tradition. Served in the casino's Restaurant Row, the buffet features 13 entrées and complimentary Champagne. None of the buffets is expensive, yet each projects an air of an extravagant feast.

Another casino staple is the bargain special. These change often, but are well-advertised and range from a 99-cent breakfast at the **CalNeva Club**, Second and Center streets, to a $5 full-course prime rib dinner at the **Sands**, 345 North Arlington. The specials change, but there is seldom a day without one or two to attract bargain hunters.

Yet another casino standby is the gourmet restaurant: No self-respecting casino manager can function comfortably without a European-trained chef directing a squad of white-hatted perfectionists in the preparation of culinary delights. The **Top of the Hilton** at the Flamingo Hilton, Second and Sierra streets, is a particularly elegant example of this kind of dining; the service is impeccable, the food delectable, and the view from the 21st floor—especially when the sun is setting beyond the white-capped Sierra and the lights of the city are twinkling below—is superb. Other casino dinner houses of distinction are the **Steak House** at Harrah's, **Le Moulin** at the Peppermill, and the **Café Gigi** at Bally's.

For many years, John Asquaga's Nugget in Sparks has been acknowledged as offering the finest casino restaurants in the Truckee Meadows. But the Nugget has lately been equalled and perhaps surpassed by the Eldorado in downtown Reno, principally because the Carano family has maintained an intense personal interest in the superb food and service in the Eldorado's fourteen kitchens and six second-floor restaurants. **La Strada** is the Eldorado's signature restaurant, serving Northern Italian cuisine at its most elegant in three distinct, inviting dining areas. Despite recognition as one of the 50 best Italian restaurants in the United States, La Strada keeps its prices moderate—subsidized somewhat by the casino plowing merrily along downstairs, perhaps. The *Wine Spectator* newsletter awarded the wine list a "Best Award of Excellence"; even the kitchen lighting here has won an award.

The house special mushroom ravioli and other varieties of fresh pasta are available for retail sale in the **Pasta Shop** nearby—the hotel produces 25 miles of spaghetti every day, and sells much of it to take-home customers. **The Eldorado Bakery** also produces more pastries than the restaurants serve. Fresh-roasted coffee—up to 100 pounds a day—is available to take home or to drink at **Tivoli Gardens**, an international adventure in design and cuisine, with Thai, Cantonese, Szechwan, Hunan, Vietnamese, Caribbean, South American, Mexican, Italian, and American selections among the 160 menu items and 80 kinds of beer from around the world. At **The Vintage**, the Continental menu highlights veal, duckling, seafood, fish, and lamb, while the extensive wine list emphasizes California fine wines. At **The Grill & Rotisserie** steaks, chicken, and ribs are wood-roasted and mesquite-grilled in a casual, library-type atmosphere, while **Choices** is an informal combination of fast-food restaurant and service deli. The **Market Place Buffet** is a local favorite for the grandeur of the spreads served from 7:00 A.M. to 2:00 P.M. and 4:00 to 11:00 P.M. daily.

DINING AWAY FROM THE CASINOS

Reno and Sparks offer an astonishing number and variety of exceptional restaurants without gambling attached. One of the best is also one of the newest: **Adele's**, a short walk south from the hotel-casinos on Virginia Street, recently opened in the Valley Bank building at the corner of Liberty Street. The style here is upscale New York/French, with splendid lunches and dinners served at tables, high-backed booths, and a bar. The menu is cosmopolitan, with a clubby, old-money atmosphere and prices to match. The chef here, who also operates long-established Adele's in Carson City, is currently Reno's most sought-after restaurateur (Tel: 702-333-6503).

Another popular mainstay in Reno is seafood: **The Rapscallion Seafood House** (Tel: 702-323-1211), 1555 South Wells Avenue at Vista Street, and **Famous Murphy's Restaurant and Oyster House** (Tel: 702-827-4111), 3127 South Virginia Street at Peckham Lane, feature seafood and pleasing surroundings. **The Oyster Bar** at John Ascuaga's Nugget (Tel: 702-356-3300) is also a favorite for seafood concoctions, especially the New York pan roasts.

An unusual dining place is **The Liberty Belle** (Tel: 702-825-1776), 4250 South Virginia Street by the Convention Center, a fine specimen of a saloon with a magnificent back bar and hearty lunch and dinner fare. It is operated by Marshall and Frank Fey, the grandsons of the man who invented the slot machine. Examples of their illustrious ancestor's handiwork—most notably the original Liberty Belle—are on display. **Ichiban Japanese Steak House & Sushi Bar** (Tel: 702-323-5550), 635 North Sierra Street at 6th Street, features the astonishing Teppanyaki-style tableside cooking involving dancing knives and flashing smiles. Try the traditional Japanese dishes as well as the steaks and lobster.

DINING AWAY FROM DOWNTOWN

You can also choose from fine restaurants serving dishes from around the world located away from the expensive center of the city. Reservations aren't necessarily required; the telephone numbers we give are more for getting directions to these somewhat scattered locations if you're not familiar with the outlying areas of Reno and Sparks. **Sapna Indian Restaurant** (Tel: 702-829-1537) offers the cuisine of northern and southern India, with masala curries spiced to order, and tandoori entrées on the dinner menu. It's in the shopping center at Kietzke and Moana, across from the Target store. **Sushi Teri**, next door to Toys R Us at 5000 Smithridge (at South Virginia Street; Tel: 702-827-9191) offers Reno's only all-you-can-eat sushi bar, with teriyaki and tempura specials also on the menu. The **Café de Thai** seems halfway to Bangkok at 3314 South McCarran and Mira Loma (Tel: 702-829-8424), and the banal shopping-center surroundings belie the artistry within. Chef Sakul is a graduate of the Culinary Institute of America, and his menu of Thai cuisine is worth the journey to the suburbs.

Que-Huong, in Sparks at 830 B Street (Tel: 702-359-5111) in the heart of old Harriman (for which see above in the Sparks section), serves light, fresh, and exotically spiced Vietnamese food. **Greek Village** at 927 West Moana is a family-operated restaurant serving lunch and dinner in traditional style, including delicious desserts (Tel: 702-826-6011), and **Elvie's Kitchenette**, in the business park at 4600 Kietzke Lane (Building 160; Tel: 702-827-1881) has Filipino specialties on the menu as well as mainstream American fare. Almost as exotic, the **Chicago Express Deli** at 1303 East Fourth Street in Reno (Tel: 702-333-0922) prides itself on soups and sandwiches, and features authentic ethnic specialties shipped fresh from "home." And **Davo's Little Brooklyn** at 424 East Fourth Street (Tel: 702-324-1011) offers a tasty sampling of Brooklyn Italian food with New York cheesecake for dessert.

If Nevada can be said to have a native cuisine other than that of the Paiute Indians or the casino buffets, it is—of all things—Basque boardinghouse fare. Each spring and autumn in the late 19th and early 20th centuries, large flocks of sheep moved between Nevada's high-mountain summer grazing lands and the broad desert valleys where they spent the winter. To manage these flocks of sheep, Scottish, Chinese, and eventually Basque herders were employed. These Basques, recruited from the Pyrénées mountain districts of France and Spain, came to take the demanding job of moving with the sheep, keeping them safe and unscattered with the help of a dog or two. For months at a time they roamed the solitary wilderness with the animals, and when they took a week off or bunked up in town between jobs, they stayed at boarding hotels kept by their fellow countrymen, where hearty meals were served family-style. Inevitably diners other than Basques were attracted to the table as well, and over the years the Basque hotels have become popular local dining places in many Nevada communities. In Reno there are three exceptional and quite different examples of the genre. The **Pyrénées Bar & Grill** (Tel: 702-329-3800), in the porched and pillared old Hardy mansion at Flint and California streets, and **Louis' Basque Corner** (Tel: 702-323-7203), at East Fourth and Evans, are actually dinner houses of some elegance, with specialty entrées and steaks, but served family-style at long tables. At the **Santa Fe Hotel** (Tel: 702-323-1891), 235 Lake Street, the style is simpler: tureens, bowls, and platters are passed up and down the long tables, and the house red wine is served in water tumblers. Be sure to bring a sheepherder's appetite to all of these spots.

Pyramid Lake

This extraordinary desert lake, a remnant of the inland sea that once covered much of the Great Basin (Utah's Great Salt Lake is another), is a little more than a half-hour's drive north from Reno via Pyramid Way (Highway 445).

Fed by the Truckee River, which is fed in turn by Lake Tahoe, Pyramid Lake is contained within a Paiute Indian reservation. It is the antithesis of Lake Tahoe, with an absolute minimum of development and no glamour at all. There are no pine forests, no casinos, and no tours (other than the brief look at the fish hatchery that maintains the populations of Lahontan cutthroat trout and *cui-ui,* a species unique to Pyramid). There is only the lake and its desert setting. Cupped by chalky pink, tan, and gray hills, Pyramid's water is such a brilliant iridescent blue under the summer sun that it can hurt your eyes just to gaze upon it, so dark and cold to look at in winter that it chills eyeballs in their sockets.

The principal attraction for visitors is the otherworldly beauty of the lake itself and the sport provided by the cutthroat trout (the minimum size that you can keep is 19 inches). Tribal permits are available for fishing and boat launching at the ranger station at Sutcliff, as is information for hiking and exploring by car. At The Needles, near the northern end of the lake, warm pools fed by hot springs provide a sort of prehistoric pleasure.

Nixon, the reservation's main town, is on the southeast shore of the lake. The road from Nixon south to Wadsworth (Highway 447) parallels the Truckee and passes by the site of the battle in which the Paiutes annihilated an invading force from Virginia City in 1860. At Wadsworth you can pick up Interstate 80 to return to Reno.

GETTING AROUND

The Reno-Cannon International Airport is served by major airlines (American, America West, Delta, Southwest, United, and USAir) with flights to and from metropolitan centers around the United States. Shuttle connections are available from the airport to hotels in Reno and to hotels and ski areas at Lake Tahoe.

There is local bus service in Reno and Sparks and in some towns at Lake Tahoe; Greyhound buses link these communities to each other and to Carson City. That makes public transportation a possibility, but—if ease, comfort, and convenience are considerations—a remote one. There is no substitute for travelling by car around the far western part of Nevada, and if your visit is in winter, late fall, or early spring, make it four-wheel drive. Reno, Carson City, and Lake Tahoe offer plenty of taxicabs, and limousines are available at short notice, but there is nothing better than the simplicity and flexibility of getting around by private car.

Amtrak sends a train a day in each direction between Chicago and San Francisco across the Sierra, with stops at Truckee and Reno (Tel: 800-872-7245).

Highway access to this part of Nevada is by Interstate 80 from San Francisco and Sacramento to the west and from Salt Lake City and northern Nevada to the east. From the west I-80 passes through Truckee (where Highways 89 and 267 proceed, respectively, to Tahoe City and King's Beach at the North Shore of Lake Tahoe) and through Reno. U.S. 395 connects Reno, Carson City, and the Carson Valley, continuing south along the east slope of the Sierra through the Owens Valley to southern California and north to northeastern California and Oregon. U.S. 50 connects the South Shore of Lake Tahoe with Placerville to the west, and to the east continues through Carson City, central Nevada, and (eventually) Baltimore, Maryland.

Summers are hot and thronged with visitors throughout the region; winters are cold and brisk and especially busy at Lake Tahoe, where the ski resorts provide the major attraction. Despite the unpredictable weather, spring and fall are perhaps the most beautiful seasons, with wildflowers blooming in May and June and the cottonwood trees blazing brilliant yellow in October.

Because pleasing visitors is the major industry in this part of the West, there are squadrons of organizations you can call when you have a question. They are devoted to helping you find your way around, and they welcome the opportunity to assist you with current information: Nevada State Commission on Tourism, Tel: (800) NEVADA-8; Lake Tahoe Visitors Authority (South Shore), Tel: (800) AT-TAHOE or (916) 544-5050; Incline Village/Crystal Bay Visitors & Convention Bureau (North Shore, Nevada side), Tel: (800) GO-TAHOE or (702) 832-1606; Tahoe North Visitor & Convention Bureau (North Shore, California side), Tel: (800) 824-6348 or (916) 583-3494; Reno-Sparks Convention & Visitors Authority, Tel: (800) FOR-RENO or (702) 827-RENO; Reno Downtown Visitors Center, Tel: (702) 329-3558; Sparks Downtown Visitors

Center, Tel: (702) 358-1976; Carson City Convention & Visitors' Bureau, Tel: (800) 638-2321 or (702) 687-7410.

ACCOMMODATIONS REFERENCE

The rate ranges given here are projections for fall 1993 through spring 1994. Unless otherwise indicated, rates are for double room, double occupancy.

▶ **Best Western Carson Station.** 900 South Carson Street, **Carson City**, NV 89701. Tel: (702) 883-0900 or (800) 528-1234; Fax: 882-7569. $45–$55.

▶ **Caesars Tahoe.** P.O. Box 5800, **Stateline**, NV 89449. Tel: (702) 588-3515 or (800) 648-3353; Fax: 586-2024. $105–$145.

▶ **Cal Neva Lodge Resort.** P.O. Box 368, 2 Stateline Road, **Crystal Bay**, NV 89402. Tel: (702) 832-4000 or (800) 225-6382; Fax: 831-9007. $69–$139.

▶ **Captain's Alpenhaus.** P.O. Box 262, **Tahoma**, CA 96142. Tel: (916) 525-5000. $65–$115.

▶ **Carson Valley Inn.** 1627 Highway 395, **Minden**, NV 89423. Tel: (702) 782-9711 or (800) 321-6983 (outside Nevada); Fax 782-7472. $49–$69.

▶ **Chollar Mansion.** P.O. Box 889, **Virginia City**, NV 89440. Tel: (702) 847-9777. $70–$125.

▶ **Circus Circus Hotel & Casino.** P.O. Box 5880, 500 North Sierra Street, **Reno**, NV 89513. Tel: (702) 329-0711 or (800) 648-5010; Fax: 329-0599. $36–$49.

▶ **Comstock Hotel & Casino.** 200 West Second Street, **Reno**, NV 89501. Tel: (702) 329-1880 or (800) 824-8167; Fax: 348-0539. $38–$64.

▶ **Comstock Lodge.** 875 South C Street, **Virginia City**, NV 89440. Tel: (702) 847-0233. $45–$65.

▶ **Donner Country Inn.** 9 Green Valley Drive, Lafayette, CA 94549 (mailing address). Tel: (916) 587-5574 or (510) 938-0685. $85.

▶ **Edith Palmer's Country Inn.** P.O. Box 758, **Virginia City**, NV 89440. Tel: (702) 847-0707. $70–$85.

▶ **Eldorado Hotel & Casino.** P.O. Box 3399, 345 North Virginia Street, **Reno**, NV 89501. Tel: (702) 786-5700 or (800) 648-5966; Fax: 348-7513. $49–$105.

▶ **Fitzgerald's Casino-Hotel.** Box 40130, 255 North Virginia Street, **Reno**, NV 89504. Tel: (702) 785-3300 or (800) 648-5022. $48–$96.

▶ **Flamingo Hilton.** 225 North Sierra Street, **Reno**, NV 89501. Tel: (702) 322-1111 or (800) 648-4882; Fax: 785-7086. $59–$109.

▶ **Gold Hill Hotel**. P.O. Box 304, **Virginia City**, NV 89440. Tel: (702) 847-0111; Fax: 847-9215. $40–$138.

▶ **The Hardwicke House**. P.O. Box 96, 99 Main Street, **Silver City**, NV 89428. Tel: (702) 847-0215. $35–$55.

▶ **Harrah's**. 210 North Center Street, **Reno**, NV 89502. Tel: (702) 786-3232 or (800) 648-3773; Fax: 586-6607. $75–$130.

▶ **Harrah's**. P.O. Box 8, **Stateline**, NV 89449. Tel: (702) 588-6606 or (800) 648-3773; Fax: 586-6607. $105–$225.

▶ **Harvey's**. P.O. Box 128, Highway 50, **Stateline**, NV 89449. Tel: (702) 588-2411 or (800) 648-3361; Fax: 588-6643. $89–$185.

▶ **Haus Bavaria**. P.O. Box 3308, 593 North Dyer Circle, **Incline Village**, NV 89450. Tel: (702) 831-6122. $72–$90.

▶ **Holiday Hotel**. P.O. Box 2700, **Reno**, NV 89505. Tel: (702) 329-0411 or (800) 648-5431; Fax: 322-4944. $48–$68.

▶ **Horizon**. P.O. Box C, **Stateline**, NV 89449. Tel: (702) 588-6211 or (800) 648-3322; Fax: 588-1344. $59–$99.

▶ **Hyatt Regency Lake Tahoe**. P.O. Box 3239, **Incline Village**, NV 89449. Tel: (702) 831-1111 or (800) 233-1234; Fax: 831-2171. $139–$229.

▶ **Inn at Incline**. 1003 Tahoe Boulevard, **Incline Village**, NV 89450. Tel: (702) 831-1052 or (800) 824-6391; Fax: 831-3016. $55–$99.

▶ **John Ascuaga's Nugget**. 1100 Nugget Avenue, **Sparks**, NV 89431. Tel: (702) 356-3300 or (800) 648-1177; Fax: 356-4198. $28–$89.

▶ **Ormsby House**. 600 South Carson Street, **Carson City**, NV 89702. Tel: (702) 882-1890 or (800) 648-0920; Fax: 885-6961. $46–$59.

▶ **Peppermill Hotel Casino**. 2707 South Virginia Street, **Reno**, NV 89502. Tel: (702) 826-2121 or (800) 282-2444; Fax: 826-5205. $44–$89.

▶ **Ponderosa Hotel & Casino**. 515 South Virginia Street, **Reno**, NV 89501. Tel: (702) 786-6820 or (800) 228-6820; Fax: 786-9431. $32–$42.

▶ **Reno Hilton**. 2500 East Second Street, **Reno**, NV 89595. Tel: (702) 789-2000 or (800) 648-5080. $49–$119.

▶ **Richardson House**. P.O. Box 2011, **Truckee**, CA 96160. Tel: (916) 587-5388. $55–$65.

▶ **Riverboat Hotel & Casino**. 34 West Second Street, **Reno**, NV 89501. Tel: (702) 323-8877 or (800) 888-5525; Fax: 348-0926. $25–$75.

▶ **Sands Hotel Casino**. 345 North Arlington Avenue, **Reno**, NV 89501. Tel: (702) 348-2200 or (800) 648-3553; Fax: 348-2226. $29–$69.

▶ **Sundowner Hotel & Casino**. 450 North Arlington Avenue, **Reno**, NV 89503. Tel: (702) 786-7050 or (800) 648-5490; Fax: 348-6074. $21–$90.

▶ **Sunnyside Lodge**. P.O. Box 5969, **Tahoe City**, CA 96145. Tel: (916) 583-7200 or (800) 822-2754; Fax: 583-7224. $75–$120.

▶ **Truckee Hotel**. P.O. Box 884, **Truckee**, CA 96160. Tel: (916) 587-4444. $60–$99.

▶ **The Virginian**. 140 North Virginia Street, **Reno**, NV 89501. Tel: (702) 329-4664 or (800) 874-5558; Fax: 329-2673. $42–$55.

▶ **Walley's Hot Springs**. P.O. Box 26, **Genoa**, NV 89411. Tel: (702) 883-6556. $85–$120.

THE
CENTRAL
COAST
MONTEREY BAY TO
SAN LUIS OBISPO

By Jacqueline Killeen

A native San Franciscan and fourth-generation Californian, Jacqueline Killeen has written about the state since 1968 for a number of guidebooks, as well as regional and national magazines. Currently a contributing editor and restaurant critic for San Francisco Focus *magazine, she is the author of* Country Inns of California.

"The greatest meeting of land and water in the world." So wrote poet Robinson Jeffers of California's central coast—a land of awesome beauty, where high mountains plunge abruptly into the sea, and a region with a vivid past, which has inspired writers from Richard Henry Dana to Jack Kerouac. Its history encompasses the settlement of California by Spanish soldiers and missionaries, the era of Mexican rule when rich *rancheros* and Yankee traders made Monterey "Queen of the West," and the boisterous saga of the whalers and fishing boats that plied the coastal waters. Later chapters involve the bohemian colonies in Carmel and Big Sur, the struggles of migrant workers in John Steinbeck's "Long Valley," and the castle of William Randolph Hearst, who brought the glitter of Hollywood to a hilltop above San Simeon.

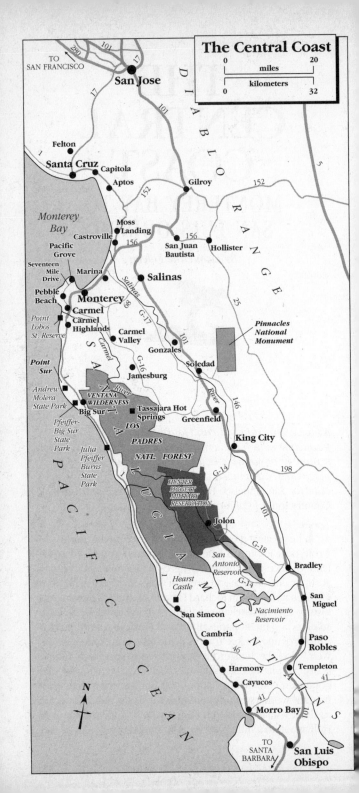

The Central Coast is also one of the world's fabled play-grounds, with diversions ranging from golf to deep-sea excursions, and from sightseeing to shopping, dining, and winery touring. The best way to explore this area is in a circular itinerary south along the ocean from Santa Cruz at the south base of the San Francisco Peninsula, through the Monterey Peninsula and Big Sur, down to Hearst Castle and San Luis Obispo. You can then return quickly back north to San Francisco via Highway 101, the inland route (mostly freeway) through the Salinas Valley.

This central section of the California coast is enormously popular with visitors and locals alike and thus can become unpleasantly crowded on peak-season weekends. If possible, plan a midweek visit to the coast, especially during the summer months.

MAJOR INTEREST

Monterey Peninsula
Historic buildings of Monterey
Cannery Row and the Monterey Bay Aquarium
Golf, tennis, and deep-sea excursions
Seventeen Mile Drive and Pebble Beach
Carmel Mission
Shops and galleries of Carmel
Dining and wine tasting
Big Sur scenery

San Simeon to San Luis Obispo
Hearst Castle
Shops and galleries of Cambria
Surfing and deep-sea fishing
San Luis Obispo and its mission

The Inland Route
Wineries
Historic missions
Steinbeck House and Steinbeck Library in Salinas
San Juan Bautista's early Californiana

THE COASTAL ROUTE TO MONTEREY

From San Francisco, Highway 1 follows the Pacific coastline all the way south to Monterey, but it's a long drive, and traffic on the two-lane road north of Santa Cruz is often congested (see Day Trips from San Francisco for details on the coast from San Francisco down to Santa Cruz). A faster and equally scenic route is from San Jose across the heavily forested Santa Cruz Mountains on Highway 17, which meets Highway 1 in Santa Cruz, about 80 miles (128 km) south of San Francisco and 43 miles (69 km) north of Monterey.

Santa Cruz

In 1791 Spanish priests founded Santa Cruz Mission on the north end of Monterey Bay to convert the Ohlone Indians who lived in the area; only a replica of the mission's chapel remains. A hundred years later, the town blossomed into a popular beach resort with a boardwalk, casino, and Victorian mansions along the shore. The **Santa Cruz Beach Boardwalk** still exists—complete with its landmark 1911 merry-go-round and its Giant Dipper roller coaster—the sole survivor among California's old-time seaside amusement parks. Unfortunately, many historic buildings in the downtown area did not survive the earthquake of 1989, which hit Santa Cruz particularly hard. Nevertheless, there is much to see and do here. Complete information is available from the Santa Cruz County Conference and Visitors Council, 701 Front Street, Santa Cruz, CA 95060; Tel: (800) 833-3494.

One of the city's weirdest attractions is **The Mystery Spot**, at 1953 North Branciforte Drive, where the laws of gravity are seemingly reversed—balls roll uphill and the like; daily tours are conducted. If you want to tarry a while in the area, consider a visit to **Roaring Camp** in nearby Felton, a re-creation of a 19th-century logging town where you can ride through the redwoods in a steam-powered narrow-gauge railroad. From May to October trains also depart from the Santa Cruz Beach Boardwalk on two-hour round-trip excursions. They run daily during the summer and holidays; weekends only at other times (Tel: 408-335-4484). Or, enjoy Santa Cruz's many facilities for pier and deep-sea fishing; **Stagnaro's Fishing Trips** at the Municipal Wharf offers daily seven-hour excursions (Tel: 408-425-7003). You'll also find fine beaches here and in the nearby resorts of Aptos and Capitola.

The Santa Cruz Mountains are home to some two dozen small family-owned wineries, such as **David Bruce** and **Bonnie Doon**, that are noted for their individualistic wines produced by nonconformist winemakers. (Bonnie Doon, which now specializes in Rhône-type wines, also produces eaux-de-vie from prunes, cherries, and pears, as well as grappa.) Most of the wineries offer tasting rooms and tours (often by appointment only). Detailed information on the wineries is available from the Santa Cruz Visitors Council.

Santa Cruz is also an important center for the performing arts. Of note are **Shakespeare Santa Cruz**, a company based at the University of California campus here that presents a summer festival of the bard's works (Tel: 408-459-2121), and the **Cabrillo Music Festival**, an internationally acclaimed two-week summer event which features classical and serious contemporary music (Tel: 408-662-2701).

STAYING IN SANTA CRUZ

For an overnight stay in Santa Cruz, your best choices in town include two bed-and-breakfast inns: ▶ **Château Victorian**, a beautifully restored and tastefully decorated Victorian near the boardwalk, and the ▶ **Babbling Brook Inn**, a wooded retreat beside a waterfall and creek; decorated in frilly country style, most of its rooms have decks and Franklin stoves.

Complete resort facilities and slightly higher prices are found at ▶ **Chaminade**, a 152-room hotel and conference center on 80 wooded acres in the hills above Santa Cruz. The guest rooms (many with private balconies or patios) are scattered in two-story structures around the main building, which was built in the 1930s as a Roman Catholic boys school. On the grounds are lighted tennis courts, a swimming pool, a fitness center, and miles of jogging trails.

The most luxurious retreat in the entire Santa Cruz area is probably the tiny ▶ **Inn at Depot Hill**, an elegant transformation of the turn-of-the-century railroad depot on a hillside above the historic beach resort of Capitola Village. Each of the eight suites or rooms is designed around a stop on a fictional train trip—Stratford-on-Avon, Paris, Côte d'Azur, Portofino—and resplendent with down comforters and featherbeds, fireplaces, patios or private gardens, outdoor hot tubs, VCRs, and even computer modems on the telephones. The inn provides its guests with breakfast, afternoon tea, wine and hors d'oeuvres, and dessert at bedtime. Capitola is known for its Begonia Festival each September, but the exotic blooms may be seen throughout the summer at the **Antonelli Begonia Gardens**, 2545 Capitola Road.

A romantic spot for dinner or Sunday brunch in Capitola is **Shadowbrook**, at 1750 Wharf Road. The restaurant, located beside a small river at the base of a cliff, is reached by funicular; Tel: 475-1511.

SOUTH TO MONTEREY

Below Santa Cruz, Highway 1 becomes freeway for a while, then narrows as it winds along the shore of Monterey Bay past the fishing village of **Moss Landing**; consider a stop here for antiques hunting in the two dozen shops that line Moss Landing Road, which parallels Highway 1. At the southern intersection of these two routes, the quaint **Moss Landing Oyster Bar** lures lovers of fresh seafood for lunch and dinner Tuesday through Sunday (Tel: 633-5302). Bird-watchers head to this area to visit **Elkhorn Slough**, a 1,300-acre wildlife sanctuary. Beyond Moss Landing, Highway 1 crosses the artichoke fields of Castroville and finally skims along the sand dunes past the Fort Ord army base to Monterey, a 40-mile (64-km) drive in total.

MONTEREY

The various communities of the Monterey Peninsula–Big Sur area are bound only by their proximity—in looks and character, each is as different from the others as a family of adopted children: historic Monterey, flaunting its Spanish-Mexican heritage; modest Pacific Grove, in the process of shedding its prim Victorian upbringing; stately Pebble Beach, looking down its aristocratic nose at the others; quaint Carmel, clinging to its image as a picturesque artists' colony; chic Carmel Valley, fighting the encroachment of suburbia; and the renegade child Big Sur, basking in its isolation and bohemian tradition.

Throughout the year, numerous cultural and sporting events occur on the Monterey Peninsula; for a calendar and a free copy of *The Official Monterey Peninsula Visitors Guide,* write to the Monterey Peninsula Chamber of Commerce, P.O. Box 1770, Monterey, CA 93942 (Tel: 408-649-1770; Fax: 649-3502). On your arrival in the area, pick up a free copy of the *Monterey Peninsula Review* for a comprehensive listing of what's happening that week.

Nestled along the hilly southern shore of Monterey Bay, the town of Monterey flourished as the political, economic, and cultural capital of Alta California under Spanish-Mexican rule (1770 to 1846), when San Francisco was scarcely more than a village. The wealthy *rancheros* built their homes here, as did the Yankee sea captains and merchants who made fortunes trading at the bustling seaport. In *Two Years Before*

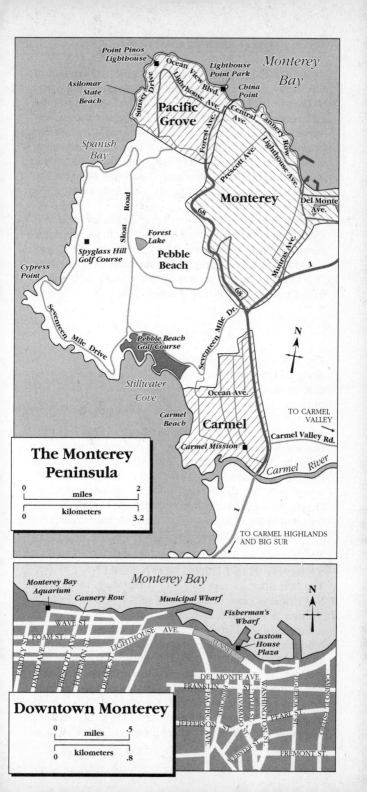

The Monterey Peninsula

Point Pinos Lighthouse

Monterey Bay

Asilomar State Beach

Spanish Bay

Ocean View Blvd.
Lighthouse Ave.
Sunset Drive
Lighthouse Point Park
China Point
Central Ave.
Cannery Row
Lighthouse Ave.

Pacific Grove

Forest Ave.
Prescott Ave.

Monterey

Del Monte Ave.

68

Munras Ave.

1

Sloat Road

Forest Lake

Spyglass Hill Golf Course

Pebble Beach

Cypress Point

Seventeen Mile Drive

Pebble Beach Golf Course

68

Seventeen Mile Dr.

Stillwater Cove

Ocean Ave.

Carmel Beach

TO CARMEL VALLEY

Carmel

Carmel Valley Rd.

Carmel Mission

Carmel River

1

TO CARMEL HIGHLANDS
AND BIG SUR

N

| 0 | miles | 2 |
| 0 | kilometers | 3.2 |

Monterey Bay

Monterey Bay Aquarium
Cannery Row
Municipal Wharf
Fisherman's Wharf

N

WAVE ST.
FOAM ST.
EARDLY ST.
DAVID AVE.
PRESCOTT AVE.
HOFMAN ST.
DRAKE ST.
LIGHTHOUSE AVE.

TUNNEL

Custom House Plaza

DEL MONTE AVE.
FRANKLIN ST.
PACIFIC AVE.
CALLE PRINCIPAL
ALVARADO ST.
TYLER ST.
WASHINGTON ST.
FIGUEROA ST.
CAMINO EL ESTERO
PEARL ST.
JEFFERSON ST.
WEBSTER ST.
FREMONT ST.

Downtown Monterey

| 0 | miles | .5 |
| 0 | kilometers | .8 |

the Mast, Richard Henry Dana described 1830s Monterey as "decidedly the pleasantest and most civilized-looking place in California." But under U.S. rule in the latter half of the 19th century, Monterey declined: The state capital was moved north, eventually to Sacramento, and San Francisco became the major port of entry. After the turn of the century the town was revived by a thriving fishing industry and then immortalized by John Steinbeck in *Cannery Row,* but the sardines have long since departed, and tourism is now the mainstay of Monterey.

From Memorial Day to Labor Day, the most effortless way to sightsee in Monterey is to leave your car in the municipal parking lot near Fisherman's Wharf and buy an all-day pass (good for unlimited rides) on **The Wave** (about one dollar). This new bus service stops at all major tourist destinations from Custom House Plaza to Cannery Row.

Old Monterey

The best way to get a historical perspective of Monterey is along the Path of History Walking Tour, a self-guided, two-mile itinerary marked by golden tiles set in the sidewalk and plaques at some 40 historic sites. Many of these adobe structures are now operated as museums with regular guided tours; during the summer actors portray historic characters in some of them. Many of the sites are associated with the **Monterey Historic Park**, which puts out maps, brochures, and booklets describing the route. You can pick up or purchase these maps at Pacific House on Custom House Plaza near Fisherman's Wharf (see below), or look for them in any of the tourist-oriented magazines here. (For more information, Tel: 408-649-7118.)

SEEING HISTORIC MONTEREY
The best place to start your tour is the **Maritime Museum and History Center** in the new $6-million Stanton Center at Custom House Plaza. It provides an in-depth view of the area's maritime history from the Spaniards' discovery of Monterey Bay through the epoch of the sardine canneries earlier in this century.

Monterey's oldest building, **The Royal Chapel**, marks the site of the mission and presidio (fort) that Father Junípero Serra and Don Gaspar de Portolá founded in 1770, as Spain's second outpost (after San Diego) on the California coast; the following year Serra moved the mission to Carmel. Mexican and Native American craftsmen built the present chapel in 1795 to replace an earlier structure destroyed by fire.

In 1822 Mexico won its independence from Spain and encouraged foreign trade with Alta California, making Monterey the official port of entry in 1829. The Mexicans collected the lucrative port duties at a waterfront **Custom House**, which now displays items from a typical ship's cargo of the 1830s. Richard Henry Dana described his own ship's store as "everything that can be imagined. From Chinese fireworks to English cart wheels . . ."

The new California trade attracted Yankees, who built two-story, balconied adobe homes during the 1830s and 1840s in a beguiling blend of New England and Spanish architecture, now known as Monterey Colonial. One of the best examples is the **Larkin House** (now a museum), built by New Englander Thomas Oliver Larkin, who became a wealthy merchant and United States consul to California. Another notable home of this era is the **Cooper-Molera Adobe**, built by Larkin's half-brother, a sea captain and trader known as Juan Bautista Cooper, who became a Mexican citizen and married the sister of General Vallejo. Exhibits in the house and gardens depict life in 19th-century Monterey. **Casa Soberanes** (also known as the House with the Blue Gate) is another handsome adobe that is furnished with a mix of modern Mexican folk art and pieces from New England and the China trade. An 1840s residence has been renamed **The Stevenson House** because an impoverished and not-yet-famous Robert Louis Stevenson rented a room here in 1879 while courting his future wife, Fanny Osbourne, and writing his essay "The Old Pacific Capital." Today the house serves as a museum of Stevenson memorabilia.

Monterey After Mexican Rule

Mexican rule of California came to an end on July 7, 1846, when Commodore John Drake Sloat of the U.S. Navy raised the Stars and Stripes over the Monterey Custom House. California was administered by U.S. military governors until the new state's constitution was drafted and signed in 1849 at **Colton Hall**, now a historical museum. Also on the property is the **Old Monterey Jail**, which Steinbeck fans will recognize as the spot frequented by Big Joe in *Tortilla Flat*. In 1847 the United States erected **Pacific House** for the Army quartermaster corps and held Sunday bull-and-bear fights in the rear walled garden. Later this large adobe was used for such disparate purposes as a tavern and a headquarters of a temperance society; today it displays exhibits of California's history and Native American artifacts. In the same period, **California's First Theater** was built as a boardinghouse and tavern; in 1850 a group of U.S. Army officers started staging plays here. The theater was reopened in 1937, and 19th-century melodramas are still performed regularly.

The mercantile center of Monterey in the 1850s was Joseph Boston and Company, later known as the **Casa del Oro** because of the gold supposedly stashed away in its safe. One of its employees in those days was a canny young Scotsman named David Jacks, who wound up owning the store—and most of Monterey County—when he and a partner purchased town lots and thousands of surrounding acres at a city auction in 1859 for $1,002.50. Jacks, however, might be best known for his marketing of Monterey Jack, the cheese made by his tenant farmers. **The Boston Store** now sells items representative of that heyday as well as dried herbs from its garden.

In the heart of old Monterey, but not listed on the Path of History tour, is the **Monterey Peninsula Museum of Art**, 559 Pacific, where collections and exhibits focus on the art of California, Asia, and the Pacific Rim, as well as international folk and tribal art. At **La Mirada** (the former Castro Adobe at 720 Via Mirada), the museum displays work by regional artists as well as decorative arts. A large new wing houses Asian exhibits.

To handle the heavy traffic of trading ships, Monterey built a new pier across from the Custom House in 1846; it is now known as **Fisherman's Wharf**. In the 1850s this wharf was home to whaling ships and later to commercial fishing vessels, which now dock at the nearby Municipal Wharf, leaving the old wharf to tourists. But even if you're turned off by the predictable array of curio shops, there are several good reasons for a stop here: One is the din of barking sea lions and seals who hang out near the end of the pier.

Dining in Monterey

On Fisherman's Wharf lovers of squid should check out **Abalonetti**, an old-time favorite that fixes calamari in every imaginable way. Near the wharf—but a world away in atmosphere—is one of Monterey's finest and most expensive dinner houses: **Fresh Cream**, recently relocated in large, elegant quarters in the Heritage Harbor building at 99 Pacific, offers French fare and dramatic views of Monterey Bay. Reservations are advised; Tel: 375-9798.

If you want to eat in an Old Monterey adobe, stop in at **Bindel's** (500 Hartnell), which was built in the 1830s by Dr. James Stokes and was the site of California's first newspaper, *The Californian*. The reasonably priced lunches feature regional specialties such as crab cakes, Castroville artichokes, and calamari; Tel: 373-3737.

A block above Cannery Row, on Wave Street, two dinner houses evoke the area's robust past. You'll find both casual and formal dining at **The Sardine Factory**: A clublike, moderately priced bar and grill occupies an historic building in front. To the rear, a pricier California-style menu is served in the intimate Victorian Captain's Room and the glass-domed Conservatory; Tel: 373-3775. Mesquite-grilled fresh seafood is the forte of the **Whaling Station Inn**, which started in a former Chinese grocery store of the Steinbeck era and now occupies most of the block; Tel: 373-3778.

Cannery Row

John Steinbeck would be horrified by much that has happened to his beloved Cannery Row, just half a mile west of Fisherman's Wharf. From the early 1900s until the 1950s the great silver-sardine boom was a boon to Monterey's economy, reaching its apex in 1945's catch of 235,000 tons. When the sardines vanished, the hulking canneries along the waterfront shut down, later to reopen as honky-tonk shopping complexes, catering primarily to collectors of flashy tee-shirts and plastic porpoises. There's even a **Spirit of Monterey Wax Museum** (700 Cannery Row), which is actually worth a visit for its colorful overview of Monterey history.

Amid the hurly-burly, however, nostalgia buffs will discover a few gems such as the handcrafted turn-of-the-century carousel in the **Edgewater Packing Company** complex; behind this cannery a wealth of railroad memorabilia awaits collectors at **The Caboose** (open only on weekends or by appointment; Tel: 373-2885). In an adjoining railroad car, an information center offers a free booklet that contains a walking tour of Cannery Row and historical background on the area. Some of the former canneries also house tasting rooms for Monterey County wines, where you can sip the varietals of the Monterey Peninsula Winery, Bargetto, Roudon-Smith, and Paul Masson.

Steinbeck might still recognize a few of his old haunts: The building at 800 Cannery Row was the Pacific Biological Laboratories of his real-life friend and fictional hero "Doc" Edward Ricketts; the Old General Store at 835 Cannery Row was Lee Chong's Heavenly Flower Grocery; and the structure at 799 Cannery Row that now houses Mackerel Jack's Trading Company was once Flora Wood's Lone Star Café.

THE MONTEREY BAY AQUARIUM

Steinbeck and Ricketts probably would approve of Cannery Row's biggest attraction: the Monterey Bay Aquarium, which draws nearly two million visitors annually. Located in a multi-million-dollar reconstruction of the former Hovden Cannery, the aquarium is home to 6,500 specimens of marine life, representing 525 species of fish, mammals, birds, and plants whose natural habitat is the two-mile-deep canyon under Monterey Bay. Notable among the exhibits are a 28-foot-high kelp forest (the world's tallest aquarium exhibit), re-creations of Monterey Bay marine habitats, and a 55,000-gallon tank where you can observe the antics of the resident sea otters. These adorable creatures, once preyed upon for their valuable pelts, were believed to be extinct until they mysteriously reappeared along the Central Coast in 1938. Within the aquarium is the **Portola Café**, which combines a cafeteria and a full-service seafood restaurant with a splendid bay view.

Staying in Monterey

Monterey has no dearth of places to stay: Most of the major hotel chains are represented, and a string of moderately priced motels lines Munras Avenue. But many discriminating—and well-heeled—travellers opt for the ▶ **Old Monterey Inn**, a Tudor mansion set in lush gardens on a wooded hillside above the town. You'll find neither television sets nor telephones in the ten exquisitely decorated bedrooms, just heaps of reading material, fireplaces, skylights, canopied beds, and garden views. A lavish breakfast is served on the patio or in the formal dining room.

If a stay in a grand hotel suits your mood, try the luxurious 290-room ▶ **Monterey Plaza**. Built over the bay at Cannery Row, the hotel is resplendent with marble floors, teak paneling, Craftsman-style architecture, and stunning bay views. Look into the many seasonal theme packages offered on the nonview rooms for a break on the rates.

One exceedingly romantic spot on Cannery Row is the ▶ **Spindrift Inn**, a small luxury hotel that echoes a pre-cannery epoch, when this beach area was a seaside resort. Wood-burning fireplaces and views of the hills or the bay grace the elegant rooms, as do European antiques and Oriental rugs.

Breakfast in bed on a silver tray? Of course. If you prefer a homey bed and breakfast to a hotel, consider ▶ **The Jabberwock**, a towered and turreted former convent with a view and a charming garden on the hillside above Cannery Row. Named after the poem from Lewis Carroll's *Alice in Wonderland,* the poem's themes are carried throughout the inn—from breakfast, which might include "razzleberry flabjous," to a volume of the famous work next to your bed.

Exploring Shore, Sea, and Air

Monterey is a pedaler's paradise: A fine bicycle path runs along the edge of the bay, with bike-rental shops en route. On Cannery Row try **Bay Bikes**, at 640 Wave, which also rents mountain and tandem bikes, and four-wheel surreys; Tel: 646-9090. Over at 299 Cannery Row, **Adventures by the Sea** rents bikes (with free hotel pickup and delivery), as well as roller skates and kayaks. Its kayak tours are a novel way to see the waterfront by sea—don't be surprised if a friendly otter jumps on your lap or a harbor seal escorts you back to shore; Tel: 372-1807. And if you want a look under the sea, **Aquarius Dive Shop**, in the Breakwater Cove Marina (32 Cannery Row), provides skin- and scuba-diving instruction, tours, and equipment rentals; Tel: 375-6605.

More conventional seagoing tours can be found at sport-fishing outlets based near the end of Fisherman's Wharf. Year-round deep-sea fishing and winter whale-watching cruises can be booked at **Monterey Sport Fishing**, Tel: (408) 372-2203, and **Randy's Fishing and Whale-Watching Trips**, Tel: (408) 372-7440.

Western Hang Gliders, on the sands at the town of Marina, offers hang-gliding lessons northeast of Monterey. Reservations and payment are required in advance; Tel: (408) 384-2622. If that's a bit too adventurous, you can still enjoy the beautiful breezes at the weekend kite flies on the dunes near Monterey, organized by **Windborne Kites**, 585 Cannery Row; call (408) 373-7422 for a schedule. Windborne will happily sell you a kite or windsock from its inventory of more than 500 models, but even kiteless participants can usually find kiters willing to lend one of theirs.

Music and Theater in Monterey

The mammoth musical event in this part of the world is the **Monterey Jazz Festival**, where Oscar Peterson, Dizzy Gillespie, and the Pancho Sanchez Latin Band have appeared on the same program in recent years. Held each September, the festival sells tickets only for the entire three-day package, with a June deadline for orders: P.O. Box Jazz, Monterey, CA 93942; Tel: (408) 373-3366. Less structured is **Dixieland Monterey**, a three-day festival held the first weekend in March, when roughly a dozen bands converge to play in various hotels and cabarets. Beyond these events, on any night of the year some form of pop music—from swing to rock—can be heard in the clubs of Cannery Row and at Monterey's hotels.

On Fisherman's Wharf, **The Wharf Theater** draws on local talent to stage productions several nights a week; these are mostly musicals ranging from *Cabaret* to Gilbert and Sullivan classics; Tel: (408) 649-2332. Across the street from the wharf, in the Custom House Plaza, **Monterey Bay Theatrefest** presents a seven-week midsummer festival of free entertainment: live music, clown troupes, poetry readings, improvisational theater, intermezzo opera, light comedy, and more. These productions are sponsored by the **Grove-Mont Theater**, which stages plays and musicals year round in its new Monterey Playhouse at 425 Washington; Tel: (408) 655-3200.

PACIFIC GROVE

In marked contrast to the Roman Catholic roots and bawdy seafaring past of Monterey, the heritage of neighboring Pacific Grove, to the west of Monterey, is puritanically Protestant. The town was founded in the 1870s as a Methodist campground on acreage donated by land baron David Jacks, whose deed prohibited gambling or consumption of alcohol on the property, and who also contributed some $30,000 toward its improvement—about 30 times what he had paid in 1859 for the entire city of Monterey. In 1879 Pacific Grove became the site of the first Chautauqua Assembly in the western United States, an annual gathering for summer education until the outbreak of World War I. During these decades, many Victorian mansions were built as boardinghouses for conference goers; other vacationers built elaborate summer homes along the rocky shore.

Ocean View Boulevard

If you come to Pacific Grove for no other reason, at least drive or cycle along Ocean View Boulevard around the rim of the peninsula, where you'll catch glimpses of sea otters, seals, and, in winter months, perhaps a migrating whale. From Monterey's Cannery Row, the road heads west, passing Stanford University's Hopkins Marine Station on China Point, once the home of a large Chinese community and the location of Chin Kee's Squid Yard in Steinbeck's *Sweet Thursday*. From here the road leads past Pacific Grove's Victorian mansions to **Lighthouse Point Park**, where a small cove shelters one of the area's few safe swimming beaches. In winter look for the swarms of monarch butterflies that migrate annually to Pacific Grove. To learn more about them and other wildlife, detour into town to the **Pacific Grove Museum of Natural History**, at Forest and Central avenues, which was founded by the Chautauqua Assembly in 1881.

Beyond town Ocean View Boulevard swings around Point Pinos Lighthouse, the state's oldest continuously operated beacon. Here the road becomes Sunset Drive to cross the sand dunes of **Asilomar State Beach**—a fine spot for picnicking or observing marine life in the tidal pools. At the end of the beach, among pines and cypresses, is the ▶ **Asilomar Conference Center**, an architectural gem you should not overlook. Julia Morgan (the architect of Hearst Castle) designed the older buildings from 1913 to 1928 in a woodsy Arts-and-Crafts style for YWCA conferences. Now owned by the state, Asilomar is still used for meetings, but independent travellers can also book rooms with budget-priced rates that include a full breakfast; the furnishings are Spartan, but the wooded seaside setting is glorious.

Staying and Dining in Pacific Grove

Many Victorian houses in Pacific Grove have been converted to bed-and-breakfast inns. Two of the loveliest, ▶ **The Green Gables Inn** and ▶ **The Gosby House Inn**, are owned and meticulously operated by the Post family, who make sure you are treated to all the extras: fresh flowers and fruit in your room; pretty, frilly furnishings; and wine and hors d'oeuvres in the afternoon. Built in the 1880s, both inns have fireplaces in most rooms, Green Gables has a dazzling view of the bay, and Gosby has whirlpool tubs in two rooms.

For most of this century, David Jacks's prohibition of alcohol in Pacific Grove inhibited the growth of restaurants, but after the ruling's repeal some restaurants began to attract diners from throughout the Monterey area. Here are three popular favorites among an abundance of choices: **Central 1-5-9**, has moved from its namesake address to 529 Central, but it still features the creative California-style cooking of chef-owner David Beckwith. Tel: 372-2235. At **Melac's**, 663 Lighthouse Avenue, French-born Jacques Melac and his Cordon Bleu–trained wife, Janet, offer a lively menu that is basically classic French, with Latin and Asian overtones. The presentation of the food is as picture-pretty as the mirrored, flowery setting; Tel: 375-1743. Finally, the enormously popular **Fandango**, at 223 17th Street, emulates a country *auberge*, with stone fireplaces and individually arranged bouquets of flowers everywhere. A few tables are outdoors, some are in intimate little rooms, others face the open kitchen, and those upstairs provide bay views. The food at lunch, brunch, and dinner is a Mediterranean mix—pastas, *cassoulet,* paella, couscous—at quite modest prices; Tel: 373-0588.

PEBBLE BEACH

A mention of Pebble Beach evokes many images: the wind-swept Lone Cypress on its isolated perch on the shore, the storybook homes of the very rich along the Seventeen Mile Drive, and some of the world's most challenging golf courses. But Pebble Beach's gilt-edged present was begotten in a humble past. The 5,300 acres of Del Monte Forest (now owned by the Pebble Beach Company) on the tip of the Monterey Peninsula southwest of Monterey and Pacific Grove, were part of the ubiquitous David Jacks's holdings until 1880, when he sold the property for five dollars an acre to the Pacific Improvement Company, which grazed its cattle there. At the turn of the century, the company built a rustic log lodge on the pebbled beach of Stillwater Cove, where Chinese fishermen harvested abalone, as a beach retreat for vacationers coming from the swank Del Monte Hotel in Monterey—a 17-mile excursion over dirt roads.

Staying and Dining at Pebble Beach

Samuel F. B. Morse (grandnephew of the telegraph inventor) forged the destiny of Pebble Beach by buying Del Monte Forest. In 1919 he built the Pebble Beach Golf Links along Stillwater Cove, as well as the most lavish showplace of the era: Del Monte Lodge, now known as ▶ **The Lodge at Pebble Beach**. Recently renovated, the lodge is still every bit the grand resort of yesteryear; its traditionally furnished rooms have wood-burning fireplaces, private balconies or terraces, and picture-postcard views across the cove to Car-

mel and Point Lobos. (Less expensive rooms face the forest.)
But if you don't care to exchange your family jewels for a
room here, you still can experience the mystique of Pebble
Beach by having afternoon tea on Havilland china by the
massive fireplaces in the **Terrace Lounge** or with a drink or
sandwich in the club-like **Tap Room**, where photos of golf's
greats peer down from the walls. Of several restaurants at
the lodge, the best is **Club XIX**. This intimate French spot is
formal and a bit stuffy at night, but it's terrific for lunch,
when less expensive bistro-style fare is served informally on
a terrace above the fabled 18th hole of the Pebble Beach
links; Tel: 624-3811.

The only other place to stay within Del Monte Forest is
▶ **The Inn at Spanish Bay**, the Pebble Beach Company's large
new resort complex beside the sand dunes on the northwest
edge of the forest. It is slightly less expensive than the lodge
and a stay at the inn allows you to use all of the lodge
facilities. The rooms are decorated in a contemporary style
and are equipped with gas-burning fireplaces, wet bars, and
decks or balconies. Rates are based on the view—there's a
$100 difference between the rooms overlooking the ocean
and those by the parking lot. Spanish Bay has several restaurants with ocean views, including **The Dunes**, which serves
breakfast, lunch, and dinner on an oceanfront terrace and in
a glass-walled dining room; big draws are the moderately
priced weeknight buffets with bagpipe music and the Friday
clambakes. But the culinary jewel is **The Bay Club**, which
turns out memorable northern Italian dinners with some
most creative touches: calamari vinaigrette served in a
radicchio cup, saffron risotto with lobster, and spinach
cannelloni with a basil-salmon stuffing, to name a few. The
check will be big, but so will the pleasure; Tel: 647-7500.

Guests at the Pebble Beach Resorts may use the athletic
facilities at two private clubs, which have tennis courts, large
swimming pools, and full fitness centers.

Sports at Pebble Beach

Golf, of course, is king at Pebble Beach, and the reigning
monarch is the **Pebble Beach Golf Course**, which many
regard as the world's premier public course for its cliffside
fairways and holes at the water's edge. Duffers pay a king's
ransom to play here—$225, including cart or caddy. Substan-
tial discounts and preferential tee times, however, are
granted to guests at the Pebble Beach Resorts, as well as at
the company's other less expensive championship courses:

Spyglass Hill Golf Course near Seal Rock and the new **Links at Spanish Bay**. Reservations for all courses are advised; Tel: (408) 624-3811 or (800) 654-9300. The Pebble Beach Company also owns the **Old Del Monte Golf Course** in Monterey, where the fees are about one-third of the charge at the least expensive courses in Del Monte Forest; Tel: (408) 373-2436. Also open to the public in Del Monte Forest is the championship 18-hole **Poppy Hills Golf Course**; Tel: (408) 625-2035. Many golf tournaments are held at Pebble Beach throughout the year, but the granddaddy of them all is the famous AT&T National Pro Am (formerly the Crosby), which pairs top pros with political and show-biz celebrities each January.

Pebble Beach is also a haven for the horsey set—the Pebble Beach Equestrian Center (Tel: 408-624-2756) conducts trail rides daily through Del Monte Forest and periodically sponsors horse shows and dressage shows. Other annual events at Pebble Beach include dog shows and regattas at Stillwater Cove, but since 1950 one of the biggest draws has been the Concours d'Elegance, an August conclave of vintage and classic cars plus classy imports at the lodge; a highlight is a Christie's auction of rare antique autos.

The Seventeen Mile Drive

This scenic drive winds along the rocky shores of Del Monte Forest from Pacific Grove to Carmel. Visitors are charged an admission fee (and given an annotated map), but the fee will be refunded if you eat at one of the Pebble Beach Resorts along the drive or pick up picnic makings at the **Pebble Beach Market** behind the lodge (there is no charge for cyclists).

From the Pacific Grove gate and Spanish Bay the road follows the edge of several private golf courses (including ultraexclusive Cypress Point). Along the way are the **seal and bird rocks**, home to numerous shore birds and herds of sea lions and harbor seals. There is a picnic area here and at Spanish Bay. Next you'll reach **Cypress Point Lookout**; gawk at the view down the coast to Point Sur Lighthouse 20 miles south. Along the coast are the famous cypress trees, which Robert Louis Stevenson described as "ghosts fleeing before the wind." From here you'll pass palatial seaside villas, most of which were designed in the 1920s by leading architects of the era, including Bernard Maybeck, Julia Morgan, and Palm Beach's Addison Mizner, in styles from Byzantine and Romanesque to Spanish Colonial Revival. You'll also see the lodge and the public swimming beach at Stillwater Cove en route to the drive's southern entrance gate in Carmel.

CARMEL-BY-THE-SEA

Across the cove from Pebble Beach and a few miles south of Monterey via Highway 1 is the wooded village of Carmel, whose picturesque architecture ranges from Mediterranean to Hansel and Gretel. Every nook and cranny of the town seems to be crammed with quaint cottages and inns, eateries, shops, and galleries—and with visitors. It's hard to imagine that only 90 years ago Carmel was just a stretch of windswept sand dunes waiting to be developed. At that time the mission (see below) had been abandoned, leaving only a few farms near the Carmel River. Then, at the dawn of the 20th century, land developers started selling lots on the dunes for $250 apiece. One of the first takers was poet George Sterling, who built a bungalow here in 1905 and soon was joined by many of his literary cronies. Mary Austin, Jack London, Upton Sinclair, Sinclair Lewis, and many lesser-known or never-known writers and artists were among the members of the "Carmel Colony." But this bit of bohemia was already breaking up in 1910 when the *Los Angeles Times* headlined a spoof on Carmel: "Hotbed of Soulful Culture . . . the Most Amazing Colony on Earth." After the literary heavies had fled Carmel, however, a number of major writers and artists settled here in later years, among them Lincoln Steffens, Robinson Jeffers, Edward Weston, and Ansel Adams.

Today Carmel carefully preserves its artsy-craftsy village-like character with strict ordinances. Neither high buildings nor glitzy signs—not even street numbers—mar the landscape, and no buses are allowed in town. For a scenic overview, drive or cycle down Ocean Avenue, the flower-bedecked main street, to the cypress-edged white sand dunes above Carmel Beach. From here Scenic Road, paralleled by a bike path, leads south on a bluff above the beach with no obstructions on the seaward side except **The Walker House**, a low-slung stone residence designed by Frank Lloyd Wright. Just beyond, at Carmel Point, is **Tor House**, the stone cottage and adjacent medieval-looking tower that Robinson Jeffers built in the early 1920s. Until his death in 1962, he wrote most of his major works here, including his play *Medea.* Tours of the house are conducted on Fridays and Saturdays by reservation only (no children under 12 allowed); Tel: (408) 624-1813 or 624-1840. Around the point the road clings to the cliffs, then leads by Carmel River State Beach, a lagoon, and a bird sanctuary before reaching the mission.

Carmel Mission

Mission San Carlos Borromeo del Río Carmel is the second oldest, and unquestionably the most important, of California's missions. In 1771 Spanish-born priest Junípero Serra moved this mission from Monterey to the fertile lands at the mouth of the Carmel River. This became his home, and from here he and his successors established the string of 21 Franciscan missions that stretches—each a day's foot-journey apart—from San Diego to Sonoma; thus Carmel became known as the Mother Mission. Father Serra lived here until his death in 1784 and is buried in the church (now a basilica). In 1988, after visiting here, Pope John Paul II beatified Serra, the final step before canonization as a saint.

The original wooden mission buildings were gradually replaced with adobe; the present sandstone church with its Moorish tower was completed in 1797, when the mission reached the height of its prosperity with a Christianized Native American population of more than 900. Then, in 1834, Mexico abruptly secularized the missions, and civil officials granted most of the lands (which Spain, before Mexico became independent, had intended to return to the Native Americans) to favored friends of the government. The Carmel mission was abandoned and gradually collapsed into ruins. Although attempts at preservation were made, serious renovation did not begin until 1931 when Harry Downie, a Catholic layman, became curator of the restoration—a project that lasted 50 years.

Today you should plan to loiter a while. Enter through a lovely courtyard, which is filled with flowers, cacti, and larger-than-life statues of saints, to the interior of the church, where a vaulted stone ceiling and carved altar tower over Serra's grave. Museum exhibits are devoted to the history of the area and the mission; of special interest are the re-creations of the padres' living quarters: dining room, library, kitchen, and the cell-like room where Serra lived in ascetic simplicity.

Shopping on Ocean Avenue

As a shoppers' mecca, only San Francisco outranks Carmel in Northern California. Conveniently, most of the town's myriad shops and galleries are located along a five-block stretch of Ocean Avenue (from Junípero to Monte Verde) and its side streets; here you will find plenty of high-quality and unusual collectibles, clothing, antiques, jewelry, artwork, crafts—you name it—from all over the world. What follows is a mere sampling.

At the head of Ocean Avenue, **Carmel Plaza** houses branches of many major stores: I. Magnin, Peck & Peck, Saks Fifth Avenue, Banana Republic, Laura Ashley, Sharper Image, and Brentano's Bookstore. Across the street, at Ocean and Mission, is a branch of **The Nature Company**, which stocks everything from naturalist books and tee-shirts to barometers to star-gazing equipment. You can pick up a free schedule here of "Discovery Events" such as exploring the tide pools of the Monterey Peninsula.

A stroll down Ocean Avenue leads to some fine clothing stores: **Derek Rayne, Ltd.** (Carmel's oldest shop, with a classy and classic selection of clothing for men and women), **Scotch House** (sweaters from Scotland), and a branch of **Lanz**. Custom-made cotton clothing in prints from Provence is the forte of **The French Collection**, along with provincial accessories for wardrobe and home. Even more awaits Francophiles at **Pierre Deux** (French country clothing, fabrics, tablewear, bedding, and such). For cookware and tableware check out **Carmel Bay Company** (which also carries gifts and posters) and **Dansk II** (a factory outlet that handles the full Dansk line at substantial discounts). Ocean Avenue haunts for collectibles include **Quilts, Ltd.** (handmade American patchworks, plus quilted apparel and gifts), **The Impulse Shoppes** (miniatures, dollhouse furnishings and accessories), and **Kris Kringle of Carmel** (bewitching ornaments, Santas, stockings, illuminated villages, and the like). A dazzling newcomer to Carmel is the **Laurel Burch Gallerie** (Ocean at Monte Verde), a fantasy world of vibrant colors: cotton shirts, silk scarves, tote bags, umbrellas, and so forth, all silk-screened by designer Laurel Burch. The shop also carries her cloisonné and cast-metal jewelry, as well as note cards, posters, and serigraphs.

Shopping in the Ocean Avenue Area

Prowl the side streets for more boutiques, many tucked into little arcades south of Ocean Avenue. Worthy of a stop on San Carlos is **The Owl's Nest** (a tiny shop brimming with a huge menagerie of artist-made teddy bears). A block down on Dolores look for **Conway of Asia** (a bazaar full of Oriental rugs, furnishings, jewelry, and objets d'art).

Lincoln Avenue holds even more treasures: **Anderlé Gallery** (a discriminating collection of primitive and Far Eastern art, wall-hangings, and furnishings), **Peter Rabbit & Friends** (clothing, stuffed animals, china, silver, and books for the friends of Beatrix Potter), **The Garden Shop** (wind chimes, fountains, and garden sculpture), and **Village Straw Shop** (if it's made of straw it's probably here).

The streets north of Ocean Avenue hold more shops and many of Carmel's art and crafts galleries. A good start for a gallery tour is the **Carmel Art Association Galleries**, on Dolores near Fifth, where works by more than 100 local artists are exhibited in eight rooms. You can also pick up a copy of the Carmel Gallery Guide here, which describes the type of work (from Neo-Impressionist to contemporary to copies of Old Masters) shown in more than 60 galleries, both in town and in Carmel Valley. Some highlights on Dolores include **Golf Arts & Imports** (paintings, books, and antiques related to the sport) and **Handworks** (jewelry, ceramics, glassware, weavings, and furniture by more than 300 American craftspeople).

Not to be missed are **The Photography West Gallery** (on Dolores just south of Ocean) and the **Weston Gallery** (on Sixth west of Dolores), which display the work of such distinguished photographers as Edward and Brett Weston and Ansel Adams.

Dining in Carmel

For a picnic, tote your basket to one of the following food stores and take cash; neither one accepts credit cards. You'll find most everything you need at **Mediterranean Market**; located at Ocean and Mission, this superb deli, grocery, and wine shop has a fine selection of sandwiches, cheeses, cold meats (even prosciutto from Parma), seafood, pasta, and fruit salads. For crusty sourdough bread and luscious pastries, head down Ocean to **Monterey Baking Company**; an adjoining deli sells croissant sandwiches.

If you need a lunch or teatime break during a shopping spree, make your way down Dolores, south of Ocean, to an old-fashioned English tearoom, the tiny **Tuck Box**, which is justifiably famous for its scones, muffins, and homemade jams and marmalades. You can buy a terrific breakfast here, too, but expect to wait in line.

At any time of the day or evening, one of the most popular spots in town for casual dining is **Casanova** at Fifth near Mission; the woodsy patio is especially beguiling on sunny days. This charming restaurant features country-style food of southern Europe at modest prices, notably a wide selection of pastas and a "Mediterranean casserole," a California version of bouillabaisse for about one-tenth what you would pay in Marseille; Tel: 625-0501.

Another hot new spot for lunch or dinner in Carmel is **Ristorante Piatti** at Sixth and Junípero, a new link in the mini-chain of upscale trattorias started by Claude Rouas in the Napa Valley (see Wine Country chapter). The menu features pastas, pizzas, and grilled items, plus a nice selection of antipasti; Tel: 625-1766. The Monterey Peninsula is not noted for its Asian food, but for lunch or dinner, **Shabu Shabu**, in Carmel Plaza, offers the romantic atmosphere of a Japanese country inn and traditional one-pot dishes cooked at your table; Tel: 625-2828.

Carmel's better dinner houses tend to be French or Italian, intimate, and fairly expensive; reservations are advised. A local classic for Italian cooking is **Raffaello**, the enterprise of a distinguished family of Florentine restaurateurs. Remo d'Agliano is host and his mother, now in her 70s, is in charge of the kitchen, turning out homemade pastas and *secondi piatti* such as garlicky prawns and tangy veal piccata in this formal dining room on Mission south of Ocean; Tel: 624-1541. Another old favorite is **The French Poodle** (Fifth and Junípero), a citadel of French haute cuisine owned and operated for some 30 years by Michele and Marc Vedrines. In the candlelit dining room, there's taped classical music, illuminated oil paintings, and a menu that goes by the book—Escoffier's; Tel: 624-8643. **Creme Carmel**, at San Carlos and Seventh, offers a more contemporary approach to French dining. The decor in the narrow, wood-ceilinged dining room is low key, with mostly banquette seating and a smattering of graphics on the wall, and the menu is decidedly Franco-Californian, with light sauces and many daily specials to reflect the seasonal bounty; Tel: 624-0444.

Hotels and Inns of Carmel

In most vacation locales only a few places stand out as exceptional among a run-of-the-mill gaggle of look-alike motels and hotels. Not so in Carmel—each of the 50-plus lodging places here is distinctive, with not a single carbon-copy branch of a chain in the lot. The diversity of these accommodations, plus the town's central location in the hub of the Monterey Peninsula, make Carmel the base of choice for many visitors.

Carmel's oldest hostelry, the ► **Pine Inn**, opened in 1902 to attract prospective real-estate buyers. Located smack on Ocean Avenue, the hotel has grown to occupy most of a block, with shops, restaurants, and a cozy bar off its turn-of-the-century lobby. Though small, the moderately priced rooms in the original building mirror the Victorian spirit. ► **La Playa Hotel**, a small resort a few blocks from the beach, is the grande dame of Carmel hotels, with beautiful gardens surrounding a pool. (A massive face-lift in the 1980s rescued this place from a dowdy middle age.) But the rates—and the accommodations—are more modest than other luxury resorts on the Monterey Peninsula (about half the tariff at Pebble Beach). Request a room with a view of the bay, or, if you're travelling with a family or another couple, consider one of La Playa's newly renovated cottages a block from the beach. These have wood-burning fireplaces, private gardens, and more pizzazz than the rooms in the hotel; most also have full kitchens. The **Terrace Room** overlooking the gardens is a lovely spot for an al fresco lunch.

Historic ► **Mission Ranch** is a 20-acre resort (with tennis courts) overlooking a meadow of grazing sheep where Carmel River enters the bay. Recently purchased and extensively renovated by former Carmel mayor Clint Eastwood, the ranch was once part of a large dairy farm. The funky old farmhouse has been transformed into a luxurious bed and breakfast and the once run-down cabins have been replaced with deluxe housekeeping cottages. There are also motel-style accommodations and a popular restaurant on the beautifully landscaped grounds.

Breakfast is included at the following small inns, as is afternoon wine or tea. The ► **Sea View Inn** is a 1920s Maybeck-style shingled house, which probably once had a view that is now blocked by pines. The eight bedrooms (some with private baths and window seats tucked in alcoves) are decorated in country chic. In the center of the shopping area, the ► **Cypress Inn**, also dating from the 1920s, might well be mistaken for the mission because of its ornate tower and Moorish-Mediterranean façade. Its 20 rooms cluster around a tiled, flower-banked courtyard and offer modern comforts such as TVs, phones, and private baths. You'll also find these amenities in the rooms at the ► **Cobblestone Inn**, along with fireplaces, refrigerators stocked with soft drinks, bowls of fruit, and flowery country furnishings.

All of the preceding small inns are located in the heart of Carmel village, an easy walk from the shops. Away from town at Carmel Point, ► **Sandpiper Inn At-the-Beach** is a favorite of visitors from abroad; the guest book of the multi-lingual owners shows names from over 70 countries. The inn is indeed at the beach, and many of the antiques-filled rooms offer fine bay views as well as fireplaces. Bicycles are available for pedaling into town.

The Performing Arts in Carmel

The Monterey Peninsula's oldest and best-known musical event is the July **Bach Festival**. Concerts, recitals, lectures, and symposia relate not only to Bach but to other Baroque luminaries; even opera and ballet are included. The highlight of the festival is a candlelit concert in the Carmel Mission basilica; other performances are held at the Sunset Cultural Center. Book well in advance: P.O. Box 575, Carmel, CA 93921; Tel: (408) 624-1521; Fax: 624-2788.

The Monterey County Symphony also performs at the Sunset Cultural Center (for reservations, Tel: 624-8511), as does the Carmel Music Society (Tel: 625-9938). Nearby, the open-air **Forest Theater** mounts productions that range from contemporary plays to an autumn Shakespeare festival; for information on all Forest Theater productions, call 624-3996. Finally, Hidden Valley Music Seminars in Carmel Valley offers year-round chamber music, opera, and dance performances; Tel: 659-3115.

CARMEL VALLEY

East of the village of Carmel, the Carmel River flows from the Santa Lucia Mountains to the Pacific for a dozen miles through a long, narrow valley. The sun usually shines here on those many days when fog veils the coast, making Carmel Valley a desirable place to live and to visit. Among those who have built homes on the oak-studded hillsides are several émigrés from Hollywood, including Doris Day, Clint Eastwood, and Merv Griffin. And the green turf of golf links—dotted with tennis courts and tiny lakes—now covers former dairy lands on the valley floor. Some of the golf and tennis centers are semiprivate clubs, but others are open to the public; check out the two 18-hole courses and modest greens fees at the **Rancho Canada Golf Club** (Tel: 624-0111) and the tennis courts and fitness center at the **Carmel Valley Racquet Club** (Tel: 624-2737).

Carmel Valley has also become a wine-producing area in

the years since William Durney planted the first vineyards in the surrounding mountains in 1968 and started making varietal wines in 1977. Although the Durney winery and most others in the area are not open to the public, **Château Julien** on Carmel Valley Road has become a major visitor's attraction. The winery's Swiss-style château is open daily for tastings of its award-winning varietals and for tours; Tel: 624-2600.

Shopping in Carmel Valley

Don't dismiss as suburban sprawl the stretch of shopping malls and apartments along Highway 1 at the foot of the valley; tucked behind the parking lots are two of the Monterey Peninsula's finest shopping centers. **The Barnyard**, in a garden setting, is a complex of rustic barn-like structures with more than 50 shops and restaurants (take Carmel Valley Road off Highway 1, turn right at Carmel Rancho Boulevard, then right at Carmel Rancho Lane). The Barnyard is home to **Thunderbird Bookshop**, a giant that claims to have the largest inventory on the West Coast and frequently hosts book-signing events. Within the bookstore and on an outside deck, the **Thunderbird Restaurant** serves soups, sandwiches, and pastries all day. Another spot for an alfresco lunch is **Silver Jones**, which cooks up lively, eclectic California cuisine.

The Barnyard's boutiques are a treasure trove of unusual jewelry, home accessories, tableware, fine arts, and collectibles. Meriting special mention are **Holly Berry** (handmade Christmas ornaments and miniatures), **Hudson & Company** (English riding apparel and tack, plus equestrian gifts), and **Succulent Gardens** (more than 500 cacti and other succulents, "living" wreaths made from succulents, unusual planters, and an extraordinary selection of wind chimes).

Just south of The Barnyard is **The Crossroads**, which was built to resemble an English village with streets and mews bordered by trees and flowers (from Highway 1, take Rio Road east). This is the locale of the **Rio Grill**, one of the peninsula's most popular eateries, with both indoor and outdoor seating. The menu is an eclectic potpourri of starters and salads (from quesadillas to Chinese chicken salad), unusual sandwiches (grilled eggplant with roasted red peppers), and light entrées such as pasta and barbecued baby back ribs. Next door to the Rio Grill is a new branch of

Chevys, the San Francisco–based chain of Mexican restaurants noted for their giant margaritas in beer mugs, do-it-yourself fajitas, and funky decor.

Among the many shops at The Crossroads are **Holiday Hutch** (decorations, toy soldiers, nativities, and ostrich-egg figurines) and **Gepetto's Collectibles** (Raggedy Anns, hand puppets, and music boxes, among the barrage of dolls and stuffed animals).

The Resorts of Carmel Valley

From Highway 1, Carmel Valley Road (route G-16) leads east past a number of resorts. In the lower valley, on the 245-acre, beautifully landscaped grounds of the Carmel Valley Golf and Country Club, ▶ **Quail Lodge** provides luxuriously appointed rooms and suites (many with fireplaces) set in one- and two-story buildings. Guests here (and members of other golf clubs with agreements with the Carmel Valley Golf Club) may use the club's championship 18-hole golf course, tennis courts, and swimming pool. (Inquire about the specially priced golf packages.) Also at the lodge is **The Covey,** an elegant, intimate dinner house facing a little lake; for reservations, call 624-1581.

Midway up the valley, the ▶ **Carmel Valley Ranch Resort** sits among the oaks on a hillside above the Carmel Valley Ranch Golf Club. The units are one- or two-bedroom deluxe suites with fireplaces, broad decks, wet bars, cathedral ceilings, and stylish contemporary furnishings. Some rooms have private hot tubs on the decks, and most have views of the valley. As at Quail Lodge, resort guests are welcome to use the links of the golf club and the pool and courts of the Carmel Valley Ranch Tennis Club.

Most of the lower reaches of Carmel Valley were developed during the last two decades, but the upper valley is a step back in time. Weathered buildings make the tiny village of Carmel Valley resemble an Old West town, and nearby ▶ **Los Laureles Lodge** revels in its history. The lodge occupies part of a large Mexican land grant where the recipe for Monterey Jack cheese was supposedly developed. Early in this century cabins were built on the property for guests of Monterey's Del Monte Hotel, who came to the valley to hunt and fish. (The lodge's main building was once the home of Muriel Vanderbilt Phelps, who raised racehorses here in the 1930s.) Although the lodge was extensively renovated in 1990, it retains its rustic country charm and reasonable room rates. Its dining room and Victorian-era bar are open to the public.

One of California's most extraordinary inns is secluded in 330 acres of mountainous terrain at the top of Carmel Valley. ► **Stonepine** was the equestrian estate of the Henry Potter Russells (he was a noted breeder of racehorses, and she was the granddaughter of Big Four railroad magnate Charles Crocker). They built an exquisite eight-bedroom château here, with fireplaces in almost every room. Those who stay at the inn today are treated as house guests in an aristocratic country home: welcoming fruit, cheese, and wine in the bedrooms, which are splendidly appointed with antiques and (in most) whirlpool tubs; afternoon tea in the enormous salon; a formal multicourse dinner in the oak-paneled dining room; a light breakfast in bed or in the sunroom. Another four guest rooms are located in the paddock house of the estate's equestrian center. Daytime diversions include a dip in the pool, tennis, croquet, and horseback riding.

Los Padres National Forest

Carmel Valley Road is a gateway to the high country of the Santa Lucia Mountains: Los Padres National Forest and the Ventana Wilderness. Within a small valley in this untamed land is the secluded **Tassajara Hot Springs**, once a watering hole for the Esselen Indians and now a monastery for the ► **Tassajara Zen Mountain Center**. From May through Labor Day, the monks welcome overnight guests for a stay in the sparsely decorated cabins, a soak in the hot mineral springs, and a taste of their internationally acclaimed vegetarian cooking (meals are included in the room rates). The bread alone will send you to nirvana. Workshops on subjects ranging from cooking to Zen are conducted throughout the summer. If you're interested in stopping by just for the day, reservations are still required; day guests should call (408) 659-2229 for reservations. (Be sure to bring a picnic lunch: The dining room is open only to overnight guests.)

Steep, winding Tassajara Road, which leads to the hot springs from Carmel Valley Road, is an 80-minute, potentially hazardous drive, especially for vehicles with automatic transmissions. A four-wheel-drive van picks up overnight guests at 11:00 A.M. daily in Jamesburg, 14 miles (22 km) north of Tassajara.

Another way to explore this backcountry is via two- to five-day horseback excursions conducted by **Ventana Wilderness Expeditions**, a venture of the pioneer Nason family, who count Esselen Indians among their ancestors (Star Route, Box 94, Carmel Valley, CA 93924; Tel: 408-659-0433).

If you continue east on Carmel Valley Road (G-16), the route will eventually connect with Highway 101 at Greenfield in the Salinas Valley, providing a long and scenic alternative for travellers heading south (allow two hours to drive from Highway 1 to Highway 101). The road meanders southeast through mountain forests and meadows, past horse farms and cattle ranches, and finally through the Arroyo Seco Canyon.

THE CARMEL HIGHLANDS

South of Carmel, Highway 1 heads down the coast past a Spanish Colonial Carmelite monastery of cloistered nuns (stop for a look at the grounds and chapel) and past Monastery Beach to **Point Lobos State Reserve**. Jutting into the Pacific, this craggy finger of land has at various times served as a cattle pasture, a whaling station, and the site of an abalone cannery, but all signs of commerce are now gone and the park's 534 acres of meadows and pine and cypress forests protect black-tailed deer, gray squirrels, brush rabbits, and a variety of birds. Sea otters, sea lions, and harbor seals play in the rocky coves, and the great gray whales swim offshore during their winter migration. A road and hiking and bicycle trails circle the point; guided walking tours are also offered (inquire at the ranger station at the park entrance).

Below Point Lobos in an exclusive residential area, the ▶ **Highlands Inn** perches on a steep hillside overlooking a spectacular stretch of shore. A historic lodge, built in 1916 of local golden granite, is the hub of the inn; marching up the hillside behind it are rows of contemporary buildings that contain handsome "spa suites" with large living rooms, fully equipped bar-kitchens, wood-burning fireplaces, broad decks, and—sitting out in the room so you can enjoy the view—oversized whirlpool tubs. (Inquire about the heavily discounted midweek rates.)

The inn is only a ten-minute drive south from Carmel, well worth the trip to admire the dramatic vista, even if it's just for drinks at sunset. Or you might consider breakfast, lunch, or dinner at Highland's **California Market**, a delightful café with modest prices, a deck, and a view of the rocky coast. For a big splurge, the inn offers prix-fixe and à la carte dinners in its **Pacific Edge** restaurant under the direction of Brian Whitmer, one of California's most talented young chefs. On his ever-changing menu, look for such imaginative concoctions as a "strudel" of baby artichokes with chevre and the juice of wild mushrooms, or marinated loin of lamb with eggplant cannelloni. Tel: 624-0471.

Highland's next-door neighbor, the ▶ Tickle Pink Inn, shares the same ocean vista but the rooms are less expensive. Some rooms have fireplaces and most have views and private decks where Continental breakfast and afternoon wine and cheese are served in sunny weather.

BIG SUR

For most of the 90 miles (144 km) from Carmel south to San Simeon, the Santa Lucia Mountains thrust almost perpendicularly out of the Pacific to heights of 5,000 feet, the result of a giant cataclysm some ten million years ago. Finding this coast impassable, the northbound Spanish colonists detoured inland to reach Monterey Bay. Homesteaders started settling here in the 1860s, but even then the area was isolated: No passable road existed until the present two-lane highway opened in 1939; telephones and electricity did not reach Big Sur until the 1950s. Today Highway 1 creeps along ledges blasted from the cliffs 1,000 feet above the shore, crosses mighty bridges spanning creeks and canyons of redwood groves, and passes above rocky coves and inlets used by bootleggers during Prohibition.

The Heart of Big Sur

The first 20 miles (32 km) south of Carmel Highlands contain few traces of civilization until the road reaches **Point Sur Lighthouse,** built in 1899 atop a rock that juts 350 feet out of the sea. On weekends, two-hour tours of the lighthouse are conducted; Tel: 625-4419. Several miles south of Point Sur, **Andrew Molera State Park** occupies part of a land grant where Captain Juan Bautista Cooper once raised cattle and supposedly smuggled in goods to avoid the customs duties at Monterey. The park is also the locale of **Molera Trail Rides,** which conducts guided horseback tours of the nearby beaches, bluffs, and redwood groves from April through November; Tel: 625-8664.

From here the road follows the Big Sur River inland for about 6 miles (10 km) through the redwood forests of the Big Sur Valley. Within the valley and then for about 4 miles

(6½ km) south, the restaurants and hostelries that comprise the heart of Big Sur are located on Highway 1; you can't miss them. You'll come first to the historic **River Inn**, where locals gather for food, drink, jazz, and poetry readings. At the inn is a grocery store for picnic provisions and the **Heart Beat of Big Sur Gallery of Gifts**, with an amazing inventory from ethnic musical instruments and tapes to handcrafted jewelry, antique birdhouses, and bronze Hindu statues.

At the southern end of the valley, the 800 acres of **Pfeiffer–Big Sur State Park** contain hiking trails and rivers stocked with steelhead. The park is named after the Pfeiffer family, early homesteaders who at the century's turn built Pfeiffer's Resort, whose guests from Carmel—a ten-hour stagecoach ride away in those days—included George Sterling and Robinson Jeffers.

STAYING AND DINING IN BIG SUR

Pfeiffer–Big Sur State Park is now the site of ► **Big Sur Lodge**, which has moderately priced overnight accommodations in woodsy cottages surrounding a mountain meadow, plus a swimming pool and sauna. Some rooms have fireplaces and/or kitchenettes, although cooking utensils are not provided. Just south of the park, adventurous travellers may want to follow an extremely narrow, winding road down Sycamore Canyon to **Pfeiffer Beach**, noted for its beauty but also for its hazardous swimming.

At the end of Big Sur Valley, Highway 1 climbs over the mountains a few miles to the coast. Here, 1,200 feet above the Pacific (and well signposted from the highway), the ► **Ventana Inn** is a serene retreat for rich hippies, nature-loving young professionals, and those who want to absorb the rugged beauty with few distractions—perhaps a walk in the redwoods, a swim in the pool, or a soak in the Japanese baths. The resort's stunning contemporary buildings overlook a mountain meadow where deer often roam. Paneled in knotty cedar, the rooms themselves exude country comfort, with handmade quilts, fireplaces or wood-burning stoves, and broad decks, some with private hot tubs. Ventana further pampers its guests with a splendid breakfast spread and afternoon wine and cheese. Across the meadow, with a terrace overlooking the Pacific, the **Ventana Restaurant** offers light California-style cooking—it's a popular lunch destination for Big Sur visitors; Tel: 667-2331.

Perched among 90 acres on a wooded ridge across from Ventana, the new ► **Post Ranch Inn** has been widely acclaimed for its sensitivity to the environment. Not a single tree was cut down to make room for the 30 woodsy and luxurious guest units, which sit on poles like treehouses among the oaks or are carved into the cliffside with unobstructed views of the ocean 1,100 feet below. Within, rooms are paneled in redwood, floored with *raja* slate from India, and decorated with furnishings handmade by local craftspeople. All have fireplaces, wet bars, and limestone whirlpool tubs—with views. Within this idyllic complex is the **Sierra Mar** restaurant, which features the regional California cooking of a noted young chef, Wendy Little. Lunch and dinner is by reservation only; Tel: 667-2200.

Just down the road from Post Ranch, the decks of **Nepenthe Restaurant** provide an even more spectacular view of the coast—perhaps the best in this land of superlative vistas. Known for its burgers and steak sandwiches, Nepenthe is built around a log cabin, which Orson Welles bought for Rita Hayworth in the 1940s but which she never occupied. In the Nepenthe complex, the **Phoenix Gift Shop** stocks a large array of handcrafted items such as jewelry, ceramics, sweaters, and patchwork quilts.

Nearby, ▶ **Deetjen's Big Sur Inn** has been putting up travellers since the 1930s. Built by a Norwegian homesteader, this rustic hostelry is now operated by a preservation foundation. The wooden cabins contain modestly priced rooms with a rudimentary Old World charm; baths are often shared, the walls are thin, and in some the only heat comes from a potbellied stove. Nevertheless the inn has a devoted clientele, as does Deetjen's restaurant, a local legend for hearty breakfasts and candlelit dinners accompanied by classical music.

Bohemian Big Sur

In the 1940s a number of San Francisco artists—among them painter Jean Varda and sculptor Beniamino Bufano—discovered that Big Sur was a peaceful and inexpensive place to work. Henry Miller moved here in 1944, and later the Beat poets of the 1950s wandered down the coast to pay homage to him. Miller, known for remaining somewhat aloof, is said to have refused to see Allen Ginsburg, although he did meet with Dylan Thomas and once invited Jack Kerouac for dinner. The latter never arrived; he got lost in the wilds of Big Sur and was discovered at dawn, asleep in a meadow near the cabin of Lawrence Ferlinghetti, poet and founder of North Beach's City Lights Bookstore.

This poetic era is now commemorated with a collection of Miller memorabilia and paintings at the **Henry Miller Memorial Library**, located on Highway 1 just south of Nepenthe in the former home of Miller's longtime friend, painter and writer Emil White. All of Miller's books are for sale here, too, including some rare editions. (Closed weekdays except in summer.) Down the road a cluster of three huge water tanks houses the **Coast Gallery**, where many of Miller's bright, fanciful watercolors are on display, along with the work of other local artists with an emphasis on marine scenes and wildlife. Also within the complex is a boutique selling handcrafted jewelry and clothing, a candlemaking studio, and a café that offers wine, sandwiches, and pastries.

Within the next 5 miles (8 km) heading south, Highway 1 passes Partington Ridge (where Miller lived until 1962) and continues to **Julia Pfeiffer Burns State Park**, where trails lead to a picnic area and McWay Canyon, the site of a 50-foot waterfall that cascades into the ocean. Beyond the park a bridge crosses Anderson Canyon, home in the early days of the Big Sur colony to Miller, White, and other artists who lived cheaply in the abandoned buildings that had once housed the convicts who built Highway 1.

A favorite pastime of the locals in those days was soaking in the waters of the natural hot springs at a cliffside resort down the road. Here—about halfway between Carmel and Hearst Castle—Michael Murphy (whose parents owned the resort) founded the ▶ **Esalen Institute**. In addition to its educational conferences and intensive study programs, Esalen holds weekend self-awareness workshops in subjects ranging from Gestalt psychology to massage to lucid dreaming. If space is available, last minute reservations (within a week of arrival) are accepted for overnight guests who do not wish to participate in workshops. Couples are given private rooms, but singles are bunked two to four per room. The fees cover room, meals, and use of the hot springs, which are closed to the public (if you're shy, be forewarned that nudity is not discouraged in the hot springs and pool). See Accommodations Reference for booking information.

About 14 miles (22 km) south of Esalen, the largely unpaved Nacimiento-Fergusson Road leaves Highway 1 to switchback east over the mountains to Highway 101, passing Mission San Antonio de Padua (see El Camino Real: The Inland Route, below). This road is recommended only for fearless drivers in perfect weather—never for recreational vehicles. Continuing south, Highway 1 follows the coast for about 38 miles (61 km) of great ocean views to San Simeon.

SAN SIMEON TO SAN LUIS OBISPO

In the southern part of the Santa Lucia range—from San Simeon down to San Luis Obispo—the mountains converge with the ocean to form a landscape more gentle than the cataclysmic Big Sur coast. For thousands of years the Chumash Indians hunted on these lands and fished along the beaches; later Mexican *rancheros* raised their cattle here, and finally dairy farms were established along the coast. But the biggest event in this pastoral nook of California was William Randolph Hearst's construction of a hilltop castle 1,600 feet above the former whaling port of San Simeon.

Hearst Castle

W. R. Hearst officially named his estate La Cuesta Encantada (The Enchanted Hill), but humbly called it "the ranch." In 1919, while living in New York, Hearst commissioned Berkeley architect Julia Morgan to design a vacation house for his family on his San Simeon lands: 240,000 acres he had inherited from his father, U.S. Senator George Hearst, whose fortune came from Nevada's Comstock Lode. The younger Hearst lavished millions on the project until 1941, when he moved away due to poor health; parts of the castle were never completed. During those years, architect Morgan spent almost every weekend at San Simeon supervising the never-ending construction.

She was probably the least famous of Hearst's weekend visitors. Although his wife and five sons did vacation at San Simeon in the early years, the later hostess-in-residence was his protégée and mistress, actress Marion Davies. Together they entertained the elite of Hollywood and the forerunners of today's jet set. Davies' co-star Clark Gable was a visitor, as were Gary Cooper and Louis B. Mayer; William Powell courted Jean Harlow here; Marie Dressler, Doris Duke, and Adela Rogers St. John were on the guest list; and at times Bob Hope kept them all laughing. On a typical weekend, 30 to 50 guests occupied the ranch's 58 bedrooms. After Hearst's death in 1951 his heirs gave the castle and 120 acres of the grounds to the state of California, and it became a state park.

SEEING HEARST CASTLE

Visitors are admitted to the estate by scheduled tour only. Daytime tours last just under two hours and offer four itineraries. First-time visitors should book Tour One, which focuses on the ground floor of La Casa Grande, the main house whose Spanish-Moorish tiled towers dominate the landscape for miles around. Throughout the house the original furnishings and priceless artworks remain intact: In the Assembly Room, Flemish tapestries hang beside a 16th-century French Renaissance fireplace, and in the Refectory festival banners from Siena flutter above Gothic tapestries. Hearst's guests dined here at a polished 300-year-old refectory table incongruously set with paper napkins (he thought they were more sanitary) and catsup bottles alongside massive silver candlesticks. This tour also visits the indoor Roman Pool, where walls are inlaid with Italian mosaic tiles; the open-air Neptune Pool, encircled with a colonnade that flanks a Greco-Roman temple; and Casa del Sol, an 18-room Spanish Renaissance villa with gilded ceilings and moldings—one of three guest cottages below the main house.

Tours Two, Three, and Four explore the castle's upstairs bedrooms, guest wing, grounds, and other guest houses. A slightly longer evening tour, offered in the spring and fall, takes in the highlights of the estate, including Hearst's personal quarters. During this tour docents dress as Hearst's guests and staff, and a newsreel in the theater depicts life at the castle in the 1930s.

Hearst Castle, unfailingly easy to find (you can see it from miles away), is the most popular visitor attraction in Northern California, so purchase your tickets well in advance during peak travel seasons. They can be charged to a major credit card by calling Mistix; Tel: (800) 444-7275. Special arrangement for wheelchair-accessible and foreign-language tours must be made directly with the castle; Tel: (805) 927-2020.

San Simeon

Below the castle, in the tiny port of San Simeon, are more Julia Morgan buildings: a mission-style warehouse, which stored Hearst's hordes of treasures, and several Mediterranean-style houses, built for the castle's construction crew (there were 93 workers on the payroll in 1929). At San Simeon Landing you can arrange sport-fishing charters, winter whale-watching excursions, and rod and reel rentals at **George's Tackle Shop**; Tel: (805) 927-1777 or (800) 762-5263. Also here is the area's oldest building: the 1852 **Sebastian Store**, which displays whaling implements and vintage photographs; lunch and breakfast are served on the patio from April to September. Just south of San Simeon, modern motels cluster around the highway. One of the most attractive is the large ▶ **Best Western Cavalier Inn**; ask for a balconied oceanfront room. For complete information on accommodations here and in nearby Cambria, contact the Cambria Chamber of Commerce (767 Main Street, Cambria, CA 93428; Tel: 805-927-3624).

Cambria

Nine miles (14 km) south of San Simeon, the picturesque village of Cambria is not only an accommodations and dining center for Hearst Castle visitors, it's a destination in its own right. Nestled in a pine-rimmed valley off Highway 1, the town is home to many artists and craftspeople, who sell their work in the town's numerous shops and galleries. But from the 1860s to the 1890s Cambria was a bustling center for whalers, quicksilver (mercury) miners, and lumberjacks, all lured by the area's abundant resources; a large Chinese colony once farmed for seaweed here, too.

SHOPPING IN CAMBRIA

A small hill divides Cambria into two villages, both filled with shops and galleries. Not to be missed in the West Village is **The Soldier Factory**, 789 Main Street, which manufactures, and sells worldwide, hand-painted toy soldiers, miniature forts, and the like; there's a small exhibit of antique toy soldiers, too. Next door, rock hounds will have a field day at **McKinney's Gems and Minerals** (777 Main). Upstairs at 775 Main is one of the Central Coast's most unusual galleries: the **Great American Characters Gallery**, which exhibits original handpainted "cels" (single-image celluloid drawings from animated cartoons) with a glittering cast that includes Bugs Bunny, Porky Pig, and Elmer Fudd.

On Main Street between the villages you'll see the **Schoolhouse Gallery**, an 1881 one-room schoolhouse that exhibits work of the local art association; in its front yard sits Cambria Jail, a tiny, windowless structure typical of the lockups for overindulgers built near saloons in the 19th century.

In the East Village, collectors will probably strike pay dirt in a cluster of boutiques on Burton Drive. Among the shops are **Pacific West Art** (contemporary jewelry, sculpture, and graphics, with an emphasis on wildlife), **Seekers** (museum-quality contemporary American glass art), and **Suma Sil Gallery** (Native American fine arts, crafts, and artifacts, including some pre-Columbian items). Don't overlook **Heart's Ease**, a small cottage filled with a vast assortment of herb lotions and potions, bulk potpourri, dried herbs and spices, herb vinegars, jams, jellies, and more.

A local success story is Linn's Fruit Bin, purveyors of preserves made from fruit grown at the Linn family farm near Cambria; there's a shop and café in town at **Linn's Main Binn** (2277 Main Street). It sells Linn's preserves and pies, as well as a distinguished selection of other foods and gifts.

STAYING IN CAMBRIA

West of the village a row of new motels rims Moonstone Beach, which is now the most desirable spot in the area for an overnight stay. One of these hostelries is ▶ **Best Western Fireside Inn By-the-Sea**, which boasts many unmotel-like amenities: gas-burning fireplaces, wet bars, and fresh flowers in the rooms; some rooms also have ocean views and whirlpool tubs. You'll also find ocean views and fireplaces, plus some rooms with patios and whirlpool tubs, at the ▶ **Blue Dolphin** and ▶ **Sand Pebbles Inn**, both of which also offer guests a Continental breakfast and afternoon tea. At ▶ **The Blue Whale Inn**, you'll receive a full breakfast (such as cheese-filled crepes) cooked and served by the resident innkeepers. Six mini-suites (decorated with canopied beds, chintz fabrics, and country pine) are sited so that each has an ocean vista from its sitting area, which has a fireplace, and a view of Hearst Castle from the glass-walled tub/shower. The castle's towers can also be spotted from one of the private decks of ▶ **The Beach House**, another small bed-and-breakfast inn. Some rooms boast fireplaces or ocean views, and in the spacious A-framed living room, telescopes and binoculars are provided for glimpsing the passing dolphins, seals, and at times even whales.

DINING IN CAMBRIA

The old-timer among Cambria's dozens of restaurants is **The Brambles Dinner House**, located in an antiques-filled 1874 house at 4005 Burton Drive and known for its prime rib with Yorkshire pudding. Reservations are advised; Tel: 927-4716. Down the street, **Robin's** serves breakfast, lunch, and dinner with home-grown produce and multi-ethnic accents from quesadillas to pasta primavera to Thai green curry; Tel: 927-5007. A favorite of locals is **Ian's**, 2150 Center Street, where you can stop for a casual bar snack of burgers or raw oysters or enjoy one of chef Ian McPhee's celebrated California-style dinners; seafood is emphasized: fresh abalone steaks, swordfish with cilantro pesto, planked salmon with mustard butter, and the like. Reserve for dinner; Tel: 927-8649.

Out at Moonstone Beach, pan-broiled fresh seafood with no frills draws the crowds to **The Sea Chest**, despite their policy of accepting neither reservations nor credit cards. Arrive early to catch the sunset over the Pacific from a table in the front room. On the outdoor terrace at **Creekside Gardens Café**, 2114 Main Street, you can choose a hearty breakfast from an extensive menu that includes omelets with heaps of country fries and Danish sausage from Solvang, a Danish enclave about 100 miles (160 km) south of Cambria on Highway 101.

There's more to do than just eat at **The Hamlet at Moonstone Gardens**, perched on a bluff above Highway 1 north of Moonstone Beach. Whether lunching on a big burger or loitering at dinner over garlicky herb-crusted rack of lamb, you can admire a glorious view of the Pacific. Within the complex a wine bar offers tastings of local wine; the gardens, gift shop, and nursery contain waterfalls, fish pools, and many exotic plants, with a focus on succulents from midget cacti to giant yucca trees; Tel: 927-3535.

Harmony

Six miles (10 km) south of Cambria on Highway 1, Harmony (population 18) is barely a speck on the map, but in the early decades of this century the **Harmony Valley Creamery** prospered by producing butter and cheese. One frequent customer was teetotaling William Randolph Hearst, who treated his guests to glasses of buttermilk on their way from the train depot at San Luis Obispo to San Simeon. The folks at Harmony claim that Pola Negri and Rudolph Valentino were among the sippers. Today the old creamery houses a bevy of crafts shops (including one that produces hand-thrown stoneware from kilns behind the shops) and a wine bar. The hamlet also shelters a tiny chapel and a glass-blowing studio, where you can watch the artisans at work. A popular place for dinner or Sunday brunch is the **Old Harmony Pasta Factory**, which serves Italian fare (including a honey-dough pizza) and some truly unusual pastas, such as (at brunch) apple-stuffed ravioli; Tel: 927-5882.

The Morro Bay Area

For some 20 miles (32 km) between Cambria and Morro Bay you'll travel south on Highway 1 as it crosses a pastoral landscape where cattle graze on hills above the ocean. Take a detour into **Cayucos**, a small resort town known for its pier fishing, scuba diving, and surfing. In the 19th century, Cayucos was a thriving little seaport; evidence of those early days remains on the town's main street, where Old West buildings hover over a wooden boardwalk guarded by a cigar-store Indian.

Beyond Cayucos, as the road approaches the fishing town of **Morro Bay**, a miniature Gibraltar looms on the seascape: Morro Rock, a rounded promontory rising 576 feet above the ocean, is home to a few of California's nearly extinct peregrine falcons. In town, Embarcadero Street is a busy marina lined with seafood cafés and restaurants, curio shops, and the berths of excursion and sport-fishing boats. Also here are the small **Morro Bay Aquarium** and the Giant Chessboard, where the pieces are two to three feet high.

South of town a eucalyptus forest covers the 2,000 acres of **Morro Bay State Park**, a wildlife sanctuary, bird-watcher's paradise, and preserve for a large rookery of the great blue heron. Just inside the park gates, surrounded by lush gardens, ▶ **The Inn at Morro Bay** overlooks Morro Bay Estuary. Decorated in French country style, many of the rooms in this deluxe resort have decks and fireplaces. The inn is also a lovely stop for lunch, as you gaze beyond the glass-walled dining room to watch seagulls perform an ongoing aerial ballet, seemingly in time with the taped classical music within.

San Luis Obispo

At Morro Bay Highway 1 turns inland for 12 miles (19 km) to San Luis Obispo, cradled in a valley between the Santa Lucia Mountains and a chain of rocky peaks (extinct volcanoes) extending to the sea. Today the town is best known as the home of California State Polytechnic University, but its historic heart is **Mission San Luis Obispo de Tolosa**, founded by Father Junípero Serra in 1772. Although the mission is only California's sixth oldest, it was the first to be topped with the now-distinctive red-tiled roof—introduced after Native Americans burned the original wooden structure by shooting flaming arrows through its thatched roof. Stop inside to visit the small museum that focuses on the history of the area, then stroll through the old town around the mission to see the restored 19th-century adobes and Victorians (a map of historic sites is available at the Chamber of Commerce, 1039 Chorro). Don't miss **Ah Louis Store** (now a Far Eastern gift shop), which in the 1880s served as general store, bank, and post office for 2,000 Chinese who built railroad tunnels through the mountains.

Behind the mission an imposing stone Romanesque structure (built in 1904) now serves as the **San Luis Obispo County Historical Museum**, and across the street the **Art Center** gallery strikes a contemporary note. In front of the mission a creek meanders through **Mission Plaza**; hovering over the creek's tree-lined banks at the plaza are the outdoor decks and patios of several restaurants, some with live music at lunchtime. Beer buffs should check out **SLO Brewing Co.**, an upstairs brew pub with a menu of burgers and other pub food at 1119 Garden Street. But for a truly fine meal head across town to **Café Roma**, at 1819 Osos Street near the train depot. You'll find patio seating weekdays and candlelight at night in this charming family-run restaurant, but the big draw is the superbly prepared Northern Italian cooking; Tel: 541-6800. The route from town to the depot leads by the Kundert Medical Building at Pacific and Santa Rosa, which was designed by Frank Lloyd Wright; around the corner on Pacific is the 1850s Dallidet Adobe and the 1889 Ramona Depot.

San Luis Obispo's many motels and inns range from the humble 1920s Motel Inn (which is the origin of the word "motel") to the outrageously gaudy Madonna Inn. A cut above them all is the ▶ **Apple Farm Inn**, a 67-room hostelry built in 1987 to look like grandma's house—a rich grandma, that is. Each room is individually decorated in a countryish, yet sophisticated, Victorian style with fireplaces throughout; Trellis Court, an adjoining motel-type building, offers rooms at modest prices as well. Behind the inn is a swimming pool and a working grist mill that grinds the flour for the breads and pancakes served at the extremely popular **Apple Farm** restaurant. It's easy to forgive some of the commercial aspects of this eatery when you taste the fresh, down-home country cooking; breakfast is truly outstanding.

EL CAMINO REAL: THE INLAND ROUTE BACK NORTH

When the Spaniards' first land expedition up the California coast was diverted by the cliffs of Big Sur, Don Gaspar de Portolá's party headed inland through the gentler mountains around **Paso Robles** and marched some 100 miles north up the Salinas Valley to Monterey Bay. The Franciscans later built their missions along this route, which they called El Camino Real (The King's Highway) to honor the king of Spain. Today Highway 101 more or less follows this road.

From San Luis Obispo, Highway 101 switchbacks up a steep grade to the Paso Robles wine country, the mountainous site of some 25 wineries. The oldest, dating back to 1882, is **York Mountain Winery**, on Highway 46 to Cambria. Most of the wineries have tasting rooms; you can pick up the free brochure "Wine Tasting in Paso Robles" at any winery for complete information. Before reaching Paso Robles, Highway 101 bypasses the 19th-century town of Templeton; leave the freeway for a few minutes for a glimpse of the re-created false-fronted buildings on Main Street—reminders of the Old West.

The Missions of the Southern El Camino Real

Ten miles (16 km) north of Paso Robles and just one block off Highway 101 is **Mission San Miguel Arcángel**, founded in 1797 (after Serra's death), the 16th in the chain. The present mission, built in the early 19th century and beautifully restored, is distinguished by an arched colonnade around its monastery courtyard and by the trompe l'oeil murals in the church. San Miguel is one of only four missions in California still tended by brown-robed Franciscan friars.

Franciscans are also in residence farther north at lovely **Mission San Antonio de Padua**, founded by Father Serra in 1771 as the third mission in the chain and at one time (in 1790 with a population of 1,092) the largest community in California. In 1773 the mission church was the site of the first Christian marriage in California—between a Spanish soldier and a Salinan Indian woman. But history and the highway long ago bypassed San Antonio, which is now surrounded by the vast Hunter Liggett Military Reservation in the Santa Lucia foothills west of Highway 101. A visit here requires an hour-long detour through vineyards and cattle farms on County Road G-18 for about 40 miles (64 km) from Camp Roberts through Jolon to King City. The mission, which has been totally restored, provides a fine picture of mission life in the 19th century and serves today as a retreat and training center for the Franciscan order. (Turn northwest onto County Road G-18 from Highway 101 one mile north of Bradley.) Another reason for taking this side trip is for a look at **Jolon Lodge**, across the road from Mission San Antonio. An imposing 70-room hacienda that Julia Morgan designed for W. R. Hearst as a hunting retreat in the 1930s, the lodge is now an army officer's club.

Salinas Valley

This is John Steinbeck's "Long Valley," where the Salinas River is bordered by flat, fertile farmlands below the eastern slopes of the Santa Lucia range. It was in this valley that he set *The Grapes of Wrath, East of Eden,* and other works. Agriculturally speaking, Salinas often translates as "lettuce," but the valley—one of the state's newest viticultural areas—is becoming increasingly noted for its Monterey County wines. Two Santa Clara County vintners in search of more acreage—Paul Masson and Mirassou—planted the valley's first post-Prohibition vineyards in 1962 between Soledad and Greenfield. When they released their first bottlings four years later, the wine world took notice. Today Monterey wines command serious respect. An interesting tasting room en route is **The Monterey Vineyards**, just off 101 at Gonzales; hourly tours are conducted. Even if you don't care to tipple, take a look at "The Story of a Winery," the exhibit here of Ansel Adams photographs. Serious wine bibbers might want to visit **Chalone Vineyards**, one of Monterey County's most prestigious wineries. Located off Highway 146 in the hills east of Soledad, it's open to the public on weekends and by appointment on weekdays; Tel: (408) 678-1717.

Farther east, Highway 146 leads to the **Pinnacles National Monument**, where eerie volcanic spires rise 600 feet above the valley. This 16,000-acre park with 30 miles of trails is popular with hikers and rock climbers, especially in the spring when wildflowers accent the otherwise barren landscape. The Chaparral Ranger Station at the west side of the park is 12 miles (19 km) from Soledad, and offers great views from the road; no automobiles are allowed to enter the park itself. Bear Gulch Visitors Center at the east side of Pinnacles is only accessible from Hollister to the north (via Highway 25) or from King City to the south (via Highway 146). There are campgrounds on either side of Pinnacles—a private one on the east side outside the park and a National Park Service one near the western entrance within the monument (closed on weekends mid-February through

May). There are also several standard motels along Highway 101. For more information on the park, Tel: (408) 389-4485.

Three miles (5 km) west of Soledad, Steinbeck's setting for *Of Mice and Men,* is **Mission Nuestra Señora de Soledad.** Founded in 1791 as the 13th link of the mission chain, the mission was reduced to ruins by years of floods and neglect. Although the chapel and one wing have been reconstructed, this is the least interesting of the missions along this route.

At the northern end of the Salinas Valley, Steinbeck's home town of **Salinas** is the commercial center for this agricultural area. A fascinating lunch stop at 132 Central Avenue is the **Steinbeck House,** a Queen Anne Victorian where the author was born and wrote some of his early works. Now magnificently restored, the Steinbeck House is operated as a restaurant by the nonprofit Valley Guild, whose volunteers help prepare and serve lunch on weekdays. The menu is fixed, the food is delicious, and reservations should be made well in advance; Tel: (408) 424-2735. The **Steinbeck Center** displays letters, photographs, and rare editions and sponsors the Steinbeck Festival in early August, a four-day blitz of films, lectures, and tours of the novelist's haunts; Tel: (408) 753-6411.

San Juan Bautista

Only a few minutes east of Highway 101, this quiet village is virtually a living museum of early Californiana, from the founding of its mission in 1797 through the 19th century. The core of this town in the hills, about 20 miles (32 km) north of Salinas, is **San Juan Bautista State Historic Park,** a group of restored buildings facing the town plaza. A self-guided tour includes visits to the Castro House, a balconied 1840s adobe built by the Mexican prefect of northern Alta California; the Plaza Hotel, a major stagecoach stop, now restored to look as it did in the 1860s; the Plaza Stable, where vintage carriages and wagons are displayed; and the Plaza Hall, which was used for public meetings and social gatherings. On the first Saturday of each month living-history events are conducted in the park; Tel: (408) 623-4881.

On the north side of the plaza, **Mission San Juan Bautista,** 15th of the 21 Franciscan missions, was once the home of 1,200 Native Americans and is one of the few missions where a priest remained in residence after secularization. The mission's church was damaged severely in the 1906 earthquake (the San Andreas Fault runs just east of town); it is now restored. The church is distinguished by three naves, and it was here that the memorable bell tower scene of the classic Hitchcock film *Vertigo* was shot. The wing that contained the kitchen and the padres' living quarters is now a museum.

A block from the plaza, antiques stores, art and crafts galleries, gift shops, and restaurants line Third Street. A landmark eatery for Old California atmosphere, **La Casa Rosa** serves a limited luncheon menu (casseroles and a soufflé) in an 1858 adobe and its gardens. You'll also find outdoor dining in a pretty setting and traditional Mexican food at **Jardines de San Juan**.

GETTING AROUND

The ideal way to explore the Central Coast is by car. In a pinch, a round-trip itinerary from San Francisco to San Luis Obispo (about 500 miles/800 km) may be made in three days, with overnight stops on the Monterey Peninsula and in the vicinity of Hearst Castle, but this would allow time only for the major sights. If you want to shorten the route you can cut back to Highway 101 from Highway 1 at Castroville, northeast of the Monterey Peninsula; just south of Cambria, Highway 46 provides a scenic drive on a good road over the mountains to Paso Robles and 101; or Highway 41 leads back to 101 from Morro Bay.

For nondrivers the Monterey Peninsula is serviced by Greyhound Bus Lines (Tel: 415-558-6789), American Eagle, Delta Skywest, United Airlines, and USAir. (Many hotels and inns offer courtesy pickups at the Monterey Peninsula Airport, which is east of Highway 1 just north of Monterey.) Once there, **The Bus** (Monterey-Salinas Transport) operates between the various peninsula towns and south to Nepenthe at Big Sur; for a schedule call (408) 899-2555. Another option is a sightseeing tour: Try **Seacoast Safaris** (1067 Sawmill Gulch, Pebble Beach, CA 93953; Tel: 408-372-1288), **Steinbeck Country Tours** (P.O. Box 22848, Carmel, CA 93922; Tel: 408-625-5107), or **Otter-Mobile Tours & Charters** (P.O. Box 2743, Carmel, CA 93921; Tel: 408-625-9782). These have a range of itineraries from short treks around the peninsula to all-day excursions that include Big Sur and Hearst Castle.

From San Francisco, daily 11-hour, round-trip tours to the Monterey Peninsula are offered by **Gray Line** (Tel: 415-558-9400 or 800-556-5660) and **Great Pacific Tour Company** (Tel: 415-626-4499). Two- and three-day bus tours to the peninsula and Hearst Castle are among the packages available through **California Parlor Car Tours** in San Francisco (Tel: 415-474-7500). And if you want to try the train, **Amtrak** has daily service from Oakland (with bus transfer from San Francisco) to Salinas and San Luis Obispo; from the latter, Amtrak operates an overnight bus tour to Hearst Castle (Tel: 800-321-8684).

ACCOMMODATIONS REFERENCE
The rate ranges given are projections for fall 1993 through spring 1994. Unless otherwise indicated, rates are for double room, double occupancy.

▶ **Apple Farm Inn.** 2015 Monterey Street, **San Luis Obispo,** CA 93401. Tel: (805) 544-2040 or (800) 374-3705; Fax: 541-5497. $105–$190 (inn), $55–$99 (Trellis Court).

▶ **Asilomar Conference Center.** 800 Asilomar Boulevard (P.O. Box 537), **Pacific Grove,** CA 93950. Tel: (408) 372-8016; Fax: 372-7227. $66–$84.

▶ **Babbling Brook Inn.** 1025 Laurel Street, **Santa Cruz,** CA 95060. Tel: (408) 427-2437 or (800) 866-1131; Fax: 427-2457. $85–$150.

▶ **The Beach House.** 6530 Moonstone Beach Drive, **Cambria,** CA 93428. Tel: (805) 927-3136 or (800) 549-6789. $120–$150.

▶ **Best Western Cavalier Inn.** 9415 Hearst Drive, **San Simeon,** CA 93452. Tel: (805) 927-4688 or (800) 826-8168; Fax: 927-0497. $59–$118.

▶ **Best Western Fireside Inn By-the-Sea.** 6700 Moonstone Beach Drive, **Cambria,** CA 93428. Tel: (805) 927-8661 or (800) 528-1234; Fax: 927-8584. $70–$130.

▶ **Big Sur Lodge.** Pfeiffer–Big Sur State Park, **Big Sur,** CA 93920. Tel: (408) 667-2171 or (800) 424-4787; Fax: 667-3110. $69–$129.

▶ **Blue Dolphin.** 6470 Moonstone Beach Drive, **Cambria,** CA 93428. Tel: (805) 927-3300. $75–$175.

▶ **The Blue Whale Inn.** 6736 Moonstone Beach Drive, **Cambria,** CA 93428. Tel: (805) 927-4647. $135–$165.

▶ **Carmel Valley Ranch Resort.** 1 Old Ranch Road, **Carmel Valley,** CA 93923. Tel: (408) 625-9500 or (800) 422-7635; Fax: 624-2858. $235–$385.

▶ **Chaminade.** One Chaminade Lane, P.O. Box 2788, **Santa Cruz,** CA 95063. Tel: (408) 475-5600 or (800) 283-6569; Fax: 476-4942. $125–$145.

▶ **Château Victorian.** 118 First Street, **Santa Cruz,** CA 95060. Tel: (408) 458-9458. $110–$140.

▶ **Cobblestone Inn.** Junípero between Seventh and Eighth, P.O. Box 3185, **Carmel**, CA 93921. Tel: (408) 625-5222; Fax: 625-0478. $95–$175.

▶ **Cypress Inn.** Lincoln and Seventh, P.O. Box Y, **Carmel**, CA 93921. Tel: (408) 624-3871 or (800) 443-7443; Fax: 624-8216. $107–$198.

▶ **Deetjen's Big Sur Inn.** Highway 1, **Big Sur**, CA 93920. Tel: (408) 667-2377. $40–$110.

▶ **Esalen Institute.** Highway 1, **Big Sur**, CA 93920. Tel: (408) 667-3000; Fax: 667-2724. $80–$125 per person (overnight room and board); $380 (weekend workshop).

▶ **The Gosby House Inn.** 643 Lighthouse Avenue, **Pacific Grove**, CA 93950. Tel: (408) 375-1287; Fax: 655-9621. $85–$150.

▶ **The Green Gables Inn.** 104 Fifth Street, **Pacific Grove**, CA 93950. Tel: (408) 375-2095. $110–$160.

▶ **Highlands Inn.** Highway 1, P.O. Box 1700, **Carmel**, CA 93921. Tel: (408) 624-3801 or (800) 682-4811; Fax: 626-1574. $225–$400.

▶ **Inn at Depot Hill.** 250 Monterey Avenue, **Capitola**, CA 95010. Tel: (408) 462-3376; Fax: 462-3697. $155–$250.

▶ **The Inn at Morro Bay.** Morro Bay State Park, **Morro Bay**, CA 93442. Tel: (805) 772-5651 or (800) 321-9566; Fax: 772-4779. $90–$210.

▶ **The Inn at Spanish Bay.** 2700 Seventeen Mile Drive, **Pebble Beach**, CA 93953. Tel: (408) 647-7500 or (800) 654-9300; Fax: 624-6357. $245–$350.

▶ **The Jabberwock.** 598 Laine Street, **Monterey**, CA 93940. Tel: (408) 372-4777. $100–$180.

▶ **The Lodge at Pebble Beach.** Seventeen Mile Drive, **Pebble Beach**, CA 93953. Tel: (408) 624-3811 or (800) 654-9300; Fax: 624-6357. $295–$450.

▶ **Los Laureles Lodge.** Carmel Valley Road, **Carmel Valley**, CA 93924. Tel: (408) 659-2233 or (800) 533-4404; Fax: 659-0481. $78–$125.

▶ **Mission Ranch.** 26270 Dolores Street, **Carmel**, CA 93923. Tel: (408) 624-6436 or (800) 538-8221; Fax: 626-4163. $95–$225.

▶ **Monterey Plaza.** 400 Cannery Row, **Monterey**, CA 93940. Tel: (408) 646-1700 or (800) 334-3999; Fax: 646-0285. $150–$280.

▶ **Old Monterey Inn.** 500 Martin Street, **Monterey**, CA 93940. Tel: (408) 375-8284 or (800) 350-2344. $160–$220.

▶ **Pine Inn.** Ocean Avenue and Lincoln, **Carmel**, CA 93921. Tel: (408) 624-3851 or (800) 228-3851; Fax: 624-3030. $85–$205.

▶ **La Playa Hotel.** Camino Real and Eighth Avenue, P.O. Box 900, **Carmel**, CA 93921. Tel: (408) 624-6476 or (800) 582-8900; Fax: 624-7966. $115–$210 (rooms), $210–$495 (cottages).

▶ **Post Ranch Inn.** Highway 1, P.O. Box 219, **Big Sur**, CA 93920. Tel: (408) 667-2200 or (800) 527-2200; Fax: 667-2824. $245–$475.

▶ **Quail Lodge.** 8205 Valley Greens Drive, **Carmel**, CA 93923. Tel: (408) 624-1581 or (800) 538-9516; Fax: 624-3726. $225–$345.

▶ **Sand Pebbles Inn.** 6252 Moonstone Beach Drive, **Cambria**, CA 93428. Tel: (805) 927-5600. $95–$175.

▶ **Sandpiper Inn At-the-Beach.** 2408 Bay View Avenue at Martin, **Carmel**, CA 93923. Tel: (408) 624-6433 or (800) 633-6433 (in California). $100–$170.

▶ **Sea View Inn.** Camino Real at Eleventh, P.O. Box 4138, **Carmel**, CA 93921. Tel: (408) 624-8778. $80–$115.

▶ **Spindrift Inn.** 652 Cannery Row, **Monterey**, CA 93940. Tel: (408) 646-8900 or (800) 841-1879; Fax: 646-5342. $149–$389.

▶ **Stonepine.** 150 East Carmel Valley Road, **Carmel Valley**, CA 93924. Tel: (408) 659-2245; Fax: 659-5160. $225–$750.

▶ **Tassajara Zen Mountain Center.** Tassajara Reservation Office, 300 Page Street, San Francisco, CA 94102. Tel: (415) 431-3771. No credit cards. $150–$240.

▶ **Tickle Pink Inn.** 155 Highlands Drive, **Carmel**, CA 93923. Tel: (408) 624-1244 or (800) 635-4774; Fax: 626-9516. $149–$259.

▶ **Ventana Inn.** Highway 1, **Big Sur**, CA 93920. Tel: (408) 667-2331 or (800) 628-6500. $170–355.

CHRONOLOGY OF THE
HISTORY OF
SAN FRANCISCO AND
NORTHERN CALIFORNIA

- **circa 10,000 B.C.**: The last Ice Age ends, having shaped the Northern California landscape known today. *Sequoia sempervirens* (Coast Redwoods), once found worldwide, survive in the coastal fog belt.
- **A.D. 1510**: The name California is used for a rich and mystic island described in a Spanish poem, *Las Sergas de Esplandián* by Garcí Ordóñez de Montalvo.
- **1542**: A Spanish ship returning from the Philippines reaches the Northern California coast; a headland is named Cabo Mendocino.
- **1579**: Sir Francis Drake beaches the *Golden Hinde* for repairs at a still undetermined Northern California bay.
- **1602**: Sebastián Vizcaíno lands at Monterey Bay. He calls it a "noble harbor," a comment that confuses later explorers.
- **1768**: New Spain officials make plans to settle California and prevent Russian intrusions there.
- **1769**: Gaspar de Portolá's expedition to find Monterey Bay reaches San Francisco Bay instead.
- **1770 (June 3)**: Father Junípero Serra celebrates the founding Mass for Monterey presidio and mission. Gaspar de Portolá, who led two expeditions north, grumps, "If the Russians want Northern California, they deserve it."
- **1775**: Spanish Lt. Juan Manuel de Ayala takes the first ship into San Francisco Bay.
- **1776**: The Presidio of San Francisco is dedicated on

September 17, the Misión San Francisco de Asís on October 4.

- **1777**: San Jose Pueblo is founded at the south end of San Francisco Bay.
- **1786**: Monterey entertains its first foreign visitor, the French explorer François de la Pérouse.
- **1792**: The first Yankee arrives in California, a gunner on a Mexican ship.
- **1808**: Russians establish a sea otter hunting base at Bodega Bay, north of San Francisco.
- **1812**: Russians found Fort Ross, 120 miles north of San Francisco Bay.
- **1820**: U.S. ships begin California trade for hides and tallow. A few Yankees begin to settle in the north.
- **1825**: California becomes a territory of now-independent Mexico.
- **1828**: Fur trapper Jedediah Smith makes the first crossing of the rugged Northern California coastal mountains.
- **1833**: Mexico secularizes the missions in California, having found that conflicts with Native Americans made the institutions too economically burdensome (Mexico would not secularize its own missions until 1857).
- **1836**: Juan Bautista Alvarado marches on Monterey and declares California a "free and sovereign state" within the Mexican Republic. Mexican control grows more and more tenuous.
- **1839**: John Augustus Sutter, a Swiss, founds Sutter's Fort, the first settlement in the interior, near the junction of the Sacramento and American rivers.
- **1840**: Yankee traders who have become Mexican citizens and married locals are by now important figures in California society.
- **1841**: John Bidwell and 36 immigrants from Missouri reach Sutter's Fort after a six-month transcontinental journey. The Russians sell Fort Ross to Sutter.
- **1842**: Commodore A.C. Jones, U.S. Navy, thinking the U.S. and Mexico are at war, occupies Monterey and claims California for the United States. He's wrong, so he apologizes and leaves town.
- **1844**: U.S. Lt. John C. Frémont's expedition arrives at Sutter's Fort. Forty-six easterners make the first wagon crossing of the Sierra Nevada.
- **1845**: Two hundred sixty-nine overland settlers arrive.

- **1846**: Sacramento Valley Yankee settlers begin the Bear Flag revolt to establish California as a republic. The U.S. declares war on Mexico and claims Monterey and Yerba Buena at San Francisco Bay in early July. Nearly 300 Mormon settlers, led by Samuel Brannan, disembark at Yerba Buena. Winter traps the Donner Party from Illinois in the Sierra Nevada.
- **1847**: Yerba Buena is renamed San Francisco; by year's end it has 200 buildings, 800 residents, and a newspaper.
- **1848**: Carpenter James Marshall finds gold on January 24 at Sutter's Mill, Coloma, near Placerville. By mid-June San Francisco is half empty. Gold-seekers arrive from Oregon, Hawaii, Mexico, Peru, Chile, and elsewhere, and an estimated $6 million worth of gold is mined by December 31. News filters east, and President Polk confirms the strike to Congress on December 5.
- **1849**: The great Rush of '49 begins. A first ship with 365 Argonauts anchors at San Francisco on February 28; by the end of the year 1,000 ships have arrived. Between spring and winter, 30,000 gold-seekers cross the continent—in all, 90,000 people came to seek their fortunes.
- **1850**: California joins the Union as a nonslave state. Forty-five thousand gold-seekers arrive by overland routes. Levi Strauss reaches San Francisco and starts stitching sturdy britches for miners. The state's Chinese population grows to 789 men and two women. Thirty steamboats ply San Francisco Bay and the valley rivers.
- **1851**: Vigilantes organize to fight crime in San Francisco. Sacramento, the settlement that engulfed Sutter's Fort, has grown to a population of 10,000.
- **1852**: San Francisco culture is launched with the arrival of singer Elisa Biscaccianti; the North Coast lumber town of Mendocino is founded, and the original Almaden and Paul Masson vineyards are planted near San Jose.
- **1853**: The first California-built steamboat takes to the water.
- **1854**: Sacramento becomes the state capital.
- **1855**: Gold production and overland arrivals decline, and California weathers a year of financial woes. The San Francisco *Alta* reports 370 murders in eight months.

- **1856**: California's first train service begins with a 22-mile route between Sacramento and Folsom. San Francisco vigilantes hang four men.
- **1857**: Fort Bragg is founded north of Mendocino. The Butterfield Overland Mail travels from Missouri to San Francisco in 24 days.
- **1858**: San Francisco and Los Angeles are linked by telegraph.
- **1860**: The first Pony Express mail reaches Sacramento; an engineer surveys a railroad route over the Sierra Nevada via Emigrant Gap and Donner Pass, and Comstock Lode silver from Nevada enriches San Francisco.
- **1861**: The telegraph links Sacramento and the East Coast.
- **1863 (January 8)**: Ground is broken in Sacramento for the Central Pacific Railroad, which thousands of Chinese will be hired to build.
- **1868**: A charter is issued for the University of California.
- **1869 (May 10)**: Northern California and the East are linked by rail as the Central Pacific Railroad and Union Pacific meet at Promontory, Utah.
- **1870**: Point Arena Lighthouse is built south of Mendocino; it topples in 1906.
- **1873**: Andrew S. Hallidie's cable car makes its first run down and up San Francisco's Clay Street.
- **1874**: California's capitol building in Sacramento is completed at the scandalous cost of $2,600,000.
- **1884**: Sarah L. Winchester, widow of the Winchester rifle fortune heir, settles in San Jose and begins house construction that will continue for 38 years.
- **1887**: Scottish gardener John McLaren is hired to tend San Francisco's Golden Gate Park; he stays 50 years.
- **1890**: Congress creates Yosemite, General Grant, and Sequoia national parks.
- **1891**: Stanford University founded at Palo Alto by Leland Stanford in honor of his dead son. Stanford endows the university with money and land.
- **1892**: Conservationist John Muir organizes the Sierra Club.
- **1898**: The first automobile in California sputters down Oakland's streets.
- **1900**: San Francisco's Fisherman's Wharf is built.

- **1903:** Jack London, California's first native-born writer of note, publishes *The Call of the Wild*.
- **1904:** A. P. Giannini opens the Bank of Italy, "a people's bank." It's now the Bank of America.
- **1906 (April 18, 5:12 A.M.):** An earthquake coming out of the sea at Point Arena and travelling 7,000 miles an hour hits San Francisco with an estimated force of 8.3 on the Richter scale. Water and gas mains burst, and fire follows. It takes 74 hours to stop the flames, which engulf 4.7 square miles. The official death toll is 450.
- **1907:** Muir Woods redwood grove becomes a national monument.
- **1908:** Seventy-seven "skyscrapers" are under construction when Theodore Roosevelt's Great White Fleet visits still-rebuilding San Francisco.
- **1913:** Congress approves the San Francisco water supply dam that floods Hetch Hetchy Valley, northern "twin" to Yosemite Valley. Automobiles are allowed into Yosemite National Park.
- **1914:** On Memorial Day, Lassen Peak begins a series of small eruptions; almost a year later, activity climaxes with a big bang as the peak blows its top.
- **1915:** San Francisco celebrates its rebirth with the Panama-Pacific International Exposition.
- **1916:** Bridge engineer Joseph Strauss says the Golden Gate can be spanned for $25 to $30 million.
- **1921:** Gaetano Merola, an opera company conductor, arrives in San Francisco and stays to organize the city's opera association. Harry Bridges arrives to work on the docks and later organizes the longshoremen.
- **1931:** Work starts on the San Francisco–Oakland Bay Bridge.
- **1932:** The San Francisco War Memorial Opera House is inaugurated.
- **1933:** Work starts on the Golden Gate Bridge. The Central Valley Project, one of the world's largest irrigation schemes, is approved.
- **1934:** Striking longshoremen, police, and strikebreakers clash at the Embarcadero on July 5. Eleven days later, 150,000 Bay Area workers stage a one-day general strike in sympathy.
- **1935:** Dust Bowl migrants, scornfully called "Oakies" and "Arkies," begin to flow into California.
- **1936 (November 15):** The San Francisco–Oakland Bay Bridge opens.

- **1937 (May 27)**: The Golden Gate Bridge opens, and 200,000 people walk across. The final cost of the bridge is $27,125,000, some $40,000 under budget.
- **1939**: *The Grapes of Wrath,* John Steinbeck's novel about migrant farm workers, enrages conservatives. The Golden Gate International Exposition opens on Treasure Island, San Francisco Bay.
- **1942**: Soon after World War II hits the U.S., the West Coast's Japanese-Americans are uprooted and sent to relocation camps. Bay Area shipyards enjoy a war effort boom; Henry Kaiser's Richmond yard will build 23 percent of America's Liberty Ships.
- **1946**: Sardine catches plummet, dooming Monterey's Cannery Row.
- **1949**: University of California employees are required to sign loyalty oaths.
- **1953**: San Francisco's Chinese go public with their New Year's celebration, inaugurating a grand parade.
- **1956**: Lawrence Ferlinghetti's City Lights Books publishes Allen Ginsberg's *Howl,* the anthem of San Francisco's Beat Generation.
- **1960**: Police turn fire hoses on students protesting House Un-American Activities Committee meeting at San Francisco City Hall.
- **1964**: A free-speech movement builds up steam at U.C. Berkeley. A 9.2 earthquake in Alaska triggers a tidal wave that hits the coast, wiping out Crescent City's waterfront.
- **1966**: Ronald Reagan is elected governor, and wife, Nancy, refuses to live in Sacramento's century-old governor's mansion. Eight thousand U.C. Berkeley students strike to protest Navy recruiters on campus.
- **1967**: Hippies celebrate the Summer of Love in San Francisco's Haight-Ashbury district. At the same time, city citizens stage what they call a "freeway revolt," refusing to allow construction of a crosstown freeway and halting work on the Embarcadero Freeway.
- **1969**: Peoples' Park riots break out in Berkeley. Ninety Native Americans occupy the deserted federal prison on Alcatraz Island.
- **1970**: San Francisco's gay and lesbian community stages its first Lesbian/Gay Freedom Day Parade, now an annual event the last Sunday in June.
- **1971**: Alice Waters opens Chez Panisse restaurant, signalling Berkeley's transformation from Radical Capital to Foodie Empire.

- **1974:** Newly elected Governor Jerry Brown, son of former Governor Edmund G. Brown, refuses to live in the luxurious Sacramento governor's mansion built by Reagan supporters. The Symbionese Liberation Army kidnaps Patricia Campbell Hearst.
- **1978:** Former City Supervisor Dan White assassinates San Francisco Mayor George Moscone and Supervisor Harvey Milk, a leader of the gay community.
- **1979:** Members of San Francisco's gay community stage "White Night" riot to protest the voluntary-manslaughter verdict in the Dan White trial as too lenient.
- **1981:** In July, the San Francisco Public Health Department begins recording reported cases of and deaths from a new disease called AIDS; by the end of April 1991, the official files list 10,414 cases and 7,221 deaths.
- **1982:** New Republican Governor George Deukmejian is willing to live in Sacramento's unused governor's mansion, but the Democratic legislature sells it.
- **1984:** San Francisco's cable-car system reopens after reconstruction, and the Monterey Bay Aquarium opens on Cannery Row.
- **1987:** San Francisco celebrates the Golden Gate Bridge's 50th birthday by reserving it for walkers for a few hours; an estimated 200,000 take part. Pope John Paul II visits San Francisco and the Carmel Mission on the Monterey Peninsula in light of Father Junípero Serra's candidacy for sainthood. The International AIDS Memorial Quilt is displayed in San Francisco's Moscone Center; it returns in 1988 and 1990.
- **1989 (October 17, 5:04 P.M.):** Minutes before the start of the third World Series game at Candlestick Park, San Francisco, an earthquake measuring 7.1 on the Richter scale hits. The 58,000 spectators at Candlestick are unscathed, but a mile of double-deck freeway in Oakland and a section of the Bay Bridge's upper roadway collapse, and houses topple and burn in San Francisco's Marina district. Seventy-five miles away, near the epicenter, 60 percent of downtown Santa Cruz is in ruins. The overall toll in Northern California: 100,000 buildings damaged or destroyed; 14,000 people displaced; 67 people killed.
- **1990:** On the 84th anniversary of the 1906 earthquake, Northern California is hit by a swarm of trem-

ors measuring 3.3 to 5.4 on the Richter scale. On the lighter side, hordes of endangered sea lions invade the pleasure boat docks at San Francisco's Pier 39 marina; the beasts enchant tourists and terrify yachtsmen who must pass the quarter-ton animals to reach their boats.

- **1991**: Demolition of San Francisco's earthquake-damaged double-deck Embarcadero Freeway begins. Pulling down the hated freeway is a postscript to the 1967 "freeway revolt" that halted construction before the road could be extended to wall off most of the city's bay shore. California is in its fifth year of drought, and on October 20 a brush fire in the dry, wooded East Bay hills burns out of control. By the time the flames die, more than 3,000 houses and apartments have been destroyed, and 28 lives lost.

- **1992**: The San Francisco Bay Area breathes a sigh of relief when the San Francisco Giants baseball team decides not to move to Florida. In November, the state elects two women to the Senate, former San Francisco mayor Diane Feinstein and former North Bay Representative Barbara Boxer. This historic first makes California the only state ever represented in the Senate by two women at the same time.

—Shirley Maas Fockler

INDEX

564   INDEX